The Early Muslim Conquest of Syria

This book narrates the battles, conquests and diplomatic activities of the early Muslim fighters in Syria and Iraq vis-à-vis their Byzantine and Sasanian counterparts. It is the first English translation of one of the earliest Arabic sources on the early Muslim expansion entitled *Futūḥ al-Shām* (The Conquests of Syria).

The translation is based on the Arabic original composed by a Muslim author, Muḥammad al-Azdī, who died in the late 8th or early 9th century C.E. A scientific introduction to al-Azdī's work is also included, covering the life of the author, the textual tradition of the work as well as a short summary of the text's train of thought. The source narrates the major historical events during the early Muslim conquests in a region that covers today's Lebanon, Israel, Palestinian Territories, Jordan, Syria, Turkey and Iraq in the 7th century C.E. Among these events are the major battles against the Byzantines, such as the Battles of Ajnādayn and al-Yarmūk, the conquests of important cities, including Damascus, Jerusalem and Caesarea, and the diplomatic initiatives between the Byzantines and the early Muslims. The narrative abounds with history and Islamic theological content.

As the first translation into a European language, this volume will be of interest to a wide range of readership, including (Muslim and Christian) theologians, historians, Islamicists, Byzantinists, Syrologists and (Arabic) linguists.

Hamada Hassanein is Assistant Professor at Prince Sattam bin Abdulaziz University (Saudi Arabia), on secondment from Mansoura University (Egypt). His academic interest is the application of linguistic theories to Arabic texts. His recent publications include *Arabic Antonymy Translation* (2017) and *Discourse Functions* (2018).

Jens Scheiner is Professor of Islamic Studies at the University of Göttingen (Germany). His research interests are the political and social history of the early and classical periods of Islam and Hadith Studies (in particular isnad-cum-matn analysis). He published on the early Muslim conquests, the cultural history of Baghdad and hadith.

Culture and Civilization in the Middle East

General Editor: Ian Richard Netton
Professor of Islamic Studies, University of Exeter

This series studies the Middle East through the twin foci of its diverse cultures and civilisations. Comprising original monographs as well as scholarly surveys, it covers topics in the fields of Middle Eastern literature, archaeology, law, history, philosophy, science, folklore, art, architecture and language. While there is a plurality of views, the series presents serious scholarship in a lucid and stimulating fashion.

55 Ibn al-Haytham's Geometrical Methods and the Philosophy of Mathematics
A History of Arabic Sciences and Mathematics Volume 5
Roshdi Rashed

56 New Horizons in Qur'anic Linguistics
A grammatical, semantic, and stylistic analysis
Hussein Abdul-Raof

57 Arabs and Iranians in the Islamic Conquest Narrative
Memory and Identity Construction in Islamic Historiography, 750–1050
Scott Savran

58 The Chaldean Catholic Church
Modern History, Ecclesiology and Church-State Relations
Kristian Girling

59 Text Linguistics of Qur'anic Discourse
An Analysis
Hussein Abdul-Raof

60 The Early Muslim Conquest of Syria
An English Translation of al-Azdī's Futūḥ al-Shām
Translated and annotated by Hamada Hassanein and Jens Scheiner

For a full list of books in the series, please go to:
https://www.routledge.com/middleeaststudies/series/SE0363

The Early Muslim Conquest of Syria

An English Translation of al-Azdī's Futūḥ al-Shām

Translated and annotated by
Hamada Hassanein and
Jens Scheiner

Routledge
Taylor & Francis Group
LONDON AND NEW YORK

First published 2020
by Routledge
2 Park Square, Milton Park, Abingdon, Oxon OX14 4RN

and by Routledge
52 Vanderbilt Avenue, New York, NY 10017

Routledge is an imprint of the Taylor & Francis Group, an informa business

British Library Cataloguing-in-Publication Data
A catalogue record for this book is available from the British Library

Library of Congress Cataloging-in-Publication Data
A catalog record has been requested for this book

ISBN: 978-0-367-23025-8 (hbk)
ISBN: 978-0-429-27801-3 (ebk)

Typeset in Times New Roman
by codeMantra

To my family
To the one I love: M. K.

Contents

List of manuscript notes xi
Acknowledgements xiii

Introduction 1

1 Summary of al-Azdī's *Futūḥ al-Shām* 2

2 The compiler-author and his work 6

The compiler-author 6
The title 9
The audience 10
The manuscripts 10
*The chains of transmission (*riwāyas*) 13*
The editions 20
Studies of al-Azdī's Futūḥ al-Shām *21*

3 Policies of translation 25

4 Translation 35

[Section I: Abū Bakr al-Ṣiddīq's preparation for attacking the Byzantines in Syria] 38
[Abū Bakr al-Ṣiddīq's appointment of the first commander] 49
Abū Bakr al-Ṣiddīq's (r.) letter to the people of Yemen 51
The report (*khabar*) [about the reaction] of the people of Yemen 52
Naming those whom Abū Bakr appointed (*ʿaqada*) as commanders of the districts (*ajnād*) 54
Shuraḥbīl b. Ḥasana's vision 56
The coming of the people of Ḥimyar to Abū Bakr al-Ṣiddīq (r.) 57
[Section II: Abū Bakr al-Ṣiddīq's dispatch of military units to Syria] 60
Khālid b. Saʿīd b. al-ʿĀṣ's march [to Syria] 64
[Heraclius's reaction to the dispatch of the Muslim units] 69
Abū ʿUbayda b. al-Jarrāḥ's (r.) march to Syria and the route he took and travelled along 72

This is Abū ʿUbayda b. al-Jarrāḥ's letter to Abū Bakr (r.) informing him of what he learned of Heraclius's, the Emperor of the Byzantines, mobilisation of the Byzantine groups and of what Abū ʿUbayda wanted to consult Abū Bakr about 73
This is Yazīd b. Abī Sufyān's letter to Abū Bakr (r.) 74
The departure of Hāshim b. ʿUtba [b. Abī Waqqāṣ] (r.) 76
The story (*qiṣṣa*) of Saʿīd b. ʿĀmir b. Ḥudhaym['s departure] 78
The coming of the Arabs to Abū Bakr (r.) 80
The arrival of Ḥamza b. Mālik al-Hamdānī 80
The arrival of Abū al-Aʿwar al-Sulamī 82
The arrival of Maʿn b. Yazīd b. al-Akhnas al-Sulamī 83
[The reaction of the people in Syria] 85
The story of Abū Bakr's (r.) plan to consult the Qurayshite people of Mecca who delayed embracing Islam [in response to] what Abū ʿUbayda b. al-Jarrāḥ had written; and [the story] about ʿUmar b. al-Khaṭṭāb's hatred of that [consultation] 86
Abū Bakr's (r.) appointment (*ʿaqd*) of ʿAmr b. al-ʿĀṣ (r.) as commander 89
Abū Bakr's letter to Abū ʿUbayda (r.) 90
[The battles of al-ʿAraba and al-Dāthina] 92
[Section III: Khālid b. al-Walīd's activities in Iraq] 93
The arrival of al-Muthannā b. Ḥāritha [al-Shaybānī] to Abū Bakr (r.) 94
[Khālid b. al-Walīd's battles in Iraq] 97
The story of deposing Khālid b. al-Walīd from [commanding the Muslim troops in] Iraq and his taking command of [the Muslim troops in] Syria 107
Khālid b. al-Walīd's march to Syria and his battles against Banū Taghlib and others along his way 109
The route which Khālid took to Syria 112
This is Khālid's letter to Banū Mashjaʿa 115
[Section IV: Conquests and battles in Syria] 119
The battle of Bosra and [the fight against] its people 119
The battle of Ajnādayn 124
Khālid b. al-Walīd's march to Damascus and his siege of its people 130
The Battle of Marj al-Ṣuffar 131
The death of Abū Bakr (r.) and his appointment of ʿUmar b. al-Khaṭṭāb (r.) as his successor [to the rule] 133
The letter from Abū ʿUbayda and Muʿādh b. Jabal to ʿUmar b. al-Khaṭṭāb (r.) 134
ʿUmar b. al-Khaṭṭāb's letter to Abū ʿUbayda b. al-Jarrāḥ (r.) concerning his [=the latter's] appointment and restitution as [chief] commander of [the troops in] Syria as well as [concerning] the deposition of Khālid b. al-Walīd (r.) 137
The conquest of Damascus and its peace-making [process] (*ṣulḥ*) 138
ʿAmr b. al-ʿĀṣ's letter to Abū ʿUbayda (r.) 141

The battle of Fiḥl 144
The story of Mu'ādh b. Jabal['s negotiation with] the Byzantines 147
Abū 'Ubayda b. al-Jarrāḥ's letter to 'Umar b. al-Khaṭṭāb (r.) informing him about the Byzantines' setting up camp in a place called Fiḥl 153
'Umar b. al-Khaṭṭāb's letter to Abū 'Ubayda b. al-Jarrāḥ (r.) 155
Abū 'Ubayda b. al-Jarrāḥ wrote [the following letter] to 'Umar b. al-Khaṭṭāb (r.) 166
Abū 'Ubayda b. al-Jarrāḥ wrote [the following letter] to 'Umar b. al-Khaṭṭāb (r.) [regarding this issue]\\235 167
'Umar (r.) wrote [the following letter] to him [in reply] 167
The Muslims' march to Ḥimṣ after they had finished [their campaigns] in Fiḥl and in the land of the River Jordan 168
The conquest of the city of Ḥimṣ and its peace-making [process] 169
Abū 'Ubayda b. al-Jarrāḥ wrote [the following letter] to 'Umar b. al-Khaṭṭāb (r.) 171
The report on how God ('a.) led the Muslims to the conquest of [central] Syria and the report on Caesar when he learned of it 174
[Prelude to the battle of al-Yarmūk] 175
The Byzantines' assembly [of an army] against the Muslims after the Muslims had driven them out of [central] Syria 175
Abū 'Ubayda b. al-Jarrāḥ's letter to 'Umar b. al-Khaṭṭāb (r.) informing him of what he knew about the Byzantines' mustering [of an army] against him 179
'Umar b. al-Khaṭṭāb's letter to Abū 'Ubayda b. al-Jarrāḥ (r.) 181
'Amr b. al-'Āṣ's letter to them [=the people of Jerusalem] 186
The story of Qays b. Hubayra [al-Murādī] during Abū 'Ubayda b. al-Jarrāḥ's consultation with the Muslims and what they said in reply to Abū 'Ubayda 191
The report on Qays b. Hubayra [al-Murādī] and some of the Muslim women 192
The speech (*khuṭba*) of Bāhān, the [chief] commander of the Byzantines, who was ordered to march to the Muslims 194
The report on what the corrupt Byzantines, [i.e.] Bāhān's companions, did to the Byzantine people of Syria, and the reason why God eliminated, exterminated and dispersed their group[s] 195
Abū 'Ubayda b. al-Jarrāḥ's setting up camp at al-Yarmūk and his request to 'Umar b. al-Khaṭṭāb (r.) for reinforcements 199
The report on Sufyān [b. 'Awf b. Mughaffal al-Azdī], Abū 'Ubayda's messenger to 'Umar (r.) 203
Mention of what happened between Khālid b. al-Walīd and Bāhān, the subordinate of the Emperor of the Byzantines 212
Khālid b. al-Walīd's reply 217
Bāhān's consultation with his companions about how to fight the Muslims, about what they [=the Muslims] have chosen for themselves and about Bāhān's letter to Caesar in that regard 219
The story of Bāhān's vision 221
Abū 'Ubayda b. al-Jarrāḥ's (r.) vision 223
A Byzantine [grand] man's vision 225

The story of the Byzantine [man] who committed what he committed and of restraining Bāhān from [punishing] him 226
The battle of al-Yarmūk 227
The story of the chieftainship of al-Ashtar, whose [more complete name] was Mālik b. al-Ḥārith al-Nakhaʿī 241
The coming of the [news of the] Byzantines' defeat to Caesar, the Emperor of the Byzantines, and what he said thereupon 244
The story of al-Ashtar [=Mālik b. al-Ḥārith al-Nakhaʿī] and Maysara b. Masrūq [al-ʿAbsī] 246
Abū ʿUbayda b. al-Jarrāḥ's letter to ʿUmar b. al-Khaṭṭāb (r.) [which he wrote] when God (ʿa.) made him triumphant over the people of al-Yarmūk 252
ʿUmar b. al-Khaṭṭāb's letter to Abū ʿUbayda b. al-Jarrāḥ (r.), [which is] the reply to his [=Abū ʿUbayda's] letter to him [=ʿUmar] 252
The story of the peace-making [process] with the people of Jerusalem and of ʿUmar's (r.) coming to Syria 253
The story of the owner of the two leaves 253
ʿUmar's (r.) speech in al-Jābiya 257
The story of Kaʿb al-Ḥabr's [conversion to] Islam (r.); may God rest him 262
ʿUmar b. al-Khaṭṭāb's return [to Medina] 265
[The aftermath of the conquest of Jerusalem] 268
Abū ʿUbayda's death; God rest his soul 268
ʿAbd al-Raḥmān b. Muʿādh b. Jabal's (r.) death 269
Muʿādh b. Jabal's will; [may] God rest his soul and be pleased with him 270
Muʿādh [b. Jabal's] appointment of ʿAmr b. al-ʿĀṣ as successor; may God's mercy, forgiveness and satisfaction be upon both of them 272
Muʿādh b. Jabal's letter to ʿUmar b. al-Khaṭṭāb concerning Abū ʿUbayda's death (r.) 272
The speech of ʿUbāda b. al-Ṣāmit [al-Anṣārī] (r.) 274
The speech of Abū al-Dardāʾ al-Anṣārī (r.) 275
The conquest of Caesarea and the appointment of Yazīd b. Abī Sufyān [as chief commander] of all the districts of Syria 276
Yazīd b. Abī Sufyān's letter to ʿUmar b. al-Khaṭṭāb (r.) 282
ʿUmar's (r.) letter to Yazīd b. Abī Sufyān (r.); may God have mercy upon him 283
Yazīd b. Abī Sufyān's death; God rest him 283

Bibliography 285
Index 291

Manuscript notes

Acknowledgements

The proverb "Many hands make light work" necessitates that we thank all the people who have lent a hand, without stint, to bring this work to light. First and foremost, we thank our former colleague Adam Walker who, in spite of undergoing a severe ordeal, spared none of his effort or time to peruse and proofread this work. We are grateful to him for his very extensive reading, insightful comments, candid feedback and critical acumen. In addition, Penelope Krumm read the final draft of the manuscript very attentively and helped us to detect some inconsistencies. We thank her warmly for her efforts. Furthermore, we express our sincerest thanks to Mohamed al-Zeiny, assistant professor at the University of Mansoura, who rectified several Arabic-related errors and clarified many misunderstandings. Moreover, the research assistants, Veronika Bruchner and Nadine Becker, deserve big thanks for including numerous corrections in the emerging manuscript, while Julia Gellert supported us in preparing the index; many thanks to her, too. Our thanks are also due to our families for their great patience with our work that took us more than eight years to finish and to colleagues and friends, notably Isabel Toral-Niehoff, Mohamed Shehata, Ahmed al-Qenawy and Muhriz al-Daghir, for their assistance and moral support. Special thanks go to the University of Göttingen, Germany, Mansoura University, Egypt, Prince Sattam bin Abdulaziz University, Saudi Arabia, and DAAD for providing funding that helped shape a big part of this project. Finally, we would like to thank all anonymous reviewers who gave us valuable feedback over the past three years. Any shortcomings that may remain are entirely the fault of the translators.

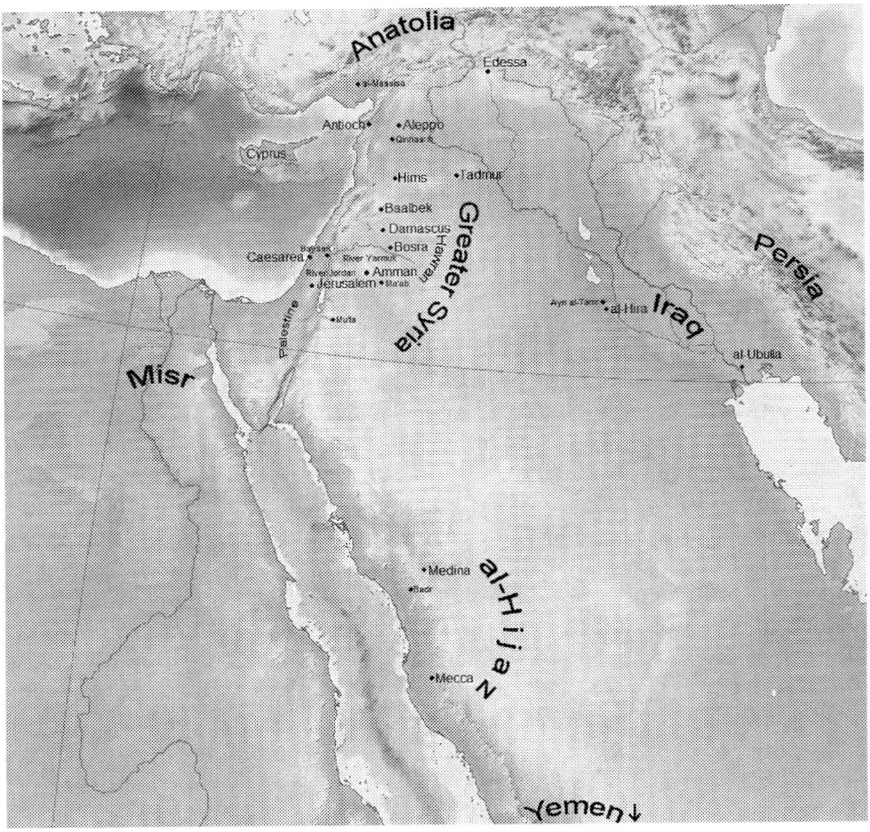

Map 0.1 Syria and the Near East (according to al-Azdī's *Futūḥ al-Shām*)

Introduction

Over the past decades, al-Azdī's *Futūḥ al-Shām* has become a main source for our understanding of the Muslim expansion in Greater Syria during the late antique period. Many scholars consider it the earliest extant historical work in Arabic, belonging to the genre of *futūḥ* (conquest) literature. Surprisingly, however, it has not been translated into any other language. For this reason and because it is widely used as a source of historical research regarding this period, we present a "precise study translation" (M. Hodgson) of the work in English. Before turning to the translation itself, we will briefly introduce the content of the work by summarising its main points (Chapter 1) and reproduce the most important information about the compiler-author of the work, its title as well as the extant manuscripts, their chains of transmission (*riwāyas*), the editions and the most important studies on the work (Chapter 2).[1] Then we will state our policies in translating the work (Chapter 3) and finally present the translated text (Chapter 4).

1 Chapter 2 is a summary of the forthcoming monograph: Scheiner, *Al-Azdī's Futūḥ al-Shām in Past and Present*. This work includes many more references and detailed argumentations on the points summarised here.

1 Summary of al-Azdī's *Futūḥ al-Shām*

Al-Azdī's *Futūḥ al-Shām* narrates the events that led to the final conquest of Greater Syria ("*al-Shām*") by several groups of people called "Arabs" or "Muslims" during 633–641 C.E.[1] In this chapter, a summary of the main events as described in *The Conquests of Syria* is provided. This summary makes use of the vocabulary and the concepts of the text, deliberately adopting al-Azdī's perspective. The whole narrative can be divided into four sections that are indicated in the summary and the translation as well. Page numbers in parentheses refer to the pages of the ʿUqla/Banī Yāsīn edition, which are also mentioned as cross-references in our translation. They will help the reader to correlate this summary with the Arabic original.

The narrative starts with a brief reference to Muḥammad's death and the "Apostasy Wars (*ridda*)" in the time of Abū Bakr (77–78), after which the latter envisaged attacking the Byzantines in Syria and started the preparations for this undertaking (Section I). Hence, Abū Bakr consulted some important companions on this issue and finally decided to do so (81–86). Having invited some Arabian tribes from Yemen to join him, he then appointed several commanders (among whom were, for example, Abū ʿUbayda b. al-Jarrāḥ and Yazīd b. Abī Sufyān) and started to dispatch them to Syria (86–108). This marks the beginning of Section II of the text. Then the focus of the narrative switches to the Byzantine Emperor, who mobilised his subjects in Syria to oppose the coming Muslims (108–111). In reply to this, Abū Bakr sent further troops to Syria, some of which were again from Yemen; others came from Mecca (116–136). The first battles occurred at al-ʿAraba and al-Dāthina (136). Then, in Section III of the text, the focus switches to Iraq, to which Abū Bakr dispatched Khālid b. al-Walīd to fight and conquer (137–142). After the Battle of al-Ubulla and the conquests of other places, Abū Bakr ordered Khālid to leave Iraq and support his fellow Muslims in Syria as chief commander (142–154). Khālid made his famous march through the

1 For a contextualisation of these developments into the wider expansion of the early Islamic state, see Donner, *Early Islamic Conquests*; Kennedy, *Arab Conquests*; Hoyland, *In God's Path*; Berger, *Entstehung*.

Syrian desert (154–162) and met Abū ʿUbayda near Damascus (162). With Khālid's arrival in Syria, Section IV begins. Therein various conquests, battles and events in Syria are mentioned. First, Khālid conquered Bosra and, together with Abū ʿUbayda, raided Damascus (165–169). Because they had learned that the Byzantines were encamped in Ajnādayn, Khālid and Abū ʿUbayda ordered the other Muslim commanders to join them, and the ensuing Battle of Ajnādayn is described (169–179). Khālid then continued his operations at Damascus (179–195). During the siege of the city, Abū Bakr died. ʿUmar succeeded him to lead the Muslim community, deposed Khālid from the chief command and appointed Abū ʿUbayda instead (184–191). After fending off a unit of Byzantine reinforcements near Baalbek (195–198), the Muslims turned towards Fiḥl, which they conquered after strong resistance from its inhabitants (199–237). In the course of fighting there, one of the Muslim leaders, Muʿādh b. Jabal, had a talk with some Byzantine commanders, in which he introduced major tenets of the Muslims' faith and their motivation for fighting against them (202–210). A second talk, in which the Byzantines offered southern Syria to the Muslims, ended in vain (210–219). The Muslims won the ensuing battle and the land of the River Jordan fell under their control (220–236). Then the Muslims turned towards Ḥimṣ, which they also conquered (237–244). Having heard about all this, Heraclius consulted his subordinate commanders and decided to dispatch a huge army under the command of Bāhān to fight the Muslims (245–247). In light of this advance, the majority of the Muslims decided to retreat southwards, returning some of their spoils to the previous owners, and met with all other Muslim units near al-Yarmūk gorge, a place in central Syria, where they camped opposite the Byzantine army (248–272). The narrative focus then shifts to the Byzantines' encampment, where Bāhān motivated his commanders and soldiers but failed to control his corrupt companions (272–278). Having asked ʿUmar for reinforcements, Abū ʿUbayda prepared the Muslims for battle (279–290). The subsequent Battle of al-Yarmūk, in which Khālid and others excelled, is narrated from several perspectives, highlighting the bravery of many individual Muslims from various tribes (290–341). The battle was interrupted by a talk between Khālid and Bāhān in which Khālid explained to Bāhān why the Muslims would fight to the end and what they would gain from this fight (294–311). Bāhān tried yet another way to negotiate peace with the Muslims, but finally realised that he would not be able to beat the Muslims militarily. Nonetheless, he marched out against them with his companions, whose corruption is again noted, and ultimately lost both the battle and his life (311–343). When Heraclius received the news about the Byzantines' defeat, he returned from Antioch to Constantinople after having bid farewell to Syria (343–346). The narrative continues to describe a conflict between al-Ashtar and Maysara b. Masrūq, two Muslim commanders who were sent north again. During his march, Maysara conquered Qinnasrīn and its hinterland but was ordered by Abū ʿUbayda to return before he was able to attack Antioch (346–351). Abū ʿUbayda appointed commanders over Ḥimṣ and Damascus and turned with the Muslims towards Jerusalem (352–354), the conquest of which is narrated next (355–366). The narration, however, is interrupted by a short story about a Muslim, called Mukhaymis, who claimed that he entered Paradise and brought two leaves from there to his companions (356–357). The inhabitants of Jerusalem requested that the caliph ʿUmar should grant them a peace treaty. Thus, ʿUmar left Medina, travelled to Syria and made his famous speech at al-Jābiya (362–365). After having granted the peace treaty, ʿUmar stayed in the Muslims' encampment near Jerusalem for some days, during which he decided a legal case concerning cooked, non-alcoholic juice, visited all the commanders and decreed a monthly livelihood for every Muslim (367–370). Before ʿUmar's return, Kaʿb b. Ḥabr's conversion from Judaism to the new faith is narrated (370–374). In the course of his journey back to Medina, ʿUmar decided more cases that have a legal dimension: one case about a man who was living with two sisters, one about some negligent taxpayers who had to stand in the sun and one about two men who shared the same wife in their daily life (375–378). The narrative then turns back to Abū ʿUbayda, whose death from the plague is described. In addition to Abū ʿUbayda's death, the deaths of ʿAbd al-Raḥmān b. Muʿādh b. Jabal and his father are narrated. Interestingly, Khālid b. al-Walīd's, ʿAmr b. al-ʿĀṣ's and Shuraḥbīl b. Ḥasana's deaths are not mentioned. Having succeeded Abū ʿUbayda in commanding the Muslims, Muʿādh b. Jabal appointed ʿAmr b. al-ʿĀṣ as his successor, while ʿUmar appointed several other people in command of the various districts and cities of Syria (379–388). Two exhortatory speeches are narrated (one by ʿUbāda b. al-Ṣāmit; the other by Abū al-Dardāʾ) (388–390) before mentioning the appointment of Yazīd b. Abī Sufyān and the subsequent conquest of Caesarea (390–401). Another conflict between two commanders, Ḥabīb b. Maslama and al-Ḍaḥḥāk b. Qays, occurred (392–396) after which Yazīd handed over the command of the troops shortly before the conquest of Caesarea to his brother Muʿāwiya b. Abī Sufyān, who finally conquered the city (399). The narrative ends with the statement

> The Muslims rejoiced over that [conquest] greatly and no enemy of them was left, either in the farthest or in the nearest parts of Syria. [Hence,] God had expelled the Polytheists from it and Syria as a whole had fallen into the hands of the Muslims,

followed by two short letters, a description of Yazīd's death and a brief summary of Muʿāwiya's (further) rule over Syria (399–403).

As this summary clearly shows, al-Azdī's *Futūḥ al-Shām* is a typical work of Muslim *akhbār* historiography. It is composed of a religiously loaded language and many traditions (*khabar*, pl. *akhbār*) that are often introduced by a chain of transmitters (*isnād*) in which the scholars who had presumably passed down the attached text are listed. Another typical feature of this genre is that the narrative depicts the events through actions and speeches of a limited number of collective actors and leading figures.[2] For example, among the Muslims who figure prominently are the caliphs Abū Bakr and 'Umar and the military commanders Abū 'Ubayda b. al-Jarrāḥ, Khālid b. al-Walīd and Yazīd b. Abī Sufyān. Among the prominent Byzantines are the Emperor Heraclius and his chief commander Bāhān. All these persons often deliver speeches in the *Futūḥ al-Shām* and correspond with others by exchange of numerous letters. Hence, speeches and letters appear as distinctive features of the narrative as well as of the whole genre.

2 For a quantitative analysis of collective and individual actors in al-Azdī's *Futūḥ al-Shām*, see Scheiner, *Scholars, Figures, and Groups*.

2 The compiler-author and his work

The compiler-author

Concerning the compiler-author of the work, there is no entry (*tarjama*) in any biographical dictionary that unambiguously refers to Abū Ismāʿīl Muḥammad b. ʿAbdallāh al-Azdī al-Baṣrī. Al-Azdī's full name, as presented here, is found in the extant manuscripts of the *Futūḥ al-Shām*. In other Arabic sources, our compiler-author is often mentioned as "Abū Ismāʿīl", "Abū Ismāʿīl al-Azdī" or "al-Azdī".[1] In this introduction, his full name is shortened to "al-Azdī".

Compared to his name, we have even less information about al-Azdī's *floruit*, because no year is mentioned for any event of his life in any Arabic source. Hence, some scholars presented arguments for what they regarded as al-Azdī's date of death, while other scholars simply picked a particular date without arguing for it. The most controversial argumentation was presented by Michaël de Goeje (1864), who quite unspecifically dated al-Azdī's *Futūḥ al-Shām* to "the time of the crusades", which has to be understood as the period between 1099 and 1291 C.E. (or between 429 and 690 A.H.).[2] He did so due to textual features within the work and on the basis of his comparison of the work with Ibn Ḥubaysh's (d. 584/1188–1189) *Kitāb al-ghazawāt*.[3] Emmanuel Sivan (1968) and Lawrence Conrad (1987) questioned this argumentation by giving some counterarguments.[4] However, it was Ella Landau-Tasseron (2000) who was able to completely refute de Goeje's theory in her study on the manuscript titled *Al-durr al-nafīs* ("*The Precious Pearls*"), in which she proved that a large part of the *Futūḥ al-Shām* was quoted by ʿUmar al-Ṭalamankī (d. 429/1037) in al-Andalus and was thus extant in the early 5th/11th century, i.e. before the Crusades (at the latest).[5]

1 See, for example, Ibn Ḥajar, *Al-iṣāba. Ed. al-Baghawī*, I, 282 (no. 8383); Ibn Ḥubaysh, *Ghazawāt. Ed. Zakkār*, I, 195, l. 2; Ibn al-ʿAdīm, *Bughyat al-ṭalab*, I, 69, l. 12–70, l. 3.

2 Henceforth, dates are given in both the Hijra- and Common Era datings in the format 429 [A.H.]/1099 [C.E.], except for publication dates or death dates of modern scholars.

3 See de Goeje, *Mémoire sur le Fotouho's-Scham* and 38–39 (for the quotation).

4 See Sivan, *L'Islam*; Conrad, *al-Azdī's History*.

5 See Landau-Tasseron, *New Data*.

The oldest argumentation for al-Azdī's date of death was provided by William Nassau Lees (1854), who studied the biographical information of (some of) al-Azdī's informants mentioned in the *Futūḥ al-Shām*'s *isnāds*. On this basis, he concluded that al-Azdī flourished in the middle of the 2nd/8th century and died "about A.H. 178 [794–795 C.E.]" or some years earlier.[6] The suggested date of death is an educated guess and it is quite unspecific. However, several later scholars adopted Lees's method, presenting more precise dates on the basis of al-Azdī's informants in the *isnāds*: For example, Akram al-ʿUmarī (1983) suggested the "final decades of the 2nd century", probably 180–200/796–815; Suleiman Mourad (2000) went for "around 190/806", i.e. perhaps 185–195/801–811, while ʿIṣām ʿUqla and Yūsuf Banī Yāsīn (2004) stated that al-Azdī died "within the years 170–175/786–791".[7] In short, on the basis of the *isnāds*, al-Azdī's date of death was placed between 170–200/786–815, i.e. in the early ʿAbbāsid period, by Lees, al-ʿUmarī, Mourad and ʿUqla and Banī Yāsīn.

A similar conclusion was reached by Muḥammad Kurd ʿAlī (1945) and Lawrence Conrad (1987) who based their arguments on the text of the *Futūḥ al-Shām*. Kurd ʿAlī accepted Lees's suggested date, which he supported with the argument that the work's literary style agrees with it.[8] Conrad, instead, focused on several textual elements and motifs in the *Futūḥ al-Shām* (e.g. the usage of the toponyms Bayt al-Maqdis and Dayr Khālid, the quotation of six prophetical *ḥadīths*, the inherent stress on *ijmāʿ* [consensus] and the opposition to Qadarī positions) and came to the conclusion that al-Azdī died between "190–205/805–820" or in "the late 2nd/early 3rd centuries".[9] Conrad's argumentation convinced several scholars and thus Walter Kaegi (1992), Josef van Ess (2001), Nancy Khalek (2010/2011) and—with some hesitation—Boaz Shoshan (2016) accepted it in their own studies.[10]

Jens Scheiner (2007) presented the period "around 210/825–826", i.e. ca. 205–215/820–830, as the death date on the basis of possible biographical information on al-Azdī's father, while ʿAbd al-Munʿim ʿĀmir (1970) suggested that al-Azdī "appeared" in the middle of the 2nd/8th century and died in 231/845–846.[11] Furthermore, Ṣāliḥ Darādaka (2008) mentioned the year

6 See al-Azdī, *Futūḥ al-Shām. Ed. Lees*, IV–V (Preface) and V (for the quotation).

7 See al-ʿUmarī, *al-Azdī wa-kitābuhū*, 69; Mourad, *al-Azdī*, 593; al-Azdī, *Futūḥ al-Shām. Ed. ʿUqla/Banī Yāsīn*, 15–16; Mourad's dating was later adopted by Mohammad Rihan (2014) (see Rihan, *Politics and Culture*, 177, n. 63; 74).

8 See Kurd ʿAlī, *Futūḥ al-Shām*, 544.

9 See Conrad, *al-Azdī's History*, 58 and 39–42 (for the quotations).

10 See Kaegi, *Byzantium*, 10–11 (Kaegi, however, did not correctly quote Conrad, who dated the work to the late 2nd/8th or early 3rd/9th century); van Ess, *Fehltritt*, 137, n. 113; Khalek, *Tall and Slender*, 111 (Khalek never explicitly mentioned a death date of al-Azdī, but accepted Conrad's conclusions, with which she was "inclined to agree" [see ibid., 111, n. 23]. She was clearer in her monograph, where she called al-Azdī's *Futūḥ al-Shām* "a late eighth- or early ninth-century text" [see Khalek, *Damascus*, 12]); Shoshan, *Historical Tradition*, 9.

11 See Scheiner, *Grundlegendes*, 12; al-Azdī, *Futūḥ al-Shām. Ed. ʿĀmir*, ك.

237/851 in this context without providing a source.[12] ʿĀmir's dating, however, was refuted by al-ʿUmarī (1983), who pointed out that it was taken from another scholar's *tarjama*.[13] Without arguing for it or specifying why, other scholars suggested the 2nd/8th century (Daniel Haneberg [1860], ʿUmar Kaḥḥāla [1960], Landau-Tasseron [2000]) or the 3rd/9th century (Aloys Sprenger [1857], Sivan [1968]) as al-Azdī's *floruit*.[14] However, most of these suggestions are unreliable, because they are too broad and not supported with any argument.

In conclusion, there seems to be a fairly widespread consensus among scholars that al-Azdī died within a period of approximately forty years, i.e. between ca. 170–210/786–825. Although this period is quite broad, it represents the sum of all efforts exerted to contextualise al-Azdī as a scholar historically. Furthermore, it is based on evidence from the *isnāds*, from the text of the *Futūḥ al-Shām* and from biographical dictionaries. In other words, on the basis of what we know (at this point), al-Azdī died sometime in the 2nd half of the 2nd/8th or at the beginning of the 3rd/9th centuries.

Given his position as a compiler-author of the early ʿAbbāsid period, there exist two argumentations for the geographic provenance of al-Azdī (and the *Futūḥ al-Shām*). Although these are two different points—a compiler-author can come from one region and compose his work after travelling in pursuit of knowledge in another—both issues are mixed in these theories. The first argument was presented by Conrad (1987), who stated that al-Azdī was Syrian (hence, his *nisba* al-Azdī which refers to the tribe of al-Azd that settled there) and that he utilised Syrian, particularly Ḥimṣī, sources for his *Futūḥ al-Shām*.[15] Van Ess (2001), Khalek (2010) and Shoshan (2016) found this argumentation convincing and followed it.[16] The second argument was presented by Mourad (2000) after Kaegi (1992) had made a brief comment in this regard.[17] According to Mourad, al-Azdī originated from Iraq (hence, his second *nisba* al-Baṣrī) and made use of Iraqi, in particular Kūfan, sources. Having evaluated the individual arguments of the two scholars, we do not find either argument completely convincing. On the one hand, *pace* Conrad Ḥimṣ is only one of the cities highlighted in the work (the others are Damascus and Jerusalem) while, on the other hand, al-Azdī's informants can be associated with various regions of the Islamicate world (not only Iraq, i.e. al-Kūfa and al-Baṣra, but also Syria and al-Ḥijāz). Therefore, we think it is best to leave the question unsettled until further evidence is brought into the debate.

12 See Darādaka, *Fatḥ Dimashq*, 8.

13 See al-ʿUmarī, *al-Azdī wa-kitābuhū*, 71–72. Unaware of al-ʿUmarī's refutation, Muḥyī al-Dīn Lāgha (2011) accepted it (see Lāgha, *Baḥth*, 2; 20).

14 See Haneberg, *Erörterungen*, 133; Kaḥḥāla, *Muʿjam al-muʾallifīn*, X, 199; Landau-Tasseron, *New Data*, 373; Sprenger, *Catalogue*, 3 (no. 31); Sivan, *L'Islam*, 197.

15 See Conrad, *al-Azdī's History*, 49–55.

16 See van Ess, *Fehltritt*, 349; Khalek, *Tall and Slender*, 111; Shoshan, *Historical Tradition*, 57.

17 See Mourad, *al-Azdī*, 591; Kaegi, *Byzantium*, 104.

The title

The title of the work under consideration here is less disputed than the compiler-author, but some variants still exist. In principle, there are four different titles that have been used in the secondary literature so far. The first is *Futūḥ al-Shām* ("The Conquests of Syria"). This title is found in some of the manuscripts and was used by Sprenger (1857) and de Goeje (1864). It is an abbreviated version of the second title: *Kitāb futūḥ al-Shām* ("The Book on the Conquests of Syria"). Lees introduced this title (in 1854) when he published the *editio princeps*.[18] The matter of adding or deleting the word *kitāb* ("book") in book titles occurs quite often in Arabic and secondary literature. Thus, we find this extended title in another manuscript as well. It was also adopted in the latest edition prepared by ʿUqla and Banī Yāsīn (2004).[19] In sum, it makes only a small difference whether one calls the work *Futūḥ al-Shām* or *Kitāb futūḥ al-Shām*.

The third title that was quite often used for the work, for example, by Baron Mac Guckin de Slane (1874), Carl Brockelmann (1937), Georges Vajda (1953/1956), Fuat Sezgin (1967) and Yvette Sauvan and Marie-Geneviève Balty-Guesdon (1995), reads *Mukhtaṣar futūḥ al-Shām* ("The Abridgement of [the Book on] the Conquests of Syria").[20] This title is found only in one manuscript (from Paris) and hence was used by all the scholars who studied this manuscript. However, it is a later addition to one of the title sheets and insinuates an intertextual relationship to the more extensive *Futūḥ al-Shām* ascribed to another scholar, i.e. al-Wāqidī. In addition, it does not represent the original title of the work, which is (*Kitāb*) *Futūḥ al-Shām* and which is also present in that manuscript. Therefore, the title *Mukhtaṣar futūḥ al-Shām* should be discarded and no longer used.

The fourth (potential) title of the work was introduced by ʿĀmir (1970) in the second edition and used later by Kaegi (1992) and Nadia El Cheikh (2004), all of whom relied on the former's edition.[21] It reads "*Taʾrīkh futūḥ al-Shām*" ("The History of the Conquests of Syria") and is not found in any extant manuscript. Although it nicely describes the content of the work, this title should be discarded, as well, because it seems to be an invention by the mentioned editor.

This leaves us with *Futūḥ al-Shām* or its prolonged form *Kitāb futūḥ al-Shām*. For reasons of brevity and because it is currently the most widely used form, we decided on *Futūḥ al-Shām* in this publication.

18 See al-Azdī, *Futūḥ al-Shām. Ed. Lees*, title sheet.

19 See al-Azdī, *Futūḥ al-Shām. Ed. ʿUqla/Banī Yāsīn*, title sheet.

20 See de Slane, *Catalogue*, 310–311; Brockelmann, *Geschichte. Supplement*, I, 208; Vajda, *Index*, 495 and idem, *Les certificats*, 27; Sezgin, *Geschichte*, I, 292–293; Sauvan/Balty-Guesdon, *Catalogue*, V, 224–227 (1664–1665).

21 See al-Azdī, *Futūḥ al-Shām. Ed. ʿĀmir*, title sheet; Kaegi, *Byzantium*, 10, n. 25; El Cheikh, *Byzantium*, 18, n. 12.

The audience

The question of the audience for which the *Futūḥ al-Shām* was written was not considered in previous studies. Unfortunately, the work includes no direct indications in this regard. Hence, we are left only with hypotheses. The *Futūḥ al-Shām* narrates a success story—a story of spectacular military as well as spiritual achievements. Accordingly, God guided and supported the Muslims in triumphing over the powerful but religiously and socially corrupt Byzantines. Islam—as defined in the *Futūḥ al-Shām*—emerges triumphant over the other religions, particularly Christianity (which is treated in very general terms in the work). This is clear in some Christians' (and Jews) conversions to the conquerors' faith, as described in the *Futūḥ al-Shām*, as well as in the military and legal subjugation of the adherents of the former religions. The narration is suffused with religious, and in particular qur'ānic, terms and concepts. From all this, we can infer that the work was directed towards a Muslim audience that shared the ideas and concepts presented therein and that would have reacted positively to this narrative. It is not clear whether the *Futūḥ al-Shām* was compiled for Muslim scholars alone or for a wider audience for religious purposes, as the chain of transmission (*riwāya*) in one of the manuscripts implies. On the one hand, only scholars, with their proficient knowledge of classical Arabic, could have understood some of the phrases contained in the text. Other stories, on the other hand, are easy to comprehend and appeal to any listener. In any case, the narrative is a vivid account that has attracted the attention of many individuals and is a fascinating text for 21st-century readers (or listeners) of any religious denomination.

The manuscripts

Although we face an absence of biographical evidence for the 2nd/8th- or early 3rd/9th-century scholar known as Abū Ismāʿīl Muḥammad b. ʿAbdallāh al-Azdī al-Baṣrī and his work titled *Futūḥ al-Shām*, the three extant manuscripts do provide a certain amount of information.[22] They include not only the name of the compiler-author and his work, on both the title and the last pages, but mention al-Azdī in the several manuscripts' chains of transmission (*riwāyas*) and in the many chains of transmitters (*isnāds*) throughout the text. Apart from this, the earliest external, i.e. non-manuscript, evidence for al-Azdī's name and work is found in Ibn Khayr al-Ishbīlī's (d. 575/1179) *Fahrasa*.[23]

The oldest extant manuscript is Paris ms 1664, which was described by Baron de Slane (1874), Brockelmann (1937), Vajda (1953/1956), Sezgin (1967), Sauvan/Balty-Guesdon (1995), Mourad (2000) and ʿUqla/Banī Yāsīn (2004).[24] According to its colophon, it was copied in Jerusalem by

22 There seems to be a fourth extant manuscript in Istanbul which I am trying to get hold of.

23 See al-Ishbīlī, *Fahrasa. Ed. Codera/Tarrago*, 238, l. 1–5.

24 See de Slane, *Catalogue*, 310–311; Brockelmann, *Geschichte. Supplement*, I, 208; Vajda, *Index*, 495 and idem, *Les certificats*, 27; Sezgin, *Geschichte*, I, 719; Sauvan/Balty-Guesdon,

Muḥammad b. Ibrāhīm al-Ghassānī (n.d.) and dates back to 22 Dhū al-Ḥijja 613/2 April 1217. This complete manuscript is divided into six parts (*juz'*) and includes three reading certificates (*samā'*) that document its transmission in the 7th/13th and possibly (but improbably) the 9th/15th century. It was obtained by Johann Michael Wansleben (1635–1679) in Cairo between 1671 and 1673 and is preserved today in the *Bibiothèque Nationale* in Paris. Paris ms 1664 forms the basis of the 'Uqla/Banī Yāsīn edition of the *Futūḥ al-Shām* and accordingly of the present translation.

The second extant manuscript is the "Kāle-Sprenger-manuscript"/Berlin ms 9767 that was described by Lees (1854) and Wilhelm Ahlwardt (1897) and that is several decades younger than Paris ms 1664.[25] Lees stated that the manuscript was "fully 600 years old" and hence dated it back to ca. the 650s/1250s. Ahlwardt falsely ascribed this almost complete manuscript to al-Wāqidī and dated it, without providing any argument but most likely on the basis of codicological grounds, to "ca. 700/1300" which is some decade later than Lee's proposed date. According to a date found in one of its *riwāyas* (other *riwāyas* are not preserved therein), the manuscript was transmitted in Alexandria in Muḥarram 573/June–July 1177 from Abū Ṭāhir al-Silafī (d. 576/1180) to his disciples, who might have lived until the mid-7th/13th century. Aloys Sprenger obtained the manuscript from "Shāh Kālè" in Delhi in 1850 (hence, the name), brought it to Europe and sold it to the Prussian King Frederick William IV's library. It is thus preserved today in the *Staatsbibliothek* in Berlin. The "Kāle-Sprenger-manuscript"/Berlin ms 9767 forms the basis for the Lees edition of the *Futūḥ al-Shām*.

The third and most recent manuscript is Paris ms 1665, which was described by Baron de Slane (1874), Brockelmann (1937), Sezgin (1967), Sauvan/Balty-Guesdon (1995), Mourad (2000) and 'Uqla/Banī Yāsīn (2004).[26] According to its colophon, it was copied in Dhū al-Qa'da 764/September 1363. This incomplete manuscript is also divided into several parts that correspond to those mentioned in Paris ms 1664. It also includes two ownership notes that document its transmission through the 10th/16th and 11th/17th centuries. According to a date found in one of its *riwāyas*, the manuscript was transmitted on Saturday, 14 Ramaḍān 635/1 May 1238 by one of al-Silafī's disciples, Jamāl al-Dīn Abū al-Faḍl Yūsuf al-Muḥāmilī, in his teaching sessions (*majālis*) in Cairo to his own disciples. The manuscript was then obtained by Gilbert Gaulmin (1585–1665) in Cairo between 1623 and 1665 and is preserved today in the *Bibliothèque Nationale* in Paris. Paris ms 1665 was consulted by 'Uqla and Banī Yāsīn as a second source of their edition of the *Futūḥ al-Shām*.

Catalogue, V, 224–227 (1664–1665); Mourad, *al-Azdī*, 578; al-Azdī, *Futūḥ al-Shām. Ed. 'Uqla/Banī Yāsīn*, 69–74.

25 See al-Azdī, *Futūḥ al-Shām. Ed. Lees*, IIIff. (Preface); Ahlwardt, *Katalog*, IX, 272.

26 See de Slane, *Catalogue*, 310–311; Brockelmann, *Geschichte. Supplement*, I, 208; Sezgin, *Geschichte*, I, 719; Sauvan/Balty-Guesdon, *Catalogue*, V, 224–227 (1664–1665); Mourad, *al-Azdī*, 578; al-Azdī, *Futūḥ al-Shām. Ed. 'Uqla/Banī Yāsīn*, 69–74.

A special case is the alleged Damascus manuscript that was described by ʿĀmir (1970).[27] It was written in the 6th/12th century and included an ownership note and a reading certificate (*samāʿ*) that documented its transmission in Alexandria in the last decades of the 6th/12th century. ʿĀmir claimed to have found the manuscript in Damascus in 1958 in a "special library". However, today the manuscript is lost (or has never existed, as several modern scholars assume). According to ʿĀmir alone, it forms the basis of his edition of the *Futūḥ al-Shām*.

In conclusion, apart from the Damascus manuscript, all extant manuscripts of the *Futūḥ al-Shām* date back to the 7th/13th and 8th/14th centuries. They were obtained from Cairo or Delhi and are said to have been transmitted in Syria (Jerusalem) and Egypt (Alexandria and Cairo). All manuscripts were transmitted by disciples of al-Silafī (d. 576/1180) according to their *riwāyas*: In Paris ms 1664, Abū al-Faḍl Jaʿfar b. ʿAlī al-Hamadhānī al-Iskandarānī (d. 636/1238) is mentioned as the disciple who transmitted the work to Nūr al-Dīn ʿAlī b. Masʿūd al-Mawṣilī al-Dimashqī (d. 704/1304), while in Paris ms 1665, the disciple is Abū al-Maymūn ʿAbd al-Wahhāb b. ʿAtīq al-Miṣrī (d. 626/1229). In the "Kāle-Sprenger-manuscript"/Berlin ms 9767, no name is provided, but from the formula *akhbaranā* (lit. "he reported to us"), one can deduce that al-Silafī had read his manuscript to a group of scholars ("us"), as well. In addition, from Ibn al-ʿAdīm's chain of transmitters, which can be interpreted as a *riwāya* of a *Futūḥ al-Shām* manuscript, one can deduce another disciple of al-Silafī's, i.e. Abū ʿAlī Ḥasan b. Aḥmad b. Yūsuf al-Ṣūfī al-Awqī (d. 630/1232), who transmitted the work to Ibn al-ʿAdīm (d. 660/1261).[28] Hence, we know by name three of al-Silafī's disciples who were responsible for distributing the *Futūḥ al-Shām* in the 7th/13th and 8th/14th centuries. Furthermore, according to the *riwāyas*, al-Silafī was directly responsible for the transmission of all extant manuscripts. Hence, the *riwāyas* point to the central role this *ḥadīth* scholar played in the transmission history of this work in the early Crusades period. It is, therefore, not too farfetched to suggest that al-Silafī was the most important scholar who promoted a *futūḥ* work on the expansion in Syria in the name of the late 2nd/8th- or early 3rd/9th-century scholar al-Azdī.[29]

In addition to their *riwāyas*, all manuscripts show a high degree of similarity in their texts and share most of the *isnāds*. This has led several previous scholars to put forward hypotheses about relationships between the manuscripts: ʿĀmir (1970), for example, argued for a close textual relationship between the "Kāle-Sprenger-manuscript"/Berlin ms 9767 and the alleged Damascus manuscript.[30] Stephen Humphreys (2001) hypothesised, in our eyes convincingly, that Paris ms 1664 and Paris ms 1665 were related recen-

27 See al-Azdī, *Futūḥ al-Shām. Ed. ʿĀmir*, ن–ل.

28 This chain is found in Ibn al-ʿAdīm, *Bughyat al-ṭalab*, I, 69, l. 12–17; 569, l. 2–8; 572, l. 15–22; III, 1336, l. 14–1337, l. 6; VII, 3150, l. 7–16.

29 For a similar assessment, see Mourad, *al-Azdī*, 582.

30 See al-Azdī, *Futūḥ al-Shām. Ed. ʿĀmir*, ن–م.

sions and that the "Kāle-Sprenger-manuscript"/Berlin ms 9767 and Paris ms 1665 could be related, as well.[31] Although only a more detailed study of all extant manuscripts can provide better evidence for these hypotheses, what has become clear thus far is that all known manuscripts of al-Azdī's *Futūḥ al-Shām* (even if we accept ʿĀmir's claim regarding the Damascus manuscript) belong to one family. Undoubtedly, Paris ms 1664 is the oldest copy, while the "Kāle-Sprenger-manuscript"/Berlin ms 9767 comes next and Paris ms 1665 is the most recent.

The chains of transmission (*riwāyas*)

Regarding the chains of transmission (*riwāyas*), which have been frequently mentioned thus far, we will take a closer look at these texts in this section. Chains of transmission are included in all three extant manuscripts as well as in some other Arabic bio-bibliographical works. They represent a continuous list of names that begins with a scholar in the 7th/13th or 8th/14th and ends with al-Azdī's name. These chains, which are mentioned either at the beginning of the manuscripts or at the beginning of the various parts of the manuscripts, claim to document the transmission of the text (or section) that follows. Hence, they have to be distinguished from other chains of names that are attached to individual traditions, so-called *isnāds* ("chains of transmitters"). In other words, the first scholar mentioned in these chains claims to have received either a physical copy of the manuscript or—more often—a permission (*ijāza*) from the aforementioned scholar to transmit the manuscript to his own disciples. In contrast, the final scholar in the chain is usually assumed to be the compiler-author of the work, the title of which is also sometimes mentioned within the chains. Accordingly, al-Azdī, as the last person mentioned in these chains of transmission, must be (and, in fact, often was) considered as the compiler-author of the *Futūḥ al-Shām*. Moreover, the *riwāyas* also provide conclusions about the transmission history of the manuscript, because they sometimes include information about the social context of the transmission (e.g. dates, places or sessions of the transmission), in addition to the names of the scholars who are said to have transmitted the manuscript. In this sense, *riwāyas* form a special source of social and educational history; therefore, the known *riwāyas* of the *Futūḥ al-Shām* will be presented here in detail.

The *riwāya* of the oldest manuscript, i.e. Paris ms 1664, reads:

> Nūr al-Dīn Abū al-Ḥasan ʿAlī b. Masʿūd [b. Nafīs] al-Mawṣilī [al-Ḥanbalī al-Dimashqī] (d. 704/1304), **the owner of the manuscript** > Abū al-Faḍl Jaʿfar b. ʿAlī [b. Hibat Allāh] al-Hamadhānī [al-Iskandarānī] (d. 636/1238) > Abū Ṭāhir Aḥmad b. Muḥammad al-Silafī (d. 576/1180) > Abū al-Ḥusayn Aḥmad b. Muḥammad b. Musbiḥ al-Muqriʾ (n.d.) > Abū

31 See Humphreys, *Notes*, seventh and eighth paragraphs.

> Isḥāq Ibrāhīm b. Saʿīd b. ʿAbdallāh [al-Tujībī al-Ḥabbāl] (d. 482/1089) > Abū al-ʿAbbās Munīr b. Aḥmad b. al-Ḥasan al-Khashshāb (d. 412/1021) > Abū al-Ḥasan ʿAlī b. Aḥmad b. Isḥāq al-Baghdādī (d. 340/951) > Abū al-ʿAbbās al-Walīd b. Ḥammād al-Ramlī (d. ca. 300/912) > al-Ḥusayn b. Ziyād al-Ramlī (n.d.) > Abū Ismāʿīl Muḥammad b. ʿAbdallāh al-Azdī al-Baṣrī (d. between 170–210/786–825).

This *riwāya* is found on the title sheet of the manuscript and includes little additional information about the manuscript's transmission except its final owner.[32] Within Paris ms 1664, however, the *riwāya* is mentioned four more times at the beginnings of parts one, two, three and four.[33] In these cases, the *riwāya* is similar to the first one but a bit shorter. It begins with the fifth transmitter:

> Abū Isḥāq Ibrāhīm b. Saʿīd b. ʿAbdallāh [al-Tujībī] al-Ḥabbāl (d. 482/1089) > Abū al-ʿAbbās Munīr b. Aḥmad b. al-Ḥasan al-Khashshāb (d. 412/1021) **by way of reading to the former while I was listening** > Abū al-Ḥasan ʿAlī b. Aḥmad b. Isḥāq al-Baghdādī (d. 340/951) **by way of reading to the former**[34] > Abū al-ʿAbbās al-Walīd b. Ḥammād al-Ramlī (d. ca. 300/912) > al-Ḥusayn b. Ziyād al-Ramlī (n.d.) > Abū Ismāʿīl Muḥammad b. ʿAbdallāh al-Azdī al-Baṣrī (d. between 170–210/786–825).

In the abbreviated versions of the *riwāya*, the mode of transmission is mentioned: "By way of reading" (*qirāʾatan*), which refers to the usual manner in which manuscripts were transmitted (i.e. aural transmission). In addition, these versions all start with the scholar Abū Isḥāq Ibrāhīm b. Saʿīd al-Ḥabbāl (d. 482/1089), who seems to have played an important role in the transmission of the manuscript. Presumably, he had a fixed text of the *Futūḥ al-Shām* at hand, which he transmitted in a full version to his student(s). If this assumption is true then the whole narrative of the *Futūḥ al-Shām* was established during Abū Isḥāq al-Ḥabbāl's life time (at the latest), which was a century before al-Silafī (d. 576/1180) transmitted his version and some fifty years after al-Ṭalamankī (d. 429/1037) made large extractions of the *Futūḥ al-Shām* for one of his historical works (that was later preserved in the *Al-durr al-nafīs* manuscript).

The *riwāya* of the second oldest manuscript, i.e. "Kāle-Sprenger-manuscript"/Berlin ms 9767, reads:

> Abū Ṭāhir Aḥmad b. Muḥammad b. Aḥmad b. Aḥmad b. Ibrāhīm al-Silafī al-Iṣfahānī (d. 576/1180) **in the port of Alexandria in Muḥarram 573/June-July 1177** > Abū al-Ḥusayn Aḥmad b. Muḥammad b. Musabbaḥ

32 See al-Azdī, *Futūḥ al-Shām. Ed. ʿUqla/Banī Yāsīn*, 75.

33 See al-Azdī, *Futūḥ al-Shām. Ed. ʿUqla/Banī Yāsīn*, 77, 126, 177, 227.

34 One variant reads: "By way of reading to the former from his book *in his house*". See al-Azdī, *Futūḥ al-Shām. Ed. ʿUqla/Banī Yāsīn*, 227.

[read: Musbiḥ] al-Muqri' (n.d.) **in Fusṭāṭ Miṣr in Dhū al-Ḥijja 515/ February-March 1122** > Abū Isḥāq Ibrāhīm b. Sa'īd b. 'Abdallāh al-Yaḥtī [read: Al-Tujībī] [al-Ḥabbāl] (d. 482/1089) > Abū al-'Abbās Munīr b. Aḥmad b. al-Ḥasan b. 'Alī b. Munīr al-Ḥashshāb [read: al-Khashshāb] (d. 412/1021) > Abū al-Ḥasan 'Alī b. Aḥmad b. 'Alī [read: Isḥāq] al-Baghdādī (d. 340/951) > Abū al-'Abbās al-Walīd b. Ḥammād al-Ramlī (d. ca. 300/912) > al-Ḥusayn b. Ziyād al-Ramlī (n.d.) > Abū Ismā'īl Muḥammad b. 'Abdallāh al-Azdī al-Baṣrī (d. between 170–210/786–825).

This *riwāya* is found only once and is not placed at the beginning of the text (as in the Paris ms 1664) but on page 35, where the second part (*juz'*) of the manuscript begins.[35] It includes two comments on the transmission history of the text.[36] Accordingly, it was read in the two religiously most important months, i.e. *Dhū al-Ḥijja* and *Muḥarram*, in Old Cairo and Alexandria in the 6th/12th century. Hence, we can deduce from this *riwāya* that the *Futūḥ al-Shām* was (publicly) read as part of religious celebrations in 6th/12th-century Egypt. This means that a complete text had to be available to Abū al-Ḥusayn al-Muqri' (n.d.) in 1122, who lived one generation after Abū Isḥāq al-Ḥabbāl.

A third *riwāya* from the 8th/14th century is found in Paris ms 1665. It is particularly interesting, because several dates and places of transmission of the text are mentioned therein. The *riwāya* reads:

> Jamāl al-Dīn Abū al-Faḍl Yūsuf b. 'Abd al-Mu'ṭī b. Manṣūr b. Najā al-Muḥāmilī (d. 642/1244) **by way of listening to the former in al-Qāhira** > [Abū al-Maymūn] 'Abd al-Wahhāb b. 'Atīq b. Wardān [al-'Āmir al-Miṣrī] (d. 626/1228) **in the latter's sessions on Saturday 14th Ramaḍān 635/1st May 1238** > Abū Ṭāhir Aḥmad b. Muḥammad b. Aḥmad b. Muḥammad b. Ibrāhīm b. Silafa al-Silafī al-Iṣfahānī (d. 576/1180) **by way of listening to the former in the latter's sessions in Alexandria on Sunday 14th Rabī' I 574/10th August 1178** > Abū al-Ḥasan [read: Abū al-Ḥusayn] Aḥmad b. Muḥammad b. Musbiḥ al-Muqri' (n.d.) **in Fusṭāṭ Miṣr** > Abū Isḥāq Ibrāhīm b. Sa'īd b. 'Abdallāh al-Nu'mānī al-Tujībī al-Ḥabbāl (d. 482/1089) **in Fusṭāṭ Miṣr** > Abū al-'Abbās Munīr b. Aḥmad b. al-Ḥasan b. 'Alī b. Munīr al-Khashshāb (d. 412/1021) > Abū al-Ḥasan 'Alī b. Aḥmad b. Isḥāq b. Ibrāhīm al-Baghdādī (d. 340/951) **by way of reading to the former while I was listening from his book in his house in [3]43/954-955**[37] > Abū al-'Abbās al-Walīd b. Ḥammād al-Ramlī (d. ca. 300/912) **literally in Sha'bān 286/August 899** > Abū Ismā'īl Muḥammad b. 'Abdallāh al-Azdī al-Baṣrī (d. between 170–210/786–825).

35 The other parts of the "Kāle-Sprenger-manuscript"/Berlin ms 9767 are indicated neither by particular phrases nor by the repetition of the *riwāya*.

36 See al-Azdī, *Futūḥ al-Shām. Ed. Lees*, 35, n. 4.

37 This date contradicts al-Baghdādī's (d. 340/951) date of death and, therefore, seems to be wrong.

This *riwāya* is found at the beginning of the incomplete and latest manuscript of the *Futūḥ al-Shām*.[38] It includes most comments on the transmission history of the text and was, therefore, used as a source by Mourad.[39] According to this *riwāya*, the manuscript was continuously transmitted from the 3rd/9th to the 7th/13th centuries in Egypt (particularly in Old Cairo, Alexandria and Mamluk Cairo).

Within Paris ms 1665, however, other versions of the *riwāya* are mentioned three more times in the place where parts two, three and four of Paris ms 1664 begin.[40] However, the new parts are not marked by special phrases, but only by the *riwāya* alone. In these three cases, the *riwāya* takes another form, which reads:

> Abū ʿAbdallāh Muḥammad b. Ḥamd b. Ḥāmid [al-Iṣfahānī] (n.d.) > Abū al-Ḥasan [ʿAlī b. al-Ḥusayn b.] al-Farāʾ [al-Mawṣilī] (d. 519/1125) **by way of writing (*kitābatan*)** > Abū Isḥāq [Ibrāhīm b. Saʿīd b. ʿAbdallāh] al-Ḥabbāl (d. 482/1089) > Abū al-ʿAbbās Munīr b. Aḥmad [al-Khashshāb] (d. 412/1021) > Abū al-Ḥasan ʿAlī b. Aḥmad b. Isḥāq al-Baghdādī (d. 340/951) **by way of reading to the former while I was listening** > Abū al-ʿAbbās al-Walīd b. Ḥammād al-Ramlī (d. ca. 300/912) > Abū Ismāʿīl Muḥammad b. ʿAbdallāh [al-Azdī al-Baṣrī] (d. between 170–210/786–825).

Apart from the information about the written transmission of the work, this *riwāya* includes two peculiarities. First, al-Ḥusayn b. Ziyād al-Ramlī, i.e. al-Azdī's usual disciple, is mentioned in only one of the three cases; he is also missing in the *riwāya* at the beginning of the manuscript.[41] We are not sure whether the dropping of al-Ḥusayn b. Ziyād's name has to be regarded as a transmission error (in three places) or whether Paris ms 1665 was transmitted similarly to the *riwāya* mentioned by Ibn Khayr al-Ishbīlī, in which al-Ḥusayn b. Ziyād is also missing.[42] However, in light of Paris ms 1664 and the "Kāle-Sprenger-manuscript"/Berlin ms 9767, both of which include the name, the former option seems more likely. Second, the *riwāya* within the manuscript differs in the first transmitters from the one found at the beginning, i.e. the two scholars Abū ʿAbdallāh Muḥammad b. al-Iṣfahānī (n.d.) and Abū al-Ḥasan ʿAlī b. al-Farāʾ al-Mawṣilī (d. 519/1125) are found neither at the beginning of the text nor in any other *riwāya*. In addition, al-Silafī's name is not included in these *riwāyas* within Paris ms 1665. It seems as if the middle parts of Paris ms 1665 were transmitted partly by other scholars compared to its first part. Of course, some interference could be at play here,

38 See al-Azdī, *Futūḥ al-Shām. Ed. ʿUqla/Banī Yāsīn*, 77, n. 2.

39 See Mourad, *al-Azdī*, 582.

40 See al-Azdī, *Futūḥ al-Shām. Ed. ʿUqla/Banī Yāsīn*, 126, n. 2; 177, n. 5; 227, n. 1.

41 See al-Azdī, *Futūḥ al-Shām. Ed. ʿUqla/Banī Yāsīn*, 177, n. 5.

42 For Ibn Khayr's *riwāya*, see below p. 18. In this case, someone must have included al-Ḥusayn b. Ziyād's name in the one place later, probably as a correction.

i.e. a scholar—say Abū al-Maymūn ʿAbd al-Wahhāb b. ʿAtīq al-Miṣrī—who knew of Paris ms 1664 adopted this manuscript's *riwāya* and attached it to the beginning of Paris ms 1665. Whatever might have happened in this case, the *riwāya* of Paris ms 1665 also highlights the role of Abū Isḥāq al-Ḥabbāl (d. 482/1089): First, he is mentioned as the last common transmitter of all *riwāyas* included in Paris ms 1665 (in fact, in all *riwāyas* discussed so far)[43]; second, in the three shorter *riwāyas* of Paris 1665, it is said that the text of the *Futūḥ al-Shām* was transmitted in writing from him to Abū al-Ḥasan ʿAlī b. al-Farāʾ al-Mawṣilī. This indicates again that a fixed text of the work most likely existed during Abū Isḥāq al-Ḥabbāl's lifetime.

In conclusion, the *riwāyas* found in the manuscripts of the *Futūḥ al-Shām* credit al-Azdī with being the compiler-author of the work, highlight the role Abū Isḥāq al-Ḥabbāl played in the transmission of a fixed text and stress the function al-Silafī had in distributing the work to a wider audience. Hence, al-Silafī, who was interested in *futūḥ* works in general, seems to have obtained a manuscript that was "edited" by Abū Isḥāq al-Ḥabbāl (d. 482/1089) and that included a *riwāya* in which al-Azdī's name was mentioned. Whether the transmission of the narrative from al-Azdī to Abū Isḥāq al-Ḥabbāl, i.e. over a period of more than 250 years, happened as indicated in the *riwāyas* is possible but difficult to prove at the moment.

Apart from the evidence found in these *riwāyas*, there is, unfortunately, no other reference to al-Azdī as the compiler-author of the *Futūḥ al-Shām* prior to the 6th/12th century. Nobody before al-Silafī in Egypt and Ibn Khayr al-Ishbīlī in al-Andalus documented this author-text relationship. This is not to say that it was not known earlier that al-Azdī compiled a *Futūḥ al-Shām* (we have seen that Abū Isḥāq al-Ḥabbāl did know about it) but that it was never written down in any biographical or bibliographical work.

However, we have plenty of evidence that the content of the *Futūḥ al-Shām* was known and was quoted before. In addition to several shorter traditions found in various Arabic historiographical works from the 2nd/8th to the 6th/12th centuries, large parts of the work were quoted by Dionysius of Tellmaḥrē (d. 230–231/845), al-Ṭalamankī (d. 429/1037) and Ibn ʿAsākir (571/1176).[44] However, none of these scholars stated that he excerpted the traditions from al-Azdī's *Futūḥ al-Shām*; either only al-Azdī is mentioned (in the case of al-Ṭalamankī) or only the work's title, *Futūḥ al-Shām*, is listed (in the case of Ibn ʿAsākir) or no information is given at all (in the case of Dionysius of Tellmaḥrē). Often, traditions about the expansion in Syria were either anonymously transmitted or ascribed to other Muslim scholars who were known to have compiled a work on *futūḥ*, such as Abū Mikhnaf, al-Qudāmī or Abū Ḥudhayfa. This lack of concrete evidence renders the information derived from the *riwāyas* of the manuscripts so important.

43 This was already observed by Humphreys (see Humphreys, *Notes*, eighth paragraph).

44 For a detailed analysis of all these passages, see Scheiner, *Al-Azdī's Futūḥ al-Shām in Past and Present* (Chapter 3).

In summing up and in light of the above, we accept the evidence found in the *riwāyas*: Al-Azdī is the compiler-author of the *Futūḥ al-Shām*, Abū Isḥāq al-Ḥabbāl (at the latest) transmitted a fixed text and al-Silafī distributed manuscripts, copies of which have been preserved until today, even though external reference to these points are available only from the 6th/12th century onward.

Apart from the above-mentioned *riwāyas* found in the manuscripts of the *Futūḥ al-Shām*, there are three other chains of transmitters that can be identified as *riwāyas*.[45] The first chain is found in Ibn Khayr al-Ishbīlī's *Fahrasa* and reads:

> Ibn Khayr al-Ishbīlī (d. 575/1179) > Abū Bakr Muḥammad b. Aḥmad b. Ṭāhir al-Ishbīlī (d. 580/1184) > Abū ʿAlī al-Ghassānī al-Qurṭubī (d. 498/1105) > Ḥakam b. Muḥammad al-Judhāmī al-Qurṭubī (d. 447/1055) > Abū Muḥammad ʿAbd al-Raḥmān b. al-Naḥḥās al-Miṣrī (d. 416/1025) > Abū al-Ḥasan ʿAlī b. Aḥmad b. Isḥāq al-Muʿaddil al-Baghdādī (d. 340/951–952) > Abū al-ʿAbbās al-Walīd b. Ḥammād al-Ramlī (d. ca. 300/912) > al-Azdī (d. between 170–215/786–825).

In his *Fahrasa*, Ibn Khayr al-Ishbīlī lists all the works he transmitted or was allowed to transmit from his teachers.[46] Thus, although there is no text transmitted together with this chain, it is likely that it still represents a *riwāya* for a *Futūḥ al-Shām* manuscript that Ibn Khayr had at hand. The analysis of this *riwāya* makes it clear that Ibn Khayr al-Ishbīlī's manuscript was neither transmitted via al-Silafī (who was a contemporary of his) nor was based on the fixed text transmitted by Abū Isḥāq al-Ḥabbāl. Furthermore, al-Ḥusayn b. Ziyād al-Ramlī is not found in the chain. In addition, when putting this *riwāya* in relation to the *riwāyas* found in the three extant manuscripts, we find that Abū al-Ḥasan ʿAlī b. Aḥmad al-Baghdādī (d. 340/951–952) is the common scholar of all the chains. Thus, if this chain is correct, along with Abū Isḥāq al-Ḥabbāl, he seemed also to have played an important role in the transmission history of the *Futūḥ al-Shām*. It has to be noted in this context that Abū al-Ḥasan al-Baghdādī is also mentioned in the two *isnāds* found in *Al-durr al-nafīs*, i.e. that he belonged to the transmitters from whom al-Ṭalamankī received some of his traditions about the expansion in Syria. However, since Ibn Khayr al-Ishbīlī did not cite an independent manuscript

45 Further rudimentary chains of transmitters are quoted in one or two cases by al-Ṭalamankī and Ibn ʿAsākir. However, it is not clear whether they can convincingly be interpreted as *riwāyas* of the *Futūḥ al-Shām* or whether they just represent *isnāds* of the respective traditions. Hence, they are not discussed here. Al-Dhahabī also mentioned a short *riwāya* when stating that his teacher Muḥammad b. Mukarram b. ʿAlī al-Ruwayfaʿī had heard (and obtained permission to transmit) al-Azdī's *Futūḥ al-Shām* from Ibn al-Makhaylī [al-Muḥāmilī?]. For al-Dhahabī's statement, see al-Dhahabī, *Muʿjam al-shuyūkh*, II, 288, l. 9.

46 See al-Ishbīlī, *Fahrasa. Ed. Codera/Tarrago*, 238, l. 1–5.

text, the scope and content of the text Abū al-Ḥasan al-Baghdādī had transmitted is difficult to specify.

The second chain of transmitters that can be identified as a *riwāya* is found in Ibn al-ʿAdīm's (d. 660/1261) *Bughyat al-ṭalab* and it reads:[47]

> Ibn al-ʿAdīm (d. 660/1261) > Abū ʿAlī Ḥasan b. Aḥmad [b. Yūsuf al-Ṣūfī] al-Awqī (d. 630/1232) **in Jerusalem** > Abū Ṭāhir Aḥmad b. Muḥammad b. Ibrāhīm al-Iṣfahānī al-Silafī (d. 576/1180) > Abū al-Ḥusayn Aḥmad b. Muḥammad b. Musbiḥ [al-Muqriʾ] (n.d.) > Abū Isḥāq Ibrāhīm b. Saʿīd [b. ʿAbdallāh al-Tujībī] al-Ḥabbāl (d. 482/1089) > Abū al-ʿAbbās Munīr b. Aḥmad b. al-Ḥasan b. Munīr al-Khashshāb (d. 412/1021) > [Abū al-Ḥasan] ʿAlī b. Aḥmad b. Isḥāq al-Baghdādī (d. 340/951) > [Abū al-ʿAbbās] al-Walīd b. Ḥammād al-Ramlī (d. ca. 300/912) > al-Ḥusayn b. Ziyād [al-Ramlī] (n.d.) > Abū Ismāʿīl Muḥammad b. ʿAbdallāh [al-Azdī] al-Baṣrī (d. between 170–215/786–825).

Because this chain of transmitters is mentioned five times by Ibn al-ʿAdīm and because the traditions quoted with it have the same wording as found in the edition of al-Azdī's *Futūḥ al-Shām*, it is very likely that this is the *riwāya* according to which Ibn al-ʿAdīm used a copy of the work. Two points can be inferred from this *riwāya*: First, Ibn al-ʿAdīm used a manuscript copy of al-Azdī's *Futūḥ al-Shām*, which was also transmitted via al-Silafī and which explains the close textual relation to the edition (and hence to the Parisian and Berlin manuscripts, respectively). Second, according to the information given in the *riwāya*, the work was read and transmitted in Jerusalem shortly after Saladin had reconquered the city. This fact then demonstrates that al-Azdī's *Futūḥ al-Shām* was quite popular in the time of the Crusades and that it also had an audience in 7th/13th-century Syria, besides Egypt.

The final chain of transmitters to be discussed in this context was provided by Ibn Ḥajar al-ʿAsqalānī (d. 852/1449) in the compilation in which he listed his teachers and their works (*mashyakha*) *Al-muʿjam al-muʾassis*.[48] It reads:

> Ibn Ḥajar (d. 852/1449) > Zaynab [bt. Aḥmad b. ʿAbd al-Raḥīm b. ʿAbd al-Wāḥid b. Aḥmad b. Manṣūr al-Maqdisī, known as] bt. al-Kamāl (d. 740/1339) **who had [received] an *ijāza* of the work from** > Sibṭ al-Silafī (d. 651/1253) > my maternal uncle Abū Ṭāhir [Aḥmad b. Muḥammad b. Ibrāhīm al-Iṣfahānī al-Silafī] (d. 576/1180) > [Abū al-Ḥusayn] Aḥmad b. Muḥammad b. [Musbiḥ] Shaykh al-Muqriʾ (n.d.) > [Abū Isḥāq] Ibrāhīm b. Saʿīd [b. ʿAbdallāh al-Tujībī] al-Ḥabbāl (d. 482/1089) > [Abū al-ʿAbbās]

47 See Ibn al-ʿAdīm, *Bughyat al-ṭalab*, I, 69, l. 12–17; 569, l. 2–8; 572, l. 15–22; III, 1336, l. 14–1337, l. 6; VII, 3150, l. 7–16.

48 See Ibn Ḥajar, *Al-muʿjam al-muʾassis*, II, 327–328.

Munīr b. Aḥmad [b. al-Ḥasan b. Munīr] al-Khashshāb (d. 412/1021) > [Abū al-Ḥasan] ʿAlī b. Aḥmad b. Isḥāq [al-Baghdādī] (d. 340/951) > [Abū al-ʿAbbās] al-Walīd b. Ḥammād al-Ramlī (d. ca. 300/912) > al-Ḥusayn b. Ziyād al-Tamīmī [read: Al-Ramlī] (n.d.) > Abū Ismāʿīl Muḥammad b. ʿAbdallāh al-Azdī [al-Baṣrī] (d. between 160–215/776–830).

Although there is, as in Ibn Khayr al-Ishbīlī's case, no text transmitted together with this chain, it is likely that it still represents a *riwāya* that relates to another *Futūḥ al-Shām* manuscript, because Ibn Ḥajar quoted many passages from al-Azdī's *Futūḥ al-Shām* that accord verbatim with the modern edition in his other works. This *riwāya* thus shows that Ibn Ḥajar's manuscript is also based on al-Silafī's and Abū Isḥāq al-Ḥabbāl's texts. Furthermore, another disciple of al-Silafī's is mentioned therein, i.e. his nephew. This shows that al-Silafī transmitted the *Futūḥ al-Shām* also within his own family.

The editions

There are three modern editions of al-Azdī's *Futūḥ al-Shām*: The *editio princeps* prepared by William Nassau Lees in 1854 on the basis of the "Kāle-Sprenger-manuscript"/Berlin ms 9767; the second edition established by ʿAbd al-Munʿim ʿĀmir in 1970 on the basis of an alleged manuscript from Damascus; and the most recent edition from 2004 prepared by ʿIṣām ʿUqla and Yūsuf Banī Yāsīn on the basis of Paris ms 1664 and Paris ms 1665.[49] A brief commentary on the advantages and disadvantages of each edition is mentioned below in order to allow the reader to assess them in a comparative manner.

Regarding Lees's edition, on the positive side, there is his sound and almost complete manuscript, which he thoroughly edited and annotated. On the negative side, it must be acknowledged that this is not a critical edition, since Lees used only one manuscript, which had some lacunae and had been damaged by bookworms. In addition, Lees's edition is quite difficult to read due to the setting of its pages.

Regarding ʿĀmir's annotated edition, the only advantage it has is that it can easily be read due to its spatial setting. Major disadvantages are the absence of the manuscript on which it is allegedly based and the fact that it is not a critical edition, because ʿĀmir did not use more than one manuscript. For these reasons, ʿĀmir's edition should no longer be used. In addition, it is superseded by the third, i.e. the ʿUqla/Banī Yāsīn edition.

The third is the most recent edition and the first annotated critical edition based on two manuscripts (as well as referencing ʿĀmir's edition). It is easy to read due to its spatial setting and its highlighting of the many headings and *isnāds*. The only disadvantages are that ʿUqla and Banī Yāsīn did not

49 See al-Azdī, *Futūḥ al-Shām. Ed. Lees*; *Ed. ʿĀmir*; *Ed. ʿUqla/Banī Yāsīn*.

use all extant manuscripts (they overlooked the Berlin manuscript) and that this edition is unavailable in many academic libraries. A reprint of this edition is, therefore, a desideratum.

In conclusion, the ʿUqla/Banī Yāsīn edition is the best choice for future studies of al-Azdī's *Futūḥ al-Shām*. This is the reason why we decided to translate it into English and make it available to a wider audience. However, before we turn to the description of our policies in this translation, a short thematic summary of the most important secondary literature should be given.

Studies of al-Azdī's *Futūḥ al-Shām*

All extant studies of al-Azdī's *Futūḥ al-Shām* can be divided in two large groups:[50] Those that focus on the *riwāyas* and *isnāds* as well as the transmitters mentioned therein and those that focus on the content of the work.

Regarding the study of the *riwāyas* and *isnāds*, many scholars have made substantial efforts to identify the persons mentioned in the *Futūḥ al-Shām* with the help of the biographical literature. Hence, Lees (1854) was able to identify twenty-four transmitters, while Mourad (2000) found forty-one transmitters in total, of whom he could identify thirty-one.[51] ʿUqla/Banī Yāsīn (2004) found forty-two transmitters for whom they could make some biographical comments.[52] However, they could find a *tarjama* relating to only twenty-two of them, as they noted in their introduction.[53] Muḥyī al-Dīn Lāgha (2011) was able to identify twenty-six persons.[54] The results of all these studies are included in our own footnotes that also comment upon each transmitter in the *riwāyas* and *isnāds*. The *isnāds* as part of the *Futūḥ al-Shām* were first studied by Lees (1854), who attached an index of all *isnāds* to his edition.[55] Then de Goeje (1864) also dedicated a large part of his *Mémoire sur le Fotouho's-Scham* to the *isnāds* included in the *Futūḥ al-Shām*. He concluded that the majority of them are incomplete, "in disorder and uncertain" and most of them include "fictive names".[56] However, many of de Goeje's arguments on this issue are no longer tenable. In full contrast to de Goeje, but without providing any argumentation, ʿĀmir states: "All *isnāds* are trustworthy and sound".[57] Such a general statement is of no help, either, and most likely debatable. Conrad (1987) counted all *isnāds* (i.e. ninety-five *isnāds* including forty-three transmitters) and found them

50 A detailed analysis of all extant studies can be found in Scheiner, *Al-Azdī's Futūḥ al-Shām in Past and Present* (Chapter 2).

51 See al-Azdī, *Futūḥ al-Shām. Ed. Lees*, 51–58; Mourad, *al-Azdī*, 589.

52 See al-Azdī, *Futūḥ al-Shām. Ed. ʿUqla/Banī Yāsīn*, 22–34.

53 The figure 22 is based on a count of all individuals on whom ʿUqla and Banī Yāsīn made such a comment.

54 See Lāgha, *Baḥth*, 3–10.

55 See al-Azdī, *Futūḥ al-Shām. Ed. Lees*, 51–58 (Isnads).

56 See de Goeje, *Mémoire sur le Fotouho's-Scham* and 22, 17 (for the quotations).

57 See al-Azdī, *Futūḥ al-Shām. Ed. ʿĀmir*, ي.

"ambiguous".[58] This ambiguity is also commented on below on pages 31–32 when we introduce our translation policies.

Regarding the content of the (more) literary parts of the *Futūḥ al-Shām*, many scholars have studied the portrayal of the various—although often repeated and not very numerous—figures mentioned therein. De Goeje (1864) and Conrad (1987) focused on Khālid b. al-Walīd;[59] de Goeje, Conrad and Khalek (2010) on Abū ʿUbayda b. al-Jarrāḥ;[60] de Goeje, Kaegi (1992) and Conrad (2002) on Heraclius;[61] and de Goeje, El Cheikh (2004) and Khalek on Bāhān.[62] In addition, van Ess (2001) and Khalek studied the portrayal of Muʿādh b. Jabal,[63] while van Ess also tackled the latter's son ʿAbd al-Raḥmān and Khalek discussed the portrayal of "the Christians".[64] In addition, individual scholars have analysed various traditions mentioned in the *Futūḥ al-Shām*. Conrad (1987), for example, stressed the depiction of Ḥimṣ,[65] while Lees focused on Khālid's desert march.[66] Rihan (2014) and Ulrich (2019) looked particularly into the representation of the tribes of ʿĀmila and al-Azd,[67] whereas Scheiner (2010) studied the conquest of Damascus[68] and Shoshan (2016) investigated ʿUmar b. al-Khaṭṭāb's takeover of Jerusalem.[69] In addition, Mourad (2011) and Ṣāyama (2009) analysed the poems in the work.[70] Lees and de Goeje treated the speeches found in the text,[71] while de Goeje, El Cheikh and Khalek focused on interreligious debates.[72] Many scholars commented on, but did not thoroughly study, the letters included in the *Futūḥ al-Shām* (e.g. Lees, de Goeje, Kurd ʿAlī [1945], al-ʿUmarī [1983] and Conrad [1987]).[73]

58 See Conrad, *al-Azdī's History*, 30–31.
59 See de Goeje, *Mémoire sur le Fotouho's-Scham*, 5–7; Conrad, *al-Azdī's History*, 39–42.
60 See de Goeje, *Mémoire sur le Fotouho's-Scham*, 5–7; Conrad, *al-Azdī's History*, 39–42; Khalek, *Tall and Slender*, 115–122.
61 See de Goeje, *Mémoire sur le Fotouho's-Scham*, 24–25; Kaegi, *Byzantium*, 11; Conrad, *Heraclius*.
62 See de Goeje, *Mémoire sur le Fotouho's-Scham*, 29–32; El Cheikh, *Byzantium*, 35–38; Khalek, *Tall and Slender*, 115–122.
63 See van Ess, *Fehltritt*, 26; Khalek, *Tall and Slender*, 115–122 (Khalek, however, seems not to have been aware of van Ess's study).
64 See van Ess, *Fehltritt*, 136–139; Khalek, *Damascus*, 54.
65 See Conrad, *al-Azdī's History*, 52.
66 See al-Azdī, *Futūḥ al-Shām. Ed. Lees*, 66–67, n. 3.
67 See Rihan, *Politics and Culture* (see also Scheiner, *Review of M. Rihan*); Ulrich, *al-Azd*.
68 See Scheiner, *Damaskus*.
69 See Shoshan, *Historical Tradition*, 112–123.
70 See Mourad, *Poetry*; Ṣāyama, *Shiʿr*.
71 See al-Azdī, *Futūḥ al-Shām. Ed. Lees*, 156, n. 2; de Goeje, *Mémoire sur le Fotouho's-Scham*, 24.
72 See de Goeje, *Mémoire sur le Fotouho's-Scham*, 25; El Cheikh, *Byzantium*, 36–37; Khalek, *Damascus*, 53.
73 See al-Azdī, *Futūḥ al-Shām. Ed. Lees*, 122, n. 2; de Goeje, *Mémoire sur le Fotouho's-Scham*, 24; Kurd ʿAlī, *Futūḥ al-Shām*, 545–549; al-ʿUmarī, *al-Azdī wa-kitābuhū*, 74; Conrad, *al-Azdī's History*, 48.

The style of the *Futūḥ al-Shām* is composed of individual traditions (*akhbār*) mostly equipped with single *isnāds* (as described by Conrad and ʿAbd al-ʿAzīz al-Dūrī [2004][74]). It includes only few prophetical traditions but makes use of a number of quotations of and references to the Qurʾān (Conrad [1987]).[75] In fact, we can speak of a qurʾānicised language, as Scheiner demonstrated in a presentation held at the Institute of Ismaili Studies in 2012.[76] The narrative of the *Futūḥ al-Shām* has been perceived as "edifying" (de Goeje, Khalek),[77] "didactic" (Conrad),[78] "entertaining" (Conrad, Khalek)[79] or as "glorifying Islam" (de Goeje, Caetani),[80] "glorifying the tribes of Yemen" (Caetani, Conrad, Shoshan)[81] and "praising al-Azd" (al-ʿUmarī, Conrad, Lāgha, Shoshan).[82] ʿĀmir (1970) found therein a "religious programme" useful to "mobilise Muslims",[83] while Conrad interpreted the work as describing actions by Muslims that succeeded through God's will and their engagement in them.[84] He also thought that the companions of the Prophet were emphasised, while Shoshan perceived a stress on the Muslims' fighting against unbelievers (*jihād*).[85] While all of these characterisations are not completely wrong, they do not individually represent the only correct interpretation. Their subjectivity aside, these assessments and characterisations call for further engagement in al-Azdī's *Futūḥ al-Shām*—be it on the basis of the Arabic original or the English translation.

In conclusion, Conrad's statement that "al-Azdi remains an outhor [sic] known to us only through the book that survives under his name"[86] is still valid today. However, after more than 150 years of research, we know a lot more about the content and transmission history of the *Futūḥ al-Shām*. If other works, such as al-Balādhurī's *Futūḥ al-buldān*, were studied with the same effort, we would now know a lot more about the literature of the *futūḥ* genre in general. What we know about al-Azdī is very limited: He was the compiler-author of the *Futūḥ al-Shām* and he died in the later decades of the

74 See Conrad, *al-Azdī's History*, 54; al-Azdī, *Futūḥ al-Shām. Ed. ʿUqla/Banī Yāsīn*, 6 (*Taqdīm*).

75 See Conrad, *al-Azdī's History*, 60.

76 This presentation has never been published. Nonetheless, we would like to express our thanks to the organisers of the conference Dr. Nuha al-Shaar and Dr. Omar Ali-de-Unzaga for giving Scheiner the possibility to present his ideas.

77 See de Goeje, *Mémoire sur le Fotouho's-Scham*, 22; Khalek, *Damascus*, 56–57.

78 See Conrad, *al-Azdī's History*, 61.

79 See Conrad, *al-Azdī's History*, 61; Khalek, *Damascus*, 18.

80 See de Goeje, *Mémoire sur le Fotouho's-Scham*, 22; Caetani, *Annali*, II-2, 1149.

81 See Caetani, *Annali*, II-2, 1151, n. 2; Conrad, *al-Azdī's History*, 53 (van Ess followed Conrad in this; see van Ess, *Fehltritt*, 349); Shoshan, *Historical Tradition*, 97.

82 See al-ʿUmarī, *al-Azdī wa-kitābuhū*, 75–76; Conrad, *al-Azdī's History*, 53; Lāgha, *Baḥth*, 12–20; Shoshan, *Historical Tradition*, 97.

83 See al-Azdī, *Futūḥ al-Shām. Ed. ʿĀmir*, ي.

84 See Conrad, *al-Azdī's History*, 39.

85 See Conrad, *al-Azdī's History*, 45; Shoshan, *Historical Tradition*, 172.

86 See Conrad, *al-Azdī's History*, 32.

2nd/8th or the first years of the 3rd/9th centuries. He thus preserved one of the oldest Muslim narratives about the events that were central to Islam's formative period. As the detailed study of the work's research history has shown,[87] al-Azdī's *Futūḥ al-Shām* was often assessed as a "deficient" source when being compared with "better" sources, such as al-Balādhurī's *Futūḥ al-buldān* or al-Ṭabarī's *Ta'rīkh*. However, such a dichotomy between "better" and "worse" narrative sources is unwarranted. Every source offers some information (and neglects some); every source has a typical narratological style and inherent source-critical problems and, therefore, is useful for some research questions, but useless for others. Consequently, sources should be assessed in relation to the research question and approach at issue and not on the basis of—often unspecified—subjective criteria of likes or dislikes. This should be the case particularly for future research on al-Azdī's *Futūḥ al-Shām*.

87 See Scheiner, *Al-Azdī's Futūḥ al-Shām in Past and Present* (Chapter 2).

3 Policies of translation

Regarding our English translation, which is based on the ʿUqla/Banī Yāsīn edition, we follow an approach labelled "precise study translation" by Marshall Hodgson. Hodgson contrasts this type of translation with, on the one hand, "re-creative translations" that are "more or less a paraphrase" of the source as well as "easily readable" and, on the other hand, with "explanatory translations" that "will stay fairly close to the text, but [...] change[ ] the mood of the work". Philologically "precise study translations" faithfully reproduce the original work in order to present "an equivalent communication of the original which readers can then interpret for themselves". To achieve this aim, such a translation "has to be maximally precise".[1] This linguistic precision, which we have pursued by several means, is our main aim in the present translation.

First, we translated the same Arabic term consistently throughout the translation. To give some examples: Whenever *nazala* (lit. "to dismount, to camp") is used in this sense, we rendered it as "to set up camp". Also the noun *ahl* (lit. "people, inhabitants") is translated consistently as "people" (e.g. "the people" or "the people of Jerusalem") rather than distinguishing between "the people of Jerusalem" and "the inhabitants of Jerusalem". Furthermore, *qāla* ("to say") is always rendered by this verb. In other words, other verbs that express this meaning, such as "to speak", "to tell" or "to state", are not used for the sake of consistency. All this may make the text sound a bit formulaic, but it has the same formulaic character of the Arabic original. This also holds true for several technical terms that are consistently rendered throughout the translation and that are, in addition, mentioned in transliteration in parentheses when they first occur. The list below includes all these expressions.

Second, we stuck to the religious terminology of the text in order to convey the original tenor or mood of the text. Thus, we have used "Messenger of God" (for Arabic *rasūl Allāh*) rather than Prophet, and we have kept the eulogies (in abbreviation) in the translation and translated, for instance,

1 See Hodgson, *Venture*, I, 67–68.

al-jāhiliyya as "pre-Islamic period" rather than "antiquity/late antiquity". If we feel that we might have departed a bit too far from the original meaning, we added the Arabic term in parentheses after the English expression, thus allowing the reader to look for a better rendering in this case.

Third, we have kept repetitive synonyms, which Arabic regularly makes use of, in the English rendering. Thus, for example, we use the phrase "they were helpless and powerless against s.o". Although both adjectives basically mean the same.

Fourth, although the syntax of the original language is usually shortened in the English rendering, we adhered to other typical features of Arabic, like changes between direct and indirect speech within one sentence, shifts of persons from, for example, first person singular to first person plural within a sentence (*iltifāt*, lit. "deictic shift") and syntactically inconsistent or incomplete clauses within a sentence (*anacoluthon*).[2]

This, of course, causes confusion in an English sentence. Although we have, as demanded by Hodgson, left these and other ambiguities of the text intact, we do want to offer the reader a readable English text. Therefore, we developed a strategy of disambiguation by using square brackets. With this tool, we polish typical features of Arabic by augmenting expressions in order to create meaningful and comprehensible English sentences. In addition, with the help of the square brackets, we also provide the reader with a possible interpretation of an ambiguous phrase. Of course, readers of Arabic may come up with other interpretations of these ambiguous phrases. A good example for the first case, i.e. the augmentation of phrases, is the following: "Abū ʿUbayda remained [in this situation] for fifteen nights". Without the addition the English sentence is not meaningful, even though the Arabic phrase is. A similar case is when we add a plural -s in square brackets to a word, as in the phrase "by the One in whose hand[s] my soul lies". The Arabic has a singular noun here; English makes more sense when the plural, i.e. hands, is used. Regarding the second case, i.e. to provide a possible interpretation, often in Arabic ambiguous personal and possessive pronouns are used. Two examples may make this point clear: Usually, the subject of the verb *qāla* (lit. "he said") is not separately expressed in Arabic. The English reader would always want to know, however, who exactly was doing the saying. To resolve this issue, we render these phrases as "he [=Abū Bakr] said", i.e. adding our interpretation in square brackets.[3] Another good example is when ambiguous pronouns are used, as in "*fa-aqbala ilay**hi** ḥattā laqiya**hū***" (lit. "he proceeded to him until he met him"). In this sentence, it is not clear who met whom. Hence, we add the nouns, technically the antecedents to

2 For an example of a deictic shift, see the translation on page 136, note 323; for an example of anacoluthon, see the translation page 205 ("When Abū ʿUbayda b. al-Jarrāḥ set up camp at al-Yarmūk…").

3 In case we were unable to name an individual as subject, we phrased "he [=the narrator] said".

which the pronouns refer in our view, in square brackets, e.g. "he [=Abū ʿUbayda] proceeded to him until he met him [=Khālid]".[4]

Being aware of these tools, the reader has two strategies for dealing with square brackets: Either a sentence can be read as if the information in the brackets was part of the original sentence, in which case a correct English sentence emerges. Or the sentence can be read excluding the brackets, in which case the reader gets a rendering that is closer to the Arabic original but may bend English grammar to some extent. This approach allows the reader to make use of the translation as an independent text, while simultaneously allowing it to be read side by side with the Arabic text. Or, as Hodgson puts it, a possible re-translation of our text "into the original language will give back the original form, without precisions or omissions".[5]

Such a re-translation is supported by the following list that includes all technical terms and their English equivalents:

ahl al-—people of [...]
ahl al-dhimma—protected people
ahl al-quwwa wa-al-shidda—men of might and toughness
ahd—pact
ʿaqada li-fulān ʿalā—to give command/authority to s.o. over
Allāh—God
Allāh al-lādhī lā ilāh illā huwa—God with whom no other deity is associated
Allāhu akbar—God is the Greatest
Allāhumma—Oh God
ʿalayhi salām (ʿs.)—Peace be upon him
amān—letter of protection
ʿāmil/ʿummāl—subordinate/s
amīr—commander
amīr al-muʾminīn—the Commander of the Believers
ammā baʿdu—regarding the matter at hand
amr—cause, matter
al-amr bi-al-maʿrūf wa-al-nahy ʿan al-munkar—commanding what is right and forbidding what is wrong
ʿan yadin wa-hum ṣāghirūn—by hand and with humility
ashrāf—noblemen
ʿaskar—army unit
aswāq—offerings
athqāl—chattels
awliyāʾ—close friends
ʿaẓīm al-Rūm—the Mighty of the Byzantines
balāʾ—performance
baṣīra—discernment

4 See al-Azdī, *Futūḥ al-Shām. Ed. ʿUqla/Banī Yāsīn*, 162, l. 1–2.
5 See Hodgson, *Venture*, I, 68.

bidʿa—innovation
biṭrīq—patrician
daʿwa—call
dhimma—protection
dimāʾ—souls
fataḥa Allāh ʿalā yad (fulān)—God leads (someone) to the conquest of
fa-idhā—lo and behold
fī āthāriha—in pursuit of them
fiʾa—company
ghadāt—early morning prayer[s]
ghāra ʿalā—to raid
ghunāʾ—competence
ḥadd—vehemence
ḥadīth—tradition
ḥajj—pilgrimage
hady—[faithful] guidance
hāl—condition, situation
al-ḥamd li-llāh—Praise be to God
ḥamida Allāh wa-athnā ʿalayhi—he praised and thanked God
khalīfa—caliph
ḥasuna islāmuhū—he excelled at Islam
ḥasbunā wa-niʿmat al-wakīl—He is sufficient for us and He is the best Upholder
hayʾa—visage
ḥayy—[sub]tribe
ilāh—deity
ʿiṣāba—company
jāhiliyya—pre-Islamic period
jamāʿa—generality
jāsha ʿalā—to march an army against
jaysh—army unit
juyūsh—troops (pl.)
jazāʾ—competence
jazaka Allāh khayran—May God reward you with [all that is] good
jihād—fighting for the cause of God
jizya—tribute
jumūʿ—groups
jund/ajnād—district/s
jund/junūd—soldier/s
juzʾ—part (of the manuscript)
kabbara—to proclaim "God is the Greatest"
katība—cavalry unit
katāʾib—military units
khabar—report
khalīfat rasūl Allāh—the successor of the Messenger of God

kharāj—tax
khayl—cavalry unit
khilāfa—caliphate
khuṭba—speech
kunya—patronymic
kuwar—provinces
la-ʿamrī—I swear upon my life
la-ʿamru Allāh—I swear by the Eternal God
lā ḥawla wa-lā quwwa illā bi-Allāh—Neither power nor strength [is obtained] except through God
mādda—matériel
maʿādha Allāh—God forbid
mujāhid—fighter for the cause of God
malik—sovereign
malik al-Rūm—the Emperor of the Byzantines
mulūk al-Rūm—the Byzantine sovereigns
mamlaka—empire
munādī—caller
nahaḍa—he got up
qaḍāʾ—decree
qāla—he said
qalīlan—for a little while
qāma fī—he rose [and stood] before
qāma ilā—he rose [and went] to
qaṣafa baʿḍahum ʿalā baʿḍ—to crash into one another
qaṣṣa—exhort
qiṣṣa—story
qatala qitālan shadīdan—to fight fiercely
Qayṣar—Caesar
qibla—direction of prayers
Rabb—Lord
raḥimahū Allāh—God rest him/May God have mercy upon him
raḥimaka/kum Allāh—May God have mercy upon you/you (pl.)
raḥmat Allāh ʿalayhi—God rest his soul
rakʿa—act of prayer
rasūl Allāh—Messenger of God
raʾy—opinion, decision
riḥḥāl—belongings
ruʾūs—chiefs
rustāq—rural surroundings
sāʿatan—for a short while
ṣālaḥa ʿalā—to make peace with
salām ʿalaykum—peace be upon you
ṣallā ʿalā al-nabī—he blessed and saluted the Prophet
sawād—arable lands

sayyid—master
shadda ʿalā—to assault
shayṭān—Satan
subḥān Allāh—Glory be to God
ṣulḥ—peace-making
sunna—normative practices
sūra—chapter
tābiʿūn—followers
taḥ aṣṣ ana—fortify [one's place] against
ṭāʾifa—party
takhallafa—remain behind
ṭūl al-qiyām—performing lengthy [prayers]
umma—community
ʿumra—minor pilgrimage
wa-Allāhi—I swear by God that
wakīl—trustee
wālī—leader, close friend
wa-salām—peace [be upon you]
wa-salām ʿalayka wa-raḥmat Allāh wa-barakātuhū—May God's peace, mercy and blessings be upon you
wayḥaka/kum—woe unto you/you (pl.)
wuḍūʿ—ritual ablution
yawm—battle-day
zakāt—the prescribed tax

For the eulogies that pervade the Arabic text, but are abbreviated and mentioned in parentheses after the expressions they belong to in the English rendering, see the following list:

- (ʿa.) accords to *ʿazza wa-jalla* ("the Almighty and Great", lit. "may He [=God] be strong and exalted"),
- (r.) equals *raḍiya Allāh ʿanhū* (lit. "may God be pleased with him"),
- (ṣ.) represents *ṣallā Allāh ʿalayhi wa-sallama* (lit. "may God bless him and grant him salvation"),
- (ʿs.) stands for *ʿalayhi salām* (lit. "peace be upon him"); regarding God's eulogies
- (t.) represents *taʿālā* ("the Exalted", lit. "may He [=God] be exalted"),
- (tt.) means *tabāraka wa-taʿālā* ("the Blessed and Exalted", lit. "may He [=God] be blessed and exalted").

Some other stylistic issues of our translation are:

1 Groups' names are usually capitalised. Hence, "the Muslims" represents *al-muslimūn* (lit. "those submitting themselves to [the one] God"),

"the Polytheists" *al-mushrikūn* (lit. "those associating [other deities] with God"), "the Emigrants" *al-muhājirūn* and "the Supporters" *al-anṣār*, etc. Tribal names composed of *Banū* (lit. "the sons of [...]") are used without the definite article "the".

2 Personal names are transliterated according to the Arabic text except for *ibn* (lit. "son of") and *bint* (lit. "daughter of") that are abbreviated to "b." and "bt.".
3 In order to facilitate the identification of the persons mentioned in al-Azdī's narrative, we provide the complete persons' names that are mentioned only in part. For example, Maysara b. Masrūq who is often referred to as Maysara in the Arabic text appears as Maysara [b. Masrūq] in the translation.
4 Furthermore, we preserve the chapter divisions of the ʿUqla/Banī Yāsīn edition and present the chapter headings that are mainly based on Paris ms 1664 in bold or italic. However, we added some headings in square brackets to help the reader navigate the text more easily.
5 Regarding the paragraphs, however, we do not follow the edition, since some traditions in it are narrated in two or more paragraphs. In these cases, we present the respective tradition in one paragraph; in other cases, we created new paragraphs as meaningful textual units.
6 ʿUqla/Banī Yāsīn's pagination is retained in the translation and indicated by "\\" and the respective page number, i.e. "\\162". Thus, a parallel reading between the translation and edition is facilitated.
7 In two cases, we divert from ʿUqla and Banī Yāsīn's typesetting: First, we attach the *basmallāh* that is usually separated from the following letter in the edition to the ensuing text. Second, we do not mention the *isnāds* in bold as the editors did.

Regarding the *isnāds* found in the *Futūḥ al-Shām*, a comment might be of use here. Usually, they are understood as a continuous chain of transmitters (i.e. al-Ḥusayn b. Ziyād > al-Azdī > A > B > C). On the basis of this assumption, al-Azdī's informants were identified and his date of death was calculated. However, the majority of *isnāds* contain the coordinator *wa-* (lit. "and") and are presented as if they were two independent strands, i.e. al-Ḥusayn b. Ziyād > al-Azdī who said *and* A > B > C who said. Take, for example, the following typical *isnād* that reads:

> *Akhbaranā* al-Ḥusayn b. Ziyād *ʿan* Abī Ismāʿīl Muḥammad b. ʿAbdallāh *qāla* ***wa-****ḥaddathanī* Yazīd b. Yazīd b. Jābir *ʿan* ʿAmr b. Muḥṣan *ʿan* ʿAbdallāh b. Qurṭ al-Thumālī *qāla* [...].[6]

The coordinator *wa-* is very rarely found within a continuous chain of transmitters, but usually introduces a second strand, as in Ibn ʿAsākir's

6 See al-Azdī, *Futūḥ al-Shām. Ed. ʿUqla/Banī Yāsīn*, 155, l. 9–156, l. 1.

TMD. In addition, it does not linguistically make a lot of sense when we consider al-Azdī's statement "and Person A told me". What does "and" refer to? To the *isnād* mentioned before? To another transmitter? Therefore, if we interpret the coordinator as referring to another strand, this will mean that al-Ḥusayn b. Ziyād's disciple, who is al-Walīd b. Ḥammād in the *riwāya* of the *Futūḥ al-Shām*, offers two strands to the following information: One stopping at al-Azdī and another stopping at ʿAbdallāh b. Qurṭ al-Thumālī. This format of the *isnāds* is, with one or two exceptions, consistently used throughout the *Futūḥ al-Shām*. The second coordinated strand usually stops at an eyewitness or a narrator who participated in the events. Therefore, it might have been added later to the text, serving as a better confirmation of a first strand that offers a huge gap between the narrator, i.e. al-Azdī, and the event. For the moment, this is only a hypothesis, but it will be of interest to all modern scholars who doubt the authenticity of eyewitness reports. This feature of the *isnāds* deserves more attention and study.

8 Still, these observations are taken into account in our translation when rendering the coordinator *wa-* as "furthermore". The above-mentioned *isnād*, for example, is thus translated as follows:

> Al-Ḥusayn b. Ziyād [al-Ramlī] reported to us on the authority of Abū Ismāʿīl Muḥammad b. ʿAbdallāh [al-Azdī], who said: **Furthermore**, Yazīd b. Yazīd b. Jābir related to me on the authority of ʿAmr b. Muḥṣan on the authority of ʿAbdallāh b. Qurṭ al-Thumālī, who said: [...].

9 Following the usual conventions, we quote dates according to the *hijrī* calendar and convert them to common-era dates.

Regarding the dating of the events, relative chronology is preferred to exact dating in the narrative. Hence, "hard" dates are rare. Only the following events are dated: the fights at al-Madāʾin are dated to 12 [=633–634], while the Battle of Ajnādayn and Abū Bakr's death are placed in 13 [=634–635]. The conquest of Damascus and the Battle of Fiḥl occurred in 14 [=635–636], whereas the Battle of al-Yarmūk is said to have happened in 15 [=636–637]. The plague of al-ʿAmwās was in 18 [=639–640] and finally the conquests of Caesarea and Jalūlāʾ are placed in 19 [640–641]. Usually dates occur after the narration of each event; most of them are mentioned *en bloc*. This could be due to a later insertion of most dates by one or more transmitters of the narrative.

10 In addition, we follow the IJMES transliteration system with some modifications. First, we do not transcribe geographical and other terms that are found in a standard English dictionary. Hence, Iraq is spelled in this way instead of al-ʿIrāq. Second, ʿAbdallāh and ʿUbaydallāh are written as one word, rather than ʿAbd Allāh and ʿUbayd Allāh. Third, the article *al-* is retained in composite phrases, such as Abū al-Walīd (rather than abbreviated to Abū l-Walīd).

11 Regarding quotations from the Qurʾān, we quote Abdel Haleem's translation because of its high legibility.
12 Furthermore, we included the following typographical conventions in the translation:

( )	Indicates the Arabic expressions that are mentioned in the original; furthermore, abbreviated eulogies are put in ( ).
[ ]	Indicates that the information between the square brackets is not mentioned in the original but is added to the text for reasons of clarity.
Italics	Indicates either emphasis placed on some expressions or the foreignness of a specific term; all transliterated Arabic terms are thus put in italics.
" "	Indicates citations from other works, most often from the Qurʾān, direct speech by various figures in the narrative and literal translations of Arabic terms.
' '	Indicates quotations or direct speech within quotations.

In addition, the translation is consistently annotated. These annotations provide biographical and geographical information about the groups, individuals and places mentioned in the Arabic text, refer to quoted qurʾānic verses and explain some difficult Arabic terms wherever necessary.

Apropos biographical information, we have annotated all the groups and individuals throughout the translation when they are first mentioned. Regarding the groups, if the group represents an Arabian tribe, we say whether the genealogists classified it as belonging to the Northern or Southern branch and mention the role the tribe plays in al-Azdī's narrative. At the end of each entry, we provide a source for further information, usually the entry in the *Encyclopedia of Islam* or Caskel's *Ǧamharat an-nasab*.

Regarding individuals, the structure of the annotations is similar. We usually provide the full name of a person, his/her date of death, the role he/she plays in al-Azdī's narrative and mention a source for this information, most often the *Encyclopedia of Islam* or important biographical dictionaries (like Ibn Saʿd's *Kitāb al-ṭabaqāt al-kabīr*, al-Bukhārī's *Al-taʾrīkh al-kabīr* or Ibn ʿAsākir's *Taʾrīkh madīnat Dimashq*). If an individual has been identified by another modern scholar, particularly William Lees, Suleiman Mourad or ʿIṣām ʿUqla and Yūsuf Banī Yāsīn, we provide this information in the footnote, as well.

Regarding the geographical terms in the notes and the translated text, we adhere to the Arabic place name, which we provide in transliteration. If the place name has a meaning, like Dayr Khālid (lit. "Khālid's monastery"), we provide the English translation in the footnote. There, we also mention the (more or less) exact location of the place on the basis of the *Encyclopedia of Islam* or Yāqūt's geographical dictionary *Muʿjam al-buldān*, both of which are also quoted as references. We have tried to keep annotations to a minimum in order not to overwhelm the reader with too much information.

In conclusion, we have sought, through this work, to provide a "precise" English translation of one of the earliest and most valuable Arabic sources on the Muslim conquest of Greater Syria, thus making available a religio-historical document on the major events during the early Muslim expansion into today's Lebanon, Israel, Palestinian Territories, Jordan and Syria. Future readership will decide whether our efforts have been successful.

4 Translation

[Manuscript note: The transmission of the work]

\\75[1] In the transmission (*riwāya*) of al-Ḥusayn b. Ziyād al-Ramlī[2] who recounted from the former [=al-Azdī].

1 We include this *riwāya* in the translation, because the editors of al-Azdī's *Futūḥ al-Shām*, ʿUqla and Banī Yāsīn, attached it to the beginning of the text. In fact, this *riwāya* occurs in one of their manuscripts, i.e. Paris no. 1664, only. See their footnote in al-Azdī, *Futūḥ al-Shām. Ed. ʿUqla/Banī Yāsīn*, 75, n. 1.

2 Al-Ḥusayn b. Ziyād al-Ramlī (n.d.) was a transmitter of *ḥadīth* and the compiler of a book on foster relationships (*al-riḍāʿ*). Conrad was able to identify him on the basis of al-Ṭūsī's *Al-fihrist* where al-Ḥusayn b. Ziyād (without the *nisba* al-Ramlī) is mentioned as having transmitted this book to al-Walīd b. Ḥammād al-Ramlī (see Conrad, *al-Azdī's History*, 58, n. 126). Conrad proposes the years 230–245/844–860 as the period of death for al-Ḥusayn b. Ziyād (see ibid., 57, 58). Mourad found another reference to al-Ḥusayn b. Ziyād in Ibn Ḥajar's *Lisān al-mīzān* (see Mourad, *al-Azdī*, 580–581). However, al-Ḥusayn b. Ziyād's *nisba* is not mentioned there, either. Combining al-Ṭūsī's and Ibn Ḥajar's information, Mourad characterises al-Ḥusayn b. Ziyād as an "ʿAlid" from al-Kūfa who flourished between the late 2nd/8th and the mid-3rd/9th century, i.e. he accepts Conrad's proposed period of death. Furthermore, Mourad speculates that al-Ḥusayn b. Ziyād resided as a trader in al-Ramla for some time, which accounts for his *nisba*. Landau-Tasseron argues that the reference in Ibn Ḥajar's *Lisān al-mīzān* is to another al-Ḥusayn b. Ziyād who "seems too early to have been the informant of al-Walīd b. Ḥammād" (see Landau-Tasseron, *New Data*, 366). Regarding the identification of al-Ḥusayn b. Ziyād al-Ramlī as ʿAlid or Shīʿī, she indirectly criticises Mourad (and Conrad) for having confused this transmitter with al-Ḥusayn b. Ziyād al-Luʾluʾī who, according to Ibn al-ʿAdīm, was the Shīʿī (see Landau-Tasseron, *New Data*, 367, n. 22). Van Ess also questions the identification of al-Ḥusayn b. Ziyād as ʿAlid and steers away from quoting Conrad's (and Mourad's) proposed date of death (see van Ess, *Fehltritt*, 348). ʿUqla and Banī Yāsīn identify him as a disciple of Jaʿfar al-Ṣādiq (d. 148/765) and hence assume that he died "at the beginning of the 3rd/9th century". In addition, they accept al-Ṭūsī's information and regard him as a Shīʿī who flourished in the 2nd/8th century and who transmitted from Jaʿfar al-Ṣādiq (d. 148/765) and ʿAlī b. Mūsā b. Jaʿfar al-Riḍā (d. 203/818) (see al-Azdī, *Futūḥ al-Shām. Ed. ʿUqla/Banī Yāsīn*, 16, 35, 51). On the basis of Ibn al-ʿAdīm's *Bughyat al-ṭalab*, Shoshan adds that al-Ḥusayn b. Ziyād was a contemporary of Fuḍayl b. ʿIyāḍ (d. 187/803) (see Shoshan, *Historical Tradition*, 9, 22, n. 75 referring to Ibn al-ʿAdīm, *Bughyat al-ṭalab*, III, 1455, l. 20–21; however, al-Ḥusayn b. Ziyād in this case is to be identified with the above-mentioned Abū ʿAlī al-Ḥusayn b. Ziyād al-Marwazī, see ibid., III, 1455, l. 3–4). In al-Azdī's narrative, al-Ḥusayn b. Ziyād is regularly mentioned as a transmitter of *ḥadīth* and as the immediate transmitter from al-Azdī. On al-Ḥusayn, see al-Ṭūsī, *Al-fihrist*, 82 (no. 220) and Ibn Ḥajar, *Lisān*, II, 284 (no. 1181).

In the transmission of Abū al-ʿAbbās al-Walīd b. Ḥammād al-Ramlī[3] who recounted from the former.

In the transmission of Abū al-Ḥasan ʿAlī b. Aḥmad b. Isḥāq b. Ibrāhīm al-Baghdādī[4] who recounted from the former.

In the transmission of Abū al-ʿAbbās Munīr b. Aḥmad b. al-Ḥasan al-Khashshāb[5] who recounted from the former.

3 Abū al-ʿAbbās al-Walīd b. Ḥammād b. Jābir al-Ramlī (d. ca. 300/912) was a transmitter of *ḥadīth* and the compiler-author of a book on the merits of Jerusalem. Conrad was able to identify him and presents his death date as "close to the end of the third century A.H." (see Conrad, *al-Azdī's History*, 57). Mourad analyses his role in the development of the *Faḍāʾil Bayt al-Maqdis* genre and mentions his date of death as "around 300/912" (see Mourad, *Note*, 34–39). Van Ess dates al-Walīd b. Ḥammād's *floruit* back to the "two latter thirds of the 3rd[/9th] century" (see van Ess, *Fehltritt*, 348). ʿUqla and Banī Yāsīn accept Conrad's death date but point out that there was a gap of ninety years between al-Ḥusayn b. Ziyād al-Ramlī's and al-Walīd b. Ḥammād's deaths. Arguing that both were from Ramla, that there were other scholars of that age and that al-Walīd b. Ḥammād is recognised as a sound scholar, they dismiss the possibility of a later extended *isnād* (*irsāl*) supposedly done by al-Walīd b. Ḥammād (see al-Azdī, *Futūḥ al-Shām. Ed. ʿUqla/Banī Yāsīn*, 35–36). In addition, they stress that al-Walīd b. Ḥammād also transmitted traditions to Abū Bishr al-Dūlābī (see ibid., 51–52). In al-Azdī's narrative, al-Walīd is regularly mentioned as a transmitter and as the second-generation transmitter after al-Azdī. On al-Walīd b. Ḥammād al-Ramlī, see Ibn ʿAsākir, *TMD*, LXIII, 121–123 (no. 7999); al-Dhahabī, *Siyar aʿlām al-nubalāʾ*, XIV, 78–79 (no. 37); al-Dhahabī, *Taʾrīkh al-islām*, vol. 291–300 H., 320 (no. 538).

4 Abū al-Ḥasan ʿAlī b. Aḥmad b. Isḥāq al-Baghdādī (d. 340/951–952) was a transmitter of *ḥadīth* in Baghdad who later travelled to Damascus and settled in Cairo. Based on Ibn al-ʿImād's *Shadharāt al-dhahab*, Vajda hypothesises that al-Baghdādī died in 419/1028 (see Vajda, *Certificats*, 27, n. 1). According to the *riwāya* of the Parisian ms 1665, ʿAlī b. Aḥmad al-Baghdādī transmitted the text from al-Walīd b. Ḥammād al-Ramlī in Shaʿbān 286/August 899 (see al-Azdī, *Futūḥ al-Shām. Ed. ʿUqla/Banī Yāsīn*, 63. This point was already mentioned by Mourad without providing a reference for his information; see Mourad, *al-Azdī*, 581). Based on al-Dhahabī's *Siyar*, Landau-Tasseron mentions his date of death as 340/951–952 (see Landau-Tasseron, *New Data*, 366; 366, n. 17). ʿUqla and Banī Yāsīn follow Landau-Tasseron's death date, which has to be accepted as the correct one (see al-Azdī, *Futūḥ al-Shām. Ed. ʿUqla/Banī Yāsīn*, 52). In al-Azdī's narrative, ʿAlī b. Aḥmad is mentioned as a transmitter of the whole manuscript 1664. On ʿAlī b. Aḥmad, see al-Khaṭīb al-Baghdādī, *Taʾrīkh Baghdād*, XI, 322 (no. 6137); Ibn ʿAsākir, *TMD*, XLI, 229–230 (no. 4782); al-Dhahabī, *Siyar aʿlām al-nubalāʾ*, XV, 474–475 (no. 267).

5 Abū al-ʿAbbās Munīr b. Aḥmad b. al-Ḥasan b. ʿAlī b. Munīr al-Khashshāb (d. 412/1022) was a reliable transmitter. Based on Ibn al-ʿImād's *Shadharāt al-dhahab*, Vajda hypothesises that al-Khashshāb died in 412/1021–1022 (see Vajda, *Certificats*, 27, n. 2). According to the *riwāya* of the Parisian ms 1665, Munīr b. Aḥmad al-Khashshāb transmitted the text from ʿAlī b. Aḥmad al-Baghdādī "in the latter's home in [3]43/[9]54–[9]55" (see al-Azdī, *Futūḥ al-Shām. Ed. ʿUqla/Banī Yāsīn*, 63. This point was already mentioned by Mourad without providing a reference for his information; see Mourad, *al-Azdī*, 581). This date, however, contradicts ʿAlī b. Aḥmad al-Baghdādī's above-mentioned date of death. Therefore, it seems to be wrong. In al-Azdī's narrative, Munīr is introduced as a transmitter of the whole manuscript 1664. On Munīr b. Aḥmad, see al-Dhahabī, *Siyar aʿlām al-nubalāʾ*, XVII, 267 (no. 163).

In the transmission of Abū Isḥāq Ibrāhīm b. Saʿīd b. ʿAbdallāh [al-Ḥabbāl][6] who recounted from the former.

In the transmission of Abū al-Ḥusayn Aḥmad b. Muḥammad b. Musbiḥ al-Muqriʾ[7] who recounted from the former.

In the transmission of Abū Ṭāhir Aḥmad b. Muḥammad al-Silafī[8] who recounted from the former.

6 Abū Isḥāq Ibrāhīm b. Saʿīd b. ʿAbdallāh al-Nuʿmānī al-Ḥabbāl (d. 482/1089) is a well-known transmitter of *ḥadīth* who lived in Cairo. According to Mourad, Ibrāhīm b. Saʿīd al-Ḥabbāl transmitted the text from Munīr b. Aḥmad al-Khashshāb in Cairo (see Mourad, *al-Azdī*, 581) while he attended Munīr's funeral and authored many books, according to Landau-Tasseron (see Landau-Tasseron, *New Data*, 374). In al-Azdī's narrative, his name of kinship (*nisba*) is given as al-Tujībī in one place and the honorific title "*al-ḥāfiẓ*" (lit. "the memoriser") is ascribed to him in four places. In al-Azdī's narrative, he is mentioned as a transmitter of the whole manuscript 1664. On Ibrāhīm b. Saʿīd al-Ḥabbāl see Brockelmann, *GAL. Supplement*, I, 572; al-Ṣafadī, *Al-wāfī. Ed. Vol. 5 S. Dedering*, 355 (no. 2433); al-Dhahabī, *Siyar aʿlām al-nubalāʾ*, XVIII, 495–503 (no. 259).

7 Abū al-Ḥusayn Aḥmad b. Muḥammad b. Musbiḥ al-Muqriʾ (n.d.) was a reciter of the Qurʾān in Cairo and one of al-Silafī teachers, according to al-Silafī. ʿĀmir mentions that he was alive in the year 513/1119–1120 without providing any documentation (see al-Azdī, *Futūḥ al-Shām. Ed. ʿĀmir*, ك). According to the *riwāya* of the Parisian ms 1665, Aḥmad b. Muḥammad al-Muqriʾ transmitted the text from Ibrāhīm b. Saʿīd al-Ḥabbāl in Cairo (see al-Azdī, *Futūḥ al-Shām. Ed. ʿUqla/Banī Yāsīn*, 54. Mourad already mentioned this point without providing a reference for his information, however; see Mourad, *al-Azdī*, 581–582). In al-Azdī's narrative, Aḥmad b. Muḥammad b. Musbiḥ is mentioned as a transmitter of the whole manuscript 1664. On Aḥmad b. Muḥammad b. Musbiḥ al-Muqriʾ, see al-Silafī, *Muʿjam al-safar*, 12–13 (no. 23).

8 Abū Ṭāhir Aḥmad b. Muḥammad b. Aḥmad b. Muḥammad b. Ibrāhīm (or Silafa) al-Silafī al-Iṣfahānī (472/1078–1079—576/1180) was a traditionalist who studied in the Niẓāmiyya *madrasa* in Baghdad and in Damascus and settled in Alexandria in 511/1117–1118. He stayed there for the rest of his life, transmitting hundreds of Arabic works. According to the *riwāya* of the "Kāle-Sprenger-manuscript", al-Silafī transmitted the manuscript to his disciples "at the port of Alexandria in Muḥarram 573/July 1177" while he himself heard it from his teacher Aḥmad b. Muḥammad al-Muqriʾ in Fusṭāṭ Miṣr in Dhū al-Ḥijja 515/February–March 1122 (see al-Azdī, *Futūḥ al-Shām. Ed. Lees*, 35, n. 4). Mourad already mentioned this point without providing a reference for his information, however (see Mourad, *al-Azdī*, 582). According to the *riwāya* of the Parisian ms 1665, al-Silafī transmitted the text to his disciple Jamāl al-Dīn Abū al-Faḍl Yūsuf b. al-Muʿṭī b. Manṣūr b. Najā al-Muḥāmilī "in [one] of his final *majālis* [held] in Alexandria on Sunday, 14th Rabīʿ I 574/30th August 1178" while he himself heard it from his teacher Aḥmad b. Muḥammad al-Muqriʾ in Miṣr (see al-Azdī, *Futūḥ al-Shām. Ed. ʿUqla/Banī Yāsīn*, 55). ʿUqla and Banī Yāsīn realised that al-Silafī was a central figure (*madār*) in the transmission of the *Futūḥ al-Shām* (see ibid., 55, 58). In fact, all known manuscripts (two from Paris, one from Berlin and one from Damascus) and the *riwāya* mentioned in Ibn al-ʿAdīm's *Bughyat al-ṭalab* (see Ibn al-ʿAdīm, *Bughyat al-ṭalab*, I, 69, l. 12—70, l. 1) name al-Silafī as a transmitter. In al-Azdī's narrative, al-Silafī is mentioned as a transmitter of the whole manuscript 1664, which indicates that al-Azdī's *Futūḥ al-Shām* is one of the many works he transmitted. On al-Silafī, see *EI*², s.v. al-Silafī (C. Gilliot).

In the transmission of Abū al-Faḍl Jaʿfar b. ʿAlī al-Hamadhānī[9] who recounted from the former.

In the transmission of its [=the book's] owner al-Shaykh al-Imām Nūr al-Dīn Abū al-Ḥasan ʿAlī b. Masʿūd al-Mawṣilī al-Dimashqī[10] who recounted from the former.

[Section I: Abū Bakr al-Ṣiddīq's preparation for attacking the Byzantines in Syria]

[Manuscript note: Part (*juz'*) I]

\\77 In the name of God, the Merciful, the Compassionate; O my Lord, facilitate [my task]! Shaykh Abū Isḥāq Ibrāhīm b. Saʿīd b. ʿAbdallāh al-Ḥabbāl reported to us: Shaykh Abū al-ʿAbbās Munīr b. Aḥmad b. al-Ḥasan b. ʿAlī b. Munīr al-Khashshāb related to us, by way of reading (*qirā'atan*) to the former while I was listening: Abū al-Ḥasan ʿAlī b. Aḥmad b. Isḥāq al-Baghdādī related to us, by way of reading to the former: Abū al-ʿAbbās al-Walīd b. Ḥammād al-Ramlī related to us: Al-Ḥusayn b. Ziyād al-Ramlī related to us: Abū Ismāʿīl Muḥammad b. ʿAbdallāh al-Azdī al-Baṣrī[11] related to us, saying: When God (t.) decreed that His Prophet (ṣ.) should die, a large number of the Arabs[12] apostatised from Islam after the Prophet's

9 Abū al-Faḍl Jaʿfar b. ʿAlī b. Hibat Allāh al-Hamadhānī (d. 636/1238) is a *faqīh* and a transmitter of *ḥadīth*. Based on Ibn al-Jazarī's *Ghāyat al-nihāya* and Ibn al-ʿImād's *Shadharāt al-dhahab*, Vajda mentions his *floruit* as 541/1146 or 546/1151—636/1238 (see Vajda, *Les certificats*, 28, n. 5). ʿUqla and Banī Yāsīn found a biographical entry on him in al-Dhahabī's *Siyar*, in which his date of birth is given as 546/1151 (see al-Azdī, *Futūḥ al-Shām. Ed. ʿUqla/Banī Yāsīn*, 56). In al-Azdī's narrative, he is mentioned as a transmitter of the whole manuscript 1664. On Abū al-Faḍl Jaʿfar b. ʿAlī b. Hibat Allāh al-Hamadhānī, see al-Dhahabī, *Siyar aʿlām al-nubalā'*, XXIII, 36–39 (no. 26).

10 Abū al-Ḥasan ʿAlī b. Masʿūd al-Mawṣilī, then al-Ḥalabī, then al-Dimashqī (d. 704/1304–1305), was famous for his legal judgements (*fatāwā*) and participated in the war against the Mongols. In al-Azdī's narrative, he is mentioned as a transmitter of the whole manuscript 1664 and as its owner. On Abū al-Ḥasan ʿAlī b. Masʿūd al-Mawṣilī, see Ibn Ḥajar, *Al-durar al-kāmina*, III, 203 (no. 2916).

11 Abū Ismāʿīl Muḥammad b. ʿAbdallāh al-Azdī al-Baṣrī is the compiler-author of *Futūḥ al-Shām*. In addition, he is mentioned in the narrative as a transmitter of most of the traditions. For further information on him, see Chapter 2.

12 In al-Azdī's narrative, the term "Arabs" is mostly used from the Byzantine perspective. Accordingly, "the Arabs" are those groups that are attacking the Byzantine territory and its Christian inhabitants. In one place, there is a mention of a prophet, i.e. Muḥammad, who came to them and promised them victory in their raids. In addition, "Arabs" is contrasted with those groups in Syria that were neither local inhabitants nor Byzantine rulers or soldiers, but fighters who supported the Byzantine army and adopted Christianity. When "Arabs" is used from the Muslim perspective, it is often contrasted with "the Emigrants" and "the Supporters" (i.e. the Muslims in general). According to al-Azdī's narrative, (some) "Arabs" come from Yemen to Abū Bakr in Medina who then dispatches them to Syria. On Arabs, see EI^2, s.v. al-ʿArab (A. Grohmann et al.); *EI. Three*, s.v. Arabs (historical) (J. Retsö) and s.v. Arabs (anthropology) (D. Eickelman).

(ṣ.) death, reneged their faith by not paying the prescribed tax (*zakāt*) and said: "We were giving our possessions[13] to Muḥammad[14]; why does Ibn Abī Quḥāfa [=Abū Bakr[15]] ask for our possessions? We swear by God not to give him any of it at all". Hence, they refused and denied to pay the prescribed tax to Abū Bakr (r.). Abū Bakr (r.) soon consulted the companions of the Messenger of God (ṣ.) about the apostates, who [=the companions of the Messenger of God] unanimously agreed\\78 to adhere to their religion and to leave the [apostatising] people to what they had chosen for themselves. They also thought that they could not stand against those among them who apostatised from Islam, because of the suffering the Messenger of God (ṣ.) had in waging many fights for the cause of God (*jihād*) against them and because of the disbelief, harm, violence, hardship and adversity he faced—not to mention their large number, vehement valour and might—before they all embraced Islam prior to his death. When they [=these people] apostatised

13 On the translation of the expression "*amwāl*, (sg. *māl*)" as "possessions", see Lane, *Lexicon*, s.v. *māl*.

14 Muḥammad's full name is Abū al-Qāsim Muḥammad b. ʿAbdallāh al-Qurashī (d. 9/632). In al-Azdī's narrative, some biographical and theological information is given about Muḥammad. Biographically, he was born in Mecca, was fought there by al-Ḥārith b. Hishām and then emigrated to Ṭayba [=Medina]. In addition, Muḥammad is said to have taught religious rules and to have fought against the Meccans at Uḥud, where he lost his front teeth. A flag of Muḥammad and many of his battle-days during which he fought against other Arabian tribes are also mentioned. These battles that, according to the narrative, gained God's support led to their subjugation and their payment of taxes to Muḥammad. Furthermore, several smaller points concerning Muḥammad are mentioned: Khālid b. Saʿīd b. al-ʿĀṣ is described as being one of Muḥammad's subordinates (*ʿummāl*); Muḥammad is said to have used to fight at noon, to have had a mosque (in Medina) and to have promised Paradise to ten persons. Finally, Muḥammad's death is briefly mentioned and a description of his personal qualities is given. Regarding the more theological information given in al-Azdī's narrative, Muḥammad is said to be the Messenger and servant of God, to be His Prophet to whom God sent down a scripture and whom God sent with the truth. Furthermore, he is the Seal of the Prophets and from the Byzantine's perspective, he is called "the Arabs' Prophet". In addition, Muḥammad is described as a blessing, mercy and honour for the Muslims, and the Polytheists are called to believe "in God and in Muḥammad". In some places, traditions (*ḥadīth*) by Muḥammad are quoted. They pertain to his triumphant religion, the patience of the Muslims, the prohibition against associating anything else with God and against torturing people, the best status of the companions of the Messenger of God and those whom God will send to Paradise. On Muḥammad, see *EI*[2], s.v. Muḥammad (F. Buhl/A. Welch/et al.).

15 Abū Bakr's full name is Abū Bakr ʿAbdallāh (or ʿAtīq) b. Abī Quḥāfa ʿUthmān b. ʿĀmir al-Taymī al-Ṣiddīq ("the Truthful") (d. 13/634). Al-Azdī's narrative commences with the so-called "Apostasy Wars" (*ridda*). In the course of these and other events, Abū Bakr is portrayed as a major figure, a decisive and advice-seeking leader and an exact follower of Muḥammad's model. According to the narrative, it was Abū Bakr who devised the stratagem to attack the Byzantines in Syria and who executed it by dispatching several units of fighters to Syria. Abū Bakr is called "successor of the Messenger of God" (*khalīfat rasūl Allāh*) in al-Azdī's narrative, and his death date is said to be 22 Jumādā II 13 [=23 August 634] after the Muslims had fought (and won) the Battle of Ajnādayn. On Abū Bakr, see *EI*[2], s.v. Abū Bakr (W. Watt).

after his death, the companions of the Messenger of God (ṣ.) feared that they would suffer what the Messenger of God (ṣ.) had suffered during his lifetime because of them. [They also feared] that they would not have the power to wage war and fight for the cause of God against them. Thus, they all agreed to adhere to their religion and to leave the people [=the apostates] to what they had chosen for themselves. So Abū Bakr (r.) said: "I swear by God that if nobody supports me, I will fight them alone until I die or they revert to Islam. And if they refuse to give me a year's poor-rate (*ʿiqāl*)[16] of what they were used to giving to the Messenger of God (ṣ.), I will fight them until I meet God". Abū Bakr (r.), along with the companions of the Messenger of God (ṣ.) and the new as well as the old Muslims,[17] kept fighting them until they all reverted to Islam and returned to what they had deserted.[18] When God had subjugated the [apostatising] Arabs, when the conquests (*futūḥ*) in all directions had ended up in [favour of] Abū Bakr (r.), and when the Arabs had felt secure with Islam, acquiesced to it and concurred unanimously with it, Abū Bakr (r.) considered attacking the Byzantines.[19] However, he kept

16 See Lane, *Lexicon*, s.v. *ʿiqāl*.

17 In al-Azdī's narrative, Muslims (lit. "those who submitted themselves to (the one) God") or simply "the people" (*al-qawm*) is the standard designation for those people to whom Muḥammad is said to have come as a Prophet and whom Abū Bakr dispatched to Syria to fight the Byzantines. In addition, those people who stayed behind in Medina are also called "Muslims". Arabian tribes are usually mentioned beside the Muslims (and not as parts of them). The Muslims are generally treated as a collective unit and are only rarely divided into subgroups, thus "the Muslims" attack, fight, conquer, etc. Sometimes military subunits are mentioned, e.g. the Muslim right or left flank, the Muslim cavalry or infantry, etc. In addition, Muslim fighters, who regularly proclaim "God is the Greatest!", are divided into common Muslims and Muslim chiefs (or masters), as well as into Muslim men and (very rarely) Muslim women, but they call themselves "brothers". At the beginning of the narrative (in the context of Abū Bakr's fighting against rebellious tribes), there is a differentiation between new and old Muslims, probably referring to the Emigrants and the Supporters. On Muslims, see *EI²*, s.v. Muslim (A. Wensinck).

18 This passage of al-Azdī's narrative refers to the so-called "Apostasy Wars" (*ridda*). This term, however, is a misnomer, because the tribes that were fought by the new Islamic state were either refusing to pay taxes to Medina (but wanted to keep the new faith) or were led by chieftains who claimed to be prophets. For a detailed outline of the events during these clashes that were a prelude to the ensuing conquests in Syria and Iraq in terms of manpower and logistics, see *EI²*, s.v. al-Ridda (M. Lecker).

19 In al-Azdī's narrative, the Byzantines (al-Rūm, lit. "the Romaeans, the Greeks") are also called "*Banū al-Aṣfar*", i.e. "the sons or children of al-Aṣfar" or "the sons or children of the blond One", non-Arabs or simply the people. The Byzantines are described as being very strong and as marching to war in large numbers. In addition, the Byzantines own fortresses in Syria and have special weaponry (such as iron masks, helmets, coats of mail, arm and breast protectors and swords). They are supported by the Christian Arabs of Syria, by the local people of Syria, e.g. from Damascus, and by religious dignitaries (such as bishops, priests and monks). In addition to fighting the Muslims as a group or in many duels, they negotiate peace and religious issues with some Muslim representatives. However, in the eyes of their Syrian subjects, the Byzantines are corrupt; they misbehave and usurp, and they appropriate as many goods as possible. The Byzantines are subdivided into their Emperor, Heraclius, their noblemen who are also called patricians

it to himself and, therefore, nobody learned about it. While he was in this [situation], Shuraḥbīl b. Ḥasana[20] came to him and said: "O successor of the Messenger of God (*khalīfat rasūl Allāh*),[21] are you considering sending soldiers to Syria[22]?" He [=Abū Bakr] said: "Yes, I have considered that but told nobody about it. But you must have asked me about it only for some personal reason". He [=Shuraḥbīl] said: "Yes, while sleeping I had a vision in which

---

(*biṭrīq*, pl. *baṭāriqa*), grand men (*ʿaẓīm*, pl. *ʿuẓamāʾ*) or sovereigns (*malik*, pl. *mulūk*), and some named Byzantine commanders, such as al-Durunjār, Wardān, Bāhān, Ibn Qanāṭir and individual Byzantine soldiers, who are rarely named (except for one called Jirja). The Byzantine army is said to have an infantry consisting of swordsmen and bowmen, several cavalry units and a navy. In addition, an Armenian unit is mentioned under the command of Jirjīs. On the Byzantines, see *EI. Three*, s.v. Byzantium (N. El Cheikh). For *Banū al-Aṣfar*, see below p. 46, n. 39.

20 Shuraḥbīl's full name is Abū ʿAbdallāh Shuraḥbīl b. Ḥasana (or b. ʿAbdallāh b. al-Muṭāḥ) al-Ghawthī (d. 18/639). Van Ess identifies the name Shuraḥbīl as a composition of "*shuraḥ bi-īl*", which means "protected by God". In al-Azdī's narrative, Shuraḥbīl figures prominently. He recognises Abū Bakr's inner wish to send troops to Syria before the latter speaks about it. Later Abū Bakr appoints Shuraḥbīl as one of the commanders. After having a vision, which Abū Bakr interprets as a sign of victory, Shuraḥbīl leaves Medina three days after the departure of Yazīd b. Abī Sufyān for Syria. Next, he appears in the vicinity of Bosra, where the advance of a Byzantine unit threatens him. However, Khālid b. al-Walīd orders Shuraḥbīl to join the Muslim troops in the Battle of Ajnādayn, after which Abū ʿUbayda sends Shuraḥbīl to support ʿAmr b. al-ʿĀṣ against another Byzantine unit that is advancing to Baalbek. Then Shuraḥbīl is depicted as an advisor to the Muslims who suggests withdrawing the Muslim army from the city of Ḥimṣ to which the Byzantines march and dispatching them to the southern borders of Syria. However, his suggestion is rejected. Lastly, Shuraḥbīl is mentioned in al-Azdī's narrative as a commander of one quarter of the Muslim army during the Battle of al-Yarmūk. On Shuraḥbīl, see *EI*[2], s.v. Shuraḥbīl b. Ḥasana (C. Bosworth) and van Ess, *Pest*, 257.

21 In al-Azdī's narrative, the phrase "*khalīfat rasūl Allāh*" (lit. "the successor of the Messenger of God") refers to persons who followed Muḥammad as political and religious leaders of the new community of the Believers. It has an intertextual reference to the Qurʾān where Adam and David are described as such and are given judicial rights over the people by God (see Q. 38:26 and 2:30). In translating the phrase, we follow a more literal approach in order not to project a later religio-political view on an earlier period in which the phrase was not yet used to describe the monarch that ruled over the Muslim community.

22 Syria, more precisely "Greater Syria", (al-Shām) is a region that is bordered by the Mediterranean to the west, the Taurus Mountains to the north, the Euphrates to the northeast, vast steppes to the east and the Arabian Peninsula to the south. In the narrative, Syria is represented as an assemblage of regions and hence called sometimes "*Bilād al-Shām*" ("the Lands of Syria"), but most often al-Shām ("Syria") is used. According to the narrative, the following regions belong to Syria (listed from north to south): The land of Qinnasrīn, the land of Ḥimṣ, the land of Damascus, the land of al-Balqāʾ, the land of Ḥawrān, the land of Bekaa, the land of the River Jordan and the land of Palestine. In addition, al-Azdī also associates the following places with Syria: Antioch, Ḥimṣ, Damascus, al-Yarmūk, Maʾāb, Ajnādayn and Ayla. In the course of his narrative, al-Azdī narrates how the Muslim troops under the command of Abū ʿUbayda b. al-Jarrāḥ, Khālid b. al-Walīd, Yazīd b. Abī Sufyān, Shuraḥbīl b. Ḥasana, ʿAmr b. al-ʿĀṣ (and others) conquered these places and subdued their inhabitants into paying taxes to the early Muslim rulers. On Syria, see *EI*[2], s.v. al-Shām, al-Shaʾm (C. Bosworth et al.).

you stood amidst a group of Muslims on a mountain; then you proceeded to walk with them until you ascended to a lofty dome-like spot (*qubba*) on the mountain. Then together with your companions, you approached the people there and descended from that dome-like spot to a soft and even (*damtha*) land—he [=the narrator] said: *Al-damtha* means "soft (*layyina*) and even, mixed\\79 with sand"—where hamlets and springs as well as fields and forts exist. Then you said: 'O Muslims, launch a raid on the Polytheists,[23] for I guarantee you victory and spoils'. I was one of them [=the Muslims], holding a banner with which I then headed towards a hamlet and I entered it. The people of the hamlet asked me for a letter of protection (*amān*) and I granted it to them. Then I came [along] and found that you had reached a great fort, which was opened up to you, whose entire people offered you peace and where you were provided with the throne. Then you sat on the throne and someone said to you: 'You are predestined to conquer [many lands] and to win many victories, so thank your Lord and remain obedient to Him'. Then he recited to you: 'When God's help comes and He opens up your way[, Prophet], when you see people embracing God's faith in crowds, celebrate the praise of your Lord and ask His forgiveness: He is always ready to accept repentance'."[24] He [=Shuraḥbīl] said: "Then I woke up".

Thereupon, Abū Bakr al-Ṣiddīq (r.) said to him: "May your eyes beam [with delight]". Then Abū Bakr (r.) shed tears and said: "Regarding the mountain on which you saw us walking until we have mounted to the lofty dome-like spot and approached the people there, it means that we will suffer hard because of these soldiers [=the Byzantines] and they will suffer too; but afterwards we will win and our cause will win. Regarding our descent from the lofty dome-like spot to the mellow level land, the fields, the forts, the springs and the hamlets, it means that we will descend to a better state of fertility and living than the one we had before. Regarding my statement to the Muslims: 'Launch a raid on the people of these hamlets, for I guarantee [you] victory and spoils', it means my dispatch of the Muslims to the Unbelievers' lands and my command to them to start fighting for the cause of God. Regarding the banner you were holding and with which you headed to one of their

23 In al-Azdī's narrative, "Polytheists" (*mushrikūn*, lit. "those who associate [other deities] with God"), refers not only to the native inhabitants of Syria or the Byzantines, but also to the native inhabitants of Iraq. "The Polytheists" are said to have fought at al-Ubulla, Ajnādayn, Damascus, Fiḥl, Ḥimṣ and al-Yarmūk. When the term "Polytheists" (rather than Byzantines) is used, there is usually a military context invoking the qur'ānic concept of fighting the Polytheists for the cause of God. In addition, "Polytheists" are those who associate another deity or god with God the One, who associate a female partner or a child with God, who worship a fire, a stone, a sun or a moon instead of God. Also those who claim that God has a child or that He is one of two [=binitarianism] or one of three [=trinitarianism] are said to be "Polytheists" in al-Azdī's narrative. Hence, in line with the qur'ānic text (and most probably inspired by it), "Polytheists" are Christians and pagan Arabs who worship idols. On Polytheists, see *EI*[2], s.v. Shirk (D. Gimaret).

24 Q. 110:1–3 (*The Qur'ān. Tr. Abdel Haleem*, 442).

hamlets, then entered it and granted them peace which they had requested from you, it means that you will certainly be one of the Muslim commanders (*umarā'*, sg. *amīr*) and God (t.) will lead you to conquests. Regarding the fort that God opened up to me, it represents a destination which God will lead me to conquer. Regarding the throne on which\\80 you saw me seated, it means that God ('a.) will surely promote me and demote the Polytheists. Regarding the one who commanded me to obey my Lord and who recited the [mentioned] chapter (*sūra*) to me, it means that he notified me of my death. For when this chapter was sent down to the Messenger of God (ṣ.), he knew that his death was decreed". Then Abū Bakr's (r.) eyes flooded with tears and he said: "I swear to command what is right and forbid what is wrong, to fight whoever withholds from the cause of God ('a.) and to deploy soldiers [to fight] against those who diverted from God (*al-'ādilūn bi-llāh*) in the East and in the West until they say 'God is One' or until they bring tribute (*jizya*) by hand and with humility (*'an yadin wa-hum ṣāghirūn*)[25]. If my Lord (tt.) decreed my death, He would find me neither negligent, slack nor abstinent from the reward [He promised] to the fighters for His cause (*mujāhidūn*)". Thereupon, he appointed commanders and sent envoys to Syria.

Al-Walīd b. Ḥammād [al-Ramlī] related to us: Al-Ḥusayn b. Ziyād [al-Ramlī] related to us on the authority of Abū Ismā'īl Muḥammad b. 'Abdallāh [al-Azdī], who said: Furthermore, al-Ḥārith b. Ka'b[26] related to me on the authority of 'Abdallāh b. Abī Awfā al-Khuzā'ī[27], a companion [of

25 The expression "*aw yu'addū al-jizya 'an yadin wa-hum ṣāghirūn*" is the first of many others remodeled on the so-called "*jizya*-verse" in the qur'ānic text, which reads "*ḥattā yu'ṭū al-jizya 'an yadin wa-hum ṣāghirūn*" (lit. "until they pay the tax and agree to submit", Q. 9:29; see *The Qur'ān. Tr. Abdel Haleem*, 118). Note that the verb "*yu'ṭū*" (lit. "they give") in al-Azdī's narrative is mostly replaced with "*yu'addū*" (lit. "they bring"). The exact meaning of the expression "*'an yadin*" is still quite unclear. In the classical Muslim exegetical tradition, "*yad*" (lit. "hand") can refer either to that of the non-Muslim who gives the *jizya* or to that of the Muslim who receives it. When "*yad*" refers to the donor, the meaning has an implication for the social status of the non-Muslim, i.e. the donor should be inferior to the receiver and should pay tribute with humility. On the basis of peace treaties that are preserved in the historiographical literature, Rubin argues that "*'an yadin*" should be understood as paying tribute "out of one's property" (see Rubin, *Quran and Tafsīr*, 140). However, due to the general qur'ānic style mimicked in al-Azdī's narrative, we accept the meaning of "the inferior donor" in our translation.

26 Al-Ḥārith b. Ka'b b. 'Amr b. 'Awf al-Anṣārī al-Najjārī, then al-Maznī, (n.d.) is a companion of the Prophet Muḥammad who was killed in al-Yamāma. Mourad identifies this person as al-Ḥārith b. Ka'b b. al-Wālibī al-Azdī; according to his sources he was an 'Alid (see Mourad, *al-Azdī*, 589). On the basis of al-Ṭabarī's *Ta'rīkh*, 'Uqla and Banī Yāsīn identify him as al-Ḥārith b. Ka'b b. Fuqaym al-Azdī al-Wālibī, who was an informant of al-Azdī and Abū Mikhnaf or as al-Ḥārith b. Ka'b al-Murādī, one of the transmitters of 'Abdallāh b. Abī Awfā, on the basis of Ibn 'Asākir's *TMD* (see al-Azdī, *Futūḥ al-Shām. Ed. 'Uqla/Banī Yāsīn*, 24; 80, n. 10). In al-Azdī's narrative, al-Ḥārith b. Ka'b is mentioned as a transmitter of four traditions. On al-Ḥārith b. Ka'b, see Ibn Ḥajar, *Al-iṣāba. Ed. al-Baghawī*, I, 594 (no. 1476), al-Ṭabarī, *Ta'rīkh*, II, 273, l. 16 and Ibn 'Asākir, *TMD*, XXXI, 31.

27 'Abdallāh b. Abī Awfā al-Khuzā'ī (d. 87/705) is the last companion of the Prophet who died in al-Kūfa. 'Uqla and Banī Yāsīn found a reference to him in Ibn 'Asākir's *TMD*,

the Prophet], who said:\\81 When Abū Bakr (r.) wanted to deploy soldiers to Syria, he invited ʿUmar [b. al-Khaṭṭāb[28]], ʿUthmān [b. ʿAffān[29]], ʿAlī [b. Abī Ṭālib[30]], Ṭalḥa [b. ʿUbaydallāh[31]], al-Zubayr [b. al-ʿAwwām[32]], ʿAbd

according to which he is one of the informants of al-Ḥārith b. Kaʿb (see al-Azdī, *Futūḥ al-Shām. Ed. ʿUqla/Banī Yāsīn*, 80, n. 11). In al-Azdī's narrative, he is said to be one of the Prophet Muḥammad's companions and a transmitter of one tradition. On ʿAbdallāh b. Abī Awfā al-Khuzāʿī, see Ibn ʿAsākir, *TMD*, XXXI, 31–50 (no. 3408).

28 ʿUmar's full name is Abū ʿAbdallāh ʿUmar b. al-Khaṭṭāb al-Qurashī al-ʿAdawī (d. 23/644). In al-Azdī's narrative, ʿUmar is once called Ibn Ḥintima after his mother Ḥintima and is mentioned as a cousin of Saʿīd b. Zayd b. ʿAmr b. Nufayl. He is given the epithets "the One who separates right from wrong or differentiates between truth and falsehood" (*al-Fārūq*) and "the Commander of the Believers" (*amīr al-muʾminīn*) and "successor" (*khalīfa*) after his appointment as successor of the young community by Abū Bakr. Al-Azdī's narrative starts with depicting ʿUmar as a close consultant of Abū Bakr. ʿUmar and Khālid b. al-Walīd's relationship is portrayed with various tensions which finally led to ʿUmar's deposition of Khālid from the chief command over Syria. After having taken over rule, which, according to the narrative, is sometimes called his "caliphate" (*khilāfa*) and which is dated thirteen months minus seven days before the conquest of Damascus and sixteen months prior to the conquest of Fiḥl, ʿUmar is depicted as giving military, administrative and moral orders and as offering advice to the Muslim troops in Syria through many letters he had sent to the commanders in Syria, in particular to Abū ʿUbayda b. al-Jarrāḥ. ʿUmar was supposed to join forces with the Muslims before the Battle of al-Yarmūk, but ended up sending reinforcements that included Abū Sufyān. Finally, ʿUmar went to Syria himself, deciding several legal issues on his way. First, he is said to have delivered a (famous) speech at al-Jābiya, then to have been well received by the Muslim troops who were besieging Jerusalem. After having written a letter of protection for the people of Jerusalem, ʿUmar judges legal cases relating to a particular cooked drink, a man living (and sleeping) with two sisters at the same time, poor taxpayers who were tormented because they could not pay their taxes and two men who were sharing the same wife. At the end of al-Azdī's narrative, ʿUmar is said to have divided Syria into districts, to have ordered Yazīd b. Abī Sufyān to conquer Caesarea and to have made him (and Muʿāwiya) commanders of all of Syria. On ʿUmar, see *EI*², s.v. ʿUmar (I) b. al-Khaṭṭāb (G. Levi Della Vida/M. Bonner).

29 ʿUthmān's full name is Abū ʿAmr (or Abū ʿAbdallāh) ʿUthmān b. ʿAffān al-Umawī (d. 35/656). In al-Azdī's narrative, ʿUthmān is portrayed as a sound advisor and supporter of Abū Bakr (recommending attacking the Byzantines in Syria) and ʿUmar (recommending marching to Jerusalem). In addition, his caliphate is said to have spanned twelve years, during which he confirmed Muʿāwiya b. Abī Sufyān's command over the newly conquered territories in Syria. On ʿUthmān, see *EI*², s.v. ʿUthmān b. ʿAffān (G. Levi Della Vida/R. Khoury).

30 ʿAlī's full name is Abū al-Ḥasan ʿAlī b. Abī Ṭālib al-Hāshimī (d. 40/660). In al-Azdī's narrative, ʿAlī is portrayed as a sound advisor of Abū Bakr and ʿUmar. ʿAlī supports Abū Bakr in carrying out his stratagem of attacking Syria, quotes a tradition from the Prophet Muḥammad in which victory is predicted and advises ʿUmar to go to Jerusalem and conclude a peace treaty with the city's inhabitants. On ʿAlī, see *EI*², s.v. ʿAlī b. Abī Ṭālib (L. Veccia Vaglieri).

31 Ṭalḥa's full name is Abū Muḥammad Ṭalḥa b. ʿUbaydallāh al-Taymī (d. 36/656). In al-Azdī's narrative, Ṭalḥa is portrayed as a sound advisor of Abū Bakr and as a supporter of ʿUthmān's opinion in the debate over sending troops to Syria. On Ṭalḥa, see *EI*², s.v. Ṭalḥa (W. Madelung).

32 Al-Zubayr's full name is Abū ʿAbdallāh al-Zubayr b. al-ʿAwwām b. Khuwaylid al-Qurashī al-Asadī (d. 36/656). In al-Azdī's narrative, al-Zubayr is portrayed as a sound advisor of Abū Bakr and as a supporter of ʿUthmān's opinion in the debate over sending troops to Syria. On al-Zubayr, see *EI*², s.v. al-Zubayr b. al-ʿAwwām (I. Hasson).

al-Raḥmān b. ʿAwf[33], Saʿd b. Abī Waqqāṣ[34], Abū ʿUbayda b. al-Jarrāḥ[35], in addition to some prominent Emigrants[36] and Supporters[37] among the people who fought in the Battle of Badr[38] and others [to come to him]. All of them, including me, entered his [house], then he said: "The blessings of God (t.) are innumerable and deeds are never equal to their rewards. Much

33 In al-Azdī's narrative, ʿAbd al-Raḥmān b. ʿAwf al-Zuhrī (d. ca. 31/652) is portrayed as a sound advisor of Abū Bakr and ʿUmar. It was he who suggested seeking support from the southern Arabian tribes for the attack on the Byzantines. On ʿAbd al-Raḥmān b. ʿAwf, see *EI²*, s.v. ʿAbd al-Raḥmān b. ʿAwf (M. Houtsma/W. Watt).

34 Saʿd's full name is Abū Isḥāq Saʿd b. Abī Waqqāṣ Mālik b. Wuhayb (or Uhayb) b. ʿAbd Manāf b. Zuhra al-Qurashī (d. between 50–58/670–678). In al-Azdī's narrative, Saʿd is portrayed as a sound advisor of Abū Bakr and his nephew Hāshim b. ʿUtba b. Abī Waqqāṣ and as a supporter of ʿUthmān's opinion in the debate over sending troops to Syria. On Saʿd, see *EI²*, s.v. Saʿd b. Abī Waḳḳāṣ (G. Hawting).

35 Abū ʿUbayda's full name is Abū ʿUbayda ʿĀmir b. ʿAbdallāh b. al-Jarrāḥ al-Fihrī (d. 18/639). In al-Azdī's narrative, he supported Abū Bakr's idea to attack Syria and hence was sent as the commander in chief of the Muslim army to Syria. When Abū Bakr ordered Khālid b. al-Walīd to depart from Iraq to Syria, he deposed Abū ʿUbayda from this position and handed it over to Khālid. However, after ʿUmar had taken office, he restituted Abū ʿUbayda as the commander in chief. Abū ʿUbayda is portrayed as a political and military leader who got along with all the other Muslims. He wrote many letters to Abū Bakr, ʿUmar and the other commanders; he took part in all the major battles and conquests in Syria (e.g. Ajnādayn, Damascus, Fiḥl, al-Yarmūk and Jerusalem) and dispatched units further north to Qinnasrīn and Anatolia. According to al-Azdī's narrative, Abū ʿUbayda died during the spread of al-ʿAmwās plague in 18/639. On Abū ʿUbayda, see *EI²*, s.v. Abū ʿUbayda ʿĀmir b. ʿAbdallāh b. al-Djarrāḥ (H. Gibb).

36 In al-Azdī's narrative, "the Emigrants" (*al-muhājirūn*, lit. "those who emigrate") represent a group of the inhabitants of Medina, are described as "noble" and are said to have regularly been consulted by Abū Bakr and ʿUmar, who were supported by them. In addition, "the Emigrants" together with Abū Bakr said farewell to the departing commanders. On this group, see *EI²*, s.v. al-Muhādjirūn (W. Watt).

37 In al-Azdī's narrative, "the Supporters" (*al-anṣār*) represent a group of the inhabitants of Medina. Its constituents, the tribes of al-Aws and al-Khazraj, are not mentioned by name. However, eight individual figures are said to have belonged to this group: (a) Abū Qatāda al-Anṣārī, who is said to have been a messenger from Abū Bakr to Abū ʿUbayda; (b) ʿUmayr b. Saʿd al-Anṣārī, who was appointed as a commander by Khālid b. al-Walīd in the Battle of al-Ḥīra; (c) Bashīr b. Saʿd al-Anṣārī, who fought with Khālid at al-Ubulla; (d) Saʿīd b. ʿAmr b. Ḥarām al-Anṣārī, whom Khālid left behind as a commander of Ṣandawdāʾ; (e) Ḥassān b. Thābit al-Anṣārī, who was a famous poet and is mentioned twice as the uncle of Shaddād b. Aws b. Thābit; (f) Abū al-Dardāʾ al-Anṣārī, whom ʿUmar appointed, after Abū ʿUbayda's death, as a commander of Damascus where he gave an exhorting speech; (g) ʿUbāda b. al-Ṣāmit al-Anṣārī, who is said to have been a "master" of the Muslims and the holder of the flag of Muḥammad, whom ʿUmar, after Abū ʿUbayda's death, appointed as a commander of Ḥimṣ where he gave an exhorting speech and who was a commander of the right flank during the conquest of Caesarea where he fought bravely; and (h) Sahl b. Saʿd al-Anṣārī, who transmitted several traditions. On this group, see *EI²*, s.v. al-Anṣār (W. Watt); s.v. al-Aws (W. Watt); s.v. al-Khazraj (W. Watt).

38 Badr is a small town that lies in a plain south-west of Medina and which is surrounded by steep hills and sand dunes. Al-Azdī mentions Badr only in the context of some early Muslims who fought during Muḥammad's famous battle there. On Badr, see *EI²*, s.v. Badr (W. Watt).

praise be to Him for what He did for you. He made you reach an accord, repaired the broken ties between you, guided you to Islam and banished Satan from you so that he no longer wanted you to associate partners with God or worship a deity other than Him. [As a result,] the Arabs are children of one mother and one father today. I want to send the Muslims out to fight the Byzantines in Syria. Whichever of them perishes, perishes as a martyr and what is retained in God's place is better for the righteous. And whichever of them survives, survives to defend the religion and to merit God's (ʿa.)\\82 reward for the fighters for His cause. This is my own opinion. Now each person should tell me his own full opinion".

ʿUmar b. al-Khaṭṭāb (r.) rose, praised and thanked God, blessed and saluted (*ṣallā*) the Prophet (ṣ.) and then said: "Praise be to God who bestows what is good upon any human creature (*khalq*) He wants. I swear by God that whenever we compete to do a good deed, you, Abū Bakr, precede us in doing it. This is God's grace, which He gives to whomever He wants. I swear by God that I wanted to see you for the opinion you have just given. You were destined by God to mention it just now. You are right; May God show [us] the paths of guidance through you. Dispatch the cavalrymen one after the other to them [=the Byzantines]; also dispatch the infantrymen one after the other and the soldiers one after the other. God (ʿa.) will surely support His religion, honour Islam and its adherents and fulfil what He promised His Messenger (ṣ.)".

Then ʿAbd al-Raḥmān b. ʿAwf rose and said: "O successor of the Messenger of God, they are the Byzantines, Banū al-Aṣfar[39], who are [as] strong as iron and [as] solid as a cornerstone. I swear by God that I do not agree on the forceful hurling of cavalry against them. Rather, dispatch the cavalry to raid the nearest parts of their land and then to return to you. Then dispatch

39 In al-Azdī's narrative, the term "Banū al-Aṣfar" (lit. "the sons or children of al-Aṣfar" or "the sons or children of the blond One") refers to the Byzantines, who are named by ʿAbd al-Raḥmān b. ʿAwf and ʿUmar b. al-Khaṭṭāb as such. Some Muslim genealogists, and in particular al-Masʿūdī, regard al-Aṣfar as the grandson of Esau and the father of Rūmīl, who is seen as the ancestor of the Greeks (Rūm). De Sacy argues that Banū al-Aṣfar is an Arabic translation of the Hebrew "*edom*" (lit. "red") which was used by Jewish scholars to designate the Roman Emperors Valerian and Titus and by extension the whole Flavian family. Von Erdmann provides a passage from Bar Hebraeus's *Taʾrīkh* for the usage of "*aṣfar*" as translation of "*edom*", but then brings forward some arguments against de Sacy's thesis. In his view, "*aṣfar*" is a translation of the Latin word "*flavus*" (lit. "yellow") which was introduced by "the Arabs" to designate primarily the Roman Flavian dynasty. Later this expression was extended to all descendants of this dynasty, including the Byzantine Emperors. Raf Praet, a graduate student from Ghent University, argued in a personal communication that "*aṣfar*" might be understood as "pale" and might, therefore, refer to Constantius Chlorus, i.e. Constantius the Pale, (d. 306) who was the father of Constantine the Great and founder of the Constantian dynasty. Consequently, Banū al-Aṣfar would refer to the descendants of Constantius, i.e. to all Byzantine Emperors. On Banū al-Aṣfar, see *EI*^{2}, s.v. Aṣfar (I. Goldziher); de Sacy, *Lettre*; von Erdmann, *Ueber*; D.[ie] Red.[aktion], *Nachträge*; Fl.[eischer], *Zwei Beilagen*; Fierro, *Al-Aṣfar*.

the cavalry [again] to make more attacks and then to return to you. If they do that several times, they will harm their enemy, gain spoils from\\83 these parts of the land and, consequently, pluck up the courage to fight them. Then you summon all the people from the farthest parts of Yemen[40] and from the lands of Rabīʿa[41] and Muḍar[42]. Then bring them all to your place [in Medina[43]]. Then you can invade them [=the Byzantines] yourself if you want. Or dispatch others to invade them if you would like to". Then he sat down and fell silent, and so did the others. Then Abū Bakr (r.) said to them: "What are your opinions; may God have mercy upon you?" ʿUthmān b. ʿAffān (r.) rose, praised and thanked God (ʿa.) for what He is worth, blessed and saluted the Prophet (ṣ.) and said: "We are of the opinion that you are a good advisor for the adherents of this religion and that you have sympathy for them. Hence, if you have an opinion of guidance, righteousness and benefit to the common [Muslims], resolve to carry it out since we neither doubt nor suspect you[r reasoning]". Ṭalḥa [b. ʿUbaydallāh], al-Zubayr [b. al-ʿAwwām], Saʿd [b. Abī Waqqāṣ], Abū ʿUbayda b. al-Jarrāḥ, Saʿīd b. Zayd [b. ʿAmr b. Nufayl[44]] and all the Emigrants and the Supporters who

40 Yemen (al-Yaman) is a region encompassing the south-western part of the Arabian Peninsula, the borders of which are not entirely clear. It is bordered by the Red Sea to the west, the Arabian Sea to the south, the Persian Gulf (or alternatively by the region of ʿUmān) to the east and it ends somewhere south of Mecca to the north. Al-Azdī does not define this region, but refers only to the many Muslim fighters who came from Yemen. On Yemen, see *EI*², s.v. al-Yaman (A. Grohmann et al.).

41 Rabīʿa is a large Northern Arabian tribe that formed a tribal federation with Muḍar and settled first in central Arabia (Najd and al-Ḥijāz), that was later dominated by the rulers of the Lakhmids in al-Ḥīra and that finally emigrated to northern Mesopotamia (Diyār Rabīʿa). In al-Azdī's narrative, Rabīʿa is depicted twice as having its abodes in Iraq and thus did not take part in the Battle of al-Yarmūk or in any other fight in Syria. Instead, they are said to have fought the Persians in Iraq. On Rabīʿa, see *EI*², s.v. Rabīʿa and Muḍar (H. Kindermann); Madelung, *Rabīʿa*.

42 Muḍar is a large Northern Arabian tribe that formed a tribal federation with Rabīʿa and settled first in western Arabia (al-Tihāma and al-Ḥijāz), from which they emigrated later to northern Mesopotamia (Diyār Muḍar). In al-Azdī's narrative, Muḍar, together with Rabīʿa, is mentioned only once. On Muḍar, see *EI*², s.v. Rabīʿa and Muḍar (H. Kindermann).

43 The well-known oasis city of Medina (al-Madīna, lit. "the town" or "the place of jurisdiction", previously Yathrib) in al-Ḥijāz is located ca. 160 km east of the Red Sea and ca. 350 km north of Mecca. It is built in a depression between two hills in the north and south and two lava beds in the east and west. In his narrative, al-Azdī depicts Medina as the political and administrative centre of the Muslims' polity. Hence, Abū Bakr and ʿUmar lived there. The Muslim troops gathered in and departed from this city and money that was collected was sent from Iraq to Medina. Al-Azdī also refers once to the emigration of Muḥammad to this city. On Medina, see *EI*², s.v. al-Madīna (M. Watt et al.).

44 Abū al-Aʿwar (or Abū Thawr) Saʿīd b. Zayd b. ʿAmr b. Nufayl b. ʿAdī b. Kaʿb b. Luʾayy al-Adawī (d. 50–51/670–671) was a companion of the Prophet Muḥammad. In al-Azdī's narrative, the following biographical information about him is given: He was a cousin of ʿUmar (see also Ibn Hishām, *Al-sīra*, 145, l. 23 for the same information), an early

attended this meeting said: "'Uthmān is right about what he has just said. Do whatever you think and we will listen and obey. We will not contradict your command, will not distrust your opinion and will not fail to answer your call and obey you".

They all said this or something like this. 'Alī b. Abī Ṭālib (r.) was one of them, but he said nothing. Abū Bakr (r.) said to him: "What is your opinion, Abū al-Ḥasan?" He said: "I am of the opinion that you are the one whose cause (*amr*) is blessed and that you are of a fortunate\\84 mind[45]. If you yourself march to them now or dispatch others to them, you will be victorious, God (t.) willing". Abū Bakr (r.) said to him: "May God bring you what is good! How do you know this?" 'Alī said: "I heard the Messenger of God (ṣ.) say: 'This religion remains triumphant over its opponents until the Hour [of Resurrection] comes while its adherents remain triumphant[, too]'". Then Abū Bakr (r.) said: "Glory be to God (*subḥāna Allāh*)! How beautiful this tradition (*ḥadīth*) is! You gladdened me; may God gladden you in this life and in the afterlife".

Then Abū Bakr (r.) rose [and stood] before the people, praised and thanked God, extolled whatever He is praiseworthy for, blessed and saluted the Prophet (ṣ.) and said: "O people, God ('a.) blessed you with Islam, honoured you with fighting for His cause and favoured you with this religion over the adherents of all the other religions. O servants of God, prepare [yourselves] to invade the Byzantines in Syria. I am going to appoint commanders for you and give them authority over you. So obey your Lord, do not disobey your commanders and make [sure that] your intention, conduct and food[46] are good. For God is with those who fear Him and those who do [what is] good". He [=the narrator, al-Khuzā'ī] said: All the people fell silent and I swear by God that nobody answered him, being in awe of attacking the Byzantines and knowing how large their numbers are and how vigorous their power is. Then 'Umar b. al-Khaṭṭāb (r.) rose and said: "O Muslims, why do you not answer the successor of the Messenger of God (ṣ.) when he calls you to that which gives you life?"\\85

Khālid b. Sa'īd b. al-'Āṣ[47] rose, praised and thanked God, blessed and saluted the Prophet (ṣ.) and his family and said: "Praise be to God who is

---

emigrant to Yathrib and one of those ten to whom Muḥammad promised Paradise. In addition, he is portrayed as having supported 'Uthmān's position during the consultation with Abū Bakr and as having commanded the cavalry in the Battles of Ajnādayn and al-Yarmūk and the infantry during the conquest of Fiḥl. Later Abū 'Ubayda appointed him as commander over Damascus. In a few places, Sa'īd b. Zayd serves as a transmitter of traditions in al-Azdī's narrative, as well. On Sa'īd b. Zayd, see EI^2, s.v. Sa'īd b. Zayd (A. Wensinck/G. Juynboll).

45 For the translation of the expression "*maymūn al-naqība*" as "fortunate mind", see Lane, *Lexicon*, s.v. *naqība*.

46 That is to say, consume only proper food as prescribed by religious laws.

47 Khālid b. Sa'īd b. al-'Āṣ al-Qurashī (d. 13/635) from Quraysh was a companion of the Prophet Muḥammad. In al-Azdī's narrative, his early conversion, his emigration to

the one and only God and who has sent Muḥammad (ṣ.) 'with guidance and the religion of truth to show that it is above all [other] religions, even though the idolaters hate it'.[48] God ('a.) will certainly fulfil His promise, strengthen His religion and destroy His enemy". Then he went to Abū Bakr (r.) and said: "We will neither contradict nor remain behind you. You are the leader (*wālī*) and the one who advises kindly. We will hasten [to you] if you call upon us to fight, obey you if you command us and answer you positively if you call us". Abū Bakr (r.) felt glad about his statement and then said to him: "May God bless you for it, my brother and friend. You embraced Islam willingly, emigrated in anticipation of a reward from God in the afterlife and escaped with your religion from the Unbelievers to the land of Abyssinia. [You did all this] so that God and His Messenger are obeyed and that the word of God is the upper one. All this was made easy for you; may God have mercy upon you".

[Abū Bakr al-Ṣiddīq's appointment of the first commander]

He [=the narrator, al-Kuzā'ī] said: Khālid b. Sa'īd [b. al-'Āṣ] became well equipped and went to Abū Bakr, who was accompanied by the largest number of the Emigrants and Supporters. He greeted Abū Bakr (r.) and said: "I swear by God that to fall down from far above or to be snatched up by the birds in the air between the sky and the earth is preferable in my eyes\\86 to delaying my answer to your call and disobeying your order. I swear by God that I am neither desirous of this life nor eager to live it any longer. [Thus,] I call upon you to bear witness that I, my brethren, my slaves and whoever follows me from my family, will be entirely devoted to [fighting for the] cause of God and battling permanently against the Polytheists until God ruins them or until we all die". Abū Bakr (r.) wished him all the best and the Muslims [prayed to God to] bestow the best upon him. Then Abū Bakr said to him: "I hope that you will be one of God's advisors (*nuṣahā'*) to His servants, by means of adhering to His book and following His Prophet's normative practices (*sunna*)". After that, he [=Khālid b. Sa'īd], his brethren, his slaves and whoever followed him from his family walked out [and were]

Abyssinia and his relation to Muḥammad are mentioned. In addition, he is mentioned as a cousin of Yazīd b. Abī Sufyān. Furthermore, Khālid b. Sa'īd is the first Muslim who spoke in favour of Abū Bakr's plan to send troops to Syria and encamped near Medina before leaving for Syria. He decided to join Abū 'Ubayda (rather than Yazīd b. Abī Sufyān), because of the former's more religious prestige. Before leaving for Syria, he advised Abū Bakr to show good conduct and was bidden farewell by the latter. The end of Khālid b. Sa'īd's fighting in Syria is not mentioned in al-Azdī's narrative, but his death as a martyr is alluded to. On Khālid b. Sa'īd, see EI^2, s.v. Khālid b. Sa'id (H. Loucel).

48 Q. 61:9 (*The Qur'ān. Tr. Abdel Haleem*, 370). Note that the verse begins with "*huwa al-lādhī arsala rasūlahū*" which is rephrased in al-Azdī's text as follows: "*huwa al-lādhī ba'atha Muḥammad (ṣ.)*".

the first to encamp. Abū Bakr (r.) ordered Bilāl[49] to call out [the following] to the people: "O people, troop [together] to fight for the cause of God against your enemy, the Byzantines, in Syria".

Abū Bakr (r.) sent [the following message] to Yazīd b. Abī Sufyān[50], to Abū ʿUbayda b. al-Jarrāḥ, to Muʿādh b. Jabal[51] and to Shuraḥbīl b. Ḥasana: "I dispatch you in the direction [of Syria], appoint you as commanders of these soldiers and will equip each of you with as many infantrymen as possible. When you all reach the land [of Syria], face the enemy and assemble for fighting them [=the enemy's military units], your commander will be Abū ʿUbayda b. al-Jarrāḥ. However, if Abū ʿUbayda could not meet you and war brought [the three of] you together, your commander would be Yazīd b. Abī

49 Bilāl's full name is Abū ʿAbdallāh Bilāl b. Rabāḥ (d. between 17–21/638–642). In al-Azdī's narrative, Abū Bakr orders Bilāl twice to call out to the people to leave for Syria. Then Bilāl asks Abū Bakr to allow him to leave, too, to which Abū Bakr agrees. Bilāl leaves Medina with Saʿīd b. ʿĀmir b. Ḥudhaym's unit. At al-Jābiya, ʿUmar tells Bilāl to call the Muslims to prayers, which he does. Hearing Bilāl's call to prayers, the people were reminded of Muḥammad's time and were emotionally affected. Finally, Bilāl informs ʿUmar that the commanders in Syria eat bird meat and fine bread, i.e. expensive foodstuffs. On Bilāl, see *EI*², s.v. Bilāl b. Rabāḥ (W. ʿArafat).

50 Yazīd's full name is Abū Khālid Yazīd b. Abī Sufyān b. Ḥarb al-Umawī (d. 18/639). In al-Azdī's narrative, he is portrayed as a major actor. His character traits are described several times and he is said to be a cousin of Khālid b. Saʿīd b. al-ʿĀṣ. Yazīd was dispatched to Syria by Abū Bakr and was appointed as second commander next to Abū ʿUbayda when all Muslim units gathered. Abū Bakr sent several units of reinforcements to Yazīd, who is said to have fought the first battles against the Byzantines in al-ʿAraba and al-Dāthina and to have operated in al-Balqāʾ, where Abū ʿUbayda ordered him to support the Muslim troops in the Battle of Ajnādayn. Then Yazīd besieged Damascus from one side and commanded one quarter of the Muslim army in the Battle of al-Yarmūk. He was then appointed by Abū ʿUbayda as commander of the district of Damascus and, after the latter's death, became chief commander by ʿUmar's order. In this role, he solved a conflict over leadership between Ḥabīb b. Maslama and al-Ḍaḥḥāk b. Qays and managed the conquest of Caesarea. Al-Azdī's narrative ends with the information that Yazīd died of an illness in Damascus and that ʿUmar appointed Muʿāwiya b. Abī Sufyān as a successor in command of Syria. On Yazīd, see *EI*², s.v. Yazīd b. Abī Sufyān (C. Bosworth).

51 Muʿādh's full name is Abū ʿAbd al-Raḥmān Muʿādh b. Jabal al-Anṣārī (18/639–640). In al-Azdī's narrative, Muʿādh is a major figure and closely related to Abū ʿUbayda b. al-Jarrāḥ. Abū Bakr dispatched him as a commander to Syria. He is also mentioned as a commander of the Muslim army's right flank in the Battle of Ajnādayn. Muʿādh praised Abū Bakr for having appointed ʿUmar as his successor and supported Abū ʿUbayda in proceeding towards Ḥimṣ. Then Muʿādh discussed religious and political issues with Byzantine representatives before the Battle of Fiḥl, in which he commanded the right flank, as he did in the Battle of al-Yarmūk. During this battle, he exhorted the Muslims and was sent later to fight in the land of the River Jordan. Muʿādh advised Abū ʿUbayda to invite ʿUmar to come to Syria and grant a peace treaty to the inhabitants of Jerusalem. He took over Abū ʿUbayda's role in leading the Muslim prayers after the latter's death. Muʿādh is said to have died of al-ʿAmwās plague. Before his death, he gave some advice to the Muslims, informed ʿUmar about Abū ʿUbayda's death and appointed ʿAmr b. al-ʿĀṣ as his successor in command of Syria. On Muʿādh b. Jabal, see Ibn Saʿd, *Kitāb al-ṭabaqāt*, VII-2, 114–115.

Sufyān. March out and prepare yourselves". Then the people [=the Muslims] went out to prepare themselves for war.

Khālid b. Saʿīd b. al-ʿĀṣ had been one of the subordinates (*ʿummāl*) of the Messenger of God. Then he had hated [to continue] taking command (*imāra*) and had asked Abū Bakr for exemption. So Abū Bakr had exempted him.

Then the people [=the Muslims] started moving out to their encampments in tens, twenties, thirties, forties, fifties and hundreds day by day until they gathered and increased in number.\\87 One day, Abū Bakr (r.) went out with many of his companions until he reached their encampment. [There] he saw a reasonable number [of fighters]. But he found the number insufficient for fighting the Byzantines and, therefore, said to his companions: "What is your opinion about those? Do you deem it wise to send them to Syria in such a [small] number?" ʿUmar b. al-Khaṭṭāb (r.) said to him: "I do not find this number satisfyingly sufficient for [fighting] the groups of Banū al-Aṣfar [=the Byzantines]". Abū Bakr (r.) drew near to his companions and said to them: "What is your opinion?" They said: "We also agree with ʿUmar". Abū Bakr (r.) said: "What about sending a letter to the people of Yemen to call them to fight for the cause of God and convince them of its [the fight's] reward?" All the companions agreed and said: "What an excellent idea!" So he wrote [the following letter] to them:\\88

Abū Bakr al-Ṣiddīq's (r.) letter to the people of Yemen

In the name of God, the Merciful, the Compassionate. From the successor of the Messenger of God (ṣ.) to any Yemenite believer and Muslim to whom my letter is read. Peace be upon you. I praise, on your behalf, God with whom no other deity is associated. Regarding the matter at hand: God (ʿa.) prescribed fighting for His cause to the Believers in His book and ordered them to troop [together], lightly and heavily armed. So he said: "Struggle for His cause with your possessions and your persons".[52] Fighting for the cause of God is a religiously prescribed duty and its reward from God is great. We called the Muslims to draw near to us in order to fight against the Byzantines in Syria. They rushed to it, encamped and went out, having good intention[s] and seeking to make the most of it. O servants of God, hurry to the duty ordained by your Lord, to one of the two good [objectives], [i.e.] martyrdom or victory, and to the spoils. God (ʿa.) does not accept words without actions from His servants, nor [does He accept] their turning away from His enemies until they profess the truth and acknowledge the rule of the book [=the Qurʾān] or until they bring tribute by hand and with humility. May God protect your religion, guide your hearts, purge your deeds and endow you with the reward [promised] to those who fight for His cause and to those who are patient (*ṣābirūn*). Peace be upon you. He sent this letter with Anas b. Mālik[53] (r.) [to the people of Yemen].\\89

52 Q. 61:11 (*The Qurʾān. Tr. Abdel Haleem*, 370).

53 Abū Ḥamza Anas b. Mālik b. al-Naḍir b. Ḍamḍam al-Khazrajī al-Najjārī (d. between 91–93/709–711) is a companion of the Prophet Muḥammad and one of the most prolific

*The report (*khabar*) [about the reaction] of the people of Yemen*

Al-Ḥusayn b. Ziyād [al-Ramlī] related to us on the authority of Abū Ismāʿīl Muḥammad b. ʿAbdallāh [al-Azdī], who said[54]: Muḥammad b. Yūsuf[55] related to me on the authority of Thābit al-Bunānī[56] on the authority of Anas b. Mālik, who said: I went to the people of Yemen, to every part (*jināḥ*) and to every tribe, and read Abū Bakr's letter to them. After I finished reading it out I said: "Praise be to God and I testify that there is no [other] deity but God (*lā ilāh illā Allāh*) and that Muḥammad is His servant and messenger. In the name of God, the Merciful, the Compassionate. Regarding the matter at hand: I am a messenger from the successor of the Messenger of God (ṣ.) to you and [also] a messenger from the Muslims. Verily, I left them encamping and nothing stops them from going to their enemy except [that they are] waiting for you. So rush to your brethren; may God have mercy upon you, Muslims".

He [=the narrator, Anas b. Mālik] said: All those to whom I read this letter and who listened to what I said responded well and said: "We will march out immediately, yet [it appeared] as if we have already [started] doing so". [I proceeded] until I reached Dhū al-Kalāʿ[57]. When I read the letter and said

transmitters of traditions. In al-Azdī's narrative, he is mentioned as a messenger, delivering a letter from Abū Bakr to the people of Yemen and as a transmitter of several traditions. On Anas b. Mālik, see *EI²*, s.v. Anas b. Mālik (A. Wensinck/J. Robson).

54 Usually, the second part of the isnād is introduced with a "*fa-*" ("furthermore"). It is missing here in the Arabic text. See also p. 56 above, where the conjunction is also missing in the same *isnād*. However, the conjunction is added to the text on p. 96 of the edition, i.e. p. 60 above.

55 Muḥammad b. Yūsuf is difficult to identify because his full name is not given by al-Azdī. We could not find a *tarjama* about him. On the basis of al-Ṭabarī's *Taʾrīkh al-rusul wa-al-mulūk wa-al-khulafāʾ*, Mourad identifies him as Muḥammad b. Yūsuf al-Anṣārī (from Banū al-Ḥārith b. al-Khazraj), who was an informant of Abū Mikhnaf (see Mourad, *al-Azdī*, 591). ʿUqla and Banī Yāsīn agree to this, but mention his *nisba* as al-Khazrajī (see al-Azdī, *Futūḥ al-Shām. Ed. ʿUqla/Banī Yāsīn*, 22; 89, n. 3). Darādaka equates him with Muḥammad b. Yūsuf b. Wāqid b. ʿUthmān al-Ḍabbī al-Faryābī (d. 212/827) (see Darādaka, *Fatḥ Dimashq*, 9). In al-Azdī's narrative, he is mentioned as a transmitter of thirteen traditions. On Muḥammad b. Yūsuf al-Khazrajī, see al-Ṭabarī, *Taʾrīkh*, I, 3233, l. 18–19.

56 Thābit al-Bunānī is difficult to identify because his full name is not given by al-Azdī. ʿUqla and Banī Yāsīn identify him as Abū Muḥammad Thābit b. Aslam al-Bunānī al-Baṣrī (d. 127/744–745), one of the main informants of Muḥammad b. Yūsuf b. Thābit al-Khazrajī and a transmitter of *ḥadīth* (see al-Azdī, *Futūḥ al-Shām. Ed. ʿUqla/Banī Yāsīn*, 22; 89, n. 4). In al-Azdī's narrative, he is mentioned as a transmitter of thirteen traditions. On Thābit al-Bunānī, see Ibn Saʿd, *Kitāb al-ṭabaqāt*, VII-2, 3–4 and al-Mizzī, *Tahdhīb al-kamāl*, IV, 342–349 (no. 811).

57 Dhū al-Kalāʿ's full name is Dhū al-Kalāʿ Ayfaʿ b. ʿAbd al-Kalāʿī (d. 106/724–725). He was a transmitter of *ḥadīth* from the generation of the Followers, whose transmission is considered reliable. ʿUqla and Banī Yāsīn found the information that he was a companion of Muḥammad, that he did not transmit *ḥadīth* and that he died in the Battle of Ṣiffīn in 38/658 (see al-Azdī, *Futūḥ al-Shām. Ed. ʿUqla/Banī Yāsīn*, 89, n. 6). In al-Azdī's narrative,

these words to him, he sent out for his horse and his weaponry, immediately rose [and stood] before his people and ordered that an encampment should be erected. He did not leave us until he and many groups of the people of Yemen hastened to encamp. When they gathered, he rose [and stood] before them, praised and thanked God (ʻa.),\\90 blessed and saluted the Prophet (ṣ.) and then said: "O people, it is the mercy and blessing of God upon you to have sent you a Messenger (ṣ.) and to have sent a book down to him. The Messenger reported God's message (*balāgh*) properly, taught you whatever would guide you [well] and prohibited whatever could corrupt you. So he taught you what you were ignorant of and aroused your interest in that which is good [for you and] in which you had no interest [before]. Then your pious brethren called upon you to fight for the cause of God against the Polytheists and to get a great reward [in return]. Whoever wants to troop can go with me now". He [=the narrator, Anas b. Mālik] said: He and many people from Yemen mustered and trooped together to Abū Bakr. He [=the narrator, Anas b. Mālik] said: We returned some days earlier than he [=Dhū al-Kalāʻ], found Abū Bakr in Medina, found the [Muslims'] encampment the same [as it had been before] at his place and found Abū ʻUbayda leading the encamping people in prayer[s].

Ḥimyar[58] [tribesmen], as well as their women and children, came to Abū Bakr, who was happy about their coming. When Abū Bakr saw them, he said: "O servants of God, have we not talked together and said: 'If Ḥimyar [tribesmen], together with their children and women, came, God would support the Muslim[s] and disappoint the Polytheist[s]?' O Muslims, rejoice over the good news. God is going to lead you to victory".

He [=the narrator, Anas b. Mālik] said: And Qays b. Hubayra b. Makshūḥ al-Murādī[59], who was one of the Arabs' [renowned] horsemen in the

his name is given as Ayfaʻ and he is depicted as coming with Ḥimyar. In addition, a member of his family is said to have first entered the city of Ḥimṣ after its conquest. On Dhū al-Kalāʻ Ayfaʻ, see Ibn ʻAsākir, *TMD*, XVII, 382–397 (no. 2110) and Ibn Ḥajar, *Al-iṣāba. Ed. al-Baghawī*, I, 262–263 (no. 578).

58 Ḥimyar is a Southern Arabian tribal federation that settled in Yemen. In al-Azdī's narrative, Ḥimyar, to Abū Bakr together with Dhū al-Kalāʻ, their women and children, are said to have gone to Abū Bakr and to have formed the majority of fighters in the Battle of al-Yarmūk, where its tribespeople were attacked on the right flank. In addition, three individual figures belonged to Ḥimyar: (a) Kaʻb b. al-Ḥabr, who was a transmitter of several traditions and who is portrayed as a former Jew who, upon reading a prophecy about the coming of Muḥammad and the conquests of the Muslims in Syria, converted to the new faith; (b) a man called Shuraḥbīl, who is said to have belonged to Ḥimyar and to have killed several Byzantine soldiers in duels and (c) an unnamed man from Ḥimyar who argued with another Muslim fighter about who was the first to have killed a Polytheist at Ḥimṣ. On Ḥimyar, see *EI*^{2}, s.v. al-Yaman (A. Grohmann/W. Brice/G. Smith/et al.).

59 Qays's full name is Abū Ḥassān Qays b. Hubayra b. Makshūḥ al-Murādī (d. 37/657–658). In al-Azdī's narrative, he is depicted as an Arab nobleman, as a renowned horseman in the pre-Islamic period and as belonging to Madhḥij. He went to Abū Bakr to be dispatched to Syria. Abū Bakr joined him to Abū ʻUbayda's troops. In Syria, Qays b.

pre-Islamic period (*jāhiliyya*) and one of their noble and strong men, came with a large company of his people to Abū Bakr, greeted him, sat beside him and said to him: "What are you awaiting in dispatching these soldiers?" Abū Bakr said to him: "We were awaiting your coming". He [=Qays b. Hubayra al-Murādī] said: "We have already come, so dispatch the people, one after the other. For this place is not the place of camels or sheep[60]". He [=the narrator, Anas b. Mālik] said: At that moment, Abū Bakr walked out [with him].\\91

*Naming those whom Abū Bakr appointed (*ʿaqada*) as commanders of the districts (*ajnād*)*

He [=Abū Bakr] summoned Yazīd b. Abī Sufyān and appointed him as a commander, summoned Zamʿa b. al-Aswad b. ʿĀmir[61], from Banū ʿĀmir b. Luʾayy[62], and said to him: "You are with Yazīd b. Abī Sufyān. Do not disobey him and do not contradict his order[s]". Then he said to Yazīd: "If you would like to assign him the command over the vanguard, do so, for he is one of the Arabs' [renowned] horsemen and one of your righteous people. I hope that he will become one of the righteous servants of God". Yazīd said: "Your good opinion and high expectation of him have endeared him to me". Then Abū Bakr walked out with him. Thereupon, Yazīd said: "O successor of the Messenger of God (ṣ.), either you ride [a horse] or allow me to walk beside you, because I hate to ride while you are walking". Abū Bakr (r.) said to him: "I will not ride [a horse] and you will not get off [yours], because I reckon my steps to be [made] for the cause of God". Then he advised him,

Hubayra usually fought with (or for) Khālid b. al-Walīd and commanded cavalry units. He is said to have killed two patricians in al-Jābiya, to have fiercely fought the Byzantines with his cavalry at Fiḥl, where he recited a poem, to have advised Abū ʿUbayda not to retreat from Syria, to have defeated the Byzantines in the land of the River Jordan and to have fought during the Battle of al-Yarmūk, where he recited another poem. In addition, he is depicted as duelling with some Byzantine soldiers and to have been mistaken for ʿAbdallāh b. Qurṭ al-Thumālī by the latter's wife. On Qays b. Hubayra, see Ibn ʿAsākir, *TMD*, XXXXVIIII, 480–497.

60 Figuratively speaking, the original Arabic text employs a part-for-whole synecdoche, i.e. pad (*khuf*) for camel and shinbone (*kurāʿ*) for sheep, goats and horses. The contextual meaning of the sentence is that "this place", i.e. Medina or al-Ḥijāz, is not suitable for wide animal husbandry, but Syria is.

61 Zamʿa b. al-Aswad b. ʿĀmir b. Luʾayy al-Qurashī (n.d.) was a cavalryman whom Abū Bakr appointed in command of the vanguard in Yazīd b. Abī Sufyān's unit. In al-Azdī's narrative, he is said to have belonged to Banū ʿĀmir b. Luʾayy and is depicted as being praised by Abū Bakr as a renowned and righteous horseman, as being positioned in the vanguard under the command of Yazīd b. Abī Sufyān and as being ordered to listen to Yazīd and not to disobey him. On Zamʿa b. al-Aswad, see Ibn Ḥajar, *Al-iṣāba. Ed. al-Baghawī*, II, 567 (no. 2817).

62 ʿĀmir b. Luʾayy is a Northern Arabian tribe that was a subtribe of Quraysh. In al-Azdī's narrative, the tribe is referred to once as Banū ʿĀmir b. Luʾayy and one individual figure is said to have belonged to it. This is Zamʿa b. al-Aswad b. ʿĀmir whom Abū Bakr put under the command of Yazīd b. Abī Sufyān. On ʿĀmir b. Luʾayy, see Caskel, *Ǧamharat*, I, 4; II, 160.

saying: "O Yazīd, I strongly recommend fear of (*taqwā*) and obedience to God to you. Favour Him [to anyone or anything else] and be afraid of Him. And when you meet the enemy and God leads you to victory, do not manacle, mutilate, maim or betray, and do not accuse [the defeated] of cowardice. Do not, you all, kill children, old men or women, do not burn palm trees or uproot them, do not cut down fruitful trees, and do not slaughter\\92 cattle except for eating [them]. You will pass by people in their hermitages who claim to have secluded themselves for [worshipping] God. Leave them to what they have secluded themselves for. You will also find others in the middle of whose heads Satan has taken up abode as if the middles of their heads were the sand grouses' nests (*afāḥīṣ al-qaṭā*)[63]. Strike the nests which they have hollowed in their heads with swords until they turn repentantly to Islam or until they bring tribute by hand and with humility. God will certainly support those who support Him and His Messengers in absentia (*bi-al-ghayb*)[64]".

Then he took his [=Yazīd's] hand and said: "I bid farewell to you and may God's peace and mercy be upon you". Then he bade him farewell and said: "You are my first commander and I have appointed you [as the leader] of some Muslim men, who are noble, neither inferior (*awzāgh*) among people—[he (=the narrator) said: *Awzāgh*] means "not low"—nor weak, nor cold-blooded in respect of religion. So keep good company with them, lay them under your protection, put them under your wing and consult them about any matter. May God improve your companionship and our successorship (*khilāfa*)". Then Yazīd left with [one] army unit for Syria.

Abū Bakr, God rest his soul[65], used to invoke God every day, morning and evening, [i.e.] after the early morning and the afternoon prayers, saying: "O God, You created us and we were nothing beforehand. Then You sent us a Messenger (ṣ.) as a mercy and a favour from You to us. Then You guided us [well] when we went astray, endeared belief to us when we were Unbelievers, multiplied us when we were few, united us when we were dispersed and empowered us when we were weak. Then You imposed fighting for Your cause on us and ordered us to fight against the Polytheists until they say: 'There is no [other] deity but God and Muḥammad is His Messenger' or until they give tribute by hand and with humility. O God, we became those who seek Your satisfaction and fight Your enemies. As for those who abandon You and worship another deity besides You,\\93 You are farther and farther above what they say. O God, make Your Muslim servants victorious over Your polytheistic enemy. O God, drive them [=the Muslims] to a resounding conquest, lead them to a great victory and give them supportive power. O God, help them [=the Muslims] to summon up their courage, make

63 For this translation, see Lane, *Lexicon*, s.v. *faḥaṣa*.

64 The Arabic prepositional phrase "*bi-al-ghayb*" serves as an ambiguous adjunct that seems to post-modify either the verb (i.e. "support") or the object of the sentence (i.e. "Him and His messengers").

65 This phrase is expressive of Abū Bakr's death. We consider it to be included as a later comment by one of the transmitters.

their feet stand firm and make their enemy quake. Furthermore, strike terror into their [=the enemies'] hearts, annihilate them all, exterminate them all, wipe out their collectivity, bequeath their land, homes and possessions to us. Be also very close to and intimate with us and improve all our affairs, intentions, decisions and responsibilities. Make us thankful for Your blessings. Forgive us and [forgive] all the Believers and Muslims, male and female, alive and dead. May God strengthen us and [strengthen] you with firm speech in the worldly life and in the afterlife, for He is the Kindest and the most Compassionate to the Believers".

Shuraḥbīl b. Ḥasana's vision

Al-Walīd b. Ḥammād [al-Ramlī] related to us: Al-Ḥusayn b. Ziyād [al-Ramlī] reported to us on the authority of Abū Ismā'īl Muḥammad b. 'Abdallāh [al-Azdī], who said: [Furthermore,] Muḥammad b. Yūsuf related to me on the authority of Thābit al-Bunānī on the authority of Anas b. Mālik, who said: When Abū Bakr, may God have mercy upon him, sent Yazīd b. Abī Sufyān to Syria, he [=Yazīd] did not depart from Medina until Shuraḥbīl b. Ḥasana came to him. Then he [=Shuraḥbīl] went to Abū Bakr, sat down beside him and said: "O successor of the Messenger of God, while sleeping I saw that you were among a large group of the Muslims.\\94 [It seemed as if] you were in Syria and we were with you. You were received there by the Christians[66] with their crosses and by the patricians with their military units (*katā'ib*) who fell upon you from all directions like the flood. Therefore, we held fast to [the statement that] 'there is no [other] deity but God' and said: 'God [alone] suffices us and is the best Trustee (*wakīl*)'. Then we looked around and, lo and behold, we were in the hamlets and the fortresses in their [=the Byzantines'] rear, on their right and on their left. And, lo and behold, a man came to us [and proceeded] until he descended to an

66 In al-Azdī's narrative, "the Christians" (*naṣārā*, sg. *naṣrānī*) are treated as a collective actor; no Christian denomination is mentioned. Once it is said that "the Christians" had crosses and that there were monks, who lived for a very long time in hermitages, but then left them when the Muslims threatened Syria. Furthermore, "the Christians" are usually said to be "Arabs" and to have supported the Byzantines in Syria. Hence, Arab Christians fought with the Byzantines at Ajnādayn, Fiḥl and al-Yarmūk and supported them in Damascus and Caesarea. However, one Christian Arab group is especially said to have abstained from helping the Byzantines against their fellow (early Muslim) Arabs. Three individual Christians are singled out in this context: (a) Abū Bashīr al-Tanūkhī, who fought for the Byzantines at al-Yarmūk, but blamed them for corruption and misbehaviour; (b) Ḥudhayfa b. 'Amr al-Tanūkhī, who reported defeat at al-Yarmūk to Heraclius; and (c) an unnamed Christian fighter who functioned as a spy for the Byzantines and entered the Muslims' encampment. In addition, some Christian Arabs are also depicted as interacting with the Muslims. For example, an unnamed Christian foot-messenger adopted the new faith at the hands of 'Umar. Or another unnamed Christian priest, dressed in a wool jubba, interrupted 'Umar during his speech at al-Jābiya. Finally, there are several Christians who are said to have converted to the new faith and then functioned as spies and messengers for the Muslims (rather than for the Byzantines). On Christians, see *EI*[2], s.v. Naṣārā (J. Fiey).

elevated point on the mountain and then he drew his palm and fingers out and, lo and behold, they were [like] a burning fire. Then he swooped down with it to the fortresses and the hamlets which he reached and which, consequently, caught a blazing fire. Then they were extinguished and turned into ashes. Afterwards, we looked at the Christians, patricians and groups whom we had met and, lo and behold, the ground collapsed with them. In response, the people [=the Muslims] raised their heads and hands to God (ʿa.), praising, glorifying and thanking Him. Then I woke up". Abū Bakr (r.) said to him: "May your eyes beam [with delight]. This is good news from God (ʿa.) which undoubtedly portends conquest, God willing. You are one of my commanders. So when Yazīd b. Abī Sufyān departs, stand by for three days and be available to march [out, too]". He [=Shuraḥbīl] did it and when the third day elapsed, he came to Abū Bakr the following day and bade him farewell. Abū Bakr said to him: "O Shuraḥbīl, did you hear my recommendation[s] to Yazīd b. Abī Sufyān?" He said: "Yes, I did". He [=Abū Bakr] said: "I do recommend the same to you. However, I recommend [to you some] qualities that I forgot to mention to Yazīd: Perform prayer[s] on time; have patience during war until you either triumph or get killed; visit the sick; attend the funerals and keep invoking God in all situations". Then Abū Sufyān [b. Ḥarb][67] said: "May God have mercy upon you, Abū\\95 Bakr. Yazīd had always taken these qualities into [his] full consideration and abided by them before he left for Syria. Now with your recommendation[s], he is [even] more committed to them, God (t.) willing". Then Shuraḥbīl said: "God is the One whose help is sought (*al-mustaʿān*) and whatever He wants to be comes into being".

Then he [=Shuraḥbīl] bade Abū Bakr farewell and set out with his army unit to Syria. The majority of the people [=the Muslims], however, stayed with Abū ʿUbayda b. al-Jarrāḥ in the military encampment, where Abū ʿUbayda was leading them in prayers and was waiting every day for Abū Bakr's order to leave. However, Abū Bakr was waiting for the Arabs to come to him from everywhere, seeking to flood Syria with the Muslims and wanting them to gather in large numbers if the Byzantines advanced on them.

The coming of the people of Ḥimyar to Abū Bakr al-Ṣiddīq (r.)

The people of Ḥimyar, together with Dhū al-Kalāʿ, whose name is Ayfaʿ, and a large number of the people of Yemen with excellent military equipment (*ʿudda*), came to Abū Bakr (r.). And so did Madhḥij[68] including Qays

67 Abū Sufyān's full name is Abū Sufyān Ṣakhr b. Ḥarb b. Umayya (d. 32/653). In al-Azdī's narrative, he is depicted as Yazīd's father who asked the latter about the progress in Syria. Abū Sufyān also requested ʿUmar to give him permission to fight against the Byzantines in Syria, which he did during the Battle of al-Yarmūk. On Abū Sufyān, see *EI*², s.v. Abū Sufyān (W. Watt).

68 Madhḥij is a Southern Arabian tribe that settled in Yemen and that adopted Judaism prior to Islam. In al-Azdī's narrative, Madhḥij, including Qays b. Hubayra al-Murādī,

b. Hubayra [b. Makshūḥ] al-Murādī, who was joined by a huge group of his people, including al-Ḥajjāj b. ʿAbd Yaghūth b. Asad[69]. And so did Ḥābis b. Saʿd al-Ṭāʾī[70] with a large number of people from Ṭayyiʾ[71]. And so did al-Azd[72] in\\96 a large number and with a huge group including Jundab b.

---

came from Yemen to Abū Bakr and is said to have fought fiercely in the Battle of al-Yarmūk. On Madhḥij, see *EI²*, s.v. Madhḥidj (G. Smith/C. Bosworth).

69 Al-Ḥajjāj b. ʿAbd Yaghūth b. Asad b. ʿAmr b. al-Ḥajjāj al-Zubaydī (n.d.) is said to have been a companion of the Prophet Muḥmmad. In al-Azdī's narrative, he is said to have come with Qays b. Hubayra and other tribespeople from Madhḥij to Abū Bakr and is depicted as a member of Zubayd who fought fiercely in the Battle of al-Yarmūk. On al-Ḥajjāj b. ʿAbd Yaghūth b. Asad, see Ibn ʿAsākir, *TMD*, XII, 100.

70 Ḥābis b. Saʿd al-Ṭāʾī (n.d.) is a companion of the Prophet Muḥammad who is said to have taken up quarters in Syria. In al-Azdī's narrative, he is mentioned as coming with a large troop of Ṭayyiʾ to Abū Bakr, seeking to fight in Syria against the Byzantines, as fighting with his unit in the Battle of Fiḥl and as holding one of the flags when the Muslims reached Ḥimṣ. On Ḥābis b. Saʿd al-Ṭāʾī, see al-Bukhārī, *Al-taʾrīkh al-kabīr*, II-1, 100 (no. 365).

71 Ṭayyiʾ is a Southern Arabian tribe that emigrated north and settled in the region of Aleppo and Qinnasrīn (Ḥāḍir Ṭayyiʾ) in the 6th century. Some members of the tribe embraced Christianity. In al-Azdī's narrative, it is said that some members of Ṭayyiʾ joined Khālid b. al-Walīd on his way to Syria and that two flags (i.e. units) belonged to Ṭayyiʾ when the Muslims reached Ḥimṣ. In addition, four individual figures are associated with Ṭayyiʾ: (a) Ḥābis b. Saʿd al-Ṭāʾī, a commander of a tribal unit, who went to Abū Bakr, fought with his unit in the Battle of Fiḥl and was one of the Muslim flag holders at Ḥimṣ; (b) Malḥān b. Ziyād al-Ṭāʾī, the uterine half-brother of ʿAdī b. Ḥātim, who went with another group of Ṭayyiʾ to Abū Bakr and was sent by the latter to Abū ʿUbayda in Syria, who fought later with Khālid b. al-Walīd against the Byzantines near Baalbek and who was among the first Muslims who reached Ḥimṣ, holding one of the Muslims' flags; (c) Hāniʾ b. Qabīṣa al-Ṭāʾī who lived in al-Ḥīra and fought against Khālid b. al-Walīd there; and (d) Rāfiʿ b. ʿAmr al-Ṭāʾī, about whom a poem was recited, who was Khālid's guide in crossing the desert and who was a commander of a flank in the fight against the Byzantines at Bosra. On Ṭayyiʾ, see *EI²*, s.v. Ṭayyiʾ (I. Shahīd).

72 Azd is a Southern Arabian tribe that consisted of three groups, i.e. Azd ʿUmān, Azd Sarāt and Asd Shanuʾa. In al-Azdī's narrative, Azd figures prominently, but is not divided into subgroups. Members of Azd flocked in great numbers to Abū Bakr, including Jundab b. ʿAmr b. Ḥumama al-Dawsī and Abū Hurayra al-Dawsī; they fought fiercely in the Battle of al-Yarmūk under the command of the latter. Nevertheless, they were killed in great numbers. Two poems are also recited, depicting Azd during this battle. In addition, the highest number of individual figures, i.e. 14, is said to have belonged to Azd: (a) ʿAbd al-Masīḥ b. ʿAmr b. Buqayla al-Azdī, the commander of the people of al-Ḥīra, who fought against Khālid b. al-Walīd and made peace with him; (b) ʿAmr b. al-Ṭufayl b. ʿAmr al-Azdī, who is depicted as Khālid b. al-Walīd's nephew and messenger with whom he sent letters to the troops in Syria and who is said to have fought with Maysara b. Masrūq al-ʿAbsī at al-Yarmūk, where he did heroic deeds and recited a poem and where he was finally killed; (c) Amna bt. Abī Bishr b. Zayd al-Aṭwal al-Azdiyya, who was the wife of ʿAbdallāh b. Qurṭ al-Thumālī; (d) al-Ḥārith b. ʿAbdallāh al-Azdī and ʿAbd al-Aʿlā b. Surāqa al-Azdī, who fought in the Battle of al-Yarmūk (and narrated some episodes about it). In addition, there were ten persons from Azd mentioned as transmitters throughout the narrative. There is, first and foremost, (a) Abū Ismāʿīl Muḥammad b. ʿAbdallāh al-Azdī al-Baṣrī, the compiler-author of the work, who is mentioned more than a hundred times. There are also (b) al-Ḥārith b. ʿAbdallāh al-Azdī and (c) ʿAbd al-Aʿlā b. Surāqa al-Azdī, who transmitted several traditions. The same holds true for the transmitters

ʿAmr b. Ḥumama al-Dawsī[73] and Abū Hurayra al-Dawsī[74]. And so did Qays[75] over whom Abū Bakr (r.) appointed Maysara b. Masrūq al-ʿAbsī[76] as commander. And so did [Qubāth] b. Ashyam[77] with Banū Kināna[78]. As for

---

(d) Abū Jahḍam al-Azdī, (e) Sufyān b. Sulaym al-Azdī, (f) Sufyān b. ʿAwf b. Mughaffal al-Azdī and (g) Rāshid b. ʿAbd al-Raḥmān al-Azdī; (h) ʿAbd al-Raḥmān b. Yazīd b. Jābir al-Azdī is mentioned as a transmitter of two while (i) Abū Ḥafṣ al-Azdī and (j) ʿAmr b. Muḥṣan b. Surāqa b. ʿAbd al-Aʿlā b. Surāqa al-Azdī transmitted one tradition. In conclusion, the entire narrative, in particular the long section on the Battle of al-Yarmūk, describes the deeds of Azd and is transmitted by numerous persons from Azd. On Azd, see *EI²*, s.v. Azd (G. Strenziok); Ulrich, *al-Azd*.

73 Jundab b. ʿAmr b. Ḥumama b. al-Ḥārith b. Rifāʿa al-Dawsī al-Azdī (n.d.) is a companion of the Prophet Muḥammad. In al-Azdī's narrative, he is depicted as coming with a large troop from Azd to Abū Bakr to fight in Syria. Hoisting a flag, he motivated his co-fighters from Azd to fight in the Battle of al-Yarmūk, where he is also said to have been killed. On Jundab b. ʿAmr, see Ibn ʿAsākir, *TMD*, XI, 316–318.

74 Abū Hurayra's full name is Abū Hurayra ʿAbdallāh (or ʿAbd al-Raḥmān) al-Dawsī al-Yamānī (d. between 57–59/676–679). He was a companion of the Prophet Muḥammad who is said to have transmitted several hundred traditions from him. In al-Azdī's narrative, he is considered to have belonged to Azd and is portrayed as a staunch fighter who fought with his tribe during the Battle of al-Yarmūk. On Abū Hurayra, see *EI²*, s.v. Abū Hurayra (J. Robson).

75 Qays (or Qays ʿAylān) is a Northern Arabian tribe that was a subtribe of Muḍar. In al-Azdī's narrative, members of Qays are said to have gone to Abū Bakr, who appointed Maysara b. Masrūq al-ʿAbsī as their commander; they are also depicted twice as having fought on the left flank during the Battle of al-Yarmūk. In addition, one individual figure belonged to Qays: (a) Qanān b. Ḥāzim al-Qaysī, who is said to have been a Muslim fighter. On Qays, see *EI²*, s.v. Ḳays ʿAylān (W. Watt et al.).

76 Maysara b. Masrūq al-ʿAbsī (d. ca. 20/640–641) was a companion of the Prophet Muḥammad. In al-Azdī's narrative, Maysara b. Masrūq al-ʿAbsī is a major figure whom Abū Bakr appointed as commander over the tribesmen of Qays, who is said to have been an Arab nobleman and a renowned horseman and whose wife is said to have sold a red tent to Khālid b. al-Walīd. Maysara is depicted as fighting heroically and commanding a military unit during the Battle of Fiḥl, as one of the first Muslims who reached the region of Ḥimṣ (and fought some Byzantine soldiers there) and as being sent later by Abū ʿUbayda to move north to Aleppo, but then soon was ordered to come back. When the Muslims heard of the coming of a huge Byzantine army, Maysara advised Abū ʿUbayda not to retreat from Ḥimṣ. He fought in the Battle of al-Yarmūk and was sent by Abū ʿUbayda again north to Qinnasrīn and the mountainous region north of the city, where he had a fight with Byzantine troops. In this battle, another commander, al-Ashtar, who did not recognise Maysara as a leader in prayers and pretended not to know who Banū ʿAbs were, challenged him. This conflict over leadership was not resolved and Maysara proceeded to Marj al-Qabāʾil, which was between Antioch and al-Maṣṣīṣa, where he was again ordered by Abū ʿUbayda to come back. On Maysara b. Masrūq, see Ibn ʿAsākir, *TMD*, LXI, 317–320.

77 Qubāth b. Ashyam b. ʿĀmir al-Laythī (n.d.) was a companion of the Prophet Muḥammad. In al-Azdī's narrative, he is depicted as the commander of the Muslim army's left flank during the Battle of al-Yarmūk and as a brave and tough fighter from Kināna. In addition, he once quotes a poem during that battle. On Qubāth b. Ashyam, see Ibn Saʿd, *Kitāb al-ṭabaqāt*, VII-2, 131.

78 Kināna is a Northern Arabian tribe from which Quraysh descended. In al-Azdī's narrative, Kināna is mentioned as Banū Kināna and Kināna and is said to have gone together

Rabīʿa, Tamīm[79] and Asad[80], they were in Iraq[81] and they had abodes there, which few of them [=these three tribes] saw. The majority of those [who came] were the people of Yemen, who thronged, inhabited and populated Syria.

[Section II: Abū Bakr al-Ṣiddīq's dispatch of military units to Syria]

Al-Walīd b. Ḥammād [al-Ramlī] related to us: Al-Ḥusayn b. Ziyād [al-Ramlī] reported to us on the authority of Abū Ismāʿīl Muḥammad b. ʿAbdallāh [al-Azdī], who said: Furthermore, Muḥammad b. Yūsuf related to me on the authority of Thābit al-Bunānī on the authority of Sahl b. Saʿd [al-Anṣārī][82]: When Abū Bakr (r.) wanted to dispatch Abū ʿUbayda b. al-Jarrāḥ, he summoned him, bade him farewell and then said to him: "Listen like the one who wants to understand what is being said to him and then does what he was ordered to do. You are marching out with the honourable people, the very respectable families of the Arabs, the righteous Muslims and the

---

with their tribal member and commander Qubāth b. Ashyam to Abū Bakr and is depicted twice as having fought on the left flank during the Battle of al-Yarmūk. On Kināna, see *EI²*, s.v. Kināna (W. Watt).

79 Tamīm (or Tamīm b. Murr) is a large Northern Arabian tribe. In al-Azdī's narrative, Tamīm is depicted twice as having its abodes in Iraq and as taking part neither in the Battle of al-Yarmūk nor during the fights in Syria. Instead, they fought against the Persians in Iraq. On Tamīm, see *EI²*, s.v. Tamīm b. Murr (M. Lecker); Kister, *Mecca and Tamīm*.

80 Asad is a Southern Arabian tribe. In al-Azdī's narrative, Asad is depicted twice as having had its abodes in Iraq and as taking part neither in the Battle of al-Yarmūk nor during the fights in Syria. Instead, Asad is said to have fought the Persians in Iraq. On Asad, see *EI²*, s.v. Asad (W. Caskel); Landau-Tasseron, *Asad*.

81 Iraq (al-ʿIrāq) is the region of lower Mesopotamia, which is distinct from upper Mesopotamia (al-Jazīra). Iraq's northern border is represented by a line between al-Anbār (on the Euphrates) and Tikrīt (on the Tigris) while the eastern border is constituted by the Zagros mountain range. In the south, Iraq is bordered by the Persian Gulf and the estuary of the two rivers Euphrates and Tigris (Shaṭṭ al-ʿArab), whereas it includes the steppe-lands on the western bank of the Euphrates to the west. In al-Azdī's narrative, "[the land of] Basra", "the land of al-Kūfa" and the "arable lands of Iraq" are mentioned as parts of the "land of Iraq". We also read that Iraq was ruled by "the Persians" and that the Arabian tribes of Rabīʿa, Tamīm and Asad had their abodes there. The major cities of Iraq are al-Kūfa, Basra, al-Ḥīra, al-Ubulla and ʿAyn al-Tamr. Hence, in al-Azdī's narrative, Iraq encompasses the steppe-lands on the western bank of the Euphrates, the marches near the Persian Gulf and the western bank of the Tigris. Regarding the conquests in Iraq, al-Azdī briefly refers to some minor events that took place under the command of Khālid b. al-Walīd and al-Muthannā b. Ḥāritha. On Iraq, see *EI²*, s.v. ʿIrāḳ (A. Miquel et al.).

82 Abū al-ʿAbbās Sahl b. Saʿd b. Mālik b. Khālid al-Anṣārī (d. 88/707) is a companion of the Prophet Muḥammad. On the basis of a manuscript of al-Dhahabī's *Tadhhīb al-tahdhīb al-kamāl*, Lees mentions that he died in 88 [=706–707] (see al-Azdī, *Futūḥ al-Shām. Ed. Lees*, 73, n. 2). In al-Azdī's narrative, he is mentioned as a transmitter of several traditions. On Sahl b. Saʿd al-Anṣārī, see al-Fasawī, *Kitāb al-maʿrifat wa-al-taʾrīkh*, I, 338 and Ibn Abī Ḥātim, *Al-jarḥ wa-al-taʿdīl*, IV, 198 (no. 853).

pre-Islamic [renowned] horsemen who were fighting for [the sake of] fury at that time, but who are fighting today for the reward and the good intention. So keep good company with whoever accompanies you, and when meting out truth make sure that people are all equals in your eyes. Seek help from God who is a sufficient Helper and trust in God who is a sufficient Trustee. March out tomorrow, God willing". Then he left him [=Abū Bakr]. When he [=Abū ʿUbayda] left, he [=Abū Bakr] said: "O Abū ʿUbayda". So he turned to him. Then he [=Abū Bakr] said to him: "O Abū ʿUbayda, I did see\\97 how the Messenger of God held you in high esteem and how he gave preference to you. In the same way I would also like you to know how much you are favoured by and endeared to me. By the One in whose hand[s] my soul lies, there is nobody else on earth, among the Emigrants or among others, whom I can equate with you or with this one, i.e. ʿUmar b. al-Khaṭṭāb (r.). I hold you in greater esteem than anybody else".

He [=the narrator, Sahl b. Saʿd al-Anṣārī] said: "Say, which of the Companions of the Messenger of God (ṣ.) was like Abū ʿUbayda? He [=Abū ʿUbayda] became toothless because, in the Battle of Uḥud[83], Ibn Qamīʾa al-Laythī[84] threw a stone at the face of the Messenger of God. So he [=Ibn Qamīʾa] broke his front right teeth in his lower jaw (*rabāʿiya*) and fractured his face to the extent that two rings from the metal chain strap of the Messenger's helmet stuck in his cheek. Then Abū ʿUbayda (r.) fell on him [=the Messenger of God], inserted his first incisor into one ring and pulled the ring out until his [=Abū ʿUbayda's] incisor also came out. Then he sank the other incisor into the second ring, pulled it out until his second incisor was plucked out, too. They [=some unnamed Muslims] said: 'We have never seen a toothless person better than Abū ʿUbayda (r.)'". Then Abū Bakr (r.) bade him [=Abū ʿUbayda] farewell and left.

On the following day, Abū Bakr (r.) walked out with a group of Muslim men until he reached Abū ʿUbayda. Then he walked with him until he came to Thaniyyat al-Wadāʿ[85]. Then, when he [=Abū Bakr] wanted to leave him

83 Uḥud is a rocky, flat mountain located ca. 5 km north of Medina and the site of a famous battle between the Prophet Muḥammad and the Meccans. It is the battle to which al-Azdī alludes when mentioning how Abū ʿUbayda b. al-Jarrāḥ is said to have saved the wounded Prophet Muḥammad from greater harm. On Uḥud, see *EI*[2], s.v. Uḥud (C. Robinson).

84 Ibn Qamīʾa al-Laythī is listed neither in Ibn Saʿd, al-Bukhārī, Ibn ʿAsākir nor in any other biographical work we could access. In al-Azdī's narrative, he is depicted as throwing a stone at the face of Muḥammad during the Battle of Uḥud, thus breaking his front right teeth in the lower jaw and fracturing his face, because two rings from the metal chain strap of Muḥammad's helmet stuck in his cheek.

85 Thaniyyat al-Wadāʿ (lit. "the Farewell Pass") is a mountainous pass overlooking Medina (to the south) which people passed on their way to Mecca. Al-Azdī mentions Thaniyyat al-Wadāʿ only once and narrates how Abū Bakr bade farewell to Abū ʿUbayda there, thus correlating the place name with an event in his narrative. On Thaniyyat al-Wadāʿ, see Yāqūt, *Muʿjam al-buldān*, I, 937.

[=Abū ʿUbayda], he said to him: "O Abū ʿUbayda, do what is good and live as a fighter for the cause of God. Die as a martyr so that God makes you hold your book[86] with your right hand and gladden your eyes in this life and in the afterlife. I swear by God that I wish\\98 you are one of the repentant (*tawwābūn*), the chosen penitents (*awwābūn*), the ascetics of this world and the desirers of the Hereafter. God has arranged what is good for you, bringing it to you by making you march with a Muslim army unit against His polytheistic enemy and [by making you] fight whoever disbelieves in Him, associates partners with him and worships another [deity] besides Him". Then Abū ʿUbayda said to him [=Abū Bakr]: "May God have mercy upon you, successor of the Messenger of God (ṣ.). I certainly testify to your grace since you became a Muslim, to your giving of sincere advice in favour of God and His Messenger (ṣ.) and to your struggle, after the [death of the] Messenger of God (ṣ.), against those who turned away from the religion of God until God brought them at your own hand into submission back to religion. We also bear witness that you are merciful to the Believers but tough on the Unbelievers. May God bless you for what He taught you and guide you in what He charged you with. If I am righteous, it is my Lord who bestowed righteousness upon me and if I am corrupt, it is He who is in charge of rendering me righteous. As for you, we see you have a claim on us to be answered if you called us and to be obeyed if you ordered us". Then he stepped back and Muʿādh b. Jabal moved towards him [=Abū Bakr] and said: "O successor of the Messenger of God (ṣ.), I truly wished to talk to you about something [that had happened] in Medina before we departed from it. But then it seemed to me that I would rather delay what I wanted to say until my farewell day so that it would be my farewell words to you". He [=Abū Bakr] said: "Proceed, Muʿādh! I swear by God that I have always known you for your wise speech, right opinion and rightly guided cause". Holding his horse's reins, shouldering his bow[87], wearing the sword[88] and attired with a turban, he [=Muʿādh b. Jabal] drew his [=Abū Bakr's] female riding camel close to him [=Muʿādh b. Jabal] and then said: "God sent Muḥammad (ṣ.) with His Message to His creatures. Then he [=Muḥammad] reported what\\99 God wanted him to report. He was also like what his Lord wanted him to be [like]. Then God decreed his death, while he was praised and accepted [among his followers]. May God [bestow] His benediction, mercy, blessings, salutations and satisfaction upon him [=Muḥammad]. He is surely

86 According to the Qurʾān, this book is a record of the good and bad deeds done by each human being in the worldly life. On the Day of Judgement, each human being will be given his or her own book to hold and read. Those who hold the book with the right hand will go to Paradise but those who hold it with the left hand will go to Hell (cf. Q. 69:19–37).

87 Bows (sg. *qaws*) in pre-Islamic and early Islamic times were usually carried, hanging over the shoulder (*tanakkaba*) (see Schwarzlose, *Waffen*, 40). As in pre-Islamic and early Islamic poetry, bows are—compared with spears and swords—less often mentioned in al-Azdī's narrative as (Muslim) weaponry (see ibid., 45).

88 The sword (sg. *sayf*) was usually carried, hanging around the neck (*taqallada*) in pre-Islamic and early Islamic times (see Schwarzlose, *Waffen*, 54–55).

Praiseworthy and Glorious. May God give him, in return for [his deeds] to his community (*umma*), the best reward that He has given to the Prophets [before]. Then God (t.) appointed you, the Truthful One (*al-ṣiddīq*), as successor over a group (*mala'*) of the Muslims, with their consent. However, some apostatised, some spread lies and some turned away from this religion. Consequently, some of us got discouraged, most of us got confused, a party of us liked flattery and meekness, but the largest group of us agreed unanimously to hold fast to their religion, to worship God until certainty [=death] comes to us, and to leave the [apostate] people to what they were heading for. You never accepted anything that the Messenger of God (ṣ.) had rejected from them. As a result, you were elevated with the Muslims, prepared [for war] in haste [and in earnest][89] against the evildoers and put pressure, together with the obedient exponents, on the disobedient opponents until whoever deviated from right returned to it and whoever indulged in wrong abandoned it. When God completed His blessings [bestowed] upon you and upon those who submitted themselves to you (*al-muslimīn bi-ka*) in this issue, you entrusted the Muslims with fighting for the cause of God against the Polytheists [in Syria] and with [pursuing] the direction in which God has doubled the reward and increased the victory and the spoils for them. Your cause is blessed and your opinion is praised and rightly guided. We and the righteous Believers ask God to forgive you, to have ample mercy on you and to strengthen your health through [your] obedience to Him. My invocation, praise and speech which you have been listening to will certainly make you more willing to do good deeds and to thank God for the blessing. I\\100 am repeating these words to the Believers so that they thank God for whatever He bestowed upon them and for what He has made for them by [giving you] the authority over them". Then each of them [=Abū Bakr and Mu'ādh b. Jabal] shook the other's hand, bade him farewell and prayed for him. Then they parted. Abū Bakr (r.) left and that army unit marched out.

The moment Abū Bakr (r.) left them, he said to Abū Qatāda al-Anṣārī[90]: "O Abū Qatāda, rush to Abū 'Ubayda b. al-Jarrāḥ, send him my greetings and say to him: 'I recommend that you treat your brother Mu'ādh [b. Jabal] well. Never reach a final decision without [consulting] him because he will not refrain from advising and guiding you [well]. Also look for Khālid b. Sa'īd b. al-'Āṣ. If you become his leader, give him all the rights that you would like to be given by him if he became yours. He has chosen marching out with you over marching out with his cousin, Yazīd b. Abī Sufyān, or with others. If something serious happens to you and you need counsel from a

89 Although the literal translation of the Arabic expression "*wa-qad shammartu*" is "to roll up one's sleeves", the figurative meaning is "to make haste". On both meanings, see Lane, *Lexicon*, s.v. *sh-m-r*.

90 Abū Qatāda's full name is Abū Qatāda b. Rib'ī al-Anṣārī (d. 54/673). In al-Azdī's narrative, he is mentioned as a messenger delivering letters between Abū Bakr and Abū 'Ubayda. On Abū Qatāda al-Anṣārī, see Ibn Sa'd, *Kitāb al-ṭabaqāt*, VI, 8–9 and Ibn 'Asākir, *TMD*, LXVII, 142–153.

person who holds strong opinions and sincere advice, consult him [=Khālid b. Saʿīd] and listen to him. This is because I have always known him as the master (*sayyid*) of the Muslims who are with you"". He [=the narrator, Sahl b. Saʿd] said: Abū Qatāda [al-Anṣārī] reached him [=Abū ʿUbayda], told him the message, then came back to Abū Bakr and said: "May God increase your righteousness. I informed him [=Abū ʿUbayda] about your message and I preserved your message to him and his message to you". Abū Bakr said: "As for mine to him, it is what you have just heard and as for his to me, bring it forward". He [=Abū Qatāda al-Anṣārī] said: "Abū ʿUbayda said: 'Send my greetings to him [=Abū Bakr] and say to him: As for the two men whom you recommended to me and whose favour for and advice to the Muslims you mentioned, I am going to hold them in the esteem you ordered. I wish, may God have mercy upon you, that you recommended me to them as you recommended them to me, because I need them more than they need me'". Abū Bakr (r.) said [to Abū Qatāda al-Anṣārī]: "As for this [wish], I have not forgotten it. I did recommend to them that they should support him, advise him and consult\\101 him about what they deem good for him and for the Muslims. Even if I had made no recommendation to any of them, I hope that they would not stop advising, considering and sympathising with the Muslims in any of their situations or in any of their matters attended by both of them. But we are obliged to recommend to them that which is good for them and which God employs to unify their cause".

Khālid b. Saʿīd b. al-ʿĀṣ's march [to Syria]

Al-Walīd [b. Ḥammād] related to us: Al-Ḥusayn b. Ziyād [al-Ramlī] reported to us on the authority of Abū Ismāʿīl Muḥammad b. ʿAbdallāh [al-Azdī], who said: Furthermore, ʿAbd al-Raḥmān b. Yazīd b. Jābir [al-Azdī][91] related to me on the authority of ʿAmr b. Muḥsan [b. Surāqa b. ʿAbd al-Aʿlā b. Surāqa al-Azdī][92] on the authority of Saʿīd b. al-ʿĀṣ [b. Abī Uḥayḥa][93]: One of the Muslim men said to Khālid b. Saʿīd b. al-ʿĀṣ, who made preparations to march out with Abū ʿUbayda b. al-Jarrāḥ: "If you march out with your cousin Yazīd b. Abī Sufyān, it will be much better [for us] than marching out

91 ʿAbd al-Raḥmān b. Yazīd b. Jābir al-Azdī (g. 154/770–771) is a famous transmitter. On the basis of a manuscript of al-Dhahabī's *Tadhhīb al-tahdhīb al-kamāl*, Lees mentions that he died between 153 and 156 [i.e. 770–772] (see al-Azdī, *Futūḥ al-Shām. Ed. Lees*, 31, n. 4). In al-Azdī's narrative, he is mentioned as a transmitter of two traditions. On ʿAbd al-Raḥmān b. Yazīd al-Azdī, see Ibn Saʿd, *Kitāb al-ṭabaqāt*, VII-2, 169–170 and al-Bukhārī, *Taʾrīkh*, III-1, 365 (no. 1155).

92 ʿAmr b. Muḥsan b. Surāqa b. ʿAbd al-Aʿlā b. Surāqa al-Azdī (n.d.) is known as a transmitter. In al-Azdī's narrative, he is mentioned as a transmitter of several traditions, as well. On ʿAmr b. Muḥsan, see Ibn ʿAsākir, *TMD*, XLVI, 330–331.

93 Saʿīd b. al-ʿĀṣ's full name is Abū ʿUthmān Saʿīd b. al-ʿĀṣ b. Abī Uḥayḥa Saʿīd b. al-ʿĀṣ al-Umawī al-Qurashī (d. 59/678–779). In al-Azdī's narrative, Saʿīd b. al-ʿĀṣ is mentioned as a transmitter of one tradition about Khālid b. Saʿīd. On Saʿīd b. al-ʿĀṣ, see *EI*^{2}, s.v. Saʿīd b. al-ʿĀṣ (C. Bosworth).

with someone else". He [=Khālid b. Sa'īd b. al-'Āṣ] said: "My cousin [=Yazīd b. Abī Sufyān] is dearer to me than that one [=Abū 'Ubayda] because of his kinship [with me], but that one is dearer to me than my cousin because of his religion. In the time of the Messenger of God (ṣ.), that one [=Abū 'Ubayda] was my brother in terms of my religion, my close associate and my previous helper against my cousin. Today I feel more intimate and more tranquil with him than with others".\\102 When Khālid [b. Sa'īd b. al-'Āṣ] wanted to leave for Syria, he put on his weapons and ordered his brothers [to do so as well]. Thus, 'Amr [b. Sa'īd b. al-'Āṣ[94]], al-Ḥakam [b. Sa'īd b. al-'Āṣ[95]] and Abbān [b. Sa'īd b. al-'Āṣ[96]], his slaves (*ghilmān*) and his clients [also] put on their weapons. Then he came to Abū Bakr (r.) after the early morning prayer[s] and prayed with him [once more]. After they had finished, he and his brothers rose [and stood] before Abū Bakr and [then] sat beside him. He [=Khālid] praised God continuously and thanked Him, blessed and saluted the Prophet (ṣ.) and then said: "O Abū Bakr, God ('a.) most rightfully honoured us, you and all the Muslims, with this religion. Right is the one who sticks to the Prophet's normative practices, who annihilates innovation[s] (*bid'a*) and whose conduct in ruling the subjects is just. Each of the adherents of this religion is obliged to do good deeds, but the leader's justice is of more general benefit. O Abū Bakr, fear God [when treating the people] whom God has put under your authority. Have mercy on the widow and on the orphan and support the weak and the oppressed. When it comes to the truth, [take care not to treat] a Muslim man better when you are pleased with him and worse when you are angry with him. Try as hard as possible not to get angry because anger begets injustice. Do not envy a Muslim when you are able to because your envy of the Muslim will make you his enemy and he will turn hostile towards you if he knows about it. Because if the leader becomes hostile towards the subjects and the subjects become hostile towards the leader, this will bring about their destruction. Be gentle with whoever does good deeds (*muḥsin*) and strict with whoever is suspected [of misbehaviour] and call a spade a spade for the sake of God".[97]

94 'Amr b. Sa'īd's full name is 'Amr b. Sa'īd b. al-'Āṣ b. Umayya b. 'Abd Shams (d. 13/634–635). In al-Azdī's narrative, 'Amr b. Sa'īd, together with the unit of his brother Khālid, left Medina and encouraged the Muslims to fight during the Battle of Fiḥl, in which he himself fought heroically. After having had a talk with 'Abdallāh b. Qurṭ al-Thumālī, he was killed by the Byzantine fighters during this battle. On 'Amr b. Sa'īd b. al-'Āṣ, see Ibn 'Asākir, *TMD*, XXXXVI, 23–28.

95 Al-Ḥakam's full name is Abū Khālid al-Ḥakam b. Sa'īd b. al-'Āṣ al-Umawī (n.d.). In al-Azdī's narrative, he is mentioned as the brother of Khālid b. Sa'īd with whom he left Medina for Syria. On al-Ḥakam b. Sa'īd, see Ibn 'Asākir, *TMD*, XV, 9.

96 Abbān's full name is Abū al-Walīd Abbān b. Sa'īd b. al-'Āṣ al-Umawī (d. 29/649–650). In al-Azdī's narrative, Abbān b. Sa'īd is said to have left Medina with the unit of his brother Khālid and to have married Umm Abbān bt. 'Utba shortly before the Battle of Ajnādayn, during which he was killed with an arrow. On Abbān b. Sa'īd, see al-Bukhārī, *Al-ta'rīkh al-kabīr*, I-1, 450 (no. 1439) and Ibn 'Asākir, *TMD*, VI, 126–141.

97 The literal translation of this sentence is "When it comes to God's rights, fear no complaint".

Then he [=Khālid b. Sa'īd b. al-'Āṣ] said: "Give me your hand, for I do not know whether or not we will meet again in this world. If God ('a.) has ordained that [we] survive [in this world], we ask Him for pardon and forgiveness. If, however, this is a departure from this life without reunion [=death], then may God bring us and you together with the Prophet (ṣ.) in the Gardens of Bliss".\\103

Then Abū Bakr (r.) shook his [=Khālid b. Sa'īd b. al-'Āṣ's] hand. Then he wept and so did Khālid and the Muslims. They thought that he [=Khālid b. Sa'īd b. al-'Āṣ] wanted martyrdom and thus they kept weeping. Then Abū Bakr (r.) said to him: "Wait for us to walk [out] with you". He said: "I do not want you to do this". He [=Abū Bakr] said: "But I do want that. And whoever of the Muslims wants it [can do so, too]". He and the people in his company rose and walked out of the dwellings of Medina. He [=the narrator, Sahl b. Sa'd al-Anṣārī] said: I have never seen a larger company of the Muslims bidding farewell to somebody than the number of those who bade farewell to Khālid b. Sa'īd [b. al-'Āṣ] and his brethren. When he [=Khālid b. Sa'īd b. al-'Āṣ] went out of Medina, Abū Bakr (r.) said to him: "You did recommend guidance to me and I got it well. I also recommend [something] to you, so listen to my recommendation and get it well[, too]. You are surely a person who has been given a precedent in Islam and a great virtue by God. The people are watching you and listening to you. You are marching out to such a great destination for the sake of remuneration and I do hope that your marching is [motivated] by a reward and bona fide intention, God willing. So strengthen the savant, teach the ignorant, blame the affluent fool, exhort the common Muslims and earmark your advice and consultation for the leader of the soldiers, inasmuch as God and the Muslims require from you. Work for God as if you were seeing him. Consider yourself dead and know that soon we shall all die. Then we will be resurrected and after that we will be interrogated and questioned. May God make us and [make] you grateful for His blessings and fearful of His curses". Then he [=Abū Bakr] shook his hand [again], bade farewell to him, then shook his brethren by the hand and bade farewell to them, one after the other, as did the Muslims. Then they summoned their camels and mounted them. They were walking with Abū Bakr (r.),\\104 [but] then they led their horses out in a neat manner. When they turned away, Abū Bakr (r.) said: "O God, protect them from [attacks coming from] their front, from their back, from their right and from their left. Remove their sins and greaten their rewards". Then Abū Bakr (r.) and the Muslims who were with him turned away.

Al-Walīd b. Ḥammād [al-Ramlī] related to us, saying: Al-Ḥusayn b. Ziyād [al-Ramlī] related to us on the authority of Abū Ismā'īl Muḥammad b. 'Abdallāh [al-Azdī], who said: Furthermore, Abū Mujāhid Sa'd[98]

98 This person is consistently called Sa'd Abū Mujāhid in al-Azdī's narrative. We inverted the two parts of his name for reasons of consistency. His full name is Abū Mujāhid Sa'd b. Mujāhid al-Ṭā'ī al-Kūfī (n.d.). In al-Azdī's narrative, he is mentioned as a transmitter of three traditions. On Sa'd, see al-Bukhārī, *Al-ta'rīkh al-kabīr*, II-2, 66 (no. 1976).

related to me on the authority of al-Muḥill b. Khalīfa[99]: Malḥān b. Ziyād al-Ṭā'ī[100], the uterine brother of 'Adī b. Ḥātim[101], came with a group of about 1,000 men from Ṭayyi' to Abū Bakr (r.) and said to him: "We came to you, longing to fight for the cause of God and aspiring to that which is good. We are the people who, as you know, fought with you against those of us who apostatised until they confirmed what they were [previously] denying. And we fought with you against those of us who apostatised until they reverted to Islam voluntarily and compulsorily. So send us, may God have mercy upon you, in the tracks of the people [=the Muslims] and choose a good commander [for us] whom we [can] join". They came to Abū Bakr (r.) after all the commanders had left\\105 for Syria. Then Abū Bakr (r.) said to him [=Malḥān b. Ziyād al-Ṭā'ī]: "I have chosen the best commander and the earliest emigrant for you all. Follow Abū 'Ubayda b. al-Jarrāḥ, for I choose him to be your company and commend his decency to you. What an excellent fellow traveller and what an excellent fellow dweller he is!"

Al-Walīd b. Ḥammād [al-Ramlī] related to us, saying: Al-Ḥusayn b. Ziyād [al-Ramlī] reported to us on the authority of Abū Ismā'īl Muḥammad b. 'Abdallāh [al-Azdī], who said: Furthermore, Abū Mujāhid Sa'd related to me on the authority of al-Muḥill b. Khalīfa on the authority of Malḥān b. Ziyād [al-Ṭā'ī], who said: I said to Abū Bakr (r.): "I am pleased with what you have chosen for me". Abū Bakr said: "Then follow him [=Abū 'Ubayda] until you catch up with him". I followed him until I caught up with him in Syria. I witnessed with him all the [battle] sites he witnessed and I never missed any of them.

Al-Walīd b. Ḥammād [al-Ramlī] related to us, saying: Al-Ḥusayn b. Ziyād [al-Ramlī] reported to us on the authority of Abū Ismā'īl Muḥammad b. 'Abdallāh [al-Azdī], who said[102]: Qudāma b. Ḥāzim b.[103] Sufyān[104] related to

99 Al-Muḥill b. Khalīfa al-Ṭā'ī (n.d.) is mentioned in al-Azdī's narrative as a transmitter of several traditions. On al-Muḥill b. Khalīfa al-Ṭā'ī, see al-Mizzī, *Tahdhīb al-kamāl*, XXVII, 290–291 (no. 5810).

100 Malḥān b. Ziyād b. Ghaṭīf al-Ṭā'ī (n.d.) is a companion of the Prophet Muḥammad. In al-Azdī's narrative, he is depicted as the uterine brother of 'Adī b. Ḥātim. He is said to have come with a second group of Ṭayyi' to Abū Bakr and to have been sent by the latter to Abū 'Ubayda in Syria. Later he fought with Khālid b. al-Walīd against the Byzantines near Baalbek and was among the first Muslims who reached Ḥimṣ, holding one of the Muslims' flags. On Malḥān b. Ziyād al-Ṭā'ī, see Ibn 'Asākir, *TMD*, LX, 258–269.

101 Abū Ṭarīf 'Adī b. Ḥātim al-Ṭā'ī (d. 66/685–686), about whom almost nothing is known, is mentioned in al-Azdī's narrative as the uterine brother of Malḥān b. Ziyād al-Ṭā'ī. On 'Adī b. Ḥātim, see Ibn Ḥibbān, *Mashāhīr 'ulamā' al-amṣār*, 44 (no. 271).

102 Here the conjunction *fa-/wa-* is also missing.

103 In light of the biographical evidence presented in the next footnote, we changed the expression "*'an*" in the edited text to "*ibn*". 'Uqla and Banī Yāsīn falsely consider "*ibn*" to be a mistake and thus changed it to "*'an*" (see al-Azdī, *Futūḥ al-Shām. Ed. 'Uqla/Banī Yāsīn*, 105, n. 14).

104 Qudāma's full name is Qudāma b. Ḥāzim b. Sufyān al-Khath'amī. He is mentioned only in al-Ṭabarī's *Ta'rīkh* and Ibn 'Asākir's *TMD* as a transmitter of traditions and a source

me: Ibn Dhī al-Sahm\\106 al-Khathʿamī[105], together with a group of people from Khathʿam[106] numbering less than 1,000 but more than 900, came from Yemen to Abū Bakr (r.) and said to him: "We left [our] homes, possessions and estates and came with our women and children to fight for the cause of God against the Polytheists. So what is your opinion about [bringing along] our children and our women? Shall we leave them [here] with you and depart, and if God disposes victory, we send for them to come to us? Or do you think that we depart with them and trust in our Lord [that they will not get hurt]?" Abū Bakr (r.) said: "O Muslims, glory be to God! Have you ever heard any of the Muslims, who marched to the land of the Byzantines and the land of Syria, mention children and women the way my brother [from] Khathʿam did? O brother [from] Khathʿam, I swear to you that if I heard what you have said while the people were [still] here with me, i.e. before they departed [to Syria], I would love to have kept their families in my custody. I would also have sent them out without their women and children who would distract and concern them until God granted them victory. However, most of the Muslims left with their offspring, so take the majority (*jamāʿat al-muslimīn*) as your example. I ask God to defend the sanctity of Islam and its adherents with His might. March out under the protection and shield of God (t.). There are commanders in Syria, whom we dispatched to it. Choose whomever you want to be your company". He [=the narrator, Qudāma b. Ḥāzim b. Sufyān] said: He [=Ibn Dhī al-Sahm] marched [out] until he caught up with Yazīd b. Abī Sufyān and accompanied him.\\107

Al-Walīd b. Ḥammād [al-Ramlī] related to us, saying: Al-Ḥusayn b. Ziyād [al-Ramlī] reported to us on the authority of Abū Ismāʿīl Muḥammad b. ʿAbdallāh [al-Azdī], who said: Furthermore, Yaḥyā b. Hāniʾ b. ʿUrwa

---

for Abū Mikhnaf and al-Qudāmī (see Mourad, *al-Azdī*, 590). We could not find a *tarjama* about him. In al-Azdī's narrative, he is mentioned as a transmitter of one tradition. On Qudāma b. Ḥāzim, see, for example, al-Ṭabarī, *Taʾrīkh*, II, 938, l. 12–13 and Ibn ʿAsākir, *TMD*, LXVIII, 32.

105 Ibn Dhī al-Sahm al-Khathʿamī (n.d.) is mentioned in al-Azdī's narrative as coming with a group of Khathʿam to Abū Bakr and as appealing to Abū ʿUbayda to settle his dispute with al-Nuʿmān b. Maḥmiyya Dhū al-Anf al-Khathʿamī over the chieftainship. After his death in battle, Abū ʿUbayda appointed his competitor al-Nuʿmān b. Maḥmiyya Dhū al-Anf al-Khathʿamī as the commander of Khathʿam. On Ibn Dhī al-Sahm, see Ibn ʿAsākir, *TMD*, LXVIII, 33.

106 Khathʿam is a Northern Arabian tribe that was a subtribe of Anmār. In al-Azdī's narrative, members of Khathʿam came from Yemen to Abū Bakr, taking their spouses and children to Medina (and further to Syria). Banū ʿAmr is mentioned as a subtribe of Khathʿam, while Khathʿam is said to have participated in the Battle of al-Yarmūk, where it was positioned on the left flank. In addition, two individual figures belonged to Khathʿam: (a) Ibn Dhī al-Sahm al-Khathʿamī, the leader of Khathʿam, who was addressed by Abū Bakr as a brother and was killed during the Battle of al-Yarmūk and (b) al-Nuʿmān b. Maḥmiyya Dhū al-Anf al-Khathʿamī, whom Abū ʿUbayda appointed as the leader of Khathʿam in Syria and who struggled with Ibn Dhī al-Sahm al-Khathʿamī for chieftainship. When the latter was killed during the Battle of al-Yarmūk, Abū ʿUbayda confirmed al-Nuʿmān b. Maḥmiyya Dhū al-Anf al-Khathʿamī as the chief. On Khathʿam, see *EI*[2], s.v. Khathʿam (G. Levi Della Vida).

[al-Murādī[107]] related to me: Abū Bakr (r.) recommended Qays b. Hubayra b. Makshūḥ al-Murādī to Abū ʿUbayda b. al-Jarrāḥ and said to him [=Abū ʿUbayda]: "You are accompanied by a man of great honour [=Qays b. Hubayra al-Murādī]. He [=Qays b. Hubayra al-Murādī] is one of the Arabs' [renowned] horsemen. The Muslims cannot do without his opinion, his consultation and his valour in war. Draw him close to you, be nice to him and show him that you neither do without him nor underestimate him. In doing so, you [can] extract his advice, effort and strife against your enemy". He [=the narrator, Yaḥyā b. Hāniʾ b. ʿUrwa] said: Thereafter, Abū Bakr (r.) summoned Qays b. Hubayra [al-Murādī] and then said to him: "I dispatch you with the commander Abū ʿUbayda, who never oppresses if he is oppressed, who always forgives if he is done evil, who keeps in touch if he is not kept in touch and who is merciful to the Believers but tough on the Unbelievers. So do not disobey his order and do not disagree with his opinion, because he orders only that which is good for you. I have already ordered him to listen to you, so give him only the order to fear God (t.). We have heard that you are an honourable and valorous chief (*raʾīs*)—a master tested in the times of the pre-Islamic ignorant people who were notorious only for [committing] sin[s]. So use your valour, toughness and succour for Islam against the Polytheists, against whoever disbelieves in God and against whoever worships another [deity] besides Him. God\\108 (ʿa.) gives a great reward, much remuneration and glory to the Muslims in return for this". He [=the narrator, Yaḥyā b. Hāniʾ b. ʿUrwa] said: Then Qays b. Hubayra [al-Murādī] said: "If I survived and God kept you alive, you would hear about my care for the Muslims and my struggle against the Unbelievers, which would make you happy, pleased and satisfied". Abū Bakr (r.) said to him: "Do that; may God have mercy upon you". He [=the narrator, Yaḥyā b. Hāniʾ b. ʿUrwa] said: When Abū Bakr (r.) learned that Qays b. Hubayra [al-Murādī] put two patricians in al-Jābiya[108] to the sword, he said: "Qays [b. Hubayra al-Murādī] is truthful, obedient and dutiful".

[Heraclius's reaction to the dispatch of the Muslim units]

Al-Walīd b. Ḥammād [al-Ramlī] related to us, saying: Al-Ḥusayn b. Ziyād [al-Ramlī] reported to us on the authority of Abū Ismāʿīl Muḥammad b. ʿAbdallāh

107 Yaḥyā's full name is Abū Dāwūd Yaḥyā b. Hāniʾ b. ʿUrwa al-Murādī (n.d.). Mourad mentions his date of death as ca. 125/743 (see Mourad, *al-Azdī*, 590). In one place, ʿUqla and Banī Yāsīn state that he died "around 128/745–746" (see al-Azdī, *Futūḥ al-Shām. Ed. ʿUqla/Banī Yāsīn*, 27; this is not repeated in the notes to the edited text; see ibid., 107, n. 3). In al-Azdī's narrative, he is mentioned as a transmitter of three traditions. On Yaḥyā b. Hāniʾ b. ʿUrwa al-Murādī, see Ibn Ḥibbān, *Al-thiqāt*, VII, 614.

108 Al-Jābiya was a huge encampment (*ḥīra*) in Jawlān located ca. 80 km south of Damascus. Hence, al-Azdī often refers to al-Jābiya as the place where Abū ʿUbayda b. al-Jarrāḥ set up camp. He also narrates the famous speech which ʿUmar b. al-Khaṭṭāb is said to have given at al-Jābiya. On al-Jābiya, see *EI*[2], s.v. al-Djābiya (H. Lammens/J. Sourdel-Thomine).

[al-Azdī], who said: Furthermore, 'Abd al-Malik b. Nawfal [b. Masāḥiq al-Qurashī][109] related to me on the authority of Abū Sa'īd al-Maqburī[110] on the authority of Hāshim b. 'Utba b. Abī Waqqāṣ[111], who said: When Abū Bakr's (r.) soldiers marched to Syria, Heraclius[112], the Emperor of the Byzantines, who [at that time] was in Palestine[113], learned of it and was told [the following]:

109 'Abd al-Malik's full name is Abū Nawfal 'Abd al-Malik b. Nawfal b. Masāḥiq al-Qurashī (n.d.). According to Mourad, he died ca. 145/762 and was Abū Mikhnaf's maternal grandfather (see Mourad, *al-Azdī*, 591). 'Uqla and Banī Yāsīn identify him on the basis of al-Mizzī's *Tahdhīb al-kamāl* as a sound *ḥadīth* scholar from Mecca who was one of the informants of al-Azdī and Abū Mikhnaf (al-Azdī, *Futūḥ al-Shām. Ed. 'Uqla/Banī Yāsīn*, 108, n. 8). In al-Azdī's narrative, he is mentioned as a transmitter of eight traditions. On 'Abd al-Malik b. Nawfal, see al-Bukhārī, *Al-ta'rīkh al-kabīr*, III-1, 434 and al-Mizzī, *Tahdhīb al-kamāl*, XVIII, 429–431 (no. 3571).

110 Abū Sa'īd's full name is Abū Sa'īd Kaysān al-Maqburī (d. 100/718). In al-Azdī's narrative, he is mentioned as a transmitter of several traditions. On Abū Sa'īd Kaysān al-Maqburī, see Ibn Sa'd, *Kitāb al-ṭabaqāt*, V, 61–62.

111 Hāshim's full name is Abū 'Umar Hāshim b. 'Utba b. Abī Waqqāṣ al-Zuhrī (d. 37/657). In al-Azdī's narrative, he is mentioned as the nephew of Sa'd b. Abī Waqqāṣ, was ordered by Abū Bakr to command reinforcements that were sent to Abū 'Ubayda and is portrayed as commander of the infantry during the Battles of Ajnādayn and al-Yarmūk and during the conquest of Fiḥl. In a few traditions, Hāshim b. 'Utba also functions as a transmitter. On Hāshim b. 'Utba, see *EI*^{2}, s.v. Hāshim b. 'Utba (Ed.).

112 Heraclius (Hiraql) (d. 20/641) was the famous Byzantine Emperor (r. 610–641) in the times of Muḥammad, Abū Bakr and 'Umar. In al-Azdī's narrative, Heraclius (sometimes called Caesar) features prominently as the mastermind behind the Byzantine defence. Heraclius is identified several times as the Emperor of the Byzantines, who knows of Muḥammad. After having learned that Abū Bakr had dispatched military units to Syria, he, while being in Palestine, started organising the defence of Syria by assembling Byzantine noblemen and Christian Arabs and calling them to fight the Muslims. In one speech, he referred to previous wars against the Sasanian Emperor Khusraw Aparwīz and against the Turks, probably identified here with the Avars or Slavs, and declared that victory was due to the Byzantines' proper conduct (later it was explained to him that the Byzantines' defeat at Ḥimṣ was brought about by their unjust behaviour and improper conduct). From Palestine, Heraclius went to Damascus, Ḥimṣ and Antioch, calling his subjects to fight. In the rest of the events during the conquest of Syria, Heraclius is said to have stayed in Antioch. There, he kept close contact with his subjects in Syria and the commanders of the units he had sent there. For example, he asked the inhabitants of Damascus in writing to keep up the defence of the city until reinforcements would reach them and he was informed by his commander Bāhān about the upcoming Battle of al-Yarmūk. In addition, Heraclius frequently sent reinforcements to various places in Syria (e.g. to Damascus, Baysān, Jerusalem, Caesarea and al-Yarmūk). Also the remnant parts of the Byzantines' units went to him in Antioch (e.g. after the defeat at Damascus and Ḥimṣ). After having lost Ḥimṣ, Heraclius wanted to leave Antioch, but the Byzantine sovereigns held him back. However, after the great loss in the Battle of al-Yarmūk, he finally did so, taking the route from Antioch to Constantinople via Edessa. In the course of this route, he turned back and bade farewell to Syria, which he believed not to be part of the Byzantine Empire anymore. On Heraclius, see Jones/Martindale/Morris, *Prosopography*, III, 586–587.

113 Palestine (Filasṭīn, lit. "the land of the Philistines") is a region, the borders of which lie in the Mediterranean in the west, between Gaza and Ayla in the south, the Jordan valley and the Dead Sea in the east and between Caesarea and Baysān in the north. In al-Azdī's

"The Arabs have advanced on you and have mustered huge groups against you, claiming that their Prophet, who was sent to them, told them that they would be victorious over the people of these lands. They came to you having no doubt\\109 that this would happen. But they marched to you with their women and children, putting all credence in their Prophet's words and saying: 'If we entered them [=the lands], we would conquer them and live with our women and children in them'". Then Heraclius said to them [=those who mentioned the last words]: "People become more valiant when they fight with faith and trust. It is too difficult for whoever opposes them to dissuade them from their opinion or divert them from their cause". He [=the narrator, Hāshim b. ʿUtba b. Abī Waqqāṣ] said: He [=Heraclius] summoned the people of the lands, the Byzantine noblemen (*ashrāf al-Rūm*) and all the Arabs who were embracing his religion [=Christianity] to his place. Then he said: "O adherents of this religion, God (ʿa.) has always been kind to you, supportive of and helpful to your religion against the bygone communities, against Khusraw[114] and the [Zoroastrian] magi (*majūs*), against the Turks (*al-Turk*)[115] who have never understood and against all the other communities. This was because you were following the scripture of your Lord and your Prophet's [=Jesus's[116]] normative practices[117]. His affair was a right path and his action was true guidance. When you exchanged and altered [your religious practices], it increased some people's greed for that which you possess. I swear by God that we have paid no attention to them but we are not afraid of being plagued by them. They

---

narrative, it is referred to as "the land of Palestine" or Palestine and is associated with the two major cities Jerusalem and Caesarea. Furthermore, it is located south of the "land of Ḥimṣ" and adjacent to "the land of the Arabs". It is usually confined by "the land of the River Jordan". Furthermore, its conquest by the Muslims under the command of ʿAmr b. al-ʿĀṣ is mentioned and Heraclius's stay there is referred to. On Palestine, see *EI*^{2}, s.v. Filasṭīn (D. Sourdel).

114 In al-Azdī's narrative, Khusraw (Kisrā) refers to the Sasanid Emperors, Khusraw Anūshirwān (r. 531–579) or Khusraw Aparwīz (r. 591–628). The Arabic term "*Kisrā*" is sometimes treated as the name of the Persian Emperors in general. Khusraw is mentioned twice: (a) in Heraclius's speech, in which the latter is said to have fought him; (b) as the superior of the commander Zādiba. On Khusraw, see *EI*^{2}, s.v. Kisrā (M. Morony).

115 Kaegi is probably correct in identifying "the Turks" with the Khazars (see Kaegi, *Byzantium*, 11). Conrad, however, interprets the term as referring to the Avars (see Conrad, *Heraclius*, 137).

116 In al-Azdī's narrative, Jesus (qurʾānic ʿĪsā b. Maryam) is depicted from both Christian and Muslim perspectives. "The Christians" say that they follow the religion of Jesus and that Jesus is the son of Mary. "The Muslims" reiterate qurʾānic concepts according to which Jesus is a servant and messenger of God, that he is just like Adam created from earth and that he foretells Muḥammad's coming. In addition, "the Muslims" are depicted as believing in Jesus as the same prophet that "the Byzantines" believe in and, parallel to Muḥammad, Jesus is said to have established normative practices (*sunan*), which the Byzantines follow. On Jesus in the Islamic context, see *EI*^{2}, s.v. ʿĪsā (G. Anawati); on Jesus in the biblical context, see *RGG4*, s.v. Jesus Christus (J. Roloff/P. Pokorny et al.).

117 In al-Azdī's narrative, the word *sunna* (lit. "custom, practice") is used as a reference to Jesus's normative practices by analogy with Muḥammad's normative practices.

marched [out] to us barefoot, naked and starving. They were driven out to your lands by rain shortage, land infertility and terrible [living] condition[s]. So advance\\110 on them and fight them in defence of your religion, your lands, your women and your children. I am leaving you [now] but I am going to reinforce you with the cavalry and the infantry you need. I have already appointed commanders over you. Listen to them and obey [them]". Then he set out for Damascus[118], repeating the same words on similar occasion[s]. Afterwards, he went to Ḥimṣ[119] repeating the same words on similar occasion[s]. Then he set out until he reached Antioch[120], stayed there, sent for the Byzantines and rallied them all to him. A [large] number of them, which nobody but God ('a.) could count, came [to him]. Their warriors, men, young men and followers (*atbāʿ*) also trooped to him. They all regarded the Arabs' advance on them as serious and feared that they [=the Arabs] would usurp their reign.\\111

Abū ʿUbayda b. al-Jarrāḥ's (r.) march to Syria and the route he took and travelled along

Abū ʿUbayda b. al-Jarrāḥ proceeded until he passed by Wādī al-Qurā[121]; then he headed to al-Ḥijr[122], the land of the Prophet Ṣāliḥ[123] ('s.), which

118 Damascus (Dimashq al-Shām) is located ca. 100 km east of the Mediterranean coast behind the Lebanon and Anti-Lebanon mountain ranges at the foot of Jabal Qāsiyūn and at the edge of the desert that extends as far as the Euphrates (to the east) and the Arabian Peninsula (to the southeast). According to al-Azdī's narrative, the conquest of Damascus happened as a double-conquest undertaken by Khālid b. al-Walīd and Abū ʿUbayda after a long siege. Whereas Khālid conquered the city by force, Abū ʿUbayda granted the inhabitants of Damascus a peace treaty which was regarded later as superior. On Damascus, see *EI*[2], s.v. Dimashḳ (N. Elisséeff) and Burns, *Damascus*.

119 Ḥimṣ is located on the eastern bank of the Orontes at the entrance to a depression of two mountains midway between Aleppo and Damascus. According to al-Azdī's narrative, Ḥimṣ was conquered by the Muslim troops after a short siege and after its inhabitants asked the Muslim troops for peace. On Ḥimṣ, see *EI*[2], s.v. Ḥimṣ (N. Elisséeff).

120 Antioch (Anṭākiya) is a town situated at the Orontes ca. 20 km east of the Mediterranean coast. In al-Azdī's narrative, it is referred to several times as the headquarters of the Byzantine Emperor Heraclius, from which he sent out several units and which he left for Constantinople after his troops were defeated. On Antioch, see *EI*[2], s.v. Anṭākiya (M. Streck/H. Gibb).

121 Wādī al-Qurā (lit. "the Valley of the Villages") is an area in al-Ḥijāz located ca. 350 km north of Medina. In al-Azdī's narrative, it is mentioned as a station of Abū ʿUbayda's and ʿUmar's trip to Syria. On Wādī al-Qurā, see *EI*[2], s.v. Wādī al-Ḳurā (M. Lecker).

122 Al-Ḥijr refers either to an area or to a small village in Wādī al-Qurā that is said to have been inhabited by the Arabian tribe Thamūd, according to Yāqūt. The "people of al-Ḥijr" (Q. 15:80) and Thamūd (e.g. Q. 7:73, 11:61) are mentioned in the Qurʾān, where it is said that God sent the Prophet Ṣāliḥ to them. In al-Azdī's narrative, this information is given, in addition to the geographic information that the village is located between al-Ḥijāz and Syria. Furthermore, it is mentioned as a station of Abū ʿUbayda's trip to Syria. On al-Ḥijr, see Yāqūt, *Muʿjam al-buldān*, II, 208.

123 Ṣāliḥ (lit. "the Pious") is a qurʾānic figure who is said to have been sent as a prophet to Thamūd. In al-Azdī's narrative, Ṣāliḥ is mentioned in the context of al-Ḥijr and its hinterland. In folklore, al-Ḥijr is sometimes identified as *Madāʾin Ṣāliḥ* (lit. "the dwellings of Ṣāliḥ"). On Ṣāliḥ, see *EI*[2], s.v. Ṣāliḥ (A. Rippin).

is located between al-Ḥijāz[124] and Syria; then [he proceeded] to Dhāt al-Manār[125], then to Zīzā'[126]; then he marched to Ma'āb[127] near Amman[128]. There the Byzantines came out to [fight] them [=Abū 'Ubayda and his unit]. But it did not take long before the Muslims vanquished them and forced them [back] into their town. Then they besieged them. The people of Ma'āb made peace with them in it [=the town]. It became the first Syrian town whose people made peace [with the Muslims]. Then Abū 'Ubayda marched [away] and when he drew near al-Jābiya, someone came to him and said: "Heraclius, the Emperor of the Byzantines, is in Antioch and he has mobilised against you unprecedented groups that none of his forefathers had ever assembled against any of the bygone communities".\\112

This is Abū 'Ubayda b. al-Jarrāḥ's letter to Abū Bakr (r.) informing him of what he learned of Heraclius's, the Emperor of the Byzantines, mobilisation of the Byzantine groups and of what Abū 'Ubayda wanted to consult Abū Bakr about

Al-Walīd b. Ḥammād [al-Ramlī] related to us, saying: Al-Ḥusayn b. Ziyād [al-Ramlī] related to us on the authority of Abū Ismā'īl Muḥammad b. 'Abdallāh [al-Azdī], who said: Furthermore, Abū Ḥafṣ al-Azdī[129] talked to me about the [following] letter from Abū 'Ubayda b. al-Jarrāḥ to Abū Bakr (r.):

In the name of God, the Merciful, the Compassionate. From Abū 'Ubayda b. al-Jarrāḥ to the servant of God Abū Bakr, the successor of the Messenger

124 Al-Ḥijāz (lit. "the Barrier") is a region in the north-western part of the Arabian Peninsula. Although the geographical borders of al-Ḥijāz are not agreed on, it is most likely bordered by al-'Aqaba and Palestine in the north, al-Ṭā'if in the east, Yemen in the south and the Tihāma (coast) in the west. In al-Azdī's narrative, no detailed information about al-Ḥijāz is given, but it is described as the Muslims' home region. On al-Ḥijāz, see *EI*², s.v. al-Ḥidjāz (G. Rentz).

125 Dhāt al-Manār (lit. "the One with the Minaret") is a location at the border between al-Ḥijāz and Syria, according to Yāqūt. In al-Azdī's narrative, it is described as a "watering place" at which Abū 'Ubayda stopped on his way from Medina to Amman. In addition, al-Azdī mentions the case of a man living in Dhāt al-Manār who married two sisters and who was scolded for this by 'Umar, when he was on his way back from Syria to Medina. On Dhāt al-Manār, see Yāqūt, *Mu'jam al-buldān*, II, 716.

126 Zīzā' is one of the villages in al-Balqā' region (i.e. in the middle part of Transjordan). In al-Azdī's narrative, it is mentioned as one of Abū 'Ubayda's stations on his way from Medina to Amman. On Zīzā', see Yāqūt, *Mu'jam al-buldān*, II, 966.

127 Ma'āb is a city in the region of al-Balqā' (i.e. the middle part of Transjordan) at the edge of Syria. In al-Azdī's narrative, it is mentioned as one of Abū 'Ubayda's stations on the route to Syria and as being located in the vicinity of Amman. Abū 'Ubayda besieged and conquered Ma'āb, which was the first city in Syria that the Muslim troops conquered. On Ma'āb, see Yāqūt, *Mu'jam al-buldān*, IV, 377.

128 Amman ('Ammān) is located ca. 30 km east of the Jordan valley. In al-Azdī's narrative, the conquest of Amman is not mentioned, but it serves to locate Ma'āb. On Amman, see *EI*², s.v. 'Ammān (G. Lankester Harding).

129 In al-Azdī's narrative, Abū Ḥafṣ al-Azdī is mentioned as a transmitter of one tradition. On Abū Ḥafṣ al-Azdī, see Ibn Ḥajar, *Lisān*, VII, 36 (no. 354).

of God (ṣ.). Peace be upon you. I praise, on your behalf, God with whom no other deity is associated. Regarding the matter at hand: We do ask God to strengthen Islam and its adherents and drive them to an easy conquest. I learned that Heraclius, the Emperor of the Byzantines, descended on one of the Syrian towns (*qarya*) called Antioch, that he sent for the people of his empire (*mamlaka*) and rallied them to him and that they trooped to him [mounted on] tractable and intractable [animals][130]. So I thought of informing you about this and of knowing your opinion about it. May God's peace, mercy and blessings be upon you.

Then Abū Bakr (r.) wrote [the following letter back] to him:

In the name of God, the Merciful, the Compassionate. Regarding the matter at hand: I received your letter and understood what you mentioned therein about Heraclius, the Emperor of the Byzantines. As for his descent on Antioch, it forecasts that he and his companions will be defeated and that God will lead you and the Muslims to conquest. As for what you mentioned about his rallying of the people of his empire and his mobilisation of groups against you,\\113 we and you foreknew that they would do so. No people would forsake their power or renounce their reign without fighting [for it]. I knew, thank God, that they would be invaded by a large number of Muslim men who love death as much as their enemy loves life, who seek a great reward from God for their fight and love fighting for the cause of God (t.) more than they [=the Byzantines] love their women's virginity and the best of their possessions. In battle, one of them [=the Muslims] is better than 1,000 of the Polytheists. Face them with your soldiers and do not be distressed by [the absence of] any of those Muslims who remained away from you, for God (t.) accompanies you. Instead, I am going to reinforce you with men until you will have obtained enough [support] and you will need no more, God willing. May God's peace and mercy be upon you.

Then he [=Abū Bakr] sent this letter with Dārim al-ʿAbsī[131] [to Abū ʿUbayda].

This is Yazīd b. Abī Sufyān's letter to Abū Bakr (r.)

In the name of God, the Merciful, the Compassionate. Regarding the matter at hand: When Heraclius, the Emperor of the Byzantines, learned of our advance on him, God struck terror into his heart. He pulled himself

130 The Arabic phrase used here "*ʿalā al-ṣaʿba wa-al-dhalūl*", a remodelling of "*rakibū al-ṣaʿba wa-al-dhalūl*", is also used as an idiomatic expression meaning "by all possible means" (see, for example, Ibn Manẓūr, *Mukhtaṣar*, XV, 55).

131 Dārim al-ʿAbsī is listed neither in Ibn Saʿd, al-Bukhārī, Ibn ʿAsākir nor in any other biographical work we could access. In al-Azdī's narrative, he is portrayed as a messenger delivering a letter from Abū Bakr to Abū ʿUbayda concerning the descent of the Byzantines on Antioch, which Abū Bakr interpreted as a sign of the Byzantines' weakness. In addition, Dārim's son Qanān b. Dārim is mentioned in the narrative.

together, took up headquarters in Antioch, appointed some of his soldiers as commanders of the Syrian cities and ordered them to fight us. They became available [there] and made preparations for fighting us. The [Christian] Arabs of Syria who were at peace [with the Muslims] (*musālimat al-Shām*) informed us that Heraclius told the people of his empire to troop [together] and that they proceeded in large numbers[132]. So give us your order and hasten to tell us\\114 your opinion on this so that we can follow it, God (t.) willing. We also ask God (t.) for [the bestowal of] victory, patience, conquest and vigour upon the Muslims. May God's peace and mercy be upon you.

Then Abū Bakr (r.) wrote [the following letter] to him [=Yazīd b. Abī Sufyān]:

In the name of God, the Merciful, the Compassionate. Regarding the matter at hand: I received your letter in which you mentioned the heading of the Emperor of the Byzantines to Antioch and God's (ʿa.) striking terror of the Muslim groups into his heart. God, praise be to Him, led us to victory by means of fear when we were [fighting together] with the Messenger of God (ṣ.) and reinforced us with His obliging angels. That religion, by virtue of which God led us to victory through fear, is the [same] religion that we call people [to embrace] today. I swear by your Lord that He will never make Muslims equal to sinners, nor will whoever attests that "There is no [other] deity but God" be equal to whoever worships other deities besides Him or worships several deities. When you face them [=the Byzantines], rush to them with whomever you have and fight them, for God (t.) will never disappoint you. God (tt.) has also told us that a small company (*fiʾa*) defeats a large company by the will of God. Nevertheless, I am reenforcing you with men\\115 followed by [more] men until you will have got enough and will need no more people, God (t.) willing; may God's peace and mercy be upon you.

He [=Abū Bakr] sent this letter with ʿAbdallāh b. Qurṭ al-Thumālī[133] [to Yazīd]. When he [=ʿAbdallāh b. Qurṭ] came to Abū Bakr (r.) [to deliver Yazīd's letter], Abū Bakr (r.) said to him: "Tell me the latest news about the people [=the Muslims]". He [=ʿAbdallāh b. Qurṭ] said to him: "The Muslims are fine. They moved into the nearest part of Syria and its people became terrified of them. We were told that the Byzantines mustered [large and many] groups (*jamma*) [for fighting] against us—he [=the narrator] said: And *al-jamma* means "the soldiers when they all gathered". We have not met our enemy yet although we are expecting and anticipating—i.e. waiting for—the encounter with it every day. If Heraclius sent [against] us no troops, Syria would not be

132 For the meaning of the idiomatic expression "*yajurrūna al-shawka wa-al-shajara*" (lit. "dragging the spikes and trees"), see Lane, *Lexicon*, s.v. *shawka*.

133 ʿAbdallāh's full name is ʿAbdallāh b. Qurṭ al-Thumālī al-Azdī (d. 56/677). In al-Azdī's narrative, he is a messenger of Abū Bakr and ʿUmar, fights in Fiḥl and Ḥimṣ and is appointed as the commander of Ḥimṣ by ʿUmar. In addition, he is a transmitter of several traditions. On ʿAbdallāh b. Qurṭ al-Thumālī, see Ibn ʿAbd al-Barr, *Al-istīʿāb*, III, 978 (no. 1634).

hard to conquer at all". Then Abū Bakr (r.) said to him: "Tell me the truth". He [='Abdallāh b. Qurṭ] then said: "Why would I not tell you the truth? Am I allowed to lie or is it proper of someone like me to lie to someone like you? If I lied to you about this, would I not be unfaithful to what I am trusted with, [as well as] to my Lord, to you and to the Muslims?" Thereupon, Abū Bakr (r.) said to him: "God forbid, you are absolutely none of these [people]". Abū Bakr (r.) wrote [and gave] the [preceding] letter to him [='Abdallāh b. Qurṭ al-Thumālī], sent him back to Yazīd and said to him: "Tell him [=Yazīd] and tell the Muslims that I am going to reinforce them with Hāshim b. 'Utba [b. Abī Waqqāṣ] and Sa'īd b. 'Āmir b.\\116 Ḥudhaym[134]". 'Abdallāh b. Qurṭ [al-Thumālī] set out with Abū Bakr's (r.) letter until he reached Yazīd. Then he [=Yazīd] read it to the Muslims who delighted in and rejoiced over it.

The departure of Hāshim b. 'Utba [b. Abī Waqqāṣ] (r.)

Al-Walīd b. Ḥammād [al-Ramlī] related to us, saying: Al-Ḥusayn b. Ziyād [al-Ramlī] reported to us on the authority of Abū Ismā'īl Muḥammad b. 'Abdallāh [al-Azdī], who said: Furthermore, Abū 'Ubāda[135] related to me on the authority of his grandfather: Abū Bakr (r.) sent for Hāshim b. 'Utba b. Abī Waqqāṣ and said to him: "O Hāshim, it is by virtue of your earnestness and your best fortune that you became one of those whose assistance is sought by the community for fighting for the cause of God against its polytheistic enemy. [You also became] one of those whose advice, loyalty, decency and valour are trusted by the leader. The Muslims have recently sent me a request for support against their polytheistic enemy. So march with your followers to them [=the Muslims] and I am going to dispatch [more] people with you. March out until you reach either Abū 'Ubayda or Yazīd". He [=Hāshim b. 'Utba b. Abī Waqqāṣ] said: "No, [I would] rather [go to] Abū 'Ubayda". He [=the narrator, the grandfather of Abū 'Ubāda] said: He went to Abū 'Ubayda. Then he [=the narrator, the grandfather of Abū 'Ubāda] said: Then Abū Bakr

134 Sa'īd's full name is Sa'īd b. 'Āmir b. Ḥudhaym al-Jumaḥī (d. 20–21/640–642). In al-Azdī's narrative, his name of kinship (*nisba*) is given as al-Qurashī and al-Jumaḥī (Jumaḥ is a subtribe of Quraysh) and he is mentioned as being ordered by Abū Bakr to lead Muslim reinforcements to Yazīd b. Abī Sufyān in Syria, where he takes part in the Battles of al-'Araba and al-Dāthina. Khālid b. al-Walīd puts him in command of the army's left flank in the Battle of Ajnādayn. Then he fights in the Battle of Fiḥl and is sent by Abū 'Ubayda as a messenger to 'Umar in Medina. From there 'Umar sends him back with reinforcements to support the Muslims in the Battle of al-Yarmūk. On Sa'īd b. 'Āmir b. Ḥudhaym, see Ibn Sa'd, *Kitāb al-ṭabaqāt*, VII-2, 122.

135 Abū 'Ubāda is difficult to identify because only his patronymic (*kunya*) is mentioned by al-Azdī but his full name is not given. Mourad identifies him as Abū 'Ubāda 'Īsā b. 'Abd al-Raḥmān b. Farwa al-Anṣārī al-Zuraqī (see Mourad, *al-Azdī*, 591). 'Uqla and Banī Yāsīn were unable to identify him (see al-Azdī, *Futūḥ al-Shām. Ed. 'Uqla/Banī Yāsīn*, 116, n. 7). In al-Azdī's narrative, he is mentioned as a transmitter of one tradition. On Abū 'Ubāda al-Zuraqī, see Ibn Abī Ḥātim, *Al-jarḥ wa-al-ta'dīl*, VI, 281–282 (no. 1559).

(r.) rose [and stood] before the people, praised and thanked God and then said: "Regarding the matter at hand: Your Muslim brethren are safeguarded, protected[136] and defended, and arrangements are made for them. God ('a.) struck terror of them into the hearts of their enemies. [Hence,] they sought refuge in their fortresses, closed\\117 their doors and shut themselves in. Their [=the Muslims'] messengers came to inform me that Heraclius, the Emperor of the Byzantines, escaped their clutches and set up camp in one of the villages in the farthermost part of Syria. They [=the Muslims in Syria] [also] sent me a message, telling me that Heraclius had dispatched soldiers from that place to [fight] them. So I decided to reinforce your Muslim brethren with soldiers from among you, by help of whom God will strengthen their backs, suppress their enemies and strike terror into their [=the enemies'] hearts. Be ready [to march out], may God have mercy upon you, with Hāshim b. 'Utba b. Abī Waqqāṣ and seek the reward and [that which is] good in return for that [march]. For if you are rendered victorious, it [=the reward] will be the conquest and spoils; but if you perish, it will be martyrdom and dignity". Then Abū Bakr (r.) returned to his home and the people started to flock to Hāshim [b. 'Utba b. Abī Waqqāṣ] until their number increased. When they numbered 1,000, Abū Bakr (r.) ordered him [=Hāshim b. 'Utba b. Abī Waqqāṣ] to march [out]. Hāshim went to Abū Bakr, greeted him and bade farewell to him. Then Abū Bakr (r.) said to him: "O Hāshim, we used to benefit from an old man's opinion, consultation and good planning and to profit from a young man's patience, valour and succour. God ('a.) gathered all these characteristics in you when you were a young [man] anticipating what would be good. When you face your enemy, be patient, persevere and know that any step you take, any amount of money you spend, or any thirst, weariness or hunger you suffer for the cause of God is rewarded by God with a good deed [written] in your record. For God never wastes the reward for those who do what is good". Hāshim [b. 'Utba b. Abī Waqqāṣ] then said: "If God wants me to be good, He causes me to be so and I will do what is good, as power is gained only through God. If I am not killed, I will kill [the enemies] and then kill [more of them] again, God willing". His uncle Sa'd b.\\118 Abī Waqqāṣ (r.) said to him: "O my nephew, do not make a stab or give a strike except for the sake of God[137]. Be informed that you imminently depart this life and shortly return to God (t.). And nothing from this life will accompany you to the afterlife except for a firm footing you gave or a good deed you did beforehand". He [=Hāshim b. 'Utba b. Abī Waqqāṣ] said: "O uncle, do not fear that, I will not do anything other than that. I would be certainly a failure and a hypocrite if I made my arrivals and departures, my comings, goings and my endeavours, my stabs with

136 For this meaning, see Ullmann, *WKAS*, s.v. *kala'a*.

137 We decided to translate the expression "*turīdu bi-hā wajḥ Allāh*" (lit. "you seek through it the face of God") in a more comprehensible manner as rendered above. On this expression, see Baljon, *To Seek*.

my spear[138] and my strikes with my sword for the sake of people [only]". Then he left Abū Bakr (r.) and followed Abū ʿUbayda until he reached him. The Muslims [there] found his arrival auspicious and rejoiced over it.

*The story (**qiṣṣa**) of Saʿīd b. ʿĀmir b. Ḥudhaym['s departure]*

He [=the narrator, the grandfather of ʿUbāda] said: Saʿīd b. ʿĀmir b. Ḥudhaym learned that Abū Bakr (r.) wanted to dispatch him [to Syria]. When Abū Bakr delayed this [process] and did not mention it to him for a couple of days, he said: "O Abū Bakr, I learned that you wanted to dispatch me to that direction but then I noticed that you went silent. Therefore, I do not know what you have finally decided. If you want to dispatch someone else, send me with him. That is fine with me. But if you do not want to dispatch anybody, I have a desire to fight for the cause of God. Thus, let me, may God have mercy upon you, catch up with the Muslims, for I was told that the Byzantines mounted a huge crowd against our brethren". Abū Bakr said: "O Saʿīd b. ʿĀmir b. Ḥudhaym, may God, the most Merciful, have mercy upon you. You have ever been, as far as I know,\\119 one of those behaving modestly, keeping contact [with others], abasing themselves [to God], working hard [for God] at the crack of dawn and remembering God very often". Then Saʿīd said: "May God (t.) have mercy upon you; God's blessings upon me are much better than what you could mention and the favour, might and grace [bestowed] upon us belong to God. I swear by God that you have ever been, as far as I know, disclosing the truth, acting with equity, showing mercy towards the Believers and toughness on the Unbelievers, ruling with justice and truth and excluding nobody in oath[s]". Then Abū Bakr (r.) said to him: "Enough, Saʿīd, enough! Get out and prepare yourself [to fight]; may God have mercy upon you. I am going to supply the Muslims with reinforcements over whom I appoint you as a commander". Abū Bakr (r.) ordered Bilāl [to cry out publicly]. So he cried out [the following statement] to the people [accordingly]: "O Muslims, get ready [to march out] with Saʿīd b. ʿĀmir b. Ḥudhaym to Syria". In a few days, 700 men got ready [to march out] with him. When Saʿīd b. ʿĀmir [b. Ḥudhaym] wanted to depart with the people, Bilāl (r.) came to Abū Bakr (r.) and said: "O successor of the Messenger of God (ṣ.), if you manumitted me in order that I stay with you and in order to prevent me from the good I want for myself, I would stay with you. But if you manumitted me for the sake of God in order to be the master of my own self and to settle on what is good for me, let me go to fight for the cause of God, because I prefer fighting for the cause of God to staying [behind with you]". Abū Bakr (r.) said to him: "God will certainly testify that I have [just] manumitted you only for His sake and that I want

138 Spear (sg. *rumḥ*) was a weapon made of wood or a pipe with two iron tips (at the top and bottom) and was used for pushing and hence piercing the opponent (see Schwarzlose, *Waffen*, 214, 217). Throughout al-Azdī's narrative, it is the only expression used to refer to a spear.

neither reward nor thanks from you. I would also not like you to abandon your own desires for my own desires as long as yours call you to obey my Lord".\\120 Bilāl said to him: "If you want me to stay, I will". Abū Bakr (r.) said to him: "As long as your desire is to fight for the cause of God, I will not order you to stay. I just wanted you to be the caller for prayers (*li-l-ādhān*). And I will surely feel lonely because of your departure, Bilāl. Separation is unavoidable—separation without reunion until the Day of Resurrection. Bilāl, do good [deeds] which will be your provision from this life [for the afterlife] and by means of which God will remember you as long as you live and enhance your reward when you die". So Bilāl said to him: "May God bless you for it, my benefactor and brother in Islam. I swear by God that it is not an innovation from you to order us to be patient with obedience to God and to adhere to the truth and the good deed[s]. I also do not want to call for prayers for [the sake of] anybody else after the [death of the] Messenger of God (ṣ.)". Then Bilāl went out with Sa'īd b. 'Āmir b. Ḥudhaym [to Syria].

Sa'īd came on his she-camel and stopped by Abū Bakr (r.), who was in company with the Muslims. Then he [=Sa'īd] said: "We are heading for this destination, so may God deem it a blessed one. O God, if you have destined us to meet again, reunite us in obedience to You. But if You have destined us to separate [forever], then [separation is due] to your mercy. Peace [be upon you]".

Then he turned and went away. Abū Bakr (r.) then said: "Servants of God, supplicate God in favour of your brother so that God accompanies and protects him. And raise your hands [in supplication]; may God have mercy upon you". Numbering more than 50 men, they raised their hands. Abū Bakr (r.) then said: "The more a number of Muslims raise their hands to their Lord in supplication to ask for something, the more He responds positively to them, as long as they do not call for disobedience or a breach of a tie of kinship". Sa'īd learned about their supplication after he had reached the land of Syria and had fought the enemy. He then said: "May God have mercy upon my brethren; I wish they had not prayed for me. I marched out, keen on and desirous of martyrdom. The moment I faced the enemy, God protected me from defeat and retreat. I was liable to martyrdom but then my long-loved desire for martyrdom was gone. When I learned that my brethren had prayed for my safety, I knew that [their prayers] were accepted and that I was safe".\\121 Abū Bakr (r.) ordered him [=Sa'īd b. 'Āmir b. Ḥudhaym] to march [out] to catch up with Yazīd b. Abī Sufyān. So he marched [out] until he caught up with him. Then he [=Sa'īd b. 'Āmir b. Ḥudhaym] witnessed with him the Battle[s] of al-'Araba[139] and al-Dāthina[140].

139 Al-'Araba, or Wādī al-'Araba, is the name of the southern part of the Jordan valley extending ca. 170 km from the southern end of the Dead Sea to the Gulf of 'Aqaba. According to al-Azdī's narrative, al-'Araba is the location of the first battle between the Byzantines and the Muslims under the command of Yazīd b. Abī Sufyān. It is unclear whether al-'Araba is conceived as a town or not. On al-'Araba, see *EI*², s.v. 'Araba (N. Glueck).

140 Al-Dāthina is an area (or a village) near Gaza in Palestine, according to Yāqūt. According to al-Azdī's narrative, it is the location of the first battle between the Byzantines

The coming of the Arabs to Abū Bakr (r.)

The arrival of Ḥamza b. Mālik al-Hamdānī

Al-Walīd b. Ḥammād [al-Ramlī] related to us, saying: Al-Ḥusayn b. Ziyād [al-Ramlī] reported to us on the authority of Abū Ismāʿīl Muḥammad b. ʿAbdallāh [al-Azdī], who said: Furthermore, ʿAbd al-Raḥmān b. Yazīd b. Jābir al-Azdī related to me on the authority of ʿAmr b. Muḥṣan on the authority of Ḥamza b. Mālik al-Hamdānī, later al-ʿUdhrī[141], that he came with a large group, [i.e.] more than 2,000 men, from Hamdān[142] to Abū Bakr al-Ṣiddīq (r.). When Abū Bakr saw their [high] number and fortitude, he delighted in [seeing] them and rejoiced over this. Then he said: "Praise be to God for what He has done for the Muslims. He [=God] is still supplying them with reinforcements from among them [=the Muslims]. With their help He strengthens their backs and destroys their enemies". He [=the narrator, Ḥamza b. Mālik al-Hamdānī] said: Afterwards, Abū Bakr (r.) ordered us to encamp in Medina. He [=the narrator, Ḥamza b. Mālik al-Hamdānī] said: I was visiting Abū Bakr frequently in the morning and in the evening while he was accompanied by a number of Emigrants and Supporters. He [=the narrator, Ḥamza b. Mālik al-Hamdānī] said: He [=Abū Bakr] treated me kindly, seated me\\122 near him and said to me: "Study the Qurʾān, perform the ritual ablution (*wuḍūʾ*), bend over and prostrate [in prayer] properly, perform the ritual prayer[s] (*ṣalāt*) on time, give the prescribed tax when it is due, advise the Muslim, desert the Polytheist and mobilise people on the day of war (*baʾs*)". I said: "I swear by God that I would exert myself to do all that you told me. I do know that you have done your best in advising me and your utmost in exhorting [me]". He [=the narrator Ḥamza b. Mālik al-Hamdānī] said: Then he [=Abū Bakr] moved out to our encampment and ordered us to prepare ourselves and get ready, to buy what we need and then rush out to our companions [in Syria]. He [=the narrator Ḥamza b. Mālik al-Hamdānī]

---

and the Muslims under the command of Yazīd b. Abī Sufyān. On al-Dāthina, see Yāqūt, *Muʿjam al-buldān*, II, 154–155 (s.v. Dāthin).

141 Ḥamza b. Mālik al-Hamdānī (n.d.) is known as the tribal leader of Hamdān and as a follower of Muʿāwiya in Jordan. In al-Azdī's narrative, he is also said to have been associated with ʿUdhra, hence taking the *nisba* al-ʿUdhrī, and is depicted as coming with a large group from Hamdān to Abū Bakr who gave him religious and military advice, called him a brother and sent him to Abū ʿUbayda in Syria. In addition, Ḥamza functions as a transmitter of several traditions in the narrative. On Ḥamza b. Mālik, see Ibn ʿAsākir, *TMD*, XI, 381.

142 Hamdān is a Southern Arabian tribe that settled north of Ṣanʿāʾ and Najrān. In al-Azdī's narrative, the members of Hamdān are said to have lived in villages and to have fought during the Battle of al-Yarmūk. In addition, two individual figures belonged to Hamdān: (a) Ḥamza b. Mālik al-Hamdānī, who is also a transmitter of traditions and who is said to have come with a large group from Hamdān to Abū Bakr, who called him a brother and sent him to Abū ʿUbayda in Syria and (b) al-Mujālid b. Saʿīd al-Hamdānī, who is a transmitter of two traditions. On Hamdān, see *EI*^{2}, s.v. Hamdān (J. Schleifer/W. Watt).

said: We mustered for that purpose and prepared ourselves quickly. When we finished, he [=Abū Bakr] sent for me and said: "O brother of Hamdān, you are noble, leading, valiant and in control of a clan. So fetch them [=the clansmen] to war and do not use them for hurting people".

He [=the narrator Ḥamza b. Mālik al-Hamdānī] said: I was accompanied by men from the villages of Hamdān, some of whom were characterised by lack of knowledge and hard-heartedness. The people of Medina were hurt by some of them and complained about it to Abū Bakr (r.) who thereupon said: "I adjure by God all the Muslims who hear my entreaties, my pleadings and my implorations to leave those people alone. Whoever sees that I have a claim on him should bear their sharp tongues and their unlikable impetuosity as long as they have not exceeded the limit. By virtue of those [tribesmen from Hamdān] and the likes of those, God (ʿa.) will destroy our enemies, the groups of Heraclius and the Byzantines. Furthermore, they are certainly your brethren. If any of you suffered their impetuosity but bore it, would that not be a better decision and a more suitable time than taking revenge on them?" The Muslims said: "Yes[, it would]". He [=Abū Bakr] said: "Indeed, they are your brethren in terms of religion and your supporters against the enemies. So, they have\\123 a claim on you to bear that [behaviour] from their side". Then he descended [from the speech platform[143]]. He [=the narrator, Ḥamza b. Mālik al-Hamdānī] said: Then he looked at me and said: "What are you waiting for? Set out with God's blessing". He [=the narrator, Ḥamza b. Mālik al-Hamdānī] said: Then I set out. He [=the narrator, Ḥamza b. Mālik al-Hamdānī] said: Before I left, I said to him: "Am I under the command of someone other than you?" He [=Abū Bakr] said: "Yes, there are three whom we appointed as commanders. Join whomever you want". He [=the narrator, Ḥamza b. Mālik al-Hamdānī] said: I marched out until I entered the nearest part of Syria. When I caught up with the Muslims, I asked them: "Which of the commanders is the best? And which of them was favoured most by the Messenger of God (ṣ.)?" They said: "Abū ʿUbayda b. al-Jarrāḥ". So I thought to myself: "I swear by God that I will never compare this man with anyone else". I proceeded and reached Abū ʿUbayda (r.), entered his [encampment] and then told him the story of my departure [from Yemen], my arrival to Abū Bakr (r.), what happened to me and to my companions in Medina, my arrival to him [=Abū ʿUbayda] and [why] I choose him over the others. He [=Abū ʿUbayda] then said: "May God bless your arrival, your fighting for the cause of God and your coming to us. May God bless you for [the benefit of] us and [bless all] the Muslims you brought to us".

143 The narrator assumes that the speaker was standing, during his speech, on something raised above the ground. Since this elevated thing is not exactly mentioned in the text, we think it to be a speaker's platform. This seems to be the case throughout the text when the verb "*nazala*" (lit. "to descend"), after the delivery of a speech, is used.

Al-Walīd b. Ḥammād [al-Ramlī] related to us: Al-Ḥusayn b. Ziyād [al-Ramlī] reported to us on the authority of Abū Ismā'īl Muḥammad b. 'Abdallāh [al-Azdī], who said: Furthermore, Abū al-Mughfil[144] related to me on the authority of 'Amr b. Muḥṣan, who said: Abū Bakr (r.) was never tired of dispatching soldiers to Syria and reinforcing the commanders by sending them more and more men in order to elevate the adherents of Islam and humiliate the adherents of polytheism.\\124

The arrival of Abū al-A'war al-Sulamī

Al-Walīd b. Ḥammād [al-Ramlī] related to us, saying: Al-Ḥusayn b. Ziyād [al-Ramlī] reported to us on the authority of Abū Ismā'īl [Muḥammad b. 'Abdallāh al-Azdī], who said: Furthermore, 'Abd al-Malik b. Nawfal b. Masāḥiq [al-Qurashī] related to me on the authority of Abū Sa'īd al-Maqburī, who said: When Abū Bakr (r.) learned of the large assembly of the Byzantines against the Muslims, nothing astonished him more than the coming of those who emigrated to him from the Arabs' land. The more they came to him, the more he sent them [out] in turn, one after the other. Among those who came [to him] was Abū al-A'war al-Sulamī[145], also known as 'Amr b. Sufyān, who then entered his [house] and said: "We came to you, not driven by dearth (*quḥma*)[146] or by lack (*'adam*)—he [=the narrator] said: *Quḥma* means "famine" and *'adam* means "pennilessness". Either we stay stationed with you if you want, or dispatch us to your polytheistic enemy, if you want". Abū Bakr (r.) said: "No, rather fight the Unbelievers and support the Muslims". Then he [=Abū Bakr] dispatched him [to Syria]. So he [=Abū al-A'war al-Sulamī] marched [out] until he reached Abū 'Ubayda (r.).\\125

144 Abū al-Mughfil is listed neither in Ibn Sa'd, al-Bukhārī, Ibn 'Asākir nor in any other biographical work we could access. 'Uqla and Banī Yāsīn suppose that he is Abū al-Mughfil Mikhnaf al-Azdī, who is mentioned in Ibn 'Asākir's *TMD* as a transmitter reporting from 'Amr b. Muḥṣan al-Azdī (see al-Azdī, *Futūḥ al-Shām. Ed. 'Uqla/Banī Yāsīn*, 34; 123, n. 9). We could not find Abū al-Mughfil there (see Ibn 'Asākir, *TMD*, XLVI, 330–331 (no. 5395) where Muḥaffif b. Yazīd b. Ma'qil is listed). In al-Azdī's narrative, he is mentioned as a transmitter of one tradition.

145 Abū al-A'war's full name is Abū al-A'war 'Amr b. Sufyān al-Sulamī (n.d.). In al-Azdī's narrative, Abū al-A'war is introduced as one of the tribal leaders who went to Abū Bakr, seeking to fight against the Byzantines in Syria. Abū Bakr dispatched him to Abū 'Ubayda there. During the conquest of Jerusalem, he welcomed 'Umar but was scolded by him for wearing Byzantine clothing. On Abū al-A'war 'Amr al-Sulamī, see Ibn 'Asākir, *TMD*, XXXXVI, 53–60.

146 On the meaning of "*quḥma*", see Lane, *Lexicon*, s.v. *q-ḥ-m*. Lane only knows of form V, i.e. "*taqaḥḥama*", which he renders as "to experience dearth, drought or sterility". Wahrmund, however, lists "*quḥma*" in his dictionary, which is translated as "hardship in years of hunger" (*Noth des Hungerjahres*); see Wahrmund, *Handwörterbuch*, s.v. *quḥma*.

The arrival of Maʿn b. Yazīd b. al-Akhnas al-Sulamī

He [=the narrator, Abū Saʿīd al-Maqburī] said: Then Maʿn b. Yazīd b. al-Akhnas al-Sulamī[147], together with about 100 men from Banū Sulaym[148], came to Abū Bakr. Then Abū Bakr (r.) said: "If these [tribesmen] were larger in number than they are, we would send them to their brethren". ʿUmar b. al-Khaṭṭāb (r.) then said to him: "I swear by God that even if they were [only] ten [persons], I would be of the opinion that you should reinforce their brethren with them. Yes, I swear by God, I am of the opinion that you reinforce them [=the Muslims] with even one man if he has got competence (*jazāʾ*)[149] and sufficiency". Then Ḥabīb b. Maslama[150] said: "I have almost the same number of men who are not affiliated to a tribe and who desire to fight for the cause of God. O successor of the Messenger of God (ṣ.), bring us and those [fighters from Banū Sulaym] together and then dispatch [all of] us [to Syria]". Abū Bakr (r.) said: "As for now, march out with all of them, and you are the commander of the people until you reach your brethren [in Syria]". The he [=Ḥabīb b. Maslama] marched out and encamped with them [=the fighters from Banū Sulaym]. Then he assembled their companions and marched [out] with all of them until he reached Yazīd b. Abī Sufyān.

147 Maʿn's full name is Maʿn b. Yazīd b. al-Akhnas b. Manṣūr al-Sulamī al-Kūfī (n.d.). In al-Azdī's narrative, he is depicted as coming with ca. 100 men from Banū Sulaym to Abū Bakr in order to fight in Syria where he joined Yazīd b. Abī Sufyān. In addition, he raided the Byzantines and fought in the Battle of al-Yarmūk. On Maʿn b. Yazīd b. al-Akhnas, see Ibn Saʿd, *Kitāb al-ṭabaqāt*, VI, 23.

148 Sulaym is a Northern Arabian tribe that was a subtribe of Qays ʿAylān. In al-Azdī's narrative, Sulaym is mentioned and referred to once as Banū Sulaym. In addition, two individual figures belonged to Sulaym: (a) Maʿn b. Yazīd b. al-Akhnas al-Sulamī, who is said to have gone, together with some members of his tribe, to Abū Bakr and who was sent forward to Yazīd b. Abī Sufyān in Syria, where he raided the Byzantines and fought in the Battle of al-Yarmūk and (b) Abū al-Aʿwar ʿAmr b. Sufyān al-Sulamī, who also went to Abū Bakr and was then dispatched to Abū ʿUbayda in Syria. There, he welcomed ʿUmar during his journey to Syria but was scolded by him for wearing Byzantine clothing. On Sulaym, see *EI*^{2}, s.v. Sulaym (M. Lecker); Lecker, *Banū Sulaym*.

149 See Lane, *Lexicon*, s.v. *jazāʾ*.

150 Ḥabīb's full name is Abū ʿAbd al-Raḥmān (or Abū Maslama) Ḥabīb b. Maslama al-Fihrī al-Qurashī (d. ca. 42/662). In al-Azdī's narrative, Ḥabīb is introduced when Abū Bakr dispatched him together with Maʿn b. Yazīd b. al-Akhnas al-Sulamī and his men to Syria where he reached Yazīd b. Abī Sufyān's unit. By order of Abū ʿUbayda, Ḥabīb collected (but later returned) the taxes of Ḥimṣ, then fought during the Battle of al-Yarmūk and was given command over Ḥimṣ by Abū ʿUbayda. After ʿUmar's deposition of him from the command over Ḥimṣ (and his nomination of ʿAbdallāh b. Qurṭ instead), Ḥabīb is presented as a strong supporter of Yazīd b. Abī Sufyān who gave him command over the vanguard during the conquest of Caesarea. After the narration of a conflict over command between Ḥabīb and his cousin al-Ḍaḥḥāk b. Qays, Ḥabīb commanded the cavalry during the conquest of Caesarea. On Ḥabīb, see *EI*^{2}, s.v. Ḥabīb b. Maslama (J. Fück).

He [=the narrator, Abū Saʿīd al-Maqburī] said: Then about 200 men from Banū Kaʿb[151], Aslam[152], Ghifār[153] and Muzayna[154] assembled, went to Abū Bakr (r.) and said: "Appoint a commander over us and send us to our brethren [in Syria]". So he [=Abū Bakr] appointed al-Ḍaḥḥāk b. Qays[155] who marched [out with them] until he reached Yazīd b. Abī Sufyān and set up camp with him.\\126

[Manuscript note: Part II]

This is the end of the first part [of the Book on the Conquests of Syria]. It is continued at the beginning of the second part by a letter from the people of the Syrian cities to the Emperor of the Byzantines, in which they inform him about the Arabs' descent upon them and ask him for reinforcements, as well as his letter [of response] to them concerning his opinion on what they wrote to him. Praise be to God alone and [may] His blessings be [bestowed] on our master Muḥammad, on his family and on all of his companions. Praise be to God, the Lord of the worlds.

151 Banū Kaʿb (or Kaʿb b. Rabīʿa) is a Northern Arabian tribe that was a subtribe of Muḍar. In al-Azdī's narrative, Banū Kaʿb is said to have gone, together with some other tribes, to Abū Bakr and to have asked him to appoint a commander over its members. He appointed al-Ḍaḥḥāk b. Qays who then marched with them to Syria. On Banū Kaʿb, see *EI*[2], s.v. Banū Kaʿb (A. Abu-Hakima).

152 Aslam is either a subtribe of Quḍāʿa or of Khuzāʿa. In al-Azdī's narrative, it is unclear which tribe is meant. Aslam is said to have gone, together with some other tribes, to Abū Bakr and to have asked him to appoint a commander over its members. He appointed al-Ḍaḥḥāk b. Qays, who then marched with them to Syria. On Aslam, see *EI*[2], s.v. Ḳuḍāʿa (M. Kister); s.v. Khuzāʿa (M. Kister).

153 Banū Ghifār is a Northern Arabian tribe that was a subtribe of Kināna. In al-Azdī's narrative, Banū Ghifār is mentioned as Ghifār and is said to have gone, together with some other tribes, to Abū Bakr and to have asked him to appoint a commander over its members. He appointed al-Ḍaḥḥāk b. Qays, who then marched with them to Syria. On Ghifār, see *EI*[2], s.v. Banū Ghifār (J. Fück).

154 Muzayna is a Northern Arabian tribe and a subtribe of Muḍar. In al-Azdī's narrative, Muzayna is said to have gone, together with some other tribes, to Abū Bakr and to have asked him to appoint a commander over its members. He appointed al-Ḍaḥḥāk b. Qays, who then marched with them to Syria. On Muzayna, see *EI*[2], s.v. Muzayna (F. Donner).

155 Al-Ḍaḥḥāk's full name is Abū Unays (or Abū ʿAbd al-Raḥmān) al-Ḍaḥḥāk b. Qays al-Fihrī (d. 64/486). In al-Azdī's narrative, al-Ḍaḥḥāk was appointed as a commander of Banū Kaʿb, Aslam, Ghifār and Muzayna by Abū Bakr, who sent him to Syria. There he met with Yazīd b. Abī Sufyān's unit. Al-Ḍaḥḥāk is then portrayed as a messenger of Abū ʿUbayda, who was ordered to tell the troops to obey Khālid b. al-Walīd. In another scene, he is depicted as entering, together with ʿAmr b. al-ʿĀṣ, Abū ʿUbayda's grave. In addition, al-Ḍaḥḥāk is presented in the course of a conflict with his cousin Ḥabīb b. Maslama over command, during which al-Ḍaḥḥāk did not follow Ḥabīb's orders. Yazīd called for al-Ḍaḥḥāk to come to him and then solved this conflict. Finally, al-Ḍaḥḥāk is mentioned as one of the commanders who fought during the conquest of Caesarea. On al-Ḍaḥḥāk, see *EI*[2], s.v. al-Ḍaḥḥāk b. Ḳays al-Fihrī (A. Dietrich).

In the name of God, the Merciful, the Compassionate.[156] Shaykh al-Ḥāfiẓ Abū Isḥāq Ibrāhīm b. Saʿīd b. ʿAbdallāh al-Ḥabbāl reported to us, saying: Abū al-ʿAbbās Munīr b. Aḥmad b. al-Ḥasan b. ʿAlī b. Munīr [al-Khashshāb] related to us, by way of reading to the former, while I was listening: Abū al-Ḥasan ʿAlī b. Aḥmad b. Isḥāq al-Baghdādī reported to us, by way of reading to the former: Abū al-ʿAbbās al-Walīd b. Ḥammād al-Ramlī related to us: Al-Ḥusayn b. Ziyād al-Ramlī reported to us, saying: Abū Ismāʿīl [Muḥammad b. ʿAbdallāh al-Azdī] al-Baṣrī related to us the letter from the people of the Syrian cities to the Emperor of the Byzantines, in which they inform him about the Arabs' descent upon them and ask him for reinforcements, as well as his letter [of response] to them concerning his opinion on what they wrote to him.

[The reaction of the people in Syria]

Abū al-ʿAbbās al-Walīd b. Ḥammād al-Ramlī related to us: Al-Ḥusayn b. Ziyād al-Ramlī related to us on the authority of Abū Ismāʿīl Muḥammad b. ʿAbdallāh al-Azdī al-Baṣrī, who said: Furthermore, ʿAbd al-Malik b. Nawfal [b. Masāḥiq al-Qurashī] related to me on the authority of his father [Nawfal] on the authority of Saʿīd b. Zayd b. ʿAmr b. Nufayl, who said: When the people of the Syrian cities saw that the Arabs advanced on them from all directions and their groups increased there [=in Syria], they dispatched their messengers to\\127 their Emperor, informing him about it and asking him for reinforcements.

He [=Heraclius] wrote to them [the following letter]:

You really made me wonder when you asked me for reinforcements and when you emphasised, [in your letters] to me, the large number of the Arabs who came to you. I know them and [I know] who came to you better [than you do]. Verily, the people of one city of yours are a hundredfold larger in number than those who came to you. So confront and fight them and do not think that I wrote this [letter] to you in order to avoid sending you reinforcements. I will certainly send you a huge number of soldiers that would congest the spacious earth.

Then the people of the Syrian cities corresponded with one another and sent for those Arabs who embraced their religion [=Christianity], calling them to fight the Muslims. They [largely] accepted their call to support them. However, some of them became furious and angry in favour of the Arabs. They preferred the Arabs' appearance to that of the Byzantines, since the latter were not firmly religious.\\128 Abū ʿUbayda b. al-Jarrāḥ learned about their exchange of messages and news and hence wrote [the following letter] to Abū Bakr (r.):

In the name of God, the Merciful, the Compassionate. Regarding the matter at hand: Praise be to God who strengthened us with Islam, honoured

156 This expression and the following chain of transmission (*riwāya*) mark the beginning of the second part of the book.

us with faith (*īmān*) and guided us of His own volition to [arrive at] the [right] decision on which other people differ. He is still guiding whomever He wants to the straight path. My spies (*ʿuyūn*) from among the common people of Syria[157] told me that the first reinforcements from the Emperor of the Byzantines had already reached them, that the people of the Syrian cities had sent their messengers to him, asking for reinforcements, and that he had written [the following message] to them: "The people of one city of yours are larger [in number] than the Arabs who came to you. So rise and fight them. My reinforcements will come to you from your rear". This is what we [=Abū ʿUbayda and the Muslims] learned about them and the Muslims are in good spirits to fight them. We were also informed that they [=the people of the Syrian cities] were preparing [themselves] to fight us. God has bestowed His victory upon the Believers and [cast] His repulsion upon the Polytheists. He certainly knows everything they do. Peace [be upon you].\\129

The story of Abū Bakr's (r.) plan to consult the Qurayshite people of Mecca who delayed embracing Islam [in response to] what Abū ʿUbayda b. al-Jarrāḥ had written; and [the story] about ʿUmar b. al-Khaṭṭāb's hatred of that [consultation]

When the letter [from Abū ʿUbayda] came to Abū Bakr (r.), the noble Emigrants and the Supporters, as well as the people of precedence (*ahl al-sābiqa*) from among them, flocked to Abū Bakr. Then he [also] invited the noble people of Mecca[158] [to the meeting], so ʿUmar said to him: "Why did you invite the people of Mecca, together with the Emigrants and the Supporters [to the meeting]?" Abū Bakr (r.) said to him: "To consult them about what Abū ʿUbayda wrote to us". Then ʿUmar (r.) said to him: "As for the Emigrants and the Supporters, they are people of consultation and advice. [But,] as for the male people of Mecca, whom we were fighting so that God's word would become the supreme [one], they were fighting us in order to extinguish God's light with their mouths and were striving to kill and humiliate us, [simply] because we said 'There are no deities other

157 We follow Fischer's interpretation in rendering the expression "*anbāṭ al-Shām*" (lit. "the Nabateans of Syria") as "common people, peasants". The term does not refer to the descendants of the Nabatean rulers. In al-Azdī's narrative, "*anbāṭ al-Shām*" are frequently said to have worked as spies and foot-messengers for the Muslim troops, bringing news about the Byzantines' activities and delivering letters between the commanders. Hence, they are likened to the Samaritans in other sources. On the Nabateans of Syria, see *EI²*, s.v. Nabaṭ (D. Graf/T. Fahd); on the Samaritans, see Pummer, *Foot-Soldiers*; on the translation, see Fischer, *Redakteurglossen*, 450–451.

158 Mecca (Makka) is located in the western part of the Arabian Peninsula in the region of al-Ḥijāz, ca. 70 km east of the Red Sea. It lies in a valley between two ranges of steep hills. In al-Azdī's narrative, it is mentioned that the Prophet Muḥammad was born in Mecca and that he appeared in public there. On Mecca, see *EI²*, s.v. Makka (W. Watt et al.).

than God' while they said 'There are deities other than God'. After God strengthened our call (*daʿwa*), authenticated our speech and made us victorious over them [=the male people of Mecca], you want [now] to give them precedence in [our] issues, consult them about them [=the issues], seek their advice and draw them closer [to us] than those who are better than they. What is the point then in giving advice to our righteous men who were fighting them for the cause of God while we give them [=the male people of Mecca] precedence over the [others] [=the righteous men]? Therefore, we are not of the opinion that they should be given such a [high] standing among us after their fight and strife against us. By God, do not ever do that at all". Abū Bakr (r.) said to him: "They excelled at Islam and I wanted to draw them close and hold them in the same honourable esteem in which they were held by their people.\\130 As for what you have just mentioned, I consider this to be [only] your opinion on this issue". He [=the narrator, Saʿīd b. Zayd b. ʿAmr b. Nufayl] said: These Qurayshite noblemen learned about this [=ʿUmar's opposition] and found it hard to accept. Then al-Ḥārith b. Hishām[159] said: "ʿUmar b. al-Khaṭṭāb (r.) had been absolutely right in his toughness against us before God guided us to Islam, but now, after God had guided us to Islam, we consider his toughness against us only as [creating] a rupture [in our relations]".

Then he [=al-Ḥārith b. Hishām], Suhayl b. ʿAmr[160] and ʿIkrima b. Abī Jahl[161] went out in the company of some noblemen from Quraysh[162] and

159 Al-Ḥārith's full name is al-Ḥārith b. Hishām b. al-Mughīra b. ʿAbdallāh b. ʿAmr al-Makhzūmī (n.d.). In al-Azdī's narrative, he is mentioned as one of the Qurayshite noblemen who went to Abū Bakr, seeking to be sent to Syria, who then blamed ʿUmar for his toughness towards him after embracing the new faith and who is said to have died in Cyprus in a battle between the Muslims and the Byzantines. On al-Ḥārith b. Hishām, see Ibn Saʿd, *Kitāb al-ṭabaqāt*, V, 329.

160 Suhayl's full name is Abū Yazīd Suhayl b. ʿAmr b. ʿĀmir b. Luʾayy al-ʿĀmirī (d. 18/639–640). In al-Azdī's narrative, he is mentioned as one of the noblemen of Quraysh who went to Abū Bakr, seeking to fight against the Byzantines in Syria and as blaming ʿUmar for being tough on him and his companions although they had embraced the new faith. He is said to have died in Cyprus in a battle between the Muslims and the Byzantines. On Suhayl b. ʿAmr, see Ibn Saʿd, *Kitāb al-ṭabaqāt*, V, 335.

161 ʿIkrima's full name is ʿIkrima b. Abī Jahl ʿAmr b. Hishām al-Makhzūmī (n.d.). In al-Azdī's narrative, he is depicted as being one of the noblemen of Quraysh who went to Abū Bakr, devoting himself to fighting against the Byzantines in Syria. He was one of those who died in Cyprus in a battle between the Muslims and the Byzantines. On ʿIkrima, see Ibn Saʿd, *Kitāb al-ṭabaqāt*, V, 329 and Ibn Ḥibbān, *Al-thiqāt*, III, 310.

162 Quraysh is a Northern Arabian tribe that took control over the sanctuary in Mecca where they settled. In al-Azdī's narrative, Banū Sahm and Banū Muḥārib b. Fihr are mentioned as subtribes of Quraysh. Members of Quraysh are associated with Mecca and are regularly referred to as noblemen who are contrasted with the Supporters and the Emigrants. ʿUmar argued explicitly against permitting these noblemen to participate in the raids on Syria, but Abū Bakr was in favour of it. Finally, the noblemen of Quraysh marched out of Medina under the command of ʿAmr b. al-ʿĀṣ. In addition, six individual figures belonged to Quraysh: (a) Suhayl b. ʿAmr and (b) ʿIkrima b. Abī Jahl are said to be

came to Abū Bakr (r.), who was accompanied by ʿUmar. Al-Ḥārith then said: "O ʿUmar, you had been absolutely right in your toughness against us before [we embraced] Islam, but now God has guided us to Islam and thus we consider your toughness against us only as [creating] a rupture [in our relations]". Then Suhayl b. ʿAmr fell on his knees and said: "O ʿUmar, it is you whom we address and whom we blame. As for the successor of the Messenger of God (ṣ.), we cleared him of [causing] rancour, spite and rupture". Then he [=Suhayl b. ʿAmr] said: "Are we not your brethren in Islam and descendants of your paternal lineage? If God has granted you, in this issue, a good footing which we have not been given\\131, [why] do you then sever [the ties of] kinship with us and belittle our rights?" ʿIkrima b. Abī Jahl also said: "If you had something to say about your hostility towards us before, today you would not be tougher on those who defected from this religion and opposed the Muslims than we".

ʿUmar (r.) then said to them: "I swear by God that I said what you have learned only as a piece of advice for those who embraced Islam before you [did] and as a means of meting out justice to you [all] and to those Muslims who are better than you". Suhayl b. ʿAmr said: "If you favour us with fighting for the cause of God, I swear by God that we will fight as much as we can. And I ask you [now] to bear witness that I totally devote myself to the cause of God". Al-Ḥārith b. Hishām said: "I also ask you to bear witness that I totally devote myself to the cause of God. I swear by God that I will certainly make every fight I engage in against the enemies of God twice as fierce as every fight I engaged in against the Messenger of God (ṣ.). And I will certainly spend, for the cause of God, twice as much as the money I spent on the war against the Messenger of God (ṣ.)". ʿIkrima b. Abī Jahl said: "I also ask you to bear witness that I totally devote myself to the cause of God". Abū Bakr (r.) then said: "O God, make them reach the best of what they hope and reward them with the best for what they do. You [three] absolutely did the right thing. God guided you [to the right decision]. God has rendered ʿUmar's blame good for them".

When they left Abū Bakr (r.), Suhayl [b. ʿAmr], who was intelligent and noble, drew near to his companions and said: "Do not worry about what you have seen. They were called [to embrace Islam] and we were also called [to do so]. They responded [promptly], but we delayed [our response]. If you

two of their noblemen; (c) Saʿīd b. ʿĀmir al-Qurashī is mentioned as a commander of one flank during the Battle of Ajnādayn; (d) Suwayd b. Kulthūm al-Qurashī is said to have encamped in Damascus (after its conquest) and to have returned the spoils to its inhabitants when the Muslims had to retreat; (e) Ḥabīb b. Maslama al-Qurashī is depicted as a commander of Ḥimṣ and, after his deposition by ʿUmar, as a supporter of Yazīd b. Abī Sufyān during the conquest of Caesarea; and (f) ʿAbd al-Malik b. Nawfal al-Qurashī is mentioned as a transmitter of several traditions. All the other members of Quraysh, e.g. Muḥammad, Abū Bakr, ʿUmar and Abū Sufyān, are not explicitly said to have belonged to this tribe. On Quraysh, see *EI*[2], s.v. Ḳuraysh (W. Watt).

knew of God's favours [that were bestowed] upon you by virtue of those who preceded you [in conversion] to Islam, life would be of no use to you. No deed done for God is better than fighting for His cause. Rush then to be between\\132 the Muslims and their enemy. Then fight the enemy [alone], without them [=the Muslims], until you die. By doing so, we may receive the reward [promised] to the fighters for the cause of God". So they marched out to fight the Byzantines. He [=the narrator, Saʿīd b. Zayd b. ʿAmr b. Nufayl] said: I was told that they [=al-Ḥārith b. Hishām, Suhayl b. ʿAmr and ʿIkrima b. Abī Jahl] died in Cyprus[163] [in a battle] between the Muslims and the Byzantines.

*Abū Bakr's (r.) appointment (*ʿaqd*) of ʿAmr b. al-ʿĀṣ (r.) as commander*[164]

Abū Bakr (r.) then summoned ʿAmr b. al-ʿĀṣ[165] (r.) and said to him: "O ʿAmr, those [=al-Ḥārith, Suhayl and ʿIkrima] are the noblemen of your [tribes]people (*qawm*) who are marching out as fighters for the cause of God. So march out and encamp [with them] until I dispatch [more] people with you [to Syria]". He [=ʿAmr b. al-ʿĀṣ] said: "O successor of the Messenger of God (ṣ.), am I not the leader of the people [=the Muslims]?" He [=Abū Bakr] said: "Yes, you are the leader of whomever I dispatch with you from here". He [=ʿAmr b. al-ʿĀṣ] said: "No, rather [I want to be] the leader of [all] the Muslims I reach". He [=Abū Bakr] said: "No[, definitely not]. Instead [you are just] one of our commanders there. When war brings you [all] together, your [chief] commander is Abū ʿUbayda b. al-Jarrāḥ". Then ʿAmr [b. al-ʿĀṣ]

163 Cyprus (Qubrus) is the largest island in the Eastern Mediterranean and lies ca. 71 km south of the southern coast of Anatolia and ca. 98 km west of the Syrian coast. In al-Azdī's narrative, Cyprus is mentioned once as the place where al-Ḥārith b. Hishām, Suhayl b. ʿAmr and ʿIkrima b. Abī Jahl died. The conquest of the island is not referred to. On Cyprus, see *EI*[2], s.v. Ḳubrus (A. de Groot).

164 The expression "*ʿaqada li-*" means "to appoint as commander by tying a flag to the person's spear". See Lane, *Lexicon*, s.v. *ʿaqada*.

165 ʿAmr's full name is Abū ʿAbdallāh ʿAmr b. al-ʿĀṣ al-Sahmī (d. 42/663). In al-Azdī's narrative, ʿAmr is portrayed as a major figure. He was dispatched to Syria by Abū Bakr but argued with both Abū Bakr and ʿUmar to be the commander in chief. Both of them, however, chose Abū ʿUbayda instead. Having been well received and held in high esteem later by Abū ʿUbayda in Syria, ʿAmr appeared in Palestine where Abū ʿUbayda ordered him to support the Muslim troops in the Battle of Ajnādayn. Left behind after the conquest of Fiḥl, ʿAmr is said to have raided the lands of the River Jordan and Palestine and to have backed up the Muslim troops' advance on Ḥimṣ. He then marched to Jerusalem to conquer it, but was ordered to meet the rest of the Muslim army in al-Yarmūk, where he took part in that battle as a commander of one section of the army. After the conquest of Jerusalem, which was executed by ʿUmar and during which ʿAmr's participation is not mentioned, Abū ʿUbayda appointed ʿAmr as a commander over Palestine. Al-Azdī's narrative ends with the information that ʿAmr entered Abū ʿUbayda's grave after the latter's death, that he ordered the people to flee from the plague in Syria and that he was appointed by Muʿādh b. Jabal as his successor. On ʿAmr, see *EI*[2], s.v. ʿAmr b. al-ʿĀṣ (A. Wensinck).

marched out and encamped [in Medina], accompanied by those noblemen from Quraysh [=al-Ḥārith b. Hishām, Suhayl b. ʿAmr and ʿIkrima b. Abī Jahl]. Then a large number of people flocked to him.

When his departure was due, he [=ʿAmr b. al-ʿĀṣ] came to ʿUmar (r.) and said to him: "O Abū Ḥafṣ, you were aware of my discernment in war and my temper in invasion (*ghazw*). You were [also] aware of the [high] standing I had in\\133 the Prophet's eyes and how he directed me to fight the Polytheists. So advise Abū Bakr to appoint me as the [chief] commander of the soldiers in Syria, because I hope that God (ʿa.) leads me to the conquest of these lands and that He will show you and the Muslims some parts of it which will gladden you". ʿUmar said to him: "I will not lie to you. I would never talk to him [=Abū Bakr] about that at all and I would not agree if he gave you command over Abū ʿUbayda, since we hold Abū ʿUbayda in much higher esteem than you". He [=ʿAmr b. al-ʿĀṣ] said: "Abū ʿUbayda would lose nothing of his grace if I became his commander". ʿUmar (r.) then said to him: "Woe unto you, ʿAmr, you really love to be in command. I swear by God that you seek only worldly honour by means of this leadership. O ʿAmr, fear God, do all your deeds only for God's sake and march out to this army unit. If you are not the [chief] commander this time, you will soon be, God willing". He [=ʿAmr b. al-ʿĀṣ] said: "Now I am satisfied". Then he went out and made preparations to march [to Syria].

When he [=ʿAmr b. al-ʿĀṣ] wanted to depart, Abū Bakr (r.) went out with him to bid him farewell and said: "O ʿAmr, you have a good opinion, experience in these causes and discernment in war. You are moving out with the noblemen of your [tribes]people and the virtuous of the Muslim men. You are going to your brethren whom you should spare neither advice nor good consultation. Perhaps one of your opinions will be laudable in war and of a blessed consequence". ʿAmr said to him: "I would rather live up to your opinion and accept your decision". Then he [=ʿAmr b. al-ʿĀṣ] bade him farewell and departed [from Medina]. He headed towards Syria and showed great competence and performance among the Muslims [in war].\\134

Abū Bakr's letter to Abū ʿUbayda (r.)

Abū Bakr (r.) wrote [the following letter] to Abū ʿUbayda:

In the name of God, the Merciful, the Compassionate. Regarding the matter at hand: I received your letter in which you mention the march of your enemies to fight you and their Emperor's letter about his readiness to reinforce them with [such] a large number of soldiers that would congest the spacious earth. I swear by the eternal God that the earth, despite its spaciousness, has already hemmed him and [hemmed] them in because of your presence in their area. I swear by God that I will never lose hope that you will soon remove him [=Heraclius] from his place, God willing. So disseminate your cavalry unit[s] into the villages and the arable lands (*sawād*), hamper them [=the Byzantines] with pieces of provisions and matériel (*māda*) but do not besiege the cities until you receive my order [to do so]. And when they oppose you, rush to [fight] them and seek God's support against them. For whenever they receive reinforcements, we will reinforce you with either an equal or a double number [of soldiers compared to theirs]. Thanks to God, you are neither [becoming] a minority nor [enduring] an ignominy. I have never seen you quailing before or fearing them. God (ʿa.) will certainly lead you to conquest, drive you to victory over your enemies and await your gratitude to see what you will do [in return]. As for ʿAmr [b. al-ʿĀṣ], I advise you to act well towards him and I advised him not to forfeit a right he sees or knows, for he has [sound] opinion and experience. [May God's] peace and mercy be upon you.

ʿAmr [b. al-ʿĀṣ] moved [away] with the people until he set up camp with Abū ʿUbayda.\\135

Al-Ḥusayn b. Ziyād [al-Ramlī] reported to us on the authority of Abū Ismāʿīl Muḥammad b. ʿAbdallāh [al-Azdī], who said: Furthermore, ʿAbd al-Malik b. Nawfal b. Masāḥiq [al-Qurashī] related to me on the authority of his father [=Nawfal b. Masāḥiq al-Qurashī[166]], who said: Ḍirār b. al-Khaṭṭāb[167], a brave and daring poet, went out with Abū ʿUbayda and said:

أبلغ أبا بكر إذا ما لقيته
بأن هرقلا عنكم غير نائم
فجيشك لا يخذل وأمرك لا يهن
ألا رب مُولّى نصره غير عاتم
Tell Abū Bakr when you meet him
That Heraclius is not shutting his eyes to what you are doing;
Your army will never be disappointed and your cause will never weaken;
O, perhaps a recruited commander [sweeps] to a resounding victory.

Al-Ḥusayn b. Ziyād [al-Ramlī] related to us on the authority of Abū Ismāʿīl Muḥammad b. ʿAbdallāh [al-Azdī], who said: Furthermore, al-Ṣaqʿab b. Zuhayr[168] related to me on the authority of ʿAmr b. Shuʿayb[169]: While ʿAmr b. al-ʿĀṣ was marching to Syria, to which he was dispatched, he was calling

166 Nawfal's full name is Abū Saʿd Nawfal b. Masāḥiq b. ʿAbdallāh al-Qurashī al-ʿĀmirī (n.d.). In al-Azdī's narrative, he is depicted as a transmitter of several traditions. On Nawfal, see Ibn Saʿd, *Kitāb al-ṭabaqāt*, V, 179–180.

167 Ḍirār's full name is Ḍirār b. al-Khaṭṭāb b. Mirdās b. Shaybān b. Muḥārib al-Qurashī (n.d.). In al-Azdī's narrative, he is depicted as a brave and daring poet who marched out with Abū ʿUbayda to Syria and recited a poem. On Ḍirār, see Ibn Saʿd, *Kitāb al-ṭabaqāt*, V, 336 and Ibn ʿAsākir, *TMD*, XXIIII, 392–400.

168 Al-Ṣaqʿab's full name is al-Ṣaqʿab b. Zuhayr b. Salīm al-Azdī al-Kūfī. He was a brother of al-ʿAlā b. Zuhayr and an uncle of Abū Mikhnaf. ʿUqla and Banī Yāsīn mention his death date as "d. before 140/757" (see al-Azdī, *Futūḥ al-Shām. Ed. ʿUqla/Banī Yāsīn*, 25). In al-Azdī's narrative, he is mentioned as a transmitter of three traditions. On al-Ṣaqʿab, see al-Mizzī, *Tahdhīb al-kamāl*, XIII, 219 (no. 2896).

169 ʿAmr's full name is Abū Ibrāhīm ʿAmr b. Shuʿayb b. Muḥammad b. ʿAbdallāh b. ʿAmr b. ʿĀṣ al-Qurashī al-Sahmī (d. 118/736). In al-Azdī's narrative, he is mentioned as a transmitter of one tradition. On ʿAmr, see Ibn Abī Ḥātim, *Al-jarḥ wa-al-taʿdīl*, VI, 238 (no. 1323) and Ibn ʿAsākir, *TMD*, XXXXVI, 75–80.

upon the nomadic passers-by to fight [with him] and many of them trooped with him. When he and those who accompanied him from Medina congregated with them [=the nomads], numbering about 2,000 men [in total], and reached Abū ʿUbayda, Abū ʿUbayda rejoiced and was on friendly terms with them. ʿAmr [b. al-ʿĀṣ] used to give good advice in war and to have discernment for [all] things.\\136 Abū ʿUbayda said to ʿAmr [b. al-ʿĀṣ]: "O Abū ʿAbdallāh, you have witnessed the day on which the Muslims were blessed with your advice and presence. In fact, I am just one of you and I will not, even if I am already your leader, make a firm decision without [consulting all of] you. So, inform me of your [=ʿAmr b. al-ʿĀṣ's] opinion every day, because I cannot do without you". He [=ʿAmr b. al-ʿĀṣ] said: "[Just] do so; may God lead you to what is good for the Muslims".

Al-Ḥusayn b. Ziyād [al-Ramlī] related to us on the authority of Abū Ismāʿīl Muḥammad b. ʿAbdallāh [al-Azdī], who said: Furthermore, Abū Jahḍam [al-Azdī][170] related to me on the authority of Abū Umāma al-Bāhilī[171], who said: I was among the soldiers of my [tribes]people whom Abū Bakr deployed with Abū ʿUbayda. So he [=Abū Bakr] recommended him [=Abū ʿUbayda] to me and recommended me to him [=Abū ʿUbayda].

[The battles of al-ʿAraba and al-Dāthina]

He [=the narrator, Abū Umāma al-Bāhilī] said: The first battle[s] were [fought] on the battle-day[s] (*yawm*) of al-ʿAraba and al-Dāthina, which were not among the great battle-days (*ayyām*). Six Byzantine commanders marched out to us. There were 500 men with each commander, so they were 3,000 men [in total]. They advanced until they reached al-ʿAraba. Then Yazīd b. Abī Sufyān sent a messenger to inform Abū ʿUbayda about that. He [=Abū ʿUbayda] then sent me, in command of 500 men, to him [=Yazīd b. Abī Sufyān]. When I went to him, he [=Yazīd] dispatched a man in command of 500 men to [join] me. Yazīd b. Abī Sufyān advanced in our tracks in a line. When we saw the Byzantines, we assaulted and defeated them, killing one of their commanders. Then they retreated and we pursued them.

170 Abū Jahḍam al-Azdī is mentioned only in al-Ṭabarī's *Taʾrīkh*. We could not find a *tarjama* about him. On the basis of a manuscript of al-Dhahabī's *Tadhhīb al-tahdhīb al-kamāl*, Lees identifies him as Mūsā b. Sālim, mawlā Ibn al-ʿAbbās, but mentions no date of death (see al-Azdī, *Futūḥ al-Shām. Ed. Lees*, 44, n. 2). ʿUqla and Banī Yāsīn identify him on the basis of al-Ṭabarī's *Taʾrīkh* as one of the informants of Abū Mikhnaf, who was alive in 83/702 (see al-Azdī, *Futūḥ al-Shām. Ed. ʿUqla/Banī Yāsīn*, 22–23; 136, n. 7). In al-Azdī's narrative, he is mentioned as a transmitter of thirteen traditions. On Abū Jahḍam, see al-Ṭabarī, *Taʾrīkh*, II, 1099, l. 14; 1100, l. 17.

171 Abū Umāma's full name is Abū Umāma al-Ṣudayy b. ʿAjlān b. Wahb al-Bāhilī (d. 86/705). According to van Ess, he was one of the last Companions of the Prophet (see van Ess, *Fehltritt*, 324). In al-Azdī's narrative, he is mentioned as one of the flag holders in the Muslim troops at Ḥimṣ. In addition, he functions as a transmitter of two traditions. On Abū Umāma, see Ibn Saʿd, *Kitāb al-ṭabaqāt*, VII-2, 131–132 and Ibn Ḥibbān, *Mashāhīr ʿulamāʾ al-amṣār*, 50 (no. 327).

They mustered [more fighters] against us at al-Dāthina. So we marched to them. Then\\137 Yazīd sent me and my companion[s] ahead of the number [of the remaining fighters] and we defeated them. Thereupon, they fled, re-grouped and received reinforcements from their Emperor.

Al-Ḥusayn b. Ziyād [al-Ramlī] reported to us on the authority of Abū Ismāʿīl [Muḥammad b. ʿAbdallāh al-Azdī], who said: Furthermore, Muḥammad b. Yūsuf related to me on the authority of Thābit [al-Bunānī] on the authority of Sahl b. Saʿd [al-Anṣārī], who said: Abū Bakr (r.) did not stop dispatching commanders and tribes to Syria, one after the other, until he thought that they [=the Muslims in Syria] received such sufficient [reinforcements] that they no longer cared for more.

[Section III: Khālid b. al-Walīd's activities in Iraq]

Al-Ḥusayn b. Ziyād [al-Ramlī] reported to us on the authority of Abū Ismāʿīl Muḥammad b. ʿAbdallāh [al-Azdī], who said: Furthermore, ʿAbdallāh[172] related to me on the authority of his father: Abū Bakr (r.) was prompted to send Khālid b. al-Walīd[173] to Iraq because al-Muthannā b.

172 ʿAbdallāh is difficult to identify because only his first name is mentioned by al-Azdī and his full name is not given. On the basis of al-Ṭabarī's *Taʾrīkh*, Mourad identifies him as ʿAbdallāh b. ʿAbd al-Raḥmān b. Abī ʿUmra al-Anṣārī al-Māzinī, one of the informants of Abū Mikhnaf. ʿUqla and Banī Yāsīn, however, identify him as ʿAbdallāh al-Azdī al-Baṣrī, "the father of the author", without providing any *tarjama* or proof for this thesis (see al-Azdī, *Futūḥ al-Shām. Ed. ʿUqla/Banī Yāsīn*, 31). In addition, on the basis of al-Iṣfahānī's *Maqātil*, they suppose that he is ʿAbdallāh b. Muḥammad al-Azdī, one of Abū Mikhnaf's informants (see ibid., 137, n. 7). In al-Azdī's narrative, he is mentioned as a transmitter of one tradition. On ʿAbdallāh b. ʿAbd al-Raḥmān b. Abī ʿUmra, see al-Ṭabarī, *Taʾrīkh*, I, 3101, l. 10–11; on ʿAbdallāh b. Muḥammad al-Azdī, see al-Iṣfahānī, *Maqātil*, 34, l. 15.

173 Khālid's full name is Abū Sulaymān Khālid b. al-Walīd b. al-Mughīra al-Makhzūmī (d. 21/642). In al-Azdī's narrative, Khālid figures prominently and is described several times in a very personal and positive manner. His good behaviour in war is usually mentioned. The narrative starts with stating that Khālid was in al-Yamāma where he had fought (and killed) Musaylima al-Kadhdhāb by Abū Bakr's order. On ʿUmar's advice, Abū Bakr then ordered Khālid to march to Iraq to support the Muslim fighters who were led by al-Muthannā b. al-Ḥāritha. Thus, Abū Bakr appointed Khālid as commander of the Muslim army there with the help of which he successfully fought several battles in Iraq (e.g. near al-Ubulla and al-Ḥīra) and conquered several places (e.g. Kaskar and Zandaward). Then Abū Bakr sent Khālid and his unit to Syria as reinforcements, confirming him as the chief commander. Then there are several traditions in the narrative about Khālid's famous desert march, in the course of which he conquered ʿAyn al-Tamr and Tadmur and which brought him to Bosra and finally to al-Ghūṭa near Damascus. In Syria, Khālid ordered all the Muslim units to meet in Ajnādayn, commanded the siege of Damascus from the Eastern Gate and conquered it by force. After having been deposed by the new ruler, ʿUmar, Khālid is portrayed as a good advisor to the new chief commander Abū ʿUbayda and as an important commander of the cavalry and staunch fighter in various military encounters. Hence, he raided the region of Baalbek, fought during the sieges of Fiḥl and Ḥimṣ and defeated the Byzantines during the Battle of al-Yarmūk, after which he pursued their fleeing units up north to Ḥimṣ and Qinnasrīn. Before fighting started, Khālid is described as having had a religious debate with the

Ḥāritha[174] was raiding the people of Persia[175] in the arable lands [of Iraq]. Abū Bakr (r.) and the Muslims learned of his [=al-Muthannā's] news and what he did to the Persians. So ʿUmar said: "Who is that one whose [heroic] deeds reach us [even] before we know [anything] about his lineage?" Qays b. ʿĀṣim[176] said to him: "As for him who is surely neither obscure nor\\138 of anonymous lineage, neither accompanied by a small number nor of weak constitution, i.e. not feeble, that [one] is al-Muthannā b. Ḥāritha al-Shaybānī".

The arrival of al-Muthannā b. Ḥāritha [al-Shaybānī] to Abū Bakr (r.)

Then al-Muthannā b. Ḥāritha came to Abū Bakr (r.) and said to him: "Dispatch me in command of my [tribes]people, who are Muslims, in order to fight with them against the people of Persia. And [I pledge that] the people of my region will suffice you". Abū Bakr (r.) did that. So al-Muthannā b. Ḥāritha led them [=his tribespeople] to Iraq and fought [together with them there]. He raided the people of Persia and the rural areas of the arable lands [of Iraq], fighting for a year or so.

Then he [=al-Muthannā b. Ḥāritha] sent his brother Masʿūd b. Ḥāritha[177] to Abū Bakr (r.). He came to him and said: "O successor of the Messenger

---

Byzantine commander Bāhān, who became quite fond of him. Al-Azdī's narrative ends with mentioning Khālid's participation in the siege of and fights in Jerusalem. Khālid's death is not mentioned therein; his epithet "Sword of God" (*sayf Allāh*) however is. On Khālid, see *EI²*, s.v. Khālid b. al-Walīd (P. Crone).

174 Al-Muthannā's full name is al-Muthannā b. Ḥāritha b. Salama al-Shaybānī (d. 14/635–636). In al-Azdī's narrative, his tribal affiliation (*nisba*), al-Shaybānī, is given and he is depicted as commanding a troop of his tribesmen in Iraq whom he rallied to Abū Bakr, seeking to fight in the arable lands of Iraq and in Persia. When Khālid b. al-Walīd reached Iraq, al-Muthannā fought together with him and freed Abjar b. Bajīr from Khālid's detention. Furthermore, al-Muthannā did not want Khālid to leave for Syria. On al-Muthannā, see *EI²*, s.v. al-Muthannā b. Ḥāritha (F. Donner).

175 Persia (Fāris) is a region in southern Iran which is bordered in the north by the region of al-Jibāl, in the east by the region of Kirmān, in the south and south-west by the Persian Gulf and in the north-west by the region of Khūzestān. In al-Azdī's narrative, Persia is used as *pars pro toto* to refer to the western provinces of the Sasanian Empire, which are called "land of Persia". It is particularly mentioned that Iraq, al-Ullays and its district and the cities of al-Madāʾin and ʿAyn al-Tamr were under Persian [=Sasanian] control. Besides the "people of Persia", some of the Sasanid commanders are named, e.g. Jābān and Farrukh-Shadād b. Hurmuz. Finally, the military conflict between the Byzantine and the Sasanian Empires and several raids and battles that took place between Khālid b. al-Walīd and al-Muthannā b. Ḥāritha and the Persian troops in this region are mentioned. On Persia, see *EI²*, s.v. Fārs (L. Lockhart).

176 Qays's full name is Abū ʿAlī Qays b. ʿĀṣim b. Sinān b. Khālid al-Minqarī (n.d.). In al-Azdī's narrative, he is depicted as informing ʿUmar about the lineage of al-Muthannā b. Ḥāritha al-Shaybānī. On Qays, see Ibn Saʿd, *Kitāb al-ṭabaqāt*, VII-1, 23–24.

177 Masʿūd b. Ḥāritha is listed neither in Ibn Saʿd, al-Bukhārī, Ibn ʿAsākir nor in any other biographical work we could access. In al-Azdī's narrative, he is mentioned as a messenger delivering letters between his brother al-Muthannā b. Ḥāritha and Abū Bakr.

of God (ṣ.), I am the messenger of my brother al-Muthannā b. Ḥāritha [sent] to you, for he is requesting that you reinforce him [with more fighters]. He has [so far] not received any reinforcements from you. If reinforcements had come to him and the Arabs had heard of that, they would have rushed to him[, too,] and God would have humiliated the Polytheists. However, I inform you, [Abū Bakr] al-Ṣiddīq, that the Persians became weary and fearful of us and that we received many letters from them in which they solicited peace from us". ʿUmar b.\\139 al-Khaṭṭāb (r.) said: "O successor of the Messenger of God (ṣ.), send Khālid b. al-Walīd to Iraq to trample, together with this man and his companions—i.e. al-Muthannā b. Ḥāritha and his companions—on them [=the Persians] but [at the same time] to stay near to [our] people in Syria. If [our] people in Syria did not need him, he should lay [persistent] pressure on the people of Iraq until God leads him to conquest. [But] if they needed him, he would be near them [and thus could march to them]". He [=Abū Bakr] said: "Well-done, well-spoken and well-decided".

Abū Bakr (r.) wrote to Khālid b. al-Walīd who was in al-Yamāma[178] and whom he had sent to [fight] Musaylima [al-Ḥanafī] al-Kadhdhāb[179]. God had led him [=Khālid b. al-Walīd] to conquest and he had killed him [=Musaylima]. So he [=Abū Bakr] wrote [the following letter to Khālid]:

In the name of God, the Merciful, the Compassionate. From the servant of God Abū Bakr, the successor of the Messenger of God (ṣ.), to Khālid b. al-Walīd as well as to the Emigrants, the Supporters and the benevolent Followers (*tābiʿūn*) who are [there] with him. Peace be upon you. I praise, on your behalf, God with whom no other deity is associated. Regarding the matter at hand: Praise be to God who fulfilled His promise, supported His religion, strengthened His proponents, humiliated His opponents and defeated the Confederates (*aḥzāb*) alone. It is God with whom no other deity is associated [and who said]: "God has made a promise to those among you who believe and do good deeds: He will make them successors to the land, as He did with those who came before them; He will empower the religion He has chosen for them; He will grant them security to replace their fear. 'They will worship Me and not join anything with Me'. Those who are defiant after that will be the rebels",[180] a promise which is unbreakable and a statement which is not doubtable. He [=God] also imposed fighting for His cause on the Believers. Hence, the Supreme Speaker [=God] said: "Fighting

178 Al-Yamāma is part of the region of Najd in the centre of the Arabian Peninsula with its major town Ḥajr. In al-Azdī's narrative, it is mentioned in the context of Khālid's fight against (and defeat of) Musaylima al-Kadhdhāb. On al-Yamāma, see EI^2, s.v. al-Yamāma (G. Smith).

179 Musaylima's full name is Abū Thumāma Musaylima b. Ḥabīb al-Ḥanafī (d. *ca.* 10/632). In Islamic historiographical works, Musaylima is given the epithet "al-Kadhdhāb" (lit. "the persistent Liar", understood as "the false prophet"). In al-Azdī's narrative, Musaylima is depicted as being fought, defeated and killed in al-Yamāma by Khālid at Abū Bakr's order. On Musaylima, see EI^2, s.v. Musaylima (W. Watt); al-Ridda (M. Lecker).

180 Q. 24:55 (*The Qurʾān. Tr. Abdel Haleem*, 224–225).

is ordained for you, though you dislike it. You may dislike something although it is good for you, or like\\140 something although it is bad for you: God knows and you do not".[181] So seek God's fulfilment of His promise to you and follow what He imposed on you, even if [in doing so] the pain would increase, calamity would worsen, distance [from home] would lengthen and you would be extremely afflicted by loss of possessions and lives (*anfus*). All of these [hardships] weigh little against God's great reward.[182] The veracious and trustworthy [Prophet] (ṣ.) told us that God (ʿa.) would resurrect the martyrs on the Day of Resurrection (*yawm al-qiyāma*) while they would be drawing their swords, receiving from God all that they would wish until all their wishes and all that which has never [even] crossed their minds (*qulūb*) would be fulfilled. What else would the martyr wish, after his entry to Paradise, except to be sent back by God (t.) to the worldly life and to be cut into pieces with scissors for the cause of God (ʿa.) in return for God's great reward? Troop [together], may God have mercy upon you, for the cause of God, whether you are lightly or heavily armed, and fight for the cause of God with your possessions and lives. It would be better for you all if you knew [that]. I ordered Khālid b. al-Walīd to march to Iraq and not to leave it until he receives [another] order from me. March with him and do not tarry behind him, because it represents a cause for which God will magnify the reward to whoever has good intention[s] for it [=the cause] and an overwhelming drive for good [deeds]. When you reach Iraq, remain there until you receive [another] order from me. May God protect us and [protect] you from the distresses of this world and of the Hereafter; may God's peace and mercy be upon you.\\141

Abū Bakr (r.) sent this letter with Abū Saʿīd al-Khudrī[183] [to Khālid] and said to him [=Abū Saʿīd]: "Do not leave him [=Khālid] until he departs from there [=Iraq] and tell him in private: 'Go to Iraq where the Muslim men are fighting against the Persians (*aʿājim*) in the tribal area (*ḥayy*) of Rabīʿa. They [=the Persians] are valiant and large in number. When you reach them, attack your polytheistic enemy together with those who accompany you. My reinforcements will reach you soon, God willing. If I send you away from

181 Q. 2:216 (*The Qurʾān. Tr. Abdel Haleem*, 24).

182 In the Arabic text, this compound sentence is syntactically ambiguous, being assigned two readings. One is already translated above and the other is as follows: So seek God's fulfilment of His promise to you and follow what He imposed on you. If it is too painful, too calamitous and too distant for you to do so, and [if] you are afflicted, in doing so, by loss of possessions and souls, [all] that will weigh little against God's great reward.

183 Abū Saʿīd al-Khudrī is listed neither in Ibn Saʿd, al-Bukhārī, Ibn ʿAsākir nor in any other biographical work we could access. In al-Azdī's narrative, he is mentioned as a messenger from Abū Bakr to Khālid, telling the latter to go to Iraq to reinforce the Muslims in their fight against the Persians there. In addition, he is mentioned as a transmitter of one tradition.

there [=Iraq], you will be the commander wherever you are [sent to]. You will have no commander other than me'".

When Khālid b. al-Walīd read this letter, he said: "This is the opinion of Ibn Ḥintima [='Umar b. al-Khaṭṭāb]. Considering that I am closely related to this tribe [=Rabī'a] and that I was their commander, he thinks that I like this position [of command] among them and thus he advised Abū Bakr to send me away from my place [=al-Yamāma]. ['Umar] b. al-Khaṭṭāb certainly convinced [him] of someone other than me—i.e. he endeared someone else to him". [However,] when Abū Sa'īd [al-Khudrī] said to him [=Khālid b. al-Walīd] [what Abū Bakr had told him], Khālid became satisfied and rose [and stood] before the people. Then he praised and thanked God ('a.), blessed and saluted the Prophet (ṣ.) and said: "Praise be to God, who is praiseworthy. I bear witness that Muḥammad is His servant and Messenger. Regarding the matter at hand: The successor of the Messenger of God (ṣ.) wrote to us in order to motivate us to be obedient to our Lord and to fight our and God's enemy. By virtue of fighting for His cause, God has accomplished our [initial] call and unified our word and our wish. Praise be to God, the Lord of the worlds. Verily, I am going out, encamping, marching [out]—God (t.) willing—and rushing [to fight]. Whoever wants the earlier or later reward must hurry out[, too]".\\142 He then descended [from the speech platform], encamped [for some days] and his companions hurried out. He left al-Yamāma on that day and proceeded until he arrived in [the land of][184] Basra[185].

[Khālid b. al-Walīd's battles in Iraq]

A man called Suwayd b. Quṭba[186] from Bakr b. Wā'il[187], to whom a few people from Bakr b. Wā'il flocked, was there, because he wanted to do in

184 The mention of "al-Baṣra" here seems to be a case of anachronism which the editors themselves stumble and comment on (see al-Azdī, *Futūḥ al-Shām. Ed. 'Uqla/Banī Yāsīn*, 142, n. 1), denoting that what is meant is not the city itself but the "land or region of Basra" in which the city of the same name was founded later during 'Umar's rule. "The land of Basra" is used some lines below in the same context.

185 Basra (al-Baṣra) is located on the western bank of lower Tigris in the estuary of the Euphrates and Tigris (Shaṭṭ al-'Arab). In al-Azdī's narrative, it is only mentioned as referring to the "land of Basra". On Basra, see EI^2, s.v. al-Baṣra (C. Pellat et al.).

186 Suwayd b. Quṭba al-Wā'ilī (n.d.), on whom nothing but his name is known, is depicted in al-Azdī's narrative as commanding a small troop from Bakr b. Wā'il, because he wanted to raid the land of Basra. He then joined Khālid in fighting the people of al-Ubulla. On Suwayd, see Ibn Ḥajar, *Al-iṣāba. Ed. al-Baghawī*, III, 270 (no. 3724).

187 Bakr (or Bakr b. Wā'il) is a Northern Arabian tribe that was part of the great tribal federation of Rabī'a (and is thus closely related to Muḍar). In al-Azdī's narrative, Bakr is mentioned as Banū Bakr b. Wā'il and as Bakr b. Wā'il. In addition, 'Ijl is said to be a subtribe of Bakr b. Wā'il and a watering place called al-Nibāj is ascribed to Bakr. In addition, three individual figures belonged to Bakr: (a) Suwayd b. Quṭba, a commander of a military unit, who supported the Muslims' fight in Iraq and who was joined by Khālid in the Battle of al-Ubulla; (b) an unnamed commander from Bakr who led a part of the cavalry during a battle with the Byzantines at Bosra; and (c) an unnamed person

the land of Basra what al-Muthannā b. Ḥāritha was doing in the land of al-Kūfa[188]. However, he could not do that, because al-Muthannā [b. Ḥāritha] had a larger number [of soldiers] and was tougher on his enemy than he [=Suwayd b. Quṭba]. Meanwhile, he [=Suwayd b. Quṭba] was [there] with a group of people, raiding and encamping. Khālid b. al-Walīd passed by him, strengthened both his cause and his decision and ordered him to stay and rally [fighters] against the Polytheists. Suwayd b. Quṭba said to him: "The people of al-Ubulla[189] rallied [fighters] against me. Hence, I presume that nothing has stopped them from coming out to [confront] me except for your presence". Then Khālid said: "Therefore, I am leaving you until they think that I have gone away and left you. Then I will return [secretly] to you to stay overnight in your encampment".

He [=Khālid b. al-Walīd] left them and departed from the land of Basra, heading towards the land of al-Kūfa. The people of al-Ubulla learned of it and thought that Khālid had left them [=Suwayd b. Quṭba and his companions]. Learning that Khālid had marched away from Suwayd [b. Quṭba] in the evening, they all [=the people of al-Ubulla] agreed to advance on Suwayd b. Quṭba. They reached them [=Suwayd b. Quṭba and his companions] in the early morning. When darkness had fallen over Khālid, he [secretly] turned back in the middle of the night\\143 and stayed in Suwayd b. Quṭba's encampment.

The people of al-Ubulla came to Suwayd [b. Quṭba] in the morning. Khālid had beforehand mobilised [his soldiers] against them during the night. So Suwayd b. Quṭba mobilised his companions and Bashīr b. Saʿd[190] mobilised a cavalry unit (*katība*)[191]. Meanwhile, he [=Khālid] mobilised another [cav-

who is mentioned as a transmitter of one tradition. On Bakr, see *EI²*, s.v. Bakr b. Wāʾil (W. Caskel); Donner, *Bakr b. Wāʾil*.

188 "The land of al-Kūfa" refers to a region to which the later-founded city of al-Kūfa belonged. Al-Kūfa is placed on the western bank of the middle Euphrates close to the ancient city of al-Ḥīra. In al-Azdī's narrative, several tribes are said to have settled in al-Kūfa, e.g. Sulaym, Thaqīf, Hamdān, Asad, al-Nakhaʿ, Kinda and Azd. On al-Kūfa, see *EI²*, s.v. al-Kūfa (H. Djait).

189 Al-Ubulla is situated on the western bank of the Tigris north of the Nahr al-Ubulla canal and functioned as a seaport in the Tigris estuary. In al-Azdī's narrative, a battle between the people of al-Ubulla and the Muslims (under the command of Suwayd b. Quṭba and Khālid b. al-Walīd) is mentioned, but not the conquest of the city itself. On al-Ubulla, see *EI²*, s.v. al-Ubulla (J. H. Kramers).

190 Bashīr's full name is Abū al-Nuʿmān (or Abū Masʿūd) Bashīr b. Saʿd b. Thaʿlaba al-Anṣārī (n.d.). In al-Azdī's narrative, he is once mentioned by the name of kinship (*nisba*) al-Anṣārī and is depicted as commanding a cavalry unit during the Battle of al-Ubulla and as having been sent by Khālid to fight the people of Bānqiyā, where he was wounded. Later, he joined Khālid in the Battle of ʿAyn al-Tamr, where he was so severely wounded that he died there. On Bashīr, see Ibn Saʿd, *Kitāb al-ṭabaqāt*, III-2, 83–84 and Ibn ʿAsākir, *TMD*, X, 283–290.

191 The Arabic expression "*katība*" is rendered as "cavalry unit" throughout the text. On this meaning, see Lane, *Lexicon*, s.v. *katība*.

alry unit] and positioned Saʿd or Saʿīd[192] b. [ʿAmr b.] Ḥarām [al-Anṣārī][193] in [command of] those [who were] in the encampment and said [to him]: "If we need you, reinforce us. Otherwise, remain [stationed] at our rear so that they [=the people of al-Ubulla] do not attack [us] from behind". Then he appointed ʿUmayr b. Saʿd al-Anṣārī[194] as the commander of the infantry.

The people of al-Ubulla came to them in the early morning. When they drew near to them, they saw [a lot of] equipment, a [large] number, [great] mobilisation and a huge group, the likes of which they had never seen before; [it was] unlike anything they had seen or known before. When they drew near to the Muslims, they got terrified by them and held back. Thereupon, Khālid said: "O Muslims, attack them, because I see the infidels [getting] terrified by you and I see from their visage that God has struck terror into their hearts". Khālid then attacked them and so did the Muslims. Then they [=the people of al-Ubulla] were seriously defeated and a great many of them were horrifically killed. God also overwhelmed a lot of them. Then Khālid said to Suwayd b. Quṭba: "I swear by God that we fought them in the battle in such a fierce [way] that they will keep dreading you as long as you remain in their lands".

Then Khālid b. al-Walīd departed from [the land of] Basra to al-Nibāj[195], a watering place belonging to Bakr b. Wāʾil. There he [=Khālid] encountered Abū Ḥajjār Abjar b. Bajīr[196], who came to him and said: "You arrived in the

192 This person is mentioned below under the name "Saʿīd". Hence, the name "Saʿd" must have been added, because the correct form seemed to have been unclear at one point during transmission. Ibn Ḥajar refers to him as Saʿd (see Ibn Ḥajar, *Al-iṣāba. Ed. al-Baghawī*, III, 70 [no. 3186]).

193 Saʿīd (or Saʿd) b. ʿAmr b. Ḥarām al-Anṣārī is a companion of the Prophet Muḥammad. In al-Azdī's narrative, he is mentioned as being stationed by Khālid as backup behind the Muslim troops to guard against any attack by the people of al-Ubulla and as a successor whom Khālid left behind in charge of Ṣandawdāʾ. On Saʿd, see Ibn Ḥajar, *Al-iṣāba. Ed. al-Baghawī*, III, 70 (no. 3186).

194 ʿUmayr's full name is ʿUmayr b. Saʿd b. ʿUbayd al-Anṣārī (n.d.). In al-Azdī's narrative, ʿUmayr is mentioned as being appointed by Khālid in command of the infantry in the fight against the people of al-Ubulla, as having been ordered to supervise the weak after the Battle of ʿAyn al-Tamr and as having fought during the conquest of Caesarea. On ʿUmayr, see Ibn Ḥajar, *Al-iṣāba. Ed. al-Baghawī*, IV, 718–719 (no. 6040).

195 Al-Nibāj is a place (i.e. a village or an oasis) south of Basra (and north of al-Yamāma) belonging to Bakr b. Wāʾil, according to Yāqūt. However, Yāqūt identifies several places called al-Nibāj that are located south of Basra. Hence, the exact identification of the place remains unclear. In al-Azdī's narrative, al-Nibāj is described as a watering place belonging to Bakr b. Wāʾil in the vicinity of the land of Basra, for which Khālid headed and where he had a dialogue on religious issues with a Christian, called Abjar b. Bajīr. In the course of this dialogue, Khālid imprisoned Abjar, who was finally released due to the intervention of his relative al-Muthannā b. Ḥāritha. On al-Nibāj, see Yāqūt, *Muʿjam al-buldān*, IV, 735–736.

196 Abū Ḥajjār Abjar b. Bajīr is listed neither in Ibn Saʿd, al-Bukhārī, Ibn ʿAsākir nor in any other biographical work we could access. In al-Azdī's narrative, he is mentioned as a Christian Arab who met Khālid at al-Nibāj and was put by him under the threat of decapitation if he did not embrace the new faith, but who was finally released thanks to al-Muthannā b. Ḥāritha's intercession. In addition, Abjar b. Bajīr recited a poem.

best [possible manner]. May God multiply the spoils for you\\144 and make you triumphant over the Persians (*al-aʿjam*)". Khālid said to him: "How brave you are [to speak to me like this]!" He [=Abjar b. Bajīr] said: "I swear by God that I speak my mind whenever I want". He [=Khālid] said: "What is your religion?" He [=Abjar b. Bajīr] said: "I embrace the religion of Jesus". He [=Khālid] continued: "Who is Jesus?" He [=Abjar b. Bajīr] said: "The son of Mary". He [=Khālid] said: "You mean ʿĪsā b. Maryam [=Jesus]?" He [=Abjar b. Bajīr] said: "Yes". He [=Khālid] said: "Then you embrace the religion of our Prophet". Then Khālid said to him: "Do you [also] believe in Muḥammad's (ṣ.) prophethood?" He [=Abjar b. Bajīr] said: "Rather, [I believe] in Jesus's prophethood". He [=Khālid] said: "Will you believe in Muḥammad's (ṣ.) prophethood, or not?" He [=the narrator] said: Then he [=Abjar b. Bajīr] fell silent. He [=Khālid] said: "Decapitate him". He [=Abjar b. Bajīr] said: "Will you kill me if I do not follow your religion?" He [=Khālid] said: "Yes, you are an Arab, are you not?" He [=Abjar b. Bajīr] said: "Yes[, I am]". He [=Khālid] said: "We kill every Arab who does not embrace our religion". He [=Abjar b. Bajīr] said: "When did you come up with this religion? Did you not come up with it a few years ago?" He [=Khālid] said: "Yes, and so was the religion of Jesus, the son of Mary (ʿs.), which he came up with first for a day, then for two, then for ten, then for twenty, then for a year, then for two years, until it existed for ages. This will also be [the case with] our religion. Either I witness that you embrace Islam now or I behead you". Then he [=Abjar b. Bajīr] remained[197] [as a detainee] with them [=the Muslims] at the watering place.

When al-Muthannā b. Ḥāritha sent his brother Masʿūd [b. Ḥāritha] to Abū Bakr (r.) to request reinforcements, Abū Bakr (r.) wrote [the following letter] and [sent it] with him [=Masʿūd b. Ḥāritha] to al-Muthannā [b. Ḥāritha]:

Regarding the matter at hand: I sent Khālid b. al-Walīd to you to the land of Iraq. Welcome him in the presence of your people, help him, support him, back him up, do not disobey his command and do not oppose his decision[s], because he is one of those whom God (t.) described in His scripture, saying: "Muḥammad is the Messenger of God.\\145 Those who follow him are harsh towards the disbelievers and compassionate towards each other. You see them kneeling and prostrating".[198] If he [=Khālid] stays with you, he will be the commander. If he leaves you, then revert to your former position. Peace be upon you.

When he [=al-Muthannā b. Ḥāritha] received this letter, he rushed immediately, overlooking everything around him, to meet Khālid in al-Nibāj. He found Abjar b. Bajīr imprisoned there. He went to him [=Khālid] and greeted him. Khālid said to him [=al-Muthannā b. Ḥāritha]: "Welcome, horseman of the Arabs and friend (*khalīl*) of each Muslim here in my place". Al-Muthannā [b. Ḥāritha] said: "I swear by God that each of [your]

197 On this meaning, see Lane, *Lexicon*, s.v. *jalasa*.
198 Q. 48:29 (*The Qurʾān. Tr. Abdel Haleem*, 336).

companions greeted me and gave me my due (*ḥaqqī*)". When al-Muthannā [b. Ḥāritha] wanted to leave for his saddlebags, he said to Khālid: "Set my cousin, Abjar b. Bajīr, free". He [=Khālid] then said: "He is an Arab man and we do not let the Arabs embrace a religion other than ours". He [=al-Muthannā b. Ḥāritha] said: "When you are finished with [dealing with] all the Arab Christians and no one is left except him, then I will serve as the guarantor (*zaʿīm*) of his [conversion to Islam] for you". So Khālid sent for him [=Abjar b. Bajīr], delivered him to him [=al-Muthannā b. Ḥāritha] and said to him [=Abjar b. Bajīr]: "I swear by God that, but for the intercession of your cousin, [i.e.] this virtuous man whose religion is better than yours, you would not have escaped my hand until either I had killed you or you had embraced Islam". He [=Abjar b. Bajīr] said: "I swear by God that if I had known that his religion is better than mine, I would have followed his". Then he [=Abjar b. Bajīr] went out, saying [the following lines of verse]:

> إن تنجني اللهم من شر خالد
> فأنت المرجّى للنوائب والكرب
> O God, if you save me from Khālid's evil
> You will be the One in whom we seek refuge [in times] of adversity and affliction.\\146

Al-Ḥusayn b. Ziyād [al-Ramlī] reported to us on the authority of Abū Ismāʿīl Muḥammad b. ʿAbdallāh [al-Azdī], who said: Furthermore, Suqayf b. Bashīr al-ʿIjlī[199] related to me: Among them [=Banū ʿIjl[200]] was a man called Madhʿūr b. ʿAdī [al-ʿIjlī[201]] who marched out in the time of al-Muthannā b. Ḥāritha and wrote [the following letter] to Abū Bakr (r.):

Regarding the matter at hand: I am a man from Banū ʿIjl, who are horseriders—i.e. who are always on horseback—and dawn-horsemen—i.e.

199 Suqayf b. Bashīr al-ʿIjlī is a transmitter from al-Kūfa. In al-Azdī's narrative, he is mentioned as a transmitter of one tradition. On Suqayf, see Ibn Abī Ḥātim, *Al-jarḥ wa-al-taʿdīl*, IV, 322 (no. 1408) and Ibn Ḥibbān, *Al-thiqāt*, VI, 436.

200 ʿIjl is a Northern Arabian tribe that was a subtribe of Bakr b. Wāʾil. In al-Azdī's narrative, it is always referred to as Banū ʿIjl and its members are characterised as famous horsemen. In addition, three individual figures belonged to ʿIjl: (a) Madhʿūr b. ʿAdī al-ʿIjlī, who asked Abū Bakr for permission to fight in the arable lands of Iraq, who was positioned by Abū Bakr under the command of Khālid with whom he moved to Syria and who is said to have moved later to Miṣr, where he owned a house; (b) Bashīr b. Thawr al-ʿIjlī, who is characterised as a nobleman and a horseman of Banū ʿIjl and as a companion of al-Muthannā b. al-Ḥāritha from ʿIjl's sister-tribe of Shaybān and who spoke badly in a statement about Syria, which he compared to Iraq; and (c) Suqayf b. Bashīr al-ʿIjlī, who is mentioned as a transmitter of one tradition. On ʿIjl, see *EI*[2], s.v. ʿIjl (W. Watt).

201 Madhʿūr b. ʿAdī al-ʿIjlī is a companion of the Prophet. In al-Azdī's narrative, he is mentioned as asking Abū Bakr for permission to fight in the arable lands of Iraq, as being positioned by Abū Bakr under the command of Khālid, with whom he moved to Syria, and as moving later to Miṣr, where he owned a house. On Madhʿūr, see Ibn ʿAsākir, *TMD*, LVII, 198–199 (no. 7295) and *EI*[2], s.v. al-Muthannā b. al-Ḥāritha (F. Donner).

who launch [mounted] raids at dawn. I am accompanied by some of my tribesmen, each of whom is better than 100 [other] men. I have some acquaintance with the region (*balad*), valiance in war and familiarity with the land. So put me in charge of the arable lands of Iraq and you will find me [and my men] sufficient for it, God willing. Peace be upon you.

Al-Muthannā b. Ḥāritha wrote [the following letter] to Abū Bakr (r.):

Regarding the matter at hand: I am informing the successor of the Messenger of God (ṣ.) that one of our [tribes]people, a man called Madhʿūr b. ʿAdī [al-ʿIjlī] from Banū ʿIjl, came with a small number of people to challenge and disobey me. I wanted to inform you of this so that you make your decision on what is going on over here. Peace be upon you.

Abū Bakr (r.) wrote [the following letter] to Madhʿūr b. ʿAdī [al-ʿIjlī]:\\147

Regarding the matter at hand: I received your letter and understood what you mentioned [therein]. You are [exactly] as you have described yourself and your tribe is a wonderful one. I have decided that you should join Khālid b. al-Walīd and remain with him, as long as he remains in Iraq and depart with him if he departs from it. [Peace be upon you.]

And he [=Abū Bakr] wrote [the following letter] to al-Muthannā b. Ḥāritha:

In the name of God, the Merciful, the Compassionate. Regarding the matter at hand: Your companion from Banū ʿIjl [=Madhʿūr b. ʿAdī al-ʿIjlī] wrote to me, enquiring about some issues, and I wrote back to him, ordering him to remain with Khālid until I make up my mind [what else to do with him]. This is my letter to you in which I order you not to leave Iraq until Khālid b. al-Walīd departs from it. When Khālid b. al-Walīd departs from it, revert to your former place. You merit every additional [reward] and deserve every favour. [May God's] peace and mercy be upon you.

Khālid b. al-Walīd advanced until he passed by Kaskar[202] and [then] Zandaward[203], which he conquered and where he provided its people with a letter of protection (*ammana*). Then he passed by Hurmuzjird[204], which he conquered[, too,] and where he [also] provided its people with a letter of protection and they [=the people] made peace with them [=the Muslims]. Then

202 Kaskar is the name of a town in Iraq located on the western bank of the Tigris, ca. 250 km southeast of Baghdad. Wāsiṭ was founded opposite it on the eastern bank. In al-Azdī's narrative, Kaskar is mentioned as a place in Iraq, which Khālid passed by. On Kaskar, see *EI*^{2}, s.v. Kaskar (M. Streck/J. Lassner).

203 Zandaward is the name of a town between Basra and Wāsiṭ, the stones of which were used for building Wāsiṭ, according to Yāqūt. In al-Azdī's narrative, Zandaward is mentioned as a place in Iraq that Khālid conquered and where he issued a letter of protection to its inhabitants. On Zandaward, see Yāqūt, *Muʿjam al-buldān*, II, 951–952.

204 Hurmuzjird is listed neither in Yāqūt's geographical dictionary nor in any other geographical work we could access. In al-Azdī's narrative, Hurmuzjird is mentioned as a place in Iraq that Khālid conquered and where he issued a letter of protection to its inhabitants.

he passed by the district of al-Ullays[205], where Jābān[206], one of the Persian grand men, marched out to [meet] him [=Khālid]. Khālid dispatched to him al-Muthannā b. Ḥāritha, who faced them [=Jābān and his troops] at Nahr al-Damm[207] where the Muslims fought them fiercely. Then God defeated them and they [=the Muslims] killed a great many of them. That river is known today as Nahr al-Damm. And he [=Khālid] made peace with the people of al-Ullays.\\148

He [=Khālid] proceeded until he [and his unit] reached the junction of the rivers where Zādiba[208], the commander of Khusraw's scouting units (*masāliḥ*)[209], met him [=Khālid] in a middle [place] between him [=Khālid] and the Arabs. Then he fought them [=Khālid and his unit] fiercely. Zādiba came out of al-Ḥīra[210] [again] to [fight] them. So Khālid sent al-Muthannā b. Ḥāritha [and his unit] as his vanguard [against him]. Then al-Muthannā [b. Ḥāritha] faced them [=Zādiba and his unit] and fought them fiercely. Khālid b. al-Walīd then advanced on them[, too]. When they [=Zādiba and his unit] saw him, they retreated. When the people of al-Ḥīra, including ʿAbd al-Masīḥ b. ʿAmr b. Buqayla al-Azdī[211] and Hāniʾ b. Qabīṣa al-Ṭāʾī[212], saw that, they marched out [in support of Zābida]. Khālid b. al-Walīd said to them: "I call upon you to [believe in] God (ʿa.), to worship Him and to [embrace]

205 Al-Ullays is, according to Yāqūt, either a place at the border of the Syrian desert and Iraq or a village in the vicinity of al-Anbār. In al-Azdī's narrative, it is characterised as a city with a district near which al-Muthannā b. Ḥāritha and some Muslim troops fought a Persian unit under the command of Jābān and which Khālid finally conquered. In addition, a raid by Khālid on Banū Taghlib and al-Namir in al-Ullays is mentioned. On al-Ullays, see Yāqūt, *Muʿjam al-buldān*, I, 354.

206 Jābān could not be identified because his full name is not mentioned by al-Azdī. In al-Azdī's narrative, he is one of the Persian grand men whom al-Muthannā b. Ḥāritha faced at Nahr al-Damm.

207 No further information on Nahr al-Damm (lit. "the River of Blood") could be obtained. In al-Azdī's narrative, Nahr al-Damm is mentioned as a name given to a canal near al-Ullays neighbouring the Euphrates. Accordingly, the canal received this name, because al-Muthannā b. Ḥāritha killed many Byzantines at this spot.

208 Zādiba could not be identified because his full name is not mentioned. In al-Azdī's narrative, he is described as the commander of Khusraw's scouting unit that came out of al-Ḥīra to fight against Khālid and his cavalry.

209 On this meaning, see Lane, *Lexicon*, s.v. *maslaḥa*.

210 Al-Ḥīra is a city located on the western bank of the Euphrates and southeast of present-day Najaf. In al-Azdī's narrative, a commander of the city is mentioned by name (i.e. Zādiba). Furthermore, al-Ḥīra's capitulation to the Muslim troops under the command of Khālid is described. On al-Ḥīra, see *EI²*, s.v. al-Ḥīra (A. Beeston/I. Shahid); Toral-Niehoff, *Al-Ḥīra*.

211 ʿAbd al-Masīḥ b. ʿAmr b. Buqayla al-Azdī (n.d.), according to al-Azdī's narrative, is mentioned as one of the inhabitants of al-Ḥīra who had a witty dialogue with Khālid. On ʿAbd al-Masīḥ, see *EI²*, s.v. Ibn Buḳayla (C. Pellat).

212 Hāniʾ b. Qabīṣa al-Ṭāʾī is listed neither in Ibn Saʿd, al-Bukhārī, Ibn ʿAsākir nor in any other biographical work we could access. In al-Azdī's narrative, he is mentioned as one of the inhabitants of al-Ḥīra who marched out to fight Khālid and made peace with him in return for paying him 100,000 dirhams.

Islam. If you agree, you will merit the same rights we merit and have the same obligations we have. If you refuse, we will come to you with some people whose love for death is much stronger than your love for life". They said: "We do not have to fight you". So they made peace with him in return for [paying him] 100,000 dirhams.

Al-Ḥusayn b. Ziyād [al-Ramlī] reported to us on the authority of Abū Ismāʿīl Muḥammad b. ʿAbdallāh al-Azdī al-Baṣrī, who said: Furthermore, Abū al-Muthannā al-Kalbī[213] related to me: ʿAbd al-Masīḥ b. ʿAmr b. Buqayla [al-Azdī]\\149 met Khālid who said to him during their meeting: "From where can I trace you?" He said: "From my father's back". He [=Khālid] asked: "From where did you come out?" He [=ʿAbd al-Masīḥ b. ʿAmr b. Buqayla] said: "From my mother's womb". He [=Khālid] continued: "Woe unto you! What are you in?" He [=ʿAbd al-Masīḥ b. ʿAmr b. Buqayla] said: "[I am] in my clothes". He [=Khālid] said: "Woe unto you! What are you on?" He [=ʿAbd al-Masīḥ b. ʿAmr b. Buqayla] said: "[I am] on the ground". He [=Khālid] said: "Woe unto you! Do you understand (*a taʿqil*)?" He [=ʿAbd al-Masīḥ b. ʿAmr b. Buqayla] said: "Yes [I hobble (*aʿqil*)] and I [also] tie".[214] He [=Khālid] said: "Woe unto you! I am speaking to you in the language of humans!" He [=ʿAbd al-Masīḥ b. ʿAmr b. Buqayla] said: "And I am giving you the answer of humans". He [=Khālid] said: "Woe unto you! Are you [looking] for peace or war?" He [=ʿAbd al-Masīḥ b. ʿAmr b. Buqayla] said: "Rather, for peace". He [=Khālid] said: "What about these fortresses that I see?" He [=ʿAbd al-Masīḥ b. ʿAmr b. Buqayla] said: "We built them for the fool until the clement [one] comes and stops him". He [=the narrator, Abū al-Muthannā al-Kalbī] said: Then they negotiated peace and agreed on 100,000 dirhams, which the people of al-Ḥīra had to pay them [=the Muslims] every year. These 100,000 dirhams were the first sum of money that reached Medina from the land of Iraq. Khālid said to the people of al-Ḥīra: "We made peace with you, provided that you commit no offence against us and that you support us against the people of Persia". They committed to that and did so. And they preferred the appearance of the Muslims to that of the Persians.\\150

Al-Ḥusayn b. Ziyād [al-Ramlī] reported to us on the authority of Abū Ismāʿīl Muḥammad b. ʿAbdallāh [al-Azdī], who said: Furthermore, al-Mujālid

213 Abū al-Muthannā al-Kalbī is mentioned in al-Ṭabarī's *Taʾrīkh* as one of the informants of Abū Mikhnaf, without the *nisba*, however. ʿUqla and Banī Yāsīn identify him as Abū al-Muthannā al-Walīd b. al-Ḥusayn al-Kalbī al-Kūfī al-Sharqī b. al-Qaṭṭāmī, who lived during the caliphate of al-Manṣūr (r. 136–158/754–775) and who was a genealogist and a transmitter of traditions, according to Ibn al-Nadīm (see al-Azdī, *Futūḥ al-Shām. Ed. ʿUqla/Banī Yāsīn*, 34; 148, n. 15). In al-Azdī's narrative, he is mentioned as a transmitter of one tradition. On Abū al-Muthannā, see al-Ṭabarī, *Taʾrīkh*, II, 517, l. 17 and Ibn al-Nadīm, *Al-fihrist*, 90, l. 8–14.

214 The term "*aʿqil*" is a polysemous pun that can be assigned two different meanings. Khālid means one ("to understand") while ʿAbd al-Masīḥ means the other ("to hobble"). This is wordplay, verbal wit, which characterises the whole debate between the two of them.

b. Saʿīd al-Hamdānī[215] and al-Qāsim b. al-Walīd[216] related to me on the authority of [ʿĀmir] al-Shaʿbī[217], who said: Banū Buqayla[218] read [out] Khālid b. al-Walīd's letter to the people of al-Madāʾin[219], which includes [the following]:

In the name of God, the Merciful, the Compassionate. From Khālid b. al-Walīd to the provincial governors[220] of the Persian people. Peace be upon whoever follows the [right] guidance. Regarding the matter at hand: Praise be to God who violated your inviolability, usurped your reign and enfeebled your guile. Whoever performs our prayer[s], turns while praying to the direction of our prayers (*qibla*) and eats our [ritually] slaughtered animals is a Muslim who merits the same rights we merit and has the same obligations we have. When this letter reaches you, send me a guarantee [in return], accept my protection (*dhimma*) and bring me tribute. Otherwise, I swear by God, with whom no other deity is associated, that I will send you people [=fighters] who love death as much as you love life. [Pease be upon you.]

When they [=the people of al-Madāʾin] received the letter and read it, they started laughing at it. That was in the year 12 [=633–634].\\151

Al-Ḥusayn b. Ziyād [al-Ramlī] reported to us on the authority of Abū Ismāʿīl Muḥammad b. ʿAbdallāh [al-Azdī], who said: Furthermore, Ismāʿīl

215 Al-Mujālid's full name is Abū ʿUmayr al-Mujālid b. Saʿīd al-Hamdānī (d. 144/762). Without citing a source, Lees mentions that al-Mujālid died in 141 [=758–759] and that he was a weak transmitter (see al-Azdī, *Futūḥ al-Shām. Ed. Lees*, 55, n. 3). In al-Azdī's narrative, he is mentioned as a transmitter of two traditions. On al-Mujālid, see Ibn Saʿd, *Kitāb al-ṭabaqāt*, VI, 243 and Ibn Ḥibbān, *Al-majrūḥīn*, III, 10–11.

216 Al-Qāsim's full name is al-Qāsim b. al-Walīd al-Hamdānī al-Kūfī (d. 141/758–759). In al-Azdī's narrative, he is mentioned as a transmitter of two traditions. On al-Qāsim, see Ibn Saʿd, *Kitāb al-ṭabaqāt*, VI, 244 and al-Bukhārī, *Al-taʾrīkh al-kabīr*, IIII-1, 167–168 (no. 747).

217 ʿĀmir's full name is Abū ʿAmr ʿĀmir b. Sharāḥīl al-Kūfī al-Shaʿbī (d. between 103–110/721–728). In al-Azdī's narrative, he is mentioned as a transmitter of several traditions. On al-Shaʿbī, see *EI²*, s.v. al-Shaʿbī (G. Juynboll).

218 Banū Buqayla is a Southern Arabian tribe that was a subtribe of Ghassān. In al-Azdī's narrative, Banū Buqayla is mentioned once when it is said that some of its members read Khālid's letter to the people of al-Madāʾin in which he asked them to submit and pay tribute. In addition, ʿAbd al-Masīḥ b. ʿAmr b. Buqayla is mentioned as having belonged to al-Azd and as being the commander of the people of al-Ḥīra, who made peace with Khālid. On Banū Buqayla, see Caskel, *Ǧamharat*, I, 229, 312; II, 207; *EI²*, s.v. Ibn Buḳayla (C. Pellat).

219 Al-Madāʾin (lit. "the cities") is an urban complex located ca. 40 km southeast of Baghdad that consisted of five adjacent cities. In al-Azdī's narrative, al-Madāʾin is mentioned only once when it is stated that Khālid wrote a letter to its inhabitants, threatening them with attack. The conquest itself, however, is not described. On al-Madāʾin, see *EI²*, s.v. al-Madāʾin (M. Streck/M. Morony).

220 The term "provincial governors" (*marāziba*, sg. *marzubān*—a term derived from Middle Persian "*marzpān*", lit. "warden of the frontier") refers to the local leaders of the Sasanian Empire who organised the defence or concluded treaties with the attacking fighters. In al-Azdī's narrative, the provincial governors are mentioned once when Khālid sent them a letter, inviting them to the new faith. The only response they gave to the letter was laughter. On the term, see *EI²*, s.v. Marzpān (J. Kramers/M. Morony).

b. Abī Khālid[221] related to me on the authority of Qays b. Abī Ḥāzim[222], who said: I saw Khālid b. al-Walīd safe at al-Ḥīra, fearing nobody and wrapped in a garment whose two ends were tautened by him to his neck. He [=the narrator, Qays b. Abī Ḥāzim] said: And I heard him [=Khālid] at al-Ḥīra saying: "Nine [of my] swords smashed in my hand on the battle-day of Mu'ta[223] and only a Yemeni blade (*ṣafīḥa yamāniyya*)[224] remained [intact] in my hand".

Al-Ḥusayn b. Ziyād [al-Ramlī] reported to us on the authority of Abū Ismā'īl Muḥammad b. 'Abdallāh [al-Azdī], who said: Furthermore, Abū Ziyād[225] related to me on the authority of 'Abd al-Malik b. al-Aswad[226]: Khālid b. al-Walīd sent Bashīr b. Sa'd to the people of Bānqiyā[227]. However, a cavalry [unit] of the Unbelievers, under the command of one of the Persian grand men called Farrukh-Shadād b. Hurmuz[228], had already reached [the city]. When they saw Bashīr [b. Sa'd] in company of about 200\\152 of his companions, they marched out to them and then pelted them with arrows[229].

221 Ismā'īl's full name is Abū 'Abdallāh Ismā'īl b. Abī Khālid (145/762–763). In al-Azdī's narrative, he is mentioned as a transmitter of two traditions. On Ismā'īl, see Ibn Sa'd, *Kitāb al-ṭabaqāt*, VI, 240 and Ibn Ḥibbān, *Al-thiqāt*, IV, 19.

222 Qays's full name is Abū 'Abdallāh (or Abū 'Ubaydallāh) Qays b. Abī Ḥāzim al-Kūfī (d. between 84–98/703–717). 'Uqla and Banī Yāsīn mention his date of death as 68/687 (see al-Azdī, *Futūḥ al-Shām. Ed. 'Uqla/Banī Yāsīn*, 151, n. 2). In al-Azdī's narrative, he is depicted as having accompanied Khālid in the battle at al-Ḥīra, in his march to Syria and his encampment at Bosra. In addition, Qays is mentioned as a transmitter of several traditions. On Qays, see Ibn Sa'd, *Kitāb al-ṭabaqāt*, VI, 44 and Ibn Ḥibbān, *Al-thiqāt*, V, 307–308.

223 Mu'ta is a town in Transjordan located ca. 30 km southeast of the Dead Sea. In al-Azdī's narrative, Mu'ta is mentioned once in reference to the Battle of Mu'ta during the lifetime of the Prophet Muḥammad. On Mu'ta, see *EI*[2], s.v. Mu'ta (F. Buhl).

224 "*Ṣafīḥa*" (lit. "blade") denotes a broad sword (see Schwarzlose, *Waffen*, 150), while swords from Yemen are considered to be particularly strong and excellent (see ibid., 128–130).

225 Abū Ziyād could not be identified because only his patronymic (*kunya*), not his full name, is mentioned. In al-Azdī's narrative, he is mentioned as a transmitter of one tradition.

226 'Abd al-Malik b. al-Aswad is listed neither in Ibn Sa'd, al-Bukhārī, Ibn 'Asākir nor in any other biographical work we could access. In al-Azdī's narrative, he is mentioned as a transmitter of one tradition.

227 Bānqiyā is a part of the region of al-Kūfa or a village at the lower Euphrates, according to Yāqūt. In al-Azdī's narrative, a clash, between some Muslim troops under the command of Bashīr b. Sa'd and a Persian cavalry unit commanded by Farrukh-Shadād b. Hurmuz is mentioned there. During this clash Bashīr was injured and Farrukh-Shadād was killed. A second Muslim deployment under the command of Jarīr b. 'Abdallāh al-Bajalī managed eventually to conquer Bānqiyā. On Bānqiyā, see Yāqūt, *Mu'jam al-buldān*, I, 483–484.

228 Farrukh-Shadād b. Hurmuz is listed neither in Ibn Sa'd, al-Bukhārī, Ibn 'Asākir nor in any other biographical work we could access. In al-Azdī's narrative, he is depicted as the commander of a Persian cavalry unit which fought Bashīr b. Sa'd while in the course of this encounter Farrukh-Shadād was killed.

229 Arrows (a collective noun, sg. *nushshāb*) signifies wooden arrows (in contrast to "pipe arrows") which, according to pre-Islamic and early Islamic poetry, originated from Iranian culture (see Schwarzlose, *Waffen*, 280–281). Hence, a couple of lines below, it is narrated twice that a "Persian man" shot an arrow (*nushshāba*) against a Muslim fighter.

So the Muslims launched an attack on them and killed Farrukh-Shadād [b. Hurmuz]. A Persian man shot an arrow at Bashīr [b. Saʿd] and injured him. He [=Bashīr b. Saʿd] returned wounded with his companions to Khālid. So Khālid sent Jarīr b. ʿAbdallāh al-Bajalī[230] to the people of Bānqiyā. Biṣbahan b. Ṣalūbā[231] came out to them [=Jarīr and his men], apologised to them for that skirmish and said to Jarīr [b. ʿAbdallāh al-Bajalī]: "That was neither my decision nor my command, but they [=the Persians] descended on my hamlets me being averse to [it]". Then he offered them [=Jarīr b. ʿAbdallāh al-Bajalī and the Muslims] peace and they agreed to make peace with him in return for 1,000 dirhams and a [shawl-like] garment (*ṭaylasān*). Jarīr [b. ʿAbdallāh al-Bajalī] wrote them a letter [of protection].

Then Abū ʿUbayda b. al-Jarrāḥ wrote [the following letter] to Abū Bakr (r.) while he [=Abū ʿUbayda] was in al-Jābiya [in Syria].

In the name of God, the Merciful, the Compassionate. Regarding the matter at hand: The Byzantines, the townspeople and those Arabs from among them who embraced their religion have mustered to fight the Muslims. But we aspire to victory and to the fulfilment of the Lord's (tt.) promise[s] and graceful habit[s] (*ʿādatahū al-ḥusnā*). I wanted to inform you of this [matter] so that you [could] make your decision on it, God willing. Peace be upon you.

The story of deposing Khālid b. al-Walīd from [commanding the Muslim troops in] Iraq and his taking command of [the Muslim troops in] Syria

[Then] Abū Bakr (r.) wrote [the following letter] to Khālid b. al-Walīd:

Regarding the matter at hand: When my letter reaches you, depart from Iraq and leave it to its people, who had [already] been there when you reached them [=al-Muthannā b. Ḥāritha's unit]. Rush swiftly with your fellow men of might (*ahl al-quwwa*), who went\\153 with you from al-Yamāma to Iraq, who accompanied you along the way and who came to you from al-Ḥijāz, until you reach Syria. Then meet up with Abū ʿUbayda b. al-Jarrāḥ and the Muslims who are [there] with him. When you meet [them], you are the [chief] commander of the whole army. Peace be upon you.

230 Jarīr b. ʿAbdallāh al-Bajalī is listed neither in Ibn Saʿd, al-Bukhārī, Ibn ʿAsākir nor in any other biographical work we could access. In al-Azdī's narrative, he is depicted as being sent by Khālid b. al-Walīd to the people of Bānqiyā. It was Jarīr to whom Biṣbahan b. Ṣalūbā apologised for the battle that occurred between the Muslims and the Persians and whom Biṣbahan asked for peace.

231 Biṣbahan b. Ṣalūbā is listed neither in Ibn Saʿd, al-Bukhārī, Ibn ʿAsākir nor in any other biographical work we could access. In al-Azdī's narrative, he is portrayed as the leader of the people of Bānqiyā who apologised to Jarīr b. ʿAbdallāh al-Bajalī for fighting and offered him peace in return for 1,000 dirhams and a shawl-like garment. Citing al-Balādhurī, Yāqūt mentions Biṣbahan b. Ṣalūbā as Buṣbuhrī b. Ṣalūbā in one context and Ṣalūbā b. Buṣbuhrī in another (see Yāqūt, *Muʿjam al-buldān*, I, 483–484 [s.v. Bānqiyā]).

ʿAbd al-Raḥmān b. Ḥanbal al-Jumaḥī[232] went to him [=Khālid] with this letter. When he [=ʿAbd al-Raḥmān b. Ḥanbal al-Jumaḥī] came to him, and before he read out the letter, Khālid said to him: "What is [hidden] behind you[r visit]?" He [=ʿAbd al-Raḥmān] said to him: "Good [news], you are ordered to march to Syria". Khālid became angry and found it hard [to accept the decision], [so] he said: "This is the work of ʿUmar who begrudges that God leads me to the conquest of Iraq".

The Persians were extremely scared of him and feared him. And whenever Khālid (r.) fell upon a polytheistic group, he was like a torture from God for them and [fought] like a lion. Khālid hoped that God would lead him to the conquest of Iraq.

When he [then] read Abū Bakr's (r.) letter and saw therein that he [=Abū Bakr] had appointed him as the [chief] commander of Abū ʿUbayda b. al-Jarrāḥ and of the entire [army in] Syria, he restrained himself [from desiring Iraq] and said: "As long as he [=Abū Bakr] made me the [chief] commander, Syria is certainly a [matching] substitute for Iraq". Bashīr b. Thawr al-ʿIjlī[233], one of the noblemen of Banū ʿIjl, a [renowned] horseman of Bakr b. Wāʾil and one of the best companions of al-Muthannā b. Ḥāritha, said to Khālid: "May God increase your righteousness. I swear by God that He has not made Syria a [matching] substitute for Iraq. [For] Iraq has more wheat and barley, more silk brocades and silk and more silver and gold than Syria. In addition, it is also ampler and wider. I swear by God that Syria as a whole is nothing but a little sidepiece of Iraq".

Al-Muthannā b. Ḥāritha hated his [=Bashīr b. Thawr al-ʿIjlī's] advice to him [=Khālid b. al-Walīd], because he [=al-Muthannā] has always wanted Khālid to go away from him and leave it [=Iraq] to him. Khālid then said: "The adherents of Islam are in Syria and the Byzantines advanced on them and prepared themselves [for fighting] them. I am going to help them and\\154 will then return to you. Stay here the way you are. When I finish what I am leaving for, I shall immediately return to you. If I slacken my pace, I hope that you neither fail nor wither. For the successor of the Messenger of God (ṣ.) is neither heedless of you all nor careless about reinforcing you with men and soldiers until God leads you to the conquest of these lands, God (t.) willing".

232 ʿAbd al-Raḥmān's full name is Abū Ḥanbal ʿAbd al-Raḥmān b. Ḥanbal al-Jumaḥī (d. 40/660). In al-Azdī's narrative, ʿAbd al-Raḥmān serves as a messenger delivering letters between Abū Bakr and Khālid and a co-fighter with the Muslims against the Byzantines at Bosra. In addition, he recites a poem in one place. On ʿAbd al-Raḥmān, see Ibn ʿAsākir, *TMD*, XXXIIII, 319–322.

233 Bashīr b. Thawr al-ʿIjlī (n.d.) was an early Islamic figure. In al-Azdī's narrative, he is mentioned as one of the noblemen of Banū ʿIjl, a renowned horseman of Bakr b. Wāʾil and one of the best companions of al-Muthannā b. Ḥāritha. He advises Khālid not to leave Iraq and not to march to Syria because the latter is regarded as much lower in rank than the former. On Bashīr, see Ibn Ḥajar, *Al-iṣāba. Ed. al-Baghawī*, I, 345 (no. 778).

Khālid b. al-Walīd's march to Syria and his battles against Banū Taghlib and others along his way

He [=the narrator] said: Then Khālid b. al-Walīd went out of al-Ḥīra and marched until he launched a raid on al-Anbār[234], then on Ṣandawdā'[235] where he left Sa'īd b. 'Amr b. Ḥarām al-Anṣārī behind [as the one in charge]. Then he descended on 'Ayn al-Tamr[236] where Bashīr b. Sa'd [suffered a] wound [that] shook him violently. Then he [=Bashīr b. Sa'd] died as martyr [there], God rest him, and was buried [there]. A scouting unit belonging to the Persians was stationed there [='Ayn al-Tamr]. One of the Persians shot an arrow at 'Umayr b. Rabbāb b. Ḥudhayfa b. Hāshim b. al-Mughīra[237], who died as martyr there, God (t.) rest him, and was buried beside Bashīr b. Sa'd al-Anṣārī.\\155

Khālid b. al-Walīd fought them [=the people of 'Ayn al-Tamr], and thus they fortified [their place] against him. He then provoked them into another fight. [Finally,] he [overcame them,] decapitated them and captured their offspring. This was the first capture [that took place] in Iraq, with Khālid capturing a great many of them. Among the captives were Abū 'Amra[238], Abū 'Abd al-A'lā al-Shā'ir[239], Sīrīn[240] the father of Muḥammad b. Sīrīn[241]

234 Al-Anbār (lit. "the Storehouse" or "Granary" in Persian) is located on the eastern bank of the Euphrates ca. 62 km west of Baghdad or 5 km north-west of al-Fallūja near Nahr 'Īsā. In al-Azdī's narrative, al-Anbār is mentioned only once in reference to a raid on the city by Khālid. On al-Anbār, see *EI²*, s.v. al-Anbār (M. Streck/A. Duri).

235 Ṣandawdā' is a place that Yāqūt could not locate. He only mentions that the place name is derived from a Lakhmid princess with the same name, that Khālid b. al-Walīd conquered it on his way from Iraq to Syria and that he left Sa'd b. 'Amr b. Ḥarām al-Anṣārī behind as a commander. The last information is also given in al-Azdī's narrative, where the place is corrupted to Ṣandaw. On Ṣandawdā', see Yāqūt, *Mu'jam al-buldān*, III, 420.

236 'Ayn al-Tamr (lit. "the Spring of the Dates") is a town on the western bank of the Euphrates located between al-Anbār and al-Kūfa. In al-Azdī's narrative, 'Ayn al-Tamr is mentioned in the course of Khālid's march from al-Ḥīra via al-Anbār to Syria. In 'Ayn al-Tamr, Khālid decapitated many people and captured and enslaved some inhabitants. On 'Ayn al-Tamr, see *EI²*, s.v. 'Ayn al-Tamr (S. El-Ali).

237 'Umayr b. Rabbāb b. Ḥudhayfa b. Hāshim b. al-Mughīra (n.d.) is a companion of the Prophet. In al-Azdī's narrative, he is mentioned as having been killed with an arrow shot by one of the Persians and then as being buried beside Bashīr b. Sa'd al-Anṣārī. On 'Umayr b. Rabbāb, see Ibn Ḥajar, *Al-iṣāba. Ed. al-Baghawī*, IV, 717 (no. 6036).

238 Abū 'Amra could not be identified because only his patronymic (*kunya*), not his full name, is mentioned. In al-Azdī's narrative, he is said to have been one of the captives captured by Khālid at 'Ayn al-Tamr.

239 Abū 'Abd al-A'lā al-Shā'ir is listed neither in Ibn Sa'd, al-Bukhārī, Ibn 'Asākir nor in any other biographical work we could access. In al-Azdī's narrative, he is mentioned as one of the captives who were captured by Khālid at 'Ayn al-Tamr in Iraq. His last name "al-Shā'ir" indicates that he might have been a poet.

240 Sīrīn (n.d.) was an early Islamic figure. In al-Azdī's narrative, Sīrīn is mentioned as having been one of the first captives whom Khālid captured in Iraq after his victory at 'Ayn al-Tamr. On Sīrīn, see *EI²*, s.v. Ibn Sīrīn (T. Fahd).

241 Muḥammad's full name is Abū Bakr Muḥammad b. Sīrīn al-Baṣrī (d. 110/728). In al-Azdī's narrative, Muḥammad is mentioned as the son of Sīrīn who was captured by Khālid after his victory at 'Ayn al-Tamr in Iraq. On Muḥammad, see *EI²*, s.v. Ibn Sīrīn (T. Fahd).

and Ḥumrān b. Abbān[242] the client (*mawlā*) of ʿUthmān b. ʿAffān (r.). There [at ʿAyn al-Tamr] Khālid [also] killed Ḥumrān [b. Abbān's] cousin, Hilāl b. Bashīr al-Namirī[243], and crucified him.

Then Khālid sent back the weak with ʿUmayr b. Saʿd al-Anṣārī, [continued to] march with 600 men and said to al-Muthannā b. Ḥāritha: "Turn [back] to your sovereignty (*sulṭān*), neither neglectful nor blameful nor listless". Khālid also sent a letter in advance of him to the people [=the Muslims] in Syria, concerning his march to them.

Al-Ḥusayn b. Ziyād [al-Ramlī] reported to us on the authority of Abū Ismāʿīl Muḥammad b. ʿAbdallāh [al-Azdī], who said: Furthermore, Yazīd b. Yazīd b. Jābir[244] related to me on the authority of ʿAmr b. Muḥṣan on the authority of ʿAbdallāh b. Qurṭ al-Thumālī,\\156 who said: When Khālid left ʿAyn al-Tamr, heading for Syria, he wrote [the following letter] to the Muslims in Syria [and sent it] with ʿAmr b. al-Ṭufayl b. ʿAmr al-Azdī[245], the son of Dhū al-Nūr[246]:

In the name of God, the Merciful, the Compassionate. From Khālid b. al-Walīd to those Believers and Muslims in the land of the West. Peace be upon you. I praise, on your behalf, God with whom no other deity is associated. Regarding the matter at hand: I ask God, who strengthened us with Islam, graced us with His religion, honoured us with His Prophet Muḥammad (ṣ.) and favoured us with faith as ample mercy from our Lord to us and as a perfect blessing from Him to us, to complete His blessing[s] upon us and upon you. O servants of God, praise God in order that He will give you more, ask him for perfect health in order that He will maintain it for you and be thankful to Him for His blessings. I received a letter from the successor of the Messenger of God (ṣ.), ordering me to march to you [to Syria]. I hastened and rushed out [and it looked] as if my cavalrymen had already appeared

242 Ḥumrān b. Abbān (d. 84/703) is an early Islamic figure. In al-Azdī's narrative, he is mentioned as a client of ʿUthmān, as one of the captives whom Khālid captured at ʿAyn al-Tamr and as the cousin of Hilāl b. Bashīr al-Namirī. On Ḥumrān, see Ibn Saʿd, *Kitāb al-ṭabaqāt*, VII-1, 108.

243 Hilāl b. Bashīr al-Namirī is listed neither in Ibn Saʿd, al-Bukhārī, Ibn ʿAsākir nor in any other biographical work we could access. In al-Azdī's narrative, he is mentioned as Ḥumrān b. Abbān's cousin and is said to have been killed and crucified by Khālid in ʿAyn al-Tamr.

244 Yazīd's full name is Yazīd b. Yazīd b. Jābir al-Azdī al-Shāmī al-Dimashqī (d. 134/751–752). In al-Azdī's narrative, he is mentioned as a transmitter of seven traditions. On Yazīd, see Ibn Saʿd, *Kitāb al-ṭabaqāt*, VII-2, 170.

245 ʿAmr's full name is ʿAmr b. al-Ṭufayl b. ʿAmr b. Dhī al-Nūr al-Azdī (n.d.). In al-Azdī's narrative, he is depicted as Khālid's nephew and messenger, with whom he sent letters to the troops in Syria and who is said to have fought with Maysara b. Masrūq in the Battle of al-Yarmūk, where he did heroic deeds and recited a poem and where he was killed. On ʿAmr, see Ibn ʿAsākir, *TMD*, XXXXVI, 105–108.

246 Dhū al-Nūr's full name is Dhū al-Nūr al-Ṭufayl b. ʿAmr b. Ṭarīf b. al-ʿĀṣ al-Azdī (n.d.). In al-Azdī's narrative, Dhū al-Nūr is mentioned as the father of ʿAmr b. al-Ṭufayl. On Dhū al-Nūr, see Ibn Saʿd, *Kitāb al-ṭabaqāt*, IIII-1, 175–177.

before you. Rejoice over the fulfilment of God's promise and the beauty of His reward. May God protect us and [protect] you with faith [from committing sins], enable us and [enable] you to adhere always to Islam and bestow upon us and [upon] you the best reward [He promised] to the fighters for His cause. Peace be upon you.

He also wrote [the following] letter [and sent it] with him [='Amr b. al-Ṭufayl b. 'Amr al-Azdī] to Abū 'Ubayda b. al-Jarrāḥ:

In the name of God, the Merciful, the Compassionate. From Khālid b. al-Walīd to Abū 'Ubayda b. al-Jarrāḥ. Peace be upon you. I praise, on your behalf, God with whom no other deity is associated. Regarding the matter at hand: I ask God to [grant] us and [grant] you safety on the Day of Fear [=Doomsday] and protection (*'iṣma*) in the worldly abode. I received a letter from the successor of the Messenger of God (ṣ.), ordering me to march to Syria, to command the soldiers there and to manage its [=Syria's] cause. I swear by God that I have never requested or desired this or wrote to him [=Abū Bakr] about it. You, may God have mercy upon you, should remain in the [same status and] position you are in [now]. Your order will never be disobeyed, your decision[s] will never be contradicted\\157 and no issue will be decided without [consulting] you. This is because you are, indeed, one of the Muslim masters, whose favour is undeniable and whose opinion is indispensable. May God complete the blessing[s] of benevolence (*iḥsān*) [bestowed] upon us and [upon] you and [may He] mercifully save us and [save] you from the torture of Fire. May God's peace and mercy be upon you.

He [=the narrator, 'Abdallāh b. Qurṭ al-Thumālī] said: When 'Amr b. al-Ṭufayl [b. 'Amr al-Azdī] came to them [=the Muslims] in al-Jābiya, he read Khālid b. al-Walīd's letter to them and delivered the [second] letter to Abū 'Ubayda. When he [=Abū 'Ubayda] read it, he said: "May God bless what the successor of the Messenger of God (ṣ.) has decided and may God return the peace-greetings to Khālid".

He [=the narrator, 'Abdallāh b. Qurṭ al-Thumālī] said: The deposition of Abū 'Ubayda was hard for the Muslims [to accept], but it [=the deposition] was the hardest for Banū Sa'īd b. al-'Āṣ[247] [to accept], because they had

247 Banū Sa'īd b. al-'Āṣ is a Northern Arabian tribe that was a subtribe of Quraysh. In al-Azdī's narrative, Banū Sa'īd b. al-'Āṣ is mentioned once in a statement that it was hard for them to accept Abū Bakr's deposition of Abū 'Ubayda from the chief command. In addition, six individual figures belonged to Banū Sa'īd b. al-'Āṣ, according to the narrative: (a) Abū Uḥayḥa Sa'īd b. al-'Āṣ, the ancestor and father of the following persons; (b) Khālid b. Sa'īd, who was the first to speak out in favour of Abū Bakr's plan to send troops to Syria and the first to encamp before leaving for Syria; (c) 'Amr b. Sa'īd b. al-'Āṣ, who left Medina, together with the unit of his brother Khālid, and encouraged the Muslims to fight during the Battle of Fiḥl, in which he himself fought fiercely. After having had a talk with 'Abdallāh b. Qurṭ al-Thumālī, he was killed by the Byzantine fighters; (d) al-Ḥakam b. Sa'īd b. al-'Āṣ, who left Medina together with the unit of his brother Khālid; (e) Abbān b. Sa'īd b. al-'Āṣ, who left Medina together with the unit of his brother Khālid; (f) Sa'īd b. al-'Āṣ b. Abī Uḥayḥa Sa'īd, who is a transmitter of one tradition about his uncle Khālid b. Sa'īd. On Banū Sa'īd, see Caskel, *Ǧamharat*, I, 9; II, 500.

volunteered and devoted themselves to the cause of God until God would make Islam triumphant. As for Abū ʿUbayda, he showed no [sign of] envy of Khālid b. al-Walīd, neither on his face nor in his words.

Then Khālid left ʿAyn al-Tamr until he launched a raid on Banū Taghlib[248] and al-Namir[249] in al-Ullays, killed [many of] them, defeated them and took some of their possessions. He [=the narrator, ʿAbdallāh b. Qurṭ al-Thumālī] said: A man from among them was having a drink from a bowl (*jafna*), saying [the following lines of verse]:\\158

ألا علّلانى قبل جيش أبى بكر
لعل منايانا قريب وما ندري
Will you give me a second drink before Abū Bakr's army [comes]?
Perhaps our deaths are near but we do not know [it].

He [=the narrator, ʿAbdallāh b. Qurṭ al-Thumālī] said: As soon as he finished his speech, one of the Muslim men attacked him with a sword and beheaded him; lo and behold, his head fell down into the bowl.

The route which Khālid took to Syria

Al-Ḥusayn b. Ziyād [al-Ramlī] reported to us on the authority of Abū Ismāʿīl Muḥammad b. ʿAbdallāh [al-Azdī], who said: Furthermore, Ḥamza b. ʿAlī[250] related to me on the authority of a man from Banū Bakr b. Wāʾil: A man from

248 Taghlib (or Taghlib b. Wāʾil) is a large Northern Arabian tribe that was a subtribe of Rabīʿa. In al-Azdī's narrative, this tribe is referred to as Banū Taghlib and is mentioned once when Khālid is said to have attacked it in al-Ullays, killed many of its members and taken their possessions. On Taghlib, see *EI*^{2}, s.v. Taghlib b. Wāʾil (M. Lecker).

249 Al-Namir (or al-Namr) is either a Northern Arabian tribe that was a subtribe of Rabīʿa (i.e. Banū al-Namir b. Qāsiṭ), or a Southern Arabian tribe that was a subtribe of Azd Sarāt (i.e. Banū al-Namir b. ʿUthmān) or a subtribe of Quḍāʿa (i.e. Banū al-Namir b. Wabara). It is not clear which of the three is referred to in al-Azdī's narrative, but since it is said that Khālid launched an attack on Banū Taghlib and al-Namir in al-Ullays in Iraq, and killed some of its members, it most likely refers here to the first one, i.e. Banū al-Namir b. Qāsiṭ. In addition, two individual figures belonged to al-Namir: (a) Hilāl b. Bashīr al-Namirī, who is said to have been Ḥumrān b. Abbān's cousin and to have been killed and crucified by Khālid in ʿAyn al-Tamr; and (b) al-Ḥārith b. ʿAbdallāh al-Azdī, who is said to have changed his affiliation to "al-Namirī". On al-Namir, see *EI*^{2}, s.v. al-Namir b. Ḳāsiṭ (M. Lecker); Caskel, *Ǧamharat*, I, 141; II, 444 (for Banū al-Namir b. Qāsiṭ) or I, 216; II, 444 (for Banū al-Namir b. ʿUthmān) or I, 279; II, 444 (for Banū al-Namir b. Wabara).

250 Ḥamza's full name is Abū al-Khaṭṭāb Ḥamza b. ʿAlī. He is mentioned only in al-Ṭabarī's *Taʾrīkh* as an informant of Abū Mikhnaf and Sayf b. ʿUmar. We could not find a *tarjama* about him. In al-Azdī's narrative, he is mentioned as a transmitter of one tradition. On Ḥamza, see al-Ṭabarī, *Taʾrīkh*, I, 2018, l. 6; 2198, l. 6.

[Banū] Muḥārib [b. Fihr[251]] called Muḥriz b. Ḥuraysh b. Ṣulayʿ[252], who was trading in al-Ḥīra and travelling frequently to Syria, said to Khālid: "When you reach Makhaḍkhaḍ[253], make [sure] that the Morning Star [=Venus] is on your right side. Then proceed towards it until the morning [comes] and you will never be confounded". He [=Khālid] tried it and found it just as described.

Then Khālid headed towards al-Samāwa [Desert][254] until he reached the Qurāqir [Valley][255]; there were two [way] stations between the Qurāqir [Valley] and Suwā[256], which [take] five nights [to reach]. They [=Khālid and the Muslims] could not find the right way and thus were directed\\159 to Rāfiʿ b. ʿAmr al-Ṭāʾī[257] who was a guide and who said to Khālid: "Leave the chattels (*athqāl*) [and the non-combatants] behind and take these desert routes if you would like to do it". Khālid did not like to leave anyone behind and said: "I received an order which must be carried out and which [says] we should stick together". He [=Rāfiʿ b. ʿAmr al-Ṭāʾī] said: "I swear by God that [even] the single rider fears for his life because of them [=the desert routes], and he would take them [=the desert routes] only if he were in danger. What about you and your company [then]?" He [=Khālid] said: "It is inevitable and

251 Banū Muḥārib b. Fihr is a Northern Arabian tribe that was a subtribe of Quraysh. In al-Azdī's narrative, two individual figures are said to have belonged to Banū Muḥārib b. Fihr: (a) Suwayd b. Kulthūm al-Qurashī, who is said to have belonged to this tribe and (b) Muḥriz b. Ḥuraysh b. Ṣulayʿ, who is said to have been trading in al-Ḥīra, travelling frequently to Syria, and, therefore, guided Khālid on his way to Syria. On Banū Muḥārib b. Fihr, see *EI*², s.v. Muḥārib (G. Levi Della Vida).

252 We read Ṣulayʿ instead of Ḍalīʿ, as written in the edition. Muḥriz b. Ḥuraysh b. Ṣulayʿ (n.d.) is an early Islamic figure. In al-Azdī's narrative, he is mentioned as a trader at al-Ḥīra who gave advice to Khālid regarding the way from Iraq to Syria. On Muḥriz, see Ibn Ḥajar, *Al-iṣāba. Ed. al-Baghawī*, VI, 278 (no. 8373).

253 Makhaḍkhaḍ is listed neither in Yāqūt's *Muʿjam al-buldān* nor in any other Arabic work we could access. In al-Azdī's narrative, Makhaḍkhaḍ is mentioned as a station during Khālid's march to Syria.

254 Al-Samāwa (lit. "the Elevated Land") is the name of the desert and steppe land between al-Kūfa and Syria. It is exactly this context of al-Azdī's narrative in which it is mentioned, i.e. when referring to Khālid's march to Syria. On al-Samāwa, see *EI*², s.v. al-Samāwa (C. Bosworth).

255 Qurāqir is a valley in al-Samāwa Desert located in Iraq, which belonged to Kalb. In al-Azdī's narrative, the Qurāqir Valley is mentioned several times as the station before Suwā during Khālid's march from Iraq to Syria. On the Qurāqir Valley, see Yāqūt, *Muʿjam al-buldān*, IV, 48–50.

256 Suwā is a watering place in al-Samāwa Desert, according to Yāqūt. Citing al-Haytham b. ʿAdī, Yāqūt also states that Suwā is a part of a long valley that starts in the desert of Basra and is inhabited by several Arabian tribes. The part of the valley belonging to the territory of Kalb is called Qurāqir Valley, while the part in the territory of Taghlib is called Suwā Valley. In al-Azdī's narrative, Suwā is mentioned several times as a station during Khālid's march from Iraq to Syria. On Suwā, see Yāqūt, *Muʿjam al-buldān*, III, 172 (s.v. Suwā); II, 635–636 (s.v. al-Dahnāʾ).

257 Rāfiʿ's full name is Abū al-Ḥasan Rāfiʿ b. ʿAmr al-Wāʾilī al-Ṭāʾī (n.d.). In al-Azdī's narrative, he is mentioned as having guided Khālid through the desert route and as having recited a poem. On Rāfiʿ, see Ibn ʿAsākir, *TMD*, XVIII, 7–19.

I am [even] more resolute [to go]". He [=Rāfi' b. 'Amr al-Ṭā'ī] said: "Whichever of you can hang water [bags] to his she-camel's ears must do so. For they [=the desert routes] destroy [all] except those whom God ('a.) protects". Then [Rāfi' b. 'Amr] al-Ṭā'ī said to Khālid: "Fetch me twenty slaughter camels that are big, fat and averse to milking (*mishān*)". He [=Khālid] did so. Then he [=Rāfi' b. 'Amr al-Ṭā'ī] made them [=the camels] thirsty and when they had a raging thirst, he watered them. When he quenched their thirst, he pierced their lips and tied them together, i.e. tugged their mouths, so that [they would] not ruminate (*la-illā tajtarra*). Then he said to Khālid: "[Now] march [out] with the horses and the equipment".

Whenever he [=Rāfi' b. 'Amr al-Ṭā'ī] set up camp, he slaughtered four of these camels, then took the water out of their bellies and watered the horses from it. The people drank from what was left for them, too. When it [=the water] was about to run out, Khālid said to Rāfi' [b. 'Amr al-Ṭā'ī], who was sore-eyed: "Woe unto you, what now?" He [=Rāfi' b. 'Amr al-Ṭā'ī] said: "You will get some [more] water, God willing".\\160 However, the people became exhausted and thirsty and their pack animals (*dawābb*) were thirsty, too. Then Rāfi' [b. 'Amr al-Ṭā'ī] said: "Look [around]! Do you find a boxthorn tree on the way?" They [=the Muslims] said: "No". He said: "[Then] we belong to God. I swear by God that you will perish and make [others] perish. Look [around again]; may you turn fatherless!"[258] They did and found it [=the boxthorn tree]. He [=Rāfi' b. 'Amr al-Ṭā'ī] immediately proclaimed "God is the Greatest!" and so did they. Then he [=Rāfi' b. 'Amr al-Ṭā'ī] said: "Dig for its root[s]". They dug and found a spring [there]. They drank until they quenched their thirst and took [all] the water they needed. Then he [=Rāfi' b. 'Amr al-Ṭā'ī] said: "I swear by God that I have never come to this watering place before, except once with my father when I was a young boy". Using *rajaz* metre, a poet said [the following lines of verse] about this [event]:

لله در رافع أنى اهتدي
فوز من قراقر إلى سوى
أرض إذا ما سارها الجيش بكي
ما سارها قبلك من إنس أرى

How excellent is Rāfi' [b. 'Amr al-Ṭā'ī] whenever he is rightly guided.[259]
A successful crossing from the Qurāqir [Valley] to Suwā.
A ground on which the army weeps if it treads on it.
I have never seen anyone else tread on it before you.[260]\\161

258 The Arabic expression "*lā abā lakum*" (lit. "may you turn fatherless") is used as a means of insult on the occasion of wishing fatherlessness on people.

259 The Arabic expression "*li-llāh darrun*" is an exclamation of praise which is translated literally as "to God be attributed one's deed" and connotatively as "what a generous man or how good one is". See Lane, *Lexicon*, s.v. *darrun*.

260 For a more poetic translation which reads "Praise to Rāfi', how he has successfully made,/ from Qurāqir [Valley] to Suwā, the desert passage./If the army march five days they fade;/ before you no human had crossed it to my knowledge", see Mourad, *Poetry*, 178–179. For

This is Khālid's letter to Banū Mashja'a

Al-Ḥusayn b. Ziyād [al-Ramlī] reported to us on the authority of Abū Ismā'īl Muḥammad b. 'Abdallāh [al-Azdī], who said: Furthermore, al-Mustanīr b. Zubayr b. Aflaḥ b. Ya'būb b. 'Amr b. Ḍarīs al-Mashja'ī[261]—[Banū Mashja'a[262]] are a [sub]tribe (*ḥayy*) of Quḍā'a[263]—related to me, saying: Khālid b. al-Walīd came from Iraq towards us, taking the route to the Qurāqir [Valley], then to Suwā, then to al-Liwā[264] and then to Quṣam[265]. [Al-Mustanīr b. Zubayr al-Mashja'ī also said:] O Mashja'a [sub]tribe, he [=Khālid] also wrote us [the following] letter, which we still have today:

In the name of God, the Merciful, the Compassionate. This is a letter from Khālid b. al-Walīd to Banū Mashja'a, who possess the watering place of Quṣam, its freshwater, its water-supplying rights and its tribespeople, i.e. the people who inhabit its [=Quṣam's] eastern part, whereas the people of al-Ghūṭa[266] possess its western part.

---

the same poem (but with different line order), see Yāqūt, *Mu'jam al-buldān*, IV, 49 (s.v. Qurāqir). Yāqūt starts with line one, then quotes line three and four, and finishes with line two.

261 Al-Mustanīr b. Zubayr b. Aflaḥ b. Ya'būb b. 'Amr b. Ḍarīs al-Mashja'ī is listed neither in Ibn Sa'd, al-Bukhārī, Ibn 'Asākir nor in any other biographical work we could access. 'Uqla and Banī Yāsīn identify him as *al-Musayyab* b. Zubayr b. Aflaḥ b. Ya'būb b. 'Amr b. Ḍarīs al-Mashja'ī about whom they also could not find a *tarjama*. However, they found a biographical entry about his great-grandfather Ya'būb (see al-Azdī, *Futūḥ al-Shām. Ed. 'Uqla/Banī Yāsīn*, 161, n. 2 referring to Ibn 'Asākir, *TMD*, LXXIV, 144). In al-Azdī's narrative, he is mentioned as a transmitter of two traditions.

262 Banū Mashja'a is a subtribe of Quḍā'a. In al-Azdī's narrative, Banū Mashja'a is mentioned twice as a subtribe of Quḍā'a, which owned the watering place of Quṣam. Khālid is said to have written a letter to them in which he acknowledged their possessions. In addition, two individual figures belonged to Banū Mashja'a: (a) Ya'būb b. 'Amr b. Ḍarīs al-Mashja'ī, who fought with Khālid in al-Ghūṭa, Bosra and Ajnādayn, but died from the wounds he suffered in the last battle; (b) al-Mustanīr b. Zubayr b. Aflaḥ b. Ya'būb b. 'Amr b. Ḍarīs al-Mashja'ī, who is a transmitter of several traditions. On Banū Mashja'a, see Caskel, *Ǧamharat*, I, 279; II, 403.

263 Quḍā'a is a large tribe. In al-Azdī's narrative, Banū Mashja'a is mentioned twice as a subtribe of Quḍā'a while some subtribes of Quḍā'a are depicted as having participated in the Battle of Fiḥl and the Battle of al-Yarmūk, where they were positioned on the left flank. On Quḍā'a, see *EI*², s.v. Ḳuḍā'a (M. Kister).

264 Al-Liwā is, according to Yāqūt, a valley that belonged to Banū Sulaym, in which a battle between Banū Tha'laba and Banū Yarbū' took place. In al-Azdī's narrative, it is mentioned as a station on Khālid's desert route from Iraq to Syria. On al-Liwā, see Yāqūt, *Mu'jam al-buldān*, IV, 366–367.

265 Quṣam is a place in the Syrian desert. According to Yāqūt, it belongs to Iraq (*min nawāḥī al-'Irāq*) and lies between al-Kūfa and Tadmur. In contrast, it is identified in al-Azdī's narrative as an oasis, the eastern part of which belonged to Banū Mashja'a, whereas its western part belonged to the people of al-Ghūṭa, i.e. it seems to be located closer to Damascus. On Quṣam, see Yāqūt, *Mu'jam al-buldān*, IV, 124.

266 Al-Ghūṭa refers to the irrigated area of gardens and fields surrounding the city of Damascus. In al-Azdī's narrative, a number of raids launched by the Muslim troops on the region are mentioned. On al-Ghūṭa, see *EI*², s.v. Ghūṭa (N. Elisséeff).

He [=the narrator, al-Mustanīr b. Zubayr al-Mashjaʿī] said: And Yaʿbūb b. ʿAmr [b. Ḍarīs al-Mashjaʿī][267] marched with him [=Khālid], who took the route to al-Ghadīr[268], then to Dhāt al-Ṣanamayn[269]. Then he [=Khālid] marched out to al-Ghūṭa, where he raided them [=the people of al-Ghūṭa], killed whomever he wanted [to kill] and gained [some] spoils. So the enemy\\162 entered Damascus and fortified [the place].

Abū ʿUbayda, who was staying at al-Jābiya, came and met him [=Khālid], descended with him on al-Ghūṭa and besieged the people of Damascus.

Al-Ḥusayn b. Ziyād [al-Ramlī] reported to us on the authority of Abū Ismāʿīl Muḥammad b. ʿAbdallāh [al-Azdī], who said: Furthermore, al-Ḥārith b. Kaʿb related to me on the authority of Qays b. Abī Ḥāzim, who said: Khālid marched out [of Iraq] with about 200 men from Bajīla[270], most of whom belonged to Aḥmas[271]. A similar good number from Ṭayyiʾ also marched out with Khālid, who was accompanied by about 300 men of the Emigrants and the Supporters, too. His [=Khālid's] companions who entered Syria with him were 850 men. Only the mighty [people] who were intent and discerning joined him, because he was assigning them tasks which, as far as they knew, only the strong and the gallant could accomplish. He marched with us until he [and we] passed by Arak[272], besieged and raided its

267 Al-Yaʿbūb b. ʿAmr b. Ḍarīs al-Mashjaʿī is listed neither in Ibn Saʿd, al-Bukhārī, Ibn ʿAsākir nor in any other biographical work we could access. Ibn Ḥajar mentions a *Yaʿqūb* b. ʿAmr with reference to al-Azdī's *Futūḥ al-Shām*, in which he is correctly said to have witnessed the Battle of Ajnādayn and have killed seven Byzantines. According to ʿUqla and Banī Yāsīn, he is the great-grandfather of the transmitter al-Mustanīr b. Zubayr b. Aflaḥ b. Yaʿbūb b. ʿAmr b. Ḍarīs al-Mashjaʿī (see al-Azdī, *Futūḥ al-Shām. Ed. ʿUqla/Banī Yāsīn*, 29). In al-Azdī's narrative, he is said to have fought with Khālid in al-Ghūṭa, Bosra and Ajnādayn, where he killed seven Byzantines. On al-Yaʿbūb, see Ibn Ḥajar, *Al-iṣāba. Ed. al-Baghawī*, VI, 708 (no. 9431).

268 Al-Ghadīr (lit. "the Pond") is most likely a watering place between Quṣam and Dhāt al-Ṣanamayn. Yāqūt mentions several places called al-Ghadīr, none of which fits the context here. In al-Azdī's narrative, al-Ghadīr is mentioned as a station on Khālid's route from Iraq to Syria, from which he proceeded to Dhāt al-Ṣanamayn. On al-Ghadīr, see Yāqūt, *Muʿjam al-buldān*, III, 776–777.

269 Dhāt al-Ṣanamayn (lit. "the One with the Two Idols") is most likely identified as al-Ṣanamān, a village between Damascus and Ḥawrān, i.e. the region south of Damascus with the major city of Bosra, according to Yāqūt. In al-Azdī's narrative, Dhāt al-Ṣanamayn is mentioned as a station on Khālid's route from Iraq to Syria, from which he proceeded to al-Ghūṭa. On al-Ṣanamān, see Yāqūt, *Muʿjam al-buldān*, III, 429.

270 Bajīla is a Northern Arabian tribe that was a subtribe of Anmār. In al-Azdī's narrative, Bajīla is mentioned once when 200 men from Bajīla are said to have joined Khālid on his desert route to Syria. On Bajīla, see *EI*^{2}, s.v. Badjīla (W. Watt).

271 Aḥmas is a Northern Arabian tribe that was a subtribe of Bajīla. In al-Azdī's narrative, it is said that 200 men from Bajīla, most of whom belonged to Aḥmas, joined Khālid on his desert route to Syria. On Aḥmas, see *EI*^{2}, s.v. Badjīla (W. Watt).

272 Arak is a small fertile city in the steppe of Aleppo, not far from Tadmur, according to Yāqūt. In al-Azdī's narrative, a raid launched by Khālid on Arak is mentioned and is said to have ended in a siege and a peace treaty. On Arak, see Yāqūt, *Muʿjam al-buldān*, I, 210 (s.v. Arak).

people and took [their] possessions. So its people fortified [the place], but he [=Khālid] did not leave them until they made peace with him.

Al-Ḥusayn b. Ziyād [al-Ramlī] reported to us on the authority of Abū Ismāʿīl Muḥammad b. ʿAbdallāh [al-Azdī], who said: Furthermore, Abū Jahḍam [al-Azdī] related to me on the authority of ʿAbd al-Raḥmān b. al-Salīk [al-Fazārī][273] on the authority of ʿAbdallāh b. Qurṭ al-Thumālī, who said: He [=Khālid] also passed by Tadmur[274] whose people fortified [the place] against him. So he surrounded them on all sides and [tried to] seize them from all directions. However, he\\163 could not catch them and, therefore, turned away from them. Their grand men held a meeting and said: "We are only of the opinion that those people who had descended upon you [and us] are those about whom we were arguing that they would triumph over us. Therefore, let them enter [the city] and make peace with them". So they sent for Khālid b. al-Walīd, allowed him to enter [the city] and made peace with him. When Khālid had turned away from them [the first time], he said to them: "I swear by God that even if you were in the clouds, we would force you [to come] down [for a fight] and we would triumph over you. We came to you because we knew that you would allow us to enter the city. And if you did not make peace with me this time and even if I turned away from this destination, I would come back to you and would not turn away from you until I had killed your fighters (*muqātila*) and captured your offspring". Then he [=Khālid b. al-Walīd] had turned and gone away. Thereafter, they sent for him and he returned to them. [Then] they allowed him to enter [the city] and made peace with him.[275]

Al-Ḥusayn b. Ziyād [al-Ramlī] reported to us on the authority of Abū Ismāʿīl Muḥammad b. ʿAbdallāh [al-Azdī], who said: Furthermore, Yazīd b. Yazīd b. Jābir related to me on the authority of ʿAmr b. Muḥṣan b. Surāqa b. ʿAbd al-Aʿlā b. Surāqa al-Azdī, who said: On his way Khālid passed by Ḥuwārīn[276], whose people became fearful of him. Most of them protected

273 ʿAbd al-Raḥmān b. al-Salīk al-Fazārī is listed neither in Ibn Saʿd, al-Bukhārī, Ibn ʿAsākir nor in any other biographical work we could access. ʿUqla and Banī Yāsīn found a reference to him in the *tarjama* of ʿAbdallāh b. Qurṭ where ʿAbd al-Raḥmān is mentioned as transmitting from the latter (see al-Azdī, *Futūḥ al-Shām. Ed. ʿUqla/Banī Yāsīn*, 162, n. 9 referring to al-Mizzī, *Tahdhīb al-kamāl*, XV, 444). In al-Azdī's narrative, he is mentioned as a transmitter of several traditions.

274 Tadmur is a city in the Syrian desert located ca. 145 km east of Ḥimṣ and ca. 240 km west of the middle Euphrates. In al-Azdī's narrative, it is mentioned as a station on Khālid's way to Syria. Khālid besieged Tadmur, but was unable to conquer it. On Tadmur, see *EI*[2], s.v. Tadmur (C. Bosworth).

275 The second expression "They allowed him to enter [the city] and made peace with him" is an exact repetition of what was mentioned some lines before. Hence, we consider it to be a transmission error.

276 Ḥuwārīn is neither listed in Yāqūt's geographical dictionary nor in any other geographical work we could access. However, it is mentioned in al-Balādhurī's *Futūḥ al-buldān* and al-Ṭabarī's *Taʾrīkh*. Al-Balādhurī calls the place "Ḥuwārīn of Sanīr" (*Ḥuwārīn min Sanīr*) and describes it—as in al-Azdī's narrative—as a station on Khālid's route from Iraq to

themselves and fortified [the place] against him. However, he raided them, drove the[ir] possessions [=the livestock] away, killed the[ir] men and remained standing [ready to fight] against them for [several] days. So they sent for those who were around them to reinforce them. They [=their neighbours] sent them reinforcements from two places: Some came to them from Baalbek[277], which is part of the land of Damascus, and some from Bosra[278], which is the [main] city of Ḥawrān[279] and [also] a part of the land of Damascus. When Khālid saw the two groups of reinforcements approaching, he moved out [of his encampment], lined the people [=the Muslims] up, moved [forward]\\164 with 200 horsemen and launched an attack on the people of Baalbek, who were [numbering] more than 2,000 men. He made them crash into one another and killed a great many of them. They stood against him only for a short while, then they retreated and entered the city [of Ḥuwārīn]. Then he galloped with his companions in commotion [towards the second group of reinforcements]. When he stood opposite to the reinforcements from the people of Bosra, who were certainly [numbering] more than 2,000, he reviewed them and then launched an attack on them. They were able to stand firm against him only for a [short] while (*fuwāqan*)[280] until he defeated them and they [=the people of Bosra] entered the city [of Ḥuwārīn, too]. [Then] the people of the city came out and pelted the Muslims with arrows. So Khālid b. al-Walīd launched an attack on them, forced them back into the city and they were defeated [for the moment]. Hence, Khālid turned away from them on that day. However, the people of the city came out to fight him the next day. So Khālid launched an[other] attack on them and defeated them [again]. When they [eventually] saw that they were helpless and powerless against him, they made peace with him.

Syria. According to al-Balādhurī, Khālid raided Ḥuwārīn and defeated some Byzantine troops which had come as reinforcements to Ḥuwārīn from Baalbek and Bosra. Al-Ṭabarī says that Ḥuwārīn is a Syrian village close to Ḥimṣ in which Yazīd b. Muʿāwiya died at the beginning of the year 64/683. On Ḥuwārīn, see al-Balādhurī, *Futūḥ al-buldān*, 112 and al-Ṭabarī, *Taʾrīkh*, II, 427, l. 20.

277 Baalbek (Baʿlabakk) is located in the Bekaa valley, a high plain between the mountains of Lebanon to the west and the Anti-Lebanon mountain range to the east. In al-Azdī's narrative, two raids in the surroundings of Baalbek are mentioned. In addition, Abū ʿUbayda granted its inhabitants a peace treaty. On Baalbek, see *EI*[2], s.v. Baʿlabakk (J. Sourdel-Thomine).

278 Bosra (Buṣrā) is located ca. 130 km south of Damascus in southern Syria. In al-Azdī's narrative, it is mentioned as the main city of Ḥawrān. In addition, a battle between Khālid and al-Durunjār occurred there, after which the inhabitants of the city asked Khālid for peace. On Bosra, see *EI*[2], s.v. Boṣrā (A. Abel).

279 Ḥawrān is the basaltic and fertile region that separates (modern) Syria from Transjordan. Its borders to the north are the lava bed and the Damascus plain (*marj*), to the east the volcanic massif of Jabal al-Durūz, to the south al-Yarmūk river and to the west the Jawlān. In al-Azdī's narrative, the region is referred to as "the land of Ḥawrān" that is part of "the land of Damascus". On Ḥawrān, see *EI*[2], s.v. Ḥawrān (D. Sourdel).

280 The Arabic term "*fuwāqan*" refers to a period of time equivalent to the interval between two milkings or sucklings of a she-camel. On this term, see Lane, *Lexicon*, s.v. *fuwāqan*.

Al-Ḥusayn b. Ziyād [al-Ramlī] reported to us on the authority of Abū Ismāʿīl Muḥammad b. ʿAbdallāh [al-Azdī], who said: Furthermore, ʿAmr b. Muḥṣan said: An infidel from among the people of Ḥuwārīn, who was one of their bravest and toughest [men], related to me [the following], saying: I swear by God that we went out [to fight] against Khālid a day after we had received reinforcements from the people of Baalbek and from those of Bosra.\\165 We went out to [meet] him [and his unit] and we were ten times larger in number than Khālid and his companions. He [=the narrator, the infidel] said: No sooner had we drawn near to them than they stormed towards us with [their] swords as if they were lion[s], defeating us in a shameful way and killing us fiercely. So we no longer went out to [meet] them until we made peace with them. I [=the narrator, the infidel] saw among us a man whom we consider [equal in strength] to 1,000 men and who used to say: "If I see their commander, I will certainly kill him". He [=the narrator, the infidel] said: When he saw Khālid, his companions said to him: "That is Khālid, the commander of those people". He [=the narrator, the infidel] said: Then the [strong] infidel attacked him and we were hoping that, on account of his might and valour, he would kill him. Just as he drew near to him, he [=the narrator, the infidel] said, Khālid promptly hit his horse and rushed it faster towards him. He [=the narrator, the infidel] said: Whenever Khālid (r.) is in war, whoever looks at him [seems] as if he becomes swollen [with fear], thrilled and panicked [by the sight of his fight]. Then he [=Khālid] confronted the [strong] infidel, unsheathed his sword across his face, struck him and removed half of his face, then cut his head off and killed him. He [=the narrator, the infidel] said: We were defeated in a shameful way until we entered our city [decimated]. Our only concern was peace and thus we made peace with them [=Khālid and his men].

[Section IV: Conquests and battles in Syria]

The battle of Bosra and [the fight against] its people

Al-Ḥusayn b. Ziyād [al-Ramlī] reported to us on the authority of Abū Ismāʿīl Muḥammad b. ʿAbdallāh [al-Azdī], who said: Furthermore, al-Ḥārith b. Kaʿb related to me on the authority of Qays b. Abī Ḥāzim, who said: I was with Khālid b. al-Walīd when he passed by [central] Syria[281] and proceeded until he encamped at Bosra, which belonged to the land of Ḥawrān and was its [main] city. When we settled\\166 and encamped [there], al-Durunjār[282],

281 The Arabic original mentions "al-Shām" here, which might also refer in this case to "Dimashq al-Shām", i.e. Damascus.

282 Al-Durunjār refers to several Byzantine commanders and is treated as a person's name in al-Azdī's narrative. In fact, the term is derived from the Greek "*droungarios*" or "*drouggarios*" which was originally applied to a commander of a cavalry unit that was established *ad hoc*, but in the early 7th century it referred to a commander of several cavalry

together with 5,000 of the Byzantine horsemen, marched out [of Bosra] and proceeded towards us. He and his companions never thought that we would be within their reach. Khālid came out [of the encampment] and lined us up. He placed Rāfiʿ b. ʿAmr al-Ṭāʾī in command of our right flank, Ḍirār b. al-Azwar[283] in command of our left flank and ʿAbd al-Raḥmān b. Ḥanbal al-Jumaḥī in command of the infantry. He also divided his cavalry in half, placing al-Musayyab b. Najaba[284] in command of one half and another man from Bakr b. Wāʾil who was with him—he [=Khālid] did not mention his name [to me]—in command of the other half. I [=the narrator, Qays b. Abī Ḥāzim] thought that he was Madhʿūr b. ʿAdī al-ʿIjlī, who moved with Khālid b. al-Walīd from Iraq to Syria. Thereafter, he [=Madhʿūr b. ʿAdī al-ʿIjlī] went to Miṣr[285], where his home is still well-known today.

He [=the narrator, Qays b. Abī Ḥāzim] said: When Khālid divided the cavalry [in half], he ordered both [parts] of it to ascend [to an elevated spot] above the people [=the Byzantines] on the[ir] right and on the[ir] left and then surge down upon them [=the Byzantines]. He [=the narrator, Qays b. Abī Ḥāzim] said: They hurried up and did so. He [=the narrator, Qays b. Abī Ḥāzim] said: Then Khālid ordered those who were with him to march towards the centre [of the Byzantine army]. So we marched towards them and I swear by God that we were [numbering] only 850 men in addition to 400 men from [Banū] Mashjaʿa, [the subtribe] of Quḍāʿa, whom Yaʿbūb [b. ʿAmr b. Ḍarīs al-Mashjaʿī], one of their [tribes]men, had brought to us. Thus, we were [numbering] more than 1,200 men.\\167

---

subunits (*banda*), each of which had its own (sub-) commander (*komes*). In al-Azdī's narrative, one al-Durunjār is said to be the Byzantine commander of Bosra who marched out against Khālid. Another al-Durunjār was sent by Heraclius with reinforcements to the inhabitants of Damascus. Two more al-Durunjārs are said to have reached Baalbek but did not continue to Damascus. Then a further al-Durunjār was the commander of Fiḥl who attacked the Muslims in the lands of the River Jordan. And an additional al-Durunjār was the commander of the left flank of the Byzantines in the Battle of al-Yarmūk. He is described as having belonged to the Byzantines' elite and as a pious man. Hence, he foresaw the Byzantines' defeat in the Battle of al-Yarmūk and wanted his head to be wrapped in order not to face the Muslims. In the end, he was killed in that battle. On *drouggarios*, see de Goeje, *Mémoire sur le Fotouho's-Scham*, 25, n. 2; Haldon, *Warfare*, 107–111.

283 Ḍirār's full name is Abū al-Azwar Ḍirār b. al-Azwar b. Mālik b. Aws al-Asadī (n.d.). In al-Azdī's narrative, he is depicted as being positioned by Khālid in command of the cavalry's left flank in the Battle of Bosra. On Ḍirār, see al-Bukhārī, *Al-taʾrīkh al-kabīr*, II-2, 339 (no. 3050) and Ibn ʿAsākir, *TMD*, XXIIII, 378–392.

284 Al-Musayyab's full name is al-Musayyab b. Najaba b. Rabīʿa al-Fazārī (d. 65/684–685). In al-Azdī's narrative, he is associated with Bakr b. Wāʾil and is depicted as being positioned by Khālid in command of half of the cavalry to fight against al-Durunjār at Bosra. On al-Musayyab, see Ibn Saʿd, *Kitāb al-ṭabaqāt*, VI, 150–151 and Ibn Ḥajar, *Al-iṣāba. Ed. al-Baghawī*, VI, 297 (no. 8429).

285 Miṣr was the capital city of the land of Egypt located on the eastern bank of the Nile and south-west of later Cairo (al-Qāhira). In al-Azdī's narrative, Miṣr is mentioned once in reference to Madhʿūr b. ʿAdī al-ʿIjlī's home there. On Miṣr, see *EI*^{2}, s.v. Miṣr (A. Wensinck et al.).

He [=the narrator, Qays b. Abī Ḥāzim] said: We were thinking [at that time that] it did not matter to Khālid whether the number of the Polytheists was large or small, because nothing has ever filled his breast [with fear] of them. He also has never cared whichever of them he would face, due to his daring [attitude] towards them, his fervour and his courage. When we approached them, they started to attack us and launched two fierce attacks on us, but we did not abandon our positions. Then Khālid shouted out in an orotund, husky and loud voice, saying: "O adherents of Islam, [display] toughness, [display] toughness, and launch, may God have mercy upon you, an attack on them. For if you fight them, reckoning and seeking [in doing] so the sake of God, they will not be able to stand against you [even] for a short while". Then Khālid launched an attack on them and so did we, together with him. I swear by God, with whom no other deity is associated, that hardly had they stood against us for a [short] while when they were defeated. We killed a great many of them during this battle. Then we pursued them in order to drive them away, assault them, strike their flank, separate them from their companions and kill them. We continued doing so until we reached the city of Bosra, which is the [main] city of Ḥawrān. Then they [=the inhabitants] shut its gates and fortified [the place] against us. Then they sent the offerings (*aswāq*)[286] out to us. So we made peace with the people of Bosra, who welcomed the Muslims whole heartedly. They solicited peace from us and thus we made peace with them. Then Khālid marched out [of the city] immediately and raided some people from Ghassān[287] who were [residing] close to Marj Rāhiṭ[288], killing and capturing a number of them. We made peace with their [=Ghassān's] common people and they embraced Islam.

Al-Ḥusayn b. Ziyād [al-Ramlī] reported to us on the authority of Abū Ismā'īl Muḥammad b. 'Abdallāh [al-Azdī], who said: Furthermore, al-Mustanīr b.

286 The Arabic term "*aswāq*" is the plural of two singular forms: "*Sūqa*" (lit. "giving") and "*sūq*" (lit. "merchandise"). In our translation, we go for the former meaning, because it fits the context more than the latter. On both forms, see Lane, *Lexicon*, s.v. *sūq* and *sūqa*.

287 Ghassān is a Southern Arabian tribe that was a subtribe of Azd. In al-Azdī's narrative, Ghassān is depicted as an enemy of the Muslims, the victim of some raids launched by Khālid near Marj Rāhiṭ, where its members were killed, captured and forced to make peace with him. Then these members of Ghassān embraced the new faith and are mentioned twice as having supported the Muslims in the Battle of Fiḥl and the Battle of al-Yarmūk, where they were positioned on the left flank. In addition, two individual figures belonged to Ghassān: (a) Abū al-Khazraj al-Ghassānī, who transmitted a tradition about his mother, who was captured by Khālid and who wanted her husband back only after his embrace of the new faith and (b) the scribe of the manuscript of *Futūḥ al-Shām*, who is said to have been called Muḥammad b. Ibrāhīm al-Ghassānī. On Ghassān, see *EI*², s.v. Ghassān (I. Shahīd).

288 Marj Rāhiṭ is the northeastern part of a semicircular plain (*marj*) located between al-Ghūṭa around Damascus and the open desert in the east. In al-Azdī's narrative, Marj Rāhiṭ is mentioned once in the statement that Khālid b. al-Walīd fought against some Ghassānids there after he had conquered Bosra. On Marj Rāhiṭ, see *EI*², s.v. Marj Rāhiṭ (N. Elisséeff).

Zubayr b. Aflaḥ b. Yaʿbūb b. ʿAmr b. Ḍarīs al-Mashjaʿī related to me:\\168 Muḥammad[289] said: Furthermore, Abū al-Khazraj al-Ghassānī[290] related to me, saying: My mother was one of those captives. He [=the narrator, Abū al-Khazraj al-Ghassānī] said: When she saw the religion of the Muslims, their [faithful] guidance, their righteousness and their decency, Islam fell into her heart and she embraced it. He [=the narrator, Abū al-Khazraj al-Ghassānī] said: My father searched for her among the captives and recognised her. So he came to the Muslims and said: "O adherents of Islam, I am your brother, I am a Muslim man and I came to you as a Muslim. And this is my wife, whom you have captured. If you decide to keep a bond with me, maintain my right, protect me and return my wife (*ahl*) to me, do it". His wife had already embraced Islam and she excelled at it. The Muslims said to her: "What do you say about your husband? He came to take you back and he [claims that he] is a Muslim". She said: "If he is a Muslim, I will return to him; but if he is not, I do not need him [anymore] and I will never go back to him". Then they delivered her to him.

Al-Ḥusayn b. Ziyād [al-Ramlī] reported to us on the authority of Abū Ismāʿīl Muḥammad b. ʿAbdallāh [al-Azdī], who said: Furthermore, Yazīd b. Yazīd b. Jābir related to me, saying: When Khālid entered al-Ghūṭa and passed through a defile (*thaniyya*), he crossed it holding a white flag called "al-ʿUqāb". Since [the day] he crossed that defile, it has been called "Thaniyyat al-ʿUqāb"[291].

Then Khālid b. al-Walīd proceeded until he stayed in a monastery known as "Khālid's Monastery", which was named after him [and remains known as such] until today. He stayed in this monastery, which is next to the Eastern Gate [of Damascus]. Abū ʿUbayda b. al-Jarrāḥ proceeded from al-Jābiya [to Damascus] until he encamped at al-Jābiya Gate. Then both [=Khālid and Abū ʿUbayda] launched raids on\\169 al-Ghūṭa and on other [places]. While they were doing so, Wardān[292], the commander of Ḥimṣ, proceeded

289 Muḥammad is probably Abū Ismāʿīl Muḥammad b. ʿAbdallāh al-Azdī. On the basis of the same identification, Mourad observes in this chain the problem that there must have been an intermediate transmitter. With the help of Ibn ʿAsākir's *TMD*, he identifies this intermediate transmitter as al-Musayyab b. al-Zubayr (see Mourad, *al-Azdī*, 590).

290 Abū al-Khazraj al-Ghassānī is an early Islamic figure. In al-Azdī's narrative, he is mentioned as a transmitter of one tradition who narrates the story about his mother, who was captured at Bosra and was set free for the sake of her husband, i.e. Abū al-Khazraj's father, who had also embraced the new faith. On Abū al-Khazraj, see Ibn ʿAsākir, *TMD*, LXVI, 105 (no. 8415) where he is listed as Abū *al-Jarrāḥ* (rather than *al-Khazraj*) al-Ghassānī. This variation is most likely due to a scribal error.

291 Thaniyyat al-ʿUqāb (lit. "the Eagle's Pass") is a mountainous pass north of Damascus on the way to Ḥimṣ. In al-Azdī's narrative, it is mentioned twice as part of al-Ghūṭa. On Thaniyyat al-ʿUqāb, see *EI*^{2}, s.v. Marj Rāhiṭ (N. Elisséeff) and Yāqūt, *Muʿjam al-buldān*, I, 936 (where a similar etymological narrative is quoted from al-Balādhurī).

292 Wardān could not be identified because only his first name, not his full name, is mentioned. According to Kaegi, the name Wardān "is strikingly similar" to the Syriac form "B[R]YRDN", both of which "could represent a popular Armenian name "Vardan" […],

with a large group of the Byzantines towards both of them, desiring to seize Shuraḥbīl b. Ḥasana at Bosra.

He [=the narrator, Yazīd b. Yazīd b. Jābir] said: Khālid and Abū ʿUbayda learned that some of the Byzantine groups had set up camp in Ajnādayn[293] and that the people of the region (*balad*) and the Arab Christians who passed by it [=Ajnādayn] rushed to them. They [=Khālid and Abū ʿUbayda] received [this] terrifying piece of news while they were standing and fighting against some people [in the land of Damascus]. They both met and consulted each other about it. Abū ʿUbayda said to Khālid: "I am of the opinion that you [should] march [out] until you reach Shuraḥbīl b. Ḥasana before the enemies, who committed themselves to [reach] him[294], do. If we assemble, we will all march [together] to them until we meet him". Khālid said to him: "The Byzantine groups are there in Ajnādayn and if we march to Shuraḥbīl b. Ḥasana, our enemy will rush in hot pursuit of us. Rather, I am of the opinion that we [should] commit ourselves to [reach] their generality and send [a letter] to Shuraḥbīl b. Ḥasana to warn him about the march of the enemy [=Wardān and his unit] towards him and to order him to meet us in Ajnādayn. [I am also of the opinion] that we send [a letter] to Yazīd b. Abī Sufyān to warn him about the march of the enemy towards him and to order him to meet us in Ajnādayn[, too,] and that we send [another letter] to ʿAmr b. al-ʿĀṣ [ordering him] to meet us in Ajnādayn[, too]. Then we [will] all fight against our enemy".\\170 Abū ʿUbayda said: "This is a sound opinion. Carry it out with God's blessing[s] and we ask God for His blessing[s]".

Al-Ḥusayn b. Ziyād [al-Ramlī] reported to us on the authority of Abū Ismāʿīl Muḥammad b. ʿAbdallāh [al-Azdī], who said: Furthermore, Muḥammad b. Yūsuf related to me on the authority of Thābit [al-Bunānī] on the authority of Sahl b. Saʿd [al-Anṣārī], who said: Khālid b. al-Walīd rose [and stood] before the people after he had decided to set out from Damascus to Ajnādayn and had learned that the Byzantines had gathered a group against him there. So he gathered the people and rose [to speak to them]. He praised and thanked God, blessed and saluted the Prophet (ṣ.) and then said: "Regarding the matter at hand: I have learned that a group of the Byzantines set up camp in Ajnādayn and that they sought help from a few people of the region and asked them for support against us. [For] they considered those who were with them [too] small in number, aiming shamefully and deceitfully for

because Heraclius made frequent use of Armenian commanders [...]" (see Kaegi, *Byzantium*, 12). In al-Azdī's narrative, he is mentioned as the commander of Ḥimṣ, who proceeded with a large troop of the Byzantines, seeking to attack Shuraḥbīl in Bosra, and as being appointed by the Byzantine troops as commander in the Battle of Ajnādayn.

293 Ajnādayn (lit. "[Place of the] Two Armies") is a site of a battle in Palestine, which was located between Ramla and Bayt Djibrin. In a-Azdī's narrative, the first major battle between the Muslim and Byzantine troops took place at Ajnādayn on 28th of Jumādā I in 13 [=30 July 634]. On Ajnādayn, see *EI. Three*, s.v. Ajnādayn (K. Athamina).

294 On a similar, but archaic, meaning of this expression, see Lane, *Lexicon*, s.v. *ṣamada*.

an increase [of men]. I swear by God that He will certainly turn the evil fortune against them and will kill them all if He wants to. Commit yourselves to [joining] us [in reaching] them, for I am writing to Yazīd b. Abī Sufyān to come with the Muslims, who accompany him, from [the land of] al-Balqā'[295] to me and to 'Amr b. al-'Āṣ to come from the land of Palestine to me. I am also writing the same to Shuraḥbīl b. Ḥasana".

[At that time] Shuraḥbīl was in Bosra and he was one [man] to whom Abū Bakr (r.) assigned the command, in addition to Yazīd and 'Amr b. al-'Āṣ, when he dispatched [all of] them to Syria. They were the commanders to whom he [=Abū Bakr] said: "If a war should bring you [all] together [in one place], the [chief] commander of the people would be Abū 'Ubayda".\\171 Abū 'Ubayda had remained their [chief] commander until Abū Bakr (r.) dispatched Khālid b. al-Walīd to them. At that time, 'Umar b. al-Khaṭṭāb disliked Abū Bakr's (r.) appointment of Khālid as the commander of Abū 'Ubayda. However, Abū Bakr (r.) did not listen to him [='Umar] and wrote [the following letter] to Abū 'Ubayda b. al-Jarrāḥ (r.):

In the name of God, the Merciful, the Compassionate. Regarding the matter at hand: I assigned Khālid the task of fighting the Byzantines in Syria. So do not disagree with him, listen to him and obey his command. I appointed him as your [chief] commander although I know that you are better than he. However, I think that he has a discerning mind in war, which you do not have. May God show us and [show] you the paths of guidance. May God's peace and mercy be upon you.

The battle of Ajnādayn

He [=the narrator] said: Khālid was a blessed leader, well-minded, well-tested, discerning in war and always triumphant. He was part of what God had arranged for the Muslims in that respect. So Khālid was in charge of the people's cause. When he wanted to depart from the land of Damascus to [meet] the Byzantines who had gathered in Ajnādayn, he wrote [and sent] the same letter [in three copies] to the [above-mentioned] commanders. [The letter reads]:

In the name of God, the Merciful, the Compassionate. Regarding the matter at hand: Some of the Byzantine groups, neither large in number nor powerful, set up camp in Ajnādayn. God will certainly shatter them, exterminate them and turn the circle of evil against them. I departed\\172 to [meet] them on the [same] day I dispatched my messenger [with this letter] to you. When he comes to you, rush to your enemy, may God have mercy upon

295 Al-Balqā' encompasses the region of a limestone plateau between Wādī al-Zarqā' and Wādī al-Mūjib in the middle part of Transjordan with 'Ammān, Ḥusbān and al-Ṣalt as its main towns. In al-Azdī's narrative, it is usually referred to as "the land of al-Balqā'" and contrasted with the adjacent "arable lands of the River Jordan". On al-Balqā', see *EI*^{2}, s.v. al-Balḳā' (J. Sourdel-Thomine).

you, with the best equipment and the sincerest intention. May God double your rewards and take the burdens off your shoulders [=forgive your sins]. May God's peace and mercy be upon you.

He sent the copies [of the letters] with the common people of Syria (*anbāṭ al-Shām*), who were accompanying the Muslims to be their spies and their foot-messengers (*fuyūj*)[296]. The Muslims were gifting and rewarding them.

He [=the narrator] said: Khālid sent for the messenger whom he dispatched to Shuraḥbīl b. Ḥasana and said: "How [well] do you know the way?" He said: "[Very well because] I am used to showing people the way". He [=Khālid] said: "Deliver this letter to him, warn him that the [Byzantine] army unit, as we were informed, wants [to march towards] him, then guide him and his companions [back], but take a different route from that of the enemy [=Wardān's unit] that had departed towards him. And hurry to him so that he comes to us in Ajnādayn [quickly]". He said: "Yes". The messenger then set out to Shuraḥbīl b. Ḥasana. Another messenger set out to ʿAmr b. al-ʿĀṣ and a [third one] to Yazīd b. Abī Sufyān. Khālid and Abū ʿUbayda marched out with the people [=the Muslims] to the people of Ajnādayn. On that day, the Muslims were rushing to them daringly.

When they departed and left, nothing alerted them except seeing the people of Damascus [moving] in their tracks in order to pursue them. They [=the people of Damascus] caught up with Abū ʿUbayda, who was [in the unit] at the rear of the people [=the Muslims]. When Abū ʿUbayda saw that they had caught up with him and surrounded him, while he was accompanied by about 200 of his companions and the Byzantines were accompanied by a large number of the people of Damascus, he fought them fiercely. Khālid received news [about this] while he was [situated] at the vanguard of the people,\\173 unaware of what Abū ʿUbayda was facing. They [=the messengers] told him about it while he was among the horsemen and the cavalry. Khālid then turned back and so did the people, together with him. Khālid rushed with the cavalry and the men of might, proceeding at a gallop, until they reached Abū ʿUbayda and his companions, who were beset by the Byzantines who were fighting them fiercely. Khālid launched an attack with his cavalry on the Byzantines, hammered some of them against the others and fought them along a distance of three miles. They [=the Byzantines and the people of Damascus] retreated until they entered Damascus.

Khālid turned away [from the battlefield], headed with the people for al-Jābiya and kept looking around and waiting for his companions to come to him. [Then] Khālid's messenger set out to [meet] Shuraḥbīl. The distance between him [=Shuraḥbīl] and the army unit that marched with Wardān from Ḥimṣ to him [=Shuraḥbīl] was only a day's march. It [=Wardān's army unit] drew near to him and Shuraḥbīl neither knew nor sensed their march towards him.

296 On this expression, see Lane, *Lexicon*, s.v. *fayj*.

Then the messenger delivered the letter to him, told him the news and urged him to depart. So he rose [and stood] before the people and said: "O people, depart to your [chief] commander, because he has headed towards the enemy of the Muslims in Ajnādayn. He wrote to me, ordering me to meet him there". Then he [=Shuraḥbīl] moved out with the people and the guide conducted them. The [Byzantine] army unit that had marched out in search of them learned about this and thus pursued them. The [following] letter came from the Byzantines who were in Ajnādayn to their commander [=Wardān], reading: "Come to us, for we will appoint you as our [chief] commander and we will fight with you against the Arabs until we cast them out of our lands". So he [=Wardān] pursued the Muslims [and Shuraḥbīl], hoping to exterminate them, to harm them and to strike one of their flank[s], thus causing damage to a party of the Muslims. He accelerated his march towards them, but he did not catch up with them. Shuraḥbīl and the Muslims who were with him reached Khālid [first].\\174 Wardān proceeded with those [men] who were with him and met the [other] Byzantine groups in Ajnādayn. Then they appointed him as their [chief] commander and so their situation improved. Yazīd b. Abī Sufyān proceeded until he met Khālid and Abū ʿUbayda. Then they marched [together] and set up camp in Ajnādayn. ʿAmr b. al-ʿĀṣ came with those Muslims who were with him and all the people [=the Muslims] gathered in Ajnādayn.

Abbān b. Saʿīd b. al-ʿĀṣ was engaged to Umm Abbān bt. ʿUtba [b. Rabīʿa[297]]. So he married her and slept with her (*dakhala ʿalayhā*) on Thursday [the wedding] night and also spent Friday night with her. The people [then] marched [out] on Saturday early morning [against the Byzantines].

Khālid b. al-Walīd came out [of his tent] and [told] Abū ʿUbayda to get off [his horse in order to command] the infantry. He [also] dispatched Muʿādh b. Jabal [to command] the right flank, Saʿīd b. ʿĀmir b. Ḥudhaym al-Qurashī [to command] the left flank and Saʿīd b. Zayd b. ʿAmr b. Nufayl [to command] the cavalry. Khālid proceeded to march through [the lines of] the people, not remaining in one place, but [went] inciting the people [everywhere]. He also gave the order to the Muslims' women to fasten their belts and to rise behind the people. They did so, supplicating God and asking Him for help. Whenever one of the Muslim men passed by them [in retreat], they lifted their children up to him and said to him: "Fight in defence of (*dūna*) your children and your women!"

He [=the narrator] said: Khālid proceeded, stopping at every tribe and every group and saying [to them]: "O servants of God, fear God and fight for God against whoever disbelieves in Him. Do not turn on your heels [=do not flee from the battlefield]. Do not wither as you face your enemy, but chase

297 Umm Abbān's full name is Umm Abbān bt. ʿUtba b. Rabīʿa bt. ʿAbd Shams al-ʿAbshamiyya (n.d.). In al-Azdī's narrative, she is mentioned as being married to Abbān b. Saʿīd b. al-ʿĀṣ and as spending with him only two nights before he got killed in the Battle of Ajnādayn. On Umm Abbān, see Ibn ʿAsākir, *TMD*, LXX, 197–199.

[them] daringly like a lion. You are free and noble. You have rejected the worldly life and thus deserve God's\\175 reward in the afterlife. Do not panic at the sight of their [=the Byzantines'] large number, for God is sending His punishment and torture down on them". Then he [=Khālid] said to the people: "O people, attack when I attack".

Al-Ḥusayn b. Ziyād [al-Ramlī] reported to us on the authority of Abū Ismāʿīl Muḥammad b. ʿAbdallāh [al-Azdī], who said: Furthermore, ʿAbd al-Malik b. Nawfal [b. Masāḥiq al-Qurashī] related to me on the authority of Abū Saʿīd al-Maqburī [something] concerning[298] Muʿādh b. Jabal, who said: "O Muslims, sell yourselves to God (ʿa.) on this day, for if you defeat them [=the Byzantines] today, you will possess these lands forever as [part of] the abode of Islam (*dār al-islām*), along with God's satisfaction and a great reward from Him (ʿa.)".

Khālid decided to fend them [=the Byzantines] off and to delay the fight until the noon prayer[s], when the winds blow. This was the time during which the Messenger of God (ṣ.) preferred to fight. But the Byzantines rushed to him [without delay] and launched two attacks on the Muslims, [one] on Muʿādh b. Jabal on the right [flank] and [another] on Saʿīd b. ʿĀmir [b. Ḥudhaym] on the left. However, none of them left [his position]. They [=the Byzantines] shot arrows at the Muslims. So Saʿīd b. Zayd b. ʿAmr b. Nufayl, [who was] ʿUmar b. al-Khaṭṭāb's (r.) [grand] cousin[299] and one of the toughest people, one of the early Emigrants and one of those ten to whom the Messenger of God (ṣ.) promised Paradise[300], called Khālid and said: "What shall we do with those infidels? They pelted us with arrows until the horses balked". Then Khālid came to the cavalry\\176 of the Muslims and said: "Attack, may God have mercy upon you, in the name of God". Then Khālid attacked them, and so did all the people. So they [=the Byzantines] could not stand against them for [more than] a while and thus they were seriously defeated. The Muslims killed them in every possible way and took possession of their encampment and whatever was therein.

298 Although the term "*ʿan*" is mostly understood in *isnāds* as "on the authority of", we render it in this case as "concerning" due to the long time gap between the two transmitters.

299 According to Lees, Saʿīd b. Zayd b. ʿAmr b. Nufayl was not ʿUmar b. al-Khaṭṭāb b. Nufayl's cousin, but his grand or second cousin. Hence, the Arabic text needs to be corrected here by adding another "*ibn*", i.e. "*wa-huwa ibn ibn ʿamm ʿUmar b. al-Khaṭṭāb*" (see al-Azdī, *Futūḥ al-Shām. Ed. Lees*, 78, n. 2).

300 The expression "*al-ʿashara al-mubashshara*" (lit. "the ten to whom the Messenger of God promised Paradise") refers to different lists mentioned in prophetical traditions in which ten of the most famous early Muslims were promised entry to Paradise for their exceptional status. In al-Azdī's narrative, out of these ten only Saʿīd b. Zayd is explicitly said to have belonged to this group. However, the remaining nine persons are also mentioned in the narrative. They are: Abū Bakr al-Ṣiddīq, ʿUmar b. al-Khaṭṭāb, ʿUthmān b. ʿAffān, ʿAlī b. Abī Ṭālib, Ṭalḥa b. ʿUbaydallāh, Zubayr b. al-ʿAwwām, ʿAbd al-Raḥmān b. ʿAwf, Saʿd b. Abī Waqqāṣ and Abū ʿUbayda b. al-Jarrāḥ. On this concept, see EI^2, s.v. al-ʿAshara al-Mubashshara (A. Wensinck).

An arrow stuck in Abbān b. Saʿīd [b. al-ʿĀṣ],[301] who had performed very well [in the battle] and had fought fiercely on that day in which his competence intensified and his [high] standing was known [to all]. Then an arrow stuck in him, but he plucked it out and wrapped his turban around it [=his wound]. His brethren carried him [to his tent] and he said to them: "Do not remove my turban from my wound, for if you removed it, my soul would follow it [=the turban]. I swear by God that I would love it to be a stone from al-Ḥumr [Mountain][302]—which is al-Summāq Mountain[303]". He died of it; God rest his soul. Then his wife, Umm Abbān bt. ʿUtba b. Rabīʿa, said: "Nothing could make me dispense with Abbān's two nights [which he had spent with me]".

Al-Yaʿbūb b. ʿAmr b. Ḍarīs al-Mashjaʿī killed seven Polytheists in Ajnādayn. He was very steadfast and tough. He was stabbed and they [=his companions] were hoping that he would recover from it [=the stab]. He remained alive for four or five days but then succumbed to it [=the stab wound]. So he asked Abū ʿUbayda to allow him to return to his family. If he recovered, he would come back to them [=the Muslims]. He [=Abū ʿUbayda] allowed him [to do this] and so he returned to his family but then died; God (t.) rest his soul. He was buried there [=in his family's home].

Salama b. Hishām al-Makhzūmī[304], Nuʿaym b. Ṣakhr b. ʿAdī[305] al-ʿAdawī, Hishām b. al-ʿĀṣ[306], the brother of ʿAmr b. al-ʿĀṣ al-Sahmī, Habbār b. Sufyān[307] and ʿAbdallāh b. ʿAmr b. al-Ṭufayl [b. ʿAmr b.] Dhī al-Nūr al-Azdī[308], then al-Dawsī, were also killed [in the battle]. They belonged to

301 As a reminder for the reader, Abbān b. Saʿīd is previously described as having married Umm Abbān (see above p. 126).

302 No exact information on the location of al-Ḥumr Mountain could be obtained. Yāqūt only mentions Jabal al-Khamr, which is also called Jabal Bayt al-Maqdis (see Yāqūt, *Muʿjam al-buldān*, II, 21). Furthermore, he claims that Jabal al-Ḥumr is near modern Shabwa in Yemen. However, it is unclear which of the two is meant here.

303 Al-Summāq Mountain (lit. "the Sumac Mountain") is a large mountainous area west of Aleppo. In al-Azdī's narrative, al-Summāq Mountain is mentioned only to identify al-Ḥumr Mountain. On al-Summāq Mountain, see Yāqūt, *Muʿjam al-buldān*, II, 21.

304 Salama's full name is Abū Hāshim Salama b. Hishām b. al-Mughīra b. ʿAbdallāh b. ʿUmar al-Makhzūmī (d. 14/635–636). In al-Azdī's narrative, he is mentioned as having been killed in the Battle of Ajnādayn. On Salama, see Ibn Saʿd, *Kitāb al-ṭabaqāt*, IV-1, 96–97.

305 Contrary to the edited text we read ʿAdī (instead of ʿUdayy). Nuʿaym b. Ṣakhr b. ʿAdī al-ʿAdawī al-Naḥḥām (n.d.) is identified as Nuʿaym b. ʿAbdallāh b. Luʾayy b. Ghālib al-Qurashī, who was an early Islamic figure. In al-Azdī's narrative, he is depicted as being killed in the Battle of Ajnādayn. On Nuʿaym, see Ibn ʿAsākir, *TMD*, LXII, 175–184 and Ibn Ḥajar, *Al-iṣāba. Ed. al-Baghawī*, VI, 499 (no. 8879).

306 Hishām's full name is Abū Maʿshar (or Abū Muṭīʿ) Hishām b. al-ʿĀṣ b. Wāʾil (n.d.). In al-Azdī's narrative, he is mentioned as a brother of ʿAmr b. al-ʿĀṣ and as one of the Muslims who were killed in the Battle of Ajnādayn. On Hishām, see Ibn Saʿd, *Kitāb al-ṭabaqāt*, IIII-1, 140–143.

307 Habbār's full name is Habbār b. Sufyān b. ʿAbd al-Asad b. Hilāl b. ʿAbdāllah (n.d.). In al-Azdī's narrative, he is mentioned as one of the Muslims who were killed in the Battle of Ajnādayn. On Habbār, see Ibn Saʿd, *Kitāb al-ṭabaqāt*, IIII-1, 100.

308 ʿAbdallāh b. ʿAmr b. al-Ṭufayl b. ʿAmr b. Dhī al-Nūr al-Azdī (d. 13/634–635) is the grandson of Dhū al-Nūr al-Ṭufayl, who died in Ajnādayn. In al-Azdī's narrative, he is depicted

the [renowned] Muslim horsemen and to the men of succour and toughness (*ahl al-najda wa-al-shidda*). They were [all] killed on that day; God rest their souls.\\177 The Muslims killed 3,000 of them [=the Byzantines] in the battle and pursued them, capturing and killing [more of] them [afterwards]. The remnants of the Byzantine army (*falal al-Rūm*) marched away and met up [with other units] in Jerusalem[309], Caesarea[310], Damascus and Ḥimṣ. They fortified [the places] in these great cities.

[Manuscript note: Part III]

[This is the end of the second part of this book. It is continued at the beginning of the third part by a letter from Khālid b. al-Walīd to Abū Bakr.]

In the name of God, the Merciful, the Compassionate.[311] Al-Shaykh al-Ḥāfiẓ Abū Isḥāq Ibrāhīm b. Saʿīd b. ʿAbdallāh al-Ḥabbāl reported to us: Abū al-ʿAbbās Munīr b. Aḥmad [b. al-Ḥasan al-Khashshāb] related to us, saying: Abū al-Ḥasan ʿAlī b. Aḥmad b. Isḥāq al-Baghdādī reported to us, by way of reading to the former: Abū al-ʿAbbās al-Walīd b. Ḥammād al-Ramlī related to us: Al-Ḥusayn b. Ziyād al-Ramlī related to us, saying: Abū Ismāʿīl [Muḥammad b. ʿAbdallāh al-Azdī] al-Baṣrī related to us, saying: Khālid b. al-Walīd wrote [the following letter] to Abū Bakr (r.) about God's (ʿa.) bestowal of victory upon him and upon the Muslims.\\178

In the name of God, the Merciful, the Compassionate. From Khālid b. al-Walīd, the Sword of God unsheathed against the Polytheists, to Abū Bakr, the servant of God and the successor of the Messenger of God (ṣ.); may God's peace be upon you. I praise, on your behalf, God with whom no other deity is associated. Regarding the matter at hand: O [Abū Bakr] al-Ṣiddīq, I inform you that we met the Polytheists, who mustered large and many groups against us in Ajnādayn. They lifted their crosses, unrolled their scriptures and swore by God not to retreat until they either exterminate us or expel us from their lands. We marched out to them, trusting in and relying on God. We stabbed them with [our] spears; then we turned to [our] swords with which we struck them. Then God (ʿa.) sent down his victory, fulfilled his promise and defeated the Unbelievers. We killed them in every direction,

---

as one of the "men of succour and toughness" and was killed in the Battle of Ajnādayn. In addition, his father ʿAmr b. al-Ṭufayl b. ʿAmr b. Dhī al-Nūr al-Azdī is also mentioned in the narrative. On ʿAbdallāh, see Ibn Ḥajar, *Al-iṣāba. Ed. al-Baghawī*, IV, 192 (no. 4849).

309 Jerusalem (Īliyāʾ) is located ca. 60 km east of the Mediterranean coast in the Judean Mountains. In al-Azdī's narrative, the city was besieged by the Muslim troops, but its inhabitants wanted to surrender it only to ʿUmar. Thereupon, ʿUmar came to Syria and granted them a peace treaty without entering the city. On Jerusalem in the Islamic period, see *EI²*, s.v. al-Ḳuds (S. D. Goitein et al.).

310 Caesarea (Qaysāriyya) was located on the Palestinian coast ca. 40 km south of Haifa. In al-Azdī's narrative, its conquest is narrated at length. Muʿāwiya b. Abī Sufyān was ordered by his brother Yazīd to besiege the city. The taking of the city marks the end of al-Azdī's narrative on the conquests of Syria. On Caesarea, see *EI²*, s.v. Ḳayṣariyya, Ḳayṣāriyya (M. Sharon).

311 This expression marks the beginning of the third part of the book, which, however, is not explicitly mentioned as such in the edition (and the manuscript Paris 1664).

in every defile and on every side (*ḥāʾiṭ*). So thank God for strengthening His religion, for humiliating His enemy and for His good deed[s] to his close friends (*awliyāʾ*). May God's peace and mercy be upon you.

Al-Ḥusayn b. Ziyād [al-Ramlī] reported to us on the authority of Abū Ismāʿīl Muḥammad b. ʿAbdallāh [al-Azdī], who said: Furthermore, Muḥammad b. Yūsuf related to me on the authority of Thābit [al-Bunānī] on the authority of Sahl b. Saʿd [al-Anṣārī], who said: The Battle of Ajnādayn was the first\\179 great battle in Syria. It occurred on Saturday 28 Jumādā I in 13 [=30 July 634] at midday. It took place twenty-four nights earlier than the death of Abū Bakr (r.).[312]

Khālid b. al-Walīd sent his letter with ʿAbd al-Raḥmān b. Ḥanbal al-Jumaḥī to Abū Bakr. He [=ʿAbd al-Raḥmān b. Ḥanbal al-Jumaḥī] proceeded with the letter until he reached Abū Bakr (r.). When Abū Bakr (r.) read it, he rejoiced over it, liked it and said: "Praise be to God who led the Muslims to victory and who gladdened me with that [victory]".

Khālid b. al-Walīd's march to Damascus and his siege of its people

Then Khālid b. al-Walīd ordered the people to march [back] to Damascus. He proceeded with the people [towards Damascus] until he set up camp there. He headed towards his monastery, where he used to stay, and set up camp there. This [monastery] is Khālid's Monastery, which has been named after him [and remains known as such] until today. It is one mile away from Damascus, in the vicinity of the Eastern Gate. Abū ʿUbayda (r.) also proceeded until he set up camp at al-Jābiya Gate, whereas Yazīd b. Abī Sufyān set up camp on another side of Damascus. They encircled it, gathered around it in large numbers and laid\\180 tight siege to its people.

ʿAbd al-Raḥmān b. Ḥanbal al-Jumaḥī arrived with a letter from Abū Bakr (r.) to Khālid b. al-Walīd. He also went to Yazīd b. Abī Sufyān, whom he used to join. Thereupon, Yazīd said to him: "Did you meet my father, Abū Sufyān [b. Ḥarb]?" He said: "Yes". He [=Yazīd] said: "Did he ask you about me?" He said: "Yes". He [=Yazīd] said: "What did you say to him?" He said: "I said to him: 'Yazīd is a firm and modest leader; he is very courageous and popular with [his] brethren; he is good company for whoever accompanies him; he exerts as much bounty as possible in [the course of] his Islam, his religion and his good manners'. Abū Sufyān [b. Ḥarb] then said: 'Just so must be the likes of him'. He [=ʿAbd al-Raḥmān b. Ḥanbal al-Jumaḥī] said: "He also asked me to write [back] to [inform] him about how our cause is faring and to inform him about our situation. I promised him that".

He [=the narrator] said: One day Khālid b. al-Walīd moved out with the Muslims and encircled the city of Damascus. They drew near to its gate[s]

312 Abū Bakr's death date is given later as 22 Jumādā II, 13 [=23 August 634]. See below p. 133.

where its people threw stones at them and pelted them with arrows from the roofs. ʿAbd al-Raḥmān b. Ḥanbal [al-Jumaḥī] then said [the following lines of verse]:

أبلغ أبا سفيان عنا فإننا
على خير حال كان جيش يكونها
وإنا على بابى دمشقة نرتمى
وقد حان من بابى دمشقة حينها

Inform Abū Sufyān [b. Ḥarb] that we are
In the best state an army has ever been in
And we are flinging [ourselves] at the two gates of Damascus;
At the two gates of Damascus, the time [for its conquest] has come.[313]

The Battle of Marj al-Ṣuffar

He [=the narrator] said: As the Muslims were fighting them [=the people of Damascus] in this way and were hoping to conquer their city, someone came to them [=the Muslims] and brought them the [latest] news, saying: "There is an army unit that was sent to you by the Emperor of the Byzantines and that has cast [its] shadow over you". Then Khālid rushed [to move out] with the people, maintaining the same [manner of] mobilisation and the same formation. He gave precedence to [saving] the chattels and the women, and Yazīd b. Abī Sufyān moved out with them. Khālid and Abū ʿUbayda stood behind the [departing] people. Then Khālid moved with the people towards that [Byzantine] army unit. Lo and behold,\\181 it was al-Durunjār who was dispatched in a company of 5,000 men of might and toughness by the Emperor of the Byzantines to help the people of Damascus. [Some of] the people of Damascus followed them [=al-Durunjār and his unit], but the Muslims turned to them. Then the men of might and toughness from among the people of Damascus moved out [of the city] to [face] them [=the Muslims] and a great many of the people of Ḥimṣ also joined them [=the people of Damascus] [in the fight]. They were more than 10,000 [in total]. When Khālid saw them, he mobilised his companions against them in the same manner he did on the battle-day of Ajnādayn. He was one of the most discerning people in war, also [gifted] with dignity, serenity and compassion for the Muslims as well as with sound judgement for them and [good] management of their cause. He positioned Muʿādh b. Jabal in command of his right flank, Hāshim b. ʿUtba [b. Abī Waqqāṣ] in command of his left flank, Saʿīd b. Zayd b. ʿAmr b. Nufayl in command of the cavalry and Abū ʿUbayda in command of the infantry. Khālid went [to the troops] and stopped at the first line [of fighters] in order to motivate the people. Then Khālid looked at the line from its beginning to its end.

313 Damascus is referred to in this poem as "Dimashqa", probably for poetic reasons.

The Byzantine cavalry launched an attack on Saʿīd b. Zayd [b. ʿAmr b. Nufayl] who was standing with a group of the Muslims on the right flank, exhorting them and praying to God. The Byzantines then attacked them, so Saʿīd faced them and fought them until he killed [some of them]. Then Muʿādh b. Jabal launched an attack on them and [also] defeated them on the [Muslims'] right flank. Khālid also attacked them on the left flank and defeated those [who were] in his vicinity. Together with the cavalry, Saʿīd b. Zayd [b. ʿAmr b. Nufayl] launched an attack on the great majority of them. God (ʿa.) then defeated them and killed a great many of them. [Then] the Muslims took hold of their encampment. The people [=the Muslims] returned triumphant [from their encampment] and killed them [=the Byzantines] in every [possible]\\182 way. The Polytheists fled aimlessly. Some of them entered the city of Damascus along with its people, others returned to Ḥimṣ while [the remainder] caught up with Caesar[314].

Al-Ḥusayn b. Ziyād [al-Ramlī] reported to us on the authority of Abū Ismāʿīl Muḥammad b. ʿAbdallāh [al-Azdī], who said: Furthermore, Yazīd b. Yazīd b. Jābir related to me on the authority of ʿAmr b. Muḥṣan: The number of their [men who were] killed in the battle on that day, i.e. on the battle-day of Marj al-Ṣuffar[315], was 500. They also killed and captured about another 500. Then the Muslims proceeded until they descended on the people of Damascus.

Al-Ḥusayn b. Ziyād [al-Ramlī] reported to us on the authority of Abū Ismāʿīl [Muḥammad b. ʿAbdallāh al-Azdī], who said: Furthermore, Yazīd b. Yazīd b. Jābir related to me on the authority of Abū Umāma [al-Bāhilī], who said: The interval between the battle-day of Ajnādayn and that of Marj al-Ṣuffar was twenty days. I calculated it and found it [to be] Thursday, 17 Jumādā II [in 13] [=18 August 634], four days earlier than the death of Abū Bakr (r.).[316]

Thereafter, all the people [=the Muslims] proceeded until they set up camp at Damascus. They then besieged its people and hemmed them in, [leaving] the people of Damascus incapable of fighting the Muslims. Khālid set up camp at the Eastern Gate at the location where he used to encamp. Abū ʿUbayda set up camp at al-Jābiya Gate, Yazīd b. Abī Sufyān at the other gate; and ʿAmr b. al-ʿĀṣ [also] at another gate.\\183 The Muslims raided whoever came out of the city. Whenever any [of them] gained a [piece of]

314 Caesar (Qayṣar) is the title of the Roman and Byzantine Emperors and is treated in Arabic as a proper name. In al-Azdī's narrative, Caesar refers to the Byzantine Emperor Heraclius. On Caesar, see EI^2, s.v. Ḳayṣar (A. Fischer/A. Wensinck et al.).

315 Marj al-Ṣuffar is the southern part of a semicircular plain (*marj*) located between al-Ghūṭa around Damascus and the open desert in the east. In al-Azdī's narrative, a battle that took place between the Byzantines and the Muslims under the command of Khālid at Marj al-Ṣuffar on 17 Jumādā II in 13 [=18 August 634] is mentioned. This battle ended with the defeat of the Byzantine troops. On Marj al-Ṣuffar, see EI^2, s.v. Marj al-Ṣuffar (N. Elisséeff).

316 In fact, it was five days before Abū Bakr's death which is dated to 22 Jumādā II, 13 [=23 August 634]. On this date, see below p. 133. 22 Jumādā II is a Tuesday. Since Abū Bakr died on Monday night, i.e. at the end of 21 Jumādā II, the calculation of four days is correct if one takes into account that "days" started at the evening before midnight at that time.

the spoils, he came with this [piece of the] spoils [into the encampment], handed it in and never permitted [himself] to loot neither little nor much of it, to the extent that he came [into the encampment] even with a hank of thread or of fleece, a hair and a needle (*misalla*) and handed them in, without permitting [himself] to loot neither little nor much of it.[317] The commander (*ṣāḥib*) of Damascus asked some of his spies about their [=the Muslims'] acts and conduct. They [=the spies] described them to him as being characterised by [their] trustworthiness and [also] described them as praying at night and performing lengthy [prayers] (*qiyām*). He [=the commander] then said: "Those [whom you described] are monks by night and lions by day. I swear by God that I am powerless against them and there is no good for me in fighting them".

He [=the narrator] said: He [=the commander of Damascus] coaxed the Muslims into making peace, but he began to deny them that which would satisfy them, and they [also] stopped pursuing what he had requested. In doing so, he withheld from making peace and from the completion [of a peace treaty], only because he learned that Caesar was mustering groups [to fight] against the Muslims and that he intended to raid them. That was what dissuaded him from accelerating the conclusion of peace.\\184

The death of Abū Bakr (r.) and his appointment of ʿUmar b. al-Khaṭṭāb (r.) as his successor [to the rule]

Abū Bakr, may God's satisfaction, mercy and forgiveness be upon him, died on Monday evening, 22 Jumādā II 13 [=23 August 634] but [beforehand] he had appointed [as his successor] the blessed ʿUmar b. al-Khaṭṭāb (r.), al-Fārūq[318], who led the conquests. He [=ʿUmar] deposed Khālid b. al-Walīd (r.) from [the command of the troops in] Syria and employed Abū ʿUbayda (r.) [instead of him].

He [=ʿUmar] wrote [the following letter] to Abū ʿUbayda (r.):

Regarding the matter at hand: Abū Bakr al-Ṣiddīq (r.), the successor of the Messenger of God (ṣ.), is dead. We belong to God and to Him we shall return; and may God rest Abū Bakr's soul, [who was] the speaker of truth, the commander of equity, the doer of [what is] good, the man of righteous character—i.e. of natural disposition (*ṭabīʿa*), by which he [=ʿUmar] refers to his [=Abū Bakr's] piety and clemency—and the intimate and simple one. We ask God (t.), by means of His mercy, for protection from all sins and we ask Him to [make us] act in obedience to Him and to [grant us] entry into His abode. [For] He is omnipotent. May God's peace and mercy be upon you.\\185

317 On a tradition that shows Muḥammad as the precursor of these activities, see Ibn Hishām, *Al-sīra*, 880, 1–11.

318 This is an epithet of ʿUmar, the literal translation of which is "the One who separates right from wrong or differentiates between truth and falsehood". On the term "*fārūq*", see Bashear, *Title "Fārūq"*.

Yarfa'[319] marched out with the letter and delivered it to him [=Abū 'Ubayda]. Abū 'Ubayda read it [out loud]. They [=Abū 'Ubayda's companions] said: "After that, we heard nothing from Abū 'Ubayda that was beneficial to those who stayed or those who left". Then Abū 'Ubayda summoned Mu'ādh b. Jabal (r.) and let him read the letter. Then Mu'ādh [b. Jabal] turned to the messenger [=Yarfa'] and said: "May God rest Abū Bakr's soul and be satisfied with him. Reveal your news. What did the Muslims [in Medina] do?" He [=Yarfa'] said: "Abū Bakr, God rest his soul, appointed 'Umar b. al-Khaṭṭāb (r.) as [his] successor". Mu'ādh [b. Jabal] said: "Praise be to God, they did well and did the right thing". Abū 'Ubayda (r.) said: "After I read the letter, only my fear that he [=Yarfa'] would meet me and inform me that the ruler is someone other than 'Umar prevented me from asking him [=Yarfa'] [about the new leader]". The messenger [=Yarfa'] [also] said: "O Abū 'Ubayda, 'Umar (r.) says to you: 'Inform me about the condition of the people and about Khālid b. al-Walīd, what kind of man he is. Also inform me about Yazīd b. Abī Sufyān and 'Amr b. al-'Āṣ, what their condition[s] and attitudes are as well as what [kind of] advice to the Muslims [they give]'". Abū 'Ubayda (r.) said: "As for Khālid, he is the best commander, the best advisor to the adherents of Islam, the most sympathetic to them, the most considerate towards them and the toughest on their infidel enemy. May God bless him for [his deeds to] them [=the Muslims]. As for Yazīd [b. Abī Sufyān] and 'Amr [b. al-'Āṣ] in offering advice,\\186 [and showing] earnestness, consideration and sympathy towards the Muslims, they are as 'Umar loves and has ever loved them to be". He [=Yarfa'] said: "Inform me [also] about your brethren Sa'īd b. Zayd [b. 'Amr b. Nufayl] and Mu'ādh b. Jabal". He [=Abū 'Ubayda] said: "They are the same as you have ever known them [to be] except that their age has increased their abstention from the worldly life and their desire for the afterlife". He [=the narrator] said: Then the messenger leapt to leave, whereupon Abū 'Ubayda (r.) said to him: "Glory be to God! Wait until we write [a letter in return and send it] with you".

The letter from Abū 'Ubayda and Mu'ādh b. Jabal to 'Umar b. al-Khaṭṭāb (r.)

Abū 'Ubayda (r.) and Mu'ādh b. Jabal (r.) wrote a single letter to him [='Umar], [which reads]:

In the name of God, the Merciful, the Compassionate. From Abū 'Ubayda b. al-Jarrāḥ and Mu'ādh b. Jabal to 'Umar b. al-Khaṭṭāb. Peace be upon you. We do praise, on your behalf, God with whom no other deity is associated. Regarding the matter at hand: We have always known you as showing much

319 Yarfa' (n.d.) is an early Islamic figure. In al-Azdī's narrative, he is mentioned as a messenger delivering a letter from 'Umar to Abū 'Ubayda containing information on Abū Bakr's death and on 'Umar's succession to the caliphate. On Yarfa', see Ibn 'Asākir, *TMD*, LXV, 67–70 (no. 8232) and Ibn Ḥajar, *Al-iṣāba. Ed. al-Baghawī*, VI, 696–697 (no. 9394).

interest in your own cause. Now you, ʿUmar, have surely become in charge of the cause of Muḥammad's (ṣ.) community, of all its red[-skinned] and black[-skinned] [members], whereby the enemy and the friend, the noble and the common and the strong and the weak are seated before you. Each of them claims a right to, or a share of, justice from you. So consider [carefully] how you would conduct yourself, ʿUmar. We do remind you of the Day [of Judgement] on which the secrets will be unearthed, the private [parts] will be uncovered, the hidden [things] will be disclosed and the faces will be humbled\\187 before an invincible King, who subjugated them [=the faces] with His omnipotence. The people have been submitting themselves to Him, awaiting His judgement, fearing His punishment and wishing for His mercy. We were also informed that in this community there would be men who would be brethren of publicity and enemies of secrecy.[320] We seek refuge in God from this [kind of men]. [We hope that] our letter will not be held in different esteem on your part than the esteem in which we held it on ours. May God's peace and mercy be upon you.

His [=ʿUmar's] messenger headed with the letter to him. Abū ʿUbayda said to Muʿādh [b. Jabal] (r.): "I swear by God that ʿUmar (r.) has not ordered us to reveal Abū Bakr's (r.) death to the people or to notify them of his departure. I do not want to mention any of this if he [=ʿUmar] himself has not mentioned it". He [=the narrator] said: Then Muʿādh [b. Jabal] said to him: "How good your decision is!" They concealed it [=the letter] and did not mention anything to the people [=the Muslims]. No sooner had they kept [it hidden] for the while [that] ʿUmar's (r.) messenger took in going [back] to him [=ʿUmar], than ʿUmar (r.) sent the messenger back to them [again] with the reply to their letter, [in which he] assigned [the command of the troops in Syria] to Abū ʿUbayda (r.) and ordered him to exhort the people. It was Shaddād b. Aws b. Thābit[321], the nephew of Ḥassān b. Thābit al-Anṣārī[322],

320 The Arabic expression "*ikhwān al-ʿalāniya aʿdāʾ al-sarīra*" (lit. "brethren of publicity and enemies of secrecy") is reminiscent of a prophetic tradition that reads: "By the end of the world, there will be people who are brethren of publicity and enemies of secrecy; [the listeners] said: 'O Messenger of God, how will this happen?'; he said: 'It will happen when they desire only one another and fear only one another'" (for this tradition, see Ibn Ḥanbal, *Musnad*, V, 378 [no. 22055]). We understand the expression "*ikhwān al-ʿalāniya aʿdāʾ al-sarīra*" as referring to people who would behave as friends in public but as enemies in secret.

321 Shaddād's full name is Abū Yaʿlā (or Abū ʿAbd al-Raḥmān) Shaddād b. Aws b. Thābit al-Anṣārī (d. between 54–58/673–678). In al-Azdī's narrative, Shaddād is mentioned as the nephew of Ḥassān b. Thābit, as a messenger delivering letters between ʿUmar and Abū ʿUbayda and as the one who counted the killed Byzantines after the Battle of al-Yarmūk. He is also depicted as an eloquent and wise Muslim who exhorted the other Muslims in Syria. On Shaddād, see Ibn Saʿd, *Kitāb al-ṭabaqāt*, VII-2, 124, al-Bukhārī, *Al-taʾrīkh al-kabīr*, II-2, 225 (no. 2591) and Ibn ʿAsākir, *TMD*, XXII, 403–418.

322 Ḥassān's full name is Abū al-Walīd Ḥassān b. Thābit b. al-Mundhir b. Ḥarām al-Anṣārī (d. between 40–54/659–673). In al-Azdī's narrative, he is mentioned twice as the uncle of Shaddād b. Aws b. Thābit. On Ḥassān, see EI^2, s.v. Ḥassān b. Thābit (W. ʿArafat).

who brought the [second] letter [to Abū ʿUbayda]. The reply to their letter [that they had sent] to ʿUmar b. al-Khaṭṭāb (r.) was [as follows]:\\188

In the name of God, the Merciful, the Compassionate. From the servant of God ʿUmar, the Commander of the Believers (*amīr al-muʾminīn*), to Abū ʿUbayda b. al-Jarrāḥ and Muʿādh b. Jabal. Peace be upon you. I praise, on your behalf, God with whom no other deity is associated. Regarding the matter at hand: I do advise you to fear God, because it [=the fear] is a pleasure for your God, good fortune for your lives and a gain for the shrewd while the helpless are negligent. I received your letter [in which] you mentioned that you have always known me as showing much interest in my own cause. Well, for all you know, this is a commendation from both of you to me. You also mentioned that I have become in charge of the cause of this community, in which the noble and the common, the enemy and the friend and the strong and the weak are seated before me, each of them claiming a share of justice [from me]. Then you asked how I would conduct myself in this situation. Certainly neither power nor strength [is obtained] except through God (*lā ḥawla wa-lā quwwa illā bi-llāh*). You also wrote to frighten me of a day to come. This will be [true] through the alternation of night and day. These two [=night and day] erode everything new, bring close everything distant and bring forth everything promised until they reach the Day of Resurrection, a day on which the secrets will be unearthed, the private [parts] will be uncovered and the faces will be humbled before an invincible King who subjugated them with His omnipotence. [You also wrote that] the people have been submitting themselves to Him, fearing His punishment, awaiting His judgement and wishing for His mercy. You also mentioned that you were informed that in this community there would be men who would be brethren of publicity and enemies of secrecy. It is not the time for that [now]. This will happen at a later time when people desire only one another and fear only one another. You also said that you sought refuge in God from [the premonition] that I[323] would hold your letter in different esteem than the esteem in which you held it. [You also wrote that] you would never deprive me of [anything] good. I seek refuge in God from [your premonition] that I would hold your letter in esteem [different from yours],\\189 because I cannot do without you both or without your opinions and advice. So be committed to writing [letters] to me, may God have mercy upon you both. May God's peace and mercy be upon both of you.

323 There is a deictic shift in person (*iltifāt*) in the text where the speaker moves from the first person plural (in direct speech) to the first person singular (in reported speech). For further information on "*al-iltifāt*", see Abdel Haleem, *Grammatical Shift* and Saifullah, *Sudden Change*.

'Umar b. al-Khaṭṭāb's letter to Abū 'Ubayda b. al-Jarrāḥ (r.) concerning his [=the latter's] appointment and restitution as [chief] commander of [the troops in] Syria as well as [concerning] the deposition of Khālid b. al-Walīd (r.)

Al-Ḥusayn b. Ziyād [al-Ramlī] reported to us on the authority of Abū Ismā'īl Muḥammad b. 'Abdallāh [al-Azdī], who said: Furthermore, Muḥammad b. Yūsuf related to me on the authority of Thābit [al-Bunānī] on the authority of al-'Abbās b. Sahl b. Sa'd[324], who said: Shaddād b. Aws [b. Thābit] came\\190 with the [letter that included the] assignment of Abū 'Ubayda [to command the troops in Syria] and delivered it to him. Suffering [from some ailment], Shaddād [b. Aws b. Thābit] [had to] stay with Abū 'Ubayda and Mu'ādh [b. Jabal], whose encampment and cause were the same and who looked after him until he recovered. Abū 'Ubayda remained [in this situation] for fifteen nights while Khālid was leading the people in prayer[s] and was commanding what is right and forbidding what is wrong. He [=Khālid] did not know yet that Abū 'Ubayda had become his commander until the [following] letter came from 'Umar b. al-Khaṭṭāb (r.) to Abū 'Ubayda, who hated to hide it:

In the name of God, the Merciful, the Compassionate. From the servant of God 'Umar, the Commander of the Believers, to Abū 'Ubayda b. al-Jarrāḥ. Peace be upon you. I praise, on your behalf, God with whom no other deity is associated. Regarding the matter at hand: You are surrounded by Muslims whose number is enough to besiege Damascus. Therefore, send your detachments to the land of Ḥimṣ, to Damascus and to other Syrian cities. Do not let my words restrict you in a way that [will cause] you [to] bare your army unit and thus your enemy will be lured into [marching towards] you. But form your opinion thoughtfully. March those whom you can dispense with and retain those whom you need with you there. Khālid b. al-Walīd must be one of those whom you retain with you there, because you cannot do without him. May God's peace, mercy and blessings be upon you.

Then Khālid said: "God rest Abū Bakr's soul. If he were alive, he would not depose me". [After] 'Umar had appointed Abū 'Ubayda as [chief] commander, Khālid said: "May God have mercy upon Abū 'Ubayda; why did he not inform me about [his] taking command of me?" Khālid went to Abū 'Ubayda (r.) and said to him: "May God have mercy upon you; you have become my commander and my leader and you have not informed me [about it, why]? You [have continued] praying behind me although the authority has become yours". He [=Abū 'Ubayda] said: "I would have never informed you of it if you had not known about it from someone else. [As you know,] worldly authority and command come to an end. We are certainly brethren and if either of us leads his brother [in prayers] or becomes his

324 Al-'Abbās's full name is al-'Abbās b. Sahl b. Sa'd al-Sā'idī al-Anṣārī (d. 120/737). In al-Azdī's narrative, he is mentioned as a transmitter of some traditions. On al-'Abbās, see Ibn Sa'd, *Kitāb al-ṭabaqāt*, V, 200.

commander, this will not do any harm to his [=the brother's] religion or to his worldly life. Conversely, the commander might be the closer of the two to temptation and the more prone to sin, because this [position] exposes him to destruction, except\\191 for those whom God protects, but they are [only a] few". Khālid, who had always been commended by and popular among the Muslims, was deposed. He had taken over command of them [when he came to Syria] and had commanded them properly. His performance, sufficiency and competence were greater than theirs [=the Muslims'].

The conquest of Damascus and its peace-making [process] (ṣulḥ)

Then Abū ʿUbayda b. al-Jarrāḥ (r.) was in charge of laying siege to Damascus and Khālid b. al-Walīd was in charge of the fight at the gate, i.e. the Eastern Gate, where he was [encamping]. He [=Abū ʿUbayda] put him [=Khālid] in charge of the cavalry on the day when the Polytheists and the Muslims gathered to fight. Then they besieged Damascus after the death of Abū Bakr (r.). When the commander of Damascus [found that he] had awaited Caesar's reinforcements for [too] long and [when he] realised that every day the Muslims were increasing in number and in strength and that they would never leave him until they would defeat him, he began to send [messengers] to Abū ʿUbayda b.\\192 al-Jarrāḥ to solicit peace from him. The Byzantines and the people of Syria preferred Abū ʿUbayda to Khālid b. al-Walīd, for Khālid was the harsher and the tougher of the two towards them. [Therefore,] a peace treaty from Abū ʿUbayda would be more preferable to them. He [=Abū ʿUbayda] was the gentler, the more attentive in listening and the closer of the two to them. They also learned that he was the first of the two to have emigrated and to have embraced Islam. The messengers of the commander of Damascus were coming to Abū ʿUbayda while Khālid was exerting persistent pressure on the gate, which he was in charge of [attacking], fighting them [=the people of Damascus] there. The commander of Damascus sent [messengers] to Abū ʿUbayda, made peace with him and opened al-Jābiya Gate to him. [At the same time] Khālid exerted persistent pressure on the Eastern Gate and opened it by force. Khālid then said to Abū ʿUbayda (r.): "Kill and capture them, because I have conquered it [=Damascus] by force". Abū ʿUbayda said: "No, I gave them a letter of protection". Khālid b. al-Walīd's command of [the troops in] Syria spanned one year and some days.

Al-Ḥusayn b. Ziyād [al-Ramlī] reported to us on the authority of Abū Ismāʿīl Muḥammad b. ʿAbdallāh [al-Azdī], who said: Furthermore, ʿAmr b. ʿAbd al-Raḥmān[325] related to me: In Dārayyā[326], Ṣafwān b. al-Muʿaṭṭal

325 ʿAmr's full name is Abū al-Ḥasan ʿAmr b. ʿAbd al-Raḥmān Duḥaym b. Maymūn al-Qurashī (n.d.). In al-Azdī's narrative, he is mentioned as a transmitter of two traditions. On ʿAmr, see Ibn ʿAsākir, *TMD*, XLVI, 243–244.

326 Dārayyā is a village in the vicinity of Damascus, located in al-Ghūṭa, according to Yāqūt, and watered by the Baradā. In al-Azdī's narrative, it is mentioned in the context

al-Khuzāʿī[327] attacked a Byzantine man dressed in Persian finery. Then Ṣafwān [b. al-Muʿaṭṭal al-Khuzāʿī] stabbed him and struck him down. His wife immediately yelled at Ṣafwān and headed towards him. Then Ṣafwān said [the following lines of verse] about this [incident]:\\193

ولقد شهدت الخيل يكثر نقعها
ما بين داريا دمشق إلى نوى
فطعنت ذا حلى فصاحت عرسه
يا ابن المعطل ما تريد لما ارى
فأجبتها أنى سأترك بعلها
بالدير منعفر المناكب بالثرى
وأرى عليه حلية فشهرتها
إنى كذلك مولع بذوى الحلى

I saw the horses stirring up a lot of dust
Between Dārayyā near Damascus and Nawā[328];
I stabbed a wearer of finery whose wife then yelled:
"O Ibn al-Muʿaṭṭal, what do you want from what I see?"
I answered her that I would leave her husband
In the monastery covered to shoulders with earth;
I saw him dressed in finery which I pulled off;
Just like that, I am fond of wearers of finery.

Then the Muslims entered Damascus and the peace-making [process] was completed.

Al-Ḥusayn b. Ziyād [al-Ramlī] reported to me on the authority of Abū Ismāʿīl Muḥammad b. ʿAbdallāh [al-Azdī], who said: Furthermore, [Abū Ṭayba] ʿAmr b. Mālik al-Qaynī[329] related to me on the authority of Adham

---

of Ṣafwān b. al-Muʿaṭṭal al-Khuzāʿī's duel with a Byzantine man. On Dārayyā, see Yāqūt, *Muʿjam al-buldān*, II, 536–537 and *EI²*, s.v. Baradā (N. Elisséeff).

327 Ṣafwān's full name is Abū ʿAmr al-Dhakwānī Ṣafwān b. al-Muʿaṭṭal al-Khuzāʿī (d. ca. 17/638 or 59/679). ʿUqla and Banī Yāsīn criticise al-Azdī for having made a mistake when ascribing the *nisba* al-Khuzāʿī rather than al-Sulamī to Ṣafwān (see al-Azdī, *Futūḥ al-Shām. Ed. ʿUqla/Banī Yāsīn*, 39; 192, n. 7). In al-Azdī's narrative, Ṣafwān is a marginal figure. He is depicted as duelling with a Byzantine fighter, in the context of which he composed a poem that is also mentioned in the narrative. Then he raided another Byzantine unit that attacked him and is said to have reached Ḥimṣ to fight its inhabitants. On Ṣafwān, see *EI²*, s.v. Ṣafwān b. al-Muʿaṭṭal (G. Juynboll).

328 Nawā is a small town in Ḥawrān at a two-day marching distance from Damascus to the south, according to Yāqūt. In al-Azdī's narrative, Nawā is mentioned as part of a poem that speaks of a group of horsemen marching from Nawā to Dārayyā. On Nawā, see Yāqūt, *Muʿjam al-buldān*, IV, 815.

329 ʿAmr b. Mālik al-Qaynī is mentioned in al-Ṭabarī's *Taʾrīkh* as one of Abū Mikhnaf's informants. We could not find a *tarjama* about him. ʿUqla and Banī Yāsīn identify him on the basis of Ibn ʿAsākir's *TMD* as one of the transmitters of Adham b. Muḥriz al-Bāhilī (see al-Azdī, *Futūḥ al-Shām. Ed. ʿUqla/Banī Yāsīn*, 25; 193, n. 5). In al-Azdī's narrative, he is given the patronymic (*kunya*) Abū Ṭayba and is mentioned as a transmitter of four

b. Muḥriz [al-Bāhilī][330] on the authority of his father Muḥriz b. Usayd al-Bāhilī[331], who said: We conquered Damascus on [a] Sunday in [the year] 14 [=635–636] after ʿUmar's (r.) [takeover of the] rule (*imāra*) had spanned seven days short of thirteen months. He [=the narrator, Muḥriz b. Usayd al-Bāhilī] said: The people of Damascus sent a messenger to Caesar who was [at that time] in Antioch to inform him [of the following]: The Arabs besieged us and hemmed us in. We were powerless against them. We fought them several times but could not [defeat] them. So if you are still in need of us and of your rule over us,\\194 reinforce us, help us and rush to us, because we are in distress and under strain. If [you do] not [do so], we will be excused [not to follow you] and we did our best [to defend your rule]. [Be aware that] the people [=the Muslims] have just offered us a letter of protection and [would] accept a small tribute from us.

He [=Caesar] sent [the following message] to them: Keep to your fortress and [continue] fight[ing] your enemy. For if you made peace with them and opened your fortress to them, they would not fulfil [their obligations] to you but would force you to renounce your religion, fight you, capture you and divide you [as spoils] among themselves. I am certainly dispatching [more] troops in the tracks of this messenger to you.

When his[332] [=Heraclius's] messenger came to them, they awaited his reinforcements and army unit[s]. When he kept them waiting and the Muslims persisted in hemming them in and besieging them tightly and when they feared that they [=the Muslims] would enter into the city to [capture] them by force, they requested peace [from the Muslims]. Abū ʿUbayda then granted them peace and completed it for them.

The [announced] army unit came from Antioch to reinforce the people of Damascus. When it reached Baalbek, they [=its commanders] received the news that Damascus had been conquered and that its people had concluded peace [with the Muslims]. This [news] was unbearable to them and they regarded it as monstrous. They wrote about it to their Emperor and

traditions. On ʿAmr, see al-Ṭabarī, *Taʾrīkh*, II, 646, l. 20–647, l. 1 and Ibn ʿAsākir, *TMD*, VII, 464.

330 Adham's full name is Abū Mālik Adham b. Muḥriz al-Bāhilī al-Ḥimṣī (n.d.). In al-Azdī's narrative, he is mentioned as the first newborn in Ḥimṣ to whom an allotment was assigned and as a fighter in the Battle of Ṣiffīn. In addition, he is described as a transmitter of several traditions. On Adham, see Ibn ʿAsākir, *TMD*, VII, 464–467 (no. 850).

331 Muḥriz's full name is Muḥriz b. Usayd b. Mālik al-Bāhilī (d. 78/699). In al-Azdī's narrative, he is mentioned as one of those who conquered Damascus and as one of the flag holders at Ḥimṣ. In addition, he functions as a transmitter of traditions about the date of the conquest of Damascus (i.e. a Sunday in the year 14 [=635–636]) and about the peace-making process with the inhabitants of Damascus. On Muḥriz, see Ibn ʿAsākir, *TMD*, LVII, 78–79 and Ibn Ḥajar, *Al-iṣāba. Ed. al-Baghawī*, VI, 277 (no. 8372) who quotes the first.

332 Here we follow the reading of manuscript *fa* ("*-hū*", i.e. "his") rather than the edition that reads "*-hum*", i.e. "their".

remained in Baalbek under the command of two al-Durunjārs. Each of them [=al-Durunjārs] commanded 5,000 and they were 10,000 [in total]. So they settled down and sent [a messenger] to their Emperor to inform him about the place where they were stationed and the news they had received about Damascus.\\195

He [=the narrator] said: When Abū ʿUbayda appeared in the vicinity of Damascus, he ordered ʿAmr b. al-ʿĀṣ to march to the land of the River Jordan[333] and to Palestine, to stay between [the two regions] and not to advance on the cities, the fortresses and the groups [there]. Instead, [he ordered him] to launch [infantry] raids on the outskirts [of the cities] and the[ir] rural surroundings (*rasātīq*), to launch cavalry raids on them from all directions and to make peace with whoever seeks to make peace with them [=the Muslims].

ʿAmr [b. al-ʿĀṣ] moved out [as ordered] until he launched attacks on the land of the River Jordan and Palestine, caused great turmoil among them [=their people] and hemmed them in very tightly. There, he learned that Damascus was conquered and that the Muslims had entered [it] to the disadvantage of them [=the inhabitants]. Terrified and horrified, the Polytheists felt sad to see all of their cities conquered. Those Byzantines who were [still] in the cities gathered and descended from their fortresses. Then the townspeople and many of the Arab Christians joined them. [Thus,] their number increased. They wrote to Caesar who was in Antioch [at that time], asking him for reinforcements. He [=Caesar] sent [a messenger] to those 10,000 who were [waiting] in Baalbek [ordering them] to march to them.

ʿAmr b. al-ʿĀṣ's letter to Abū ʿUbayda (r.)

ʿAmr b. al-ʿĀṣ wrote [the following letter] to Abū ʿUbayda:

In the name of God, the Merciful, the Compassionate. Regarding the matter at hand: The Byzantines deemed the conquest of Damascus monstrous and [thus] gathered [forces] from the regions of the River Jordan and Palestine. Then they wrote to one another, contracted with one another, made agreements with one another, encamped [together] and mutually swore to God not to return to their women and children until they had forced the Arabs [to get] out of their lands. But God will certainly belie their statement and their hope and will never\\196 pave a way for the Unbelievers at the expense of the Believers. Write me [a letter regarding]

333 Jordan (al-Urdunn) refers to the River Jordan and the regions adjacent to this shallow river's course. In al-Azdī's narrative, the term is usually used in the expressions "land of the River Jordan" (*arḍ al-Urdunn*) or "lands of the River Jordan" (*bilād al-Urdunn*) distinguishing the region from "the land of al-Balqāʾ", Palestine and "the lands of Damascus". Fiḥl and the surrounding area belong to this region, i.e. "the land of the River Jordan" that is stretched to some areas in (today's) Transjordan. In addition, "the arable lands of the River Jordan" are mentioned. The term probably refers to the Jordan valley proper. On Jordan, see *EI*², s.v. al-Urdunn (F. Buhl/C. Bosworth et al.).

your opinion on this issue. May God guide your cause rightly, lead you to the right path and uphold your guidance. May God's peace and mercy be upon you.

'Amr [b. al-'Āṣ's] messenger came with this letter [to Abū 'Ubayda]. Abū 'Ubayda (r.) had beforehand consulted his companions (r.), had mustered them to march together with them [=the Muslims] to Ḥimṣ and had said: "God ('a.) did conquer this city [=Damascus], which is one of the greatest Syrian cities. So I decided to march to Ḥimṣ, hoping that God ('a.) would lead us to conquer it[, too]. 'Amr [b. al-'Āṣ] is right there behind us, and thus we need not be afraid that they [=the Byzantines] will come to [attack] us from behind". [Thereupon,] Khālid b. al-Walīd, Yazīd b. Abī Sufyān, Mu'ādh [b. Jabal] and the other chiefs of the Muslims said to him: "You are right and you made the right decision. March with us to them". When all of them had reached this decision, they received 'Amr b. al-'Āṣ's (r.) letter. After Abū 'Ubayda had read it, he gave it to Khālid and said: "Something that we have not expected happened [nearby]". Then they read the letter to all the Muslim attendants. Then Yazīd b. Abī Sufyān said: "Supply 'Amr [b. al-'Āṣ] with reinforcements from your side and order him to fight the people [=the Byzantines] while you stick to your place where you are [now]". He [=Abū 'Ubayda] said: "What is your opinion, Khālid?" He [=Khālid] said: "I suggest that you [first wait and] see what the army unit that has set up camp at Baalbek will do. If they [=the Byzantines] move from there [=Baalbek] and march to our brethren, you should also march to your brethren and bring them together with the whole group of the people [=the Muslims]. [However,] if they stay [there] and do not\\197 leave, you should reinforce 'Amr [b. al-'Āṣ], dispatch fighters against those [Byzantines in Baalbek] and stick to your place". He [=Abū 'Ubayda] said to him: "What an excellent opinion!" Abū 'Ubayda summoned Shuraḥbīl b. Ḥasana and said to him: "March to 'Amr [b. al-'Āṣ] and do not disagree with his order[s] or with his decision[s]. I am surely sending [some soldiers] to distract this army unit at Baalbek from you while I am reinforcing you with the men you need".

Shuraḥbīl marched out in command of 2,800 men and reached 'Amr [b. al-'Āṣ], who was in command of 2,500 men. Abū 'Ubayda (r.) said to Khālid: "Nobody can stand against that army unit which has set up camp at Baalbek except for I, you or Yazīd". Then Khālid (r.) said to him: "No, I [would] rather march to them". He [=Abū 'Ubayda] said: "They are yours [to deal with]". Abū 'Ubayda dispatched him in command of 5,000 horsemen and went out with him to bid him farewell. He walked with him a little and Khālid said to him: "Go back, may God have mercy upon you, to your encampment". He [=Abū 'Ubayda] said to him: "O Khālid, I do recommend to you the fear of God and when you face the people [=the Byzantines], do not negotiate with them, do not delay [fighting them] in their fortresses and do not let them eat, drink or wait for the arrival of their reinforcements. When you face them, fight them [immediately]. For if you defeat them, their hope[s] will fade, their spirits will weaken and their expectation[s] will [miserably] collapse. But if you need reinforcements, keep me informed [of this] until you receive the reinforcements you need. And if you need me to come to you myself, I will come to you, God willing". Then he took his hand, bade farewell to him, said to him: "Peace be upon you" and left.

Caesar's messenger reached those who were stationed at Baalbek. He ordered them to catch up with those [soldiers] who were gathered in Baysān[334] [in the land of the River Jordan]. So they marched out to those who were in Baysān, taking out with them a lot of people—i.e. from among the people of Baalbek—who embraced their religion. Many of the people of Ḥimṣ [also] went to them in furious defence of their religion and in fear of [seeing] their [other] cities conquered as Damascus was conquered.\\198 Numbering more than 20,000, they [=the people of Ḥimṣ] marched out and headed towards their groups in Baysān.

Khālid went on marching until he reached Baalbek. He was told that they [=the Byzantines] had [already] headed towards ʿAmr [b. al-ʿĀṣ] and the Muslims who were with him. Then Khālid raided the region of Baalbek, killed all the men he caught, captured the offspring he found and took plentiful sheep, cows, goods and spoils with him. Then he returned to Abū ʿUbayda and informed him of the news. [Now,] all the Muslims agreed that Abū ʿUbayda should march with all the people [=the Muslims] towards the Byzantine army. So Abū ʿUbayda ordered Khālid [to move out], who [accordingly] moved with 1,500 horsemen ahead of Abū ʿUbayda. He also ordered him to hasten [his] march to ʿAmr [b. al-ʿĀṣ] and his companions so that God would strengthen their backs by virtue of him [=Khālid] and to show the Byzantines that the Muslims had already reached them. So Khālid rushed in hot pursuit of the Byzantines and caught up their rear [fighters], whereas their front [fighters] had already entered their encampment. So he [=Khālid] launched an attack on their rear [fighters], killing a great many of them, and took lots of their chattels. However, some of them managed to retreat until they entered their encampment. Then Khālid proceeded until he set up camp with his cavalry close to ʿAmr [b. al-ʿĀṣ]. The Muslims [there] rejoiced over their [=Khālid and his unit's] coming to them. Prior to Khālid's arrival, ʿAmr [b. al-ʿĀṣ] would lead his companions, who were with him, in prayer[s] while [after his arrival] Khālid led the cavalrymen, with whom he came, in prayer[s].\\199

334 Baysān is a city in the Jordan valley located ca. 30 km south of Lake Tiberias. In al-Azdī's narrative, the Battle of Fiḥl which occurred between the Muslim troops under the command of Khālid and Abū ʿUbayda and the Byzantine troops near Baysān and which ended with the annihilation of the Byzantines is mentioned. On Baysān, see *EI²*, s.v. Baysān (J. Sourdel-Thomine).

The battle of Fiḥl

He [=the narrator] said: When the Byzantines [that had left Baalbek] learned that Abū ʿUbayda was heading towards them, they turned towards Fiḥl[335], which was part of the land of the River Jordan and set up camp [there]. The Muslims proceeded all together until they set up camp near them, and so did Lakhm[336], Judhām[337], Ghassān, ʿĀmila[338], al-Qayn[339] and some [sub]tribes from Quḍāʿa, who had joined the Muslims, thus increasing their number, and had gone with them into their encampment. The Christian people of the region started to write letters to the Muslims, while setting one foot forward and the other backward, saying: "O Muslims, we love you more than the Byzantines, even if they embrace our religion. You are more faithful and kinder to us, more reluctant to oppress us and [hence] better rulers over us. But they gained control over our cause and our homes". [Thereupon,] the Muslims said to them: "This [plea] will not help you in dealing with us unless you demand our protection. For if we defeat you, we will have the right to kill you, capture your offspring and enslave you. But if you receive protection from us, it will save you from all these [calamities] and from us, and we will make peace to your advantage". They [=the Christian people of

335 Fiḥl is located east of the Jordan valley and ca. 12 km southeast of Baysān. In al-Azdī's narrative, the conquest of Fiḥl occurred after a long battle between the Muslims and the Byzantines, in the course of which the inhabitants of Fiḥl filled a moat with water in order to keep the Muslims at bay. Only after the conquest of "the land of the River Jordan" did the inhabitants of Fiḥl ask the Muslims for a peace treaty, which was granted to them. On Fiḥl, see *EI*², s.v. Faḥl (F. Buhl/D. Sourdel).

336 Lakhm is a Southern Arabian tribe which, according to some genealogists, is regarded as a Northern Arabian tribe. In al-Azdī's narrative, Lakhm is depicted twice as having joined the Muslims in the Battle and conquest of Fiḥl and twice as having sided with the Muslims in the Battle of al-Yarmūk. On Lakhm, see *EI*², s.v. Lakhm (H. Lammens/I. Shahid).

337 Judhām is a Southern Arabian tribe that, according to some genealogists, is reckoned to be a Northern Arabian tribe. In al-Azdī's narrative, Judhām is depicted twice as having joined the Muslims in the Battle and conquest of Fiḥl and twice as having sided with the Muslims in the Battle of al-Yarmūk. In addition, the watering place Dhāt al-Manār is said to have belonged to a subtribe of Judhām, called Ḥadas, and two unnamed messengers from Judhām are mentioned. On Judhām, see *EI*², s.v. Judhām (C. Bosworth); Hasson, *Judhām*.

338 ʿĀmila is a Northern Arabian tribe that, according to some genealogists, is regarded as a Southern Arabian tribe. In al-Azdī's narrative, ʿĀmila is depicted twice as having joined the Muslims in the Battle and conquest of Fiḥl and twice as having sided with the Muslims in the Battle of al-Yarmūk. On ʿĀmila, see *EI*², s.v. ʿĀmila (H. Lammens/W. Caskel). See also Rihan, *Politics and Culture* and on Rihan's work, see Scheiner, *Review of M. Rihan*.

339 Al-Qayn (or Banū al-Qayn) is a Southern Arabian tribe that belonged to the tribal federation of Quḍāʿa. In al-Azdī's narrative, al-Qayn (once referred to as Banū al-Qayn) is depicted twice as having participated in the Battle and conquest of Fiḥl. In addition, one individual figure belongs to al-Qayn: ʿAmr b. Mālik al-Qaynī, who is mentioned as a transmitter of several traditions. On al-Qayn, see *EI*², s.v. al-Ḳayn (W. Watt).

the region] were lying in hiding to ambush the Muslims and were awaiting what Caesar would do [to help them]. For they were informed that he had sent for the farthermost people of his lands and for all the people of his empire, who had embraced their religion and who were around him [=Caesar]. They [=these new troops] were coming to them and descending upon them [=the Christian people of the region] every day while they [=the Christian people] were lying in hiding to ambush the Muslims and were awaiting what he [=Caesar] would do in this [situation]. [Thus,] the Byzantines formed a large army [whose number ranged] from\\200 30,000 to 40,000 [soldiers] with the fellow residents of the region and those adherents of their religion who had joined them.

When the Muslims descended upon them [=the Byzantine troops], nothing was more preferable to them [=the Muslims] than rushing them [into a fight]. However, nothing was more preferable to the Byzantines than holding off the Muslims, because they were hoping for [more] reinforcements from their [supreme] commander [=Caesar] and because the Muslims did not have the same plenty and sufficiency as the Byzantines did. When the Polytheists found that the Muslims were patient and persevering and that God was leading them to victory, they started to dig a moat (*miyāh*) between them and the Muslims in order to hold them off. They feared that if they rushed the Muslims [into a fight], they would run into severe trouble or suffer shameful defeat. Therefore, they kept fending and holding them [=the Muslims] off as much as they could. The Muslims[, however,] went wading hurriedly through the moat, which they [=the Polytheists] had dug against them, and squelched through the mud. When the Byzantines saw them doing this and [saw] that nothing could stop them [from advancing], they marched out [of the city], encamped and set their minds on fighting. Every day they were increasing [in number] and receiving reinforcements from the rural surroundings and the villages, as well as from those who embraced their religion. When Abū ʿUbayda learned of this, he ordered the Muslims [to attack], saying: "Launch a raid on them. Launch a raid on the people of the villages, arable lands and rural surroundings". They did so and thus cut off their [=the Byzantines'] [access] to matériel and provisions. When Ibn al-Juʿayd[340] saw this, he came to Abū ʿUbayda, who made peace with him regarding the arable lands of the River Jordan. He [=Abū ʿUbayda] [also] wrote a letter [of protection] to him. However, the Byzantines were [still] increasing [in number] in their encampment every day while the Muslims were yearning to confront them.\\201

340 Ibn al-Juʿayd could not be identified because his full name is not mentioned. In al-Azdī's narrative, he is mentioned as a commander of the people of "the arable lands of the River Jordan" and as seeking a letter of protection from Abū ʿUbayda for this region. In addition, he is depicted as the leader of the people of Jerusalem, who received another letter of protection from ʿUmar for this city.

He [=the narrator] said: One day, Ṣafwān b. al-Muʿaṭṭal al-Khuzāʿī and Maʿn b. Yazīd b. al-Akhnas al-Sulamī moved out with their cavalry, launched a raid and, as a result, gained lots of spoils. When they turned back [to their encampment], the Byzantines intercepted them and they fought each other fiercely. Both [parties] numbered about 100 horsemen in total.

Al-Durunjār also marched out with 5,000 men. Then they [=the Muslims] attacked them, withstood them and sought God's reward for their fight against them. Then the Byzantines subdued them and appropriated their spoils. Then Ḥābis b. Saʿd al-Ṭāʾī came [forward] with about 100 men from Ṭayyiʾ and attacked them [=the Byzantines]. They withdrew not so far, then launched a [counter-]attack on him [=Ḥābis b. Saʿd al-Ṭāʾī] and repelled him and his companions until they [=the Byzantines] forced them [Ḥābis and his companions] to join the [other] Muslims. Miscalculating [the situation], they [=the Byzantines] left, thinking then that it was a triumph for them although they did not kill anybody and did not defeat any group. When they left for their belongings and their encampment, they sent [the following message] to Abū ʿUbayda:

Get out—you, your companions and the Arab adherents of your religion—of our lands that yield wheat and barley, fruits (*fawākih*), grapes and vegetables (*thimār*). You do not deserve to inhabit them [=the lands]. Go back to your lands, the lands of misery and distress. Otherwise, we will come to you with what you are powerless against and we will not turn away from you as long as you are still blinking an eye[341].

Abū ʿUbayda (r.) replied to it [=their message] [with the following letter]:

As for your statement "Get out of our lands; you deserve neither to be their inhabitants nor [to gain] what they produce", I swear upon my life that we will never leave them after God has brought humiliation on you through us in them [=these lands]\\202 and bequeathed them to us, pulling them out of your hands and ceding them to us. These lands are the lands of God and [all] humans (*ʿibād*) are the servants of God. God is the King of kings who cedes reign to whomever He wants, strips of reign whomever He wants, elevates whomever He wants and humiliates whomever He wants. As for your statement that our lands are "the lands of misery and distress", you are right and we are not ignorant of what you have said. Just so are they [=the lands], but God has replaced ours with the lands of a decent living, low price[s], flowing rivers and plentiful fruits. So never think that we will depart from them or turn away from them until we exterminate you and expel you from them. So, stand against us, for I swear by God that if you do not come to us, we will spare you the burden [of coming to us] and come to you [instead]. And if you stand against us, we will not leave until we annihilate and eliminate you [all], God willing.

341 We understand the Arabic expression "*wa-fīkum ʿayn taṭrufu*" (lit. "and you are still blinking an eye") as carrying the meaning "to be still alive".

The story of Muʿādh b. Jabal['s negotiation with] the Byzantines

They [=the Byzantines] sent [another messenger] to Abū ʿUbayda (r.) [asking him] to send them a man [in order to negotiate with them]. So Abū ʿUbayda sent one.\\203 He [=the narrator] said: When the [first messenger] returned to them [with Abū ʿUbayda's reply], they became sure of the earnestness and vehemence (*ḥadd*) of the people [=the Muslims]. So they sent [the following message] to Abū ʿUbayda, saying: "Send us one of your righteous men whom we may ask about what you want, what you seek and what you call for, [one] whom we can inform about our own [aims] and [through whom] we can invite you to [your good] fortune if you agree". Abū ʿUbayda sent them Muʿādh b. Jabal (r.), who went to them on his horse. When he drew near to them, he dismounted from his horse, gripped its bridle and reached them, leading his horse. They said to one of their servants: "Hurry to him and hold his horse". When the servant went to hold his horse, he [=Muʿādh b. Jabal] said: "God forbid! I hold my horse [myself] and I do not want anybody else to hold it". He kept walking towards them while they were lying on rugs, carpets and cushions, the sight of which almost dazzled [the eyes] (*taghshā*). When he drew near such attire, suddenly a man rose to his feet and said to him: "Give me your horse to hold it for you and draw near to sit with these sovereigns (*mulūk*) in their gathering, because not everybody is allowed to sit with them. They did learn of your righteousness and grace among those to whom you belong. They [=the sovereigns] hate to sit and talk to you while you are standing. So sit with them". Muʿādh [b. Jabal] (r.) said to the interpreter: "Our Prophet (ṣ.) ordered us not to stand before anybody God created, but to stand only before God for prayer[s], for worship and for seeking Him. So my standing [position] is not for you. Rather, I stand because it is too grave to walk on such carpets and sit on such cushions that you have all to yourselves to the exclusion of your weak people and the adherents of your religion. For they [=the carpets and cushions] are a type of worldly adornment and vanity. God has renounced the worldly life, disparaged it and prohibited transgression and excess in [leading] it. So I will sit right here on the [bare] ground. As for you, tell me about your need from [there] where you are [seated] and place the interpreter between me\\204 and you to help me understand what you will say and help you understand what I will say". Then he caught the head of his horse and sat on the ground right beside the carpet. They said to him: "If you come closer and sit with us, it will be more honourable to you. Your sitting with these sovereigns on such furnishings is a [special] honour [we pay] to you. However, your sitting on the ground is an act which [only] the servant chooses for himself. [By doing so,] we see you only abasing yourself". The interpreter related to him what they said. Then Muʿādh [b. Jabal] (r.) got on his knees, turned his face to the people [=the Byzantines] and said to the interpreter: "Say to them: 'If the honour, which you have invited me to, belongs only to you to the exclusion of the likes of you [=the common people], it then represents [nothing] but the worldly life that God has induced [the Muslims] to renounce. It is an honour to you in this world [only] and this honour is yours [alone]. We are in no need of worldly honour, [worldly] vainglory or anything else that distances us from our Lord. If you claim that these gatherings and this worldly life, which your [elite] grand men have in their possession (*aydī*) and which you have all to yourselves to the exclusion of your weak people, represent an honour in the eyes of God (t.) to whoever holds them, then this is a false claim and an unjust deed. What God (ʿa.) possesses will not be obtained by mistake or by acting against what the Prophets—may God bless them all—have reported, on the authority of God (ʿa.), about the abstention from the worldly life. As for your statement that my sitting and bending down is an act that [only] the servant chooses for himself, I have surely acted in the same way that the servant chooses for himself. For I am only one of God's servants. I sat on God's carpet [=the ground] and I have never had any of God's possessions (*māl*) to myself alone to the exclusion of my brethren [who are among the] close friends of God. As for\\205 your statement that I have abased myself in my sitting [on the ground], if this is the case, it is [so] in your eyes [alone], but it is not so in the eyes of God. I do not care how my standing (*manzila*) looks in your eyes if it looks differently in the eyes of God. If you also said that [it is] God's servants [who] always show such a demeanour, then you would have made a clear error, because the servants whom God loves most are those who humble themselves to God, who stay close to His [other] servants, who do not indulge themselves in the worldly life and who do not forsake their share in the afterlife'".

He [=the narrator] said: When the interpreter rendered this [speech] to them, they looked at one another, understood [the words], wondered at what they heard from him and said to their interpreter: "Say to him: 'Are you the best of your companions?'" When the interpreter rendered [it] to him, Muʿādh [b. Jabal] (r.) thereupon said: "God forbid if I would say so. I [just] hope I am not the worst of them". He [=the narrator] said: They fell silent, not talking to him for a short while but talking to one another. When they grew silent, not talking to him for a short while, he said to their interpreter: "Ask them if they still need to talk with me; if not, I leave them". The interpreter said this to them, so they turned to him [=Muʿādh b. Jabal] and said to the interpreter: "Say to him: 'Tell us what you want [from us], what you call [people] to and what made you enter our lands and leave the land of Abyssinia, which is not far from you[r homeland], and [what made you enter also] the land of Persia, whose king and his son perished and whose people are ruled by women today. As for us, our Emperor is still alive and our soldiers are great and large [in number]. [Even] if you conquered one of our cities, one of our villages, one of our fortresses\\206 or defeated our army unit[s], would you think that you triumphed over our [entire] army, ceased our war against you or got rid of those of us who were remaining behind, while our numbers are as [many as] the stars in the sky and the pebbles on the earth? And tell us how you deem fighting us lawful while you believe in our Prophet and in our scripture?'" After they had said this and the interpreter had rendered it to Muʿādh [b. Jabal], they fell silent. Muʿādh [b. Jabal] said to the interpreter: "Did they finish?" He [=the interpreter] said to him: "Yes". He [=Muʿādh b. Jabal] said: "Make them understand that the first thing[s] I [want to] mention are to praise God, with whom no other deity is associated, and then to bless His Prophet Muḥammad (ṣ.). And [tell them] that the first thing[s] I call you to are to believe in God alone and in Muḥammad (ṣ.), to perform our prayer[s], to turn [your faces] towards the direction of our prayers, to adhere to our Prophet's (ṣ.) normative practices, to break the cross (*ṣalīb*) and to give up drinking wine and eating pork. Thereafter, you would become part of us as we become part of you. You [also] would become our brethren in [terms of] our religion, meriting the same rights we merit and having the same obligations we have. But if you refuse [all of this], you [must] bring us tribute every year by hand and with humility. [Only] then will we turn away from you. If you refuse these two things, we will not accept from you anything of what God (ʿa.) has created [in return for leaving Syria]. [In this case,] come out to [fight] us 'till God judges between us. He is the best of all judges'.[342] This is what we tell you [to do] and what we call you to.\\207 As for your statement 'What made you enter our lands and leave the land of Abyssinia, which is not far from you[r homeland] and [what made you enter also] the land[343] of Persia whose king perished', I shall inform you about this. We started fighting you only because you are [located] nearer to us than they [=the Persians] and because you are all the same in our eyes. [Furthermore,] our scripture [=the Qurʾān] has not told us to restrain ourselves from [fighting] them, but God (ʿa.) has revealed [a verse] to our Prophet (ṣ.) in His scripture, saying: 'You who believe, fight the disbelievers near you and let them find you standing firm'.[344] And you are nearer to us than they [=the Persians]. Therefore, we started fighting you. A party of us have also marched to them [=the Persians] and they are fighting them [now]. I hope that God will lead them [=the Muslims] to triumph, conquest and victory. As for your statement 'Our Emperor is alive, our soldiers are great [in number] and our numbers are [as many as] the stars in the sky and the pebbles on the earth' [which you said] to make us despair of advancing on you, it is not up to you to decide this matter. But it is up to God (ʿa.) to decide all matters and everything is within His grasp and under His might. So if God wants something [to exist], He simply says to it: 'Be' and it is [existent]. If Heraclius is your 'king', our king is God (ʿa.), who created us. And our [chief] commander is [just] one of us whom we appoint [as chief commander] over us if he treats us according to the scripture of our Lord and our Prophet's normative practices (ṣ.), whom we depose if he does otherwise, whose hand[s]

342 Q. 7:87 (*The Qurʾān. Tr. Abdel Haleem*, 100).
343 Here the translation follows the variant in footnote 1 (*arḍ*) and not the edited text (*ahl*).
344 Q. 9:123 (*The Qurʾān. Tr. Abdel Haleem*, 127).

we chop off if he steals, whom we whip if he commits adultery,\\208 who gets equally insulted if he insults one of us, who lets himself be retaliated [by the one he insulted] if he has hurt him, who neither conceals [anything] from us nor looks down upon us, nor appropriates our spoils which God has bestowed upon us and in [the division of] which he is just like any of us. As for your statement 'Our soldiers are large [in number]', even if they became greater and larger [in number] than the stars in the sky and the pebbles on the earth, we will neither trust nor rely on them [=the numbers], nor will we hope to triumph over our enemy through them [=our numbers]. Instead, we free ourselves from might and power, rely on God ('a.) and trust in our Lord. For how often did a small force, strengthened and enriched by God, defeat a large force with God's permission? And how often was a large force debased and humiliated by God? [For] God (t.) said: 'How often a small force has defeated a large army with God's permission; and God is with the patient!'[345] As for your statement 'How do you deem fighting us lawful while you believe in our Prophet and our scripture?' I shall inform you about this. We believe in your Prophet [=Jesus] as well as bear witness and say that he is one of God's servants and one of God's messengers [only] and that he 'In God's eyes is just like Adam[346]: He created him from dust, said to him, 'Be', and he was'.[347] We do not say that he is God. We do not say, either, that he is one of two [=binitarianism] or one of three [=trinitarianism], or that He has a son or He has a spouse or a child or there are other gods associated with Him. There are no other deities but He; 'He is far above what they say'.[348] You speak monstrously about Jesus. If you spoke about him the way we do, believed in the prophethood of our Prophet (ṣ.) [=Muḥammad] the way you find him [mentioned] in your scripture and [believed in him] the way we believe in your Prophet and [if you] admitted what\\209 he [=Jesus] had brought from God and [if] you professed the oneness of God, we would not fight you [any more]. Instead, we would make peace with you, support you and fight with you against your enemy".

He [=the narrator] said: When Muʿādh [b. Jabal] finished speaking to them, they said to him: "We see nothing but a [great] distance between us and you. Only one thing remains [to be talked about] and we offer it to you [now]. If you accept it from us, it will be good for you. But if you refuse [it], it will be bad for you. We offer you [the land of] al-Balqāʾ and the arable lands of the River Jordan that are adjacent to your land, provided that you keep away from the rest of our land and our cities and that we sign a

345 Q. 2:249 (*The Qurʾān. Tr. Abdel Haleem*, 29).

346 Adam (Ādam) is a biblical and qurʾānic figure. In al-Azdī's narrative, he is only mentioned once in this qurʾānic quotation. On Adam in the Islamic context, see *EI²*, s.v. Ādam (J. Pedersen). On Adam in the biblical context, see *RGG4*, s.v. Adam/Eva (G. Anderson/D. Apostolos-Cappadona).

347 Q. 3:59 (*The Qurʾān. Tr. Abdel Haleem*, 38–39).

348 Q. 17:43 (*The Qurʾān. Tr. Abdel Haleem*, 177).

letter [for peace] with you, in which we name your best and most righteous [people] and in which we bind you with pledges and covenants not to demand any [further parts] of our land except for the [parts] we both agreed on. In addition, the Persians are yours. Fight them and we will be on your side to help you [in fighting] against them until you kill and defeat them". Muʿādh [b. Jabal] said: "All of that which you have just offered us is already in our possession. If you gave us all that you possess and that we have not conquered yet, but deprived us of one of the three options (*khiṣāl*) which I have [just] described to you, we would never do it". He [=the narrator] said: So they got angry and said: "We make a step to [reach an agreement with] you but you keep your distance from us. Go [back] to your companions. We swear by God that we do hope to disperse you in the mountains tomorrow". Muʿādh [b. Jabal] (r.) said: "As for [our dispersal in] the mountains, no [definitely not]. But I swear by God that\\210 either we all get killed one after the other or we force you to leave your land in shame and with humility".

Then Muʿādh [b. Jabal] left for Abū ʿUbayda (r.) and told him what they had said to him and what he had replied to them. Remaining in this [situation], they [=the Byzantines] sent a[nother] man to Abū ʿUbayda b. al-Jarrāḥ to inform him about them, saying: "You did send us a man who neither accepted half [of our offer] nor wanted peace. We do not know whether or not this was your decision. We want to send you one [negotiator] from among us to offer you half [of what we possess] and solicit peace from you [in return]. If you accept this [offer] from him, it will be good for you and [also] for us. However, if you refuse [it], we consider this [to be] only bad for you". Abū ʿUbayda said to them [=the Byzantines] [through this messenger]: "Send whomever you want". So they sent to him a tall, red[-skinned] and blue[-eyed] man who came to Abū ʿUbayda. When he drew near to the Muslims, he could not distinguish Abū ʿUbayda from his companions, not knowing whether or not he was [sitting] among them, [because] he did not see the [usual] decor of a commander's place. Thus, he said to them [=the Muslims]: "O Arabs, where is your commander?" They said: "He is right there". He looked [around] and, lo and behold, it was Abū ʿUbayda sitting on the ground, shouldering the bow and holding arrows (*ashum*)[349] [in his hand], which he was flipping. The messenger said to him: "Are you the [chief] commander of those people?" He said: "Yes". He [=the messenger] said: "Why are you sitting on the ground? What if you were leaning on a cushion or if [you were] lying on a carpet, would it grant you benevolence in the eyes of God or deprive you\\211 of it?" Abū ʿUbayda (r.) said to him: "God (ʿa.) is not ashamed of [speaking] the truth. I will certainly speak to you about what you have just said and I will certainly tell you the truth of it. I no longer have a

349 Arrows (sg. *sahm*) signifies a "pipe arrow" which, according to pre-Islamic and early Islamic poetry, was considered to be of an Arabian origin (see Schwarzlose, *Waffen*, 280–281).

dinar or a dirham and I have nothing now except for my bow, my weapon[350] and my sword. Yesterday, I needed [to spend] a sum [of money] but I did not have it. So I borrowed the sum from this brother of mine—i.e. Muʿādh [b. Jabal]—who possessed it and lent it to me. If I had a carpet or a cushion, I would not sit on it [alone] on the ground to the exclusion of my brethren and companions while seating my Muslim brother[s], who, although I do not know it, might be better than I in the eyes of God. We [all] are the servants of God. We [all] walk on the ground, sit on the ground, eat on the ground and lie on the ground. And nothing of it will detract anything from our deeds in the eyes of God. On the contrary, by virtue of this God increases our rewards and elevates our rank[s]. In addition, by means of it, we humble ourselves before our Lord. [Now,] tell us your need which you came for".

The Byzantine [messenger] said to him: "God loves nothing more than peace-making and hates nothing more than oppression and corruption. You entered our lands in which you spread corruption and injustice. It is said: 'No sooner had a people spread oppression and corruption on earth than God cast mass destruction on them'. I [want to] offer you something which will bring you [good] fortune if you accept it. We give each of you two dinars and a garment, give you [=Abū ʿUbayda] 1,000 dinars and give your [supreme] commander—[the narrator said:] they mean ʿUmar (r.)—2,000 dinars, provided that you turn away from us [and retreat]. If you want, we will [also] offer you the land of al-Balqāʾ and the\\212 arable lands of the River Jordan that are adjacent to your land, provided that you leave our cities, our land and our villages and that we write a [peace] treaty between both of us, in which we bind each other by solemn oaths to fulfil it and keep what each of us promises to God".

He [=the narrator] said: Abū ʿUbayda praised God and thanked Him for all that He is worth, blessed and saluted the Prophet (ṣ.) and said [to the messenger]: "God (ʿa.) sent to us, as mercy from Him to the worlds, a Messenger and a Prophet to whom He sent down a wise scripture, whom He ordered to call people to worship their Lord and who said to them: 'God (ʿa.) is the one Deity, the Almighty and Wise, the Supreme and Glorious, the Creator of everything and nothing is equal to Him'. Thus, he [=the Prophet] ordered them [=the people] to unitarianise God with whom no other deity is associated [=to profess His unity or oneness], to ascribe neither a spouse nor a son to Him, to take no deities [other] than Him and to [believe] that anything other than Him, who people worship, is His creation. He [=the Prophet] (ṣ.) also ordered us [to call for his religion], saying: 'When you go to the Polytheists, invite them to believe in God and in His Messenger and to confirm what God (ʿa.) has revealed to him. Whoever believes and acknowledges

350 "*Silāḥ*" (lit. "weapon") most likely refers here to the spear, since bow, spear and sword were the three main weapons used in pre-Islamic and early Islamic times (see Schwarzlose, *Waffen*, 38).

[this] becomes your brother in [terms of] religion, meriting the same rights you merit and having the same obligations you have. Offer tribute to those [people] who reject [all of] this until they bring it by hand and with humility. [However,] if they refuse to believe [in God and His Messenger] or to bring tribute, kill and fight them. Your casualty who sacrifices himself [for this aim] is a martyr in the eyes of God and [will reside] in the Gardens of Bliss.\\213 Your enemy's casualty, however, [will reside] in the Fire'. If you accept [one of the two options] you have heard from me, it will be good for you. But if you refuse [them], come out to us until God judges between us, for He is the best of [all] judges".

Thereupon, the Byzantine [messenger] said: "You refuse [all offers] except for this?" Abū 'Ubayda (r.) said to him: "Yes". Then the Byzantine [messenger] said to him: "I swear by God that in this [case] I verily foresee that you would wish you had accepted less than what we had offered you". The Byzantine [messenger] left, lifting his hands towards heaven while saying: "O God, we did them justice but they rejected [our offer]. O God, make us victorious over them". Abū 'Ubayda leapt from his place, walked over to the people and said: "O people, rise in the morning [and stand] under your flags and in your lines [in order to fight]". Thus, they rose in the morning and marched out, mobilised and lined up.\\214

Abū 'Ubayda b. al-Jarrāḥ's letter to 'Umar b. al-Khaṭṭāb (r.) informing him about the Byzantines' setting up camp in a place called Fiḥl

He [=the narrator] said: Abū 'Ubayda wrote [the following letter] to 'Umar (r.):

In the name God, the Merciful, the Compassionate. From Abū 'Ubayda b. al-Jarrāḥ to 'Umar, the servant of God and the Commander of the Believers. Peace be upon you. I praise, on your behalf, God with whom no other deity is associated. Regarding the matter at hand: The Byzantines arrived [in the land of the River Jordan] and then a party of them set up camp in Fiḥl, together with its [=Fiḥl's] people. The people of the land and those Arabs who embrace their religion rushed to them. Together with their followers, they marched an army (*jāsha*) against us. They sent [the following message] to me, saying: Get out of our lands that produce wheat, barley, fruits and grapes. You do not deserve to inhabit them. Go back to your lands—the lands of misery and distress. If you do not do so, we will march with those whom you cannot stand against to [fight] you. For we gave God the promise that we would not turn away from you while you were still blinking an eye. I sent [the following message back] to them[, saying]: As for your statement "Get out of our lands; you do not deserve to inhabit them", I swear upon my life that we will never leave them after we have entered them and after God has led us to inherit them from you and dispossessed you of them. The[se] lands are the lands of God [alone] and humans are [only] His servants. God is the King of kings who cedes reign to whomever He wants, strips of reign whomever He wants, elevates whomever He wants and humiliates whomever He wants. As for what\\215 you mentioned about our lands and your claim that they are "the lands of distress and misery", you are right; but God has replaced our lands with your lands, the lands of decent living, low price[s] and plentiful fruits. So never think that we will depart from them or turn away from them. Rather, rally [your soldiers] against us. We swear by God to spare you the burden of coming to us, for we will certainly come to you if you do not come to us. Before rushing to [fight] them, I [just] wrote [this letter] to you [='Umar], trusting in God ('a.), accepting His decree and being certain of His victory. May God protect us, you and the Believers from the conspiracy of every conspirer and from the envy of every envier; may God lead the adherents of His religion to a resounding victory, lead them to an easy conquest and provide them with supporting sovereignty from His side. [Peace be upon you.]

Abū 'Ubayda gave the letter to one of the common people of Syria [who was] one of [their] foot-messengers and said [to him]: "Rush with this letter to the Commander of the Believers [='Umar]". Then he [=Abū 'Ubayda] rushed with the Muslims who were with him to the Byzantines and approached them. Then the Muslim cavalry confronted them, but they [=the Byzantines] did not come out [from their encampment] to them and did not confront them on that day. [Therefore,] on that day, the Muslims turned away from them and there was no [real] fighting between them.\\216

[In the meantime,] the foot-messenger departed with the letter to 'Umar (r.). Abū 'Ubayda b. al-Jarrāḥ had dispatched him [=the foot-messenger] at the beginning of the day. He [=the foot-messenger] went [out] with the letter until he reached 'Umar (r.). As soon as he came to him, he [='Umar] said to him: "Woe unto you, have you known or learned any news about the Muslims, because Abū 'Ubayda wrote to me [in the letter you have just delivered], mentioning that he had written [this letter] to me [just] before he got up [and went] to the Polytheists?" He [=the foot-messenger] said: "[Yes, because] I did not leave [Abū 'Ubayda] on that [particular] day until the Muslims returned [from confronting the Byzantines]. They had marched [out] to them [=the Byzantines] and their [=the Muslims'] cavalry had confronted and approached them, but they [=the Byzantines] had not come out to [meet] them and had not confronted them [in return]. So the Muslims had turned away and had entered their encampment in the best spirits, in the best state and with the greatest daring [to fight] against their enemy". He [='Umar] said: "As for you, what detained you [from leaving] before the late evening on that day, and [why] did you not bring me the letter [earlier], although Abū 'Ubayda (r.) had delivered it to you [and had dispatched you] at the beginning of the day?"\\217 He [=the foot-messenger] said: "I expected that you would ask me the [question about the Muslims' performance] which you have just asked. So I preferred to have knowledge of what [I expected] you would ask me about". Then 'Umar (r.) said to him: "Woe unto you, what is your religion?" He said: "Christian". He ['Umar] considered him wise and said: "Woe unto you, will your [sound] mind, which I observe, guide you to embrace Islam?" ʿUmar (r.) invited him to [embrace] Islam and said: "Woe unto you, embrace Islam for it is better for you". He [=the foot-messenger] then embraced Islam at the hand[s] of ʿUmar and excelled at it. ʿUmar (r.) then said: "Praise be to God who guides the people He wants, if He wants, to Islam and instils the knowledge of Islam in their hearts".\\218

ʿUmar b. al-Khaṭṭāb's letter to Abū ʿUbayda b. al-Jarrāḥ (r.)

Then he [=ʿUmar] wrote [the following letter and sent it] with him [=the foot-messenger] to Abū ʿUbayda:

In the name of God, the Merciful, the Compassionate. From the servant of God and the Commander of the Believers, ʿUmar, to Abū ʿUbayda b. al-Jarrāḥ. Peace be upon you. I praise, on your behalf, God with whom no other deity is associated. Regarding the matter at hand: I got your letter about the Byzantines' trooping to you, setting up camp where they descended, sending you their letter which they had sent [regarding their offer to you], as well as your writing to them in reply to what they asked you about. You had a good argument and you were rightly guided. If you get this letter from me while you are triumphant [over the Byzantines], we shall often remember the benevolence of our Lord (ʿa.) towards us and towards you. But if you get it while a misfortune or an injury is befalling you, do not wither, grieve, resign or surrender, for you will certainly gain the upper hand. It [=Syria] is God's abode, which He will surely lead you to conquer in confirmation of our Messenger's (ṣ.) saying "Have patience, for God is with the patient". Be informed that when you face your enem[ies], lean on God [in your fight] against them; and [since] He knows that you are honest, He will grant you victory over them. When you face them [=the enemies], say "O God, you have been the Supporter of your religion, the Cherisher of your close friends and their Supporter before and now. O God, undertake [arrangements for] their [=the Muslims'] victory, grant them success, do not\\219 let them rely [only] on themselves and thus fail, and be, with your mercy, their Arranger and their Defender. You are certainly the Patron (*walī*) and the Praiseworthy. [Peace be upon you.]".

The [foot-]messenger came with this letter to Abū ʿUbayda, who had [already] sent out Khālid in command of the cavalry after the day on which he [=Abū ʿUbayda] had marched [out] to the Byzantines, who had not come out to them [=Abū ʿUbayda and his unit]. So he sent out Khālid in command of the cavalry to them the following day. Abū ʿUbayda did not march out in command of the infantry on that day. A large [Byzantine] cavalry [unit] marched out to Khālid and headed towards him. So Khālid said to Qays b. Hubayra al-Murādī—who was one of the most valorous, the most crushing and the most persevering [fighters] against the enemy, next to Khālid—"March out to them". Qays b. Hubayra [al-Murādī] marched out to them [=the Byzantines], launched several attacks on them, and they also attacked him. Qays [b. Hubayra al-Murādī] fought them fiercely. Then another large Byzantine cavalry [unit] came [forward] whereupon he [=Khālid] said: "O Maysara b. Masrūq, march out to them[, too]". Maysara [b. Masrūq al-ʿAbsī] marched out [to them], fought them fiercely, attacked them and they also attacked him. Then another huge Byzantine cavalry [unit], which was larger than the [previous] two cavalry [units] together, marched out to them under the command of one of their grand men and patricians. He came [forward] and when he drew near to Khālid, he ordered half of his cavalry to launch an attack on Khālid and his companions [and they did that accordingly]. However, neither Khālid nor his companions fell back. Then he also ordered the other half to launch an attack on Khālid [and his companions] and they did so. However, [again] none of them fell back. Then he gathered them [=the cavalry units] all and all together launched an attack on Khālid [and his companions]. However, [once more] none of them left [his position]. When\\220 the Byzantine [patrician] saw that, he turned [back]. Thereupon, Khālid said to his companions: "Nothing has remained from the Byzantines' earnestness, vehemence or power except that which you have just seen. O adherents of Islam, launch with me one [further] attack, pursue them and do not lose sight of them; may God have mercy upon you". Then Khālid together with those who were with him launched an attack on them and exposed those [Byzantines] who were adjacent to him [to further attacks]. Then Qays b. Hubayra [al-Murādī] launched an attack on those [Byzantines] who were adjacent to him, defeated and exposed them[, too]. Maysara b. Masrūq [al-ʿAbsī] also launched an attack on those [Byzantines] who were adjacent to him and defeated them. [All] the Muslims pursued them, [continued] killing them and made [some of] them crash into one another until they drove them out [and back] to their encampment and their group[s]. On that day, the Muslim cavalry turned away from their [=the Byzantines'] cavalry [only] after having gained a victory over them. The Byzantines saw languishment and defeat befalling them. It [=the defeat] broke them up, weakened their cause and they became extremely terrified of the Muslims. The Muslims left for their encampment contentedly and flocked to Abū ʿUbayda (r.), delighted by the support that God (ʿa.) had shown them against their enemy and that had led them to defeat the cavalry of the Polytheists. Then Khālid said to Abū ʿUbayda: "Our defeat of the Polytheists' cavalry struck terror into the hearts of everyone. [Now] everyone's heart is terrified and frightened of getting defeated by us once again. Keep attacking those people early tomorrow morning as long as the terror of this defeat is still in their hearts. However, if you delay fighting them for a few days, the terror of this\\221 defeat will leave their hearts and they will forget it and dare [to fight again] against us". Thereupon, Abū ʿUbayda said: "Rush [to fight them] tomorrow morning with God's blessing".

Al-Ḥusayn b. Ziyād [al-Ramlī] reported to us on the authority of Abū Ismāʿīl Muḥammad b. ʿAbdallāh [al-Azdī], who said: Furthermore, Abū Ṭayba ʿAmr b. Mālik al-Qaynī related to me, saying: My fellow [tribes] people, Banū al-Qayn, attended the battle-day[s] of Fiḥl and so did Lakhm, Judhām, Ghassān, ʿĀmila and Quḍāʿa, together with the Muslims. A great many of those tribesmen were there, by virtue of whom the Muslims became more powerful against their enemy. He [=the narrator, ʿAmr b. Mālik al-Qaynī] said: Nothing was favoured more by the Byzantines than procrastinating and fending off war in order to wait for reinforcements and nothing was favoured more by the Muslims than fighting and rushing to them.

Al-Ḥusayn b. Ziyād [al-Ramlī] reported to us on the authority of Abū Ismāʿīl Muḥammad b. ʿAbdallāh al-Azdī al-Baṣrī, who said: Furthermore, Abū Jahḍam [al-Azdī] related to me on the authority of ʿAbd al-Raḥmān b. al-Salīk [al-Fazārī] on the authority of ʿAbdallāh b. Qurṭ al-Thumālī, who said: That morning when we marched out to [fight] the people of Fiḥl, Abū ʿUbayda had left [his tent] in the remaining one third of the night before and kept mobilising the people and inciting them [to fight], until morning [came]. When the morning came, he led the people in prayer[s]. During the prayer[s], [the night] was [still] closer to dark than to daylight. [Then] he positioned Muʿādh b. Jabal in command of his right flank, Hāshim b. ʿUtba [b. Abī Waqqāṣ] in command of his left flank, Saʿīd b. Zayd b. ʿAmr b. Nufayl in command of the infantry and Khālid b. al-Walīd in command of the blessed cavalry. Then Abū ʿUbayda marched [out] with the people [=the whole army] who started moving in a solemn procession gradually and slowly. Abū ʿUbayda b. al-Jarrāḥ rode [his horse] and reviewed the line [of fighters] from start to finish, stopping at every flag and every tribe to exhort (*yaquṣṣu*) the people and motivate them, saying: "O servants of God, merit\\222 victory from God through patience, for God is with the patient. O servants of God, I herald good news to you: Martyrdom for those who will be killed and victory and spoils for those who will survive. However, set your minds on fighting [the enemy], stabbing with the spears, striking with the swords, shooting arrows[351] [with the bow] and grabbing opponents in arm-to-arm fighting (*muʿānaqat al-aqrān*). I swear by God that anything from Him can be obtained only by showing obedience to Him, by having patience in adverse circumstances and by seeking His satisfaction. You will get this [reward] only through God".

The Muslims were keen on facing their enemies and rushing to [fight] them. Khālid b. al-Walīd advanced with the cavalry until he approached the Byzantines. When they saw him, they all marched out to him with their whole cavalry and infantry [after] they [had] said: "The Arabs are more skilful on horseback than we and our cavalry cannot stand theirs. So march out to the Muslims with all the cavalry and all the infantry". Khālid had defeated their cavalry the day before and that was why they were forced to

351 Arrows (a collective noun, sg. *nabl*) signifies wooden arrows (in contrast to "pipe arrows") which, according to pre-Islamic and early Islamic poetry, were considered to be of Arabian origin (see Schwarzlose, *Waffen*, 280–281).

march out with such a [huge] mobilisation [now]. They [=the Byzantines] marched out in five lines, whose two ends were invisible, numbering about 50,000 [men]. In the first line, they placed a cavalryman between two infantrymen: One of them was an archer and the other a spearman. Then they set up the two flanks [of the army] (*mujannibatān*)[352] and lined up another three lines of the infantry against the Muslims. Then they moved [forward] towards the Muslims. The first of the Muslims to have faced them in advance was Khālid b. al-Walīd [who was] in command of the cavalry. He did not slacken [his] advance on them. They[, however,] started marching [directly] to him, pelting him with arrows and thus he and his companions started retreating. [As] the Byzantines were advancing on them [=Khālid and his cavalry], Khālid and his cavalry started to retreat until the cavalry reached their [=the Muslims'] [first] line. [As a result,] the rears of the cavalry pushed [back] the fronts of the [Muslim] infantry.\\223

Then Khālid sent [the following message] to Qays b. Hubayra al-Murādī[, saying]: "March out with your cavalry [unit] until you reach their [=the Byzantines'] left flank and then launch an attack on it". He also said to Maysara b. Masrūq al-ʿAbsī: "Stand with your cavalry [unit] opposite to their [first] line and attach it to you as one single cavalry unit. When you see us launching an attack on them and [see] their line[s] collapsing, launch an attack on those of them who are adjacent to you". [Then] Khālid divided his cavalry into three [units]: He placed one third under the command of Qays b. Hubayra al-Murādī, another one third under the command of Maysara [b. Masrūq] al-ʿAbsī while Khālid [himself] was in command of its [remaining] one third. Then he marched out with one third of the cavalry until he reached their [=the Byzantines'] right flank and surmounted it. When he surmounted [it] and rose above them [=the Byzantines], they sent the cavalry [unit] of theirs up to him to keep Khālid and his companions busy. Khālid let them [do so] and when they drew near to him, he said [to his companions]: "God is the Greatest! He made them [=the Byzantines' cavalry unit] move out of their infantry to[wards] you". In fact, Khālid had wanted to bring them out of their infantry. Then he said to his companions: "Assault them". Then Khālid intercepted and assaulted them and so did his companions together with the whole cavalry. Then God defeated them and they [=Khālid and his companions] stabbed them with spears and swords wherever they wanted and lots of them were struck down before they could get [back] to their right flank.

[In the meantime,] Qays b. Hubayra [al-Murādī] went up to their left flank and they sent a huge cavalry [unit] out to him just as they had done with Khālid [on their right flank]. Then Qays [b. Hubayra al-Murādī] launched an attack on them [=the cavalry unit's members], defeated them and struck

352 See Lane, *Lexicon*, s.v. *al-mujannibatān*.

them [dead] until he reached their [=the Byzantines'] left flank and killed a great many of them.\\224

He [=the narrator] said: Wāthila b. al-Asqaʿ[353] was one of Qays b. Hubayra [al-Murādī's] cavalrymen. [At one point,] one of their [=the Byzantines'] great patricians intercepted him [=Qays]. So Wāthila [b. al-Asqaʿ] stepped out to [fight] him while saying [the following lines of verse] during his attack:

ليث وليث فى مجال ضنك
كلاهما ذو أنف ومعك
أجول جول صارم فى العرك
مع ظفرى بحاجتى وتركى
أو يكشف الله قناع الشك

A lion with a lion in a narrow place;
Both have pride and with you
I round like a staunch fighter;
Either I fulfil my need and leave
Or God removes the mask of doubt.

Then he [=Wāthila b. al-Asqaʿ] launched an attack on the patrician and struck him dead. Then they [=Qays's cavalrymen] all launched an attack until they forced them [=the Byzantines] back to their encampment and he [=Wāthila b. al-Asqaʿ] stood opposite to them.

Al-Ḥusayn b. Ziyād [al-Ramlī] reported to us on the authority of Abū Ismāʿīl Muḥammad b. ʿAbdallāh [al-Azdī], who said: Furthermore, ʿAbd al-Malik b. Nawfal [b. Masāḥiq al-Qurashī] related to me on the authority of Rabīʿa al-ʿAnzī[354] on the authority of Hāshim b. ʿUtba [b. Abī Waqqāṣ], who said: I swear by God that we were, at the beginning of that day, the most sympathetic towards our cavalrymen. Then God (ʿa.) rendered us victorious over them [=the Byzantines]. [Strictly,] we only saw God rendering our cavalrymen victorious over theirs.

Hāshim b. ʿUtba b. Abī Waqqāṣ [=the narrator] said: I summoned the people to [come to] me, ordered them to fear God, dismounted [from my horse], waved my flag and then said: "I swear by God that I will never take it [=the flag] back until I will have set it up within their line[s]. Whoever wants to

353 Wāthila's full name is Abū al-Asqaʿ (or Abū Muḥammad or Abū Shaddād) Wāthila b. al-Asqaʿ b. Kaʿb b. ʿĀmir (d. between 83–85/702–705). In al-Azdī's narrative, he is mentioned as one of Qays b. Hubayra's cavalrymen who attacked one of the Byzantine patricians, struck him dead and recited a poem while doing so. On Wāthila, see Ibn Saʿd, *Kitāb al-ṭabaqāt*, VII-2, 129 and Ibn ʿAsākir, *TMD*, LXII, 343–354.

354 Rabīʿa al-ʿAnzī is a transmitter of traditions. We could not find a *tarjama* about him. ʿUqla and Banī Yāsīn found him mentioned in al-Mizzī's *Tahdhīb al-kamāl* as informant of ʿAbd al-Malik b. Nawfal (see al-Azdī, *Futūḥ al-Shām. Ed. ʿUqla/Banī Yāsīn*, 224, n. 5 referring to al-Mizzī, *Tahdhīb al-kamāl*, XVIII, 429). In al-Azdī's narrative, he is mentioned as a transmitter of one tradition.

follow me [in this task] can do so. However, whoever wants to remain behind can do so". He [=the narrator, Hāshim b. ʿUtba b. Abī Waqqāṣ] [also] said: By the One with whom no other deity is associated, I saw none of my [fellow] flag followers remaining behind when I reached their [first] line. Then they [=the Byzantines] showered us with arrows, so we got\\225 on [our] knees and protected [ourselves] against them with the leather shields[355]. Then I drew near [to my fellow fighters] with my flag and said to my companions: "Assault them. I will sacrifice myself for you, for it [=the sacrifice] is the spoils in the worldly life and in the afterlife". Then I assaulted [them] and so did they [=the companions] together with me. Then I faced one of their grand men who came towards me. I stabbed him with the spear and he fell dead. Then we [all] fought them with swords within their line[s] for a short while. Then Khālid b. al-Walīd launched an[other] attack on their left flank and killed [many of] them quickly, fiercely and devastatingly. The Byzantines' lines collapsed from the [attacks from the] side of Khālid b. al-Walīd (r.) and from mine. Abū ʿUbayda [also] rushed to them with the infantry and the people and ordered one of Khālid's cavalry units that was adjacent to him to launch an attack on the Polytheists [and it did that accordingly]. [Thus,] they were defeated.

Al-Ḥusayn b. Ziyād [al-Ramlī] reported to us on the authority of Abū Ismāʿīl Muḥammad b. ʿAbdallāh [al-Azdī], who said: Furthermore, ʿAmr b. Mālik [al-Qaynī] related to me on the authority of his father [=Mālik], who said: Among us was a man whom we held in great esteem and who had a high status. [Once] I thought to myself: "I knew that this Arab fellow—i.e. Abū ʿUbayda—is an honest man. I swear by God that I will certainly go to him, accompany him and learn from him". He [=the narrator, the father of ʿAmr b. Mālik al-Qaynī] said: I used to go to him and move out with him to his encampment whenever he moved out. On the [battle-]day [of Fiḥl], he [=the father of ʿAmr b. Mālik al-Qaynī] went to Abū ʿUbayda and stayed by him, not leaving him. He [=the narrator, the father of ʿAmr b. Mālik al-Qaynī] said: I swear by God that I have really seen him exhorting us, saying: "Be the servants and close friends of God, make your desire for what God (t.) retains [in the afterlife] stronger than your desire for the worldly life. Do not be so dependent [on the worldly life] that you fail [to reach this aim]. Make\\226 [sure that] each of you would be a sufficient support for his peer. Fight daringly like the one who fights daringly to seek the reward of God (tt.) and do not let your enemies who face you [now] be more patient with their wrong than you are with your right [attitudes]". Then he [=Abū ʿUbayda] got up and marched with them [=the Muslims] to them [=the Byzantines]. The Muslims also got up with him under their flags peacefully, discerningly, meekly and decently. And Qays b. Hubayra [al-Murādī] launched an attack on their left flank and made them crash into one another.

355 "*Daraq*" (sg. *daraqa*, lit. "shield") signifies a shield made of (cow) skin without wooden elements (see Schwarzlose, *Waffen*, 353, 355).

Al-Ḥusayn b. Ziyād [al-Ramlī] reported to us on the authority of Abū Ismā'īl Muḥammad b. 'Abdallāh [al-Azdī], who said: Furthermore, Yaḥyā b. Hāni' b. 'Urwa al-Murādī related to me: Qays b. Hubayra [al-Murādī] fractured three swords and broke some teen number (*biḍ'ata 'ashar*)[356] of spears on that day. [While] he was fighting, he said [the following lines of verse]:

لا يبعدن كل فتى كرار
ماضى الجنان خشن صبار
حبوتهم بالخيل فى الأدبار
تقدم إقدام الشجاع الضارى
Combative lads never run away
But remain valorous, hard and patient;
Their creeping with the horses in the rear
Is as daring as the brave predator.

Maysara b. Masrūq [al-'Absī] also launched an attack [on the Byzantines]. He was [good] company and was righteous.\\227

[Manuscript note: Part IV]

This is the end of the third part of the Book of the Conquests of Syria. It is continued in the fourth part [by the following tradition]: Al-Ḥusayn b. Ziyād [al-Ramlī] reported to us on the authority of Abū Ismā'īl Muḥammad b. 'Abdallāh [al-Azdī], who said: Furthermore, al-Naḍir b. Ṣāliḥ[357] related to me on the authority of Sālim b. Rabī'a[358], who said: On that day, Maysara b. Masrūq [al-'Absī] launched an attack [on the Byzantines] while we were with him in the cavalry. Then we launched an attack on the [Byzantine army's] centre while the Byzantines' lines started collapsing on their left and their right flanks. Praise be to God alone and [may] His blessings be upon Muḥammad and his family.

In the name of God, the Merciful, the Compassionate. Shaykh Abū Isḥāq Ibrāhīm b. Sa'īd b. 'Abdallāh al-Ḥāfiẓ al-Tujībī al-Ḥabbāl reported to us, saying: Abū al-'Abbās Munīr b. Aḥmad b. al-Ḥasan[359] b. 'Alī b. Munīr al-Khashshāb reported to us: Abū al-Ḥasan 'Alī b. Aḥmad b. Isḥāq b. Ibrāhīm

356 The Arabic lexeme "*biḍ'*" is a tentative number ranging between *three* and *nine* and can be combined with the cardinal number *ten* as in "*biḍ'ata 'ashar*" (a number ranging from *thirteen* to *nineteen*), with *twenty* as in "*biḍ'ata wa-'ishrūn*" (a number ranging from *twenty-three* to *twenty-nine*) and so forth. On the meaning of "*biḍ'*", see Lane, *Lexicon*, s.v. *biḍ'*.

357 Al-Naḍir's full name is Abū Zuhayr al-Naḍir b. Ṣāliḥ al-'Absī (n.d.); he is a transmitter. According to Mourad, he transmitted from Abū Mikhnaf (Mourad, *al-Azdī*, 589–590). 'Uqla and Banī Yāsīn state that he was a young man in 77/696 (see al-Azdī, *Futūḥ al-Shām. Ed. 'Uqla/Banī Yāsīn*, 32; 227, n. 2). In al-Azdī's narrative, he is mentioned as a transmitter of one tradition. On al-Naḍir, see Ibn Abī Ḥātim, *Al-jarḥ wa-al-ta'dīl*, VIII, 477.

358 Sālim b. Rabī'a (n.d.) is an early Islamic figure. In al-Azdī's narrative, he is mentioned as fighting a Byzantine during the Battle of Fiḥl and as a transmitter of two traditions. On Sālim, see al-Bukhārī, *Al-ta'rīkh al-kabīr*, II-2, 113 (no. 2144) and Ibn 'Asākir, *TMD*, XX, 39–138.

359 We changed the edited text (al-Ḥusayn) to al-Ḥasan, since this is the form that usually occurs in the manuscripts.

al-Baghdādī reported to us, by way of reading from his book to the former in his [own] house: Abū al-ʿAbbās al-Walīd b. Ḥammād al-Ramlī related to us, saying: Al-Ḥusayn b. Ziyād al-Ramlī reported to us, saying: Abū Ismāʿīl Muḥammad b. ʿAbdallāh al-Azdī al-Baṣrī related to us, saying: Furthermore, al-Naḍir b. Ṣāliḥ related to me on the authority of Sālim b. Rabīʿa, who said: On that day, Maysara b. Masrūq [al-ʿAbsī] launched an attack [on the Byzantines] while we were with him in the cavalry. Then we launched an attack on the [Byzantine army's] centre while the Byzantines' lines started collapsing on their left and their right flanks. The collapse had not yet reached the centre, so they stood [firmly] against us [there] and fought us fiercely. Maysara [b. Masrūq al-ʿAbsī] then dismounted from his horse and I [=Sālim b. Rabīʿa] also dismounted from my horse, which moved off and went away. Then Maysara took hold of one of the Byzantines and they fought each other for a short while until Maysara struck him down and killed him. Then another [Byzantine soldier] assaulted Maysara and took hold of him. They fought each other for a short while until he struck down Maysara; he sat on his chest and assailed him.\\228 So I struck the Byzantine's face with the sword and swept his skull away. He fell dead and Maysara leapt [to his feet]. [Yet another] one of them came to me and struck me such a severe blow that stunned me. Maysara [b. Masrūq al-ʿAbsī] saw him, struck him [with the sword] and killed him. Many of them [=the Byzantines] caught up with us and surrounded us, so we thought: "We swear by God that this is [our] destruction". We had barely turned [around] when, lo and behold, we heard the Muslims calling and proclaiming "God is the Greatest!" Lo and behold, their [=the Muslims'] lines approached us and, lo and behold, the [Muslims'] flags reached us. Thus, God strengthened our backs by virtue of our brethren and they [=the Byzantines] vanished [and went] away from us. Khālid b. al-Walīd launched an attack on their right flank and hammered them against one another until they entered their encampment.

Al-Ḥusayn b. Ziyād [al-Ramlī] reported to us on the authority of Abū Ismāʿīl Muḥammad b. ʿAbdallāh [al-Azdī], who said: Furthermore, ʿAbd al-Malik b. Nawfal b. Masāḥiq [al-Qurashī] related to me on the authority of his father [=Nawfal b. Masāḥiq al-Qurashī]: On that day, Khālid engaged in such a fierce fight that none of the Muslims has ever engaged in before. This [=Khālid's fight] was the only topic (*ḥadīth*) and the only example (*mathal*) [to be mentioned] for those who witnessed it. He intercepted their lines and group[s] and launched an attack on them until he mingled with them. He fought them until he dispersed, defeated and killed a great number of them. He [=the narrator, Nawfal b. Masāḥiq al-Qurashī] said: I heard someone claiming that on that day he [=Khālid] killed eleven of the Byzantine patricians and their tough and brave men. [While] he was fighting them, he said [the following lines of verse]:

اضربهم بصارم مهند
ضرب صليب الدين هادى مهتد
لا واهن القول ولا مفند

Strike them with an Indian-made sword[360];
A strike of a staunchly religious, guiding and guided [person]
Whose argument is neither weak nor refutable.\\229

Al-Ḥusayn b. Ziyād [al-Ramlī] reported to us on the authority of Abū Ismā'īl Muḥammad b. 'Abdallāh [al-Azdī], who said: Furthermore, Muḥammad b. Yūsuf related to me on the authority of Thābit [al-Bunānī] on the authority of Sahl b. Sa'd [al-Anṣārī], who said: On that day, Mu'ādh b. Jabal was one of the most valorous people. And he was saying: "O adherents of Islam, [what you are doing] today is for the days to come. So lower your eyes, may God have mercy upon you, and rush upon your enemy daringly like a lion. Do not leave your flags. Do not abandon your lines, but goad them violently. And do not let their spoils or what is there in their encampment distract you from [fighting] them. For I fear that they might have a turning point [in battle] and that you would not be able to make a firm stand anymore if you dispersed and their spoils distracted you. Chase them so that you do not see them assembled or [standing] in line[s] [anymore]". Then the Muslims marched under their flags and in their lines, according to what he [=Mu'ādh b. Jabal] had described to them. The Byzantine lines started to collapse and retreat while the Muslim cavalry forced them back, killing them, attacking them and not veering away from them. They killed about 5,000 of them in the battle and about 2,000 [more] when they entered their encampment. They [=the Byzantines] moved out [of the encampment], crushed and defeated. The Muslim cavalry was still pursuing and killing them until they stormed into Fiḥl, which overlooked water pits below. Then they fortified [the place]. The Muslims captured about 2,000 of them. Then the Muslims [went] killing them and Abū 'Ubayda proceeded until he entered their encampment and took hold of what was therein.

Al-Ḥusayn b. Ziyād [al-Ramlī] reported to us on the authority of Abū Ismā'īl Muḥammad b. 'Abdallāh [al-Azdī], who said: Furthermore, Yazīd b. Yazīd b. Jābir related to me on the authority of 'Amr b. Muḥṣan[361] on the authority of 'Abdallāh b. Qurṭ al-Thumālī,\\230 who said: On that day, before the defeat of the Polytheists, I passed by 'Amr b. Sa'īd b. al-'Āṣ, who was accompanied by seven or eight Muslims and was ahead of them, [moving] towards the enemy and saying: "Believers, when you meet the disbelievers in battle, never turn your backs on them. If anyone does so on such a day—unless manoeuvring to fight or to join a fighting group—he incurs

360 "*Ṣārim muhannad*" (lit. "a sharp sword made according to Indian fashion") signifies a sword with an excellent blade (see Schwarzlose, *Waffen*, 128, 112).

361 The edition reads "'Abdallāh b. Muḥṣan". However, we consider it a transmission error and thus corrected it to "'Amr b. Muḥṣan", because the *isnād* mentions "'Amr b. Muḥṣan" frequently as the immediate transmitter before Yazīd b. Yazīd b. Jābir. 'Uqla and Banī Yāsīn are of the same opinion, but kept the name 'Abdallāh in their edition (see al-Azdī, *Futūḥ al-Shām. Ed. 'UqlalBanī Yāsīn*, 229, n. 7).

the wrath of God, and Hell will be his home, a wretched destination!"[362] Then he said: "But I swear by God that Paradise is a great destiny. To whom will it be [given]? I swear by God that it will be [given] to those who will sell themselves to God today and fight for His cause". Then he [also] said: "O adherents of Islam, [come] to me—I am ʿAmr b. Saʿīd b. al-ʿĀṣ—and do not flee. For if you do so, God sees you. God certainly detests whomever He sees fleeing from supporting His religion. So be ashamed if God sees you obeying His most detested creature, who is the most accursed Satan, and disobeying Him, who is the most Merciful". ʿAbdallāh b. Qurṭ [al-Thumālī] [=the narrator] said: The enemy launched an atrocious attack on us and separated me from my companions. I reached ʿAmr b. Saʿīd [b. al-ʿĀṣ] while he was saying these words and I thought to myself: "I swear by God that I do not find, today in this encampment, any man who is an earlier companion of or closer to the Messenger of God (ṣ.) than this man".\\231 He [=the narrator, ʿAbdallāh b. Qurṭ al-Thumālī] said: Having a spear with me, I drew near him [=ʿAmr b. Saʿīd b. al-ʿĀṣ] while he was beset with a group of the Byzantines. He [=the narrator, ʿAbdallāh b. Qurṭ al-Thumālī] said: Then I launched an attack on them [=the Byzantines] and killed one of them. Then I reached him [=ʿAmr b. Saʿīd], stood [still] with him and then said to him: "O [great-grand] son of Abū Uḥayḥa[363], do you know me?" He [=ʿAmr b. Saʿīd b. al-ʿĀṣ] said to me: "Yes, brother of Thaqīf[364]". I said to him: "You have not gone far [from being right]. They [=Thaqīf tribesmen] are [our] brethren, neighbours and allies, but I am [your] brother of Thumāla[365]; I am ʿAbdallāh b. Qurṭ [al-Thumālī]". He said to me: "Welcome, you are my brother in [terms of] Islam and this is the closest relation [we can have]. I swear by God that if I am summoned for testimony [on your behalf], I will certainly testify for you—and God suffices as a testifier. And if I am summoned for intercession, I will

362 Q. 8:15–16 (*The Qurʾān. Tr. Abdel Haleem*, 111).

363 Abū Uḥayḥa's full name is Abū Uḥayḥa Saʿīd b. al-ʿĀṣ al-Umawī al-Qurashī. In al-Azdī's narrative, he is mentioned as the ancestor of ʿAmr b. Saʿīd b. al-ʿĀṣ (and his brothers al-Ḥakam, Abbān and Khālid). According to the genealogical tradition, Abū Uḥayḥa is ʿAmr's great-grandfather. On Abū Uḥayḥa, see Ibn ʿAsākir, *TMD*, XXXXVI, 10 and LXVI, 457.

364 Thaqīf is a Northern Arabian tribe that was a subtribe of Muḍar. In al-Azdī's narrative, Thaqīf is mentioned once when ʿAbdallāh b. Qurṭ is falsely addressed as a member of Thaqīf. On Thaqīf, see *EI²*, s.v. Thaḳīf (M. Lecker).

365 Thumāla is a Southern Arabian tribe that was a subtribe of Azd. In al-Azdī's narrative, members of Thumāla are mentioned once as being brethren, neighbours and allies of Thaqīf. In addition, one individual figure belonged to Thumāla, i.e. ʿAbdallāh b. Qurṭ al-Thumālī, who was a messenger from Abū Bakr to Yazīd and from Abū ʿUbayda to ʿUmar and who was married to Amna bt. Abī Bishr al-Azdiyya. ʿAbdallāh b. Qurṭ is said to have fought a Byzantine unit, to have been one of the first men who reached Ḥimṣ, who entered Damascus with Abū ʿUbayda during the Muslims' retreat and who was given command over Ḥimṣ for one year by ʿUmar. Furthermore, ʿAbdallāh b. Qurṭ is a transmitter of several traditions throughout the narrative, some of which describe his own deeds. On Thumāla, see *EI²*, s.v. Azd (G. Strenziok).

certainly intercede [with God] on your behalf". He [=the narrator, ʿAbdallāh b. Qurṭ al-Thumālī] said: I looked at his face and, lo and behold, he had a sword strike on his eyebrow and his eyes were full of blood. Lo and behold, he was unable to blink or to open his eyelids because of the blood. He [=the narrator, ʿAbdallāh b. Qurṭ al-Thumālī] said: I said to him: "Anticipate good news, for God (ʿa.) will certainly cure you from this strike and bestow victory upon the Muslims". He [=ʿAmr b. Saʿīd b. al-ʿĀṣ] said: "As for the victory on behalf of the adherents of Islam, God has already bestowed it [upon them], so rush [to get your share of it]. As for me, God has made this strike bring about [my] martyrdom and has granted me another one similar to it. I swear by God that I would like it [=the wound]\\232 to be as wide as Abū Qubays [Mountain][366]. I swear by God that but for [my fear] that some of those whom you see around me might be killed, I would have rushed to [fight] this enemy [with the wound] [=the Byzantines] and would have fought them with the wound until I meet my Lord". Then he [=ʿAmr b. Saʿīd b. al-ʿĀṣ] said: "O my brother, God's (ʿa.) reward for martyrdom is great and those who lead the worldly life seldom depart it unharmed". He [=the narrator, ʿAbdallāh b. Qurṭ al-Thumālī] said: In no time a group of them [=the Byzantines] launched a severe attack on us. So he walked to them with a sword [in his hand] and fought them for a short while. While he was facing these people, the dust was stirred up between them. Then we attacked them, striking many of them dead. Lo and behold, we found ʿAmr b. Saʿīd [b. al-ʿĀṣ] thrown to the ground and stabbed more than thirty times. When they [=the Byzantines] had seen him and his severe fighting, they had become angry with him, committed themselves to him and cut him [into pieces] with their swords until he was killed; God rest his soul. Saʿīd b. al-Ḥārith b. Qays[367] and al-Ḥārith b. al-Ḥārith [b. Qays[368]] [=his brother], who were from the Qurayshite [subtribe of] Banū Sahm[369], were also killed. The Muslims gained control over the land [around Fiḥl] and conquered it. The survivors from among the enemy ended up [taking refuge] in the fortresses. God killed a great many of them and a part [of

366 Abū Qubays Mountain is a hill on the eastern edge of Mecca. In al-Azdī's narrative, it is mentioned only metaphorically by stressing its width. On Abū Qubays Mountain, see *EI*^{2}, s.v. Abū Ḳubays (G. Rentz).

367 Saʿīd's full name is Saʿīd b. al-Ḥārith b. Qays b. ʿAdī b. Sāʿd b. Sahm (d. 15/636–637). In al-Azdī's narrative, he is said to belong to Banū Sahm and is mentioned as one of those killed at Fiḥl. On Saʿīd, see Ibn Saʿd, *Kitāb al-ṭabaqāt*, IV-1, 144.

368 Al-Ḥārith's full name is al-Ḥārith b. al-Ḥārith b. Qays b. ʿAdī al-Qurashī (n.d.). In al-Azdī's narrative, he is said to belong to Banū Sahm and is mentioned as one of those killed at Fiḥl. On al-Ḥārith, see Ibn ʿAsākir, *TMD*, XI, 405.

369 Banū Sahm is a Northern Arabian tribe that was a subtribe of Quraysh. In al-Azdī's narrative, Banū Sahm is also mentioned as such. In addition, three individual figures belonged to Banū Sahm: (a) ʿAmr b. al-ʿĀṣ, who is one of the major commanders and is usually associated with the command over Palestine, (b) Saʿīd b. al-Ḥārith b. Qays and (c) al-Ḥārith b. al-Ḥārith b. Qays, who were killed (probably during the Battle of Fiḥl). On Banū Sahm, see Ibn Saʿd, *Kitāb al-ṭabaqāt*, IV-1, 139–145 and Caskel, *Ǧamharat*, I, 4, 25; II, 498.

the Byzantine army] was defeated.\\233 The Muslims fell persistently on the fortresses after they had gained control over the arable lands of the River Jordan, its mainland and what was therein. Then the Byzantines asked them [=the Muslims] to [allow them to] descend [from the fortresses] to them and to offer them protection.

Abū ʿUbayda b. al-Jarrāḥ wrote [the following letter] to ʿUmar b. al-Khaṭṭāb (r.)

In the name of God, the Merciful, the Compassionate. From Abū ʿUbayda b. al-Jarrāḥ to the servant of God and the Commander of the Believers, ʿUmar. Peace be upon you. I praise, on your behalf, God with whom no other deity is associated. Regarding the matter at hand: Praise be to God who bestowed His victory upon the Believers and [cast] His punishment upon the Unbelievers. I [write to] inform the Commander of the Believers, may God increase his righteousness, that we faced the Byzantines, who mustered large groups against us, who descended upon us from the mountaintops and who [came to us from] the seacoasts, thinking that nobody could defeat them. They appeared to us and assailed us [near Fiḥl]. But we trusted in God, raised our desire for Him and said: "God is enough for us and He is the best Upholder". We then rushed towards them with our cavalry and infantry. The fight between the two armies took place for a long period in the daytime. God granted martyrdom to some of the Muslim men, one of whom was ʿAmr b. Saʿīd b. al-ʿĀṣ, and struck the faces of the Polytheists [=He vanquished them]. [Then] the Muslims pursued them, killing and capturing them until they [=the Polytheists] took refuge in their fortresses. The Muslims then took hold of their encampment and gained control over their land. Then God caused them [=the Polytheists] to descend from their fortresses and struck\\234 terror into their hearts. O Commander of the Believers, you and the Muslims at your side should praise God for strengthening His religion and bringing about triumph over the Polytheists. Pray to God, you all, that He bestows [His] full blessing upon us. Peace be upon you.

When the people of Fiḥl realised that the Muslims had conquered the land, i.e. the land of the River Jordan, they solicited peace from them on the condition that they [=the Muslims] do not kill them, that they leave them (*anfusahum*) intact, that they [=the people of Fiḥl] bring tribute, that whichever of them is a Byzantine [soldier] should catch up with the [other] Byzantines and evacuate the lands (*bilād*) of the River Jordan and [finally] that whichever of them [=the Byzantines] loves to stay can stay, but should bring tribute[, too]. So the Muslims [agreed to] make peace with them. They wrote a letter [of protection] for them and made peace with them. Those of them who were Byzantine [soldiers] moved out towards the Byzantines' [headquarters] in that year. [However,] whoever had dwelled in that land before [continued to] dwell in the hamlets (*ḍiyāʿ*), to marry and to have children there. Those who had stayed in the fortresses [also continued to] stay [there] on the condition that they would bring tribute. As for the people of the River

Jordan, the people of the [arable] land[s] and the hamlets, the Muslims took [hold] of them by force, without [making] peace. Later the Muslims differed over [how to deal with] them. A party of them said: "We divide them up [among us]" whereas another party said: "We leave them [untouched]".

Abū ʿUbayda b. al-Jarrāḥ wrote [the following letter] to ʿUmar b. al-Khaṭṭāb (r.) [regarding this issue]\\235

In the name of God, the Merciful, the Compassionate. Regarding the matter at hand: God, the Owner of grace, favour and great blessings, led the Muslims to the conquest of the land of the River Jordan. A party of the Muslims were of the opinion that its people should be allowed to bring tribute to them and to continue inhabiting the[ir] land[s] [in return] whereas another party of them were of the opinion that they [=the people] should be divided up [among them]. So Commander of the Believers, write us your decision on this [issue]; may God continue granting you success in all matters. [Peace be upon you.]

ʿUmar (r.) wrote [the following letter] to him [in reply]

In the name of God, the Merciful, the Compassionate. From the servant of God and the Commander of the Believers, ʿUmar, to Abū ʿUbayda b. al-Jarrāḥ. Peace be upon you. I praise, on your behalf, God with whom no other deity is associated. Regarding the matter at hand: I received your letter in which you mentioned God's strengthening of the adherents of His religion, His abandonment of His enemy and His sparing us the burden of [fighting] those who opposed us. Praise be to God for His benevolence to us in what has passed by and for His good deeds to us in what has elapsed. [God is the One] who protected all\\236 the Muslims and honoured a party of the Believers with martyrdom. We congratulate them on [having obtained] their Lord's satisfaction and on His generosity to them. We ask Him not to deprive us of their [=the martyrs'] reward and to protect us from going astray after their departure. For they certainly advised [people well] for [the sake of] God, fulfilled their obligations, worked for [the sake of] their Lord and paved [the way to Paradise] for themselves. I have also understood what you mentioned about the Muslims' [taking] control over the land [of the River Jordan] and over its people, [in the context of which] a party said: "We let its people continue inhabiting the[ir] land[s], provided that they bring tribute to the Muslims", whereas another party said: "We divide them up [among us]". I considered what you have written to me in this respect and I have a different opinion on what you have asked me about. I am of the opinion that you let them stay [in their lands], impose tribute on them and divide it between the Muslims. Furthermore, they should continue inhabiting the land [in return], because they know it much better and can handle it much better than others. What do you think [would happen] if we took its people and divided them up between us? Who would be left for the Muslims after our departure [with them]? I swear by God that they [=the Muslims] would not then find any person with whom they would talk and who would talk to them and they would not benefit from anything made with this person's own hand[s]. [In contrast,] the Muslims will be nourished by those [=the inhabitants of the lands] as long as they stay alive. When we perish and they perish, our children will [in turn] be nourished by their children as long as they live and they will remain servants (*ʿabīd*) to the adherents of Islam as long as Islam remains triumphant. So impose tribute on them [=the people of the land of the River Jordan], refrain from capturing them and prevent the Muslims from oppressing or harming them and from devouring their possessions if there is no legal basis [for this]. [Peace be upon you.] \\237

The Muslims' march to Ḥimṣ after they had finished [their campaigns] in Fiḥl and in the land of the River Jordan

Al-Ḥusayn b. Ziyād [al-Ramlī] reported to us on the authority of Abū Ismāʿīl Muḥammad b. ʿAbdallāh [al-Azdī], who said: Farwa—or Qurra—b. Luqayṭ[370] related to me on the authority of Adham b. Muḥriz al-Bāhilī on the authority of his father [=Muḥriz b. Usayd al-Bāhilī], who said: Abū ʿUbayda summoned the Muslim chiefs and their cavalrymen who were with him and assembled them after we had triumphed over Fiḥl and had finished [our campaign] at the River Jordan and its [arable] land. The people of Jerusalem had already fortified [their place] against us while large [Byzantine] groups had assembled in Caesarea, together with its people, who were still great in number. [In this situation,] Abū ʿUbayda said [to the Muslim commanders]: "O adherents of Islam, God (ʿa.) has been benevolent towards you, covered you with great health and ample security, made you triumphant over the Byzantine patricians, led you to the conquest of fortresses, citadels, hamlets and cities, caused you to be the owners of this abode—[i.e.] the abode of [the Byzantine] Emperors—and made it your dwelling. I wanted to rush with you to [fight] the people of Jerusalem or those of Caesarea. But I hated to march to them while they were in the heart of their cit[ies] protecting and fortifying [their places]. When I was to descend on them [in this situation], I [also] feared that they would receive [some] soldiers as reinforcements. [However,] I have devoted myself to [fighting] them in order to conquer the[ir] land[s]. I do not know, perhaps those who already became obedient in order to me [in these lands] would return to [support] them [=the people

370 Farwa b. Luqayṭ al-Azdī al-Ghāmidī (n.d.) is only mentioned in al-Ṭabarī's *Taʾrīkh* as a transmitter of traditions and a source for Abū Mikhnaf (see Mourad, *al-Azdī*, 589). We could not find a *tarjama* about him. On the basis of Ibn ʿAsākir's *TMD*, ʿUqla and Banī Yāsīn state that Farwa b. Luqayṭ lived in 77/696 and that he is mentioned as a transmitter from Adham b. Muḥriz al-Bāhilī (see al-Azdī, *Futūḥ al-Shām. Ed. ʿUqla/Banī Yāsīn*, 28; 237, n. 1). In al-Azdī's narrative, he is also mentioned as a transmitter of two traditions. However, a transmitter of or commentator on the manuscript was not sure of the correct punctuation and vocalisation of Farwa's name. Hence, he mentioned the alternative reading "b. Qurra" twice. On Farwa, see al-Ṭabarī, *Taʾrīkh*, II, 941, l. 3 and Ibn ʿAsākir, *TMD*, VII, 464.

of Jerusalem and Caesarea] and breach the contract between me and them if they see me preoccupied with [advancing upon] them [=the people of Jerusalem and Caesarea]. Therefore, I decided [instead] to march [north]\\238 to Damascus until I reach its [hinter]land and to march to those of them [=the people in the hinterland of Damascus] who had already become obedient to me. Then I [would continue to] march [north] to Ḥimṣ. For if we managed to oust their sovereign from his place wherein he is positioned [right now] and God exiled him from that place, each hamlet or city in Syria would [in turn] make peace [with us], conclude a peace treaty, give tribute and enter into [a state of] obedience [to us]". Thereupon, all the Muslims said: "What a great decision you have [made]! Carry it out and march with us [to Ḥimṣ] if it seems [appropriate] to you". He [=Abū ʿUbayda] summoned Khālid b. al-Walīd, who has been available in times of calamity and hardship, and said to him: "March out [north], may God have mercy upon you, with the cavalry". Then Khālid moved out with the cavalry and left ʿAmr b. al-ʿĀṣ behind as successor to the land of the River Jordan and as commander of a party of the people of the land of Palestine, the two of which are adjacent to the Arabs' land. He [=ʿAmr b. al-ʿĀṣ] then seized control over it [=the land of Palestine] and stayed there. Khālid proceeded until he descended on Damascus. Its people, who had [already] made peace with the Muslims, welcomed him. Then Abū ʿUbayda came [to Damascus] the following day, so they also went out to welcome Abū ʿUbayda the way he liked [it]. He stayed [there] for two or three days.

Then he ordered Khālid to march [out] until he reached Baalbek and the land of Bekaa[371]. [Khālid did so] and conquered the land of Bekaa. [Then] he headed towards Baalbek and descended on them [=its inhabitants]. Some of their infantrymen went out to him, so he [=Khālid] sent them about fifty of the Muslim cavalrymen, including Malḥān b. Ziyād al-Ṭāʾī and Qanān b. Ḥāzim al-Qaysī[372], who launched an attack on them and crammed them into the[ir] fortress. When they [=the people of Baalbek] saw this, they sent a request for peace [to the Muslims]. Abū ʿUbayda granted it to them and wrote them a letter [of protection].\\239

The conquest of the city of Ḥimṣ and its peace-making [process]

Afterwards, Abū ʿUbayda moved out towards Ḥimṣ. So the people of Ḥimṣ sent a huge group [of fighters] out to him. Then they faced him [and the

371 Bekaa (al-Biqāʿ) is an elongated high valley between the mountains of Lebanon and the Anti-Lebanon. In al-Azdī's narrative, the Bekaa valley is mentioned once as "the land of Bekaa". On Bekaa, see *EI*², s.v. al-Biḳāʿ (J. Sourdel-Thomine).

372 Qanān b. Ḥāzim al-Qaysī is listed neither in Ibn Saʿd, al-Bukhārī, Ibn ʿAsākir nor in any other biographical work we could access. ʿUqla and Banī Yāsīn assume that he could be Qanān b. *Dārim al-ʿAbsī* who is mentioned by Ibn ʿAsākir as one of Muḥammad's companions and as a fighter during the conquest of Baalbek (see al-Azdī, *Futūḥ al-Shām. Ed. ʿUqla/Banī Yāsīn*, 238, n. 7 referring to Ibn ʿAsākir, *TMD*, XXXXVIIII, 358–360). In al-Azdī's narrative, he is depicted as one of the cavalrymen whom Khālid sent to launch an attack on the people of Baalbek.

Muslims] in Jūsiya[373]. Abū ʿUbayda threw Khālid b. al-Walīd [and his cavalry] into fighting them. Khālid marched [to them] and when he looked at them, he said: "O adherents of Islam, [display] toughness, [display] toughness". Then Khālid launched an attack on them and so did the Muslims together with him. Defeated, they [=the people of Ḥimṣ] fled until they entered their city. Khālid b. al-Walīd sent [out] Maysara b. Masrūq al-ʿAbsī, who faced a large cavalry unit of theirs at a small river near Ḥimṣ. He chased them for a short while, then launched an attack on them and defeated them.

One of the Muslim men from Ḥimyar, who was called Shuraḥbīl[374], advanced [upon them] and some of their [=Ḥimṣ's] cavalrymen intercepted him. He launched an attack on them alone and killed seven of them. Then he arrived at a river beneath Ḥimṣ, which is adjacent to Dayr Misḥal,[375] and reached the water. He dismounted from his horse and watered it. Seeing a single man [alone], about thirty cavalrymen from among the people of Ḥimṣ proceeded and came towards him. Upon seeing this, he urged his horse [forwards], crossed the water towards them, hit his horse and launched an attack on them [during which] he killed the first cavalryman, followed by the second, then the third, then the fourth, then the fifth. Thereupon, they fled and he pursued them alone. He continued to kill [some of] them, one after the other, until he killed eleven of them by the time he reached Dayr Misḥal. They rushed into the heart of the monastery and so did he together with them. The people of the monastery pelted him with stones until he was killed; God rest him.\\240

Malḥān b. Ziyād al-Ṭāʾī, ʿAbdallāh b. Qurṭ al-Thumālī and Ṣafwān b. al-Muʿaṭṭal al-Khuzāʿī proceeded until they reached the city [of Ḥimṣ]. They started going around it, wishing that its people would come out to them, but they did not. So [all] the Muslims went [there] and set up camp at al-Rastan Gate. Al-Naḍir b. Shifā[376] claimed that a man from among them, who was

373 Jūsiya is a village located ca. 30 km south of Ḥimṣ with several springs, according to Yāqūt. In al-Azdī's narrative, a battle between Abū ʿUbayda as well as Khālid and the people of Ḥimṣ is mentioned there; the former won in this battle. On al-Jūsiya, see Yāqūt, *Muʿjam al-buldān*, II, 154.

374 Shuraḥbīl could not be identified because only his first name, not his full name, is mentioned. In al-Azdī's narrative, he is said to have belonged to Ḥimyar and to have killed several Byzantine soldiers in a single fight. Shuraḥbīl is a typical southern Arabian name, being a composition of "*shuraḥ bi-īl*" that means "protected by God". On this etymology, see van Ess, *Pest*, 257.

375 Dayr Misḥal (lit. "the Misḥal monastery") is, according to Yāqūt, a monastery located between Ḥimṣ and Baalbek. In al-Azdī's narrative, it is located close to Ḥimṣ. The inhabitants of the monastery killed Shuraḥbīl, a fighter in the Muslim army, there. On Dayr Misḥal, see Yāqūt, *Muʿjam al-buldān*, II, 702.

376 Al-Naḍir b. Shifā is listed neither in Ibn Saʿd, al-Bukhārī, Ibn ʿAsākir nor in any other biographical work we could access. ʿUqla and Banī Yāsīn deduce from al-Azdī's text that his *nisba* was al-Ḥimyarī (see al-Azdī, *Futūḥ al-Shām. Ed. ʿUqla/Banī Yāsīn*, 32). In al-Azdī's narrative, he is mentioned as a transmitter of one tradition.

a member of Dhū al-Kalā''s family, was the first to have entered the city—[i.e.] the city of Ḥimṣ—because he had launched an attack through al-Rastan Gate and nothing made him turn his face back until he had passed through the Eastern Gate. Lo and behold, he found himself within the heart of the city. When he realised this, he hit his horse [and turned] back promptly until he went out through al-Rastan Gate. Lo and behold, he found himself [again] in the encampment of the Muslims.

The Muslims besieged them [=the people of Ḥimṣ] tightly. Then they started saying to the Muslims: "March to the Emperor [of the Byzantines]. If you triumph over him, we will all be your servants". He [=the narrator] said: Abū ʿUbayda remained with the people at al-Rastan Gate. The Muslims dispatched the cavalrymen to different parts of their [=the people of Ḥimṣ's] land; they [=the cavalrymen] gained lots of spoils from them [=the people of Ḥimṣ] and cut off their [access to] matériel and provisions. The siege [of the city] turned tighter and they [=the people of Ḥimṣ] feared captivity. So they sent [a messenger] to the Muslims, soliciting peace from them. The Muslims made peace with them [=the people of Ḥimṣ] and wrote a letter of protection [to safeguard] their lives, their possessions and their churches, on the conditions that they host the Muslims for one day and night and that they [=the Muslims] do not inhabit their lands. They [=the people of Ḥimṣ] also made peace for the entire [hinter]land of Ḥimṣ, on the condition that they [=its inhabitants] are obligated to pay [the Muslims] 170,000 dinars. The Muslims accepted this [condition] from them and completed the peace[-making process]. [As a result,] they [=the people of Ḥimṣ] opened the gate[s] of the city [for them]. The Muslims entered the city and [they all] assured one another's safety.\\241

Abū ʿUbayda b. al-Jarrāḥ wrote [the following letter] to ʿUmar b. al-Khaṭṭāb (r.)

In the name of God, the Merciful, the Compassionate. From Abū ʿUbayda b. al-Jarrāḥ to the servant of God ʿUmar, the Commander of the Believers. Peace be upon you. I praise, on your behalf, God with whom no other deity is associated. Regarding the matter at hand: O Commander of the Believers, praise be to God who bestowed [as spoils] upon us and upon you the best district (*kūra*) in Syria in terms of people and citadels, the largest in number, in group and in yield, the most repressive to the Polytheists and the easiest for the Muslims to conquer. O Commander of the Believers, may God increase your righteousness, I inform you that we reached the land of Ḥimṣ, where the Polytheists were [stationed] in large numbers, but the Muslims drove them [to defeat] with extreme vigour. When we entered their lands, God (ʿa.) struck terror into their hearts, weakened their malice and clipped their nails [=vanquished them]. [Thus,] they requested peace [from us] and acquiesced in bringing tribute. We accepted [this] from them and thus refrained from [continuing to fight] them. They opened the[ir] fortresses to us and had us write them a letter of protection. [Then] we directed our cavalries towards the place of their Emperor and his soldiers. So we ask God, the King of kings and the Supporter of soldiers, to strengthen the Muslims with His victory and to make the errant Polytheist confess to his sin. Peace be upon you.

When his letter came to ʿUmar, he [=ʿUmar] wrote him the [following letter] in reply:

Regarding the matter at hand: I received your letter in which you ordered me to thank God (t.) for the land He bestowed [as spoils] upon us and the citadels he led us to conquer, for empowering us over the lands, for making [good plans] for us\\242 and [for] you and for granting us and [granting] you the best performance [in war]. Therefore, endless and boundless praise be to God. You also mentioned that you directed the cavalries towards the lands where the Emperor of the Byzantines and their groups were stationed. Do not do this. Rather, send for your cavalries [to come back], attach them to you[r troops] and wait until this year comes to an end and we make our decision and seek help with all our matters from God, the Possessor of majesty and honour; peace [be upon you].

When this letter reached Abū ʿUbayda, he summoned the Muslim chiefs and said to them: "I sent Maysara b. Masrūq [al-ʿAbsī] in advance towards Aleppo[377] while I wanted to attack and raid [a part of] the Byzantine land down the roads. I wrote to the Commander of the Believers about this [plan] and he wrote back [ordering me] to withdraw my cavalries and to lie in wait for them [=the Byzantines] this year until he makes his decision [regarding further actions]". They said to him: "The Commander of [both] the Believers and the Muslims did not spare you any opinion or anything good". So he [=Abū ʿUbayda] sent a messenger and a foot-messenger with [the following] letter [to Maysara b. Masrūq al-ʿAbsī], saying:

Regarding the matter at hand: When my messenger meets you, come [back] with him and leave what I have directed you to [do] until we make a decision and see what our caliph (*khalīfa*) will command. Peace be upon you.

Maysara [b. Masrūq al-ʿAbsī] came [back] with his companions until he reached Abū ʿUbayda in Ḥimṣ and remained with him [there]. Abū ʿUbayda b. al-Jarrāḥ marched out [of the city] and encamped together with the people [nearby]. Then he summoned Khālid b. al-Walīd and said to him: "March [back] to Damascus and set up camp there together with 1,000 of the Muslims while I remain here and ʿAmr\\243 b. al-ʿĀṣ remains where he is [=the land of the River Jordan and Palestine] so that there will be a party of the Muslims in each part of Syria. This will strengthen us more [in fighting]

377 Aleppo (Ḥalab) is located at the north-western end of the Syrian inland plateau. In al-Azdī's narrative, it was conquered by Abū ʿUbayda. On Aleppo, see *EI*^{2}, s.v. Ḥalab (J. Sauvaget).

against them [=the Byzantines] and make it [=Syria] easier for us to control". Then Khālid marched out with 1,000 men until he reached it [=Damascus] while Suwayd b. Kulthūm b. Qays b. Khālid al-Qurashī[378], then [belonging to] Banū Muḥārib b. Fihr, was in [control of] it [=Damascus]. In command of 500 men, Abū ʿUbayda [remained] behind him [=Khālid] at [some distance from] Damascus. Khālid came to it [=Damascus] and encamped at one of this city's gates while Suwayd b. Kulthūm [b. Qays b. Khālid al-Qurashī] had set up camp in its centre.

Al-Ḥusayn b. Ziyād [al-Ramlī] reported to us on the authority of Abū Ismāʿīl Muḥammad b. ʿAbdallāh [al-Azdī], who said: Furthermore, Abū Mujāhid Saʿd related to me on the authority of al-Muḥill b. Khalīfa: Both Malḥān b. Ziyād al-Ṭāʾī and Ḥābis b. Saʿd al-Ṭāʾī were flag holders when the Muslims reached Ḥimṣ. The Muslims reached it with nine flags the first day they set up camp there. Two of them [=the flags] belonged to Ṭayyiʾ, who had [good] equipment, fortitude and power when meeting the Polytheists.

Al-Ḥusayn b. Ziyād [al-Ramlī] reported to us on the authority of Abū Ismāʿīl Muḥammad b. ʿAbdallāh [al-Azdī], who said: Furthermore, Farwa—or Qurra—b. Luqayṭ related to me on the authority of Adham b. Muḥriz al-Bāhilī, who said: The first flag[holder] that entered the land of Ḥimṣ and roamed around its [main] city was that of Maysara b. Masrūq al-ʿAbsī. Abū Umāma [al-Bāhilī] also had a flag and so did my father [=Muḥriz b. Usayd al-Bāhilī]. The first of the Muslim men to have killed one of the Polytheists at Ḥimṣ was my father[, though]. If it was not [he], it must have been a man from Ḥimyar who also launched an attack with my father [simultaneously].\\244 During their attack[s], each of them killed one of the Polytheists. My father used to say: "I am the first Muslim who killed one of the Polytheists at Ḥimṣ. I did not notice this man from Ḥimyar, but [when] I launched an attack he [did so, too]. Each of us killed one of them in our attack[s]".

Adham [b. Muḥriz al-Bāhilī] [=the narrator] said: I am the first newborn in Ḥimṣ and I am the first newborn to whom an allotment was assigned there. Holding a shoulder blade (*katf*) in my hand [for writing], I used to go to the elementary school (*kuttāb*) [there] to learn and I [later] witnessed [the Battle of] Ṣiffīn[379] and fought [in it].

378 Suwayd's full name is Suwayd b. Kulthūm b. Qays b. Khālid al-Fihrī al-Qurashī (n.d.). In al-Azdī's narrative, he is said to belong to Banū Muḥārib b. Fihr and is depicted as being positioned in command of Damascus when Khālid reached it, as being ordered by Abū ʿUbayda to encamp in the centre of Damascus and as returning to the inhabitants of Damascus the taxes he had collected from them beforehand. On Suwayd, see Ibn Ḥajar, *Al-iṣāba. Ed. al-Baghawī*, III, 228 (no. 3610).

379 Ṣiffīn is a village located ca. 100 m west of the bank of the Euphrates near Raqqa. In al-Azdī's narrative, Adham b. Muḥriz al-Bāhilī is said to have taken part in the famous battle there. On Ṣiffīn, see *EI*[2], s.v. Ṣiffīn (M. Lecker).

The report on how God (ʿa.) led the Muslims to the conquest of [central] Syria and the report on Caesar when he learned of it

Al-Ḥusayn b. Ziyād [al-Ramlī] reported to us on the authority of Abū Ismāʿīl Muḥammad b. ʿAbdallāh [al-Azdī], who said: Furthermore, Abū Jahḍam [al-Azdī] related to me on the authority of ʿAbd al-Malik[380] b. al-Salīk [al-Fazārī] on the authority of ʿAbdallāh b. Qurṭ al-Thumālī, who said: [After the conquest of Ḥimṣ,] Abū ʿUbayda b. al-Jarrāḥ encamped with us around Ḥimṣ for about eighteen nights. He dispatched his subordinates throughout the land of Ḥimṣ and remained calm in his encampment. The vanquished units of the Byzantines departed from Fiḥl until they reached the Emperor of the Byzantines in Antioch. Some of the Byzantine cavalrymen\\245 and a number of their grand men and owners of riches (*amwāl*), wealth and might, who had settled in Syria, left [their homes] and entered Caesarea, whereas the people of Palestine fortified [their places] in Jerusalem. When the vanquished units came to Heraclius [who was] in Antioch, he summoned one of their grand men and a number of their [renowned] horsemen and [infantry] men. They came in to [meet] him and he said to them: "Woe unto you, tell me about those people whom you confront[ed]. Are they not humans like you?" They said: "Yes[, they are]". He [=Heraclius] said: "Are you larger in number or are they?" They said: "We are a hundred times as many as they are. Wherever we faced them, we were larger in number than they were". He said: "Woe unto you, [then] why were you defeated whenever you faced them?" They fell silent. An old man from among them rose and said: "O Emperor, I tell you how it came [about]". He [=Heraclius] said: "Tell me then". He [=the old man] said: "When we launch an attack upon them, they have patience and when they launch an attack upon us, they do not cower[381]. But we cower when we launch an attack upon them and we have no patience when they launch an attack upon us". He [=Heraclius] said: "Woe unto you, why are you as you have [been] described and they are as you have claimed [them to be]?" The old man said: "I have figured out where these [attitudes] came from". He [=Heraclius] said to him: "From where?" He [=the old man] said: "From [the fact] that the people [=the Muslims] perform prayer[s] during the night, fast during the day, uphold a pact (*ʿahd*), command what is right, forbid what is wrong, oppress nobody and establish equity among them whereas we drink wine, fornicate, commit the illicit (*ḥarām*), break a pact, usurp [power],\\246 oppress [people], command what makes God wrathful, forbid what makes Him satisfied and establish corruption on earth". He [=Heraclius] said: "I swear by God that you have told me the truth. I swear by God that I am going to depart from this town and leave this

380 ʿAbd al-Malik seems to be an error in the chain of transmitters, because it is ʿAbd *al-Raḥmān* b. al-Salīk who is always mentioned in the *isnāds*.

381 On the meaning of the phrase "*kadhdhaba*" as to in "cower", see Ibn Manẓūr, *Lisān*, I, 709.

land [immediately]. There is no good for me in accompanying you [all] while you are like that". The old man said to him: "O Emperor, I adjure you, for God's sake, not to leave Syria, which is the Arabs' earthly paradise, and [not to] depart from it without fighting and exerting [yourself]!" He [=Heraclius] said: "You [all] fought them more than once in Ajnādayn, Fiḥl, Damascus, at the River Jordan, in Palestine and Ḥimṣ and in more than one place. In all these [places], you lost, retreated and were defeated". The old man said to him: "O Emperor, I adjure you, for God's sake, not to leave [Syria] while you are surrounded by Byzantines [whose number is] as many as pebbles, [grains of] dust and motes and who have not been faced by any of them [=the Muslims] yet. Then [do] you want to depart from it and return with all these [Byzantines] before fighting [them]?" He [=the narrator] said: While the old man was saying this to him, the delegation of the people of Caesarea and that of Jerusalem came to him [=Heraclius].

[Prelude to the battle of al-Yarmūk]

The Byzantines' assembly [of an army] against the Muslims after the Muslims had driven them out of [central] Syria

Al-Ḥusayn b. Ziyād [al-Ramlī] reported to us on the authority of Abū Ismāʿīl Muḥammad b. ʿAbdallāh [al-Azdī], who said: Furthermore, Abū Jahḍam [al-Azdī] related to me on the authority of ʿAbd al-Malik[382] b. al-Salīk [al-Fazārī] on the authority of ʿAbdallāh b. Qurṭ [al-Thumālī]: Just after the battle-day of Fiḥl, the people of Jerusalem and the people of Caesarea advised one another and agreed unanimously to dispatch a delegation to the Emperor of the Byzantines, Heraclius, [who was] in Antioch. [They also agreed] to inform him about their adherence to his cause and about their resumption of obedience to him and their opposition to, and hatred of, the Arabs and to request reinforcements and support from him; otherwise, they would surrender to them [=the Muslims]. When he [=Heraclius] received [news of] this decision, he decided to send [reinforcing] soldiers [to them] and to remain in Antioch. Thus, he sent [messengers] to [various places in] the Byzantine Empire (*Rūmiyya*)[383], to Constantinople[384] and to those people of

382 See footnote 380.

383 In al-Azdī's narrative, the Byzantine Empire is usually referred to as "empire" (*mamlaka, dār mamlaka*) of Heraclius, but once it is also called *Rūmiyya* (lit. "the Greeks' abode"). On the Byzantine Empire, see *EI. Three*, s.v. Byzantium (N. El Cheikh), and on the Greeks (*Rūm*) in Arabic sources, see EI^2, s.v. Rūm (N. El Cheikh et al.).

384 Constantinople (Qusṭanṭīniyya) was the capital of the Eastern Roman (later, the Byzantine) Empire. In al-Azdī's narrative, the city is mentioned three times: Once when Heraclius called for further military support and twice in the context of his return to it after his troops were defeated in Syria. On Constantinople, see EI^2, s.v. (al-) Ḳusṭanṭīniyya (J. Mordtmann).

al-Jazīra[385] and Armenia[386] who had been part of his soldiers and who had embraced his religion. He also wrote to his subordinates to rally to him all those people of his empire who had attained puberty\\247 and those who were above that [age] up to the old men. They came to him [in so large] a number that the earth could not carry. Jirjīs[387], the ruler of Armenia, also came to him with 30,000 [men]. The people of al-Jazīra also hurried to him and so did the adherents of his religion and all those of them who were obedient to him.

[Then] he [=Heraclius] summoned Bāhān[388], one of their [=the Byzantines'] grand and tough men, and gave him command over 300,000 men and dispatched his commanders and soldiers with him. He also ordered rewards [to be paid] for them. He gave 200,000 dirhams to Bāhān and then gave the commanders 100,000 dirhams—[i.e.] 100,000 dirhams to each of them. Then he said to them: "If you get together [to fight], your [chief] commander will be Bāhān". He [=Heraclius] also said: "O Byzantines, the Arabs seized control of [central] Syria. But they will not be satisfied with it until they appropriate the farthest parts of your lands. They will not be satisfied with the

385 Al-Jazīra is a region and low-lying plateau in upper Mesopotamia. It is bordered by Syria in the west, Armenia in the north and northeast, Azerbaijan in the east and Iraq in the south. In al-Azdī's narrative, al-Jazīra is mentioned as a source of people that supported the Byzantine troops. On al-Jazīra, see *EI*[2], s.v. al-Jazīra (M. Canard).

386 Armenia (Armīniya) or "Greater Armenia" encompasses a region delimited by Anatolia (to the west), Azerbaijan and the southern Caspian region (to the east), the Pontic region and the Caucasus (to the north) and the Upper Tigris area (to the south). In al-Azdī's narrative, Armenia is mentioned as a source of people that supported the Byzantine troops. On Armenia, see *EI*[2], s.v. Armīniya (M. Canard).

387 In this place, the name of the person seems to be misspelled as Jirjīs, so we changed it to the name Jirjīs, which is used throughout the narrative. Jirjīs could not be identified because his full name is not mentioned. Jirjīs could be an Arabic form of Sergius. Instead, Kaegi identifies "Jarajis" (which seems somehow related to Jirjīs) as "George" (see Kaegi, *Byzantium*, 131). In al-Azdī's narrative, Jirjīs is depicted as "the ruler of Armenia", who supported Heraclius's army with 30,000 fighters, and as being positioned by Bāhān, together with Ibn Qanāṭir, in command of the army's right flank in the Battle of al-Yarmūk. In addition, Jirjīs argued with Ibn Qanāṭir because the latter gave the former orders.

388 Bāhān (or Vāhān) is an Armenian Byzantine general who organised and fought the Battle of Yarmūk for Heraclius. In al-Azdī's narrative, Bāhān is depicted as one of the Byzantines' grand and tough men, as a sovereign (*malik*) and as the chief commander of the Byzantine army, over which Heraclius gave him command. With this army Bāhān expelled the Muslims from Qinnasrīn, Ḥimṣ and Damascus and set up camp at al-Yarmūk, wanting to be on good terms with the Muslims. Hence, he invited a Muslim representative to negotiate an agreement on Syria. However, the negotiation between Bāhān and Khālid during the Battle of al-Yarmūk failed. After talking to his fellow noblemen, Bāhān had a vision about imminent defeat in battle, but he continued to fight the Muslims. Bāhān is also depicted as having realised that the Byzantines misbehaved and oppressed the local people, but when he wanted to punish one of them for that, he was held back by his fellow noblemen. Finally, he was killed in the Battle of al-Yarmūk. On Bāhān, see *EI*[2], s.v. Yarmūk (C. E. Bosworth/W. Kaegi).

land and the cities, nor with wheat and barley, nor with gold and silver until they capture [your] sisters and mothers as well as [your] daughters and wives and enslave the free as well as the sovereigns' children. Therefore, defend your women's domicile[s] (*ḥarīm*), your sovereignty (*sulṭān*) and your empire (*dār mamlakatikum*)". Then he dispatched them to the Muslims.

He [=the narrator, ʿAbdallāh b. Qurṭ al-Thumālī] said: Spies came from their side and informed [us] of what their Emperor Heraclius had said, of his [=Bāhān's] march to us, of their [=the Byzantines'] assembly [of soldiers to fight] against us and of his [=Heraclius's] summoning those from among them and from among other [people] who were adherents of their religion and obedient to them [=the Byzantines]. When Abū ʿUbayda learned of their news, their number, their multitude and their march with the other soldiers, who were adherents of their religion and obedient to them, he decided not to conceal this [news] from the Muslims and to consult them about it to see which decision their majority would finally come to.\\248 Thus, he summoned the Muslim chiefs, the [most] serious-looking (*dhū al-hayʾa*) and the [most] righteous of them. Then he rose, praised God (ʿa.), thanked Him and blessed and saluted the Prophet (ṣ.). Then he said: "Regarding the matter at hand: O Believers, God (ʿa.), praise be to Him, blessed you and bestowed great blessings upon you, fulfilled the promise to you, strengthened you with victory and showed you what pleased you everywhere. Your polytheistic enemy has marched [out] in a large number to you. Based on what my spies have told me, they have trooped to you with the largest Byzantine deployment [ever]. They came to you by land and by sea until they marched out to their [supreme] commander [=Heraclius] [who was] in Antioch. Then he dispatched three army units to you, each of which comprised [so many] men whom only God could count. I did not like to let you deceive yourselves or to conceal the news about your enemy from you. Then [I would like you to] advise me with your opinions and I advise you with mine, because I am just like any of you". Yazīd b. Abī Sufyān rose, praised and thanked God, blessed and saluted the Prophet (ṣ.) and then said to him [=Abū ʿUbayda]: "[What] an excellent decision! May God have mercy upon you for not hiding from us what you learned about our enemy. I [will] give you my advice. If it is right, it will be what I have intended. If it is different from what will [finally] be advised, I did not intend anything bad for the Muslims. I am of the opinion that you encamp with all the Muslims at the [main] gate of the city of Ḥimṣ and send women, sons and children into the city. Then keep the city at our backs. Then send for Khālid b. al-Walīd to come [back] from Damascus to you and send for ʿAmr b. al-ʿĀṣ to come from the lands of the River Jordan and the land of Palestine to you[, too]. Then you and all the Muslims who are with you [can] face them [=the Byzantines]". Shuraḥbīl b. Ḥasana rose, praised and thanked God, blessed and saluted the Prophet (ṣ.) and then said: "Regarding the matter at hand: This is a situation in which [a piece of] advice to the Muslims is inevitable. [Even] if any of us differs [in opinion] with a brother of his, each of us has to exert himself and make an effort to advise\\249 the

Muslims. Now I have an opinion other than that of Yazīd and I swear by God that he [=Yazīd] is in my eyes one of the [soundest] advisors to all the Muslims. However, I find it absolutely imperative to advise you on what I think to be good for the Muslims. I am not of the opinion that you should send the Muslims' offspring [into the city to stay] with the people of Hims [in it] while they embrace the religion of our polytheistic enemy that has already marched [out] towards us. [For] I fear that if war breaks out between us and them and we get completely involved in it, they [=the people of Ḥimṣ] will break their pact with us, fall upon our offspring and use them to curry favour with our enemy". Abū ʿUbayda said to him [=Shuraḥbīl]: "God has already humiliated them [=the people of Ḥimṣ] in favour of you [all] and they prefer your sovereignty to that of your enemy. As for what you have just mentioned and of which you have just warned us, I am going then to expel the people [of Ḥimṣ] from the[ir] city, let our offspring settle down in it [instead] and send some of the Muslim men into it to stand guard over its walls and gates. As for us, we remain in our place until our brethren come to us". Thereupon, Shuraḥbīl b. Ḥasana said to him: "Neither you nor we have the right to expel them [=the people of Ḥimṣ] from their houses after we have made peace with them regarding their houses and their possessions on the condition that we do not expel them". Then Abū ʿUbayda turned to the generality of the people around him and said: "What is your opinion; may God have mercy upon you [all]?" They [=the Muslims] said: "We are of the opinion that you remain [here at Ḥimṣ], write to the Commander of the Believers to inform him of the Byzantines' trooping towards us and send for those Muslim brethren of yours who are [also] in Syria to come to you [in order to fight the Byzantines]". Abū ʿUbayda said: "The matter is greater and graver than you think it [to be] and I believe that the people [=the Byzantines] are going to rush [to fight] against you before the Commander of the Believers receives your news".\\250 Thereafter, Maysara b. Masrūq [al-ʿAbsī] rose, went to him [=Abū ʿUbayda] and then said to him: "O [chief] commander, may God increase your righteousness. We are not the owners of citadels, fortresses or cities. Instead, we are the owners of open land and deserted areas. If they [=the Byzantines] have already marched [out] to us as you stated, take us out of the Byzantines' lands, cities, fortresses and citadels [and return with us] to our lands or to any of their [open] lands that resemble our own. Then bring your people, who are farthest away, to you and dispatch [a messenger] to the Commander of the Believers so that he reinforces you". Thereupon, all of the Muslim chiefs who attended the meeting said: "What Maysara b. Masrūq [al-ʿAbsī] has just proposed is the [best] opinion". [However,] Abū ʿUbayda's opinion was that they should stay and not leave. But he did not like them to disagree and hoped for a good [outcome] and blessed [results] from their consensus. So Abū ʿUbayda said to them: "Be ready and available until I reach my [final] decision".

He [=Abū ʿUbayda] then sent for Ḥabīb b. Maslama, whom he had employed for [collecting] the tax (*kharāj*) and said to him: "Review the tax of Ḥimṣ which you have collected and keep it [apart] until you receive my command concerning it. Do not [continue to] collect [it] from the rest of the people [of Ḥimṣ] until I command you to do so". He [=Ḥabīb b. Maslama] did [what he was ordered to do]. When he [=Abū ʿUbayda] wanted to depart, he summoned Ḥabīb b. Maslama [again] and said to him: "Return what we have taken to those people of the land [of Ḥimṣ] whom we made peace with. As long as we do not protect them, we should not\\251 take anything [as tax] from them. Then say to them: 'We are upholding the peace [treaty] that we have made with you and will not revoke it until you break and revoke it [yourselves]. We return your possessions to you, because we hate to take your possessions while we do not protect your lands. Instead, we will withdraw to another part of the land [of Syria] and send for our brethren to come to us and then we face our enemies and fight them. If God makes us triumphant over them, we will uphold your pact with us to your benefit until you request otherwise'". In the morning, he [=Abū ʿUbayda] ordered the people [=the Muslims] to leave for Damascus. Then Ḥabīb b. Maslama summoned the people from whom he had collected the possessions and began to return [their possessions] to them, informing them of what Abū ʿUbayda had said. The people of the land [of Ḥimṣ] then started to say to them [=the Muslims]: "May God bring you back to us and may God curse the Byzantines who were dominating us. We swear by God that if they were you, they would not have returned [anything] to us. Rather, they would have extorted [our goods from] us and looted all our possessions they could find".\\252

Abū ʿUbayda b. al-Jarrāḥ's letter to ʿUmar b. al-Khaṭṭāb (r.) informing him of what he knew about the Byzantines' mustering [of an army] against him

Al-Ḥusayn b. Ziyād [al-Ramlī] reported to us on the authority of Abū Ismāʿīl Muḥammad b. ʿAbdallāh [al-Azdī], who said: Furthermore, Abū Khaddāsh[389] related to me on the authority of Sufyān b. Sulaym al-Azdī[390] on the authority of Sufyān b. ʿAwf b. Mughaffal [al-Azdī[391]], who said: The following night Abū ʿUbayda b. al-Jarrāḥ sent me from Ḥimṣ to Damascus and said: "Go to the Commander of the Believers, send him my greetings and

389 Abū Khaddāsh is difficult to identify because only his patronymic (*kunya*), not his full name, is mentioned. We could not find a *tarjama* about him. On the basis of a manuscript of al-Dhahabī's *Tadhhīb al-tahdhīb al-kamāl*, Lees identifies him as Ḥabbān b. Zayd al-Sharʿabī from Ḥimṣ (see al-Azdī, *Futūḥ al-Shām. Ed. Lees*, 138, n. 2). In al-Azdī's narrative, he is mentioned as a transmitter of three traditions.

390 Sufyān b. Sulaym al-Azdī is mentioned only in Ibn ʿAsākir's *TMD* as a transmitter from Sufyān b. ʿAwf al-Azdī. We could not find a *tarjama* about him. In al-Azdī's narrative, he is mentioned as a transmitter of several traditions. On Sufyān, see Ibn ʿAsākir, *TMD*, XXI, 347.

391 Sufyān b. ʿAwf b. Mughaffal al-Azdī (d. between 52–54/672–674) is identified as ʿAmr b. ʿAbdallāh b. Mālik b. Naṣr al-Azdī al-Ghāmidī. In al-Azdī's narrative, he is mentioned as a messenger delivering letters between Abū ʿUbayda and ʿUmar. In addition, he is a transmitter of several traditions. On Sufyān, see Ibn ʿAsākir, *TMD*, XXI, 347–352.

tell him about what I have seen and observed, about what the spies brought to our knowledge, about the large number of the enemy settling in your [=the messenger's] place and [finally] about the Muslims' decision to withdraw from [fighting] them [=the Byzantines]".

He wrote [the following letter and sent it] with him [=the messenger] to him [='Umar]:

Regarding the matter at hand: My spies came to me from the land of our enemy, [more precisely] from the village where the Emperor of the Byzantines resided, and told me that the Byzantines had already headed towards us and mustered against us the largest groups that they have never mustered against any of the [former] communities (*umam*) that existed before us. I summoned the Muslims and conveyed this news to them, consulting them about their view[s]. They unanimously agreed to withdraw from [fighting] them [=the Byzantines] until we receive your decision [regarding this matter]. Thus, I dispatched to you a man who knows what we agreed on, so ask him about whatever you want. He is\\253 knowledgeable about it and we consider him trustworthy. We seek help from God, the Omnipotent and the Omniscient. He is sufficient for us and He is the best Trustee. Peace be upon you.

Sufyān [b. ʿAwf b. Mughaffal al-Azdī, the narrator] said: When I came to the Commander of the Believers, I extended the greetings to him. Then he said to me: "Inform me about the people". I informed him about their righteousness and about God's defence of them. Then he took the letter and read it, after which he said to me: "Woe unto you, what have the Muslims done?" I said: "May God increase your righteousness. I marched out from their encampment from Ḥimṣ at night and left them while they were saying: 'We will perform the early morning prayer[s] (*ghadāt*) and then leave for Damascus'. They all agreed to [do] this".

He [=the narrator, Sufyān b. ʿAwf b. Mughaffal al-Azdī] said: He [=the Commander of the Believers] looked as if he hated it [=their decision] to the extent that I could read hatred in his face. Then he said: "What a good father you have got (*li-llāh abūka*)![392] Why did they withdraw from [fighting] their enem[ies] after God had made them triumphant over them in more than one place of theirs? Why did they leave a land after they had appropriated it and after God had led them to the conquest of it until it fell into their hands? I fear that they made a bad decision, which would end in failure and thus embolden their enemy [to fight] against them". He [=the narrator, Sufyān b. ʿAwf b. Mughaffal al-Azdī] said: I said: "May God increase your righteousness, the attendee (*shāhid*) does see what the absentee (*ghāʾib*) does not. The [supreme] commander [=Heraclius] of the Byzantines has already mustered the largest groups against us, which neither he nor

392 The Arabic phrase "*li-llāh abūka*" (lit. "[the goodness of] your father is due to God") is said on the occasion of expressing approval and praise and means "It is God who made your father bring to life someone good like you". On this phrase, see Lane, *Lexicon*, s.v. *Abū*.

any of his predecessors has ever mustered against any of our predecessors. Some of our spies told us that one of their army units passed by the[ir] encampment at the foot of a mountain. They then descended from the defile to their encampment at midday. They did not finish [descending to their encampment] until the evening. Nor did they finish [descending] until midnight. This is just one of their army units. So what do you think, may God increase your righteousness, about the [size of the] rest of them?" He [=the narrator, Sufyān b. ʿAwf b. Mughaffal al-Azdī] said: Then he [=the Commander of the Believers] said: "Were it not that I might have hated their decision and their withdrawal from their cause but then I see God have chosen the better\\254 for them in the end, I would be [still] averse to their decision". Then he said to me: "Tell me, did they all agree to turn back?" He [=the narrator, Sufyān b. ʿAwf b. Mughaffal al-Azdī] said: I said: "Yes". [Thereupon,] he [=the Commander of the Believers] said: "Thank God for that. I hope that God has unified their opinion[s] for what is good [in the end], God willing". He [=the narrator, Sufyān b. ʿAwf b. Mughaffal al-Azdī] said: I said: "O Commander of the Believers, strengthen the Muslims with reinforcements, which should reach them from your side before the battle [against the Byzantines begins]. For this battle is the decisive one (*fayṣal*) between us and them. If God makes us victorious and triumphant over them on this occasion, the Byzantines will perish just as [the peoples of] ʿĀd[393] and Thamūd[394] had perished". He [=the narrator, Sufyān b. ʿAwf b. Mughaffal al-Azdī] said: Then he said to me: "Rejoice and herald good news to the Muslims when you reach them. Take this letter from me to Abū ʿUbayda b. al-Jarrāḥ and to the Muslims and inform them that Saʿīd b. ʿĀmir b. Ḥudhaym is coming with reinforcements to them, God willing".

ʿUmar b. al-Khaṭṭāb's letter to Abū ʿUbayda b. al-Jarrāḥ (r.)

He [=ʿUmar] wrote [the following letter to him]:

In the name of God, the Merciful, the Compassionate. From the servant of God, ʿUmar, the Commander of the Believers, to Abū ʿUbayda b. al-Jarrāḥ and those Emigrants, Supporters, benevolent Followers (*al-tābiʿūn*

393 ʿĀd is an ancient Arabian tribe mentioned in the Qurʾān. In al-Azdī's narrative, ʿĀd is referred to three times: (a) in a speech by a fighter who predicts the annihilation of the Byzantines as it happened to ʿĀd; (b) in a speech by Abū al-Dardāʾ, who addresses ʿĀd's wealth, which covered the entire Arabian Peninsula from Bosra to Aden; and (c) in a quotation from the qurʾānic text (Q. 89:6–14) during prayers led by Abū ʿUbayda. On ʿĀd, see *EI*², s.v. ʿĀd (F. Buhl).

394 Thamūd is an ancient Arabian tribe mentioned in the Qurʾān. In al-Azdī's narrative, Thamūd is referred to three times: (a) in a speech by a fighter who predicts the annihilation of the Byzantines as it happened to Thamūd; (b) in a speech by Abū al-Dardāʾ, who addresses Thamūd's wealth, which covered the entire Arabian Peninsula from Bosra to Aden; and (c) in a quotation from the qurʾānic text (Q. 91:11–12) during prayers led by Abū ʿUbayda. On Thamūd, see *EI*², s.v. Thamūd (I. Shahīd).

bi-iḥsān) and fighters for the cause of God who are there with him. Peace be upon you.\\255 I praise, on your behalf, God with whom no other deity is associated. Regarding the matter at hand: I have learned about your departure from the land of Ḥimṣ to the land of Damascus and about your abandonment of the lands that God led you to conquer, thus relinquishing them to your enemy and moving out of them willingly. [At first,] I hated your decision and your act. But then I asked your messenger if this was the opinion of all of you and he claimed that it was the opinion of the best (*khiyār*), the smartest and the [entire] generality of you. So I have realised that God (ʿa.) would unify your opinion[s] only [in cases] of success, rightfulness and guidance in this life and in the afterlife. This reduced the hatred that I had previously felt inside as a result of your turning back from them [=the conquered lands]. Your messenger asked me for reinforcements for your benefit, so I am [sending out] reinforcements to you before my letter is read to you. I am dispatching reinforcements from my side to yours, God (t.) willing. Know that it was neither due to the vastness of [our] group that we defeated [other] huge group[s], nor was it due to the vastness of [our] group that God (t.) bestowed victory upon us. [Rather,] God might sometimes forsake large groups and thus they wither, diminish and fail [to win]. Their multitude does them no good and God might sometimes render a small company victorious over a large one of\\256 the enemies of God (t.). Then God (t.) has bestowed His victory upon you and [cast] His torture and punishment upon His enemies and the polytheistic enemies of the Muslims. Peace be upon you.

Al-Ḥusayn b. Ziyād [al-Ramlī] reported to us on the authority of Abū Ismāʿīl Muḥammad b. ʿAbdallāh [al-Azdī], who said: Furthermore, Abū Khaddāsh related to me on the authority of Sufyān b. Sulaym [al-Azdī] on the authority of ʿAbdallāh b. Qurṭ [al-Thumālī], who said: After we had performed the early morning prayer[s] at Ḥimṣ, we marched out with Abū ʿUbayda until we reached Damascus, where Khālid b. al-Walīd was stationed. [Thus,] we left the land of Ḥimṣ, where we no longer owned any abodes, after we had conquered it, had assured its people of their protection, had written a letter [of protection] between us and them and had concluded a peace agreement with them regarding it [=the land of Ḥimṣ].

He [=the narrator, ʿAbdallāh b. Qurṭ al-Thumālī] said: When we entered Damascus, Khālid b. al-Walīd came to us and we united our encampment and his [turning them] into one. Then Abū ʿUbayda met with Khālid in private, informed him about the news, the people's advice to him, the journey [to Damascus] and [Maysara b. Masrūq] al-ʿAbsī's opinion on this [matter]. Then Khālid said: "Indeed, [as far as I remember] the decision was to remain in Ḥimṣ until we fight them [=the Byzantines] there. But as long as you all have reached a unanimous opinion on one thing, I hope that God has unified your opinion[s] only on what is good for you". Abū ʿUbayda remained at Damascus for two days and ordered Suwayd b. Kulthūm [b. Qays b. Khālid] al-Qurashī to return to the people of Damascus, [i.e. those] who were assured of their protection and with whom peace was made, what he had collected from them. He [=Suwayd b. Kulthūm b. Qays b. Khālid al-Qurashī] returned to them [=the people of Damascus] what he had taken from them and the Muslims said to them: "We are upholding the pact that was [made] between us and you. We are also committed to [carrying out our obligations mentioned] in the letter of protection [that we presented] to you and fulfilling for you the peace treaty which we offered you before".\\257 Abū ʿUbayda then gathered his companions and said to them: "What is your opinion? Advise me!" Thereupon, Yazīd b. Abī Sufyān said: "I am of the opinion that you march out [of Damascus] until you set up camp in al-Jābiya. Then you send for ʿAmr b. al-ʿĀṣ to come to you with the Muslims who are with him. Then we stand alert for the people [=the Byzantines] until they come to us. We fight them and seek God's help against them". Thereafter, Shuraḥbīl b. Ḥasana said: "Since we have [already] relinquished [to them] the part of their land that we [wanted to] relinquish, I am of the opinion that we hand it all over to them, leave it to them [completely] and establish between us [and them new] borders that lie between their land and ours. Thus, we draw near to our caliph and to our reinforcements. If some [of these] reinforcements, which we hope would help us against our enemy, reach us, we will fight them [=the Byzantines] in case they come to us. Otherwise, we will advance upon them if they turn away from us [in retreat]". Some of the Muslim men [then] said: "This, may God increase your righteousness, is a good idea. So accept it and resort to it, because it will have, God willing, a good outcome". [Thereupon,] Muʿādh b. Jabal said: "May God increase your righteousness. Would these people want, from their enemy, something more harmful or harsher to them than that which you want [to do] to yourselves? [Why do] you relinquish to them a land which God led you to conquer, [a land] where a number of the Byzantine sovereigns and valiant leaders (*ṣanādīd*) were killed and [a land] where God destroyed their powerful soldiers! If the Muslims evacuate it, surrender it to them and return to the same state in which they were before, it will be much harder for the Muslims to re-enter it after having departed from it. Is it proper of you to depart from it and leave it, and [also] leave [the land of] al-Balqāʾ and [the land of] the River Jordan [that are still in your hands] after\\258 you have collected the tax[es] in return for [your obligation to] defend them? I swear by God that if you depart from it and then you want to re-enter it after [your] departure from it, you will certainly go through [a great deal of] hardship in [doing] so". Then Abū ʿUbayda said: "I swear by God that he [=Muʿādh b. Jabal] is truthful and righteous. We should not leave a community [of people] who paid us a tax and with whom we concluded a pact until we are excused by God for being unable to defend them any further. If you agree, we will set up camp in al-Jābiya and send for ʿAmr b. al-ʿĀṣ to come to us. Then we will stand alert for the people [=the Byzantines] [to come] until we face them there". Thereupon, Khālid b. al-Walīd said to him: "[Do] you [think that] if you were in al-Jābiya, you would be in a better position than the one you are in right now?" He [=the narrator] said: While they remained in this [situation], pondering over decision [making],

ʿAbdallāh b. ʿAmr b. al-ʿĀṣ[395] came to Abū ʿUbayda with the [following] letter from his father:

In the name of God, the Merciful, the Compassionate. Regarding the matter at hand: The people of Jerusalem and many of those [living] in the [land of the] River Jordan, with whom we have made peace, broke the pact between us and them. They also stated that the Byzantines had headed collectively[396] towards [central] Syria and that you had relinquished [some] land to them, departed from it and turned away from it. This [act] encouraged them to oppose me and the Muslims on my side. [Hence,] they exchanged letters, reached a mutual agreement and made a pact to march towards me. [Now,] write your opinion [on this issue] to me. If you want to come to me, I will wait for you until you arrive. But if you want to set up camp somewhere in Syria, or in any other land, and that I come to you, let me know [that this is] your opinion and I will come to you. I will then march to you wherever you are. If [you do] not [want me to come], send me reinforcements\\259 that will help me [to fight] against my enemy [here] and to handle what is adjacent to me. For they [=the people of Jerusalem and the land of the River Jordan] have spread lies about us, circulated rumours about us and prepared for [fighting] us. If they find a [sign of] weakness in us, or see an opportunity [to attack] us, they will not negotiate with us [but fight us]. Peace be upon you.

Abū ʿUbayda b. al-Jarrāḥ wrote [the following letter back] to him [=ʿAmr b. al-ʿĀṣ]:

In the name of God, the Merciful, the Compassionate. Regarding the matter at hand: ʿAbdallāh b. ʿAmr [b. al-ʿĀṣ] came to me with your letter in which you mentioned the liars' spreading of lies, their readiness for [confronting] you and their daring [to fight] against you, owing to their knowledge of our turning away from the Byzantines and our relinquishment of [parts of] the land to them. Praise be to God, this [withdrawal] was neither because of a weakness in the Muslims' insights [into the matter], nor because of [their] powerlessness against their enemy. Rather, it was the scheme of their [=the Muslims'] great majority against their polytheistic enemy to lure them out of their cities, fortresses and citadels, to assemble all the Muslims, [including] those who are on the flanks [of Syria] and those who are near them [=the Byzantines], to wait for the reinforcements to come to them and then to fight them [=the Byzantines], God willing. Their [=the Muslims'] cavalry had already gathered, their horsemen had become fully prepared and we trusted in God's bestowal of victory upon His close friends, [His] fulfilment of His promise, [His] enhancement of His religion and [His] humiliation of

395 ʿAbdallāh's full name is Abū Muḥammad ʿAbdallāh b. ʿAmr b. al-ʿĀṣ (n.d.). In al-Azdī's narrative, he is introduced as a messenger delivering letters between his father, ʿAmr b. al-ʿĀṣ, and Abū ʿUbayda. On ʿAbdallāh, see Ibn Saʿd, *Kitāb al-ṭabaqāt*, IIII-2/VII-2, 8–13/189–190.

396 The Arabic idiomatic expression "*qaḍḍ wa-qaḍīḍ*" (lit. "with gravel and pebbles") is employed here in a non-compositional manner to mean "collectively, wholly and fully".

the Polytheists until none [of them] would [be able to] defend his mother, his wife or himself [and] until they [=the Byzantines] would climb the tops of the mountains [in escape], would fail to defend the fortresses, incline to peace and request peace-making [from us]. [This is] God's practice (*sunnat Allāh*) that took place before, [for]: "You will find no change in God's practices".[397] So inform the Muslims around you that I am, God willing, coming to them with all the adherents of Islam. [Tell them] to increase the[ir] trust in God and not to show your [opposing] warriors and enemies any [signs of] weakness, feebleness or\\260 failure. For they will disparage you and summon up the[ir] courage [to fight] against you. May God honour us and [honour] you with His victory and bestow His vigour and forgiveness upon us and upon you. Peace be upon you.

Abū ʿUbayda said to ʿAbdallāh b. ʿAmr [b. al-ʿĀṣ]: "Extend my greetings to your father, report to him that I am following you [immediately], and also inform the Muslims [there] of this. O ʿAbdallāh b. ʿAmr, be one of those by virtue of whom God strengthens the Muslims' backs and increases their trust in Him and with whom they associate themselves. You are one of the [Prophet's] companions and God has given to the companions, thanks to their companionship with the Messenger of God (ṣ.), priority over the other Muslims. Do not depend on your father in this respect. On the one side, motivate the people, promise them victory and tell them to be patient, while your father is doing the same on the other side". He [=ʿAbdallāh] said: "I hope that you will hear [of me] in this regard what pleases you, God willing". He [=the narrator] said: He [=ʿAbdallāh b. ʿAmr b. al-ʿĀṣ] and his father did [as ordered] and thus had [received] a reward, [showed] competence and spite against the Polytheists and [displayed] toughness and might against the Muslims' enemy. Then ʿAbdallāh [b. ʿAmr b. al-ʿĀṣ] left with Abū ʿUbayda's letter until he came with it to his father who read it [out] to the people.

Then ʿAmr b. al-ʿĀṣ rose and gathered those Muslims who were with him. He praised and thanked God (ʿa.), blessed and saluted the Prophet (ṣ.) and then said:\\261 "Regarding the matter at hand: [May] God's (ʿa.) protection (*dhimmat Allāh*) cease to cover any man from among the people of [the land of] the River Jordan who adheres to our pact, but controls a man from among the people of Jerusalem, harbours him in his residence and has not brought or delivered him to us. Verily, each of the adherents to our pact [in the land of the River Jordan] should not remain [inactive], but should prepare himself and get ready to march with me to [fight] the people of Jerusalem. For I do want to march [out] to them and set up camp at their place. Then I will not leave them until I kill their fighters and capture their offspring, or they bring tribute by hand and with humility". Then he [=ʿAmr b. al-ʿĀṣ] called the Muslims to set out for Jerusalem and marched about two miles towards the land of Jerusalem. He then took up quarters [there], encamped and said to the

397 Q. 33:62 (*The Qurʾān. Tr. Abdel Haleem*, 271).

people of [the land of] the River Jordan: "Send the offerings out to us". Thereupon, his callers announced: "Verily, protection ceases to cover any of the protected men [from the land of the River Jordan] who refuses to come out with his weaponry in order to stay with us in our encampment and await our command to him". Then he [='Amr b. al-'Āṣ] gave the order to all the protected people to flock to him [and they did so]. Hence, they marched out [of their houses] with their equipment and weaponry. Then he sent to them his son 'Abdallāh [b. 'Amr b. al-'Āṣ], who reached them and instructed them to encamp. 'Abdallāh [b. 'Amr b. al-'Āṣ], together with 500 Muslim men, set up camp with them. [By mobilising them,] he [='Amr b. al-'Āṣ] wanted to divert the [attention of the] people of the River Jordan from spreading lies and [also wanted] to inform the people of Jerusalem that he intended to march towards them and descend upon them. Thus, [he wanted] to strike terror into their hearts, [make] them preoccupied with [protecting] themselves and their fortresses from the [upcoming] raid on them and [cause] them to engage in handling their own [matters]. As a result [of this], the traders from among the people of the River Jordan and those from Jerusalem who stayed with a close friend or a relative there [=the land of the River Jordan] marched out [of their safe havens],\\262 rushed to Jerusalem and said to them [=the people of Jerusalem]: "This is [an act of] 'Amr b. al-'Āṣ, who has already headed towards you and marched with the people [=the Muslims] to you". Therefore, they [=the people of Jerusalem] gathered [in the city] from everywhere, exchanged letters [in this regard] and everyone who went to them from [the land of] the River Jordan started to inform them only of his [='Amr b. al-'Āṣ's] march [to them] and his encampment [nearby]. Thus, they [=the people of Jerusalem] were sure that he [='Amr b. al-'Āṣ] wanted [to raid] them and, for this reason, they became extremely panicked and increasingly frightened and scared.

'Amr b. al-'Āṣ's letter to them [=the people of Jerusalem]

It [reads]: In the name of God, the Merciful, the Compassionate. From 'Amr b. al-'Āṣ to the patricians of the people of Jerusalem. Peace be upon whoever follows the guidance, believes in God the Almighty, with whom no other deity is associated, and in [His Prophet] Muḥammad (ṣ.). Regarding the matter at hand: We do extol our Lord in the best [possible] way and thank Him abundantly for showing us [His] mercy [by sending] His Prophet (ṣ.), by honouring us with His message, by dignifying us with His religion, by gracing us with obedience to Him and by dignifying us with [belief in] His oneness (*tawḥīd*) and sincerity of knowing Him. Praise be to Him. We neither make anything equal to Him nor worship a deity other than Him, for that would be an outrageous thing to say. Glory [be] to God whom we praise. May the praise to Him be exalted. Praise be to God, who has divided you into sects and split up your religion into [different] parties because of the unbelief [you have] in your Lord. Each\\263 party is happy with what they [=its members] have. Some of you claim that God has got a son[398]; others claim that God is one of two [=binitarianism]; and [yet] others claim that God is one of three [=trinitarianism]. Away (*buʿd*), away (*suḥq*)[399] with whoever associates a partner to God! [For] God is definitely far above what they say [about Him]. Praise be to God who killed your patricians, usurped your power, expelled your sovereigns from these lands, bequeathed your land[s], houses and possessions to us, humiliated you because of your unbelief in Him, your polytheism and rejection of the [true] belief, in God and in His messenger, which we invited you to. Thus, God inflicted hunger, fear, humiliation and disgrace on you in return for what you had done. When you receive this letter from me, convert to Islam and you will be safe. If [you do] not [do that], come to us so that I write you a letter of protection for your lives and possessions and [thus] conclude a pact with you, [according to which] you should bring me tribute by hand and with humility. If [you do] not [do that, too], I swear by God, with whom no other deity is associated, to assault you with one cavalry after another and one infantry after another, and not to turn away from you until I kill [your] fighters, capture [your] offspring and [until] you become a community that [once] came into existence, but then looks as if it had never existed [before].

He sent this letter with a Christian foot-messenger to them [=the people of Jerusalem] and said to him: "Rush back to me [with their reply] because I will be waiting for you". When he [=the foot-messenger] came to them [=the people of Jerusalem], they said to him: "Woe unto you, what is [hidden] behind you[r visit]?" He said: "I do not know [anything] except that this man sent me with this letter to you, dispatched his soldiers to you and said [to me]: 'Nothing stops me from advancing [further] on them except waiting for your [=the Christian foot-messenger's] return'". They said to him: "Give us\\264 a period of respite (*sāʿa*) during the daytime, for we are waiting for our spy to come to us from the [side of the] Arabs' [chief] commander [=Abū ʿUbayda], who is in Damascus [right now], and from the [side of the] the [Byzantine] Emperor's army that has headed towards us. So we will see what he will report back to us. If we think that we can stand against the Arabs, we will not make peace with them. [However,] if we fear that we cannot stand against them, we will do what the people of the River Jordan and the others [in Syria] have done. We are just like the other people of Syria". Hence, the infidel [=the Christian foot-messenger] stayed until the evening. Then the messenger of the people of Jerusalem, whom they had sent to spy for them, returned and told them that Bāhān [=Heraclius's chief commander]

398 The sentence "*anna Allāha waladan*" (lit. "God [...] a son") seems to be grammatically incorrect, probably due to a problem with the transmission. The correct reading should have been "*anna Allāha wālidun*" (lit. "God is a father") or "*anna li-llāh waladan*" (lit. "God has a son"). We have chosen the latter meaning, because it is more frequent.

399 The two Arabic words "*buʿd*" and "*suḥq*" are synonymous, the usage of which represents a typical feature of the narrative's style.

was approaching [them] in command of three army units [sent out] by the Emperor of the Byzantines, each of which included more than 100,000 fighters. [He also told them] that when the Arabs learned of those groups that marched against them, they realised that they would not be able to stand against those who were heading towards them and thus they retreated. The first Arabs had entered the land of Qinnasrīn[400] [before] but they [=the advancing Byzantine troops] expelled them from it. Then they [=Bāhān and the Byzantine troops] went to the land of Ḥimṣ and expelled them [=the Arabs] from it[, too]. Then they went to the land of Damascus and [also] expelled them from it. Then the Arabs headed towards [the land of] the River Jordan, [where] their companion who had written to you [was stationed], while the Byzantines were pursuing them and driving them fiercely and rapidly to those lands in your vicinity. They [=the people of Jerusalem] deemed this a herald of good news, rejoiced over it, summoned the infidel [messenger] who had been sent by ʿAmr b. al-ʿĀṣ to them and said to him: "Go [back] with our letter to your companion". They wrote [the following letter and sent it] with him [to ʿAmr b. al-ʿĀṣ]:\\265

Regarding the matter at hand: You wrote a letter to us in which you commended yourself and blamed us for what we have embraced. Whoever speaks falsely neither benefits himself nor harms his enemy with it [=the falsehood]. We understood what you called us to. Those who had already marched [out] to you are our sovereigns and adherents of our religion. If God makes them triumphant over you, this will be His [customary] act [which He had often done] in our favour in ancient times (*al-qadīm*). If, however, He afflicts us with your triumph over us, we swear upon our lives that we will concede [power] to you in humiliation. And we will be just like those brethren of ours over whom you [already] triumphed and who then submitted to you and gave you that which you requested. [Peace be upon you.]

The [Christian foot-]messenger came with this letter to ʿAmr b. al-ʿĀṣ, who said to him: "What delayed you [from coming back]?" The messenger told him the news. With the letter he had written to them [=the people of Jerusalem] and the groups he had mustered against them, ʿAmr [b. al-ʿĀṣ] had intended to dissuade them from mustering [troops] against him and from launching a raid on him, [but then] he learned of the Byzantines' trooping towards the Muslims. No sooner had the day [on which the messenger met ʿAmr b. al-ʿĀṣ again] elapsed than Khālid b. al-Walīd arrived in the vanguard of Abū ʿUbayda [in the land of the River Jordan]. Abū ʿUbayda had moved with the Muslims out of the land of Damascus towards the lands

400 Qinnasrīn was located ca. 25 km south of Aleppo on the right bank of the Quwayq. In al-Azdī's narrative, it is usually referred to in the expression "the land of Qinnasrīn". Once, the etymology of the name is given as "*qinnu nasrin*" (lit. "eagle's coop"), which may be derived from Syriac "*qanā*" (lit. "fundament, base") and "*nzarā*" (lit. "the chirping or twittering"), i.e. "the chirping's base". On Qinnasrīn, see *EI*[2], s.v. Ḳinnasrīn (N. Elisséeff).

of the River Jordan [earlier], had ordered ʿAbd al-Raḥmān b. Ḥanbal [al-Jumaḥī] to call out to the people to march to the lands of the River Jordan [who had done so], had also ordered Khālid b. al-Walīd to move in command of his vanguard [to it, and he had done so] and had ordered Shuraḥbīl b. Ḥasana [and all the other units] to march to lands of the River Jordan[, too]. He [=Abū ʿUbayda as well as the whole army] proceeded until he set up camp at al-Yarmūk[401]. ʿAmr [b. al-ʿĀṣ] also came [to him] and set up camp with him.\\266

Al-Ḥusayn b. Ziyād [al-Ramlī] reported to us on the authority of Abū Ismāʿīl Muḥammad b. ʿAbdallāh [al-Azdī], who said: Furthermore, Mālik b. Qusāma b. Zuhayr[402] related to us on the authority of one of the Byzantine men, called Jirja[403]—he [=the narrator] said: He [=Jirja] had just converted to Islam and had excelled at it—who said: I was [a soldier] in that army unit which the Emperor of the Byzantines had dispatched under the command of Bāhān from Antioch [towards the Muslims]. We came in such a large number that only God (t.) could count, thinking that none of the people would defeat us. We then forced the first [unit of the] Arabs out of the land of Qinnasrīn and advanced in their tracks until we [also] forced them out of the land of Ḥimṣ. Then we advanced [further] in their tracks until we forced them out of Damascus. He [=the narrator, Jirja] said: All those Christians who were embracing our religion caught up with us to the extent that [even] a monk descended from his hermitage, where he had spent a long period of his lifetime, and departed from it. He descended [from there] and came to fight with us for his religion in fury and in defence of it. He [=the narrator, Jirja] said: The Arabs in Syria, who were bound to obey Caesar, fell into three categories: One category included those who were embracing the [other] Arabs' religion and were [siding] with them. Another category included Christians who had determination for Christianity and were [sid-

401 Al-Yarmūk is an eastern tributary of the River Jordan located ca. 9 km south of Lake Tiberias. In al-Azdī's narrative, the famous battle between the Muslim and Byzantine troops is narrated in detail. Al-Yarmūk refers to the plateau to the north of the river from which the Byzantine soldiers fell into the river's gorge. Alternatively, "al-Wāqūṣa" (lit. "the neck-breaker") is mentioned as a name for the river. On al-Yarmūk, see *EI*^{2}, s.v. Yarmūk (C. E. Bosworth/W. Kaegi).

402 Mālik b. Qusāma b. Zuhayr al-Māzinī al-Tamīmī is listed neither in Ibn Saʿd, al-Bukhārī, Ibn ʿAsākir nor in any other biographical work we could access. His father is known as a transmitter who died during the time of al-Ḥajjāj. In al-Azdī's narrative, Mālik is mentioned as a transmitter of one tradition. On Mālik's father Qusāma b. Zuhayr al-Māzinī al-Tamīmī, see Ibn Abī Ḥātim, *Al-jarḥ wa-al-taʿdīl*, VII, 147 (no. 817).

403 Jirja (or Jirjīs) is an early Islamic figure and a Byzantine convert. In al-Azdī's narrative, he is depicted as a Christian soldier in the unit that Heraclius sent from Antioch under the command of Bāhān. Jirja is also portrayed as a messenger from Bāhān to Abū ʿUbayda, requesting him to send them a sound-minded man whom they would ask for a compromise. Jirja had a long debate with Abū ʿUbayda on Jesus and Muḥammad and finally embraced the new faith. On Jirja, see Ibn Ḥajar, *Al-iṣāba. Ed. al-Baghawī*, I, 533 (no. 1281).

ing] with us. The [third] category included Christians who did not have such determination for Christianity and who thus said: "We hate to fight the adherents of our religion and we [also] hate to support the non-Arabs[404] [=the Byzantines] against our people [=the Arabs in Syria]".\\267

The Byzantines proceeded in pursuit of the adherents of Islam, of whom they were petrified and terrified. But when they witnessed them relinquishing the lands and leaving to them what they had conquered, [all] this, in addition to their [huge] number that has never been gathered against any other [enemy] before, encouraged them [to fight] against them [=the Muslims].

Al-Ḥusayn b. Ziyād [al-Ramlī] reported to us on the authority of Abū Ismāʿīl Muḥammad b. ʿAbdallāh [al-Azdī], who said: Furthermore, Abū Maʿshar[405] reported to me: When the Byzantines advanced on the Muslims and drew near to them, Abū ʿUbayda summoned the Muslim chiefs and consulted them. [Thus,] Yazīd b. Abī Sufyān said to him: "I am of the opinion that you and the Muslims [should] withdraw [further], that you set up camp with them in Ayla[406], remain there, send [a messenger] to the Commander of the Believers to inform him about the number[s] of our enemy that have already marched towards us, and that you wait for reinforcements to reach us [there]". Then ʿAmr b. al-ʿĀṣ said: "In my eyes, Ayla is a[n unsuitable] village just like any of the other Syrian villages (*qurā al-Shām*). [Thus,] in contrast, I am of the opinion that we [should retreat and] set up

404 Non-Arabs is a loose translation of the Arabic term "*ʿajam*" which refers to people whose way of speaking Arabic is incomprehensible or obscure in regard to pronunciation and grammar. In many Arabic sources, "*ʿajam*" refers to people from Iran. In al-Azdī's narrative, however, "*ʿajam*" is sometimes used to designate the Byzantines and sometimes the Persians. The term is used three times: (a) to separate the Christian Arabs in Syria from the Byzantines whom they are said to have supported; (b) in a speech delivered by Abū Sufyān before the Battle of al-Yarmūk in which he says that the Muslims are "in the non-Arabs' abode" (*dār al-ʿajam*), most likely referring to Byzantine Syria; and (c) in the Muslims' attempt to increase ʿUmar's status "among the non-Arabs", most likely designating the people of Syria, by offering him white clothes to wear. On non-Arabs, see *EI*^{2}, s.v. ʿAdjam (F. Gabrieli).

405 Abū Maʿshar is difficult to identify because his full name is not mentioned. He could be Abū Maʿshar Najīḥ al-Sindī (d. 170/786) who is renowned for putting emphasis on dating historical events. However, according to Mourad, Abū Maʿshar could also be Abū Maʿshar Ziyād b. Kulayb al-Taymī al-Nakhaʿī al-Ḥanẓalī al-Barrāʾ (d. 117/735–736) (see Mourad, *al-Azdī*, 589). ʿUqla and Banī Yāsīn, who mention both possibilities, present Abū Maʿshar Ziyād b. Kulayb *al-Tamīmī's* date of death as "120–127/737–744" (see al-Azdī, *Futūḥ al-Shām. Ed. ʿUqla/Banī Yāsīn*, 30; 267, n. 3 [al-Taymī]). In al-Azdī's narrative, Abū Maʿshar is mentioned as a transmitter of two traditions. On Abū Maʿshar al-Sindī, see *EI*^{2}, s.v. Abū Maʿshar Nadjīḥ b. ʿAbd al-Raḥmān al-Sindī (J. Horovitz/F. Rosenthal); *EI. Three*, s.v. Abū Maʿshar al-Sindī (J. Scheiner). On Abū Maʿshar al-Nakhaʿī, see Ibn Saʿd, *Kitāb al-ṭabaqāt*, VI, 230 and Ibn Ḥibbān, *Al-thiqāt*, VI, 327.

406 Ayla is a city at the Gulf of ʿAqaba located at the northern shore of the Red Sea. In al-Azdī's narrative, Ayla is mentioned twice in passing and is described as a Syrian town. On Ayla, see *EI*^{2}, s.v. Ayla (H. Glidden).

camp in Qarḥā'[407] to be stationed in our land [=al-Ḥijāz] close[r] to our reinforcements. When the reinforcements then reach us, we will rush to [fight] the people [=the Byzantines]". He [=the narrator, Abū Maʿshar] said: Khālid b. al-Walīd was silently listening to what they were saying and recommending to him [=Abū ʿUbayda]. He [=Khālid], may God have mercy upon him, was the one to whom, and to whose decision[s], they used to resort when a calamity or a disaster occurred. He [=Khālid] did not fear anything and nothing concerning the Byzantines frightened him[, either]. [It appeared] as though he was getting more courageous [to fight] against them and more desirous to advance on them whenever he learned something [new] about them. Therefore, Abū ʿUbayda said to him: "O Khālid, what is your opinion [in this regard]?" He said: "I swear by God, I am of the opinion that if we fight them by virtue of number\\268 and might, they are larger and mightier than we and we are then powerless against them. But if we fight them in the name of God and for His cause, I do not think that their entire number, even if they were [to number] the whole population of the earth, would help them against us at all". Then he [=Khālid] became angry and said to Abū ʿUbayda: "Would you obey what I tell you to do?" He [=Abū ʿUbayda] said to him: "Yes". [Then] he [=Khālid] said: "Leave what is behind your door under my command and leave the people [=the Byzantines] to me. I hope that God will render me victorious over them". Thereupon, he [=Abū ʿUbayda] said: "[It is] done". He [thus] left that [=which was behind his door] [the Muslim troops] under his command. Khālid (r.) was one of the best performing, most competent, most blessed and most fortunate-minded people [from among the Muslims], and they [=the Byzantines] were easier for him [to kill] than flies.

The story of Qays b. Hubayra [al-Murādī] during Abū ʿUbayda b. al-Jarrāḥ's consultation with the Muslims and what they said in reply to Abū ʿUbayda

Al-Ḥusayn b. Ziyād [al-Ramlī] reported to us on the authority of Abū Ismāʿīl Muḥammad b. ʿAbdallāh [al-Azdī], who said: Furthermore, Yaḥyā b. Hāni' b. ʿUrwa [al-Murādī] related to me: When Abū ʿUbayda consulted the people, someone—he [=the narrator] has not mentioned his name—said to him [=Abū ʿUbayda]: "Verily, if you march out until you set up camp with us in Qarḥā' and al-Ḥijr and we [all] wait for our reinforcements there, this will be a blessed camp".\\269 He [=the narrator, Yaḥyā b. Hāni' b. ʿUrwa] said:

407 Qarḥā' is most likely to be identified as Qarḥā which is, according to Yāqūt, a town in Wādī al-Qurā. Qarḥā' could also refer to Qurḥ (or Qarḥ), which was the market place of Wādī al-Qurā. Qarḥā' is not likely to be identified as al-Qarḥā', because this is, according to Yāqūt, a village of Banū Muḥārib in Baḥrayn. In al-Azdī's narrative, Qarḥā' is described as part of "the Muslims' land", i.e. al-Ḥijāz, to which also Wādī al-Qurā belongs. On Qarḥā', Qarḥā and Qurḥ, see Yāqūt, *Muʿjam al-buldān*, IV, 53–54.

Then Qays b. Hubayra [al-Murādī] said to him [=Abū ʿUbayda]: "May God never return us to Syria if we relinquish [more parts of] it to them than the parts thereof [that we have already] relinquished to them. Would you leave such gushing springs, never-ending rivers, [abundant] crops, grapes, wine and leavened bread (*khamīr*), gold, silver and silk and return to eating dabb lizards, to wearing abas[408] and to [a life of] suffering and misery? And you then claim that our men who were killed in battle will enter Paradise and will be granted bliss beyond comparison. Why do you make claim to Paradise while you flee and withdraw from it and [want to] go to Qarḥāʾ and al-Ḥijr? May God neither accompany nor protect whoever marches [back] to them". Thereupon, Abū ʿUbayda said to him: "You have spoken the truth, Qays. Do you want to return to your lands and leave to those people the fortresses, dwellings and possessions which God led you to conquer and granted to you as spoils and which He pulled out of their [=the Byzantines'] hands? Do you [really] want later to leave and depart from them, [seeking] to return to them again and to fight them [=the Byzantines] over them [once more] after God had spared you the burden of pulling them out of their [=the Byzantines'] hands? I swear by God that this [retreat] is a misleading opinion". Thereupon, Khālid said: "May God reward you with [all that is] good, Qays. Your opinion accords with mine and I swear by God that we are neither departing nor withdrawing from these lands until God judges between us [and them], for He is the best of [all] judges". Then Maysara b. Masrūq al-ʿAbsī rose and said to Abū ʿUbayda: "May God increase your righteousness. Do not leave your place where you are [stationed right now], but trust in God and fight your enemy [here]. I hope that God leads you to victory over them [=the Byzantines]. If you departed from them [=the lands of the River Jordan], I fear that you would never return to them. Why\\270 would we relinquish these lands to them after we had fought them [=the Byzantines] over them [=the conquered lands] until we had expelled them and had killed their patricians and horsemen on the battle-days of Ajnādayn and Fiḥl?" Thereafter, Abū ʿUbayda said: "I am not going to leave [my place] and I have just assigned what is behind the door to Khālid b. al-Walīd. I am [staying here] with you, not leaving this land until God judges between us [and them], for He is the best of [all] judges".

The report on Qays b. Hubayra [al-Murādī] and some of the Muslim women

Al-Ḥusayn b. Ziyād [al-Ramlī] reported to us on the authority of Abū Ismāʿīl Muḥammad b. ʿAbdallāh [al-Azdī], who said: Furthermore, al-Ḥārith b. Kaʿb related to me on the authority of ʿAbd al-Raḥmān b. al-Salīk al-Fazārī on the authority of ʿAbdallāh b. Qurṭ [al-Thumālī], who said: When the

408 An aba is a cloak-like, woolen wrap that is occasionally striped. See Wehr, *Wörterbuch. Tr. Milton Cowan*, s.v. *ʿabāʾ*.

Byzantines proceeded in their [=the Muslims'] tracks, they [did nothing] except insult, assault and punish [the people of the lands] we had conquered [previously] but then had relinquished. Then the people of the land [of central Syria] said to them [=the Byzantines]: "You deserve the blame more than we. You debilitated our cause, failed [to help us], abandoned us and left [us alone]. Some people against whom we were powerless came to us [and subdued us]". Being certain of their [=the people of the land's] truthfulness, they [=the Byzantines] turned away from them [=the people]. They [=the Byzantines] went on pursuing the Muslims' tracks until they set up camp in a place belonging to al-Yarmūk [region], called Dayr al-Jabal[409], which was located close to the Muslims[' encampment]. Meanwhile the Muslims had placed their women and children on a mountain behind their backs.

He [=the narrator, ʿAbdallāh b. Qurṭ al-Thumālī] said: Then Qays b. Hubayra [al-Murādī] passed by some of the Muslim women who were congregating. When they saw him, Amna bt. Abī Bishr b. Zayd al-Aṭwal al-Azdiyya[410] rose [and went] to him. She was under [a marital bond with] ʿAbdallāh b.\\271 Qurṭ al-Thumālī. He [=Qays b. Hubayra al-Murādī] was the most similar of God's creatures to him [=ʿAbdallāh b. Qurṭ al-Thumālī] in war, and his horse also resembled the latter's horse and everything else relating to it, as did his weapons, his stature—i.e. his height—and his physique. [Thus,] she [=Amna bt. Abī Bishr al-Azdiyya] thought that he [=Qays b. Hubayra al-Murādī] was her husband. [When he came to the women's place,] she rose[, went] to him and said: "Listen, I will sacrifice myself for you". He [=the narrator, ʿAbdallāh b. Qurṭ al-Thumālī] said: Qays [b. Hubayra al-Murādī] knew that she mistook him for her husband. Thus, he said: "I think you mistook me [for your husband]". Then the woman [=Amna bt. Abī Bishr al-Azdiyya] said, "Shame on me!" and steered away from him. Thereupon, he [=Qays b. Hubayra al-Murādī] said: "O woman, and I also address all the [other] women [here] whoever they are, may God make ugly any woman who lies down for her husband if he does not fight in defence of her after her enemy has already descended upon her yard. If he [=the husband] wants that [=lying] with her, she should throw dust in his face and say to him: 'Get out and fight in defence of me, otherwise I will not be your wife [anymore] if you do not defend me'. I swear upon my life that nobody would flee in such

409 Dayr al-Jabal (lit. "the Monastery of the Mountain") is neither listed in Yāqūt's geographical dictionary nor in any other geographical work. However, it is mentioned in the *Futūḥ al-Shām* ascribed to al-Wāqidī, indicating the close relationship between al-Azdī's text and this work. In analogy to al-Azdī's narrative, the *Futūḥ al-Shām* ascribed to al-Wāqidī states that the Byzantine troops "set up camp at a monastery, which was called Dayr al-Jabal and which was in the vicinity of al-Ramāda and Jawlān". On this passage, see al-Wāqidī, *Futūḥ al-Shām*, I, 228.

410 Amna bt. Abī Bishr b. Zayd al-Aṭwal al-Azdiyya is listed neither in Ibn Saʿd, al-Bukhārī, Ibn ʿAsākir nor in any other biographical work we could access. In al-Azdī's narrative, she is portrayed as having mistaken Qays b. Hubayra for her husband ʿAbdallāh b. Qurṭ, owing to the similarities between the two in appearance. She and the other women were told by Qays to compel their husbands to defend them.

a situation except their [=the women's] cowardly, mean and evil husbands". Then he [=Qays b. Hubayra al-Murādī] left. Thereupon, the woman [=Amna bt. Abī Bishr al-Azdiyya] said: "O how ashamed of him I am! I rose [and went] to him, thinking that he was my husband. I rose [and went] to him to intercept him, thinking that he was [ʿAbdallāh] Ibn Qurṭ [al-Thumālī]. Yesterday, he had only a light dinner, because he preferred to retain [the rest of] his dinner for two of his brethren who dined in his dwelling. So I prepared lunch for him [today] and [interrupted him because I] wanted him to come [back] home and have lunch [with me]".

Al-Ḥusayn b. Ziyād [al-Ramlī] reported to us on the authority of Abū Ismāʿīl Muḥammad b. ʿAbdallāh [al-Azdī], who said: Furthermore, Mikhnaf b. ʿAbdallāh [b. Yazīd b. al-Mughaffal][411] related to me on the authority of ʿAbd al-Raḥmān b. al-Salīk [al-Fazārī] on the authority of ʿAbdallāh b. Qurṭ [al-Thumālī], who said: When\\272 the Byzantines set up camp in the place where they descended, we secretly sent some people of the land [of the River Jordan] into their encampment [to spy for us]. They had been Christians but they converted to Islam and excelled at it. We ordered them to enter into their encampment, conceal their Islam[ic faith] and report their [=the Byzantines'] news [to us]. They were doing so. He [=the narrator, ʿAbdallāh b. Qurṭ al-Thumālī] said: They [=the Byzantines] remained [stationed] opposite to us for some days, [perhaps] three or four. They neither asked us about anything, nor did we ask them about anything. Neither did they confront us, nor did we confront them. While we were in this [situation], we heard a loud voice, a great clamour and high-pitched sounds. We thought that the people [=the Byzantines] wanted to advance on us, so we prepared ourselves [for war] and got ready [to fight]. Then we let our spies enter their encampment to report any news to us. He [=the narrator, ʿAbdallāh b. Qurṭ al-Thumālī] said: No sooner had a little [while] passed than they returned to us and informed us that they [=the Byzantines] had received a message from the Emperor of the Byzantines, heralding good news to them about a [prospective] division of possessions among them and about the coming of reinforcements to them. Hence, they had rejoiced over this [good news] and had raised [the] cheers for him [=the Emperor] [that we had heard].

*The speech (*khuṭba*) of Bāhān, the [chief] commander of the Byzantines, who was ordered to march to the Muslims*

Thereafter, their sovereign Bāhān rose [and stood] before them [=the Byzantine soldiers]. So they flocked to him and he said to them: "Indeed, God still supports, strengthens and makes your religion triumphant over whoever

411 Mikhnaf's full name is Mikhnaf b. ʿAbdallāh b. Yazīd b. al-Mughaffal. He is listed only in Ibn ʿAsākir's *TMD* as a transmitter from ʿAbd al-Aʿlā b. Surāqa. We could not find a *tarjama* about him. In al-Azdī's narrative, he is mentioned as a transmitter of two traditions. On Mikhnaf, see Ibn ʿAsākir, *TMD*, XXXIII, 411.

opposes you. Some people [=the Muslims] had already marched to you, wanting to spoil your religion and usurp your lands, dwellings and possessions while you[r] number [is as many as] the pebbles, the [grains of] dust and the motes. I swear by God that there are about 400,000 fighters of yours in this valley, including\\273 your followers, [your] supporters, the people of your lands who flocked to you and those adherents of your religion who are with you [now]. So do not be frightened by the case of those people [=the Muslims], for their number is rather small. In addition, they are the people of suffering and misery and most of them are nude and hungry whereas you belong to sovereigns and their offspring and you are the owners of fortresses and castles, equipment and power as well as weaponry and horses (*kurāʿ*)[412]. So do not leave this land while they [=the Muslims] are [still] blinking an eye [and] until you destroy them or you perish". Thereupon, their [=the Byzantines'] patricians rose [and went] to him [=Bāhān] and said: "Give us your order[s] and see what we will do". [Then] he [=Bāhān] said [to them]: "Get ready until I give you the order [to attack]".

The report on what the corrupt Byzantines, [i.e.] Bāhān's companions, did to the Byzantine people of Syria, and the reason why God eliminated, exterminated and dispersed their group[s]

Al-Ḥusayn b. Ziyād [al-Ramlī] reported to us on the authority of Abū Ismāʿīl Muḥammad b. ʿAbdallāh [=al-Azdī], who said: Furthermore, Abū Jahḍam al-Azdī[413] related to me on the authority of a man from Tanūkh[414] who was accompanying Bāhān and carrying the patronymic Abū Bashīr[415] and who said: I was Christian and I supported Christianity against the Arabs. Thus, I proceeded with the Byzantines. Whenever we started passing by any of the people of the land [of Syria], we found them the highest praisers of the

412 The expression "*kurāʿ*" (lit. "shinbone") refers by way of a *pars pro toto* relation to sheep, goats, camels and horses. We have chosen the last meaning, i.e. "horses", because it fits best the military context of the sentence. See Ullmann, *WKAS*, s.v. *kurāʿ*.

413 The name "Abū al-Jahm al-Azdī" is corrected here as "Abū Jahḍam al-Azdī" in light of two other *isnāds* in the text in which Abū Jahḍam al-Azdī transmitted on the authority of "a Byzantine man". According to ʿUqla and Banī Yāsīn, Abū *al-Jahm* al-Azdī is not found in any biographical dictionary (see al-Azdī, *Futūḥ al-Shām. Ed. ʿUqla/Banī Yāsīn*, 33), which supports our correction.

414 Tanūkh is a Southern Arabian tribe that was, according to some genealogists, a subtribe of Quḍāʿa. In al-Azdī's narrative, two individual figures belonged to Tanūkh: (a) Abū Bashīr al-Tanūkhī and (b) Ḥudhayfa b. ʿAmr, who are said to have been Christians. While Abū Bashīr is depicted as a companion of the Byzantine commander Bāhān and a supporter of the Byzantine troops at al-Yarmūk, Ḥudhayfa is said to have been the messenger who falsely reported victory to Heraclius after the lost Battle of al-Yarmūk. On Tanūkh, see *EI*^{2}, s.v. Tanūkh (I. Shahīd).

415 Abū Bashīr al-Tanūkhī is listed neither in Ibn Saʿd, al-Bukhārī, Ibn ʿAsākir nor in any other biographical work we could access. In al-Azdī's narrative, he is mentioned as a transmitter of several traditions.

Arabs in everything relating to their cause and conduct. He [=the narrator, Abū Bashīr al-Tanūkhī] said: The Byzantines arrived [in Syria] and began to spread corruption in the land, to show misconduct and disobedience to their commanders until the [local] people cried for help against them and the villagers complained about them. They did not\\274 stop drinking wine and committing adultery. A group of the people of the land, from among the protected people (*ahl al-dhimma*), came with a deflowered slave girl to their sovereign [to complain about recurrent violations]; another group complained about their sheep being [recurrently] slaughtered and a [third] group complained about being [recurrently] ruined and looted. When Bāhān saw this and [saw] what they [=the Byzantines] were doing, he rose [and stood] before [the people] to deliver a speech and said: "O adherents of this religion, God's evidence against you will be indisputable, for he had sent you a messenger and had revealed a book to you [as guidance]. In addition, your messenger [=Jesus] did not desire this worldly life, induced you to abstain from it and ordered you neither to desire it nor to oppress anyone. Verily, God does not like the oppressors and you are now [very] oppressive. What will be your excuse before God tomorrow after you have abandoned His command, the command of His prophet and the book of your Lord, which he had brought to you? This is your enemy that has fallen upon you, killing your fighters and capturing your offspring while you are [still] committing sins, not desisting from [committing] them [=the sins] for fear of [God's] punishment. If God pulled your sovereignty out of your hands and made your enemy triumphant over you, who would be blameworthy [for wrongdoing] except you? So fear God and restrain yourselves from oppressing people".

Thereafter, a man from among the people of the land rose [and went] to him [=Bāhān] and aired a complaint. He [=the narrator, Abū Bashīr al-Tanūkhī] said: He spoke [to him] in their tongue [=Syriac or Greek] but I understood their speech. He [=the man] said: "O sovereign, may you live long and may we sacrifice ourselves to protect you against odious incidents. I am one of the people of the land, one of the protected people, and I owned some sheep which I thought to be 100 ewes or a little less and which my son was tending. One of your fellow grand men passed by us and pitched his tent\\275 beside them [=the sheep]. Then he took what he needed from them and his companions looted the rest. My wife came [out] to him, or [perhaps] he [=the man] said 'my daughter', complained to him about his companions' looting of my sheep and said to him: 'As for what you took for yourself, let it be yours. But as for what your companions took, send for them to return our sheep to us'. When he [=the grand man] saw her, he ordered her to be taken into his erected [tent] (*binā'*) where she stayed for a long time with him. When her son saw this, he approached the door of the erected [tent] and peeked [into it]. Lo and behold, he saw his [=the grand man's] fellow having sex with his mother or his sister while she was weeping. Thereupon, the lad shouted out loud. So he [=the grand man] gave the order to kill him [=the lad] and he was killed [accordingly]. They [=some witnesses] informed me of this and I [promptly] came to my [dead] son. So he [=the grand man] gave the order to some of his fellows to fall upon me and to strike me with a sword and they did so. I fended them off with my [bare] hand but they severed it". Then Bāhān said to him: "Do you recognise him [=the grand man]?" He [=the man] said: "Yes". He [=Bāhān] said: "Where is he?" He [=the man] said: "There he is, one of your grand men". He [=the narrator, Abū Bashīr al-Tanūkhī] said: That grand man, who had done this to the man, became angry and some of his companions, among whom he was known for [his] prestige and honour, also became angry on his behalf. More than 200 of his companions came [forward], fell upon the appealer and struck him with their swords until he died. Then they returned [to their places] while Bāhān was watching what they did. He said [to them] in his own tongue [=Greek]: "I am completely shocked! How come the mountains do not stir, the seas do not gush forth, the earth does not quake and the sky does not thunder because of this sin that you have committed while I am investigating your heinous deeds that you did and while I am seeing and hearing [you]? If you believe that these weak and oppressed people have a God who retaliates for them and helps the oppressed to take revenge on the oppressor, be certain of retribution. From now on He is hastening your destruction.\\276 If you do not believe this, I swear by God that you will be, in my eyes, worse than dogs and donkeys. I swear upon my life that you are doing the deeds of those who do not believe [in God]. Certainly, God is indignant at your deeds and will cause you to trust only in yourselves. As for me, I call upon God to bear witness that I am innocent of your acts and you will see the consequence of oppression, where it [=oppression] will take you and to which destiny it will drive you". Then he descended [from the speech platform].

[Manuscript note: Part V]

This is the end of the fourth part [of the Book of the Conquests of Syria]. It is continued at the beginning of the fifth part by the remainder of Abū Bashīr al-Tanūkhī's tradition. Praise be to God, the Lord of the Worlds.\\277

In the name of God, the Merciful, the Compassionate. Shaykh Abū Isḥāq Ibrāhīm b. Sa'īd b. 'Abdallāh[416] al-Ḥabbāl reported to us: Abū al-'Abbās Munīr b. Aḥmad b. al-Ḥasan b. 'Alī b. Munīr [al-Khashshāb] reported to us by way of reading to the former while I was listening: Abū al-Ḥasan 'Alī b. Aḥmad b. Isḥāq al-Baghdādī reported to us by way of reading to the former: Abū al-'Abbās al-Walīd b. Ḥammād al-Ramlī reported to us, saying: Al-Ḥusayn b. Ziyād [al-Ramlī] reported to me: Abū Ismā'īl Muḥammad b. 'Abdallāh [al-Azdī] related to us, saying: This is the rest of the tradition [narrated] by Abū Bashīr al-Tanūkhī [the Christian], who said: We [=Abū Bashīr and the Byzantines] set up camp near the Muslims and we were scared of them. We learned that their Prophet (ṣ.) had said to them: "You are going

416 In the edited text, "b. 'Abdallāh" and "b. Sa'īd" are inverted. However, we have reversed their order in our translation for reasons of consistency.

to triumph over the Byzantines". They [=the Muslims] had fought us more than once and had triumphed over us every time. However, whenever we considered our [large] number and [numerous] groups, our spirits were strengthened [again] and we thought that an army like ours was invincible. He [=the narrator, Abū Bashīr al-Tanūkhī] said: Bāhān remained [in his encampment at al-Yarmūk] for some days, dispatching messengers to all the Byzantines around him and ordering them to bring the offerings to his companions. They did so and [yet] it did not harm the Muslims, because [the land of] the River Jordan was in their hands and [so] they were supplied with abundant [provisions]. When Bāhān, the [chief] commander of the Byzantines, realised that it neither harmed them [=the Muslims] nor diminished their [resources] and that they were satisfied with [the yield from the lands of] the River Jordan, he dispatched a huge cavalry to approach them from behind—a cavalry commanded by a grand patrician who was one of their grand men and who wanted to surround them [=the Muslims] with his soldiers from all sides. But the Muslims knew what they [=the Byzantines] planned [to do]. Thus, Abū ʿUbayda summoned Khālid b. al-Walīd and dispatched him in command of 2,000 horsemen [to the Byzantines' cavalry]. Khālid headed out until he intercepted the infidel [=the grand man]. When he faced him, Khālid dismounted to [go to] the infantry and sent Qays b. Hubayra [al-Murādī] in command of the cavalry [to fight the grand man and his cavalry]. Qays [b. Hubayra al-Murādī] launched an attack on them and they fought each other fiercely. Qays [b. Hubayra al-Murādī] as well as the Muslim cavalry launched another attack on their [=the Byzantines'] cavalry and defeated it until he pushed it back to the [Muslims'] infantry that was [headed by] Khālid. Khālid marched [forward]\\278 with the infantry and when he drew near the patrician, he launched a fierce attack with [the people of] his flag on them [=the patrician and his cavalry], as did the Muslims together with him. They struck them with their swords until they were dispersed and defeated. They [=the Muslims] also killed a great many of them.

[Thereupon,] Qays [b. Hubayra al-Murādī] said to a man from Banū Numayr[417], in whose direction the patrician was fleeing from defeat: "O brother of Banū Numayr, do not let the patrician escape, because I swear by God that I have exhausted my horse [in chasing] this enemy today until my horse can no longer gallop". Thereupon, the man from [Banū] Numayr [moved forward to] attack him [=the patrician], galloping in pursuit of him for a short

417 Numayr is a Northern Arabian tribe that is regarded as a subtribe of either Asad or Tamīm or Hamdān. Numayr is also somehow related to Banū ʿĀmir. In al-Azdī's narrative, Numayr is called Banū Numayr and two individual figures are said to have belonged to Numayr: (a) Mukhaymis b. Ḥābis b. Muʿāwiya, who is said to have been a horseman and to have been temporarily admitted into Paradise and (b) an unnamed fighter who was ordered by Qays b. Hubayra to catch and kill a fleeing Byzantine patrician. However, this fighter could do so only after the patrician had been severely wounded by Qays b. Hubayra. On Numayr, see *EI*[2], s.v. Numayr (G. Levi Della Vida).

while until he caught up with him. When the patrician saw him approaching and constraining him, the patrician turned to him. Both of them tussled with their swords, but the swords did not harm [either of them]. [Then] each of them clasped the other and they both fell [from their horses] to the ground [where] they fought each other for a short while. Then the man from [Banū] Numayr knocked him [=the patrician] flat and sat on his chest, between his legs. The patrician squeezed him while he was [fighting] like a lion. Hence, he restrained the movement of the man from [Banū] Numayr. Qays [b. Hubayra al-Murādī] saw them [like this]. So he proceeded until he stopped next to them and said: "O brother of Banū Numayr, have you killed the man, God willing?" He said: "No [I have not]. I swear by God that I can neither move nor strike him with anything, while he squeezes me with his thigh[s] and clutches my hands". Thereupon, Qays [b. Hubayra al-Murādī] dismounted[, went] to him and struck him [=the patrician], severing one of his hands. Then he left him [=the patrician], turned away and said to the man from [Banū] Numayr: "[Now,] he is yours". The man from [Banū] Numayr rose and struck him with his sword until he killed him [=the patrician]. [Then] Khālid b. al-Walīd passed by him [=Qays b. Hubayra al-Murādī] and said to him: "O Qays, who is this [man] and who killed him?" Thereupon, Qays [b. Hubayra al-Murādī] said to him: "This man from [Banū] Numayr killed him". However, he did not tell him [=Khālid] what he himself had done to him [=the patrician].\\279

Abū ʿUbayda b. al-Jarrāḥ's setting up camp at al-Yarmūk and his request to ʿUmar b. al-Khaṭṭāb (r.) for reinforcements

Al-Ḥusayn b. Ziyād [al-Ramlī] reported to us on the authority of Abū Ismāʿīl Muḥammad b. ʿAbdallāh [al-Azdī], who said: Furthermore, Abū Jahḍam [al-Azdī] related to me on the authority of ʿAbd al-Raḥmān b. al-Salīk [al-Fazārī] on the authority of ʿAbdallāh b. Qurṭ [al-Thumālī]: Muʿādh b. Jabal, and some of the Muslim men who were with him, said to Abū ʿUbayda b. al-Jarrāḥ when he came from Damascus to his encampment at al-Yarmūk: "Why do you not write [a letter] to the Commander of the Believers to inform him about those army units that have marched towards us and to ask him for reinforcements?" He [=Abū ʿUbayda] said: "Yes, certainly". Then he wrote [the following letter] to him [=ʿUmar]:

Regarding the matter at hand: I inform the Commander of the Believers, may God honour him, that the Byzantines had set out towards the Muslims, by land and by sea, leaving behind nobody who would be able to carry a weapon. They had marched out with [their] priests and bishops and the monks had descended from the[ir] hermitages to [join] them, too. They also had asked the people of Armenia and al-Jazīra to march with them. [Then] they had come to us, numbering about 400,000 men. When I had learned of their situation, I did not like to let the Muslims deceive themselves [regarding the Byzantines' number] or to conceal from them [=the Muslims] what I had learned of them [=the Byzantines]. So I disclosed the news to them, explained the situation to them and asked them for their opinion[s]. The Muslims were of the opinion that they [should] withdraw to one of the [southern] lands of Syria and then tell our outermost and farthest [troops] to join us so that our entire army gathers in this location until reinforcements [sent] by the Commander of the Believers [also] reach us.

Therefore, o Commander of the Believers, hurry, hurry up [dispatching] men, one after another, [to us]. Otherwise, reckon the Believers as dead should they stand [against the Byzantines] and also [reckon] their religion [as inferior] if they dispersed [from the battlefield]. For\\280 that which they [=the Muslims] will not be able to fight against has reached them. [They would be able to fight against it] only if God reinforced them with His angels or sent them succour from His side. Peace be upon you.

When this letter reached him, ʿUmar summoned the Emigrants and the Supporters and read Abū ʿUbayda's letter to them. Thereupon, the Muslims wept bitterly, raised their hands [in supplication] and requested God (ʿa.) to support, protect and defend them [=the Muslims at al-Yarmūk]. Their sympathy for them [=the Muslims at al-Yarmūk] intensified and they said: "O Commander of the Believers, dispatch us to our brethren and appoint whomever you want as commander over us, or [you] march [out] with us to them. We swear by God that if they were killed, there would be no good [for us] in life after their death".

Al-Ḥusayn b. Ziyād [al-Ramlī] reported to us on the authority of Abū Ismāʿīl Muḥammad b. ʿAbdallāh [=al-Azdī], who said: Furthermore, Mikhnaf b. ʿAbdallāh [b. Yazīd b. al-Mughaffal] related to me on the authority of ʿAbd al-Raḥmān b. al-Salīk [al-Fazārī] on the authority of ʿAbdallāh b. Qurṭ [al-Thumālī], who said: I was the one who came with Abū ʿUbayda's letter to ʿUmar. He [=the narrator, ʿAbdallāh b. Qurṭ al-Thumālī] said: All the Emigrants and Supporters to whom I came showed much concern and sympathy for the Muslims [in Syria], fearing that destruction would befall them. I have not seen any of them more concerned or sympathetic than ʿAbd al-Raḥmān b. ʿAwf, or more iteratively saying: "O Commander of the Believers, march [out] with us. For if you go to Syria, God is going to strengthen the Believers' hearts and terrify the Unbelievers' hearts". He [=the narrator, ʿAbdallāh b. Qurṭ al-Thumālī] said: However, the companions of the Messenger of God (ṣ.) unanimously agreed that ʿUmar should remain behind but dispatch reinforcements and act as a supporter of the Muslims. Thus, ʿUmar said to ʿAbdallāh b.\\281 Qurṭ [al-Thumālī]: "How long [was the distance] between the Muslims and the Byzantines on the day you marched out to me?" He [=the narrator, ʿAbdallāh b. Qurṭ al-Thumālī] said: I said: "[It took] three or four nights [to march] between their nearest [troop] and the [first unit of the] Muslims, but five nights between their generality and the generality of the Muslims". Thereupon, he [=ʿUmar] said: "Impossible! [I do not know] when our succour would reach those people".

He [=the narrator, ʿAbdallāh b. Qurṭ al-Thumālī] said: Then ʿUmar wrote [the following letter and sent it] with me to Abū ʿUbayda (r.):

Regarding the matter at hand: [Our] brother from Thumāla [=ʿAbdallāh b. Qurṭ al-Thumālī] came to me with your letter in which you informed me of the Byzantines' trooping towards the Muslims by land and by sea and of their marching [out] with their bishops, priests and monks against you. Our Lord, who is praised by us, who arranges [our matters] for us and [who is] the Great Bestower of constant grace and blessing upon us, had [fore-]seen the situation of these bishops and monks when He sent Muḥammad (ṣ.) with the truth, strengthened him with victory and aided him with [striking] terror [into the hearts of] his enemies to be victorious [over them]. For He [=God], who never breaks His promise, said: "It is He who has sent His Messenger with guidance and the religion of truth, to show that it is above all [other] religions, however much the idolaters may hate this".[418] So do not be terrified of the multitude of those [Byzantines] who have come to you. For God has surely disowned them, and those who are disowned by God deserve to find [their] multitude useless, [deserve] to be caused by God (ʿa.) to trust only in themselves and [deserve] to be forsaken by Him. Do not feel worried about the small number of the Muslims in comparison to the Polytheists, for God accompanies you and whoever God accompanies [receives] no little [but great support]. Stay where\\282 you are until you face your enemies and fight them. Ask God (ʿa.) to make you triumphant over them, for God suffices as a helper, patron and supporter. I also understood your statement "Reckon the Muslims as dead should they stand [against the Byzantines] and also [reckon] their religion [as inferior] if they dispersed [from the battlefield]. For that which they [=the Muslims] will not be able to fight against has reached them. [They would be able to fight against it] only if God reinforced them with His angels or sent them succour from His side". I swear by God that if you had not [made an] exception in this [statement], you would have misbehaved. I swear upon my life that if the Muslims stand against them [=the Byzantines], have patience and get injured, what God retains [for them in heaven] will be better for the pious. [For] God (ʿa.) said: "There are men among the Believers who honoured their pledge to God: Some of them have fulfilled it by death, and some are still waiting".[419] Therefore, blessed are the martyrs. Those Muslims with you, who understand [what] God (ʿa.) said, should take as an example those [fighters] who were struck down (*muṣarraʿūn*) around the Messenger of God (ṣ.) in his battles. Those who fought [with the Messenger] for the cause of God neither withered nor feared death on God's side. Those [of his companions] who remained behind neither weakened nor succumbed to their disastrous predicament. Rather, they

418 Q. 9:33 (*The Qurʾān. Tr. Abdel Haleem*, 119).
419 Q. 33:23 (*The Qurʾān. Tr. Abdel Haleem*, 268).

modelled themselves on them [=the fighting companions] and [also] fought for the cause of God against whoever opposed them and abandoned their religion. [Thus,] God (ʿa.) has praised [these] people for their patience, saying: "Many Prophets have fought, with large bands of godly men alongside them who, in the face of their sufferings for God's cause, did not lose heart or weaken or surrender: God loves those who are steadfast. All they said was: 'Our Lord, forgive us our sins and our excesses. Make our feet firm, and give us help against the disbelievers', and so God gave them\\283 both the rewards of this world and the excellent rewards of the Hereafter: God loves those who do good".[420] As for the reward of the worldly life [mentioned in these verses], it is spoils and conquest. As for the reward of the Hereafter, it is forgiveness and Paradise. Thus, read out my letter to the people and order them to fight for the cause of God and to remain as patient [as mentioned in the verses] so that God bestows the reward of the worldly life and the best reward of the afterlife upon them. As for your statement "what they are powerless against has reached them", if you are powerless against them, God is powerful over them and He will [always] be powerful. I swear by God that if we had fought the people [=the Byzantines] with our [limited] power, strength and multitude [alone], it would have been too hard [to defeat them] and they would have annihilated and destroyed us. However, we trust in God, our Lord, [turn] to Him by ridding ourselves of power and strength and ask Him for victory and mercy. [By doing so] you are victorious in any situation, God willing. Therefore, show God [your] sincere intentions, raise your desire[s] to Him "and be steadfast, more steadfast than others; [and] be ready; always be mindful of God, so that you may prosper".[421] [Peace be upon you.]

ʿAbdallāh b. Qurṭ [al-Thumālī] [=the narrator] said: ʿUmar gave me this letter and ordered me to travel [to the Muslims] quickly, saying to me: "When you reach the Muslims, march through their lines and stop at those [groups] of them that are [assembled] under each flag. [Then] inform them that you are my messenger to them and say to them: "ʿUmar sends you his greetings and says to you: "O adherents of Islam, face [your enemies] sincerely, attack them daringly as lions, strike their heads with [your] swords and count them [as being of] less value than motes. For we know that you are victorious over them. So do not be terrified of your enemy's multitude and do not yearn for those [companions] of yours who have not joined you [in fighting]"""". He [=the narrator, ʿAbdallāh b. Qurṭ al-Thumālī] said: I mounted my riding camel and rushed [to Syria] for fear that I would not catch up with the people and would miss the [upcoming] battle. He [=the narrator, ʿAbdallāh b. Qurṭ al-Thumālī] said: I finally reached Abū ʿUbayda on the [very] day when Saʿīd b. ʿĀmir b. Ḥudhaym al-Jumaḥī entered with 1,000 Muslim men, who had been sent by ʿUmar to Abū ʿUbayda, into his [=Abū ʿUbayda's]

420 Q. 3:146–148 (*The Qurʾān. Tr. Abdel Haleem*, 154).
421 Q. 3:200 (*The Qurʾān. Tr. Abdel Haleem*, 49).

encampment. He [=the narrator, ʿAbdallāh b. Qurṭ al-Thumālī] said: This encouraged\\284 the Muslims who rejoiced over [the arrival of] their reinforcement[s]. I came to them [delivering] ʿUmar's (r.) letter to Abū ʿUbayda who read it [out] to the people. Then they rejoiced over his [=ʿUmar's] opinion [given] to them, over his ordering them to have patience, over heralding good news to them about [their] conquest and over wishing them a reward for that [=their fight].

The report on Sufyān [b. ʿAwf b. Mughaffal al-Azdī], Abū ʿUbayda's messenger to ʿUmar (r.)

Al-Ḥusayn b. Ziyād [al-Ramlī] reported to us on the authority of Abū Ismāʿīl Muḥammad b. ʿAbdallāh [al-Azdī], who said: Furthermore, Abū Khaddāsh related to me on the authority of Sufyān b. Sulaym al-Azdī on the authority of ʿAbdallāh b. Qurṭ [al-Thumālī], who said: When he [=Abū ʿUbayda] received [the news] that the Byzantines had advanced on him with what they [=the Muslims] were powerless against, Abū ʿUbayda sent Sufyān b. ʿAwf [b. Mughaffal] al-Azdī during the night from Ḥimṣ to ʿUmar to inform him of this news and to ask him for reinforcements. Then Abū ʿUbayda moved out with the people in the [following] morning, marching to Damascus and then to al-Yarmūk. Sufyān b. ʿAwf [b. Mughaffal al-Azdī] came to ʿUmar (r.) and informed him of the [latest] news. Saʿīd b. ʿĀmir b. Ḥudhaym was staying with ʿUmar (r.) [in Medina]. Abū Bakr al-Ṣiddīq (r.) had [previously] dispatched Saʿīd b. ʿĀmir b. Ḥudhaym [in command] of an army unit to Syria. So he had stayed with Abū ʿUbayda until the Battle of Fiḥl occurred.\\285 He had witnessed it and fared well in it. When Abū ʿUbayda had finished its proceedings (*amr*), he said to Saʿīd b. ʿĀmir b. Ḥudhaym: "I wrote a letter to the Commander of the Believers, in which I inform him of God's good deed[s] for us and of His [bestowal of the] conquest upon us. I want to send this letter only with a veracious and reliable man who will inform the Commander of the Believers about the matter as it [really] is. I would also like the man to be one of those whom the Commander of the Believers trusts and with whose righteousness he is familiar". Thereupon, Saʿīd b. ʿĀmir b. Ḥudhaym said to him: "You have just found him". Abū ʿUbayda said: "Who is it?" He [=Saʿīd b. ʿĀmir b. Ḥudhaym] said: "Me. The Commander of the Believers is already familiar with me. In addition, I considered asking your permission for [going on] pilgrimage (*ḥajj*) after God had endowed us with fighting for His cause against those Polytheists and [with] victory over them. Since this need [of yours] has arisen, give me your letter, which I will deliver on your behalf. Then I leave to [perform] pilgrimage and hope to come [back] to you as soon as possible, God willing". Abū ʿUbayda said: "I swear upon my life that you are the trustworthy, reliable and honest one among us [I was looking for]". Thus, he had written [the letter], [handed it over] to him and dispatched him to the Commander of the Believers. He [=Saʿīd b. ʿĀmir b. Ḥudhaym] had come with this letter to the Commander of the Believers.

Then he had performed his pilgrimage, returned to ʿUmar and stayed with him until Sufyān b. ʿAwf [b. Mughaffal al-Azdī] came from Ḥimṣ to him [=ʿUmar] to inform him of the Byzantines' trooping to them [=the Muslims] and of what they advanced with [to fight] against them and to ask him [=ʿUmar] for reinforcements. He [=ʿUmar] summoned Saʿīd b. ʿĀmir b. Ḥudhaym and dispatched him [in command] of 1,000 Muslim men [back to Syria]. He [=Saʿīd b. ʿĀmir] proceeded with them until they all entered the encampment of Abū ʿUbayda b. al-Jarrāḥ (r.).

Al-Ḥusayn b. Ziyād [al-Ramlī] reported to us on the authority of Abū Ismāʿīl [Muḥammad b. ʿAbdallāh al-Azdī], who said: Furthermore, ʿAbd al-Malik b. Nawfal b. Masāḥiq al-Qurashī related to me on the authority of Abū Saʿīd al-Maqburī, who said: ʿUmar (r.) [planned to] send Saʿīd b. ʿĀmir [b. Ḥudhaym] in [command of] an army unit consisting of 1,000 or 2,000 [men] to al-Yarmūk in Syria. He then summoned him and said: "O Saʿīd b. ʿĀmir [b. Ḥudhaym], I appointed you as commander of this army unit. However, you are not better than any\\286 man among them except that you are more fearful of God than he. So do not besmirch their [=the Muslims'] honour, do not beat their bodies (*abshār*), do not belittle the weak among them and do not show preference to the strong among them. Be a follower of the truth and do not follow overwhelming desire. For if I heard about you that which pleases me, I would not deprive you of what you like [to have]". He [=Saʿīd b. ʿĀmir b. Ḥudhaym] said to him [=ʿUmar]: "O Commander of the Believers, you have advised me and I have listened to you. Now listen to my advice to you". He [=ʿUmar] said: "Proceed". He [=Saʿīd b. ʿĀmir b. Ḥudhaym] said: "O Commander of the Believers, fear God [in your dealings] with the people and do not fear the people [in your dealings] with God. Wish for close and distant Muslims that which you wish for yourself and for your household but do not wish for close and distant Muslims what you do not wish for yourself and for your household. Stick to the indubitable cause so that God protects you against that which troubles you and aids you in your cause and in that which He assigns to you. Do not decide on one case with two different judgements and, as a result, your word and your decision become incongruous, truth becomes conflated with falsehood and the matter becomes unclear to you. Run into trouble [to discover] the truth wherever you find it and call a spade a spade".[422] ʿUmar (r.) bowed his head for a long time while holding a rod on which he leaned his forehead. Then he raised his head with tears trickling down his cheeks and said: "O Saʿīd, what a good father you have got![423] Who can do [all] that you have just mentioned?" He [=Saʿīd b. ʿĀmir b. Ḥudhaym] said: "Whoever has around his neck what God

422 The English idiomatic phrase "call a spade a spade" is the pragmatic equivalent of the Arabic expression "*lā taʾkhudhaka fī llāh lawmata lāʾim*" (lit. "Do not fear anybody's reproach when it relates to God").

423 The commendatory expression "*li-llāh abūka*" (lit. "[the goodness of] your father is due to God") means "It is God who made your father bring to life someone good like you".

has hung around yours\\287 should not be remiss. You are obliged to give order[s] and you will be [either] obeyed or disobeyed. Then you will have ended up [having] evidence [for the truth] and the [disobedient] people will have ended up [committing] sin[s]".

Al-Ḥusayn b. Ziyād [al-Ramlī] reported to us on the authority of Abū Ismāʿīl [Muḥammad b. ʿAbdallāh al-Azdī], who said: Furthermore, al-Ajlaḥ b. ʿAbdallāh[424] related to me on the authority of [ʿĀmir] al-Shaʿbī who, concerning Saʿīd b. ʿĀmir [b. Ḥudhaym]'s advice to ʿUmar (r.), said something similar or almost similar. He [=ʿĀmir al-Shaʿbī] [also] said: "And he [=ʿUmar] sent him to Syria". However, he did not mention al-Yarmūk [in particular].

Al-Ḥusayn b. Ziyād [al-Ramlī] reported to us on the authority of Abū Ismāʿīl Muḥammad b. ʿAbdallāh [al-Azdī], who said: Furthermore, Abū Jahḍam [al-Azdī] related to me on the authority of Sufyān b. Sulaym al-Azdī on the authority of al-Ḥārith b. ʿAbdallāh al-Azdī, later al-Namirī,[425] who said: When Abū ʿUbayda b. al-Jarrāḥ set up camp at al-Yarmūk and joined his most distant parts [of the army] to his and [when] the Byzantine groups came out in large numbers[426] to us, carrying their crosses, accompanied by [their] priests, monks, bishops and patricians [and] being exhorted by their monks and motivated by their patricians, they [=the Byzantines] proceeded and set up camp in Dayr al-Jabal. When they advanced in such [large] groups towards the Muslims, the Muslims became afraid of them. Thus, nothing was more preferable to them [=the Muslims] than marching away from them [=the Byzantines] and withdrawing from their lands until they would receive reinforcements with whose help they would reckon that they would be able to stand against the approaching Byzantines.\\288

He [=the narrator, al-Ḥārith b. ʿAbdallāh al-Azdī] said: [At this point] Abū ʿUbayda summoned the people and consulted them. All the people whom he consulted advised him to depart from Syria [and withdraw to the south], except Khālid b. al-Walīd, who advised him to stay [there] and said to him: "Leave the people [=the Byzantines] to me, leave the [whole] matter to me, and give me the command over what is behind your door. For I will

424 Al-Ajlaḥ's full name is Abū Ḥujayya al-Ajlaḥ b. ʿAbdallāh al-Kindī al-Kūfī (n.d.). ʿUqla and Banī Yāsīn mention his date of death as 145/762 (see al-Azdī, *Futūḥ al-Shām. Ed. ʿUqla/Banī Yāsīn*, 30; 287, n. 3). In al-Azdī's narrative, he is mentioned as a transmitter of one tradition. On al-Ajlaḥ, see Ibn Saʿd, *Kitāb al-ṭabaqāt*, VI, 244 and al-Bukhārī, *Al-taʾrīkh al-kabīr*, I-2, 68 (no. 1711).

425 Al-Ḥārith b. ʿAbdallāh al-Azdī is listed neither in Ibn Saʿd, al-Bukhārī, Ibn ʿAsākir nor in any other biographical work we could access. ʿUqla and Banī Yāsīn identify him as the transmitter al-Ḥārith b. ʿAbdallāh *al-Kūfī* (d. 65/687) who is mentioned in al-Dhahabī's *Taʾrīkh al-islām* (see al-Azdī, *Futūḥ al-Shām. Ed. ʿUqla/Banī Yāsīn*, 287, n. 5; 299, n. 12 referring to al-Dhahabī, *Taʾrīkh al-islām*, vol. 61–80 H., 89–90 [no. 20]). In al-Azdī's narrative, he is mentioned as a fighter in the Battle of al-Yarmūk and as a transmitter of several traditions.

426 The Arabic expression "*yajurrūna al-shawka wa-al-shajara*" (lit. "they drag spines and trees") is an idiom that means "in huge numbers, collectively or as a whole".

suffice you, with God's permission, in handling this enemy [alone]". Thereupon, Abū ʿUbayda said to him: "The people [=the Byzantines] are yours". So he [=Abū ʿUbayda] left the people [=the Byzantines] to him [to handle]. He [=the narrator, al-Ḥārith b. ʿAbdallāh al-Azdī] said: Qays b. Hubayra al-Murādī had the same opinion as Khālid b. al-Walīd about remaining in the land of Syria. None of the Muslims were equal to both of them in war or in valour. He [=the narrator, al-Ḥārith b. ʿAbdallāh al-Azdī] said: Then Khālid marched out with the people in the highest spirits (*riʿa*), with the greatest ease, the best visage, the truest discernment to face their enemy and the firmest self-assuredness to fight them. He [=the narrator, al-Ḥārith b. ʿAbdallāh al-Azdī] said: Khālid lined them up in three lines, forming a right flank and a left flank. Then Khālid came to Abū ʿUbayda and said to him: "Whom would you appoint [as commander] of your right flank?" He [=Abū ʿUbayda] said: "Muʿādh b. Jabal". Thereupon, he [=Khālid] said: "He is qualified for that [position] and is a sufficient and reliable [fighter]. So put it under his command". Hence, Abū ʿUbayda gave the order to Muʿādh [b. Jabal] to stand on the right flank [and he did so]. Then Khālid said: "Whom would you appoint as commander of the left flank?" [Thereupon,] he [=Abū ʿUbayda] said: "More than one". He [=Khālid] said: "Then put it under the command of Qubāth b. Ashyam if you agree". Abū ʿUbayda gave the order [to Qubāth b. Ashyam] to stand on the left flank [and he did so]. On that [flank] Kināna and Qays were positioned. Qubāth b. Ashyam was from Kināna and he was brave and valorous.\\289 [Then] Khālid said: "I take command of the cavalry and you appoint whomever you want as commander of the infantry". He [=Abū ʿUbayda] said: "God willing, I will put it under the command of the one whose retreat or flight [from war] is not feared. I put it [=the infantry] under the command of Hāshim b. ʿUtba b. Abī Waqqāṣ". [Thereupon,] he [=Khālid] said: "Well-spoken, well-done and well-said". Abū ʿUbayda said: "O Hāshim, dismount [from your horse], for you are [now] the commander of the infantry and I am [fighting] with you". [Then] Khālid said to Abū ʿUbayda: "Send for the followers of each flag and order them to obey me". So Abū ʿUbayda summoned al-Ḍaḥḥāk b. Qays and ordered him to do that. Al-Ḍaḥḥāk [b. Qays] marched through the [lines of the] people, saying to them: "Your [chief] commander Abū ʿUbayda orders you to obey what Khālid b. al-Walīd instructs you to do". Thereupon, the people said: "We listen and obey". Al-Ḍaḥḥāk [b. Qays] also passed by Muʿādh b. Jabal and ordered him to obey Khālid b. al-Walīd[, too]. Thereupon, Muʿādh [b. Jabal] said: "We listen and obey". Then he [=Muʿādh b. Jabal] looked at the people and said: "Verily, I swear by God that if you obey him [=Khālid], you will have obeyed the one with a blessed cause, a fortunate mind, great competence and of sound assumption and intention".

Al-Ḍaḥḥāk [b. Qays] said: I spoke to Khālid about Muʿādh b. Jabal's words [regarding him] and said to him: "I heard Muʿādh [b. Jabal] praising you and saying such and such about you". So he [=Khālid] said to me: "May God have mercy upon my brother Muʿādh [b. Jabal]. Verily, I swear by God that if he loves me, I do also love him for the sake of God. He and his companions have had precedents [in Islam] that we will never attain, reach or obtain. Congratulations to them on what God has privileged them with thereof". Al-Ḍaḥḥāk [b. Qays] said: Then I met Muʿādh [b. Jabal] and told him what I had said to Khālid and what Khālid had said in reply to me. Thereupon, Muʿādh [b. Jabal] said: "Verily, I do hope that God (ʿa.) has given him the best reward for his patience in fighting against the Polytheists, for his toughness on them, for his strife against them with his discernment and sincere intention and for his support of his religion.\\290 [I also hope] that by doing [all] this he will be one of the best doers among us". Then I met Khālid [again] [and reported] this [speech to him, too]. Thereupon, he said: "Nothing is difficult for God".

He [=the narrator, al-Ḥārith b. ʿAbdallāh al-Azdī] said: Then Khālid marched through the lines, stopping where the followers of each flag were stationed and said: "O adherents of Islam, patience is strength and retreat is a failure. With patience you are rendered victorious, for the patient have the upper hand. Verily, the weak falsifier (*mubṭil*) ends up in failure and the truth teller (*muḥiqq*) never fails, [because] he knows that God is with him and [because] he defends God's sanctities and fights for Him. If he [=the truth teller] goes to God, God will surely honour his rank and praise his endeavour. Verily, God is thankful and loves the thankful". He [=the narrator, al-Ḥārith b. ʿAbdallāh al-Azdī] said: He [=Khālid] kept stopping where the followers of each flag were stationed, exhorting them, inciting them and raising their desire [to fight] until he passed by all the people. Then he gathered the Muslim cavalry around him and summoned Qays b. Hubayra b. Makshūḥ al-Murādī [to come to him]. He [=Qays b. Hubayra] was assisting him, sharing the same opinion with him and resembling him in his steadfastness, his toughness, his courage and his daring against the Polytheists. Then Khālid said to him: "You are [one of] the [renowned] Arabs' horseman and only few of those who will witness this battle-day are equal to you in my eyes. So march out with me as part of this cavalry". He [=Khālid] also sent for Maysara b. Masrūq al-ʿAbsī, who was one of the Arabs' noblemen and [renowned] horsemen. He also summoned ʿAmr b. al-Ṭufayl b. ʿAmr [b.] Dhī al-Nūr al-Azdī, later al-Dawsī, who then [also] marched out with him. Qays [b. Hubayra al-Murādī] was valorous, tough and brave. Thus, he [=Khālid] said: "March out with me". So they [all] marched out with him. Thereafter, they divided the cavalry into four parts and he [=Khālid] then dispatched each of them in command of a quarter. Khālid [also] marched out, commanding a quarter of the Muslim cavalry, until he drew near the largest encampment of the Byzantines, where\\291 Bāhān was stationed. When the Byzantines saw them, they were panicked by their march to them, [because] they [=the Byzantines] had advanced [without resistance] and it had been said to them: "The Arabs want to depart from the land of Syria and to relinquish it to you". This [news] had left a [positive] impression on them and they had become greedy for it [=the land of Syria], hoping that there would be no fighting between them [and the Muslims]. This [hope] was confirmed to them [=the Byzantines] when they [=the Muslims] had withdrawn ahead of them, driven [out] by them and relinquishing to them the land[s] and the cities, in which they [=the Byzantines] had been defeated[427] [and which were located] between them and al-Yarmūk, [i.e.] Damascus, Ḥimṣ and their surroundings. When they saw Khālid approaching them with [his] cavalry, they were scared [to death]. They marched out under their flags, [carrying] their cross and accompanied by [their] priests, monks and patricians. Then they formed twenty lines whose two ends were not visible. They then marched a huge cavalry out to the Muslims, one that was a hundred times bigger than that of the Muslims. When their cavalry drew near to the Muslims' cavalry, one of their patricians and courageous men moved out [of his line], asking for a duel by intercepting the Muslims' cavalry. Thereupon, Khālid said: "Would a man [from among you] go out to [duel with] him? Either one of you moves out to [meet] him or I go to [duel with] him [myself]". A good many of the Muslims swiftly stepped out towards him [=Khālid] to go to him [=the patrician] [for the duel]. Maysara b. Masrūq [al-ʿAbsī] [also] wanted to move out to [fight] him, but Khālid said to him: "You are an old man and this Byzantine is a young man. I do not want you to go out to [duel with] him, because an old man can hardly stand against a young man. Stay with us in your cavalry unit, may God have mercy upon you, for you are, as far as I know, known for good performance\\292 and great competence [in battle]". ʿAmr b. al-Ṭufayl [b. ʿAmr al-Azdī] [also] wanted to move out to [fight] him, but Khālid said to him: "O my nephew, you are a young boy and I fear that you cannot stand against him".

Al-Ḥārith b. ʿAbdallāh al-Azdī [=the narrator] said: I was [stationed] in Khālid's cavalry that marched out with him and I said [to him]: "I will move out to [duel with] him". Thereupon, he [=Khālid] said: "As you wish". When I started to move out to [fight] him, Khālid said to me: "Have you ever duelled with a man before?" I said: "No". He [=Khālid] said: "Then do not go out to [duel with] him". Then Qays b. Hubayra [al-Murādī] said: "O Khālid, [it looks] as if you are roving around me". He [=Khālid] said: "Yes, if you went out to [duel with] him, I do hope that you would kill him. [However,] if you do not go out to [fight] him, I will certainly go out to [duel with] him [myself]". Thereupon, Qays [b. Hubayra al-Murādī] said: "No, I am going out to [duel with] him". Then Qays b. Hubayra [al-Murādī] went out to [fight] him, saying [the following lines of verse]:

سائل نساء الحى فى حجالها
ألست يوم الحرب من أبطالها
ومقعص الأقران من رجالها

427 Due to the absence of vowels, the root *gh-l-b* can be assigned two meaningful readings here, one is passive (*ghulibū*, see the text above) while the other is active (*ghalabū*) and is translated as "which they [=the Muslims] conquered".

I am asking the tribeswomen in their canopies:
"Am I not, on this battle-day, one of its heroes?"
And the opponent slain *in situ* is one of its men.

Then he [=Qays b. Hubayra al-Murādī] went out to [fight] him. When he drew near to him, he [=Qays b. Hubayra al-Murādī] hit his horse. Then Qays [b. Hubayra] attacked him and did not tarry [long] until he struck him with the sword upon his head, [thus] cutting the weaponry [=a helmet] that was on him and splitting his head. Lo and behold, the Byzantine fell dead between the forelegs of his horse. He [=Qays b. Hubayra al-Murādī] proclaimed "God is the Greatest!" and so did the Muslims. Thereupon, Khālid said: "After [this] you will see nothing but triumph (*fatḥ*). O Qays, attack them".\\293 Then Khālid came to his companions and said: "Attack them. I swear by God that they will never succeed after their first horseman has been covered in dust". He [=the narrator, al-Ḥārith b. ʿAbdallāh al-Azdī] said: Then we launched an attack on them [=the Byzantines], on those of them who were adjacent to us and on their [advancing] cavalry that was stationed at the front of their lines. Their lines were as wide as the mountains. Qays [b. Hubayra al-Murādī] [also] said: Then we attacked them and thus dispersed their cavalry [men] until they caught up with the[ir infantry] lines. Khālid and his companions also attacked those [Byzantines] who were adjacent to them and dispersed them until they forced them back to the[ir] lines. ʿAmr b. al-Ṭufayl [b. ʿAmr] al-Azdī and Maysara b. Masrūq al-ʿAbsī, together with their companions, also launched an attack [on them] until they pushed them back to the[ir] lines, [i.e.] to the lines of the Polytheists. Then Khālid ordered his cavalry[men] to turn away from them [=the Byzantines] [and they did so]. After that, he [=Khālid] moved [forward] with them until he joined the generality of the Muslims. [On that day,] God showed them [=the Muslims] the pleasure [of triumph] over the Polytheists.

He [=the narrator, al-Ḥārith b. ʿAbdallāh al-Azdī] said: [After this defeat] the Byzantine patricians blamed one another, saying: "Not many cavalrymen of your enemy came to you, yet they dispersed your cavalry [unit]s on all sides". Then some of their [=the Byzantines'] cavalry units marched [out again], one after the other, and covered the ground like the night and the flood as if they were black locusts (*al-jarād al-aswad*). The Muslims thought that they [=the Byzantines] would engage [in a fight] with them. [Thus,] the Muslims rushed daringly towards them. They [=the Byzantines] proceeded and when they approached the generality of the Muslims, drawing closer to them and to their cavalry, they stopped for a short while. [For] they [=the Byzantines] became afraid of them [=the Muslims] and their hearts were filled with fear of them [=the Muslims]. Then Khālid said to the Muslims: "We had turned away from them but triumph over them is ours and defeat (*dabra*) is theirs. Thus, stand firmly against them for a short while. If they advance [further] on us, we will fight them and if they withdraw from [fighting] us, triumph and superiority over them will be ours". Then they [=the Byzantines] began to advance [further] on the Muslims, but retreated later while the Muslims stood silent in their lines and under their flags.\\294 None of them uttered a word except to invoke God inwardly and to ask Him for support against His enemy. When the Byzantines witnessed their [=the Muslims'] situation and their cavalry, infantry, their [firm] lines and [display of] vehemence, earnestness, patience and silence, God struck terror into their hearts. Thus, they [again] stood facing them for a short while and then turned away from them, returning to their encampment.

He [=the narrator, al-Ḥārith b. ʿAbdallāh al-Azdī] said: Their patricians, commanders, grand men and horsemen flocked to Bāhān who was the [chief] commander of their generality. Thereupon, Bāhān said to them: "I formed an opinion and I am telling you about it. Those people descended on your lands, rode your animals, ate your food and wore your clothes. It is more appropriate for them to die than leave whatever you might provide from your decent living and from your worldly life, the like of which they have never seen before. [Therefore,] I have decided, if you may agree, to ask them to send us a sound-minded man from among them, with whom we can speak and negotiate, and to appease them [=the Muslims] with something that causes them to return to their families. Perhaps this will make them leave our lands. If they did so, what they would demand of us would be little compared with what we fear [=defeat and loss]. It would also help us to fend off the jeopardy of a battle which you do not know whether it would be [turning out] against us or in our favour". Thereupon, they said to him: "Well-spoken and well-decided for our generality. Put your decision into action". Then he [=Bāhān] dispatched one of their elites and grand men, called Jirja, to Abū ʿUbayda. He [=Jirja] came to Abū ʿUbayda and said to him: "I am a messenger from Bāhān, the subordinate of the Emperor of the Byzantines, [who is in command] of Syria and of these\\295 soldiers. He [=Bāhān] says to you: 'Send me, from among you, the man who was the commander before you [had been the commander]. For it was mentioned to me that this man is of sound mind and noble origin among you. We also heard that the minds of the people of noble decent are better than the minds of the others. We [are going to] tell him [=this man] what we want [from you] and ask him about what you want [from us]. Thus, if something good or satisfactory for both of us transpires between us, we will accept it and be thankful to God for it. But if no agreement is made between us and you, fighting will break out thereafter'". Abū ʿUbayda summoned Khālid, told him what the Byzantine [messenger] came for and said to Khālid: "Meet them [=the Byzantines] and call them to [embrace] Islam. If they agree, it will be their [good] fortune and they would become a community meriting the same rights we merit and having the same obligations we have. But if they refuse [to convert], grant them an offer to bring tribute by hand and with humility. If they [also] refuse [that], inform them that we will fight them and ask God for help [in our fight] against them until He judges between us and them, for He is the best of [all] judges".

He [=the narrator, al-Ḥārith b. ʿAbdallāh al-Azdī] said: Their messenger, this Byzantine [grand man], came at sunset [to the Muslims' encampment]. He stayed [there] only for a little while until it was the time for prayer.

Thus, the Muslims rose to perform their prayer[s]. When they finished their prayer[s], Khālid said to the Byzantine [grand man]: “The night has fallen over us, but when the morning comes, I will go to your [chief] commander, God willing. So return to him [now] and inform him of this”. The Muslims kept waiting for the Byzantine [grand man] to depart to his [chief] commander, return to him and inform him of what they had said in reply to his [message]. However, the Byzantine [grand man] did not start leaving [his place] and began to watch some of the Muslim men\\296 praying, imploring God and supplicating to Him. Then ʿAmr b. al-ʿĀṣ said: “Verily, their messenger who was sent to you is obsessed”. Thereupon, Abū ʿUbayda said [to ʿAmr]: “Not at all, do you not see how he is looking at those who are praying?” The Byzantine [grand man] kept setting his eyes [on those who were praying], not turning his sight away from them. Thereupon, Abū ʿUbayda said: “I swear by God that I do hope He has struck faith into his [=the Byzantine grand man’s] heart, endeared it to him and apprised him of its grace”. The Byzantine [grand man] remained in this [situation] for a little while, then came to Abū ʿUbayda and said [to him]: “O man, tell me when you entered this religion and when you called the people to [embrace] it”. Thereupon, Abū ʿUbayda said: “We were called to [embrace] it some twenty years ago. Some of us embraced Islam when the Messenger [of God] came to them while some embraced it thereafter”. Then he [=the Byzantine grand man] said: “Had your Messenger ever told you that another messenger would come after him?” He [=Abū ʿUbayda] said: “No, rather he told us that there would be no other Messenger after him. He also told us that Jesus, the son of Mary, had foretold his [=Jesus’s] people his [coming] [=the coming of the Messenger of God]”. [Thereupon,] the Byzantine [grand man] said: “I am one of the testifiers [for that]—[i.e.] that Jesus, the son of Mary, had foretold us [the coming of] the cameleer (*rākib al-jamal*), and I think he is only your companion [=Muḥammad]”. The Byzantine [grand man] also said: “Tell me what your companion [=Muḥammad] said about Jesus, the son of Mary, and what you all say about him?” [Thereupon,] Abū ʿUbayda said: “Our companion’s [=Muḥammad’s] statement is the same as God’s (ʿa.) statement, which is the truest and the most proper one. [For example,] God (ʿa.) says about Jesus, the son of Mary: ‘In God’s eyes Jesus is just like Adam:\\297 He created him from dust, said to him: “Be”, and he was’.[428] Furthermore, God (t.) says [about him]: ‘People of the Book, do not go to excess in your religion, and do not say anything about God except the truth: The Messiah, Jesus, [the] son of Mary, was nothing more than a messenger of God, His word, directed to Mary, a spirit from Him’ to the end of the verse; and [then he continues] to His saying: ‘The Messiah would never disdain to be a servant of God, nor would the angels who are close to Him’”.[429] When the interpreter rendered this to him in Greek (*rūmiyya*) and reached this point [of his speech],

428 Q. 3:59 (*The Qurʾān. Tr. Abdel Haleem*, 38–39).
429 Q. 4:171–172 (*The Qurʾān. Tr. Abdel Haleem*, 66).

he [=the Byzantine grand man] said: "I testify that this is characteristic of Jesus himself and I also testify that your Prophet is truthful, that he is the one about whom Jesus foretold us and that you are truthful people". He [then] said to Abū ʿUbayda: "Summon to me two of your companions who are among the first [converts] to Islam and whom you consider the best of those who are with you". So Abū ʿUbayda summoned Muʿādh b. Jabal and Saʿīd b. Zayd b. ʿAmr b. Nufayl and said to him [=the Byzantine grand man]: "These are two of the most graceful Muslims and of the first converts to Islam". Then the Byzantine [grand man] said to them and to Abū ʿUbayda: "Will you guarantee me Paradise if I convert to Islam and fight with you?" Thereupon, they said to him: "Yes, if you converted to Islam, stuck firmly [to it], did not change [your new faith] until you die and adhered to [all of] this, you would surely be one of the people of Paradise". Then he [=the Byzantine grand man] said: "I want you to bear witness that I am [from now on] one of the Muslims". Thus, he converted to Islam and the Muslims rejoiced over his [embrace of] Islam. They shook his hand, wished him the best and said to him: "If we send our messenger to your [chief] commander tomorrow while you are still with us, they will think that we detained you from [going to] them. Thus, we [must] fear that they will detain our companion [in return]. If you want, go to them tonight and conceal your [conversion to] Islam from them until we dispatch our messenger to them tomorrow and\\298 [continue doing so until] he leaves [them] and [until] we see what will happen between us and them. If our messenger returns to us, come [back] to us afterwards. How dear to us you are, how much we need you and how precious to us you are! You are now to each of us like a brother from the same mother and father". He [=the Byzantine grand man] said: "[In what you suggested] you have certainly made the best decision". Then he set out, stayed overnight with his companions [in the Byzantine's encampment] and went to Bāhān and said to him: "Tomorrow the people's [=the Muslims'] messenger whom you asked for will come to you". When the Byzantine [grand man] rose in the morning the next day and Khālid left Bāhān returning to his companions, the Byzantine [grand man] proceeded until he caught up with the Muslims. After he had converted to Islam, he excelled at it, gave succour against and caused damage to the Polytheists [before he died]; God (t.) rest him.

Mention of what happened between Khālid b. al-Walīd and Bāhān, the subordinate of the Emperor of the Byzantines

When they [=the Muslims] rose the next morning, Khālid b. al-Walīd sent [forth] his own red leather dome-like tent (*qubba*)[430] that he had bought from Maysara b. Masrūq al-ʿAbsī's wife for 300 dinars. It [=the tent] was pitched for him in the Byzantines' encampment. Then Khālid marched out until he

430 For "*qubba*" meaning "grand red tent", see Dozy, *Supplément*, s.v. *qabba*.

came to [and entered] it and stayed therein for a short while. Khālid was a tall, handsome, fortitudinous and venerable man. Whoever looked at him had his breast filled [with awe of him] and came to realise that he was one of the [renowned] horsemen and one of their [=the Muslims'] bravest and toughest [people].

Bāhān, the [chief] commander of the Byzantines, sent [a messenger] to Khālid while he was inside his dome-like tent that was pitched for him[, saying]: "Come to meet me". He [=Bāhān] had lined up for him [=Khālid], along his way, ten lines [of soldiers] on his right and ten lines on his left,\\299 [equipped] with iron masks, helmets, coats of mail, arm and breast protectors and swords. Nothing of them [=the soldiers] was seen except the pupils [of their eyes]. Behind those lines he [=Bāhān] had lined up a huge cavalry whose two ends were invisible. By doing so, he wanted to show him [=Khālid] the Byzantines' equipment and their [high] number in order to terrify him with that and to rush him into [accepting] what he wanted to offer him. Khālid[, however,] was indifferent to what he saw in [regard to] their visage and multitude. To him they [=the Byzantines] were of less value than dogs. When he drew near to Bāhān, he [=Bāhān] welcomed him and said in his own tongue [to him]: "[Come] right here to me and sit with me, since it was mentioned to me that you are of noble descent among the Arabs and one of their bravest men. [For] we love brave men who have a noble descent. It was also mentioned to me that you have a [sound] mind and sincerity. The sound-minded man avails one with his [wise] words while the sincere man keeps his word and fulfils his promise". [Then] he [=Bāhān] seated his interpreter between him and Khālid. He [=the interpreter] was translating what he [=Bāhān] was saying to Khālid, who was sitting next to him.

Al-Ḥusayn b. Ziyād [al-Ramlī] reported to us on the authority of Abū Ismāʿīl Muḥammad b. ʿAbdallāh [al-Azdī], who said: Furthermore, Abū Jahḍam [al-Azdī] related to me on the authority of Sufyān b. Sulaym [al-Azdī] on the authority of al-Ḥārith b. ʿAbdallāh al-Azdī, who said: I was Khālid b. al-Walīd's friend and I hardly left his [side]. He [=the narrator, al-Ḥārith b. ʿAbdallāh al-Azdī] said: He [=Khālid] was one of those who used to consult me when\\300 something happened to him and I used to offer him my best advice. He [=the narrator, al-Ḥārith b. ʿAbdallāh al-Azdī] said: Thus, Khālid said to me: "I have ever known you to have an auspicious opinion. Whenever you gave me a piece of advice, I found it leading only to success in the end".

He [=the narrator, al-Ḥārith b. ʿAbdallāh al-Azdī] said: The day Khālid went to the Byzantines' encampment, he said to me: "Set out with me". So I set out with him. When we entered their encampment, where his dome-like tent had been pitched, and when Bāhān had sent for him to meet him, he [=Khālid] said to me: "Come with me". Thereupon, I said to him: "The people wanted you [only] and I do not think they will [also] invite me to go with you to them". [However,] he [=Khālid] said [again] to me: "Come [with me]", so I [finally] went with him. When we approached Bāhān, who was surrounded by thousands of men, one behind the other, nothing of whom was seen except their eyes and who were holding posts, the interpreter, accompanied by two men, came to us and said: "Which of you is Khālid?" Khālid said: "Me". Thereupon, he [=the interpreter] said: "You come [with us], but this [one] goes back". Then Khālid rose and said [to them]: "This man is one of my companions and I cannot do without his opinion". Thus, he [=the interpreter] returned to Bāhān and informed him [of this]. He [=Bāhān] said: "Let him [=the companion al-Ḥārith] come with him [=Khālid]". He [=the narrator, al-Ḥārith b. ʿAbdallāh al-Azdī] said: Then we walked towards him. Yet, hardly had we taken five or six steps when about ten [soldiers] came [to us] and said to al-Ḥārith b. ʿAbdallāh [al-Azdī]: "Lay down your sword". However, they said nothing to Khālid. He [=the narrator, al-Ḥārith b. ʿAbdallāh al-Azdī] said: I waited to see what Khālid would say to me, but Khālid said to them: "He will never lay his honour [=the sword] down from his neck.[431] You sent for us, so we came to you. If you let us both [come], we will sit with you and listen to you. But if you refuse [that], clear our way so that we [can] leave you". [Once again] the interpreter returned to Bāhān and informed him [of this]. Thereupon, he [=Bāhān] said: "Let them both [come with their swords]". He [=the narrator, al-Ḥārith b. ʿAbdallāh al-Azdī] said: We reached him [=Bāhān] and he welcomed Khālid [warmly] and seated him with him. He [=al-Ḥārith b. ʿAbdallāh al-Azdī] said: I proceeded and sat on cushions laid out for people [in a place] near both of them, where I could hear their negotiation[s]. When Bāhān said to Khālid: "It was mentioned to me that you are a man of noble descent among the Arabs and one of their bravest men; it was also mentioned to me that you have a [sound] mind and sincerity; the sound-minded man avails one with his [wise] words while the sincere man keeps\\301 his word and fulfils his promise" [and] when the interpreter rendered this to him, Khālid said [in reply]: "Our Prophet (ṣ.) said to us: 'Religion is one's nobility and whoever has no religion has no nobility'. He [=the Prophet] also said to us: 'The most favoured and best bravery in this life and in the afterlife is the bravery shown in obedience to God ('a.)'. As for your mentioning that I had been given a [sound] mind and sincerity, if I have been given these [two], it is God's blessing and grace upon us and it is He whom we always praise [in gratitude for it]. Our Prophet (ṣ.) also said to us: 'When God ('a.) created the mind (*ʿaql*), preordained [it], shaped [it] and finished creating it, He said to it: "Come", so it came. Then He said to it: "Go", so it went. Then He said to it: "By my Almightiness and Majesty, none of my creatures which I have created is dearer to me than you. Through you I am praised, through you I am worshipped, through you I am recognised, through you obedience to me is obtained and through you my Paradise is entered"'". Then he [=Khālid] [also] said: "Sincerity comes only from the

431 Khālid's statement reflects the high esteem for swords in pre-Islamic and early Islamic times as well as the fact that swords were usually carried and hung around the neck. On both points, see Schwarzlose, *Waffen*, 54–55.

mind. So whoever has no mind has no sincerity and whoever has no sincerity has no mind". Thereupon, Bāhān said to him: "You are the most sound-minded of the people of the earth. Only outstanding men say, grasp and discern that which you have just said". Then Bāhān said to Khālid: "If you are such [a wise person], tell me [more] about you. Would you [even] need advice from this man who came with you?" Khālid wondered about this [question] and said to him: "There are more than 2,000 [men] in our encampment.\\302 Neither the opinion nor the advice of any of them is dispensable". Thereafter, Bāhān said to him: "We have neither thought that [this is the case with] you nor considered you [to behave like] this". Then Khālid said to him: "Neither all that you think [of us] nor all that we think [of you] is right". Thereupon, Bāhān said to him: "You are correct". Then Bāhān said to Khālid: "The first thing I [want to] say to you is to call you to friendship and concord with me". Thereupon, Khālid said to him: "How would we achieve this between me and you while we share one land, which neither I nor you want to leave before it falls into the clutches of either of us?" Then Bāhān said to him: "Perhaps God will make peace between us and you without shedding blood or killing anyone". Khālid said: "If God (t.) wants [this], He does [so]". Then Bāhān said to him: "I do want to shorten the [personal] distance between me and you and talk to you like a brother speaking to his brother. Your red dome-like tent appeals to me and I would like you to give it to me, because I have never seen a prettier and better dome-like tent than it. Take whatever you want in return for it. Ask me for whatever you like and it will be yours. Just give me this dome-like tent, because it is nicer than [the tents] we have". Thereupon, Khālid said to him: "It is yours; take it and I want none of your belongings [in return]". Al-Ḥārith b. ʿAbdallāh [al-Azdī] said: "I swear by God that I thought he would [only] ask for it to have a [closer] look at it, but, lo and behold, he [really] took it".\\303 Then Bāhān said to him: "If you want, we will start to talk to you [about our offer]; but if you want [to start], talk [about yours first]". Thereupon, Khālid said to him: "Whatever [it is], I do not care. As for me, I am sure that you already know and have also been told what I am requesting, demanding and calling for. Your companions and those of you who faced us in Ajnādayn, in Marj al-Ṣuffar, in Fiḥl, in your cities and in your fortresses [surely] came to [inform you] about that. As for you, I do not know what you want to say. So if you want to speak [first], speak; but if you want me to start, I will speak [first]". Then Khālid [made up his mind and] said to him: "Speak then". Thereupon, Bāhān said to him: "Praise be to God who made our Prophet the best of [all] Prophets, our Emperor the best of [all] emperors and our community the best of [all] communities". When he came to this point, Khālid spoke to the interpreter and interrupted the speech of the Byzantines' [chief] commander, saying: "And praise be to God who made us believe in our Prophet, in your Prophet and in all the Prophets and made the commander, to whom we assigned our matters, a man like us. For if he [=the commander] claims to be given rule over us, we depose him from [ruling over] us. We also do not think that he has gained any superiority over any Muslim man except if he is more fearful [of God] and more righteous than he [=the Muslim man] in the eyes of God. And praise be to God who made our community the best of [all] communities [because] it commands right and forbids wrong, confesses sin[s], asks God to forgive it [=the sin], worships God alone and associates nothing else with Him. Now say whatever you want". After [hearing] that, Bāhān's face turned pale and he remained [silent] for a little while. Then Bāhān said: "Praise be to God who tested [our performance in war] and then made it a good performance for us, made us rich [when we were] poor, rendered us victorious over the [other] communities, strengthened us [in such a way] that we cannot be humiliated and protected us from\\304 [undergoing] injustice and thus our women's domicile[s] have become untouchable. We are neither happy nor discontented with what God strengthened us with and [what He] gave to us from our worldly life. Nor do we oppress people [in respect to it]. O Arabs, we had neighbours from among you, with whom we had good [relations of] neighbourhood, whom we held in the greatest esteem, whom we preferred to others, with whom we maintained the [mutual] pact and whom we gave a choice from [any of] our lands to settle wherever they wanted. They used to live [in them] safely and leave [them] safely. [Thus,] we were thinking that all the Arabs who were not our neighbours would thank us for what we had given to their brethren and what we had done for them. In contrast, we saw nothing from you except that you suddenly advanced on us with [your] cavalry and infantry, fighting us over our fortresses and desiring to triumph over us in our [own] lands. This had also been wanted from us before you [did it], by those whose number was [even] bigger than yours and who had a greater stratagem and stronger soldiers [than you]. [However,] we forced them out of them [=the lands], but they had not left us [until] they were killed or taken captive. [The people of] Persia wanted that [=the lands] from us, too, and you know what God (ʿa.) did to them. The Turks also wanted that from us, so we faced them more ferociously than we had faced [the people of] Persia [and finally defeated them]. Other people than you, from the east and the west, who had vigour, power and great soldiers, wanted [that from] us, too. [But] God [also] led us to triumph over all of them and arranged [victory] for us against them. None of the[se] communities was easier [to fight] or less dangerous to us than you. In contrast, all of you are [only] shepherds of sheep and camels, owners of rocks and stones and [endurers of] misery and suffering. Therefore, you greedily desire that we relinquish our lands to you. How awful your greed for us is! We also thought that nothing drove you to our lands, while all the prestigious and vast\\305 communities around us guard against our multitude and our vehement bravery, except for the infertility of [your] land and the lack of rain that have been inflicted upon you. You wreaked havoc in our lands and spread all [forms of] corruption. You rode our animals which are not like yours, wore our clothes which are not like yours—the Byzantines' white clothes look like silver plates—ate our food which is not like yours, gained [some spoils] from us and [finally] filled your hands with red gold, white silver and sumptuous goods. [Nevertheless,] we are meeting you now and all that [I have mentioned] belongs to us, although it fell in your hands. However, we give it to you, [if] you get out with it and depart from our lands. If your egos reject [everything] except to covet and to ravage and you want us to give you more from our treasuries by means of which the weak among you become strong and the absent one sees himself returning to his household with [something] good, we will do [that, too]. [Hence,] we will decree 10,000 dinars to the [chief] commander among you [personally], decree the same to you, decree 1,000 dinars, [again] 1,000 [dinars], to your chiefs and decree 100 dinars, [again] 100, to all your companions, provided that you swear solemnly binding oaths to us not to come back to our lands any more". Then he [=Bāhān] fell silent.\\306

Khālid b. al-Walīd's reply

Then Khālid b. al-Walīd (r.) said [to Bāhān]: "Praise be to God with whom no other deity is associated". When the interpreter rendered his statement "Praise be to God with whom no other deity is associated" to him [=Bāhān], he [=Bāhān] raised his hands to heaven and then said to Khālid: "How excellent is what you said!" Then Khālid [continued and] said: "I testify that Muḥammad (ṣ.) is the Messenger of God". When the interpreter rendered [this] to him [=Bāhān], he [=Bāhān] said: "[Only] God knows [whether this is correct], I do not know; perhaps he [=Muḥammad] is as you say". The interpreter told Khālid [of this comment]. Then Khālid, may God have mercy upon him, said: "Regarding the matter at hand: As for all that you have mentioned about your people, including wealth and might, protection of [your] women's domicile[s], triumph over [former] enemies and dominion over the lands, we already know [all of this]. We also know all that you mentioned about your [former] kindness towards your [Arab] neighbours from among us. [You did] that [only] for a cause with which you were nourishing your worldly life. Your nourishment was [also] in their favour and your benevolence to them was [just] for the aggrandisement of your rule and your might. Do you not see that two thirds or half of them [=the Arab neighbours] embraced your religion, thus fighting with you against us [only for that reason]? As for reminding us of shepherding camels and sheep, you can hardly see any of us hating it. And whoever hates it [=shepherding] is not superior to whoever does it. As for your statement 'We are the owners of rocks and stones and [endurers of] misery and suffering', our situation, I swear by God, is just as you have described [it] and we neither deny nor disown it. We were in an [even] worse and more distressful [condition] than what you have mentioned.

[Now,] I am going to tell you our story, present our cause to you and call you to your [good] fortune if you would accept [it].\\307 Verily, we, the Arabs, were one of these communities whom God—praise be to Him—caused to reside in a place on earth where there are no running rivers and where there exists only meagre vegetation. Most of our lands are wastelands and deserts. Therefore, we were the owners of stone- and loam-made [houses] and ewes and camels, [and the endurers of] straitened livelihood and persistently unceasing distress. [Thus,] we were severing the ties of our kinship and killing our children for fear of destitution. The strong among us were devouring the weak and so were our majority [devouring] our minorit[ies]. No tribe of ours could feel safe from [being attacked by] another except for four months per year. [In addition,] we were worshipping, other than God, deities (*arbāb*) and idols (*aṣnām*), which we sculpted with our own hands from stones, which we selected with our own eyes, which neither harmed [us] nor benefited [us] and before which we were prostrating [ourselves]. While we were in this situation, on the brink of a fire pit [=hell], those of us who died, died as Polytheists and fell into the Fire whereas those of us who survived, survived as Unbelievers, [because they had] associated partners with their Lord and had severed the ties of their kinship. Then God sent us a Messenger from our own core, our nobility, our elite, our high-ranking people and from the best of us, who called us to [believe in] God alone, to worship [only] Him, not to associate anything else with Him and to uproot the [deified] rivals whom the Polytheists were worshipping rather than Him. [Thus,] he [=the Messenger] said to us: 'Do not take a deity, a close associate or a supporter other than God as your Lord. Do not assign to Him either a female partner or a child. Do not worship, other than Him, a fire, a stone, the sun or the moon. Be satisfied with Him as [your] Lord and as God rather than [looking for] something else [to worship]. Be His close friends, call [other people] to [worship] Him and to seek Him'. He [=the Messenger] also said: 'Fight those who took other deities besides God; and [fight] all those who claimed that God has a child or that He is one of two [=binitarianism] or one of three [=trinitarianism] until they say: "There is no [other] deity but God alone who has no partner" and until they embrace\\308 Islam. If they do so, you will be forbidden to shed their blood [anymore and violate] their possessions and their honour, except on the basis of a law. [For] they would [have become] your brethren in [terms of] religion, meriting the same rights you merit and having the same obligations you have. However, if they refuse to embrace your [former] religion and adhere to their religion, offer them [to pay] tribute which they should bring by hand and with humility. If they do so, accept [it] from them and turn away from them. However, if they [also] refuse [that], fight them. Whichever of you is killed will be a living, provided-for martyr in God's place and God would let him enter Paradise. [In contrast,] whichever of your enemies is killed will be killed as an Unbeliever and will go into Fire, remaining therein forever'". Then Khālid said: "This is, I swear by God with whom no other deity is associated, the religion of God with whom no other deity is associated. God had ordained it [=the religion] to His Prophet (ṣ.), whereupon he had taught [it] to us and had ordered us to call [other] people to [embrace] it. Thus, we are calling you [now] to what our Prophet (ṣ.) had called [us] to and to what he had ordered us to call [other] people to. Hence, we are calling you to [embrace] Islam. Furthermore, [we are calling you] to testify that there is no [other] deity but God and that Muḥammad is His servant and His Messenger, to perform the ritual prayer[s], to give the prescribed tax and [finally] to acknowledge [the words] that had come [down] from God (ʿa.). If you do [all of this], you will be our brethren in Islam, meriting the same rights we merit and having the same obligations we have. However, if you refuse [to convert], we offer you to bring [us] tribute by hand and with humility. If you do [so], we will accept it from you and turn away from you. However, if you [also] refuse to do [that], I swear by God that people who are keener on death than you are on life will come to [fight] you. [In this case] march out [to fight] us in the name of God so that we put you to trial before God. For the earth belongs to God who bequeaths it to whichever servant [of His] He wants whereas the [happy] ending is only for those who fear God". Then Khālid fell silent.

Then Bāhān said: "As for [the first option, i.e.] our conversion to your religion, you would hardly find any of these people abandoning his religion to embrace yours. As for [the second option, i.e.] bringing tribute [to you]"—after he breathed a deep sigh which was heavy\\309 and hard for him [to let out]—he [went on] saying: "All those whom you see [here] will [rather] die before they bring tribute to any of the [other] people. [For] they [=the Byzantines] are [used to] collecting tribute, not to giving it. As for your [third] statement: 'March out [to fight] until God judges between us', I swear upon my life that these people and these groups came out to you only to put you to trial before God. And as for your statement: 'For the earth belongs to God who bequeaths it to whichever servant [of His] He wants', you are right. I swear by God that this land over which we fight each other had belonged to one of the communities that existed before we [did]. [Then] we fought them over it and expelled them from it. Beforehand it had also belonged to other people who had been expelled from it by those whom we had fought over it. Therefore, come out to [fight] us in the name of God, for we are marching out to [fight] you [as well]".

Al-Ḥārith b. ʿAbdallāh al-Azdī [=the narrator] said: When Bāhān finished his speech, Khālid leapt and stood up, as did I simultaneously. He [=Khālid] passed by his dome-like tent and left it to him [=Bāhān]. We moved until we departed from their encampment. He [=the narrator, al-Ḥārith b. ʿAbdallāh al-Azdī] said: The Byzantines' commander [again] sent [some] men with us until they led us out of their encampment and protected us. He [=the narrator, al-Ḥārith b. ʿAbdallāh al-Azdī] said: We returned to Abū ʿUbayda and Khālid told him the news and reported to them [=Abū ʿUbayda and the Muslims] that fighting\\310 would break out between [the Byzantines and] them. He [=Khālid] said to the people: "O people, be ready [to fight] like people who believe they are going to fight in a short while and then they fight".

Bāhān's consultation with his companions about how to fight the Muslims, about what they [=the Muslims] have chosen for themselves and about Bāhān's letter to Caesar in that regard

Al-Ḥusayn b. Ziyād [al-Ramlī] reported to us on the authority of Abū Ismāʿīl Muḥammad b. ʿAbdallāh [al-Azdī], who said: Furthermore, Abū Jahḍam al-Azdī related to me on the authority of a Byzantine man, who said: I was with Bāhān in their [=the Byzantines'] encampment. He [=the narrator, Abū Jahḍam al-Azdī] said: He [=the Byzantine man] [later] converted to Islam and excelled at it. He [=the Byzantine man] said: [After his negotiations with Khālid] Bāhān wrote a letter to Caesar in which he informed him of his situation, his companions' situation and the Muslims' [new] situation. The day Khālid left them, he [=Bāhān] gathered his companions and said: "Tell me your opinion on the cause of these people. I [tried] to frighten them off but I do not think that they are frightened. I also tried to arouse their greed but they are not greedy. [Then] I wanted them to turn back and depart from our land in all direction[s], but they are not turning back. [Thus, I think that] the people [=the Muslims] only want to destroy you, exterminate you, usurp your reign, devour your lands, capture your children and women and take your possessions. Hence, if you are free [men], fight for your reign (*sulṭān*) and protect your women's domicile[s], your women, your children, your lands and your possessions".\\311 Thereupon, the patrician men rose, one after the other, informing him [=Bāhān] that each of them was eager to die for his land and for his reign. They said to him: "If you want, rise with us [to fight the Muslims]". Thereupon, Bāhān said to them: "How would we, in your opinion, fight them? For we are more than ten times larger in number than they are. We are about 400,000 [in number] while they are, give or take, about 30,000". Some of them [=the patricians] said: "Send to them 100,000 [soldiers] every day in order to fight them while the remainder stay at rest. [In the meantime,] we march our children and chattels to the sea so that we will no longer have anything that concerns or distracts us. One hundred thousand of us will fight them every day. While they [=the Muslims] are subject to death, injuries, suffering, hardship and distress on a single day, we will be fighting only once every four days. If they defeat 100,000 of us on one day, more than 200,000 will remain undefeated [to continue fighting them]". Some others said: "No, rather we are of the opinion that if they march out to [fight] us, you dispatch ten of your companions to each one of them. We swear by God that if you send ten against one [man], they will certainly defeat him". Bāhān then said to them [=the patricians]: "This cannot happen. How would I manage to confront each one of them with ten of my companions? And how would I be able to separate each of them from his companion so that I [can] send [against] him ten from my side? This cannot happen". He [=the narrator, the Byzantine man] said: Finally, their unanimous decision was that\\312 they all march out to fight them [in one stroke]. They would not turn away from them until God judges between them [and the Muslims]. He [=the narrator, the Byzantine man] said: All the Byzantines agreed on this [plan].

He [=the narrator, the Byzantine man] said: [Then] Bāhān wrote [the following letter] to Caesar:

Regarding the matter at hand: O Emperor, we ask God for [bestowing] victory upon you, upon your soldiers and upon the inhabitants of your empire as well as for [bestowing] glory upon your religion and upon the people under your reign. You dispatched me [in command] of [such] a [large] number [of soldiers] that only God could count. I came to the people [=the Muslims], sent [a messenger] to them and frightened them off but they do not frighten; I aroused their greed, but they are not greedy; [then] I scared them but they are not scared; [after that,] I asked them [to make] peace [with me on certain conditions], but they did not accept [them]; and [finally,] I offered them a reward in return for their departure, but they did not [agree to] do it[, either]. Your soldiers are extremely scared of them and I fear that frustration will have overwhelmingly befallen all of them and terror will have entered into their hearts. However, I know some of them [=the Emperor's soldiers] who are not escaping from their enemy, who are not doubtful about their religion and who will never flee [from a fight] until they become either triumphant or killed when they face them [=the Muslims]. [Thus,] I gathered the decision makers (*ahl al-raʾy*) from among my companions and the advisors for our reign and for our religion. They are unanimous that they should all rush to [fight] them [=the Muslims] on one single day and should not quit [fighting] them until God judges between us and them.\\313

The story of Bāhān's vision

He [=the narrator] said: Bāhān had a vision and he wrote about it in the [following] letter to the Emperor of the Byzantines, saying:

Someone came to me in my sleep and said to me: "Do not fight these people, because they will destroy and defeat you". When I awakened from my sleep, I thought he [=the unnamed figure] was [sent] by Satan who wanted to sadden me, so I chased him away. If he were Satan [himself], I chased him away. However, if he were not Satan, the case [of the Muslims] became clear to me. Therefore, Emperor, dispatch your chattels, your servants and your possessions [immediately] and march them to the farthest part of your lands and wait [there] for [the outcome of] our battle [against the Muslims]. If God makes us triumphant over them, you should thank God who has strengthened your religion and defended your reign. However, if they triumph over us, accept God's decree (*qaḍāʾ*) and know that this worldly life is [as] transient for you as it had been for those who had existed before we [did]. [In this case] do not be sorry for what you have lost and do not be happy about [all those] thing[s] which are [still] in your hands. Hurry to your strongholds and [rush to defend] your empire (*dār al-mamlaka*); do what is good for your subjects and for [your] people so that God will do what is good for you [in return]; show mercy to the weak and the poor so that you will be shown mercy [in return]; and behave humbly towards God so that He will elevate you [in return], for God does not love the haughty. Peace [be upon you].

He [=the narrator] said: After [the consultation with his peers] Bāhān marched out to [fight] the Muslims on a foggy and drizzling day and formed against them [=the Muslims] twenty lines whose two ends were invisible. Then he positioned [commanders] over his right and left flanks. Thus, he positioned Ibn Qanāṭir[432] over his right flank together with Jirjīs [who was] in [command of] the people of Armenia and he positioned al-Durunjār,\\314 who was one of their [=the Byzantines'] elites and their pious men, over his left flank. Then they [all] moved towards the Muslims. When the Muslims saw them swarming like locusts and filling the earth like the widths of the mountains, they rushed to their flags. Khālid b. al-Walīd, Yazīd b. Abī Sufyān, ʿAmr b. al-ʿĀṣ and Shuraḥbīl b. Ḥasana [immediately] went to Abū ʿUbayda. They were the commanders to whom Abū Bakr al-Ṣiddīq (r.) had given command and whom he had dispatched to Syria. Thus, they came to Abū ʿUbayda, who was accompanied by Muʿādh [b. Jabal] and with whom he never parted. Then they said to him: "Those [=the Byzantines] marched [out] to [fight] us on such a rainy day. We are of the opinion that we should not march out to [fight] them on it [=the rainy day] except when they come [very close] to us and break into (*laṭṭa*) our encampment or force us [to do] that [by other means]". [Thereupon,] he [=Abū ʿUbayda] said: "You are absolutely right". He [=the narrator] said: [Then] Abū ʿUbayda moved out [of his tent] with Muʿādh b. Jabal and they lined up the people [=the Muslims], mobilised them and put them in their positions. The Byzantines proceeded in the rain but [soon] stopped for a short while to wait for it [to stop]. When they realised that it would neither cease nor stop [raining], they returned to their encampment.

He [=the narrator] said: [Then] al-Durunjār, who was a pious man among them [=the Byzantines], called one of the Arab men who embraced Christianity and said to him: "Enter the encampment of those people [=the Muslims] and check how their conduct is, how their state is, what their activities are, what they are doing and how they are behaving [towards others]. Then report [all of] it to me". That man moved out [of the Byzantines' encampment] until he entered the encampment of the Muslims who did not reject him because he was one of the Arabs [in terms of] his tongue and his face. He stayed overnight in their encampment until the morning [came] and found the Muslims praying the whole night\\315 as if they were [doing so] at day. Then he rose in the morning and [also] spent most of his day [there]. Then he moved out [of the encampment, went back] to him [=al-Durunjār] and said to him: "I have come to you from [the encampment of] the people who stand the whole night praying, who fast during the day, who command what is right and forbid what is wrong and [who are] monks by night but lions by day. [For example,] if their sovereign steals [something] in their presence, they cut off [his hand]. If he fornicates, they stone him

432 Ibn Qanāṭir could not be identified because his full name is not mentioned by al-Azdī. In al-Azdī's narrative, he is depicted as a commander in the Byzantine army during the Battle of al-Yarmūk and as being blamed by Jirjīs, the ruler of Armenia, for giving him orders to attack the Muslims. De Goeje regards Ibn Qanāṭir as a misreading of Būqināṭir, an Arabicised version of the Greek *Buccinator* (see de Goeje, *Mémoire sur la conquête* (2nd ed.), 106, n. 4).

because of their love for truth and because of their choice of it [=truth] over a passing fancy". Thereupon, he [=al-Durunjār] said: "If those people are as you have claimed [them to be] and as you have described them, the earth's interior would be [a] better [place] for whoever wants to fight and face them than its surface [is]".

On the next day, [which was] also a foggy day, they [=the Byzantines] marched out [of their encampment again]. [Previously,] some Arab men who were Christians had gone to the Muslims and had embraced Islam. Thereafter, Abū ʿUbayda and Khālid b. al-Walīd had said to them: "[Go back and] enter the Byzantines' encampment, [but] conceal your Islam from them and report their news [back] to us. If [you do so,] you will get a reward for this and [also] God will reckon it on your behalf as fighting for His cause. By doing so, you further defend the sanctity of Islam and uncover the fallacy of the Polytheists". Then they had departed and entered the Byzantines' encampment and after half of the night had passed by, they returned to Abū ʿUbayda b. al-Jarrāḥ and said to him: "The people [=the Byzantines] have already lit fires and are mobilising [fighters] against you, in preparation to fight and approach you in the early morning. If you are [going] to do [something], do it now". Thus, Abū ʿUbayda, Muʿādh b. Jabal, Khālid b. al-Walīd, Yazīd b. Abī Sufyān\\316 and ʿAmr b. al-ʿĀṣ moved out [of their tents], mobilised the people and lined them up [for fighting]. They continued doing so until the morning.

Abū ʿUbayda b. al-Jarrāḥ's (r.) vision

Al-Ḥusayn b. Ziyād [al-Ramlī] reported to us on the authority of Abū Ismāʿīl [Muḥammad b. ʿAbdallāh al-Azdī], who said: Furthermore, al-Ṣaqʿab b. Zuhayr related to me on the authority of al-Muhājir b. Ṣayfī al-ʿUdhrī[433] on the authority of Rāshid b. ʿAbd al-Raḥmān al-Azdī[434], who said: On that day, Abū ʿUbayda b. al-Jarrāḥ led us in the early morning prayer in his encampment. [It was] the early morning in which we met the Byzantines [for a fight] at al-Yarmūk. During the first act of prayer (*rakʿa*)[435], he recited [the

433 Al-Muhājir b. Ṣayfī al-ʿUdhrī is mentioned only in Ibn ʿAsākir's *TMD* as a transmitter from Rāshid b. ʿAbd al-Raḥmān al-Azdī. In al-Azdī's narrative, he is mentioned as a transmitter of several traditions. On al-Muhājir, see Ibn ʿAsākir, *TMD*, XVII, 460 (where his name is spelled as al-Muhāṣir b. Ṣayfī al-ʿUdhrī).

434 Rāshid b. ʿAbd al-Raḥmān al-Azdī is an early Islamic figure. In al-Azdī's narrative, he is mentioned as a Muslim fighter against the Byzantines in the Battle of al-Yarmūk and as a transmitter of two traditions. On Rāshid, see Ibn ʿAsākir, *TMD*, XVII, 460–461 (no. 2119).

435 A "*rakʿa*" (lit. "a bending of the body") is a sequence of actions during the Muslim ritual prayers that involves standing, bending and prostrating while uttering some religious formulas. Here it is approximately translated as "an act of prayer". On *rakʿa*, see *EI*², s.v. Rakʿa (Ed.).

following verses of the Qur'ān]: "By the day break, by the ten nights [...]".[436] When he came to God's ('a.) words: "Have you[437] considered how your Lord dealt with [the people of] 'Ād, of Iram, [the city] of lofty pillars[438], whose like has never been made in any land" [and] to His words: "Your Lord is always watchful",[439] I [=Rāshid b. 'Abd al-Raḥmān al-Azdī] thought to myself: "I swear by God that we are going to triumph over the people [=the Byzantines] because of what God has put into his [=Abū 'Ubayda's] mouth"; and I profusely rejoiced over that [prospective triumph]. [Then] I said [aloud]: "I swear by God that our enemy equals this [annihilated] community [='Ād] in [terms of] unbelief, multitude and sinning".\\317

He [=the narrator, Rāshid b. 'Abd al-Raḥmān al-Azdī] said: Then during the second act of prayer, he [=Abū 'Ubayda] recited [the following verses:] "By the sun and by its brightness [at forenoon] [...]". When he came to God's (a.) words: "In their arrogant cruelty, the people of Thamūd called [the messenger sent to them] a liar, when the most wicked man among them rose [against him]"[440] [and recited them] to the end of the chapter—he [=the narrator, Rāshid b. 'Abd al-Raḥmān al-Azdī] said:—I thought to myself: "I swear by God that this is [yet] another one [=community that was annihilated]. If this omen is true, God will certainly pour a scourge of torture on them [=the Byzantines] and will certainly cast destruction upon them as He had inflicted destruction on the people of those [bygone] centuries". He [=the narrator, Rāshid b. 'Abd al-Raḥmān al-Azdī] said: When Abū 'Ubayda finished his prayer[s], he turned with his face to the people [=the Muslims] and said: "O people, rejoice over the good news, for during my [last] night I saw what the sleeper sees: Some men came to me and welcomed me warmly while I was wearing a white garment. They summoned to me some of you whom I know and then said to us: 'Advance on your enemy and do not fear them, for you are superior [to them]'. [I also saw] that we marched to the encampment of our enemy. When they saw us approaching them, they split [in half] towards us like the splitting of a head. We proceeded until we entered their encampment and they turned away in flight". Thereupon, the people [=the Muslims] said to him [=Abū 'Ubayda]: "May God increase your righteousness. May your eyes beam [with delight]. This is a herald of good news from God. May God herald to you the best news".\\318

Then Abū Marthad al-Khawlānī[441] said [to the Muslims]: "I also, may God increase your righteousness, had a vision which is surely [a herald of]

436 Q. 89:1–2 (*The Qur'ān. Tr. Abdel Haleem*, 420).

437 The 2nd-person pronoun "you" refers here most likely to the Prophet Muḥammad.

438 On the translation of "*Iram dhāt al-'imād*" (lit. "Iram with the pillars") and on its identification as a city (in contrast to the designation of a tribe), see *EI*², s.v. Iram (W. Watt).

439 Q. 89:6–14 (*The Qur'ān. Tr. Abdel Haleem*, 420).

440 Q. 91:11–12 (*The Qur'ān. Tr. Abdel Haleem*, 423).

441 Abū Marthad al-Khawlānī (n.d.) is an early Islamic figure. In al-Azdī's narrative, he is portrayed as informing the Muslims of a vision he had, in which God supported the

good news from God. [Last] night I saw what the sleeper sees: We marched out towards our enemy and when we faced each other in battle, God poured huge white birds from heaven on them—[birds] that had talons like lions' claws and that were pouncing from heaven as eagles [do]. When they [=the birds] approached one of the Polytheists, they struck him a blow that caused him to fall dead. [It looked] as if the people [=the Muslims] were saying: 'O Muslims, rejoice over the good news, because God has supported you with angels'". He [=the narrator, Rāshid b. 'Abd al-Raḥmān al-Azdī] said: The Muslims then rejoiced over this [auspicious] vision and were pleased with it. Then Abū 'Ubayda said [to them]: "I swear by God that this is [another herald of] good news from Him. Tell [all] the people about this vision, because the likes of such visions encourage the Muslim, enhance his belief [in God] and embolden him to face his enemy". He [=the narrator, Rāshid b. 'Abd al-Raḥmān al-Azdī] said: This vision and Abū 'Ubayda's vision spread among the Muslims who rejoiced over them [both] and considered them [to be heralds of] good news.

A Byzantine [grand] man's vision

Al-Ḥusayn b. Ziyād [al-Ramlī] reported to us on the authority of Abū Ismā'īl [Muḥammad b. 'Abdallāh al-Azdī], who said: Furthermore, Abū Jahḍam al-Azdī related to me on the authority of a Byzantine man who related to me [the following] during the caliphate of 'Abd al-Malik b. Marwān[442]: One of the Byzantine grand men went to Bāhān in the morning of the day on which he [=Bāhān] marched out to [fight] the Muslims at al-Yarmūk. Then he [=the Byzantine grand man] said [to him]:\\319 "I had a vision and I want to tell you about it". He [=Bāhān] said: "Proceed". [Thereupon,] he [=the Byzantine grand man] said: "I saw that tall men came from heaven down to us. The height of each of them was greater than the range of his eyesight. They pulled our swords out of their scabbards and [pulled away] the tips of our spears from their [two] ends.[443] Then they tied us all up and thereafter said to us: 'Escape [from here] because most of you will perish'. We promptly started escaping [from the place], with some of us falling on their faces, some becoming petrified, unable to leave their places, and some untying their manacles and running so hastily that we would not see them [anymore]". Thereupon, Bāhān said to him [=the Byzantine grand man]: "As for those [of

Muslims with angels in their fight against the Polytheists. On Abū Marthad, see Ibn Ḥajar, *Al-iṣāba. Ed. al-Baghawī*, VI, 284 (no. 8393).

442 'Abd al-Malik's full name is Abū al-Walīd 'Abd al-Malik b. Marwān al-Umawī al-Qurashī (d. 86/705). He is the famous Umayyad ruler. In al-Azdī's narrative, he is introduced as a "caliph" and his "caliphate" is used as a means of historical dating. On 'Abd al-Malik, see *EI*², s.v. 'Abd al-Malik b. Marwān (H. Gibb); Robinson, *'Abd al-Malik*.

443 Spears (sg. *rumḥ*) in pre-Islamic and early Islamic times used to have two iron tips, "*asinna*" (sg. *sinān*, lit. "spearhead"), denoting the two ends (see Schwarzlose, *Waffen*, 229).

us] whom you saw falling on their faces and those whom you saw becoming petrified and unable to move or leave their places, they are those who will perish. As for those [of us] whom you saw untying their manacles and running so hastily that you would not see them [anymore], they are those who will survive". Then Bāhān said to him: "As for you, I swear by God that you will never get away safe from me [again], because your face is the face that portended evil [news] and caused despair of [all that is] good. Are you not the one who was the toughest of the people on me concerning the cause of the [grand] man who killed one of the protected people [and had raped his wife]? I wanted to execute him [=this grand man] in retribution for him [=the protected man], but you were one of the toughest on me with respect to his cause until I adjourned one of God's prescribed punishments (*ḥadd*) and abandoned it. I had the right to carry it out, but you, with a group of fools, interfered [when I wanted to solve the issue] between me and him [=the grand man]. So I grudgingly left him [untouched] lest I cause a rift\\320 in your group, that I divide you or that you beat one another [because of this]. As for [what I can do] now, I thought to myself: '[Why not] to die?', but I [want to] face the people [=the Muslims] in a short while [instead]. Disperse now if you want to or assemble [to fight them] if you want to. However, I will turn to God (t.) in repentance of having abandoned the prescribed punishment on that [very] day. I could and should have executed him [=the grand man] even if you would have killed me [together] with him". Then he [=Bāhān] gave the order to behead him [=the Byzantine grand man who had the vision] [and he was beheaded]. Then he sent for the Byzantine [grand man] who had killed the protected man (*dhimmī*), but he [=the Byzantine grand man] escaped from him. Thus, he [=Bāhān] could not apprehend him.

The story of the Byzantine [man] who committed what he committed and of restraining Bāhān from [punishing] him

Al-Ḥusayn b. Ziyād [al-Ramlī] reported to us on the authority of Abū Ismāʿīl [Muḥammad b. ʿAbdallāh al-Azdī], who said: Furthermore, Abū Jahḍam [al-Azdī] related to me, saying: [At one point] I asked the Byzantine [man]: "What was the story of that Byzantine [murderer]?" He [=the Byzantine man] said: "[Once] one of the Byzantine patricians, who was one of their grand and tough men, stayed in the house of one of the protected people, fell upon the protected man's wife and had sexual intercourse with her. Her husband came [forward] to stop him, but he [=the Byzantine patrician] killed him. Therefore, his [=the husband's] brother rushed out and appealed to their chief commander Bāhān for help against him [=the Byzantine patrician] [after] he had told him [=Bāhān] about his news. Thereafter, Bāhān summoned him [=the Byzantine patrician] and said: 'Is what that [man] claims true?' He [=the Byzantine patrician] said: 'Yes'. Thereupon, he [=Bāhān] said: 'What forced you to do what you have done?' He [=the Byzantine patrician] said: 'Verily, she was my slave girl and her husband is my slave. Do you want to stop me from having [sexual] pleasure with my [own] slave girl? Or would you rather execute me in retribution for my slave?' [Thereupon,] Bāhān said to him: 'In meting out justice I should execute you in retribution for him [=the slave] and I should protect their [=the slaves'] women\\321 from the likes of you'. [Immediately] many of the foolish and evil Byzantine men rose and said: 'Will you execute one of our grand men and noblemen in retribution for one of our slaves?' So they prevented him [=Bāhān] from [doing] that. That man whom Bāhān [finally] killed was one of the toughest among them on Bāhān on that day. Then Bāhān said to them [=the Byzantine men]: 'As for you, you [all] did a heinous thing, disobeyed your Lord and made Him angry with you. If He gets angry with people, He will take revenge on them'. Then he turned away from them. The brother of the killed [man], however, said to Bāhān: 'Since you did not help me [to take] revenge on them, I will seek revenge against them from the King of Heaven'".

The battle of al-Yarmūk

This is the battle in which God destroyed the Polytheists, chased them away, led the Muslims to conquest, strengthened them and humiliated their enemy.

Al-Ḥusayn b. Ziyād [al-Ramlī] reported to us on the authority of Abū Ismā'īl Muḥammad b. 'Abdallāh [al-Azdī], who said: Furthermore, al-Ṣaq'ab b. Zuhayr related to me on the authority of al-Muhājir b. Ṣayfī [al-'Udhrī] on the authority of Rāshid b. 'Abd al-Raḥmān al-Azdī, who said: Bāhān came out to us [=the Muslims] on the battle-day of al-Yarmūk, [which was] a foggy day. He marched out to us in command of twenty lines numbering about 400,000 fighters. He positioned Ibn Qanāṭir in command of his right flank and positioned\\322 Jirjīs, the ruler of Armenia, with him. He [also] positioned al-Durunjār, who was one of their [=the Byzantines'] pious men, in command of his left flank. Then he [=Bāhān] advanced on the Muslims like the night and the flood (*al-layl wa-al-sayl*). The Muslims had become self-assured to fight the Polytheists and God had relieved (*sharaḥa*) their breasts and encouraged their hearts to face their enemy. Thus, they had the strongest insight, the best intention, the greatest reckoning and the staunchest keenness on confronting them [=the Byzantines]. Then Abū 'Ubayda led them out, positioned Mu'ādh b. Jabal in command of his right flank and Qubāth b. Ashyam in command of his left flank. He also positioned Hāshim b. 'Utba b. Abī Waqqāṣ in command of the infantry and Khālid b. al-Walīd in command of the cavalry. The [other] commanders were Yazīd b. Abī Sufyān commanding one quarter [of the army], Shuraḥbīl b. Ḥasana commanding the [second] quarter, 'Amr b. al-'Āṣ commanding the [third] quarter and Abū 'Ubayda commanding the [fourth] quarter.

The people [=the Muslims] marched out [of their encampment] according to their flags. Among them were the Arabs' noblemen and their [renowned] horsemen from among their [male] people and their tribes. Among the [latter] were al-Azd numbering one third of the people, Ḥimyar forming the majority of the people, as well as Hamdān, Khawlān[444], Madhḥij, Khath'am, Quḍā'a, Lakhm, Judhām, 'Āmila, Ghassān, Kinda[445] and Ḥaḍramawt[446] together with a group from Kināna. However, the great majority of the people were from Yemen. Neither Asad, Tamīm nor Rabī'a attended it [=the battle] on that day, [for] their dwellings were not there [in Syria], but in Iraq. Therefore, they fought the Persians in Iraq.\\323 When the Muslims came into their [=the Byzantines'] view, Abū 'Ubayda walked through [the lines of] the Muslims and then said [to each of them]: "O servants of God, support God so that He supports you and makes your feet stand firm [in return], for God's promise [of support] is the truth. O Muslims, be patient, for patience is salvation from unbelief, satisfaction to the Lord and refutation of shame—i.e. an abolition [of shame]. Thus, do not leave your lines, do not take one step towards them and do not start fighting them; [rather,] point your spears [against them], protect yourselves with the leather shields and keep silent and still, except for invoking (*dhikr*)[447] God, until I give you the order [to attack], God willing".

He [=the narrator] said: Mu'ādh b. Jabal [also] went out to motivate the people, saying: "O reciters of the Qur'ān, memorisers of the scripture, supporters of [God's] guidance and proponents of the truth, I swear by God that wishes [alone] do not guarantee the obtainment of God's mercy or entry to His Paradise. In addition, God gives forgiveness and ample mercy only to the truthful who trust in what God ('a.) has promised them. Have you not listened to God's ('a.) statement [in which this is mentioned]: 'God has made a promise to those among you who believe and do good deeds: He will make them successors to the land, as He did with those who came before them'[448]

444 Khawlān is a Southern Arabian tribe that was, according to some genealogists, a subtribe of Quḍā'a. In al-Azdī's narrative, Khawlān is said to have fought in the Battle of al-Yarmūk, in which it was attacked on the right flank. In addition, one individual figure belonged to Khawlān: Abū Marthad al-Khawlānī, who had a vision in which God supported the Muslims with strong birds against the Polytheists. On Khawlān, see *EI*², s.v. Khawlān (A. Grohmann/A. Irvine).

445 Kinda is a Southern Arabian tribe. In al-Azdī's narrative, Kinda is said to have participated in the Battle of al-Yarmūk. Although he is not explicitly called al-Kindī, one individual figure belonged to Kinda: Shuraḥbīl b. Ḥasana who left Medina three days after the departure of Yazīd b. Abī Sufyān to Syria. Then he appeared in the vicinity of Bosra and fought in the Battle of Ajnādayn and is mentioned as a commander of one quarter of the Muslim army during the Battle of al-Yarmūk. On Kinda, see *EI*², s.v. Kinda (I. Shahīd/F. Beeston); Leube, *Kinda*.

446 Ḥaḍramawt is a Southern Arabian tribe. In al-Azdī's narrative, Ḥaḍramawt is always mentioned together with Kinda and/or Ḥimyar and is said to have fought in the Battle of al-Yarmūk. Its members were attacked on the right flank, but they stood firm. On Ḥaḍramawt, see *EI*², s.v. Ḥaḍramawt (F. Beeston/G. Smith/et al.).

447 The Arabic term "*dhikr*" (lit. "mentioning, remembrance") involves a unweary oral repetition of a litany of commendatory phrases in remembrance of God. On *dhikr*, see *EI*², s.v. Dhikr (L. Gardet).

448 Q. 24:55 (*The Qur'ān. Tr. Abdel Haleem*, 224).

up to the head of the [next] verse? You will be victorious, God willing[, if you adhere to the following verse:] 'Obey God and His Messenger, and do not quarrel with one another, or you may lose heart and your spirit may desert you. Be steadfast: God is with the steadfast'.[449] Also, be ashamed if your Lord should see you fleeing from your enemy while you are in His grasp and under His mercy. Moreover, none of you has a shelter or refuge other than His.\\324 Nor does any of you gain reinforcement from anyone other than God". Thereafter, he [=Muʿādh b. Jabal] started walking through the [other] lines, inciting and exhorting them [=the Muslims] [, too]. Then he left for his position.

Al-Ḥusayn b. Ziyād [al-Ramlī] reported to us on the authority of Abū Ismāʿīl [Muḥammad b. ʿAbdallāh al-Azdī], who said: Furthermore, Muḥammad b. Yūsuf related to me on the authority of Thābit [al-Bunānī] on the authority of Sahl b. Saʿd al-Anṣārī, who said: ʿAmr b. al-ʿĀṣ also passed by the people [=the Muslims] on that day and started exhorting, inciting and rousing them, saying: "O people, lower your gaze, get on your knees, point your spears [against your enemy] and stick to your positions and lines. If your enemy attacks you, allow them a period of respite and when they approach the [spear] tips[450], leap on their faces as the lion does. By the One who loves truth and rewards for it, abhors falsehood and punishes for it and rewards with benevolence, I learned that the Muslims would conquer it [=Syria], one hamlet after another and one castle after the other. Do not be terrified of their [huge] groups or numbers, because if you are resolutely tough on them, they will certainly panic as little partridges (*ḥajal*)[451] do".

Al-Ḥusayn b. Ziyād [al-Ramlī] reported to us on the authority of Abū Ismāʿīl [Muḥammad b. ʿAbdallāh al-Azdī], who said: Furthermore, Muḥammad b. Yūsuf related to me on the authority of Thābit [al-Bunānī] on the authority of Sahl b. Saʿd al-Anṣārī: [One day,] Abū Sufyān b. Ḥarb had asked ʿUmar b. al-Khaṭṭāb (r.) for permission to fight against the Byzantines in Syria. Thus, he had said to him [=ʿUmar]: "I would like you to allow me to march out to\\325 Syria to volunteer my possessions, to support the Muslims [there], to fight the Polytheists and to be there with a group of the Muslims whom I will spare neither [my] advice nor [anything] good". Thereupon, ʿUmar had said to him: "O Abū Sufyān, I allow you [to do that]. May God accept your fighting for His cause, bless your decision and enhance your reward for what you have intended to do". Then Abū Sufyān [b. Ḥarb] had prepared himself with the best [of his] equipment and in the best visage. Then he had departed with many Muslims who had also moved out voluntarily. Abū

449 Q. 8:46 (*The Qurʾān. Tr. Abdel Haleem*, 113).

450 "*Aṭrāf al-asinna*" (lit. "the ends of the spearheads") is an expression both parts of which refer to the tip of the spear (see Schwarzlose, *Waffen*, 229).

451 The Arabic term "*ḥajal*" can be assigned two meanings, thus designating two quite distinct species of birds: "Partridges" (our translation) or "bobwhites". On the first meaning, see Lane, *Lexicon*, s.v. *ḥajal*.

Sufyān [b. Ḥarb] had kept good company with them until they had reached the generality of the Muslims [in Syria]. The day when the Muslims were to march out to their enemy at al-Yarmūk, Abū Sufyān [b. Ḥarb] [also] walked through [the lines of] the people [=the Muslims] and stopped at the followers of each flag and of every group to urge, motivate and exhort them, saying: "O Muslims, you are now in the non-Arabs' abode (*dār al-ʿajam*), separated from [your] families and away from the Commander of the Believers and the Muslims' reinforcements. I swear by God that you are now facing an enemy whose number is [very] large, whose rage is hard on you and to whom you have done much harm [as you did] to their women, to their children, to their possessions and to their lands. I swear by God that nothing will save you from them today and you will not obtain God's satisfaction [at all] except through truthful confrontation and patience in times of adversity. Thus, protect yourselves with your swords, seek proximity to your Creator by means of them [=the swords] and make them [=the swords] the fortresses to which you resort and in which you protect yourselves". He [=the narrator] said: Abū Sufyān [b. Ḥarb] fought fiercely and performed well on that day.\\326

He [=the narrator] said: [Then] the Byzantines advanced on the Muslims, hastening in procession with [their] crosses. They came [to them] with the[ir] bishops, priests, monks, patricians and horsemen, making a noise like thunder. Most of them had pledged allegiance to [fight to] death and 30,000 of them aligned [themselves], ten by ten, into a chain so that they could not flee. When Khālid b. al-Walīd saw them coming, he went to the Muslims' women who were stationed on an elevated hill within the encampment, and said: "O Muslims' women, whenever you see a man retreating because of defeat [to the encampment], kill him". Thus, they took the tent poles promptly, drew near to the Muslims and said [to them]: "You are not our husbands [any longer] if you do not defend us today". [Then] Khālid came to Abū ʿUbayda (r.) and said to him: "Those [=the Byzantines] came in large number[s] in earnestness, with vehemence and toughness. [They think] that nothing would resist [them]. Moreover, the Muslims' cavalry[men] are not many. I swear by God that my cavalry would not stand [firm] at all because of the severity of their attack, their cavalry and their infantry". At that time Khālid b. al-Walīd's cavalry was positioned in front of the lines of the Muslims who were [grouped] in three lines. Khālid [then] said: "I am of the opinion that I [should] divide my cavalry [in two] so that I take command of one [part] and Qays b. Hubayra [al-Murādī] of the other. Then our [two] cavalries should stand behind the right and left flanks [of the infantry]. If they launch an attack on the people [=the Muslims] and then the Muslims stand firm, God will strengthen them [=the Muslims] [even more] and make their feet stand [even] firm[er] [with the cavalries at their backs]; gratitude is [due] to God (t.). But if it is\\327 the opposite, we will [immediately] launch an attack with our horses—which were resting—on them, [i.e.] on their right and left flanks [simultaneously]. When the severity and power of their cavalry wane, their generality disperses and they break their lines and become scattered, we will then launch [another] attack on them while they are in such a [bad] situation. At this time, I hope that God will lead us to triumph over them and encircle them with evil". [In addition,] he [=Khālid] said to Abū ʿUbayda: "As for you, I am of the opinion that you [should] place Saʿīd b. Zayd [b. ʿAmr b. Nufayl] in your position while you stand [in command of] a good group right behind him so that you become a backup to the Muslims". Abū ʿUbayda accepted his advice and said: "Do what God has shown you and I will do what you have just mentioned". Then Abū ʿUbayda ordered Saʿīd b. Zayd [b. ʿAmr b. Nufayl] to stand in his position [and he did so]. [Thereafter,] Abū ʿUbayda mounted his horse and marched through [the lines of] the people [=the Muslims], [once more] motivating and advising them to fear God and to be patient. Then he left and stood behind the people to act as their backup.

The Byzantines [continued to] approach like sheets of [darkness at dead of] night and when they were opposite the [Muslims'] right flank, Muʿādh b. Jabal cried out to the people [=the Muslims], saying: "O Muslim servants of God, those [fighters] are ready to attack you fiercely. I swear by God that nothing can resist them except for truthful confrontation and patience in [times of] distress". Then he dismounted from his horse and said: "Whoever wants to take my horse to fight on it can take it". His son ʿAbd al-Raḥmān b. Muʿādh [b. al-Jabal][452], a pubescent youth, promptly leapt towards him and said: "O father, I wish I would be more useful to the Muslims as a horseman than I am as an infantryman. However, you, father, are more useful as an infantryman than you are as a horseman. For the majority\\328 of the Muslims are infantrymen and so if they see you patient and perseverant [as a fellow infantryman], they will be patient and [will] persevere[, too,] God willing". Thereupon, Muʿādh b. Jabal said to him: "O son, may God lead me and [lead] you to what He likes and what He desires". [On that day,] Muʿādh [b. Jabal] and his son engaged in such a [fierce] battle in which many of the Muslims had never engaged [before].

He [=the narrator] said: Then the Byzantines spurred one another and called one another [to fight forcefully]. The bishops and the monks also exhorted them. [Thus,] they drew near to the Muslims. When Muʿādh [b. Jabal] suddenly heard that [noise] from their side, he said: "O God, make their feet quake, terrify their hearts and bestow tranquility (*sakīna*) upon us, make us keep the word of piety (*taqwā*), make us love the confrontation and make us satisfied with [Your] decree".

He [=the narrator] said: Bāhān, the [chief] commander of the Byzantines, marched out [of his encampment] and walked through [the lines] of

452 ʿAbd al-Raḥmān's full name is ʿAbd al-Raḥmān b. Muʿādh b. Jabal al-Anṣārī (n.d.). Van Ess regards him as a "sheer literary character". In al-Azdī's narrative, ʿAbd al-Raḥmān is described as a young lad who fought with his father in the Battle of al-Yarmūk and died of al-ʿAmwās plague later on. On ʿAbd al-Raḥmān, see Ibn Ḥajar, *Al-iṣāba. Ed. al-Baghawī*, V, 47–48 (no. 6237) and van Ess, *Fehltritt*, 136.

his companions, prepared himself [and them for fighting] and [also] ordered them to [have] patience and to fight for their offspring, their possessions, their reign and their lands. After that, he issued [an order] to the commander of the left flank to launch an attack upon them [=the Muslims]. It was al-Durunjār who was in command of it and he was a pious man. Then the patricians and the chiefs who were with him said [to him]: "Your commander [just] ordered you to launch an attack upon them". He [=the narrator] said: The patricians [next to al-Durunjār] prepared themselves [for war] and then launched a fierce attack on the right flank [of the Muslims], which included al-Azd, Madhḥij, Ḥaḍramawt, Ḥimyar and Khawlān. However, they stood firm when they clashed [with the Byzantine's left flank] and fought [it] fiercely. Then [some of] the Byzantines fell upon them like mountains and displaced the Muslims from the right flank to the centre (*qalb*) until a party of the Muslims withdrew to the[ir] encampment. But the majority of the people [=the Muslims] stood firm, did not fall back and fought under their flags without withdrawal. On that day, Zubayd[453] did not withdraw, either. It [=the tribe of Zubayd] was positioned on\\329 the right flank and it included al-Ḥajjāj b. ʿAbd Yaghūth [b. Asad], the father of ʿAmr b. al-Ḥajjāj[454], who shouted: "O men, o men[455], [come to me]". Numbering about 500 of the toughest men, they flocked to him and launched a fierce [counter-] attack on the Byzantines. They did not cease until they merged [into a fight] with the Byzantines, then fought [them] fiercely and distracted them from pursuing those Muslims who were withdrawing [to their encampment]. After having fallen back, Ḥimyar, Ḥaḍramawt and Khawlān also launched a fierce attack on them and then made their way back to their positions until they stood in the [same] line[s] where they had stood [before].

Holding poles (*al-ʿanāhir*)—he [=the narrator] said: *Al-ʿanāhir* means "tent poles"—the women received the defeated Muslims who were fleeing and started hitting their faces with them.

Al-Ḥusayn b. Ziyād [al-Ramlī] reported to us on the authority of Abū Ismāʿīl [Muḥammad b. ʿAbdallāh al-Azdī], who said: Furthermore, Muḥammad b. Yūsuf related to me on the authority of Thābit [al-Bunānī] on the authority of Sahl b. Saʿd [al-Anṣārī], who said: Khawla bt. Thaʿlaba b. Mālik b. al-Dakhsham[456] took one of those poles and moved towards the defeated

453 Zubayd is a Southern Arabian tribe. In al-Azdī's narrative, Zubayd is depicted as fighting in the Battle of al-Yarmūk on the Muslims' right flank. In addition, one individual figure belonged to Zubayd: Al-Ḥajjāj b. ʿAbd Yaghūth b. Asad b. ʿAmr b. al-Ḥajjāj al-Zubaydī, who also took part in this battle. On Zubayd, see Caskel, *Ǧamharat*, I, 270; II, 608.

454 ʿAmr's full name is ʿAmr b. al-Ḥajjāj al-Zubaydī (n.d.). In al-Azdī's narrative, he is mentioned as the son of al-Ḥajjāj b. ʿAbd Yaghūth. On ʿAmr, see Ibn Ḥajar, *Al-iṣāba. Ed. al-Baghawī*, IV, 619 (no. 5811).

455 The Arabic expression "*khayfān [min al-nās]*" means "a multitude of men". On this expression, see Lane, *Lexicon*, s.v. *khayfān*.

456 Khawla bt. Thaʿlaba b. Mālik b. al-Dakhsham (n.d.), the wife of Aws b. al-Ṣāmit, is an early Islamic figure. In al-Azdī's narrative, she is depicted as holding one of the tent poles

[and withdrawing Muslims], declaiming [the following lines of verse] in the *rajaz* metre, saying:

يا هاربا عن نسوة تقيات
رميت بالسُم وبالمنيات
فعن قليل ما ترى سبيات
غير حظيات ولا رضيات

O fleer from [defending] God-fearing women,
May you be shot with poison and death;
In a little [while] you will see captive women
Neither favoured nor satisfied.

He [=the narrator] said: Al-Azd also stood firm and engaged in such a [fierce] fight that none of the [other] tribes has ever engaged in [before]. A [great] number of them [=members of al-Azd] were killed, the likes of which have never been killed in any [other] tribe [before].\\330

On that day, ʿAmr b. al-Ṭufayl [b. ʿAmr b.] Dhī al-Nūr [al-Azdī] also proceeded, saying: "O al-Azd, [take care that] the Muslims do not get attacked from your side [=the right flank]". Then he started striking [the Byzantine soldiers] with his sword and advancing on them [=the Byzantines], saying [the following lines of verse]:

قد علمت دوسُ ويشكرُ تعلم
أنى إذا الأبيضُ يوما مُظلِم
وعرَّدَ النكْسُ وفرَّ الأيهم
أنى عفر فى الوقاع ضيغمُ

Daws[457] knew and Yashkur[458] also knows
That, if the blank sword[459] is darkened [with blood] one day
And the coward escaped and the brave fled,
I am a very strong lion in the battles.

---

and moving towards the retreating Muslims, pushing them back to fight while reciting a poem. On Khawla, see Ibn Saʿd, *Kitāb al-ṭabaqāt*, VIII, 275–277.

457 Daws is a Southern Arabian tribe that was a subtribe of al-Azd. In al-Azdī's narrative, Daws is mentioned once in a poem. In addition, three individual figures belonged to Daws: (a) Jundab b. ʿAmr b. Ḥumama al-Dawsī, who is mentioned as one of the two commanders of Azd who led its members to Abū Bakr and as a flag holder during the Battle of al-Yarmūk. In addition, he encouraged the people during this battle, recited a poem about al-Azd and was killed there; (b) Abū Hurayra al-Dawsī, the second leader of al-Azd, who went to Abū Bakr and who also fought in the Battle of al-Yarmūk and encouraged the people to fight; and (c) ʿAbdallāh b. ʿAmr b. al-Ṭufayl b. ʿAmr b. Dhī al-Nūr al-Azdī, who is depicted twice as having changed his affiliation to "al-Dawsī" and who recited a poem about Daws. On Daws, see *EI*[2], s.v. al-Azd (G. Strenziok).

458 Yashkur is a Northern Arabian tribe that was a subtribe of Bakr b. Wāʾil. In al-Azdī's narrative, Yashkur is mentioned once in a poem together with the Southern Arabian tribe of Daws. On Yashkur, see *EI*[2], s.v. Bakr b. Wāʾil (W. Caskel).

459 In pre-Islamic and early Islamic poetry, "*al-abyaḍ*" (lit. "the white [one]") was used to refer to a sword with a blank blade (see Schwarzlose, *Waffen*, 171–172). This is the meaning we follow here.

He [='Amr b. al-Ṭufayl b. 'Amr al-Azdī] fought fiercely and killed nine of their [=the Byzantines'] toughest [fighters]. Then he was killed; God rest him. Hoisting a flag, Jundab b. 'Amr b. Ḥumama [al-Dawsī] [also] said [to his fellow tribesmen]: "O al-Azd, only those who fight will both survive and be safe from sin and shame. Verily, the [one] killed [in battle] is a martyr but the one who flees today is a failure". Then he [=Jundab b. 'Amr b. Ḥumama al-Dawsī] started saying [the following lines of verse]:

يا معشر الأزد اجتذاذ الأقيال
هيهات هيهات وقوف للحال
لا يمنع الراية إلا الأبطال
O al-Azd, [rush] to cut off the chieftains;
Never, never is the situation static;
Nobody protects the flag except the heroes.

He [=Jundab b. 'Amr b. Ḥumama al-Dawsī] fought fiercely [on that day] until he was killed; God rest him. Moreover, Abū Hurayra [al-Dawsī] shouted: "O blessed one[s], o blessed one[s], [come forward]". Then al-Azd flocked to him [=Abū Hurayra al-Dawsī].\\331

Al-Ḥusayn b. Ziyād [al-Ramlī] reported to us on the authority of Abū Ismā'īl Muḥammad b. 'Abdallāh [al-Azdī], who said: Furthermore, Mikhnaf b. 'Abdallāh b. Yazīd b. al-Mughaffal related to me on the authority of 'Abd al-A'lā b. Surāqa [al-Azdī][460], who said: On that day, I reached Abū Hurayra [al-Dawsī] while he was saying [as motivation for his tribesmen]: "Prepare yourselves well for the houris (*al-ḥūr al-'ayn*)[461] and be desirous of proximity to your Lord in the Gardens of Bliss. In [other] times of good deeds, you will not be loved more by your Lord than in this [battle] time. Verily, [all] the patient will enjoy their own graceful reward".

He [=the narrator] said: Then al-Azd flocked to him [=Abū Hurayra al-Dawsī] and clashed with the Byzantines. I swear by the One with whom no other deity is associated that we saw the earth revolving with the Byzantines in one orbit (*majāl*) as the quern does. But the Byzantines neither left [their positions] nor fell back and [some of] them fell upon them [=the Muslims] like mountains. I have never seen a time in which more skulls were falling, more wrists were dropping or more palms were flying down than in this time. I swear by God that we scared them [=the Byzantines] in an evil

460 'Abd al-A'lā's full name is Abū 'Abd al-Raḥmān 'Abd al-A'lā b. Surāqa al-Azdī al-Qurashī (?) al-Baṣrī (n.d.). In al-Azdī's narrative, 'Abd al-A'lā is a transmitter of one tradition, in which he describes his deeds during the Battle of al-Yarmūk. On 'Abd al-A'lā, see Ibn 'Asākir, *TMD*, XXXIII, 411–416.

461 The Arabic expression "*al-ḥūr al-'ayn*" (lit. "eyes with a marked contrast of white eyeballs and black irises") refers to voluptuously beautiful black-eyed maidens who, according to Muslim belief, will be gifted to the inhabitants of Paradise. See Lane, *Lexicon*, s.v. *ḥawar*.

way and they scared us, too. We remained in this [situation for a while] and most of the fight was [concentrated] on [our] right flank. However, those in the centre were also facing what we were facing. But [because of] the people's [=the Byzantines'] fury, vehemence, earnestness and rage against us, and [because] we were at the edge of the right flank, we faced in their fight [against us] what nobody else has ever faced [before]. I swear by God that while we were fighting them like that, about 20,000 of them [=the Byzantines] entered into our encampment from behind, but God protected us from falling back.\\332

He [=the narrator] said: [Then] Khālid b. al-Walīd, God rest him,[462] launched an attack on them [=those Byzantines who entered the Muslims' encampment], made them crash into one another and smashed about 10,000 of them in the [Muslims'] encampment. However, the rest of them entered into the Muslims' tents inside the encampment, [some] wounded and some unwounded. Then Khālid b. al-Walīd (r.) went out with his cavalry [to the Byzantines], expelling and killing all those Byzantines who were close to our encampment. When he was opposite us, Khālid brought his cavalry[men] together and then said [to them]: "O adherents of Islam, nothing remains from the people's [=the Byzantines'] earnestness, fight and might except what you have [just] seen. Thus, [display] toughness, [display] toughness. By the One in whose hand[s] my soul lies, God will certainly grant you triumph over them this time [again]". Hearing such words from Khālid, each of the Muslims was encouraged [to continue to fight] against them [=the Byzantines]. He [=the narrator] said: Then Khālid intercepted the [bulk of the] Byzantines, of whom more than 100,000 were next to him. In command of about 1,000 horsemen only, he launched an attack on them. He [=the narrator] said: I swear by God that no sooner had they been attacked than God dispersed their assembly. He [=the narrator] said: We also launched a fierce attack on whichever [unit] of their infantry was adjacent to us. Thus, they [=the Byzantines] were put to flight and we pursued them, killing them the way we wanted. [Finally,] their left flank could not protect [itself] against our right flank.

[Manuscript note: Part VI]

This is the end of the fifth part of the Book on the Conquests of Syria. [It is continued at the beginning of the sixth part by a tradition about the wrapping of al-Durunjār].\\333

In the name of God, the Merciful, the Compassionate. Shaykh Abū Isḥāq Ibrāhīm b. Sa'īd b. 'Abdallāh al-Ḥabbāl reported to us, saying: Abū al-'Abbās Munīr b. Aḥmad b. al-Ḥasan al-Khashshāb reported to us, saying: Abū al-Ḥasan 'Alī b. Aḥmad b. Isḥāq b. Ibrāhīm al-Baghdādī reported

462 The phrase "God rest him" signals, here (as in several other cases), that Khālid b. al-Walīd (or the respective person) has died. Since he is presented alive in the following pages, it must have been added by one of the transmitters of the narrative and hence represents a later perception of Khālid.

to us, saying: Abū al-ʿAbbās al-Walīd b. Ḥammād al-Ramlī related to us, saying: Al-Ḥusayn b. Ziyād al-Ramlī reported to us, saying: Abū Ismāʿīl Muḥammad b. ʿAbdallāh al-Azdī al-Baṣrī related to us, saying: Then Khālid reached al-Durunjār, who said to his companions: "Wrap cloths[463] around me. I wish I did not [start to] fight those people [=the Muslims] today". They wrapped the cloths around him. Thereupon, he said: "I wished that God had spared me the war against those people [=the Muslims]. [I also wished] that I had not seen them and they had not seen me and that I had not triumphed over them and they had not triumphed over me; this is a bad day". He took no heed until the Muslims fell upon him and killed him.

While he was on the right flank of the Byzantines[' army], Ibn Qanāṭir said to Jirjīs, the ruler of Armenia: "Attack them". Thereupon, he [=Jirjīs] said to him: "You order me to attack them while I am a commander just like you!" Ibn Qanāṭir then said to him: "You are a commander, [too,] but I am your commander and you are ordered to obey me". Thus, they both quarreled [about this issue]. He [=the narrator] said: Finally, Ibn Qanāṭir launched a fierce attack on the Muslims' left flank where Kināna, Qays, Lakhm, Judhām, Khathʿam, Ghassān, Quḍāʿa and ʿĀmila were positioned. They were [stationed] between the Muslims' left flank and the centre. Accordingly, the Muslims were put to flight and the [fighters at the] left flank withdrew from its lines. But the followers of the flags (*ahl al-rāyāt*) and the [surrounding] defenders (*ahl al-ḥifāẓ*) stood firm and fought [back] fiercely. The Byzantines closely pursued the Muslims who were fleeing until they entered [all] together the [Muslims'] encampment and the Muslim women met them with the tent poles with which they were striking their faces.\\334

Al-Ḥusayn b. Ziyād [al-Ramlī] reported to us on the authority of Abū Ismāʿīl Muḥammad b. ʿAbdallāh [al-Azdī], who said: Furthermore, my father[464] related to me on the authority of Makīla b. Ḥanẓala b. Ḥawya[465] on the authority of his father Ḥanẓala b. Ḥawya[466], who said: I swear by God that [during this attack] I was on the left flank and, lo and behold, some of the Byzantine men [mounted] on Arab horses passed by us, but they did not

463 This probably refers to special cloths that are wrapped around the deceased in preparation for burial. We thank Adam Walker for pointing this out to us.

464 ʿUqla and Banī Yāsīn interpret the expression "*abī*" (lit. "my father") as a reference to al-Azdī's father ʿAbdallāh al-Azdī. However, they did not find a *tarjama* about him (see al-Azdī, *Futūḥ al-Shām. Ed. ʿUqla/Banī Yāsīn*, 15; 334, n. 1).

465 Makīla b. Ḥanẓala b. Ḥawya is listed neither in Ibn Saʿd, al-Bukhārī, Ibn ʿAsākir nor in any other biographical work we could access. ʿUqla and Banī Yāsīn refer to Ibn ʿAsākir's *TMD* where *Maklaba* b. Ḥanẓala b. Ḥawya is mentioned (see al-Azdī, *Futūḥ al-Shām. Ed. ʿUqla/Banī Yāsīn*, 334, n. 2 and Ibn ʿAsākir, *TMD*, LX, 235–236 [no. 7624]). In al-Azdī's narrative, Makīla is said to be the son of Ḥanẓala b. Ḥawya, on whose authority he transmits one tradition.

466 Ḥanẓala's full name is Ḥanẓala b. Ḥawya al-Kinānī. In al-Azdī's narrative, he is mentioned as a staunch fighter who killed a Byzantine and as a transmitter of several traditions. On Ḥanẓala, see Ibn ʿAsākir, *TMD*, XV, 321–322 (no. 1820).

look like the Byzantines, because they resembled us more [in appearance]. I have never forgotten what one of them said [to us]: "O Arabs, hurry [back] to Wādī al-Qurā and to Yathrib".[467] He [=the narrator, Ḥanẓala b. Ḥawya] said: He [=the Byzantine men who resembled the Arab] also said [the following lines of verse]:

في كل حـين فئة تغير
نحن لنا البلقاء والسدير
هيهات يأبى ذلك الأمير
والملك المتوج المحبور

Every time a company raids;
[The land of] al-Balqā' and al-Sadīr[468] are ours;
It is impossible for that commander to refuse [this]
And for the crowned exhilarated king, too.

He [=the narrator, Ḥanẓala b. Ḥawya] said: I attacked him [=the Byzantine resembling an Arab] and he attacked me. We both tussled with our swords but they [=the swords] were of no avail to us. He [=the narrator, Ḥanẓala b. Ḥawya] said: Then I clasped him [=the Byzantine man] until we fell [off our horses] together. Thereafter, we fought each other for a while [on the ground]. Then we both separated. He [=the narrator, Ḥanẓala b. Ḥawya] said: I glanced at his neck and something [that looked] like the lace of a sandal appeared on it. Then I walked towards him and targeted this spot with my sword. I swear by God that I did not miss it and I cut it [=the neck]. [Thereupon,] he fell down [to the ground], so I struck him [again] until I killed him.\\335 I proceeded to my horse which had run away, but which my people had captured for me. Hence, I went along until I mounted it. He [=the narrator, Ḥanẓala b. Ḥawya] said: On that day, Qubāth b. Ashyam fought fiercely and started saying [the following lines of verse]:

إن تفقدوني تفقدوا خير فارس
لدى الغمرات والرئـيس المحاميا
وذا فخر لا يملأ الهول نحره
ضروبا بنصـل السيف أروع ماضيا

467 Yathrib is the late antique name of Medina. For geographical details, see p. 47, n. 43 or *EI*², s.v. al-Madīna (M. Watt et al.).

468 Yāqūt gives three explanations of al-Sadīr: (a) a river, (b) a palace in the vicinity of al-Ḥīra and (c) an Arabicised form of the Persian "*seh dalah*" (lit. "three martens"). According to Beeston/Shahid and Massignon who all quote Yāqūt's (second) tradition, al-Sadīr is one of the palaces of the Lakhmid rulers in al-Ḥīra adjacent to the castle of al-Khawarnaq. According to Yāqūt, al-Sadīr is also a region that lies between the river of al-Ḥīra, Najaf and Kaskar. This fits most the usage of the term "al-Sadīr" in al-Azdī's narrative that is mentioned once in a line of verse in which al-Sadīr is contrasted with "the land of al-Balqā'". On al-Sadīr, see Yāqūt, *Mu'jam al-buldān*, III, 59–61; *EI*², s.v. al-Ḥīra (A. Beeston/I. Shahid); *EI*², s.v. al-Khawarnaḳ (L. Massignon).

If you lose me, you will have lost the best horseman
For hardships and for the defending chief;
[He] has pride and terror never fills his breast
Making with the sword[469] the most marvellous history.

He [=the narrator, Ḥanẓala b. Ḥawya] said: Also on that day, he [=Qubāth b. Ashyam] smashed three spears and broke two swords. Whenever he broke a sword or smashed a spear, he used to say: "Who is going to provide a [new] sword or a [new] spear—for the cause of God—as an aid for a man who has detained himself with God's close friends and who has promised God neither to flee nor to leave [his position], but to fight the Polytheists until God makes the Muslims triumphant or until he dies?" He [=Qubāth b. Ashyam] was one of the best performers [in war] among the people on that day. [On the same day,] Abū al-Aʿwar al-Sulamī dismounted [from his horse] and said [to the tribesmen from Qays who were positioned at the left flank near Qubāth]: "O Qays, have some patience and [seek] some of the reward [of God], for patience is an honour and a noble deed in this world and a mercy and a virtue in the Hereafter. So be patient and persevere".\\336

Al-Ḥusayn b. Ziyād [al-Ramlī] related to us on the authority of Abū Ismāʿīl Muḥammad b. ʿAbdallāh [al-Azdī], who said: Furthermore, al-Ḥakam b. Jawwās b. al-Ḥakam b. al-Mughaffal[470] related to me on the authority of ʿAmr b. Muḥṣan on the authority of Ḥabīb b. Maslama, who said: On the battle-day of al-Yarmūk, we had to resort to Saʿīd b. Zayd [b. ʿAmr b. Nufayl]. Saʿīd's goodness is due to God! On that day, Saʿīd was [fighting] like a lion. I swear by God that he got on his knees and when they [=the Byzantines] drew near to him, he leapt into their faces like a lion. Then he stabbed the first of the people [=the Byzantines] with his flag and killed him. I swear by God that he then continued fighting on foot like a brave valiant man fighting on horseback.

He [=the narrator, Ḥabīb b. Maslama] said: Yazīd b. Abī Sufyān was one of the most competent and best performing people [in war], and so was his father. While inciting and exhorting the people [=the Muslims], his father passed by him [=Yazīd] and said [to him]: "O son, you are in command of a flank of the Muslims' army (*amr*)—[i.e.] Yazīd was in command of a quarter of the people [=the Muslims] at that time—and every Muslim in this valley is obliged to fight. How should it be then for the likes of you who are in command of the Muslims' affairs? Those [who are in command] are the worthiest of fighting for the cause of God, of patience and of advice. O son, fear God, act nobly for your cause and do not let any of your companions

469 "*Naṣl al-sayf*" (lit. "the blade of the sword") was used in the pre-Islamic and early Islamic poetry to refer to the blade or the sword as a whole (see Schwarzlose, *Waffen*, 163), too.

470 Al-Ḥakam b. Jawwās b. al-Ḥakam b. al-Mughaffal is listed neither in Ibn Saʿd, al-Bukhārī, Ibn ʿAsākir nor in any other biographical work we could access. In al-Azdī's narrative, he is mentioned as a transmitter of one tradition.

be more desirous of the afterlife, more patient\\337 in war, more damaging to the Polytheists, more painstaking against Islam's enemy or a better performer [on the battlefield] than you are in their eyes". Thereupon, he [=Yazīd] said: "O father, I swear by God that I will do [all of this]". Then Yazīd fought fiercely on the flank where he was positioned.

He [=the narrator, Ḥabīb b. Maslama] said: A group of the Byzantines also launched a fierce attack on ʿAmr b. al-ʿĀṣ [and his unit]. Thus, his companions were put to flight, yet ʿAmr [b. al-ʿĀṣ] stood firm, duelled with them extensively and fought them fiercely. Then his companions came back to him. He [=the narrator, Ḥabīb b. Maslama] said: I heard Umm Ḥabība bt. al-ʿĀṣ[471] say: "May God make ugly [every] man who runs away from [defending] his spouse. May God make ugly [every] man who runs away from [defending] his daughter". He [=the narrator, Ḥabīb b. Maslama] said: I also heard some [other] Muslim women say: "O Muslims, fight because you will no longer remain our husbands if you do not defend us". They [=the women] took the tent poles and whenever a fleeing Muslim [man] passed by them, they attacked him in order to strike his face and force him back to the generality of the Muslims.

Shuraḥbīl b. Ḥasana also fought fiercely in his quarter [of the army] where he was positioned. He was amid the people [=the Muslims], stationed next to Saʿīd b. Zayd [b. ʿAmr b. Nufayl]. [At one point in the battle,] he started calling [out to the people], saying: "God has purchased the persons and possessions of the Believers in return for the Garden—they fight in God's way: They kill and are killed—this is a true promise given by Him",[472] to the end of the verse. Thereupon, he [=Shuraḥbīl] said: "Where are those who sell their lives to God in order to seek His satisfaction? Where are those who yearn for His proximity in His abode?" Then many people flocked to him and the centre [of the army] remained [firm] and its fighters (*ahl*) who were [stationed there] with Saʿīd b. Zayd [b. ʿAmr b. Nufayl] were not put to flight. In addition, Abū ʿUbayda was a backup to the Muslims from behind.\\338

When Qays b. Hubayra [al-Murādī] saw that the Byzantines had launched a fierce attack on the Muslim cavalry [that was] next to the [Muslims'] left flank, he intercepted the Byzantines with his cavalry, which had [previously] been a part (*shaṭr*) of Khālid b. al-Walīd's cavalry. Then he made them [=the Byzantines] crash into one another, and the [withdrawing] Muslims [from the left flank] returned in pursuit of the Byzantines, fighting them [and killing them]. Khālid b. al-Walīd also launched an attack on the Byzantines [who were] next to him on the right flank of the Muslims. So he launched an attack and then struck them [with his sword] until he forced them [back]

471 Umm Ḥabība bt. al-ʿĀṣ, the sister of ʿAmr b. al-ʿĀṣ, is listed neither in Ibn Saʿd, al-Bukhārī, Ibn ʿAsākir nor in any other biographical work we could access. In al-Azdī's narrative, she is mentioned as praying to God to make ugly any Muslim fighter who flees from the battlefield and who no longer defends his spouse or daughter and as joining women in hitting the retreating fighters with tent poles to force them back to the battlefield.

472 Q. 9:111 (*The Qurʾān. Tr. Abdel Haleem*, 126).

to their lines. When Khālid saw that Qays b. Hubayra [al-Murādī] had put the Byzantines, who were next to him, to flight and that the [recovering] Muslims had launched a fierce attack on them[, too,] he [=Khālid b. al-Walīd] attacked the Byzantines who were next to him and made them crash into one another. [Then] all of the Muslims advanced on them [=the Byzantines] little by little. When they drew near to them, they launched an[other] attack on them and thus the Byzantines started tearing down their lines and began to flee. [Immediately thereafter,] Abū ʿUbayda sent [a message] to Saʿīd b. Zayd [b. ʿAmr b. Nufayl] that [said]: "Attack them". So he [=Saʿīd b. Zayd b. ʿAmr b. Nufayl] promptly attacked them while all the Muslims also launched a fierce attack on them. Thus, God vanquished the Byzantines and enabled the Muslims to overcome them.[473] Then they [=the Muslims] killed them the way they wanted and none of them [=the Byzantines] could protect himself from any of the Muslims. Khālid b. al-Walīd (r.) reached al-Durunjār after he [=al-Durunjār] had ordered his companions to wrap his head in a garment. Then Khālid (r.) said: "I wish I were able to see him". Thereupon, the Muslims struck him [=al-Durunjār] [with their swords] until they killed him while his head was wrapped in the garment. He was averse to fighting the Muslims, because of their description and characterisation in the books he used to read. [For] he was one of their [=the Byzantines'] pious men.\\339 He [=the narrator] said: The Muslims pursued them [=the Byzantines], killing them by all means. They [=the Byzantines] jostled, one against the other, until they reached a place overlooking abysses beneath them. Then they started falling heedlessly therein. [For] it was a foggy day and, therefore, the last of them did not know what the first [who fled] was facing. They were receding into them [=the abysses] until about 100,000 men fell into them. [Later] they could be counted only with reeds (*qaṣab*). Abū ʿUbayda dispatched Shaddād b. Aws b. Thābit, the nephew of Ḥassān b. Thābit [al-Anṣārī], to count them the day after the battle. When he counted them with reeds, he found those who had fallen down in these abysses [totalled] more than 80,000. Since then [these] abysses have been called al-Wāqūṣa[474] [and have remained known as such] until today. [They were so-called] because they [=the Byzantines] had their necks broken therein, unaware of their fall into them until the fog cleared. [Only] then did they take a different direction [in their flight]. After [many of them] had fled, the Muslims killed about 50,000 of them [later] in the battle.

473 We interpret the two Arabic expressions "*ḍaraba Allāh wujūh al-Rūm*" (lit. "God struck the Byzantines' faces") and "*manaḥa Allāh al-muslimīna aktāfahum*" (lit. "God granted the Muslims their shoulders") as being idiomatically employed to mean "God vanquished them" and "God enabled the Muslims to overcome them", respectively.

474 Al-Wāqūṣa (lit. "the Neck-Breaker") is a valley in Syria in Ḥawrān, according to Yāqūt. In al-Azdī's narrative, al-Wāqūṣa is the name of some abysses into which the Byzantine soldiers fell during the Battle of al-Yarmūk. On al-Wāqūṣa, see Yāqūt, *Muʿjam al-buldān*, IV, 893–894.

In command of the cavalry, Khālid b. al-Walīd (r.) pursued them [=the Byzantines], killing them in every valley, on every defile, on every mountain and in every direction [he could find them]. He continued killing them until he reached Damascus. [There] the people of Damascus went out to him, received him [well] and said to him: "We are upholding the pact that was [made] between us and you". Thereupon, Khālid said to them: "Yes, uphold your pact". Then Khālid pursued them [=the Byzantines] and went on killing them in the villages, valleys, mountains, on the defiles, in the plains, on the hills and in every direction [they fled to]. Thus, he continued killing them until he reached Ḥimṣ.\\340 [There] the people of Ḥimṣ went out to him and said to him exactly what the people of Damascus had said to him [before]. [Thereupon,] he [=Khālid] said to them: "We [also] uphold [the pact] that was [concluded] between us and you".

[In contrast,] Abū ʿUbayda came to the Muslims who were killed, may God rest them and reward them with the best [in return] for [their good deeds to] Islam and its adherents, and buried them. When he finished that [=burying them], al-Nuʿmān b. Maḥmiyya Dhū al-Anf al-Khathʿamī[475] went to him and said: "Give me command over my [tribes]people". So he [=Abū ʿUbayda] gave him the command over them [=the tribespeople]. As a result of this issue, a man from his [=al-Nuʿmān's] tribe of Banū ʿAmr[476], called Ibn Dhī al-Sahm [al-Khathʿamī], whom the Khathʿam [tribespeople] had [previously] appointed as their chief and their commander, went [to complain] to him [=Abū ʿUbayda]. They [=al-Nuʿmān and Ibn Dhī al-Sahm] appealed to Abū ʿUbayda to [settle] their dispute over the chieftainship. Abū ʿUbayda put them off until they would be done with their war and fight against the Byzantine enemy; then he would consider their case. When the people [=the Muslims and the Byzantines] met and fought [each other], Ibn Dhī al-Sahm [al-Khathʿamī] was killed and martyred on that day. Thus, Abū ʿUbayda appointed al-Nuʿmān b. Maḥmiyya Dhū al-Anf [al-Khathʿamī] as commander of Khathʿam.\\341

The story of the chieftainship of al-Ashtar, whose [more complete name] was Mālik b. al-Ḥārith al-Nakhaʿī

He [=the narrator] said: Al-Ashtar, whose [more complete name] was Mālik b. al-Ḥārith al-Nakhaʿī[477], [also] came to Abū ʿUbayda and said to

475 Dhū al-Anf al-Nuʿmān b. Maḥmiyya al-Khathʿamī (n.d.) is an early Islamic figure. In al-Azdī's narrative, he is depicted as disputing with Ibn Dhī al-Sahm al-Khathʿamī over the command of Khathʿam but the former was given the command by Abū ʿUbayda upon the death of the latter in the Battle of al-Yarmūk. On al-Nuʿmān, see Ibn Ḥajar, *Al-iṣāba. Ed. al-Baghawī*, VI, 499 (no. 8877).

476 Banū ʿAmr is a Northern Arabian tribe that was a subtribe of Khathʿam. In al-Azdī's narrative, it is mentioned once as a tribal group that supported al-Nuʿmān b. Maḥmiyya Dhū al-Anf al-Khathʿamī's claim for chieftainship. On Banū ʿAmr, see Caskel, *Ǧamharat*, I, 224; II, 345.

477 Mālik's full name is Abū Ibrāhīm Mālik b. al-Ḥārith al-Nakhaʿī (d. 37–38/658–659), known as al-Ashtar (lit. "the one with inverted eyelids"). In al-Azdī's narrative, Mālik

him: "Give me command over my [tribes]people". So he [=Abū ʿUbayda] appointed him as the commander [of al-Nakhaʿ]. His story was the same as that of [al-Nuʿmān b. Maḥmiyya Dhū al-Anf] al-Khathʿamī. He went to his [tribes]people, who were commanded by [another] man from among them. Thus, al-Ashtar [=Mālik b. al-Ḥārith al-Nakhaʿī] appealed to Abū ʿUbayda to [settle] their dispute over the chieftainship. Then Abū ʿUbayda summoned al-Nakhaʿ[478] [tribespeople] and said to them: "Which of these two do you prefer and like [more] to be your chief?" Thereupon, they [=al-Nakhaʿ tribespeople] said: "Both of them are honourable, agreeable to us and reliable among us". Abū ʿUbayda then said: "What do I do [now] with both of you?" Then he [=Abū ʿUbayda] came to al-Ashtar and said [to him]: "Where were you when this one was given the command?" [Thereupon,] he [=al-Ashtar] said: "I was in Medina with the Commander of the Believers (r.). Then I came [later] to you [=the Muslims]". He [=Abū ʿUbayda] said: "You came to this one while he was the chief of your companions". He [=al-Ashtar] said: "Yes". [Then] he [=Abū ʿUbayda] said: "You should not dispute your cousin after the generality of your [tribes]people had accepted him [as commander] before your coming to them". Al-Ashtar [=Mālik b. al-Ḥārith al-Nakhaʿī] said: "He is agreeable, honourable and worthy of that [=the chieftainship]. However, I am also worthy of the chieftainship. Thus, he can succeed me to the chieftainship of my [tribes]people and I take rule over them [from now on] as this one has been ruling them [until now]". Thereupon, Abū ʿUbayda said: "Postpone this [suggestion] today until this battle takes place. If you both get martyred, what God retains [for you] is better for both of you [than being a chief]. However, if one of you perishes and the other survives, the survivor will be the chief of his [tribes]people. In case you both survive, we let you [=al-Ashtar] succeed him [to the chieftainship], God willing". Al-Ashtar said [about this proposal]: "I agree". When the battle took place

---

is identified as al-Ashtar. He struggled with a competitor for the leadership of al-Nakhaʿ and, after the latter died in the Battle of al-Yarmūk, he was appointed commander over the tribe by Abū ʿUbayda. During the same battle, Mālik is said to have killed eleven Byzantine patricians and engaged in two hard duels with Byzantine fighters while pursuing the remnants of the army to the north of Syria. Meeting Maysara b. Masrūq and his unit, Mālik did not subdue himself under Maysara's leadership in prayers, but led the prayers of his unit himself. After that, he returned to Abū ʿUbayda. On Mālik, see *EI*^{2}, s.v. al-Ashtar (L. Veccia Vaglieri).

478 Al-Nakhaʿ is a Southern Arabian tribe that was a subtribe of Madhḥij. In al-Azdī's narrative, Nakhaʿ is mentioned three times, always in connection with its leader Mālik b. al-Ḥārith al-Nakhaʿī: (a) Mālik is one of the two individual figures said to belong to Nakhaʿ. He is depicted in a struggle for the leadership of al-Nakhaʿ. After his competitor died in the Battle of al-Yarmūk, he was appointed as its commander by Abū ʿUbayda. During the same battle, Mālik is said to have killed several Byzantines and to have pursued the remnants of the army to the north. Meeting Maysara b. Masrūq and his unit, Mālik did not subdue himself under Maysara's leadership; (b) Mālik's daughter Umm al-Nuʿmān bt. Mālik is also mentioned in the narrative. Mālik married her to his cousin in return for the latter's sword. On al-Nakhaʿ, see Caskel, *Ǧamharat*, I, 258; II, 444.

[later], the first [unnamed] chief of al-Nakhaʿ was martyred. He [=the narrator] said: Al-Ashtar went [to Abū ʿUbayda] and then Abū ʿUbayda gave him the command [over his tribespeople].\\342

Al-Ḥusayn b. Ziyād [al-Ramlī] related to us on the authority of Abū Ismāʿīl Muḥammad b. ʿAbdallāh [al-Azdī], who said: Furthermore, Abū ʿAbdallāh b. al-Ḥusayn[479] related to me: Al-Ashtar was one of their [=the Muslims'] fortitudinous and tough men and one of their mighty people and their supporters. On the battle-day of al-Yarmūk, he killed eleven of their [=the Byzantines'] patricians [during battle] and [another] three of them in a duel before they [all] were put to flight. [Then] al-Ashtar [=Mālik b. al-Ḥārith al-Nakhaʿī] joined Khālid b. al-Walīd when the latter pursued the Byzantines and when they [=the Byzantines] were fleeing. When they [=al-Ashtar, Khālid b. al-Walīd and the Muslims] reached Thaniyyat al-ʿUqāb in the land of Damascus, which was a pass (*mahbaṭ*) from which whoever came from Ḥimṣ descended and which thus lay in al-Ghūṭa, [i.e.] the Ghūṭa of Damascus, a large group of the Byzantines were [waiting] on Thaniyyat al-ʿUqāb. When they [=al-Ashtar, Khālid and the Muslims] reached that Byzantine group, they [=the members of this group] started pelting the Muslims with rocks from above. In command of [a number of] Muslim infantrymen, al-Ashtar then proceeded towards them. Lo and behold, ahead of the Byzantines was one of their grand and tough men, who was a giant and stout [person]. Al-Ashtar went to him and when he drew near to him, al-Ashtar leapt [towards him], so both he and the Byzantine ended up erect on a level rock and both tussled with their swords. [Then] al-Ashtar struck the Byzantine [man]'s palm and swept it away. The Byzantine [man] also struck al-Ashtar's palm with his sword, but he did not do any harm to him. They clasped each other. Then al-Ashtar pushed him from the top of the rock, so they both fell off it and then rolled down. While gripping the infidel, not leaving him, and rolling down with him, al-Ashtar started saying: "Say, 'My prayer[s] and sacrifice, my life and death, are all for God, Lord of all the Worlds; He has no partner. This is what I am commanded, and I am the first to devote myself to Him'".[480]\\343 He [=al-Ashtar] kept repeating this until they [both] reached a level spot on the mountain and a stable [position]. When they both settled [there], al-Ashtar jumped on the Byzantine [man] and killed him. Then he shouted at the people [=the Muslims] to pass by. So the people [=the Muslims] passed by [him]. When the Byzantines saw that and [saw] that al-Ashtar had killed their companion, they cleared the mountain road to the people [=the Muslims] and fled. Abū ʿUbayda proceeded in the tracks of Khālid until the former reached Ḥimṣ. [There] he ordered Khālid to head for the land of Qinnasrīn. So Khālid proceeded ahead of him.

479 Abū ʿAbdallāh b. al-Ḥusayn could not be identified in Ibn Saʿd, al-Bukhārī, Ibn ʿAsākir or in any other biographical work we could access. In al-Azdī's narrative, he is mentioned as a transmitter of one tradition.

480 Q. 6:162–163 (*The Qurʾān. Tr. Abdel Haleem*, 93).

The coming of the [news of the] Byzantines' defeat to Caesar, the Emperor of the Byzantines, and what he said thereupon

Al-Ḥusayn b. Ziyād [al-Ramlī] related to us on the authority of Abū Ismāʿīl [Muḥammad] b. ʿAbdallāh [al-Azdī], who said: Furthermore, ʿUbaydallāh b. al-ʿAbbās[481] related to me, saying: The [news of the] defeat [in the Battle of al-Yarmūk] reached the Emperor of the Byzantines while he was in Antioch. The first to have come to him was one of the defeated [grand] men who informed him of the Byzantines' defeat. [Thereupon,] he [=the Emperor] said [to him]: "I knew that they [=the Muslims] would defeat you". He [=the narrator, ʿUbaydallāh b. al-ʿAbbās] said: Some of those who were sitting with him said: "How did you know that, Emperor?" He [=the Emperor] said: "From [the fact] that they love death as [much as] you love life and they desire the afterlife\\344 more than you desire the worldly life. Thus, they will remain triumphant as long as they stay like that, [not] changing [the religious laws] as you did and [not] breaking [the pacts] as you did".[482]

Al-Ḥusayn b. Ziyād [al-Ramlī] related to us on the authority of Abū Ismāʿīl [Muḥammad b. ʿAbdallāh al-Azdī], who said: Furthermore, Abū Jahḍam al-Azdī related to me on the authority of ʿAbd al-Raḥmān b. al-Salīk al-Fazārī on the authority of ʿAbdallāh b. Qurṭ al-Thumālī, who said: When [the news of] the defeat [in the Battle of al-Yarmūk] reached Caesar—[and] the first [person] to have come to him was one of the Byzantine [grand] men—he [=Caesar] said to him: "What happened to you over there?" Thereupon, he [=the grand man] said to him: "Good [things], Emperor. God (ʿa.) defeated them and made them perish". He [=the narrator, ʿAbdallāh b. Qurṭ al-Thumālī] said: Those who were around him [=the Emperor] rejoiced over that [news], delighted in it and howled [with delight]. Thereupon, he [=the Emperor] said to them: "Woe unto you, this is a liar. Do you not see his looks, which are the looks of a defeated [person]? Ask him what made him come. I swear upon my life that he is not a[n official] messenger. If he were not [from among the] defeated, he should have been staying with his commander [over there]". Thereafter, it did not take long before another [man] came. He [=the Emperor] said to him: "Woe unto you, what happened to

481 ʿUbaydallāh's full name is Abū Muḥammad ʿUbaydallāh b. al-ʿAbbās b. ʿAbd al-Muṭṭalib b. Hāshim (d. between 85–87/704–706). In al-Azdī's narrative, he is mentioned as a transmitter of one tradition. On ʿUbaydallāh, see *EI*², s.v. ʿUbaydallāh b. al-ʿAbbās (C. Bosworth).

482 The Arabic expression "*wa-la*" (lit. "will certainly do") is normally used to emphasise the occurrence of prospective events. However, this reading actually contradicts the complimentary words said by the Emperor of the Byzantines about the Muslims. That is why we consider it a transmission error and read it instead as "*wa-lā*" (lit. "will not do")—a reading which complies with and complements the commendatory words. The point is that the Byzantines were defeated because they loved life more than death and desired the worldly life more than the afterlife and because they changed their religious laws and broke their pacts.

you over there?" [Thereupon,] he [=the second man] said to him: "God defeated the enem[ies] and destroyed them". Heraclius then said to him: "If God had made them perish, what made you come [here]?" He [=the narrator, ʿAbdallāh b. Qurṭ al-Thumālī] said: His [=the Emperor's] companions rejoiced [again] and said: "He told you the truth, Emperor". Thereupon, he [=the Emperor] said to them: "Woe unto you, do you deceive yourselves? I swear by God that if those [Byzantines] had triumphed and won, they would not have come and galloped on their horses to you, and the message as well as good news [of victory] would have come first [to you]".\\345

He [=the narrator, ʿAbdallāh b. Qurṭ al-Thumālī] said: Then they remained in this [situation] until an Arab man called Ḥudhayfa b. ʿAmr[483] from Tanūkh appeared on his Arabian horse [and stepped in] to them. He was a Christian. Thereupon, Caesar said: "I think that the bad news is [coming only] with this [man]". When he [=the Arab Christian] drew near to him, he [=Caesar] said to him: "What [news] do you have?" He [=the Christian Arab] said: "Evil [news]". [Thereupon,] he [=Caesar] said: "Your face is the one that portends evil". Then he [=Caesar] looked at his companions and said: "Bad news brought by a bad man from a bad people". He [=the narrator, ʿAbdallāh b. Qurṭ al-Thumālī] said: He [=Caesar] remained in this [situation] until one of the Byzantine grand men [also] came to him. The Emperor said to him: "What happened to you over there?" He [=the grand man] said: "Evil [things], we were defeated". [Thereupon,] he [=the Emperor] said: "What did your commander Bāhān do?" He [=the grand man] said: "He [fought until he] was killed". He [=the Emperor] said: "[And what happened to] so-and-so and so-and-so and so-and-so?"—[thus] he mentioned the names of a number of his commanders, patricians and Byzantine horsemen. He [=the grand man] said: "They were [all] killed". Thereupon, he [=the Emperor] said to him: "I swear by God that you are too malicious, too wicked and too infidel to defend a religion or fight for a worldly life". Then he [=the Emperor] said to his guarding soldiers (*shuraṭ*): "Bring him down [to me]". So they brought him down and fetched him [to the Emperor]. Then he [=the Emperor] said to him: "Were you not the toughest of the people on me concerning the cause of Muḥammad, the Arabs' Prophet, when his letter and his messenger came to me? I wanted to accept what he had called me to and to embrace his religion. However, you were the toughest of the people on me until I refrained from what I had wanted therefrom. Now, [why] did you not fight Muḥammad's people and his companions in defence of my reign with the same [toughness] I received from you when you stopped me from embracing his religion? Cut off his neck". Then they [=the guarding soldiers] brought him [=the grand man] forward and cut off his neck. Thereafter, he [=the Emperor] called his

483 Ḥudhayfa b. ʿAmr is listed neither in Ibn Saʿd, al-Bukhārī, Ibn ʿAsākir nor in any other biographical work we could access. In al-Azdī's narrative, he is mentioned as a Christian Arab from Tanūkh who went to Heraclius, reporting defeat in the Battle of al-Yarmūk to him.

companions for departure, returning to Constantinople. When he got out of Syria and was close to the land of the Byzantines, he turned his face towards Syria\\346 and said: "O Syria, peace be upon you! [This is] a [farewell] greeting from a departing person (*muwaddi'*) who realises that he will never return to you again". Then he [=the Emperor] headed towards his land, looked at it and said: "Woe betide a land like you, how beneficial to your enemy you are, because of the pasture, fertility and good [inherent] in you!"

Al-Ḥusayn b. Ziyād [al-Ramlī] related to us on the authority of Abū Ismā'īl [Muḥammad b. 'Abdallāh al-Azdī], who said: Furthermore, 'Amr b. 'Abd al-Raḥmān related to me: When he [=Heraclius] departed from Antioch, he proceeded until he stayed in Edessa[484], which he left for Constantinople. Meanwhile, Khālid embarked on pursuing the Byzantines until he entered the land of Qinnasrīn. When he reached Aleppo, the people of Aleppo fortified [their place] against him. Abū 'Ubayda also arrived [near Aleppo] and descended on them [=the people of Aleppo]. Thus, they solicited peace and a letter of protection from the Muslims. Abū 'Ubayda accepted [that request] from them, made peace with them and wrote them a letter of protection.

The story of al-Ashtar [=Mālik b. al-Ḥārith al-Nakha'ī] and Maysara b. Masrūq [al-'Absī]

Al-Ḥusayn b. Ziyād [al-Ramlī] reported to us on the authority of Abū Ismā'īl Muḥammad b. 'Abdallāh [al-Azdī], who said: Furthermore, al-Ḥasan b. 'Ubaydallāh[485] related to me: [One day,] al-Ashtar said to Abū 'Ubayda: "Dispatch a cavalry unit with me [as commander] so that I [can] pursue the people's [=the Byzantines'] tracks and head towards their land, because I have [sufficient] competence and performance". Thereupon, Abū 'Ubayda said to him: "I swear by God that you are\\347 entitled to [receive] all that is good". So he [=Abū 'Ubayda] dispatched him [=al-Ashtar] in command of 300 horsemen [to the north] and said to him: "Do not go [too] far in pursuit [of the Byzantines] and stay close to me". Then al-Ashtar marched out [of the Muslims' encampment] and proceeded to launch raids [on them] at a distance of one day's, two days' march or so from him [=Abū 'Ubayda]. Then Abū 'Ubayda summoned Maysara b. Masrūq [al-'Absī] and dispatched him [to the north, too,] in command of 2,000 horsemen. He [=Maysara] passed by

484 Edessa (*al-Ruhā*) is located in eastern Anatolia, ca. 250 km northeast of Aleppo and ca. 160 km north of Raqqa. In al-Azdī's narrative, Edessa is mentioned only once as part of Heraclius's departure route from Antioch via Edessa to Constantinople. On Edessa, see *EI*^{2}, s.v. al-Ruhā (E. Honigmann/C. Bosworth et al.).

485 Al-Ḥasan's full name is Abū 'Alī al-Ḥasan b. 'Ubaydallāh b. Aḥmad b. 'Abdallāh al-Azdī. On the basis of al-Dhahabī's *Siyar*, 'Uqla and Banī Yāsīn, however, identify him as al-Ḥasan b. 'Ubaydallāh b. 'Urwa al-Nakha'ī al-Kūfī (d. 139/756), who was a trustworthy transmitter (see al-Azdī, *Futūḥ al-Shām. Ed. 'Uqla/Banī Yāsīn*, 346, n. 4 referring to al-Dhahabī, *Siyar a'lām al-nubalā'*, VI, 144–145 [no. 55]). In al-Azdī's narrative, he is also mentioned as a transmitter of one tradition. On al-Ḥasan, see Ibn 'Asākir, *TMD*, XIII, 129.

Qinnasrīn, started looking at it on a mountain and said: "What is this?" Thereupon, he was told its name in Greek (*rūmiyya*). He [=Maysara] then said: "It is just as [you said] and I swear by God that it looks like an eagle's coop (*qinnu nasrin*)". Then he pursued the people [=the Byzantines] until he traversed the mountainous passes [into Anatolia]. [When] al-Ashtar learned that he [=Maysara] had traversed the mountainous passes [leading into Anatolia], he headed towards him until he caught up with him. Lo and behold, Maysara [b. Masrūq al-ʿAbsī] was standing [in formation to fight] against a group of the Byzantines that were many [more than his unit]. Maysara was in command of 2,000 Muslim horsemen while those [Byzantines] were more than 30,000. Thus, he [=Maysara] became worried about those [companions] who were with him and feared that he and his companions might be annihilated. While they were in this [situation], al-Ashtar, in command of 300 horsemen from al-Nakhaʿ, appeared before them. When Maysara's companions saw them, they proclaimed "God is the Greatest!" and so did al-Ashtar and his companions. [Then] al-Ashtar [=Mālik b. al-Ḥārith al-Nakhaʿī] launched an attack upon them [=the Byzantines] from his position and so did Maysara [from his side] until they put them [=the Byzantines] to flight. They [=the Byzantines] jostled, one [against] the other, and thus they [=the Muslims] vanquished them. They [=the Byzantines] rushed headlong [into disaster] and the Muslim cavalry pursued them, killing them until they [=the Byzantines] reached an elevated place. They [=the Byzantines] ascended it [=the place] and some of their infantrymen came down to the Muslims' cavalry and pelted them [with arrows]. When the Byzantine infantrymen pelted them [with arrows], the Muslims stopped and said to one another: "Leave them [alone], for they are defeated". [Thus,] the Byzantines started going their own ways and one of their grand men moved ahead with a large number of their infantrymen. Then they began pelting the Muslim cavalry[men] [with arrows again] from an[other] elevated place. He [=the narrator, al-Ḥasan b. ʿUbaydallāh] said: The Muslims' cavalry was [still] standing [in formation to fight] against them when a red[-skinned], giant and stout man from among the Byzantines dismounted [from his horse] and intercepted the Muslims so that one of them would go out to [duel with] him. He [=the narrator, al-Ḥasan b. ʿUbaydallāh] said: I swear by God that none of them went out to [fight] him. At last, al-Ashtar said to them: "None of you will go out to [face] this\\348 infidel?" Thereupon, nobody uttered a word. He [=the narrator, al-Ḥasan b. ʿUbaydallāh] said: Then al-Ashtar dismounted [from his horse] and went out to [duel with] him. Each of them walked towards the other. Al-Ashtar was wearing a coat of mail and a helmet and so was the Byzantine [man]. When they both drew near to each other, al-Ashtar assaulted him and they both tussled with their swords. Then the Byzantine [man]'s sword fell down on al-Ashtar's head, thus cutting the helmet and rushing down into his head until it was about to stick into the bone. Al-Ashtar's strike, in contrast, fell on the Byzantine [man]'s shoulder, but his sword did not cut anything of the Byzantine['s armour]. He [=al-Ashtar] had only struck him so hard that he had weakened him and overburdened his shoulder. Then they both separated from each other. When al-Ashtar saw that his sword had done nothing [to him], he turned away, walked [back] the way he was looking until he reached the line[s] [of the Muslims] with blood running down his beard and face. [There] he said: "May God shame this sword". His companions [quickly] went to him, so he said [to them]: "I need some henna". They immediately brought it to him and he [=al-Ashtar] put it on his wound, then wrapped it with a piece of cloth. Then he moved his jawbones, snapped his molars together and then said: "How hard my jawbones, my head and my molars are!" Then he [=al-Ashtar] said to his cousin: "Hold my sword and give me yours". Thereupon, he [=the cousin] said to him: "Leave my sword to me, may God have mercy upon you, because, I do not know, I may need it". He [=al-Ashtar] then said to him: "Give it to me and Umm al-Nuʿmān[486]—i.e. his [=al-Ashtar's] daughter—is yours". He [=the narrator, al-Ḥasan b. ʿUbaydallāh] said: So he [=the cousin] gave it to him. Then he [=al-Ashtar] moved to return to the Byzantine [man], so his people said to him: "We implore you for God's sake to confront this infidel". Thereupon, he [=al-Ashtar] said: "I swear by God to march out to [fight] him and either he kills me or I kill him". Then they left him and he moved out to [continue duelling with] him.\\349 When al-Ashtar drew near to him [=the Byzantine man], he [=al-Ashtar] assaulted him wrathfully. They both tussled [again] with their swords and al-Ashtar struck him on his shoulder, thus cutting what was on it [=the armour] until the sword stuck [deep] into his lung. The Byzantine [man]'s strike, in contrast, fell on al-Ashtar's shoulder, thus cutting the coat of mail but then stopped without doing any harm to him. The Byzantine, however, fell dead and the Muslims proclaimed "God is the Greatest!" They then launched an attack upon the line[s] of the Byzantines' infantry, which started splitting [up] and pelting the Muslims [with arrows] from above. They remained in this [situation] until the evening [came] and the night separated them. When the evening fell upon them, the caller of [Maysara b. Masrūq] al-ʿAbsī called for prayers. When he [=the caller] announced [the prayers], Maysara b. Masrūq al-ʿAbsī stepped forward and led his companions in prayer[s]. Al-Ashtar also moved to the front [position] of his companions and led them in prayer[s]. When he [=al-Ashtar] started leaving [after the prayers], Qanān b. Dārim al-ʿAbsī[487] went to him and said: "O leader (*ṣāḥib*) of this cavalry [unit], what prevented you from coming to and praying with the commander Maysara b. Masrūq al-ʿAbsī?"

486 Umm al-Nuʿmān bt. Mālik b. al-Ḥārith al-Nakhaʿī is listed neither in Ibn Saʿd, al-Bukhārī, Ibn ʿAsākir nor in any other biographical work we could access. In al-Azdī's narrative, she is mentioned as being gifted by al-Ashtar Mālik b. al-Ḥārith to his cousin in return for a sword that the former needed to duel with a Byzantine.

487 Qanān b. Dārim al-ʿAbsī is an early Islamic figure. In al-Azdī's narrative, he is depicted as blaming al-Ashtar Mālik b. al-Ḥārith for not praying with the commander Maysara b. Masrūq al-ʿAbsī and as pretending not to know who al-Nakhaʿ tribe was. On Qanān, see Ibn Ḥajar, *Al-iṣāba. Ed. al-Baghawī*, VI, 284 (no. 8393).

Thereupon, al-Ashtar said: "Who is Maysara b. Masrūq?" He [=Qanān b. Dārim al-ʿAbsī] said: "[He is] Maysara b. Masrūq al-ʿAbsī". Thereupon, al-Ashtar said [to him]: "What is ʿAbs[488] and who are Banū ʿAbs[489]?" He [=Qanān b. Dārim al-ʿAbsī] said: "Glory be to God, you do not know what ʿAbs is and who Banū ʿAbs are?" Al-Ashtar then said: "No, I swear by God that I do not know [that]". Then [Qanān b. Dārim] al-ʿAbsī said to him: "Who are you then?" He [=al-Ashtar] said: "I am Mālik b. al-Ḥārith". He [=Qanān b. Dārim al-ʿAbsī] said: "Which [tribe] are you from?" He [=al-Ashtar] said: "From al-Nakhaʿ". [Thereupon, Qanān b. Dārim] al-ʿAbsī said: "I swear by God that I have never heard of al-Nakhaʿ before".\\350 Thus, some of al-Ashtar's companions became angry. So al-Ashtar said to his companions: "What made you angry? As for me, I swear by God that I did not lie and I think [that] this man was honest[, too]". Then al-Ashtar said [to Maysara b. Masrūq al-ʿAbsī]: "O servant of God, what prevented me from praying with you is that I was appointed as commander of this cavalry [unit] and nobody else was appointed as my commander nor was I ordered to obey anybody else. So I am not willing to accept as my commander [a person] whom I was not ordered to obey, nor should [a person] who was not ordered to obey me wish to be my commander. Therefore, after I perform the early morning prayer[s], I will leave [you], God (t.) willing". They [=al-Ashtar and Maysara] spent the whole night guarding one another. When they rose in the morning and he [=al-Ashtar] performed the early morning prayer[s], al-Ashtar left with his companions. Maysara [b. Masrūq al-ʿAbsī] also left [and marched] until he reached Marj al-Qabāʾil[490], which was located in the region of Antioch and al-Maṣṣīṣa[491]. Then he turned back [to Syria].

488 ʿAbs b. Baghīḍ is the alleged ancestor of Banū ʿAbs. He is alluded to in al-Azdī's narrative. On ʿAbs, see Caskel, *Ǧamharat*, I, 92; II, 135–136.

489 Banū ʿAbs is a Northern Arabian tribe that was a subtribe of Ghaṭafān. In al-Azdī's narrative, Banū ʿAbs is mentioned as the tribe of Maysara b. Masrūq. In addition, three individual figures belonged to Banū ʿAbs: (a) Maysara b. Masrūq al-ʿAbsī, a major figure, who is depicted as fighting heroically and commanding a military unit in several battles, who was also the head of two exploratory units up north, one to Aleppo and the other to Qinnasrīn and the mountainous region north of the city, but who was ordered to come back twice by Abū ʿUbayda; (b) Dārim al-ʿAbsī who was a messenger sent by Abū Bakr to Abū ʿUbayda; and (c) Qanān b. Dārim al-ʿAbsī, his son, who was a messenger from Maysara to al-Ashtar. On Banū ʿAbs, see *EI*[2], s.v. Ghaṭafān (J. Fück).

490 Marj al-Qabāʾil is listed neither in Yāqūt's geographical dictionary nor in any other geographical work we could access. However, it is mentioned in the *Futūḥ al-Shām* ascribed to al-Wāqidī as the place of a raid in a mountainous region (*ghazwat Marj al-Qabāʾil dākhil al-durūb*). In addition, it is called a "wide plain" (*marj wāsiʿ*). In his *Bughyat al-ṭalab*, Ibn al-ʿAdīm describes Marj al-Qabāʾil as lying between Antioch and al-Maṣṣīṣa. These citations show the close connection between al-Azdī's narrative, Ibn al-ʿAdīm's work (at least this passage) and the one ascribed to al-Wāqidī, since al-Azdī also locates Marj al-Qabāʾil in the regions of Antioch and al-Maṣṣīṣa. On Marj al-Qabāʾil, see al-Wāqidī, *Futūḥ al-Shām*, II, 3–4, 9 and Ibn al-ʿAdīm, *Bughyat al-ṭalab*, 571, l. 23.

491 Al-Maṣṣīṣa is a town in Cilicia on the western bank of the Jayḥān, located ca. 30 km east of Adana. In al-Azdī's narrative, al-Maṣṣīṣa is mentioned in the context of Maysara

When Abū ʿUbayda learned that they [=al-Ashtar and Maysara b. Masrūq al-ʿAbsī] took [separate] ways [into Anatolia], he pitied them and became extremely worried, regretting having sent them in pursuit of the Byzantines. He [=the narrator] said: While he [=Abū ʿUbayda] was seated among his companions, deeming their [=al-Ashtar's and Maysara's] arrival [back to him too] slow and regretting having dispatched them, [someone] came and heralded good news [to him] about al-Ashtar's arrival. Al-Ashtar came to him and informed him of the situation they had [faced], their confrontation with that [Byzantine] army unit, their [=the Muslims'] triumph over them [=the Byzantines] and what God had done for them [=the Muslims]. However, he did not mention his duel with the Byzantine [man] he had killed until someone else informed him [=Abū ʿUbayda] [about it]. [Then] he [=Abū ʿUbayda] asked him [=al-Ashtar] about Maysara b. Masrūq [al-ʿAbsī] and his companions. Thus, he told him about the direction in which he [=Maysara] had headed. He also told him that only pity for his [own] companions and [fear] of defeat, after the triumph they had gained, had stopped him [=al-Ashtar] from [allowing] his companions to join him [=Maysara b. Masrūq al-ʿAbsī]. Thereupon, he [=Abū ʿUbayda] said [to him]: "You have done the right thing and I do not wish you were with them right now, but I wish they were [here] with you".\\351 He [=the narrator] said: Then he [=Abū ʿUbayda] summoned some of the people of Aleppo and said [to them]: "Fetch me a guide who is acquainted with the route[s] [into the Byzantine territory] and offer him a reward, provided that he should track this [man's] [=Maysara b. Masrūq al-ʿAbsī's] cavalry [unit], which we dispatched in pursuit of the Byzantines [into that direction]. He should pursue them [=the cavalrymen] until he catches up with them, and should then order them to come [back] to me the moment he meets them". He [=Abū ʿUbayda] waited only for a short while until they [=the people of Aleppo] brought three guides to him and said: "These [guides] are acquainted with the route [into the Byzantine territory], dare [to take] it fearlessly and [can] guide [people] along it [very well]. They are going to march out in pursuit of your cavalry[men] until they convey your order to them". He [=the narrator] said: Then Abū ʿUbayda wrote [the following letter] to Maysara [b. Masrūq al-ʿAbsī]:

Regarding the matter at hand: When my messenger reaches you and you see my letter, come [back] to me [immediately] and do not stop for anything, because the safety of one Muslim man is dearer to me than all the Polytheists' possessions. Peace be upon you.

They [=the guides] took his letter, then marched out [of the encampment] with it until they met him [=Maysara b. Masrūq al-ʿAbsī] after he had come down from the mountainous passes and after God had shielded, protected

b. Masrūq's advance to the Byzantine territory and for the purpose of locating Marj al-Qabāʾil. On al-Maṣṣīṣa, see *EI*[2], s.v. al-Maṣṣīṣa (E. Honigmann).

and saved him and his companions. They [=the guides] then delivered Abū ʿUbayda's letter to him. When he [=Maysara] read it, he said: "May God reward such a commander of the Muslims with [what is] good. What a sympathetic [man] and what a [good] advisor he is!" His [=Abū ʿUbayda's] messengers who had headed towards him [=Maysara b. Masrūq al-ʿAbsī] proceeded until they reached Abū ʿUbayda [again] and heralded good news to him about their [=the Muslims'] safety and about their departure [back to him]. Then he [=Abū ʿUbayda] praised God for that and remained [where he was situated] until Maysara b. Masrūq [al-ʿAbsī] reached him. [Thereafter,] he [=Abū ʿUbayda] wrote a letter of protection to the people of Qinnasrīn and then ordered his caller to announce departure to Jerusalem [and he did so].\\352

He [=Abū ʿUbayda] positioned Khālid b. al-Walīd ahead of his [=Abū ʿUbayda's] vanguard in front of him and continued marching until he [=Abū ʿUbayda] reached Ḥimṣ. Then he [=Abū ʿUbayda] dispatched Ḥabīb b. Maslama al-Qurashī [to the city of] Ḥimṣ to [take] command [of it]. The land of Qinnasrīn was [also] placed at that time under [the rule of] the commander of Ḥimṣ and was [thus] called "Ḥimṣ al-Jund al-Muqaddam" because it was closer to the Byzantines than to [the land of] Damascus, [the lands of the] River Jordan and Palestine, all of which were [to the] south of (*warāʾ*) it. Then he [=Abū ʿUbayda] marched out of Ḥimṣ and passed by Damascus, over which he appointed Saʿīd b. Zayd b. ʿAmr b. Nufayl as commander. Then he [=Abū ʿUbayda] moved out [of Damascus] until he passed by the River Jordan, where he took up quarters and encamped. He dispatched messengers to the people of Jerusalem and said [to them] [=the people of Jerusalem]: "Come out to [meet] me so that I can write you a letter of protection [to safeguard] your lives and your possessions. We will maintain [our pact] with you as we have done with the others [in Syria]". However, they slackened [their reply] and refused [the offer in the end]. He [=the narrator] said: Then Abū ʿUbayda wrote [the following letter] to them:

In the name of God, the Merciful, the Compassionate. From Abū ʿUbayda b. al-Jarrāḥ to the patricians of the people of Jerusalem and [to] its [=Jerusalem's] inhabitants. Peace be upon whoever follows the [true] guidance and believes in God the Great and in His Messenger. Regarding the matter at hand: We call upon you to testify that there is no other deity but God, that Muḥammad is His servant and Messenger, that the [last] Hour is undoubtedly coming and that God will resurrect those who are in the graves. If you testify to [all of] this, we will be prohibited from [shedding] your blood and [taking] your possessions and you will become our brethren in terms of religion. But if you refuse [to testify to this], confirm to us that you will give tribute by hand and with humility. If you [also] refuse [to do that], I will advance on\\353 you with people whose love for death is stronger than yours for life, for drinking wine and for eating pork. [In this case] I will not leave you, God willing, until I kill your fighters and capture your offspring.

Abū ʿUbayda b. al-Jarrāḥ's letter to ʿUmar b. al-Khaṭṭāb (r.) [which he wrote] when God (ʿa.) made him triumphant over the people of al-Yarmūk

He [=the narrator] said: He [=Abū ʿUbayda] wrote [the following letter] to the Commander of the Believers, ʿUmar b. al-Khaṭṭāb (r.), when God made him [=Abū ʿUbayda] triumphant over the people of al-Yarmūk and [when] he marched out in pursuit of them [=the Byzantines]:

In the name of God, the Merciful, the Compassionate. From Abū ʿUbayda b. al-Jarrāḥ to the servant of God, ʿUmar, the Commander of the Believers. Peace be upon you. I praise, on your behalf, God with whom no other deity is associated. Regarding the matter at hand: Praise be to God who destroyed the Polytheists, who rendered the Muslims victorious and who had taken care of their [=the Muslims'] cause in earlier times, had demonstrated their success and had strengthened their call. Blessed be God, the Lord of the worlds. I [hereby] inform the Commander of the Believers, may God honour him, that we faced the Byzantines [who fought] in large numbers, the likes of which had never been faced by the Arabs before. They came [to us] thinking that none of the people would defeat them.\\354 Then they fought a fierce battle against the Muslims, the like of which had never been fought against the Muslims before. But God granted patience to the Muslims and [eventually] bestowed victory upon them. God killed them [=the Byzantines] in every hamlet, on every defile, in every valley, on every mountain and on every plain. The Muslims pillaged their [=the Byzantines'] encampment and took as spoils their possessions and baggage [which were] therein. Then the Muslims and I pursued them until I reached the farthest parts of the lands of Syria. I dispatched my subordinates to the people of Syria. I also sent [messengers] to the people of Jerusalem, calling them [=the people of Jerusalem] to [embrace] Islam. If they agree[, things will be fine]. If not, they have to bring us tribute by hand and with humility. However, if they [also] refuse [this], I will march to them and descend on them. Then I will not leave them until God leads the Muslims to conquest, God willing. Peace be upon you.

ʿUmar b. al-Khaṭṭāb's letter to Abū ʿUbayda b. al-Jarrāḥ (r.), [which is] the reply to his [=Abū ʿUbayda's] letter to him [=ʿUmar]

Then ʿUmar wrote [the following letter] to him [=Abū ʿUbayda]:

From the servant of God, ʿUmar, the Commander of the Believers, to Abū ʿUbayda b. al-Jarrāḥ. Peace be upon you. I praise, on your behalf, God with whom no other deity is associated. Regarding the matter at hand: Your letter came to me and I understood what you mentioned therein about God's destruction of the Polytheists, His support for the Believers and [the favours] He did to His close friends and obedient people. So praise God for His good deed[s] for us, ask Him to complete that [=His good deeds] by thanking Him. Then know that you triumphed over your enemy neither by means of [large] number[s] nor by means of [good] equipment, neither with power nor\\355 with strength, but only with God's help, support, blessing[s] and favour[s]. Might, blessing and great favour belong to God [alone]. Blessed be God, the best Creator, and praise be to God, the Lord of the worlds. Peace [be upon you].

The story of the peace-making [process] with the people of Jerusalem and of 'Umar's (r.) coming to Syria

He [=the narrator] said: Then Abū 'Ubayda waited for the people of Jerusalem [to reply] but they refused to go to him and make peace with him. So he marched towards them until he set up camp near them, besieged them tightly and hemmed them in from all sides. Then they marched out to him one day and fought the Muslims for a while. The Muslims assaulted them later from every direction and [also] fought them for a while. Finally, they [=the people of Jerusalem] were defeated and they [=the Muslims] entered into their fortress. Those who were ordered to fight them were Khālid b. al-Walīd and Yazīd b. Abī Sufyān, each of them on one side [of the city]. Sa'īd b. Zayd [b. 'Amr b. Nufayl] learned of this [=the fight against the people of Jerusalem] while he was in command of Damascus. So he wrote [the following letter] to Abū 'Ubayda (r.):

In the name of God, the Merciful, the Compassionate. From Sa'īd b. Zayd [b. 'Amr b. Nufayl] to Abū 'Ubayda b. al-Jarrāḥ. Peace be upon you. I praise, on your behalf, God with whom no other deity is associated. Regarding the matter at hand: I swear upon my life that I do not prefer you or your companions to me when it comes to fighting for the cause of God and [when it comes to] that which brings me closer to the satisfaction of my Lord ('a.).\\356 Thus, when my letter comes to you, dispatch to your district [of Damascus] whoever is more desirous of [governing] it than I; then he shall govern it for you the way you wish. For I [want to] come to you very soon, God willing. Peace be upon you.

He [=the narrator] said: When [t]his letter reached Abū 'Ubayda, he said: "I testify that he [=Sa'īd b. Zayd b. 'Amr b. Nufayl] certainly [wants to] do it". He [=Abū 'Ubayda] then said to Yazīd b. Abī Sufyān: "Be sufficient to me for [governing the district of] Damascus". Thereafter, he [=Abū 'Ubayda] sent him [=Yazīd] [out] to it [=the district of Damascus]. So Yazīd marched to it and took command of it.

The story of the owner of the two leaves

He [=the narrator] said: Among the Muslims was a man from Banū Numayr called Mukhaymis b. Ḥābis b. Mu'āwiya[492]. He was a brave horseman

492 Mukhaymis's full name is Mukhaymis b. Ḥābis b. Mu'āwiya al-Numayrī (n.d.). In al-Azdī's narrative, he is mentioned as a horseman from Banū Numayr. He disappeared for some days until he was thought to be dead. Then he re-appeared, holding two leaves from

known for [his] righteousness among the people. [Once] his companions had not seen him for some days. Thus, they went searching for him and asking about him, but they were not told anything about him. When they despaired of [finding] him, they thought that he had perished and that he had been assassinated. One day, while they were sitting [together], he appeared [again] and came to them. They became extremely happy about his [return]. He [=the narrator] said: Lo and behold, there were two leaves [of a tree] in his hand. The people [=the Muslims] had never seen greener, wider, longer, better-looking or better-smelling [leaves] than these two. [On his return] his companions said to him: "Where have you been?" [Thereupon,] he said:\\357 "I fell into a well and walked within it until I reached a planted garden which had everything in it. My eyes have never seen the likes of what was therein in any other place [before] and I do not think that God (ʿa.) has ever created any other [garden] similar to it. I stayed there all those days on which you did not see me, in an incomparable bliss, in an unparalleled view and in so pleasant a smell that nobody has ever found a more pleasant smell than it [before]. While I was in this [situation], someone came to me, took my hand and led me out of it [=the garden] to you. Beforehand I had taken these two leaves from a tree under which I was sitting. [Although I left the garden,] the two leaves remained in my hand". So the people [=the Muslims] came and took them [=the two leaves] [in their hands], smelled them and found in them a very pleasant smell that they had never found in anything else before. Thus, the people of Syria claimed [later] that he [=Mukhaymis b. Ḥābis b. Muʿāwiya] had been admitted into Paradise and those [two] leaves were [presents] from Paradise. They also said: "The successors [to the caliphate] deposited the two leaves in the [Muslims'] treasury".

He [=the narrator] said: When Abū ʿUbayda besieged the people of Jerusalem and they realised that he would not leave them and thought that they were powerless against fighting him, they said to him: "We [want to] make peace with you". [Thereupon,] he [=Abū ʿUbayda] said: "I accept peace from you". [Then] they said: "But send [a letter] to your caliph ʿUmar so that he becomes the one who issues us a pact, makes peace with us and writes us a letter of protection". Abū ʿUbayda accepted that [request] from them and started writing [a letter to ʿUmar].\\358

[Sometime earlier,] Abū ʿUbayda had dispatched Muʿādh b. Jabal [to be] in command of [the land of] the River Jordan. Seldom had Muʿādh [b. Jabal] left Abū ʿUbayda because of his desire to fight for the cause of God. Seldom had Abū ʿUbayda decided on a matter without [hearing] Muʿādh [b. Jabal]'s opinion. But he sent for Muʿādh [to return]. When Muʿādh [b. Jabal] reached him, he [=Abū ʿUbayda] informed him of what the people [of Jerusalem]

a garden that he had discovered. His fellow Muslims thought that he had been let into Paradise and that he obtained the two leaves from there. On Mukhaymis, see Ibn Ḥajar, *Al-iṣāba. Ed. al-Baghawī*, VI, 282 (no. 8383).

solicited from him. So Mu'ādh [b. Jabal] said to him: "You should write to the Commander of the Believers and ask him to come to you. Perhaps he will come to you, but then those [people might] refuse to make peace [with him]. Thus, his march will have been a burden rather than a favour [for him]. Therefore, do not write to him until you get confirmation from those [people] and have them swear solemn oaths that if you ask the Commander of the Believers to come to them, and if you write him about this [matter] and he consequently comes to them, grants them a letter of protection and writes them a peace treaty, they should [definitely] accept that and make peace with him [in return]". So Abū 'Ubayda urged them [=the people of Jerusalem] to swear solemn oaths [in this regard]. So they swore oaths that if 'Umar, the Commander of the Believers, came to them, descended upon them, granted them a letter of protection to [safeguard] their lives and possessions and wrote them a document in this respect, they would certainly accept that, bring tribute [to the Muslims] and enter into what the people of Syria had entered into. After they had done so, Abū 'Ubayda wrote [the following letter] to 'Umar (r.), the Commander of the Believers:\\359

In the name of God, the Merciful, the Compassionate. From Abū 'Ubayda b. al-Jarrāḥ to the servant of God, 'Umar, the Commander of the Believers. Peace be upon you. I praise, on your behalf, God with whom no other deity is associated. Regarding the matter at hand: We surrounded Jerusalem and they [=its inhabitants] thought that they would find relief and hope in temporisation. Because of it [=the temporisation] God only increased [their] distress, need, weakness and misery. When they realised this, they asked us to give them what they had previously been reluctant and averse to [ask]. In fact, they also solicited peace from us, provided that the Commander of the Believers should come to them to be the guarantor of their protection and the writer of their letter [of protection]. However, we feared that you, Commander of the Believers, would come [to us] and then the people [of Jerusalem] would betray [us] and renege [their promise]. Consequently, your march, may God increase your righteousness, would be a burden rather than a favour [for you]. Thus, we pressed them into agreements solemnised by their oaths that if you came to them and granted them protection for their lives and their possessions, they would certainly accept that, bring tribute [to the Muslims] and enter into what the protected people had entered into. They did [so] and we had them swear oaths concerning that. Therefore, if you, Commander of the Believers, decide that [it is suitable] for you to come to us, do it. For there will be a reward, a benefit and safety (*'āfiya*) for the Muslims in your march. May God show you guidance and simplify your cause. Peace be upon you.

When his [=Abū 'Ubayda's] letter reached 'Umar (r.), he gathered the Muslim chiefs around him, read out to them Abū 'Ubayda's letter [which was sent] to him and consulted them about what Abū 'Ubayda had written to him. Thereupon, 'Uthmān b. 'Affān said to him:\\360 "May God increase your righteousness. God ('a.) humiliated them [=the people of Jerusalem], besieged them, hemmed them in, showed them what He did to their groups and their sovereigns, killed whom He killed from among their leaders and led the Muslims to conquer some of their lands. Thus, every day they have been getting weaker, more miserly (*azalan*)—he [=the narrator] said: And *al-azal* means "hard life"—more humiliated, needier, more distressed and more coerced. If you [decide now to] stay and not [to] march to them, they will know that you deem them and their cause unimportant and that you undervalue, not overvalue, their cause. Consequently, they [=the people of Jerusalem] would remain [stable] only for a little while until they [either] resign from [their] reign or give tribute by hand and with humility. Apart from that, [if you stay] the Muslims would besiege them [further] and hem them in until they [finally] give [tribute] with their own hands". Thereupon, ʿUmar said: "What are your opinions? Does any of you [all] have another opinion?" Thereupon, ʿAlī b. Abī Ṭālib (r.) said: "Yes, Commander of the Believers, I have another opinion". He [=ʿUmar] said: "What is it?" He [=ʿAlī] [then] said: "O Commander of the Believers, they [=the people of Jerusalem] asked you for something (*manzila*) which brings on their humiliation and humbleness, but which is [at the same time] a triumph (*fatḥ*) and an honour for the Muslims. They are offering [this] to you now in a swift and peaceful manner. The only [obstacle] between you and [the realisation of] that [issue] is that you just go to them. [In addition,] Commander of the Believers, there will be a reward for you in [return for] your going to them, [for undergoing] all the thirst and all the hunger, for traversing every valley, every pass and every defile and for every cost you will spend until you go to them, God willing.\\361 If you depart to them, there will be security and safety as well as peace and conquest because of your departure to them. You cannot also be sure that, if they despair of your acceptance of peace [requested by them] and of your departure to them, they will keep to their fortresses and perhaps reinforcements from [the side of] our enemy will come to them and join them in their fortresses. Thus, warfare and fighting for the cause of God against them will cause the Muslims [additional] calamity and hardship and will result in the prolongation of their siege. The Muslims will stand [firm] against them and, consequently, a form of exhaustion and hunger will befall them. Perhaps the Muslims will also draw near to their fortresses, so they [=the people of Jerusalem] will pelt them with arrows or throw stones at them. If any of the Muslim men were killed [in this attack], you would wish you could ransom [this] Muslim man with your march to Maqṭaʿ al-Turāb[493]. Indeed, the [killed] Muslim man would deserve that [march] from his brethren". Thereupon, ʿUmar (r.) said: "ʿUthmān [advised us] well regarding the stratagem of the enemy [in Jerusalem] while ʿAlī [advised us] well regarding the consideration for the adherents of Islam". Then he [=ʿUmar] said: "March [out]

493 Maqṭaʿ al-Turāb (lit. "the Intersection of Dusty [Roads]") is neither listed in Yāqūt's geographical dictionary nor in any other geographical work we could access. In al-Azdī's narrative, Maqṭaʿ al-Turāb is mentioned in a speech by ʿAlī, in which ʿUmar is obliged to go to this place to achieve peace.

in the name of God, because I am [also] encamping and marching [out]". The people's [=the Muslims'] noblemen, the Arabs' respected households, the Emigrants and the Supporters marched out with him. ʿUmar also took al-ʿAbbās b. ʿAbd al-Muṭṭalib[494] out with him.

Al-Ḥusayn b. Ziyād [al-Ramlī] reported to us on the authority of Abū Ismāʿīl Muḥammad b. ʿAbdallāh [al-Azdī], who said: Furthermore, ʿAbd al-Malik b. Nawfal [b. Masāḥiq al-Qurashī] related to me on the authority of Abū Saʿīd al-Maqburī: During his march [to Syria], ʿUmar (r.) used to\\362 sit with his companions as soon as he [had finished] performing the early morning prayer[s], turning his face and then saying to them: "Praise be to God who strengthened us with Islam, honoured us with faith and honoured us with Muḥammad (ṣ.), by virtue of whom He guided us away from error, united us after separation, reconciled our hearts, rendered us victorious over the enemies, granted us control over the lands and bonded us together as mutually loving brethren. Therefore, servants of God, praise God for these blessings. Ask Him [for] more [blessings], [ask him] to [enable you to] thank Him for them and [ask him] to complete these blessings in which you are wallowing. For God certainly increases [one's] desire for Him and completes His blessing[s] upon the thankful". He [=the narrator] said: ʿUmar did not stop [repeating] this statement every morning on his [way] back and forth [to the place of prayers].\\363

ʿUmar's (r.) speech in al-Jābiya

Al-Ḥusayn b. Ziyād [al-Ramlī] reported to us on the authority of Abū Ismāʿīl Muḥammad b. ʿAbdallāh [al-Azdī], who said: Furthermore, ʿAṭāʾ b. ʿAjlān[495] related to me on the authority of Abū Naḍra[496] on the authority of Abū Saʿīd al-Khudrī: ʿUmar moved towards his destination until he reached al-Jābiya. Then he rose [and stood] before the people and said: "Praise be to God, the Ever-Praiseworthy, who is praised for [His] protection, the Ever-Glorious, the Ever-Forgiving and the Ever-Loving. Whichever servant He wants to

494 Al-ʿAbbās's full name is Abū al-Faḍl al-ʿAbbās b. ʿAbd al-Muṭṭalib b. Hāshim b. ʿAbd Manāf (d. 32/653). In al-Azdī's narrative, al-ʿAbbās is mentioned once as having accompanied ʿUmar on his way to Jerusalem. On al-ʿAbbās, see *EI*², s.v. al-ʿAbbās b. ʿAbd al-Muṭṭālib (W. Watt).

495 ʿAṭāʾ's full name is Abū Muḥammad ʿAṭāʾ b. ʿAjlān al-Baṣrī al-ʿAṭṭār (n.d.). Mourad mentions his date of death as "d. ca. 135/752" (see Mourad, *al-Azdī*, 591). In al-Azdī's narrative, he is presented as a transmitter of three traditions. On ʿAṭāʾ, see al-Bukhārī, *Al-taʾrīkh al-kabīr*, III-2, 476 (no. 3034).

496 Abū Naḍra could not be identified because only his patronymic (*kunya*), not his full name, is mentioned by al-Azdī. ʿUqla and Banī Yāsīn identify him as Abū Naḍra al-Mundhir b. Mālik al-Kūfī (d. 108/727) on the basis of al-Dhahabī's *Taʾrīkh al-islām* (see al-Azdī, *Futūḥ al-Shām. Ed. ʿUqla/Banī Yāsīn*, 363, n. 3 referring to al-Dhahabī, *Taʾrīkh al-islām*, vol. 101–120 H., 301 (no. 305). In al-Azdī's narrative, he is presented as a transmitter of one tradition.

guide becomes rightly guided. 'But you will find no protector to lead to the right path those He leaves to stray'".[497] He [=the narrator] said: Lo and behold, in his [='Umar's] place [at that time] was one of the Christians' priests, dressed in a wool jubba.[498] He [=the narrator] said: When 'Umar (r.) had said: "Whichever servant God [wants to] guide becomes rightly guided", the Christian said [in return]: "I testify [to that]". He [=the narrator] said: When 'Umar (r.) had said: "But you will find no protector to lead to the right path those He leaves to stray", he [=the narrator] said: The Christian pulled his jubba off his chest and then said [in return]: "God forbid! God does not lead astray whoever wants guidance [from Him]". Thereupon, 'Umar (r.) said: "What did God's enemy, this Christian, say?" They [=the Muslims] said: "He said: 'God [always] guides rightly and leads nobody astray'". 'Umar then raised his voice and resumed his speech, repeating his former statement, and so did the Christian [repeat his retort] as before. So 'Umar (r.) got angry and said: "I swear by God that if\\364 he repeats it [=his statement] [again], I will certainly cut off his neck". He [=the narrator] said: The infidel understood it and fell silent. He [=the narrator] said: Then 'Umar (r.) resumed his speech and said: "Whoever God guides has no misguider and whoever God misguides has no guider". He [=the narrator] said: Then the Christian kept quiet. Thereafter, he [='Umar] said: "Regarding the matter at hand: I heard the Messenger of God (ṣ.) say: 'The best of my people are those who will follow you [=Muḥammad's companions], then those who will follow them. Then falsehood will spread until one will bear witness although he will not be asked for it and swear an oath although he will not be asked for it[, either]. Whoever wants the ease of Paradise must adhere to the [main] group [of Muslims] (*jamā'a*) and pay no attention to those who have deviated. Verily, if a man and a woman get alone together, except that he is her unmarriageable relative (*maḥram*), their third [company] is Satan'".

He [=the narrator] said: Then he [='Umar] left al-Jābiya for Jerusalem. So the Muslims [there] went out to welcome him. Abū 'Ubayda marched out with all the people [=the Muslims] to him and drove out a workhorse for him to ride. 'Umar (r.) came [to Jerusalem] [sitting] on his camel [that was equipped] with a saddle and a yearling ram-leathered cover (*ṣuffa*)[499]. [This way] he reached a ford (*makhāḍa*). They [=the Muslims] came [forward], rushing towards him, but he said to the Muslims: "[Stay] in your places". Then 'Umar (r.) dismounted from his camel and seized his camel's leash,

497 Q. 18:17 (*The Qur'ān. Tr. Abdel Haleem*, 184).

498 A jubba is a kind of outer garment the exact size and length of which varies from one region to another. On this term and the diverse meanings, see Lane, *Lexicon*, s.v. *jubba* and Dozy, *Vêtements*, s.v. *jubba*. Dozy draws the attention to several *ḥadīths* according to which a wollen jubba is worn during raids (see ibid., 107).

499 A "*ṣuffa*" is "an appurtenance of a horse's saddle [...] a thing with which it is covered, between the *qarabūsān*, which are its fore and hinder parts". On this term, see Lane, *Lexicon*, s.v. *ṣuffa*.

which was made of fibre. He [=ʿUmar] then walked through the water ahead of his camel until\\365 he passed the water [and reached] Abū ʿUbayda's companions. Lo and behold, there was a workhorse with them, which they had put aside [from the spoils]. They said: "O Commander of the Believers, ride this workhorse, because it is more suitable and easier for you to ride [than a camel]. In addition, we do not like the protected people to see you in such shape as we are seeing you [now]". They [=Abū ʿUbayda's companions] [also] welcomed him with white clothes. ʿUmar (r.) dismounted [again] from his camel, rode the workhorse but left the clothes [untouched]. However, when the workhorse ambled with him, he dismounted from it and said [to the Muslims]: "Take this [horse] away from me, for this is a devil and I fear that he will change my heart". [Then] they [=the Muslims] said: "O Commander of the Believers, if you wear these white clothes and ride this workhorse, it will be more manly, more memorable and better for fighting for the cause of God". Thereupon, ʿUmar (r.) said to them: "Woe unto you, do not seek honour in something other than that which God has honoured you with; [otherwise,] you will be humiliated in consequence". Then he [continued] marching together with the Muslims until he reached Jerusalem and set up camp there. Some of the Muslim men including Abū al-Aʿwar al-Sulamī came to him [=ʿUmar] after they had worn the Byzantines' clothes and [thus] resembled them in visage. [To this] ʿUmar (r.) said: "Throw dust at their [=the Muslim men's] faces until they return to our visage, our customs (*sunna*) and our clothes". They [=other Muslims] [also] had displayed [clothes made of various] sorts of silk brocade. [Regarding them,] he [=ʿUmar] gave an order to rip them [=the clothes] off them [and it was done]. Thereupon, Yazīd b. Abī Sufyān said to him: "O Commander of the Believers, our pack-and-riding animals and clothes are many, our living is decent, our prices are low and the Muslims' situation is as you like it [to be]. So if you wear some of these white clothes, ride any of these vigorous animals and provide the Muslims with some of this abundant food, it will make [your] reputation more widespread, your appearance nicer and your [standing] greater among the non-Arabs (*aʿājim*)".\\366 Thereupon, he [=ʿUmar] said to him: "No, Yazīd. I swear by God that I will not give up the visage I had when I left my companion[s]; I will not get dressed for the sake of the people [here] in a way which, I fear, will disgrace me in the eyes of my Lord. Nor do I want my cause to greaten in the eyes of the people, but lessen in the eyes of God". ʿUmar (r.) never changed the original visage he had had during the life of the Messenger of God (ṣ.) and the life of Abū Bakr until he departed this life.

He [=the narrator] said: When ʿUmar (r.) had set up camp with the people [=the Muslims] who were at Jerusalem and he had reassured the people [of their cause], Abū ʿUbayda dispatched [the following message] to the people of Jerusalem: "Descend to the Commander of the Believers and enter into an agreement [with him] for [the benefit of] yourselves". Thus, Ibn al-Juʿayd and a number of their [=the people of Jerusalem's] grand men descended to him, so ʿUmar (r.) wrote them a letter of protection and peace. When they [=Ibn al-Juʿayd and the grand men] took hold of their letter and they were granted protection, all the people [=the Muslims, Ibn al-Juʿayd and the grand men] mingled with one another.

[Then] Abū ʿUbayda appointed ʿAmr b. al-ʿĀṣ as the commander of Palestine. ʿUmar stayed [in Jerusalem] for some days [during which] ʿAmr b. al-ʿĀṣ said to him: "O Commander of the Believers, the people of these lands bring us a juice which they press [from some fruits] and cook before it ferments. They bring it in a sweet state as if it was an inspissated juice (*rubb*) that they cook until two thirds of it evaporates and one third remains. [Are we allowed to drink it?]" Thereupon, ʿUmar said to them [=the people of the region]: "How do you prepare it?" Then he looked at him [=ʿAmr b. al-ʿĀṣ] and said: "I think there is nothing wrong with it". They [=the people of the region] said: "We press it [from some fruits] and then take it before it ferments and cook it until two thirds of it evaporates and one third remains". Thereupon,\\367 ʿUmar (r.) said: "[Hence,] the illicit parts (*ḥarām*) of it evaporate while the licit part (*ḥalāl*) of it remains". Then he [=ʿUmar] said [to ʿAmr]: "O ʿAmr, drink it, for there is nothing wrong with it". He [=ʿUmar] also said [about the drink]: "[It looks] as if it were the camels' tar (*ṭilāʾ al-ibil*)" and thus it was called "the Tar (*al-ṭilāʾ*)" on that day. He [=the narrator] said: Thereafter, ʿUmar (r.) wrote [the following letter] about it [=the drink] to ʿAmmār b. Yāsir[500]:

Regarding the matter at hand: I went down to the land of Syria and they [=the people near Jerusalem] brought me one of their drinks. I asked them about it: "How do you prepare it?" They told me that they cook it until two thirds of it evaporate and one third of it remains, that is, when its foam (*rubya*), alcoholic vapour (*rīḥ junūn*) and what is illicit in it evaporate, but what is licit and good thereof remains. Hence, order those Muslims who are there with you to use it as one of their drinks. Peace [be upon you].

He [=the narrator] said: All the commanders of the districts requested a visit from ʿUmar (r.), for whom each [of them] made preparations and who was asked [by each of them] for a visit to his dwelling (*raḥl*). ʿUmar acquiesced [to that] in honour of them. He visited them [all] except Abū ʿUbayda, who did not request a visit from him. So ʿUmar (r.) said to him: "All the commanders of the districts requested a visit from me except you". Thereupon, Abū ʿUbayda said: "O Commander of the Believers, I feared that if I requested a visit from you, you would squeeze your eyes [with tears] in my tent (*bayt*)". He [=ʿUmar] said: "Despite this, invite me to visit [you]". He [=Abū ʿUbayda] said: "Then [come and] visit me". He

500 ʿAmmār's full name is Abū al-Yaqẓān ʿAmmār b. Yāsir b. ʿĀmir b. Mālik b. Qaḥṭān al-ʿAnsī (d. 37/657–658). In al-Azdī's narrative, he is mentioned as receiving a letter from ʿUmar who recommended to him the drink that was introduced to him by the people of Jerusalem after ʿUmar had made sure of its legitimacy. On ʿAmmār, see Ibn ʿAsākir, *TMD*, XXXXIII, 348–435.

[=the narrator] said: 'Umar went to him in his tent, in which there was nothing except the felted mat (*labad*) of his horse, which, lo and behold, was his [sleeping] mattress, his saddle and his cushion.\\368 And lo and behold, there were dry chunks [of bread] in an aperture in his tent. He [=Abū 'Ubayda] fetched them and put them on the ground in front of him [='Umar]. He also fetched him [='Umar] grounded salt and a pottery tankard of water. When 'Umar saw this, he wept. Then he [='Umar] drew him [=Abū 'Ubayda] close to him and said: "You are my brother and all of my companions receive something from this worldly life and it [=the worldly life] in turn gets something back from them, except you". Thereupon, Abū 'Ubayda said to him [='Umar]: "Did I not tell you that you would squeeze your eyes [with tears] in my tent?"

He [=the narrator] said: Then 'Umar (r.) rose [and stood] before the people, praised and thanked God for what He is worth, blessed and saluted the Prophet (ṣ.) [and] then said: "O adherents of Islam, God fulfilled the promise [given] to you, made you victorious over the enemies, bequeathed the[ir] lands to you and gave you power over the land. So show only thankfulness to your Lord in return. Take care not to commit sins, for the commission of sins is a denial of the blessings. Hardly had people shown ingratitude for what God had bestowed upon them, not resorting to repentance later, when they were stripped of their might and their enemy was given authority over them". Then he [='Umar] descended [from the speech platform] and the prayer[s] were due. So 'Umar said: "O Bilāl, will you not call us to prayer; may God have mercy upon you?" Thereupon, Bilāl said: "O Commander of the Believers, I swear by God that I had decided not to call for prayer[s] for the sake of anyone else after [the death of] the Messenger of God (ṣ.), but I will obey you today if you order me to [call for] these prayer[s] only". When Bilāl [then] called for prayer[s] and the companions heard his voice, they remembered their Prophet (ṣ.) and hence they wept bitterly. On that day, none of the Muslims wept longer than Abū 'Ubayda b. al-Jarrāḥ and Mu'ādh b. Jabal (r.). [They wept] until 'Umar (r.) said to them both: "Enough [with weeping], you both; may God have mercy upon you". When 'Umar (r.) finished his prayer[s], Bilāl rose, [went] to him and said: "O Commander of the Believers, I swear by God that the commanders of your districts in Syria eat nothing but bird meat and fine bread, which [none of] the common Muslims can find". So 'Umar (r.) said to them [=the commanders]: "[Is] what \\369 Bilāl said true?" Thereupon, Yazīd b. Abī Sufyān said to him: "O Commander of the Believers, the prices in our lands are low and we obtain here what Bilāl has just mentioned for the same [amount of money] we spent on nourishing our dependents in al-Ḥijāz". 'Umar (r.) then said: "Nay, I swear by God not to leave this place (*'arṣa*) until you guarantee to me [the provision of] monthly livelihoods to [all] the Muslims". Then he [='Umar] said: "Consider how much a man needs to be sated [per day] and what suffices him every day!" They [=the commanders] said to him: "Such and such [an amount per day]". Thereupon, he [='Umar] said: "How much is that per month?" They said: "Two *jarībs*[501] [of grain] in addition to an appropriate [amount] of\\370 oil and vinegar at the beginning of each crescent moon [=monthly]". Finally, they [=the commanders] guaranteed to him [the provision of] this [amount of food]. Then he [='Umar] said: "O Muslims, this is for you in addition to your grants (*uʿṭiyāt*). If what I have imposed on your commanders for you is fulfilled and given to you every month, this is what I like [to happen]. However, if they do not do it, inform me in order that I depose them from [commanding] you and put others in command of your cause". He [=the narrator] said: This [regulation] remained in practice for a long period of time until some evil commanders cut it off and deprived them [of it].

The story of Kaʿb al-Ḥabr's [conversion to] Islam (r.); may God rest him

Al-Ḥusayn b. Ziyād [al-Ramlī] reported to us on the authority of Abū Ismāʿīl Muḥammad b. ʿAbdallāh [al-Azdī], who said: Furthermore, ʿAṭāʾ b. ʿAjlān related to me on the authority of Shahr b. Ḥawshab[502]: Kaʿb al-Ḥabr's[503] [conversion to] Islam took place when ʿUmar (r.) reached Syria. He [=Kaʿb b. al-Ḥabr] reported to me [the details of] how it took place and how his situation was [at that time].

He [=the narrator, Shahr b. Ḥawshab] said: Kaʿb al-Ḥabr's father was one of the adherents of the Torah who believed in the Messenger of God (ṣ.) and [at the same time] was one of their scholars and rabbis. Kaʿb [b. al-Ḥabr] said: "He was also one of the people who were most knowledgeable about what\\371 God had revealed in the Torah to Moses[504] and about the Prophets' scriptures. And he hid none of what he knew from me. That was before the sending (*mabʿath*) of the Prophet (ṣ.). When he [=the father] was

501 "*Jarīb*" is a particular measure of corn, such as wheat, whose quantity differs from one region to another and thus sometimes weighs 10,000 or 3,600 cubits. On this term, see Lane, *Lexicon*, s.v. *jarīb*.

502 Shahr's full name is Abū ʿAbd al-Raḥmān Shahr b. Ḥawshab al-Ashʿarī (d. between 98–118/716–737). In al-Azdī's narrative, he is mentioned as a transmitter of several traditions. On Shahr, see Ibn Saʿd, *Kitāb al-ṭabaqāt*, VII-2, 158.

503 Kaʿb's full name is Abū Isḥāq Kaʿb b. Mātiʿ b. Haysuʿ (or Haynūʿ) al-Ḥabr. He is the famous early Islamic figure of Jewish origin who embraced the new faith, probably in 17/638. "Al-Ḥabr" (or "al-Aḥbār" as he is more often called) is the Arabic rendering of "*ḥāber*" (Hebr.), a Babylonian title for Jewish scholars. In al-Azdī's narrative, he is depicted in a story that recounts how Kaʿb embraced the new faith. His father told him about two hidden sheets in which the sending of the Prophet Muḥammad was mentioned. Thanks to these two sheets, Kaʿb embraced the new faith at the hands of ʿUmar, who was in Syria at that time. In addition, Kaʿb functioned as transmitter of several traditions in the narrative. On Kaʿb, see *EI*², s.v. Kaʿb al-Aḥbār (M. Schmitz).

504 Moses (Mūsā b. ʿImrān) is the famous biblical and qurʾānic figure. In al-Azdī's narrative, Moses is mentioned twice as having received the Torah from God. On Moses in the Islamic context, see *EI*², s.v. Mūsā (B. Heller/D. Macdonald); on Moses in the biblical context, see *RGG4*, s.v. Mose (E. Otto/W. Kraus et al.)

at death's door, he summoned me and said: 'O my son, you know that I would not hide from you anything that I know. However, I concealed two sheets [of paper] from you, in which the sending of a prophet is mentioned and his time is imminent. I disliked to inform you about this, because I had the fear that, after my death, one of those [known] liars would emerge and you would follow him and tear them [=the two sheets] from your scripture. Thus, I put both of them into this aperture which you see [over there] and coated them with clay [to seal the aperture]. Do not touch them or view them nowadays, but leave them in their place until that Prophet (ṣ.) emerges. When he emerges, follow him and have a look at them [=the two sheets], for God will certainly bestow [many] more good [things] upon you by [doing all] this'". Kaʿb [b. al-Ḥabr] said: "When my father died, nothing was dearer to me than the [swift] completion of the funeral ceremony so that I [could] look at what was [written] on the two sheets. [Immediately after] the funeral ceremony had ended, I opened the aperture and took out the two sheets. Lo and behold, [the following] was written thereon:

Muḥammad [is] the Messenger of God (ṣ.), the Seal of the Prophets. [There will be] no [other] Prophet after him. His birth is in Mecca and his emigration is to Ṭayba [=Medina][505]. He is neither rude, harsh nor vociferant[506] in the markets. He does not repay evil for evil, but repays good for evil. He forgives, pardons and remits [sins]. His community are the constant praisers (*ḥammādūn*), who praise God for all glories and in all situations, whose tongues are smoothened by [proclaiming] "God is the Greatest!", whose Prophet (ṣ.) is supported by God against all those who oppose him, who wash their orifices (*furūj*) with water, wear loincloth[s] (*izār*) around their waists and [learn] their holy scriptures (*anājīl*) by heart, who eat their Eucharists in their stomachs and are rewarded for [eating] them and whose mutual mercy among one another\\372 is like the mutual mercy among children of the [same] parents. They [=the community members] are the first to enter Paradise on the Day of Resurrection and the first to be brought close (*al-sābiqūn al-muqarrabūn*) [to God], the intercessors and the interceded-for (*al-shāfiʿūn wa-al-mushaffaʿ lahum*)'.

He [=Kaʿb] said: "When I read this, I thought to myself: 'I swear by God that my father did not teach me anything better than this'. I remained with it [=the knowledge] as long as God wanted and I waited, after [the death of] my father, until the [foretold] Prophet (ṣ.) was sent [out by God]. The lands between us [=Kaʿb and the Prophet] were so distant and separate [from each other] that I could not go to him". He [=Kaʿb] said: ["One day,] I learned

505 On the identification of Ṭayba as Medina, see the prophetical tradition mentioned in al-Balādhurī's *Futūḥ al-buldān* (*Ed. de Goeje*, 11, l. 13–15 and *Tr. Hitti/F. Murgotten*, 26); for another tradition, see also al-Hamadhānī's *Kitāb al-buldān*, 23, l. 2.

506 This is read as "*ṣakhkhāb*" instead of "*sakhkhāb*", because *ṣād* and *sīn* are said to be used interchangeably in words with *khāʾ* as a second radical. On this term, see Lane, *Lexicon*, s.v. *sakhaba*.

that the Prophet (ṣ.) had emerged in Mecca and that he would appear [to humankind] one time and disappear at another. So I said [to myself]: 'He is the one', yet I was fearful of the liars about whom my father had warned and alarmed me. So I started seeking to ascertain and find out [the truth about the Prophet]". He [=Kaʿb] said: "I remained with that [attitude] until I learned that he [=the Prophet] had gone to Medina. Then I thought to myself: 'I wish that he is the one [I have read about]'. Later I was [also] informed of his episodes (*waqāʾiʿ*) [that were] in his favour sometimes and against him sometimes. I then started to seek out the way to him, but I was not destined [to meet him] until I learned later that he (ṣ.) had died. [At this point] I thought to myself: 'Perhaps he is not the one whom I thought [to be]'. Then I learned that a successor (*khalīfa*) had taken his place and only a little [while] passed before his [=the successor's] soldiers came to us [to Syria]. [Now] I thought to myself: 'I will not embrace this religion until I know that they [=the soldiers] are those whom I was anticipating and awaiting. I will observe their conduct, their deeds and the consequence [of their acts]'". He [=Kaʿb] said: "Hence, I kept refraining from and delaying [any further actions] in order to ascertain [the truth about these people] and find [evidence for this issue] until ʿUmar b. al-Khaṭṭāb (r.) came to us [to Jerusalem?]. When I saw the Muslims' prayer[s], fasting, piety, fulfilment of the pact and what\\373 God has arranged for them against the[ir] enemies, I knew that they were those whom I was waiting for. So I thought of embracing Islam [at that time]". He [=Kaʿb] said: "I swear by God that I was on my roof one night and, lo and behold, one of the Muslim men was praying and reciting God's scripture [=the Qurʾān] until he came to [the following] verse, raising his voice: 'People of the Book, believe in what We have sent down to confirm what you already have before We wipe out [your sense of] direction, turning you back, or reject you, as We rejected those who broke the Sabbath: God's will is always done'".[507] He [=Kaʿb] said: "When I heard this verse, I swear by God that I feared that I would not awaken in the morning and that my face would take the place of my nape [=fear of death]. So nothing was dearer to me than [awakening in] the morning. When the morning came, I went to ʿUmar (r.) and [finally] converted to Islam".

Al-Ḥusayn b. Ziyād [al-Ramlī] related to us on the authority of Abū Ismāʿīl Muḥammad b. ʿAbdallāh [al-Azdī], who said: Furthermore, ʿAṭāʾ [b. ʿAjlān] related to me on the authority of Shahr b. Ḥawshab on the authority of Kaʿb [b. al-Ḥabr], who said: I said to ʿUmar (r.) as he was departing from Syria: "O Commander of the Believers, in the scripture of God (t.) it is written that these lands which were inhabited by the Israelites[508] would be conquered for

507 Q. 4:47 (*The Qurʾān. Tr. Abdel Haleem*, 55).

508 Israelites (*Banū Isrāʾīl*, lit. "the Sons (or Children) of Israel") is the qurʾānic designation of the Jewish people. In al-Azdī's narrative, Israelites is used twice: (a) to refer to the lands of Syria as a region that was inhabited by the Israelites (according to "the scripture of God") and (b) in a reference to the punishments (e.g. plague, flood, locusts, lice, frogs

one of the righteous men who is merciful towards the Believers and tough on the Unbelievers, whose privacy (*sirr*) is like his public appearance, whose public appearance is like his privacy, whose words do not\\374 contradict his actions, in whose eyes the close and the distant are equal in terms of rights and whose followers are monks by night and lions by day, show mercy to one another, contact one another and sacrifice themselves for one another". Thereupon, ʿUmar (r.) said to him [=Kaʿb]: "May your mother be bereft of you, is what you have just said right?" He [=Kaʿb] said: "Yes, I swear by the One who revealed the Torah to Moses and who hears what I am saying, it is absolutely right". ʿUmar, God rest his soul, [then] said: "Praise be to God, who strengthened, dignified, honoured and showed mercy to us by virtue of Muḥammad (ṣ.) and by virtue of His own mercy that encompasses everything". He [=the narrator, Shahr b. Ḥawshab] said: Kaʿb [b. al-Ḥabr] was one of the Yemenite Arabs who belonged to Ḥimyar.\\375

ʿUmar b. al-Khaṭṭāb's return [to Medina]

Then ʿUmar marched out of Syria, heading towards Medina.

Al-Ḥusayn b. Ziyād [al-Ramlī] reported to us on the authority of Abū Ismāʿīl [Muḥammad b. ʿAbdallāh al-Azdī], who said: ʿAmr b. Mālik [al-Qaynī] related to me, saying: ʿUmar (r.) proceeded towards Medina and passed by one of the watering places of Judhām, which was governed by a group from among them called Ḥadas[509]. The watering place was called Dhāt al-Manār. He [=ʿUmar] was informed about a man, at the watering place, who was [living] with two sisters. ʿUmar (r.) sent for him, so he was brought [to ʿUmar]. Then he [=ʿUmar] said to him [=the man]: "Who are these two women [living] with you?" He [=the man] said: "My wives". [Thereupon,] he [=ʿUmar] said: "What is the relationship between the two of them?" He [=the man] said: "They are sisters". ʿUmar (r.) [then] said to him: "What is your religion? Are you not a Muslim?" He [=the man] said: "Yes[, I am]". He [ʿUmar] said: "Did you not know that this is illicit for you [to do]?" He [=the man] said: "No, I swear by God I did not know that and is it [really] not licit for me [to do it]?" Then ʿUmar (r.) said to him: "You liar, I swear by God that it is illicit for you [to do] and either you let one of them go or I will certainly behead you. I swear by God that if I had known that you had married them while you knew that it is illicit in our religion, I would surely have beheaded you before uttering a word [about the issue] to you". Thereupon, he [=the man] said to him: "O ʿUmar, are you serious?" He [=ʿU-

---

and blood) which God inflicted on the Israelites when they were in Egypt, a reference which relates intertextually to the Old Testament (2 Moses 7–11). On the Israelites, see EI^2, s.v. Banū Isrāʾīl (S. Goitein).

509 Ḥadas is a Southern Arabian tribe and a subtribe of Lakhm. In al-Azdī's narrative, however, Ḥadas is mentioned once as a subtribe of Judhām that was in charge of the watering place called Dhāt al-Manār. On Ḥadas, see Caskel, *Ǧamharat*, I, 290; II, 247.

mar] said: "Yes, I swear by God with whom no other deity is associated that I am certainly serious about what you have heard; either you let\\376 one of them go or I will surely behead you". Thereupon, he [=the man] said: "May God deform this religion. I swear by God that I have gained nothing good from it". Thereupon, ʿUmar (r.) said: "Draw him near to me", so they drew him near to him. He [=ʿUmar] struck him some blows over his head with the whip (*dirra*) and then said to him: "O enemy of God, do you insult God's religion that He has chosen for His angels, His messengers and the best of His creatures?" Then he [=ʿUmar] released him and said to him: "Let one of them [=the wives] go". Thereupon, the man said: "How to make a choice between the two of them?" ʿUmar (r.) said: "Cast lots between both of them". He [=the man] then said: "Both of them are equally dear [to me] and honourable". Then they [=the Muslims] cast lots between both of them and he retained the one upon whom the lots were drawn. He [=ʿUmar] then said to him: "Stay away from the other [woman]". Then ʿUmar (r.) summoned him and said to him: "Listen to what I say!" He [=the man] said: "Say whatever you like". [Thereupon,] he [=ʿUmar] said: "We would certainly kill whoever embraced Islam and converted to our religion but abandoned it later on. So take care not to relinquish Islam and be aware that if I should hear that you are back to [your improper] relationship with the sister of your wife, with whom you [just] broke, or that you drew near to her after I had cast lots between both of them, I will [definitely] stone you".

Al-Ḥusayn b. Ziyād [al-Ramlī] related to us on the authority of Abū Ismāʿīl [Muḥammad b. ʿAbdallāh al-Azdī], who said: Furthermore, Hishām b. ʿUrwa [b. al-Zubayr[510]] related to me on the authority of his father [=ʿUrwa b. al-Zubayr[511]], who said: When ʿUmar (r.) returned from Syria to Medina, he passed by [some] people who were forced to stand in the sun and over whose heads oil was being poured. Thus, he [=ʿUmar] said: "What about these [people]?" They [=local tax officers] said: "[They are] the people on whom the tax has been imposed, but they have withheld it. So they are tormented for that until they bring the tax imposed on them [to us]".\\377 Thereupon, ʿUmar (r.) said: "What do they [=the taxpayers] say [regarding the payment]?" They [=local tax officers] said: "They say: 'We do not find anything to give'". ʿUmar (r.) then said: "Leave them [=the taxpayers] [alone] and do not burden them with what they cannot give or what they cannot afford. For I heard the Messenger of God (ṣ.) say: 'Do not torment people, for those who torment people in the [worldly] life will be tormented by God

510 Hishām's full name is Abū al-Mundhir Hishām b. ʿUrwa b. al-Zubayr b. al-ʿAwwām (146/763–764). In al-Azdī's narrative, he is mentioned as a transmitter of traditions. On Hishām, see Ibn Saʿd, *Kitāb al-ṭabaqāt*, VII-2, 67.

511 ʿUrwa's full name is Abū ʿAbdallāh ʿUrwa b. al-Zubayr b. al-ʿAwwām al-Qurashī al-Asadī (d. between 93–94/711–713). In al-Azdī's narrative, ʿUrwa is mentioned in an *isnād* as a transmitter of traditions to his son Hishām on ʿUmar's return from Jerusalem to Medina. On ʿUrwa, see *EI*^{2}, s.v. ʿUrwa b. al-Zubayr (G. Schoeler).

on the Day of Resurrection'". Then he [='Umar] sent [a messenger] to them [=the taxpayers], freed them, threatened the one who did this to them and ordered him not to go back [to them]. Then he [='Umar] headed for Medina.

Al-Ḥusayn b. Ziyād [al-Ramlī] related to us on the authority of Abū Ismā'īl [Muḥammad b. 'Abdallāh al-Azdī], who said: Furthermore, al-Mujālid b. Sa'īd al-Hamdānī related to me on the authority of 'Āmir al-Sha'bī: 'Umar (r.) proceeded [towards Medina] and when he reached Wādī al-Qurā, he set up camp near some people [living there]. Then he was informed that an old man at the watering [place] had a wife and that a young man had come to him [=the old man] and said to him: "Do you agree to share your wife with me and [in return] I will suffice to shepherd, water and goad your camels? She would be mine for a whole day (*yawm wa-layla*) and yours for [another] whole day". Thereupon, the old man said to him [=the young man]: "Yes, I do [agree to this]". Thus, they were both [living] like that [when 'Umar came to the place]. Then 'Umar (r.) sent for them. They came to him and he asked them, saying: "What is your religion?" Thereupon, they [=the old and the young men] said: "[We are] Muslims". 'Umar (r.) [then] said: "What is that which I have learned about you?" They said: "What is it?" Then 'Umar informed them [of it] and they did not deny it. Thereafter, 'Umar (r.) said to them: "Do you not know that this is illicit according to the Islamic religion and that it should not be done?" Thereupon, they said: "Nay, we swear by God that we did not know [this]". Then 'Umar (r.) said to the old man: "Woe unto you, what prompted you to carry out this shameful act that, to my knowledge, neither a righteous man nor [even] a debauchee has ever done [before]?" Thereupon, he [=the old man] said to him: "I am an\\378 old man and I have become weak. I have no son on whom I can rely and on whom I can depend. [Thus,] I thought [to myself]: 'This is a man who is able to shepherd and water [the camels] whereas I am too weak to do so nowadays. He suffices [to spare me] the burden [of shepherding them]'. As for your telling me that this is illicit, I will completely refrain from it [henceforth]". Then 'Umar (r.) said to him: "O old man, take your wife's hand, for she is your own wife and nobody else should have access to her". Thereafter, he [='Umar] said to the young man: "As for you, take care that I should not hear that you dispute with them over any of the watering [places]. For, if I learn that you are in dispute with them over any of the watering [places], I swear by God to behead you". [Thereupon,] he [=the young man] said: "I will do [as you wish]". He [=the narrator] said: Those people were Jews by descent.

Then 'Umar (r.) proceeded towards Medina [until he reached it]. The people [of Medina] welcomed and congratulated him on the victory and the conquest [of Jerusalem]. Then he came [forward] and entered the Mosque of the Messenger of God (ṣ.), where he performed two acts of prayer near the pulpit. Then he ascended the pulpit and the people [=the Muslims] flocked to him. He then rose, praised and thanked God, blessed and saluted the Prophet (ṣ.) and said: "O people, God has decreed a commandment for this community to praise and thank Him. So He strengthened their call, unified their word (*kalima*), manifested their triumph, made them victorious over the enemies, honoured them, gave them power over the land and bequeathed the Polytheists' lands, dwellings and possessions to them. So express [your] thanks to God\\379 so that He shall give you more, and praise Him for His blessings upon you so that He shall continue them for you. May God cause us and you to join the grateful". Then he [=ʿUmar] descended [from the pulpit].

[The aftermath of the conquest of Jerusalem]

Abū ʿUbayda's death; God rest his soul

He [=the narrator] said: The Muslims stayed in Syria under the command of Abū ʿUbayda b. al-Jarrāḥ. He [=Abū ʿUbayda] stayed there for three [more] years after ʿUmar (r.) had marched out of it [=Syria]. Then he [=Abū ʿUbayda] died, God rest him, of the plague of al-ʿAmwās[512], which had befallen the people of Syria and of which many people had died. He [=the narrator] said: When Abū ʿUbayda was afflicted with the plague in [the lands of] the River Jordan, where his grave [still] exists, he summoned the Muslims. When they came into [his dwelling] to [see] him, he [=Abū ʿUbayda] said [to them]: "I am making a recommendation to you. If you accept it, you will stay in good [conditions] as long as you live and after you perish: Perform the prayer[s], pay the prescribed tax, fast, give alms, perform the [major] pilgrimage (*ḥajj*) and the minor pilgrimage (*ʿumra*), keep in contact with one another, love one another, be truthful to your commanders, do not deceive them and do not be obsessed with the worldly life. [Even] if a person's life was prolonged for 1,000 years, it would not be possible for him to escape from the [imminent] death which I [have reached] as you [can] see. God has prescribed death to the children of Adam. So they will [all] die. However, the cleverest of them is the one who is the most obedient to his Lord and the keenest on doing [good deeds in preparation] for his Doomsday (*yawm al-maʿād*)". Thereafter, he [=Abū ʿUbayda] said: "O Muʿādh, lead the people in prayer[s]". So Muʿādh [b. Jabal]\\380 led the people in prayer[s] and [then] Abū ʿUbayda died; may God's mercy, forgiveness and satisfaction be upon him as well as upon all the companions of the Messenger of God (ṣ.). Thereafter, Muʿādh b. Jabal rose [and stood] before the people [=the Muslims] and said: "O people, show God sincere repentance for your sins. For if a servant meets God (ʿa.) repenting his sin, God is obliged to forgive him his sins. Whoever is in debt must repay it, for a servant is bound by his debt. Whichever of you has broken with a Muslim must meet him [again], be reconciled with him when

512 Al-ʿAmwās was a small town located ca. 30 km west of Jerusalem. In al-Azdī's narrative, al-ʿAmwās is mentioned in the context of the so-called plague of al-ʿAmwās, of which the two Muslim commanders Abū ʿUbayda and Muʿādh b. Jabal died. On al-ʿAmwās, see *EI*[2], s.v. ʿAmwās (J. Sourdel-Thomine).

he meets him and shake hands with him. This is because a Muslim should not desert his Muslim brother for more than three days. That would be a heinous thing to do in the eyes of God (t.). O Muslims, you mourn for a man [=Abū ʿUbayda] who, I swear by God, I claim to be the most youthful, the most warm-hearted, the farthest from calamity, the most advisory for the people, the most sympathetic and the most affectionate servant [of God] I have ever seen, compared with the [other] servants of God. So ask God to [bestow] mercy upon him and come to perform the [funeral] prayer[s] on his [=Abū ʿUbayda's] behalf. May God forgive him the sins he committed earlier and [those] he committed later. I swear by God that you will never have a commander like him after his [death]". Then the people [=the Muslims] assembled and Abū ʿUbayda was taken out [of his dwelling]. Muʿādh [b. Jabal] moved ahead [of the funeral procession] and performed the [funeral] prayer[s] on his [=Abū ʿUbayda's] behalf. When he [=Muʿādh b. Jabal] took him to his grave, he, ʿAmr b. al-ʿĀṣ and al-Ḍaḥḥāk b. Qays entered his [=Abū ʿUbayda's] grave [all together]. After they had laid him in his grave, had got out of it and had thrown earth upon him, Muʿādh [b. Jabal] said: "God rest you, Abū ʿUbayda. I swear by God that\\381 I will certainly praise you with what I know. I swear by God that I will never speak falsely [about you], lest God cast [His] wrath upon me. I swear by God that you [=Abū ʿUbayda] were, as far as I know, one of those who invoke God very often, one of those who walked humbly on earth; one of those who used to say 'Peace [be upon you]' when the ignorant addressed them, one of those who spent the night prostrating and standing [in prayers performed] for their Lord and one of those who neither squandered nor gave niggardly, but maintained a just balance between [the two] when they spent [something]. I swear by God that you were, as far as I know, one of the humble and modest and one of those who had mercy upon the orphan and the poor and abhorred the rough and the arrogant". None of the people [=the Muslims] was more mournful for the loss and death of Abū ʿUbayda or more sorry for him than Muʿādh b. Jabal.

ʿAbd al-Raḥmān b. Muʿādh b. Jabal's (r.) death

He [=the narrator] said: [After that,] Muʿādh [b. Jabal] led the people [=the Muslims] in prayer[s] for some days. However, the plague became more severe and deaths increased among the people. When ʿAmr b. al-ʿĀṣ (r.) saw this, he said: "O people [=the Muslims], this plague is the punishment with which God had tortured the Israelites, in addition to the flood (*ṭūfān*), the locusts (*jarād*), the lice (*qummal*), the frogs and the [transformation of water into] blood". He [=ʿAmr b. al-ʿĀṣ] ordered the people to flee from it [=the plague]. Muʿādh [b. Jabal], however, was informed of ʿAmr [b. al-ʿĀṣ's] statement and said [to the Muslims]: "What made him [=ʿAmr b. al-ʿĀṣ] speak about something that he is not knowledgeable about?" Then Muʿādh [b. Jabal] came [forward] and ascended the pulpit, praised and thanked God for what He is worth, blessed and saluted the Prophet (ṣ.) and then mentioned the plague (*wabāʾ*), saying: "It [=the plague] is not as ʿAmr [b. al-ʿĀṣ] has described [it]. Rather, it is a mercy [sent to you] from your Lord,\\382 a prayer [for you] from your Prophet and [a means of] death of the righteous [people who lived] before you. O God, give Muʿādh and his household the largest share of it [=the plague]". Then he [=Muʿādh b. Jabal] prayed and returned to his house. Lo and behold, he found his son ʿAbd al-Raḥmān infected by the plague. When he [=ʿAbd al-Raḥmān b. Muʿādh b. Jabal] saw him [=Muʿādh b. Jabal], he said: "O father, 'this is the [sign of] truth from your Lord, so do not be one of those who doubt'".[513] [Thereupon,] he [=Muʿādh b. Jabal] said [to him]: "O my son, 'God willing, you will find me steadfast'".[514] Thereafter, he [=ʿAbd al-Raḥmān b. Muʿādh b. Jabal] stayed [alive] only a little while [longer] until he died, God (t.) rest him. Muʿādh [b. Jabal] performed the [funeral] prayer[s] on his behalf and then buried him, too. When Muʿādh [b. Jabal] returned to his house, he was [also] infected by the plague and his pain got worse [over time]. His companions [then] started visiting him frequently. He [=the narrator] said: When his companions went to him, he proceeded towards them and said: "Do [good] deeds while you are having a period of respite, a life [to live] and some remaining lifetime before you [reach the Day of Judgement], on which you would wish [to go back to life] to do a [good] deed, but [on which] you would find no way to do so. [Therefore,] spend from what you have [now] for what comes later, before you perish and leave all that as an inheritance to those who will come after you [depart]. Know that you would have none of your possessions except what you eat, drink, wear, spend, give and expend [for your daily life]. Anything other than that is [left] for [your] inheritors". He [=the narrator] said: When his [=Muʿādh b. Jabal's] pain got worse, he [=Muʿādh b. Jabal] kept saying: "O Lord, throttle me so hard that I witness [that] You know that I love you".\\383

Muʿādh b. Jabal's will; [may] God rest his soul and be pleased with him

He [=the narrator] said: [One day,] a man came to him [=Muʿādh b. Jabal] during his illness and said to him: "O Muʿādh, teach me something from which God will make me benefit before you leave me. Thereafter, neither will I see you nor will you see me [again], nor will I find anyone like you [later]. Then I may need to ask people about that which will benefit me after you [depart], but I will not find the likes of you among them [to teach me]". Thereupon, Muʿādh [b. Jabal] said [to him]: "Not at all, the righteous Muslims—praise be to God—are many and God will never forsake the adherents of this religion". Then he [=Muʿādh b. Jabal] said to him: "Take from

513 Q. 3:60 (*The Qurʾān. Tr. Abdel Haleem*, 39).
514 Q. 37:102 (*The Qurʾān. Tr. Abdel Haleem*, 287).

me [now] what I order you [to do]: Be one of those who fast during the day, one of those who pray in the middle of the night, one of those who ask [God] for forgiveness at the early dawn and one of those who invoke God very often [and] in any situation. Furthermore, do not drink wine, do not fornicate, do not disrespect your parents, do not devour the orphan's possession[s], do not flee from advancing [on your enemy], do not consume usurious interest (*ribā*), do not abandon the prescribed ritual prayer[s], do not neglect the prescribed tax, maintain ties of kinship, be merciful towards the Believers, do not oppress a Muslim, perform the [major] pilgrimage as well as the minor pilgrimage and fight for the cause of God. [Only] then will I support [your claim] to Paradise".

Al-Ḥusayn b. Ziyād [al-Ramlī] related to us on the authority of Abū Ismāʿīl [Muḥammad b. ʿAbdallāh al-Azdī], who said: Furthermore, Abū Janāb al-Kalbī[515] and al-Qāsim b. al-Walīd related to me, saying: When Muʿādh [b. Jabal] was at death's door, he said to his slave girl: "Woe unto you, look out, have we reached the morning yet?" She looked out and said: "Not yet". Then he left her for a while and then said to her: "Look out [again]". She looked out and said: "Yes[, we have reached it now]". Thereupon, he [=Muʿādh b. Jabal] said: "I seek refuge in God from a night whose morning [leads] to the Fire". He then said: "Welcome death, welcome [to] a visitor who came in [times of] need. Whoever regrets [not having done good deeds in this life] will be unsuccessful [in the afterlife]". Then he [=Muʿādh b. Jabal] said: "O God, you certainly know that I have never loved to stay in this world for the sake of [enjoying] the running rivers or the growing trees. Instead, I have ever loved to stay\\384 for the sake of enduring the long night and long hours of daytime, for the sake of bearing the midday thirst in the excruciating heat and for the sake of vying with religious scholars (*ʿulamāʾ*) to engage in the circles of invocation [of God] (*ḥalaq al-dhikr*)". When the moment of his [=Muʿādh b. Jabal's] death drew near, ʿAbdallāh b. al-Daylamī[516] approached him and said to him: "O Muʿādh, may God have mercy upon you. Perhaps we and you will never meet [again] at all". [Thereupon,] Muʿādh [b. Jabal] said [to his companions]: "Seat me", so they seated him, [with] a man sitting behind his back [to lean on]. Muʿādh [b. Jabal] rested his back on the man's chest and then said: "How evil this moment of deceit is!" He [=Muʿādh b. Jabal] also said: "The Messenger of God (ṣ.) told me a tradition which

515 Abū Janāb's full name is Abū Janāb Yaḥyā b. Abī Ḥayya al-Kalbī al-Kūfī (d. 147/764–765). On the basis of a manuscript of al-Dhahabī's *Tadhhīb al-tahdhīb al-kamāl*, Lees identifies him as Yaḥyā b. Abī Uḥayya al-Kalbī al-Kūfī and mentions that he died between 147 and 150 [=764–767] (see al-Azdī, *Futūḥ al-Shām. Ed. Lees*, 244, n. 2). In al-Azdī's narrative, he is mentioned as a transmitter of one tradition. On Abū Janāb, see Ibn Saʿd, *Kitāb al-ṭabaqāt*, VI, 250 and al-Mizzī, *Tahdhīb al-kamāl*, XXXI, 284–290 (no. 6817).

516 ʿAbdallāh b. al-Daylamī is listed neither in Ibn Saʿd, al-Bukhārī, Ibn ʿAsākir nor in any other biographical work we could access. In al-Azdī's narrative, he is said to have fought with Muʿādh b. Jabal and prayed for him when the latter was on deathbed, suffering terribly from al-ʿAmwās plague.

I hid from you lest you rely on it. But now I will not hide it from you [any longer]. I heard the Messenger of God (ṣ.) say: ‘God sends to Paradise and saves from the Fire only those servants of God (‘a.) who die while testifying that there is no [other] deity but God, the only God who has no [other divine] partner, that Muḥammad is His servant and Messenger, that the Hour is undoubtedly coming and [finally] that God will resurrect those [who are] in the graves, while believing in the Messengers and in the truth of what these had brought, and while believing in Paradise and the Fire’”. At that moment he [=Mu‘ādh b. Jabal] died; God rest him.

[Sometime earlier,] he [=Mu‘ādh b. Jabal] had appointed ‘Amr b. al-‘Āṣ as [his] successor. Thus, ‘Amr b. al-‘Āṣ performed the [funeral] prayer[s] on his [=Mu‘ādh b. Jabal's] behalf, entered [into] his grave and laid him in his resting place. Some of the Muslim men also entered [Mu‘ādh's grave] with him [=‘Amr b. al-‘Āṣ]. When ‘Amr [b. al-‘Āṣ] came out of his [=Mu‘ādh b. Jabal's] grave, he said: “O Mu‘ādh, God rest you, for you were, as far as we have known you, one of the Muslims' [sincere] advisors and one of\\385 their best and most outstanding [men]. Then you were educating the ignorant, tough on the corrupt and merciful towards the Believers. I swear by God that nobody like you will be appointed as successor after you”.

Mu‘ādh [b. Jabal's] appointment of ‘Amr b. al-‘Āṣ as successor; may God's mercy, forgiveness and satisfaction be upon both of them

Al-Ḥusayn b. Ziyād [al-Ramlī] related to us on the authority of Abū Ismā‘īl [Muḥammad b. ‘Abdallāh al-Azdī], who said: Furthermore, Abū Ma‘shar related to me: When Mu‘ādh [b. Jabal] was at death's door, he appointed ‘Amr b. al-‘Āṣ as successor [in command] of the people [=the Muslims] and all [lands] of Syria. His [=Mu‘ādh b. Jabal's] and Abū ‘Ubayda's deaths occurred during al-‘Amwās plague. Many people of them [=the Muslims] also died of it, God rest them. That was in [the year] 18 [=January 639-January 640]. The Battle of Ajnādayn was on Saturday, two nights before the end of Jumādā al-Ūlā, in 13 [=30 July 634]. Then the conquest of Damascus was on Sunday, 15 (*niṣf*) Rajab 14 [=3 September 635]. The Battle of Fiḥl was on Saturday, eight nights before the end of Dhū al-Qa‘da in 14 [=9 December 635], during the 16th month of ‘Umar b. al-Khaṭṭāb's (r.) rule. The Battle of al-Yarmūk, in which the Byzantines were destroyed and annihilated, occurred five nights after the beginning of Rajab in 15 [=13 August 636].\\386

Mu‘ādh b. Jabal's letter to ‘Umar b. al-Khaṭṭāb concerning Abū ‘Ubayda's death (r.)

Al-Ḥusayn b. Ziyād [al-Ramlī] related to us on the authority of Abū Ismā‘īl [Muḥammad b. ‘Abdallāh al-Azdī], who said: Furthermore, Muḥammad b. Yūsuf related to me on the authority of Thābit al-Bunānī: When Abū

'Ubayda died, Mu'ādh [b. Jabal] wrote [the following letter] to 'Umar b. al-Khaṭṭāb, notifying him of Abū 'Ubayda's death. He wrote:

From Mu'ādh b. Jabal to the servant of God, 'Umar, the Commander of the Believers. Peace be upon you. I praise, on your behalf, God with whom no other deity is associated. Regarding the matter at hand: Reckon [among the dead] a man who was faithful to God and in whose eyes God was great; [a man] who was dear to us and to you, Commander of the Believers—[i.e.] Abū 'Ubayda b. al-Jarrāḥ. May God forgive him the sins [he committed] earlier and those [he committed] later. We belong to God and to Him we shall return. We reckon him [as having been martyred] in anticipation of God's reward and we trust in God on his behalf. I wrote [this letter] to you after [his] death while the plague had [rapidly] spread among the people, and [ultimately] nobody could escape his appointed time [of death]. Whoever has not died [yet] is going to die. May God make what He retains for us better than the worldly life. Whether God causes us to survive or perish, [we pray that] He would reward you with His mercy, forgiveness, satisfaction and Paradise [for your good deeds] to the Muslims in general, to our elite and to our common people. [May God's] peace and mercy be upon you.

He [=the narrator, Thābit al-Bunānī] said: I swear by God that no sooner had 'Umar b. al-Khaṭṭāb (r.) received the letter and read it than he wept bitterly and notified those who were sitting with him of Abū 'Ubayda's death. He [=the narrator, Thābit al-Bunānī] said: I have never seen the generality of the Muslims\\387 mourning for a man from among them [as much] as they mourned for Abū 'Ubayda b. al-Jarrāḥ. He [=the narrator, Thābit al-Bunānī] said: I swear by God that hardly had a few days passed when a [second] letter arrived from 'Amr b. al-'Āṣ in which he announced Mu'ādh b. Jabal's death; God rest his soul. He [='Amr b. al-'Āṣ] wrote [the following letter]:

From 'Amr b. al-'Āṣ to the servant of God, 'Umar, the Commander of the Believers. Peace be upon you. I praise, on your behalf, God with whom no other deity is associated. Regarding the matter at hand: [Recently,] Mu'ādh b. Jabal, God rest him, died. Death [of the plague] swept through the [encampment of the] Muslims and they asked for my permission to move away from it [=the plague] to the [open] countryside (*barr*). But I know that the staying of whoever stays [where the plague prevails] will not draw him nearer to his appointed time [of death], nor will the escape of whoever escapes from it [=the plague] draw him farther from his appointed time [of death] or preclude [the occurrence of] his fate (*qadar*). [May God's] peace and mercy be upon you.

He [=the narrator, Thābit al-Bunānī] said: When 'Umar (r.) learned of Mu'ādh [b. Jabal's] death, right after his knowledge of Abū 'Ubayda['s death], he [also] mourned for him [=Mu'ādh b. Jabal] bitterly. 'Umar, may God have mercy upon him, and the Muslims wept [a lot] and grieved bitterly over him. 'Umar (r.) [then] said: "God rest Mu'ādh [b. Jabal]. I swear by God that He has eliminated abundant knowledge from this community with Mu'ādh's death. Many a time have we accepted a piece of sincere advice from him and seen it [=the advice] lead to good [consequences] and blessings. Many a time have we profited from his knowledge and [many a time] has he guided us to good [things]. May God reward him with the reward [He gives to] the righteous".\\388

He [=the narrator, Thābit al-Bunānī] said: When ʿUmar, God rest him, learned of Abū ʿUbayda's and Muʿādh [b. Jabal's] deaths, he divided the Syrian provinces (*kuwar*) [among the remaining commanders]. Thus, he dispatched ʿAbdallāh b. Qurṭ al-Thumālī [to be] the [new] commander of Ḥimṣ, over which he had beforehand ruled for one year, and deposed Ḥabīb b. Maslama from [ruling] it [=Ḥimṣ]. He also appointed Abū al-Dardāʾ al-Anṣārī[517] [as chief commander] of Damascus. Furthermore, he appointed Yazīd b. Abī Sufyān [as chief commander] of the [Muslim] soldiers that were [stationed] in Syria and [ordered] him in writing to march to Caesarea. ʿAbdallāh b. Qurṭ [al-Thumālī] remained in command of Ḥimṣ [only] for one year. Then ʿUmar became angry with him and, therefore, deposed him. Later he became pleased with him [again] and sent him back to [be the commander of] Ḥimṣ. [In the meantime,] ʿUmar (r.) had dispatched ʿUbāda b. al-Ṣāmit al-Anṣārī[518]—the holder (*ṣāḥib*) of the Prophet's (ṣ.) flag who was a participant on the battle-day of Badr (*badrī*), a participant in the ʿAqaba Pledge of Allegiance (*ʿaqabī*) and a representative [of the Medinan tribes] during this pledge (*naqīb*)—[as commander] of Ḥimṣ when he [=ʿUmar] had deposed ʿAbdallāh b. Qurṭ [al-Thumālī].

The speech of ʿUbāda b. al-Ṣāmit [al-Anṣārī] (r.)

Al-Ḥusayn b. Ziyād [al-Ramlī] related to us on the authority of Abū Ismāʿīl [Muḥammad b. ʿAbdallāh al-Azdī], who said: Furthermore, Abū Jahḍam al-Azdī related to me on the authority of ʿAbd al-Raḥmān b. al-Salīk al-Fazārī, who said: When ʿUbāda b. al-Ṣāmit [al-Anṣārī] came to the people of Ḥimṣ, he rose [and stood] before the people to deliver a speech. He praised and thanked God, blessed and saluted the Prophet (ṣ.) and then said: "Regarding the matter at hand: Verily, the worldly life is a present [transitory] pleasure, from which the pious as well as the corrupt are consuming. Verily, the

517 Abū al-Dardāʾ's full name is Abū al-Dardāʾ ʿUwaymir al-Anṣārī al-Khazrajī (n.d.). In al-Azdī's narrative, he was appointed by ʿUmar as the commander of Damascus and he delivered an exhortatory speech to the Muslim fighters in Damascus. On Abū al-Dardāʾ, see *EI²*, s.v. Abu 'l-Dardāʾ (A. Jeffery).

518 ʿUbāda's full name is Abū al-Walīd ʿUbāda b. al-Ṣāmit b. Fihr b. Thaʿlaba al-Anṣārī (d. 34/654–655). In al-Azdī's narrative, he is mentioned as the holder of the Prophet's flag in the Battle of Badr, as a participant in the ʿAqaba Pledge of Allegiance and as a representative of the Medinan tribes during this pledge. He is also depicted as having been appointed by ʿUmar as the commander of Ḥimṣ after the deposition of ʿAbdallāh b. Qurṭ al-Thumālī. He delivered an exhortatory speech to the Muslims there. Positioned by Yazīd b. Abī Sufyān in command of the army's right flank, he also fought during the conquest of Caesarea. On ʿUbāda, see Ibn Saʿd, *Kitāb al-ṭabaqāt*, III-2, 93–94, 148.

afterlife is a true promise where a mighty King [=God] makes [fair] judgement[s]. Verily, your deeds are going to be shown to you. So whoever does a good [deed] equal to the weight of an atom will see it [later] and whoever does a bad [deed] equal to the weight of an atom will see it[, too]. Verily, the worldly life has its [own] offspring\\389 and the afterlife has its [own] offspring. So be part of the offspring of the afterlife and do not be part of the offspring of the worldly life, for every mother will be followed by her own offspring on the Day of Resurrection".

Then he [=ʿUbāda b. al-Ṣāmit al-Anṣārī] said to Shaddād b. Aws [b. Thābit]: "O Shaddād, rise and exhort the people [=the Muslims]". Shaddād [b. Aws b. Thābit] was articulate and gifted with an [expressive] tongue and [great] wisdom, as well as with erudition and eloquence. Then Shaddād [b. Aws b. Thābit] rose, praised and thanked God, blessed and saluted the Prophet (ṣ.) and then said [to the people]: "Regarding the matter at hand: O people, reconsult God's scripture [=the Qurʾān] even if many people have deserted it. You have seen only part of what leads to good and only part of what leads to evil. God has collected all that is entirely good and retained it in Paradise and has also collected all that is entirely evil and retained it in the Fire. Verily, Paradise is hard and difficult [to attain] and the Fire is easy and simple [to enter]. Verily, Paradise is encircled by aversion and patience and the Fire is encircled by desire and lust. [Hence,] whoever uncovers the veil of aversion and patience finds [himself] on the brink of Paradise, and whoever is on the brink of Paradise becomes one of its inhabitants. [However,] whoever uncovers the veil of desire and lust finds [himself] on the brink of the Fire, and [whoever is on the brink of the Fire] becomes one of its inhabitants. Verily, [if you] act truthfully, you will hold the rank of the adherents of the truth on the Day [of Resurrection] when [everything] will be judged only according to the truth".

The speech of Abū al-Dardāʾ al-Anṣārī (r.)

Al-Ḥusayn b. Ziyād [al-Ramlī] related to us on the authority of Abū Ismāʿīl [Muḥammad b. ʿAbdallāh al-Azdī,] [who said]: Ismāʿīl b. Abī Khālid related to me on the authority of Qays b. Abī Ḥāzim: [One day,] Abū al-Dardāʾ al-Anṣārī rose [and stood] before the people of Damascus to deliver a speech, praised and thanked\\390 God, then blessed and saluted the Prophet (ṣ.) [and] then said: "Regarding the matter at hand: O people of Damascus, listen to the speech of a brother of yours who [wants to] impart advice to you. Why are you collecting that which you will not consume, building that which you will not inhabit and wishing for that which you will not obtain? Those who existed before you [also] collected extensively, built expansively and wished [profoundly] for later, but they died sooner. So their deeds became vain, their dwellings graves and their wishes delusion[s]. Verily, [the people of] ʿĀd and Thamūd had beforehand filled [the land] between Bosra and Aden[519] with possessions, children and blessings. But who would buy from me what they have left [behind] for two dirhams?"

The conquest of Caesarea and the appointment of Yazīd b. Abī Sufyān [as chief commander] of all the districts of Syria

He [=the narrator] said: Then ʿUmar b. al-Khaṭṭāb (r.) wrote [the following letter] to Yazīd b. Abī Sufyān:

Regarding the matter at hand: I appointed you as [chief] commander of all the districts of Syria and I wrote them [=the districts' commanders] [letters ordering] that they should listen to you, obey you and never disobey any of your orders. [Now] march out [of the place you are in], encamp with the Muslims and then advance with them to Caesarea. Then set up camp there and do not depart from there until God leads you to its conquest. For what you [all] have conquered in the land of Syria should not have been conquered while the people of Caesarea are still [living] there. They are your enemy and they are adjacent to you. Furthermore,\\391 Caesar [=Heraclius] will still be greedy for Syria as long as one of his obedient followers remains unharmed there. If you conquer it [=Caesarea], God will cut off his hopes for the entire [land of] Syria. God (ʿa.) will do this to him and [will] arrange [the best] for the Muslims, God willing. [Peace be upon you.]

So Yazīd b. Abī Sufyān marched out [of his place] and encamped with the Muslims. Then he received [a copy of] [the following] letter from ʿUmar (r.), [who had sent identical copies] to the [other] commanders of the districts:

Regarding the matter at hand: I appointed Yazīd b. Abī Sufyān as [chief] commander of all the districts of Syria and ordered him to advance on the people of Caesarea. So do not disobey his order[s] or disagree with his opinion[s]. Peace [be upon you].

Yazīd b. Abī Sufyān wrote [the following letter] in [identical] copies to the [other] commanders of the districts:

Regarding the matter at hand: I [hereby] order the [immediate] dispatch of the people [=the Muslims] [to my encampment] as I want to march with them to Caesarea. So take one [Muslim] man out of every three and hasten to dispatch them [all] to me, God willing. Peace [be upon you].

He then waited only a little [while] until the[se] soldiers [chosen] from all of the districts flocked to him.\\392 When they congregated at his [=Yazīd's] place, Yazīd b. Abī Sufyān rose, praised and thanked God for what He is worth, blessed and saluted the Prophet (ṣ.) and then said [to them]: "Regarding the matter at hand: A letter from the Commander of the Believers, ʿUmar

519 Aden (ʿAdan) is a town located on the south coast of the Arabian Peninsula. In al-Azdī's narrative, Aden is mentioned once in order to define the Arabs' land. On Aden, see *EI*[2], s.v. ʿAdan (O. Löfgren).

the blessed and the Distinguisher (*fārūq*)[520], came to me, urging me to march to Caesarea and to call them [=its people] either to [embrace] Islam or to enter into what [=the pact] the provincial people of Syria had entered into and then bring me tribute by hand and with humility. However, if they refuse [both], I will descend upon them and never leave them until I kill their fighters and capture their offspring. So march [out] to them, may God have mercy upon you. I do hope that God will collect the spoils for you in the worldly life and in the afterlife". Then he [=Yazīd] said to the people [=the Muslims]: "[Now] set out". Thereupon, Ḥabīb b. Maslama said to [some] men around him: "I swear by God that your commander [only recently] started to praise ʿUmar and what would stop him from [doing] that after he [=ʿUmar] had appointed him as [chief] commander of the entire Syria?" He [=the narrator] said: Shortly thereafter, the messenger of Yazīd b. Abī Sufyān came to him [=Ḥabīb b. Maslama,] [saying]: "March [out as commander of] the vanguard because I have appointed you as commander of it. Then advance until you descend upon the people of Caesarea and I will be the quickest to pursue you and catch up with you". He [=Ḥabīb b. Maslama] then marched [out as commander of] the vanguard [that consisted] of a huge group of the Muslims. Later he started to say: "May God have mercy upon ʿUmar. Verily, I swear by God that he has always been knowledgeable about men since he appointed Yazīd b. Abī Sufyān as [chief] commander of Syria. I swear by God that he knew his sufficiency, competence and grace". Al-Ḍaḥḥāk b. Qays heard his [=Ḥabīb b. Maslama's] first [negative] and second [positive] statements, but kept silent, saying nothing to him [=Ḥabīb b. Maslama], and hated what he [=Ḥabīb b. Maslama] said.\\393 Ḥabīb b. Maslama was a good man, but some kind of envy that [sometimes] overwhelms people had overwhelmed him when ʿUmar (r.) had appointed Yazīd as [chief] commander of Syria. Al-Ḍaḥḥāk b. Qays, together with some of his companions, was part of the vanguard. While they [=al-Ḍaḥḥāk and his companions] were marching and getting extremely hungry, they passed by a river. So al-Ḍaḥḥāk b. Qays and his companions descended to the bank of the river, which was near to a village in which a large number of the Muslims' enemies resided. They stayed [in a place] close to it [=the village] and placed chunks [of bread] they had onto a shield[521]. They [=al-Ḍaḥḥāk and his companions] were eating some of these chunks and drinking some of the water while each of them was holding the reins of his horse. While they were in this [situation], Ḥabīb b. Maslama[, their commander,] passed by and became worried about them. He then said

520 ʿUmar's epithet "*fārūq*" is usually understood as referring to "the one who distinguishes truth from falsehood" or "the true faith from the false". In addition, it is associated with the Syriac term *pārōqā* (lit. "saviour, redeemer"). On *fārūq*, see *EI*², s.v. ʿUmar (I) b. al-Khaṭṭāb (G. Levi Della Vida/M. Bonner).

521 "*Turs*" (lit. "shield") is the generic term for this weapon. Schwarzlose points out that the term signifies a shield made partly of wood, in contrast to a "*daraqa*" (lit. "shield") that is made only of animal skin (see Schwarzlose, *Waffen*, 355).

to them: "You endangered [yourselves] when you descended to the bank of this river [which is] close to this village [of your enemy]. Did you not fear that an enemy of yours might come out of this village to you, against whom you would be so powerless that it would bring about your destruction?" Thereupon, al-Ḍaḥḥāk b. Qays said to him [=Ḥabīb b. Maslama]: "God ('a.) protected us [from that] and praise be to Him. Besides, not all that is feared and dreaded occurs". He [=Ḥabīb b. Maslama] told them to set out and reprimanded them. Al-Ḍaḥḥāk [b. Qays] got angry [because of this] and said: "We neither set out by your order nor please your eye [by doing so]". Thereupon, Ḥabīb [b. Maslama] said to him [=al-Ḍaḥḥāk]: "Verily, I swear by God to inform the [chief] commander [=Yazīd] about your disobedience, your disagreement and your objection to his order". So al-Ḍaḥḥāk [b. Qays] said: "Then\\394 I will inform him of something that will harm you". Ḥabīb [b. Maslama] did not know what al-Ḍaḥḥāk [b. Qays] wanted to tell [Yazīd] for he [=Ḥabīb b. Maslama] forgot what he had said about Yazīd [earlier]. Thus, Ḥabīb [b. Maslama] proceeded to Yazīd, complained to him about al-Ḍaḥḥāk b. Qays, about his [=al-Ḍaḥḥāk's] disobedience to his [=Yazīd's] order and his gruff reply to him [=Ḥabīb b. Maslama] during their argument. Thereupon, Yazīd, who was patient, wise, clement and of good conduct, [who] was giving preference to welfare (*'āfiya*), was cherished among the Muslims, was one of the early Emigrants and [one] of the best companions of the Messenger of God (ṣ.), said to Ḥabīb [b. Maslama]: "Go [away] and I will send for him [=al-Ḍaḥḥāk b. Qays], chide him for what he did, blame him for it and extremely reproach him face to face. For I hate to bring you [and him] together and then an ugly dispute will break out between the two of you and something [bad], which I would dislike for both of you, will happen between you". So Ḥabīb [b. Maslama] left and Yazīd sent for al-Ḍaḥḥāk b. Qays. When he [=al-Ḍaḥḥāk b. Qays] came to him, he [=Yazīd] reproached him, rebuked him in a [sharp] tongue and said to him: "I appointed your cousin as commander of the vanguard and he told me that he passed by you and your companions, worried about you and [thus] ordered you [all] to save yourselves. But you started [to address] him impatiently, using bad words and obscene language. You really misbehaved in that situation if you did what he [=Ḥabīb] mentioned [to me]". Thereupon, al-Ḍaḥḥāk [b. Qays] said to Yazīd: "May God increase your righteousness. In fact, the bad speaker who talked obscenely, acted abominably and said what he should not have said is Ḥabīb b. Maslama. What I did and said to him was because of something [I had] in my breast against him, due to something he said about you. For he criticised you and criticised the Commander of the Believers [in two of his previous statements]. I decided neither to mention it to you, nor to tell you about it until I saw him initiating [hostilities against me] by backbiting me in front of you and by wanting to criticise me.\\395 When the Commander of the Believers gave you [chief] command over the districts of Syria and you rose [and stood] before the Muslims and praised the Commander of the Believers and some of the Muslims around him, he [=Ḥabīb b. Maslama] said: 'What would stop you from praising him [='Umar] after he had appointed you as [chief] commander of the districts of Syria?' He said this in envy of you and in disapproval of the Commander of the Believers. [Thus,] he criticised his [='Umar's] decision after he [='Umar] had appointed you as [chief] commander of Syria. [This is] as if he saw you unworthy of [taking] command. But you, may God increase your righteousness, are worthy of [taking] command of Syria and of what is better than Syria. But when you appointed him [=Ḥabīb b. Maslama] as commander of the vanguard, he changed his previous [negative] words, took them back and said [positive words about 'Umar]: 'May God have mercy upon 'Umar. Verily, I swear by God that he has always been knowledgeable about men since he appointed Yazīd b. Abī Sufyān as [chief] commander of Syria. I swear by God that he ['Umar] knew his [=Yazīd's] competence, sufficiency and grace'. Speaking this way [and changing his statements], he [=Ḥabīb b. Maslama] was like, may God increase your righteousness, the hypocrites who 'are content if they are given a share, but angry if not'".[522] He [=al-Ḍaḥḥāk b. Qays] [then] said to him [=Yazīd]: "Bring him face to face with me, may God increase your righteousness, and I will make him admit to [having said] both of these statements". Yazīd fell silent for a while and then said: "I will not bring you [and him] together, but I will accept from you the best [thing] you can do and forgive you the worst [thing] you may do". Then he [=Yazīd] said: "I would like nothing to happen between you and him except [all that is] good. [Therefore,] 'be mindful of God, in whose name you make requests of one another. Beware of severing the ties of kinship: God is always watching over you'".[523] He [=the narrator] said: Thereafter, they [=some Muslims] went to Ḥabīb b. Maslama and mentioned that [=al-Ḍaḥḥāk's accusations] to him. This was hard for him [to take], [but] then he said: "What did Yazīd say [about this]?" Thereupon, they told him about his [=Yazīd's] noble words. So he [=Ḥabīb b. Maslama] said: "I swear by God that he is honourable and of noble descent (*maḥtad*)"—[the narrator said:] And *al-maḥtad* means "the origin [of a person]". Then he [=Ḥabīb b. Maslama] met him [=Yazīd]. Yazīd was\\396 the gladdest [person] and [showed] him [=Ḥabīb b. Maslama] the most cheerful face. He [=Yazīd] did not blame him [=Ḥabīb b. Maslama] for anything until Yazīd b. Abī Sufyān died; God rest him.

He [=the narrator] said: [Then] Ḥabīb b. Maslama marched out in command of his vanguard to Caesarea. Groups of the Byzantine patricians, horsemen and valorous [fighters], all the Christians who hated embracing the Islamic religion, those who hated [bringing] tribute [to the Muslims] and the Byzantine people from the areas that were [still] fighting the Muslims were [all stationed] there [=at Caesarea]. Therefore, there were many troops at Caesarea [that had witnessed] great earnestness and extreme vehemence.

522 Q. 9:58 (*The Qur'ān. Tr. Abdel Haleem*, 121).
523 Q. 4:1 (*The Qur'ān. Tr. Abdel Haleem*, 50).

When Ḥabīb b. Maslama advanced in command of the vanguard and drew near to the fortress, some cavalrymen and infantrymen from Caesarea marched out to him and pelted them [=the Muslims] with arrows[524] and bolts. Their cavalry launched an attack upon the Muslims, so Ḥabīb b. Maslama as well as his cavalry retreated until he reached Yazīd b. Abī Sufyān [and the main army of the Muslims]. Yazīd then dismounted and positioned ʿUbāda b. al-Ṣāmit al-Anṣārī in command of his right flank, positioned al-Ḍaḥḥāk b. Qays in command of his left flank and restored Ḥabīb b. Maslama [to the command] of the cavalry. Yazīd b. Abī Sufyān marched [out] in command of the infantry and launched an attack upon them [=the people of Caesarea]. Then they [=the Muslims] fought extensively and fiercely and he [=Yazīd] sent al-Ḍaḥḥāk b. Qays [the following message]: "Launch an attack upon their right flank", so he [=al-Ḍaḥḥāk] attacked them [there], defeated them and killed a great many of them. Then he [=Yazīd] sent ʿUbāda b. al-Ṣāmit [al-Anṣārī] [the following message]: "Launch an attack upon their left flank", so he [=ʿUbāda b. al-Ṣāmit al-Anṣārī] attacked them [there] but they stood firm against him. He fought them extensively and killed a great many of them. They [=the two units on this flank] then separated and ʿUbāda b. al-Ṣāmit [al-Anṣārī] returned to his position [on the Muslims' right flank] and motivated, exhorted and encouraged his companions, saying: "O adherents\\397 of Islam, I am the most youthful of the leaders and [by now] the longest living [of them]. I was predetermined by God (ʿa.) to stay alive until I fought with you against this enemy. [Today] I ask God to grant me and [grant] you the best reward [he gives] to the fighters for His cause. I swear by God, in whose hand[s] my soul lies, that whenever I launched an attack with a company of the Believers on a group of the Polytheists, they [=the Polytheists] [always] evacuated the place (*ʿarṣa*) to us and God [always] led us to triumph over them except [in this case] with you [today]. What [do you think would happen] if you launched an attack with me on those [people of Caesarea], not steering away from them? [Remember] when ʿUmar (r.) learned about the atrocious fight of the people of al-Yarmūk against you, he said: 'Glory be to God. If they [=the people of al-Yarmūk] stood firm against them [=the Muslims], I would only think that the Muslims had improperly [divided up and] obtained the spoils (*ghallū*)'. [Then] he [=ʿUmar] said: 'If they [=the Muslims] had not improperly [divided up and] obtained the spoils, they [=the people of al-Yarmūk] would not have stood firm against them and they [=the Muslims] would have triumphed [over them] without any burden'. Therefore, I swear by God that I am fearful of two [bad] qualities that you [=the Muslims] [might] have: [First,] you might [have] improperly [divided up and] obtained the spoils or [second,] you were not sincere to God (ʿa.) in your [previous] attack on them [=the people of Caesarea]. Thus, launch with

524 "*Nabl wa-al-nushshāb*" (lit. "arrows") signify both wooden arrows of Arabic and Iranian origins.

me [another] assault on them [=the people of Caesarea] [now], may God have mercy upon you, when I [start to] assault. Nay, I swear by God that I will not return to my position [again], God willing, and I will not leave them [=the people of Caesarea] until God defeats them or I die amidst them". Then he [=ʿUbāda b. al-Ṣāmit al-Anṣārī] launched an[other] attack on them [=the people of Caesarea] and the [Muslims'] right flank also launched an attack with him on the left flank of the Byzantines. They [=the Byzantines and the people of Caesarea] stood firm against them until they fought each other with spears, tussled with the swords and the horses' necks mixed. When ʿUbāda b. al-Ṣāmit [al-Anṣārī] saw this, he dismounted [from his horse to fight on foot]. Then ʿUmayr b. Saʿd al-Anṣārī[525] called out to the Muslims, saying: "O adherents of Islam, ʿUbāda b. al-Ṣāmit [al-Anṣārī], the master of the Muslims and the holder of the flag of the Messenger of God (ṣ.) dismounted and walked [towards the enemy], [saying]: 'Attack, attack; towards God's mercy and Paradise! Fear the consequences of flight, which lead to the Fire'".\\398 Then the Muslims came [forward] to ʿUbāda b. al-Ṣāmit [al-Anṣārī] while he was fighting against those [of the people of Caesarea and the Byzantines] who had surrounded him. So they [=the Muslims] launched an attack upon them, made them crash into one another, removed them from their positions and then assaulted them [again].

Ḥabīb b. Maslama also launched an attack upon those of them [=the people of Caesarea] who were adjacent to him. Then Yazīd b. Abī Sufyān, as well as the generality of the Muslims, launched an attack upon them. Consequently, they [=the people of Caesarea] were badly defeated and the Muslims stuck their weapons [=spears] and swords wherever they liked and pursued them, killing them the way they wanted until they forced them [back] into their fortress. They [=the Muslims] killed a great many of their chiefs, patricians and horsemen. Then they [continued] standing [heavily armed] against them [=the people of Caesarea], besieged them, cut them off from their matériel, hemmed them in and laid an extremely tight siege to them. When the distress [of the siege] on them [=the people of Caesarea] lasted long, they blamed one another and said: "March out with us towards them to fight them until we either triumph over them or die honourably". Thus, they got ready in their city and marched out mobilised while the Muslims were heedless, not realising and not knowing that they [=the people of Caesarea] were marching out to them. Beforehand the Muslims had humiliated them, forced them back [into their city] and hemmed them in until they [=the people of Caesarea] were exhausted. [Therefore,] they [=the Muslims] thought that they [=the people of Caesarea] had become too feeble and weak to march out to them [again]. Thus, the Muslims were warned [of the imminent attack] only when all the people of Caesarea [suddenly attacked and]

525 We read this middle name as "Saʿd" rather than "Saʿīd", because the former is more frequently mentioned in other places of the text.

fought them with the[ir] swords on one side of their encampment. So the Muslims engaged in [another] atrocious battle (*jawla*).\\399

Then Yazīd b. Abī Sufyān marched swiftly out [of the encampment] towards them [=the people of Caesarea] and when he drew near to them, he fought them extensively while the Muslims' cavalry and infantry gathered around him. The [other] people [=the Muslims] marched out [of the encampment] according to their flags and their lines. When the Muslims [flocked] in large numbers to him, he [=Yazīd] ordered the cavalry to launch an attack upon them [=the people of Caesarea] [and they did so]. The infantry also rushed to [fight] them [=the people of Caesarea] and then launched an attack upon them. So they were badly and seriously defeated [again] and they [=the Muslims] killed them horridly until they [=the people of Caesarea] jostled, one against the other, and some of them went aimlessly [away] without entering the city while some others re-entered the city. In this battle, God killed about 5,000 of them. When Yazīd saw the sort of disgrace and death that God inflicted upon them and the humiliation He drove them into, he said to [his brother] Muʿāwiya[526]: "[Continue to] beleaguer it [=Caesarea] until you conquer it". [Then] Yazīd turned away from it [=Caesarea] whereas Muʿāwiya [b. Abī Sufyān] beleaguered it only for a short while. He [=Muʿāwiya] hemmed them in [again] until God (t.) led him to the conquest [of the city]. That [was] in 19 [=January 640-January 641]. Its [=Caesarea's conquest] and the [conquest of] Jalūlāʾ occurred in the same year. The Muslims rejoiced over that [conquest] greatly and no enemy of them was left, either in the farthest or in the nearest parts of Syria. [Hence,] God had expelled the Polytheists from it and Syria as a whole had fallen into the hands of the Muslims.\\400

Yazīd b. Abī Sufyān's letter to ʿUmar b. al-Khaṭṭāb (r.)

Yazīd b. Abī Sufyān wrote [the following letter] to the Commander of the Believers, ʿUmar (r.), [and sent it] with two men from Judhām; may God have mercy upon them:

In the name of God, the Merciful, the Compassionate. Regarding the matter at hand: The decision of the Commander of the Believers [=Abū Bakr] concerning [the attack on] the people of Syria was one to which he was rightly guided by God and by virtue of which God [also] rightly guided

526 Muʿāwiya's full name is Abū Yazīd Muʿāwiya b. Abī Sufyān al-Umawī al-Qurashī (d. 60/680). In al-Azdī's narrative, Muʿāwiya appears out of a sudden during the conquest of Caesarea when Yazīd ordered him to finalise its siege and when Caeserea was conquered by him. Shortly before his death, Yazīd appointed Muʿāwiya as his successor in chief command of Syria. This decision was confirmed by ʿUmar who is said to have not deposed him during his further rule. Lastly, Muʿāwiya's rule under ʿUthmān and ʿAlī, his participation in the first civil war and his own rule as caliph are mentioned. On Muʿāwiya, see *EI*[2], s.v. Muʿāwiya I (M. Hinds).

whoever accepted it. May God bless [it] [=the decision] in his [=Abū Bakr's] favour and in the favour of his obedient followers. I do inform the Commander of the Believers [=ʿUmar] that we had faced the people of Caesarea more than once. Each time God caused their earnestness to be the lowest and their stratagem to be the frailest, bringing about [our] triumph over them. So when they saw that God had broken their spirit[s], humiliated them, inflicted disgrace and shame upon them and killed their valiant [fighters], their horsemen and their sovereigns, they were forced [to stay] in their fortresses and were petrified within their [own] city. Then we laid long siege to them, cut off their matériel and provisions and hemmed them in extremely tightly. When they were exhausted by languishment and distress, God led us to its [=Caesarea's] conquest. Praise be to God, the Lord of the worlds and [may God's] peace and mercy be upon you.\\401

ʿUmar's (r.) letter to Yazīd b. Abī Sufyān (r.); may God have mercy upon him

ʿUmar (r.) wrote [the following letter] to him [=Yazīd] [in reply]:

In the name of God, the Merciful, the Compassionate. From the servant of God, ʿUmar, the Commander of the Believers, to Yazīd b. Abī Sufyān. Peace be upon you. I praise, on your behalf, God with whom no other deity is associated. Regarding the matter at hand: Your letter reached me and I understood what you mentioned therein about the conquest [of Syria and Caesarea bestowed] on the Muslims. So praise be to God, the Lord of the worlds. Thank God so that He gives you more and completes His blessing[s] upon you. For God spared you the burden of [fighting] your enemy, extended the means of living for you, gave you power over the lands [of Syria] and granted you some of all that you had requested from Him. If you count God's blessings [on you], you will never be able to enumerate them. Man (*al-ʿinsān*) is truly unjust and very ungrateful. Peace be upon you.

Yazīd b. Abī Sufyān's death; God rest him

When this letter came to Yazīd b. Abī Sufyān, he read it out to the Muslims. So they praised and thanked God for that which He had bestowed upon them, [that which] He had planned for them and [that which] He had done well for them. [Thereafter,] Yazīd b. Abī Sufyān proceeded until he set up camp in Damascus. He stayed [there] only for one [more] year until he died, God rest him.

He [=the narrator] said: [Thus,] the whole of Syria\\402 was placed onto the straight path and no enemy of the Muslims was [left] there. [Then] a severe illness befell him [=Yazīd]. When it [=the illness] became too hard to bear and he [=Yazīd] was at death's door, he wrote [the following letter] to ʿUmar (r.):

In the name of God, the Merciful, the Compassionate. Regarding the matter at hand: I have written this letter to you as, according to my thinking, I am [beginning] the first day of the afterlife and [ending] the last day of the worldly life. May God reward you with [all that is] good in return for [your good deeds to] us and to the Muslims. May He make His Paradises (*jannāt*) a home, destination and resting place for us and for you. Now, dispatch whomever you like to [accomplish] your operation in Syria. As for me, I have just appointed Muʿāwiya b. Abī Sufyān as [my] successor in command of them [=the Muslims]. [Peace be upon you.]

When his [=Yazīd's] letter came to ʿUmar (r.), he [=ʿUmar] mourned for him bitterly and wrote to Muʿāwiya about his [appointment as chief] commander of Syria. He [=ʿUmar] established him [=Muʿāwiya] [as chief commander] over it [=Syria] for four years and ʿUmar (r.) died while Muʿāwiya was still [in command] of Syria. He [=ʿUmar] had not deposed him [=Muʿāwiya] from it [=Syria] until he [=ʿUmar] (r.) died. Then ʿUthmān [b. ʿAffān] (r.) took over [the caliphate] and confirmed him [=Muʿāwiya] [as ruler] over it [=Syria] for twelve [more] years until ʿUthmān (r.) died. Then the [first] civil war (*fitna*) broke out, during which Muʿāwiya fought ʿAlī [b. Abī Ṭālib] (r.) for five years. Then Muʿāwiya became the caliph [of the Muslims] for nineteen years. He was a leader in Syria and a caliph for forty years [in total]: Four years during the caliphate of ʿUmar (r.), twelve years during the caliphate of ʿUthmān (r.), he fought ʿAlī (r.) for five years and served as caliph for nineteen years [thereafter]. This makes up forty years, but God knows best what is right.\\403

[Manuscript note: The colophon of the work]

[Copying] the Book on the Conquests of Syria (*kitāb futūḥ al-Shām*) is [now] accomplished. Praise be to God alone. May His blessings and peace be upon Muḥammad and his family. This manuscript was completed on Sunday evening, 22 Dhū al-Ḥijja 613 [=2 April, 1217]. This was done in the honourable [city of] Jerusalem (*al-Quds*), handwritten by Muḥammad b. Ibrāhīm al-Ghassānī[527]; may God forgive him, [forgive] whoever peruses it [=the book] and [forgive] the male and female Muslims [in general]. And praise be to God, the Lord of the worlds.

527 Muḥammad b. Ibrāhīm al-Ghassānī is not listed in any biographical work we could access. In al-Azdī's narrative, he is mentioned as the scribe of the *Futūḥ al-Shām* manuscript. Regarding Muḥammad b. Ibrāhīm al-Ghassānī, Sauvan and Balty-Guesdon tentatively (but plausibly) refer to al-Ṣafadī, *Al-wāfī. Ed. Vol. 2 S. Dedering*, 27–28 (no. 277). Therein it is said that al-Ghassānī was called Ibn al-Jāmūs, that he was educated at *Mashhad al-Ḥusayn* in Cairo and that he preached in Jerusalem.

Bibliography

Abdel Haleem, M. A. S.: Grammatical Shift for the Rhetorical Purposes. Iltifat and Related Features in the Qur'an. In: *Bulletin of the School of Oriental and African Studies* 55 (1992), pp. 407–432.

Abū al-Faraj al-Iṣfahānī, ʿAlī b. al-Ḥusayn: *Maqātil al-Ṭālibiyyīn. Ed. A. Ṣaqr.* Beirut ca. 1980.

Ahlwardt, Wilhelm: *Verzeichnis der arabischen Handschriften.* 10 vols. Berlin 1887–1899. [Reprint Hildesheim 1980–1981].

Al-Azdī, Muḥammad b. ʿAbdallāh: *Futūḥ al-Shām. Ed. ʿI. ʿUqla/Y. Banī Yāsīn as: Kitāb al-futūḥ al-Shām.* Irbid 2004.

Al-Azdī, Muḥammad b. ʿAbdallāh: *Futūḥ al-Shām. Ed. ʿA. ʿĀmir as: Taʾrīkh futūḥ al-Shām.* Cairo 1970.

Al-Azdī, Muḥammad b. ʿAbdallāh: *Futūḥ al-Shām. Ed. W. Lees as: The Fotooh al-Shām. Being an Account of the Moslim Conquests in Syria by Aboo Ismāʿaīl Mohammad bin ʿAbd Allah al-Azdī al-Baçrī, Who Flourished about the Middle of the Second Century of the Mohammadan Era.* Calcutta 1854. [Reprint Osnabrück 1980].

Al-Balādhurī, Aḥmad b. Yaḥyā: *Futūḥ al-buldān. Tr. P. Hitti/F. Murgotten as: The Origins of the Islamic State.* 2 vols. New York 1916–1924. [Reprint New York 1968–1969].

Al-Balādhurī, Aḥmad b. Yaḥyā: *Futūḥ al-buldān. Ed. M. de Goeje as: Liber Expugnationis Regionum. Auctore Imámo Ahmed ibn Jahja ibn Djábir al-Beládsorí.* Leiden 1866. [Reprint Frankfurt 1992].

Baljon, Johannes M.: "To Seek the Face of God" in Koran and Ḥadīth. In: *Acta Orientalia* 21 (1953), pp. 254–266.

Bashear, Suliman: The Title "Fārūq" and Its Association with ʿUmar I. In: *Studia Islamica* 72 (1990), pp. 47–70.

Berger, Lutz: *Die Entstehung des Islam. Die ersten hundert Jahre. Von Mohammed bis zum Weltreich der Kalifen.* München 2016.

Betz, Hans D. (ed.): *Religion in Geschichte und Gegenwart. Handwörterbuch für Theologie und Religionswissenschaft.* 9 vols. Tübingen 2008.

Bibliothèque National/Département des Manuscrits (ed.): *Catalogue des manuscripts arabes. Partie 2: Manuscript musulmanes. Tome V: 1465–1685. Edited by Yvette Sauvan/Marie-Geneviève Balty-Guesdon.* Paris 1995.

Brockelmann, Carl: *Geschichte der arabischen Litteratur.* 2 vols. 2nd ed. Leiden 1943–1949. [1st ed. Berlin 1897–1902].

Brockelmann, Carl: *Geschichte der arabischen Litteratur. Supplement.* 3 vols. Leiden 1937–1942.

Al-Bukhārī, Muḥammad b. Ismāʿīl: *Al-taʾrīkh al-kabīr. Ed. Dāʾirat al-mārif al-ʿuthmāniyya.* 4 vols. Hyderabad 1941–1959.

Burns, Ross: *Damascus. A History.* London 2005.

Caetani, Leone: *Annali dell'Islām.* 10 vols. Milan 1905–1926. [Reprint Hildesheim 1972].

Caskel, Werner: *Ǧamharat an-nasab. Das genealogische Werk des Hišām Ibn-Muḥammad al-Kalbī.* 2 vols. Leiden 1966.

Conrad, Lawrence I.: Heraclius in Early Islamic Kerygma. In: Gerrit J. Reinink/Bernard Stolte (eds.): *The Reign of Heraclius (610–641). Crisis and Confrontation.* Leuven 2002, pp. 113–156.

Conrad, Lawrence I.: Al-Azdī's History of the Arab Conquests in Bilād al-Shām. Some Historiographical Observations. In: Muḥammad ʿA. al-Bakhīt [=Bakhit] (ed.): *Proceedings of the Second Symposium on the History of Bilād al-Shām During the Early Islamic Period Up to 40 A.H./640 A.D. The Fourth International Conference on the History of Bilad al-Sham (1985). Vol. 1: English and French Papers.* Amman 1987, pp. 28–62.

Darādaka, Ṣāliḥ M.: Fatḥ Dimashq. Dirāsa fī al-riwāyāt al-taʾrīkhiyya. In: *Al-majalla al-Urdunniyya li-taʾrīkh wa-al-āthār* 2 (2008), pp. 1–20.

de Goeje, Michaïl J.: *Mémoire sur la conquête de la Syrie.* 2nd ed. Leiden 1900.

de Goeje, Michaïl J.: *Mémoire sur le Fotouho's-Scham atribué a Abou Ismaïl al-Baçri.* Leiden 1864.

de Sacy, Silvestre: Lettre a M. le Redacteur du Journal Asiatique. In: *Journal Asiatique* 3. serie, 1 (1836), pp. 94–96.

de Slane, Baron William Mac Guckin: *Catalogue des manuscrits arabes.* Paris 1883–1895.

Al-Dhahabī, Muḥammad b. ʿUthmān: *Siyar aʿlām al-nubalāʾ. Ed. Sh. al-Arnaʾūṭ/B. Maʿrūf.* 25 vols. 11th ed. Beirut 1998.

Al-Dhahabī, Muḥammad b. ʿUthmān: *Muʿjam al-shuyūkh. Ed. M. al-Hayla.* Al-Ṭāʾif 1988.

Al-Dhahabī, Muḥammad b. ʿUthmān: *Taʾrīkh al-islām wa-wafayāt al-mashāhīr wa-al-aʿlām. Ed. ʿU. Tadmurī.* 52 vols. Beirut 1987–2000.

D.[ie] Red.[aktion]: Nachträge und Berichtigungen. In: *Zeitschrift der Deutschen Morgenländischen Gesellschaft* 3 (1849), pp. 363–364.

Donner, Fred M.: *The Early Islamic Conquests.* Princeton 1981.

Donner, Fred M.: The Bakr b. Wāʾil Tribes and Politics in Northeastern Arabia on the Eve of Islam. In: *Studia Islamica* 51 (1980), pp. 5–38.

Dozy, Reinhart P.: *Supplément aux dictionnaires arabes.* 2 vols. Leiden 1881. [Reprint Beirut 1991].

Dozy, Reinhart P.: *Dictionnarie détaillé des noms des vêtements chez les Arabes.* Amsterdam 1845.

El Cheikh, Nadia M.: *Byzantium Viewed by the Arabs.* Cambridge, MA 2004.

Al-Fasawī, Yaʿqūb b. Sufyān: *Kitāb al-maʿrifa wa-al-taʾrīkh. Ed. A. al-ʿUmarī.* 3 vols. Baghdad 1974–1976 [=1394–1396].

Fierro, Maribel: Al-Aṣfar. In: *Studia Islamica* 77 (1993), pp. 169–181.

Fischer, A.: Redakteurglossen. In: *Zeitschrift der Deutschen Morgenländischen Gesellschaft* 59 (1905), pp. 442–456.

Fleet, Kate/Krämer, Gudrun/Matringe, Dennis/Nawas, John A./Rowson, Everett (eds.): *Encyclopaedia of Islam. Three.* Leiden 2007.

Fl.[eischer, Heinrich]: Zwei Beilagen. In: *Zeitschrift der Deutschen Morgenländischen Gesellschaft* 3 (1849), p. 381.

Gibb, Hamilton A./Lewis, Bernard/van Donzel, Johannes et al. (eds.): *Encyclopaedia of Islam.* 2nd ed. 12 vols. Leiden 1960–2004.

Haldon, John: *Warfare, State and Society in the Byzantine World, 565—1204.* London 1999.

Al-Hamadhānī, Aḥmad Ibn al-Faqīh: *Mukhtaṣar kitāb al-buldān. Ed. M. de Goeje as: Compendium libri Kitāb al-Boldān auctore Ibn al-Fakīh al-Hamadhānī.* Leiden 1885. [Reprints Leiden 1967 and Frankfurt 1992].

Haneberg, Daniel: Erörterungen über Pseudo-Waqidi's Geschichte der Eroberung Syriens. Abhandlungen der Akademie der Wissenschaften München, Philosophisch-philologische Classe. Bd. 9. München 1860.

Hasson, Isaac: Judhām entre la "Jāhiliyya" et l'Islām. In: *Studia Islamica* 81 (1995), pp. 5–42.

Hodgson, Marshall G.: *The Venture of Islam. Vol. 1: The Classical Age.* Chicago 1974.

Hoyland, Robert: *In God's Path. The Arab Conquests and the Creation of an Islamic Empire.* Oxford 2015.

Humphreys, Richard S.: Some Notes on the Futuh al-Sham of al-Azdi al-Basri. In: *H-Net Discussion Networks,* 27 Juni 2001. Retrieved from https://lists.h-net.org/cgi-bin/logbrowse.pl?trx=vx&list=h-mideast-medieval&month=0106&week=d&msg=ByFFHOleN49zfKJKWjz2/g&user=&pw= (27 Juni 2001).

Ibn ʿAbd al-Barr, Yūsuf b. ʿAbdallāh: *Al-istīʿāb fī maʿrifat al-aṣḥāb. Ed. ʿA. al-Bajāwī.* 4 vols. Cairo ca. 1960.

Ibn Abī Ḥātim al-Rāzī, ʿAbd al-Raḥmān: *Kitāb al-jarḥ wa-al-taʿdīl. Ed. Maṭbaʿat majlis dāʾirat al-maʿārif al-ʿuthmāniyya.* 9 vols. Hyderabad 1952–1953 [=1371–1373]. [Reprint Beirut 1952–1953].

Ibn al-ʿAdīm, Kamāl al-Dīn ʿUmar b. Aḥmad: *Bughyat al-ṭalab fī taʾrīkh Ḥalab. Ed. S. Zakkār.* 9 vols. Damascus 1988.

Ibn ʿAsākir, ʿAlī b. al-Ḥasan: *Taʾrīkh madīnat Dimashq. Ed. ʿU. al-ʿAmrawī/A. Shīrī.* 80 vols. Beirut 1995–2001 [=1415–1421].

Ibn Ḥajar al-ʿAsqalānī, Aḥmad b. ʿAlī: *Al-muʿjam al-mufahras aw tajrīd asānīd al-kutub al-mashhūra wa-al-ajzāʾ al-manthūra. Ed. M. Shakkūr al-Ḥājjī.* Beirut 1998 [=1418].

Ibn Ḥajar al-ʿAsqalānī, Aḥmad b. ʿAlī: *Lisān al-mīzān. Ed. Dāʾirat al-maʿrifat al-niẓāmiyya.* 7 vols. Beirut 1986 [=1406].

Ibn Ḥajar al-ʿAsqalānī, Aḥmad b. ʿAlī: *Kitāb al-iṣāba fī tamyīz al-ṣaḥāba. Ed. ʿA. al-Baghawī.* 8 vols. Cairo 1970–1972.

Ibn Ḥajar al-ʿAsqalānī, Aḥmad b. ʿAlī: *Al-durar al-kāmina fī aʿyān al-miʾa al-thāmina. Ed. M. Jād al-Ḥaqq.* 5 vols. Cairo ca. 1966.

Ibn Ḥanbal, Aḥmad: *Al-musnad. Ed. Sh. al-Arnaʾūṭ.* 50 vols. Beirut 1993–2001. [Reprint Beirut 2008].

Ibn Ḥibbān al-Bustī, Muḥammad: *Kitāb al-majrūḥīn min al-muḥaddithīn wa-al-ḍuʿafāʾ wa-al-matrūkīn. Ed. M. Zāyid.* 3 vols. Mecca [1976].

Ibn Ḥibbān al-Bustī, Muḥammad: *Kitāb al-thiqāt. Ed. Maṭbūʿāt dāʾirat al-maʿārif al-ʿuthmāniyya.* 9 vols. Hyderabad 1973–1983 [=1393–1403].

Ibn Ḥibbān al-Bustī, Muḥammad: *Kitāb mashāhīr ʿulamāʾ al-amṣār. Ed. M. Fleischhammer as: Die berühmten Traditionarier der islamischen Länder.* Cairo 1959.

Ibn Hishām, ʿAbd al-Malik: *Al-sīra al-nabawiyya. Ed. F. Wüstenfeld as: Das Leben Muhammed's nach Muhammed Ibn Ishâk bearbeitet von Abd el-Malik Ibn Hischâm. Aus den Handschriften zu Berlin, Leipzig, Gotha und Leyden.* 3 vols. Göttingen 1858–1860.

Ibn Hubaysh, ʿAbd al-Raḥmān b. Muḥammad: *Kitāb al-ghazawāt. Ed. S. Zakkār as: Ghazawāt Ibn Hubaysh.* 2 vols. Beirut 1992 [=1412].

Ibn Manẓūr, Muḥammad b. Mukarram: *Mukhtaṣar taʾrīkh Dimashq li-bn ʿAsākir. Ed. R. al-Naḥḥās.* 29 vols. Damascus 1984–1990.

Ibn Manẓūr, Muḥammad b. Mukarram: *Lisān al-ʿarab. Ed. Dār Ṣādir.* Beirut 1955–1956.

Ibn al-Nadīm, Muḥammad b. Isḥāq: *Al-fihrist. Ed. G. Flügel as: Kitāb al-Fihrist.* 2 vols. Leipzig 1871–1872. [Reprint Beirut 1966].

Ibn Saʿd, Muḥammad: *Kitāb al-ṭabaqāt al-kabīr. Ed. E. Sachau et al. as: Ibn Saad. Biographien Muhammeds, seiner Gefährten und der späteren Träger des Islams bis zum Jahre 230 der Flucht.* 9 vols. Leiden 1904–1940.

al-Ishbīlī, Muḥammad b. Khayr: *Fihrist mā rawāhu ʿan shuyūkhihī min al-dawāwīn al-muṣannafa fī ḍurūb al-ʿilm wa-anwāʿ al-maʿārif. Ed. F. Codera y Zaidín/J. Ribera y Tarragó as: Index des livres et maitres de Abou Bequer Ben Khair.* 2 vols. Zaragosa 1894–1895. [Reprint Bagdad 1963].

Jones, Arnold H./Martindale, John R./Morris, J.: *The Prosopography of the Later Roman Empire.* 3 vols. Cambridge 1971–1992.

Kaḥḥāla, ʿUmar R.: *Muʿjam al-muʾallafīn. Tarājim musannifī al-kutub al-ʿarabiyya.* 15 vols. Damascus 1957–1961. [Reprint Beirut 1983].

Kaegi, Walter E.: *Byzantium and the Early Islamic Conquests.* Cambridge 1992.

Kennedy, Hugh: *The Great Arab Conquests. How the Spread of Islam Changed the World We Live in.* Philadelphia, PA 2008.

Khalek, Nancy: *Damascus after the Muslim Conquest. Text and Image in Early Islam.* Oxford 2011.

Khalek, Nancy: 'He was Tall and Slender, and His Virtues were Numerous'. Byzantine Hagiographical Topoi and the Companions of Muḥammad in al-Azdī's Futūḥ al-Shām. In: Arietta Papaconstantinou/in collaboration with M. Debié and H. Kennedy (eds.): *Writing 'True Stories'. Historians and Hagiographers in the Late Antique and Medieval Near East.* Turnhout 2010, pp. 105–123.

Al-Khaṭīb al-Baghdādī, Aḥmad b. ʿAlī: *Taʾrīkh Baghdād aw Madīnat al-Salām. Ed. Dār al-kutub al-ʿilmiyya.* 14 vols. Beirut 1986.

Kister, Meʾir J.: Mecca and Tamīm. (Aspects of Their Relations). In: *Journal of the Economic and Social History of the Orient* 8 (1965), pp. 113–163.

Kurd ʿAlī, Muḥammad: Makhṭūṭāt wa-maṭbūʿāt. Futūḥ al-Shām. In: *Majallat al-Majmaʿ al-ʿilmī al-ʿarabī bi-Dimashq* [=*Revue de l'Académie Arabe de Damas*] 20 (1945 [=1364]), pp. 544–549.

Lāgha, Muḥyī al-Dīn: Baḥth fī mawārid kitāb futūḥ al-Shām li-Abī ʿAbdallāh al-Azdī. In: *Bulletin de Mawārid* 16 (2011), pp. 196–212.

Landau-Tasseron, Ella: New Data on an Old Manuscript. An Andalusian Version of the Works Entitled Futūḥ al-Shām. In: *al-Qanṭara* 21 (2000), pp. 361–380.

Landau-Tasseron, Ella: Asad from Jahiliyya to Islam. In: *Jerusalem Studies in Arabic and Islam* 6 (1985), pp. 1–25.

Lane, Edward W.: *An Arabic-English Lexicon. Derived from the Best and the Most Copious Eastern Sources.* 8 vols. London 1863–1893. [Reprint Beirut 1997].

Lecker, Michael: *The Banū Sulaym. A Contribution to the Study of Early Islam.* Jerusalem 1989.

Leube, Georg: *Kinda in der frühislamischen Geschichte.* Würzburg 2017.

Madelung, Wilferd F.: Rabīʿa in the Jāhiliyya and in Early Islam. In: *Jerusalem Studies in Arabic and Islam* 28 (2003), pp. 153–170.

Al-Mizzī, Abū al-Ḥajjāj Yūsuf: *Tahdhīb al-kamāl fī asmāʾ al-rijāl. Ed. B. ʿAwwād Maʿrūf.* 35 vols. Beirut 1983–1992 [=1403–1413].

Mourad, Suleiman A.: Poetry, History, and the Early Arab-Islamic Conquests of al-Shām (Greater Syria). In: Ramzi Baalbaki/Saleh S. Agha/Tarif Khalidi (eds.): *Poetry and History. The Value of Poetry in Reconstructing Arab History.* Beirut 2011, pp. 175–193.

Mourad, Suleiman A.: On Early Islamic Historiography. Abū Ismāʿīl al-Azdī and his Futūḥ al-Shām. In: *Journal of the American Oriental Society* 120 (2000), pp. 577–593.

Mourad, Suleiman A.: A Note on the Origin of Faḍāʾil Bayt al-Maqdis Compilations. In: *al-Abḥāth* 44 (1996), pp. 31–48.

Pummer, Reinhard: Foot-Soldiers on the Byzantines of Spies for the Muslims? The Role of Samaritans in the Muslim Conquest of Palestine. In: Carmel McCarthy/John F. Healey (eds.): *Biblical and Near Eastern Essays. Studies in Honour of Kevin J. Cathcart.* London 2004, pp. 280–296.

Al-Qurʾān. Tr. M. Abdel Haleem as: The Qur'an. A New Translation. Oxford 2004.

Rihan, Mohammad: *Politics and Culture of an Umayyad Tribe. Conflict and Factionalism in the Early Islamic Period.* London 2014.

Robinson, Chase F.: *ʿAbd al-Malik.* Oxford 2007. [Reprint Oxford 2012].

Rubin, Uri: Quran and Tafsīr. The Case of "ʿan yadin". In: *Der Islam* 70 (1993), pp. 133–144.

Al-Ṣafadī, Khalīl b. Aybak: *Al-wāfī bi-al-wafayāt. Ed. vol. 2 S. Dedering.* 30 vols. Stuttgart 1949.

Ṣāyama, Ibtisām M.: *Shiʿr al-fatḥ al-islāmiyya li-bilād al-Shām fī ʿahd al-khalīfatayn Abī Bakr wa-ʿUmar. [MA Thesis].* Ghaza 2009 [=1430].

Sayfullāh, M. S.: Sudden Change in Person and Number. Neal Robinson on *Iltifat.* Retrieved from https://www.islamic-awareness.org/quran/text/grammar/robinson (n.d.).

Scheiner, Jens: *Al-Azdī's Futūḥ al-Shām in Past and Present. A Study of the Work's Research History, Parallel Passages and Extant Manuscripts.* Piscataway [forthcoming].

Scheiner, Jens: Scholars, Figures, and Groups in al-Azdī's Futūḥ al-Shām. In: Sebastian Günther (ed.): *Knowledge and Education in Classical Islam. Religious Learning between Continuity and Change.* Leiden [forthcoming].

Scheiner, Jens: Review of: M. Rihan: Politics and Culture of an Umayyad Tribe. Conflict and Factionalism in the Early Islamic Period. London 2014. In: *Der Islam* 93 (2016), pp. 312–315.

Scheiner, Jens: *Die Eroberung von Damaskus. Quellenkritische Untersuchung zur Historiographie in klassisch-islamischer Zeit.* Leiden 2010.

Scheiner, Jens: Grundlegendes zu al-Azdīs Futūḥ aš-Šām. In: *Der Islam* 84 (2007), pp. 1–16.

Schwarzlose, Friedrich W.: *Kitāb as-silāḥ. Die Waffen der alten Araber aus ihren Dichtern dargestellt. Ein Beitrag zur arabischen Alterthumskunde, Synonymik und Lexicographie nebst Registern.* Leipzig 1886. [Reprint Hildesheim 1982].

Sezgin, Fuat: *Geschichte des arabischen Schrifttums.* 17 vols. Leiden 1967–2015.

Shoshan, Boaz: *The Arabic Historical Tradition and the Early Islamic Conquests. Folklore, Tribal Lore, Holy War.* London 2016.

Al-Silafī, Abū Ṭāhir Aḥmad b. Muḥammad: *Muʿjam al-safar. Ed. Shīr M. Zamān.* Islamabad 1988.

Sivan, Emmanuel: *L'Islam et la Croisade. Idéologie et propagande dans les réactions Musulmanes aux Croisades.* Paris 1968.

Sprenger, Aloys: *A Catalogue of the Bibliotheca Orientalis Sprengeriana.* Gießen 1857.

Al-Ṭabarī, Abū Jaʿfar Muḥammad b. Jarīr: *Taʾrīkh al-rusul wa-al-mulūk. Ed. M. de Goeje et al. as: Annales quos scripsit Abu Djafar Mohammed ibn Djarir at-Tabari.* 15 vols. Leiden 1879–1901. [Reprint Beirut 1965].

Toral-Niehoff, Isabel: *Al-Ḥīra. Eine arabische Kulturmetropole im spätantiken Kontext.* Leiden 2014.

Al-Ṭūsī, Muḥammad b. al-Ḥasan: *Al-Fihrist. Ed. M. Ṣādiq.* 2nd ed. Najaf 1960 [=1380].

Ullmann, Manfred/et al.: *Wörterbuch der klassisch arabischen Sprache. Vol. 1: [Kāf]; Vol. 2: [Lām].* 2 vols. Wiesbaden 1970–2009.

Ulrich, Brian J.: *Arabs in the Early Islamic Empire. The Fashioning of al-Azd under the Caliphate.* Edinburgh 2019.

al-ʿUmarī, Akram Ḍ.: al-Azdī wa-kitābuhū "Futūḥ al-Šām". In: idem (ed.): *Dirāsāt taʾrīkhiyya.* Medina 1983, pp. 69–79.

Vajda, Georges: *Les certificats de lecture et de transmission dans les manuscrits arabes de la Bibliothèque nationale de Paris.* Paris 1956.

Vajda, Georges: *Index général des manuscripts arabes musulmans de la Bilbiothèque nationale de Paris.* Paris 1953.

van Ess, Josef: *Der Fehltritt des Gelehrten. Die "Pest von Emmaus" und ihre theologischen Nachspiele.* Heidelberg 2001.

van Ess, Josef: Die Pest von Emmaus. Theologie und Geschichte in der Frühzeit des Islams. In: *Oriens* 36 (2001), pp. 248–267.

von Erdmann, Franz: Ueber die sonderbare Benennung der Europäer, Benu-l-asfar (Nachkommen des Gelben), von Seiten der Westasiaten. In: *Zeitschrift der Deutschen Morgenländischen Gesellschaft* 2 (1848), pp. 237–241.

Wahrmund, Adolf: *Handwörterbuch der arabischen und deutschen Sprache.* Gießen 1898. [Reprint Graz 1970].

Al-Wāqidī, Muḥammad b. ʿUmar: *Futūḥ al-Shām. Ed. Ḥ. al-Ḥājj.* 2 vols. Cairo n.d.

Wehr, Hans: *Wörterbuch für die Schriftsprache der Gegenwart. Tr. J. Milton Cowan as: A Dictionary of Modern Written Arabic (Arabic—English).* 4th ed. Wiesbaden 1979.

Yāqūt al-Rūmī, Abū ʿAbdallāh Yāqūt b. ʿAbdallāh: *Muʿjam al-buldān. Ed. F. Wüstenfeld as: Jaqut's geographisches Wörterbuch.* 6 vols. Leipzig 1866–1873. [Reprint Leipzig 1924].

Index

Note: Page numbers followed by “n” denote endnotes.

Abbān b. Sa'īd b. al-'Āṣ 65, 65n96, 126, 128
al-'Abbās b. 'Abd al-Muṭṭalib 257, 257n494
al-'Abbās b. Sahl b. Sa'd 137, 137n324
'Abd al-A'lā b. Surāqa al-Azdī 234, 234n460
'Abdallāh 93, 93n172
'Abdallāh b. Abī Awfā al-Khuzā'ī 43, 43n27
'Abdallāh b. 'Amr b. al-'Āṣ 184, 184n395, 185
'Abdallāh b. 'Amr b. al-Ṭufayl b. 'Amr b. Dhī al-Nūr al-Azdī 128, 128n308
'Abdallāh b. al-Daylamī 271, 271n516
'Abdallāh b. Muḥammad al-Azdī *see* 'Abdallāh
'Abdallāh b. Qurṭ al-Thumālī 31–32, 75, 75n133, 76, 110–112, 117, 157, 163–165, 170, 174, 175, 177, 182, 192, 199–203, 244–245; ~ 's appointment as commander of Ḥimṣ 274; ~ 's wife 193
'Abd al-Malik b. al-Aswad 106, 106n226
'Abd al-Malik b. Marwān 225, 225n442
'Abd al-Malik b. Nawfal b. Masāḥiq al-Qurashī 70, 70n109, 82, 85, 91, 127, 159, 162, 204, 257,
'Abd al-Malik b. al-Salīk 174, 174n380, 175; *see also* 'Abd al-Raḥmān b. al-Salīk al-Fazārī
'Abd al-Masīḥ b. 'Amr b. Buqayla al-Azdī 103, 103n211; ~ 's dialog with Khālid 104
'Abd al-Raḥmān b. 'Awf 44–45, 45n33, 46, 200
'Abd al-Raḥmān b. Ḥanbal al-Jumaḥī 108, 108n232, 120, 130, 189; ~ 's citation of a poem 131
'Abd al-Raḥmān b. Mu'ādh b. Jabal 4, 231, 231n452; ~ 's death 269–270
'Abd al-Raḥmān b. al-Salīk al-Fazārī 117, 117n273, 192, 244, 274
'Abd al-Raḥmān b. Yazīd b. Jābir al-Azdī 64, 64n91, 80
Abdel Haleem, M. A. S. 33, 285
Abjar b. Bajīr al-'Ijlī *see* Abū Ḥajjār Abjar b. Bajīr
Abode/s 60, 182; God's ~ 133, 155, 239; non-Arabs' ~ (dār al-'ajam) 190n404, 230; ~ of Islam (dār al-islām) 127; ~ of the Byzantine Emperors 168; Satan's ~ 55; worldly ~ 111
'Abs 249, 249n488
Abū al-'Abbās Munīr b. Aḥmad b. al-Ḥasan al-Khashshāb 14–16, 19–20, 36, 36n5, 38, 85, 129, 161, 197, 235; ~ 's funeral 37n6
Abū al-'Abbās al-Walīd b. Ḥammād al-Ramlī 14–16, 18–20, 32, 36, 36n3, 38, 43, 56, 60, 64, 66–69, 73, 76, 80, 82, 85, 129, 162, 197, 236
Abū 'Abd al-A'lā al-Shā'ir 109, 109n239
Abū 'Abdallāh b. al-Ḥusayn 243, 243n479
Abū 'Abdallāh Muḥammad b. Ḥamd b. Ḥāmid al-Iṣfahānī 16
Abū 'Alī al-Ghassānī al-Qurṭubī 18
Abū 'Alī Ḥasan b. Aḥmad b. Yūsuf al-Ṣūfī al-Awqī 12, 19
Abū 'Amra 109, 109n238
Abū al-A'war 'Amr b. Sufyān al-Sulamī 82, 82n145, 238, 259
Abū Bakr 2–3, 5, 26, 32, 38, 39n15, 43, 51, 70, 74–75, 85, 96–97, 100–102, 130, 203, 259; ~ as al-Ṣiddīq 39n15, 42, 51, 57, 63, 80, 95, 127n300,

129, 133, 203, 222; ~ asks people of Yemen for support 51–54; ~ as servant of God 73, 95, 129; ~ as Successor of the Messenger of God 28, 39n15, 41, 46, 48, 51, 52, 54, 56, 62, 73, 78, 83, 88, 89, 95, 97, 102, 108, 110, 111, 129, 133; ~ in poems 91, 112; ~ interprets dreams 42, 57; ~ 's appointment of commanders 49–50, 54–56, 59, 124, 222; ~ 's appointment of Khālid as chief commander 107–108, 111; ~ 's consideration of attacking the Byzantines 40–41, 282; ~ 's consultation with leading Companions 44–48; ~ 's death 133–135, 137; ~ 's death (as means of dating) 130, 132, 138; ~ 's dispatch of Abū ʿUbayda 60–62; ~ 's dispatch of commanders 62–69, 76–84, 86–90, 92, 93, 94, 95; ~ 's role during the *ridda* wars 39–40
Abū Bakr Muḥammad b. Aḥmad b. Ṭāhir al-Ishbīlī 18
Abū Bashīr al-Tanūkhī 195, 195n415, 196–198
Abū al-Dardāʾ al-Anṣārī 4, 274, 274n517, 275
Abū al-Faḍl Jaʿfar b. ʿAlī al-Hamadhānī al-Iskandarānī 12–13, 38, 38n9
Abū Ḥafṣ *see* ʿUmar b. al-Khaṭṭāb
Abū Ḥafṣ al-Azdī 73, 73n129
Abū Ḥajjār Abjar b. Bajīr 99, 99n196; ~ 's dialog with Khālid 100–101
Abū al-Ḥasan *see* ʿAlī b. Abī Ṭālib
Abū al-Ḥasan ʿAlī b. Aḥmad b. Isḥāq al-Baghdādī 14–16, 18–19, 20, 36, 36n4, 38, 85, 129, 161–162, 197, 235
Abū al-Ḥasan ʿAlī b. al-Ḥusayn b. al-Farāʾ al-Mawṣilī 16–17
Abū al-Ḥasan ʿAlī b. Masʿūd al-Mawṣilī 38, 38n10
Abū Ḥudhayfa Isḥāq b. Bishr 17
Abū Hurayra al-Dawsī 59, 59n74, 234
Abū al-Ḥusayn Aḥmad b. Muḥammad b. Musbiḥ al-Muqriʾ 13, 15, 19, 37, 37n7
Abū Isḥāq Ibrāhīm b. Saʿīd b. ʿAbdallāh al-Tujībī al-Ḥabbāl 14–20, 37, 37n6, 38, 85, 129, 161, 197, 235
Abū Ismāʿīl Muḥammad b. ʿAbdallāh al-Azdī al-Baṣrī 1–2, 10, 12, 23–24, 35, 38, 38n11, 43, 52, 56, 60, 64, 66–70, 73, 76, 80, 82, 85, 87, 91–93, 101, 104–106, 110, 112, 115–117, 119, 121–123, 127, 129–130, 132, 137–139, 156–157, 159–163, 168, 173–175, 179, 182, 189–192, 194–195, 197, 199–200, 203–205, 213, 219, 223, 225–227, 229, 232, 234, 236, 238, 243–244, 246, 257, 262, 264–267, 271–272, 274–275; ~ as compiler-author 6–8, 10, 13, 17–18, 23, 38n11; ~ as part of the *riwāyas* 13–20; ~ 's role in *isnāds* 31–32
Abū Jahḍam al-Azdī 92, 92n170, 117, 157, 174–175, 195, 199, 205, 213, 219–220, 225–226, 244, 274
Abū Janāb al-Kalbī 271, 271n515
Abū Khaddāsh 179, 179n389, 182, 203
Abū al-Khazraj al-Ghassānī 122, 122n290
Abū Marthad al-Khawlānī 224, 224n441
Abū Maʿshar 190, 190n405, 191, 272
Abū al-Maymūn ʿAbd al-Wahhāb b. ʿAtīq b. Wardān al-ʿĀmir al-Miṣrī 12, 15, 17
Abū Mikhnaf al-Azdī 17, 43n26, 52n55, 68n104, 70n109, 91n168, 92n170, 93n172, 104n213, 112n250, 139n329, 161n357, 168n370; ~ 's grandfather 70n109; ~ 's uncle 91n168
Abū al-Mughfil 82, 82n144
Abū Muḥammad ʿAbd al-Raḥmān b. al-Naḥḥās al-Miṣrī 18
Abū Mujāhid Saʿd 66, 66n98, 67, 173
Abū al-Muthannā al-Kalbī 104, 104n213
Abū Naḍra 257, 257n496
Abū Qatāda al-Anṣārī 63, 63n90, 64
Abū Qubays Mountain 165, 165n366
Abū Saʿīd al-Khudrī 96, 96n183, 97, 257
Abū Saʿīd al-Maqburī 70, 70n110, 82–84, 127, 204, 257
Abū Sufyān b. Ḥarb 57, 57n67, 88n162, 130, 230; ~ in a poem 131; ~ 's dispatch to Syria 229–230; ~ 's son 238
Abū Ṭāhir Aḥmad b. Muḥammad al-Silafī 11–20, 37, 37n8; ~ 's nephew 20
Abū ʿUbāda 76, 76n135; ~ 's grandfather 76–78
Abū ʿUbayda b. al-Jarrāḥ 2–5, 22, 26–27, 45, 45n35, 47, 53, 57, 64–65, 67, 69, 74, 76, 78, 81–82, 85–86, 90–92, 107, 141–143, 147, 171–174, 177–179, 241–243, 250–251; ~ as chief commander 45n35, 89, 124, 137–138, 151, 178, 187, 206, 217, 269; ~ at al-Jābiya 116; ~ converting a Christian 211–212; deposition

of ~ 108, 111–112; ~ favoured best by Muḥammad 81; mourning for ~ 269, 273; ~ 's appointment of ʿAmr as commander 260; ~ 's death 268–269, 272–274; ~ 's debate with a Byzantine 151–153; ~ 's dispatch to Syria 50, 60–63; ~ 's funeral 269; ~ 's participation in the Battle of Ajnādayn 123–128; ~ 's participation in the Battle of Fiḥl 144–146, 153–163, 166; ~ 's participation in the Battle of Marj al-Ṣuffar 131–132; ~ 's participation in the Battle of al-Yarmūk 179–211, 219, 222–223, 224, 227–241, 252–253; ~ 's participation in the conquest of Aleppo 246; ~ 's participation in the conquest of Damascus 122, 130, 132, 138–140; ~ 's participation in the conquest of Ḥimṣ 168–171; ~ 's participation in the conquest of Jerusalem 253–261; ~ 's rescue of the Prophet Muḥammad 61; ~ 's route to Syria 72–73; ~ 's tent 157, 222, 223, 260–261; ~ 's victory in the Battle of Maʾāb 73; ~ 's vision 223–225
Abū Uḥayḥa Saʿīd b. al-ʿĀṣ 164, 164n363; ~ 's great-grandson 164
Abū Umāma al-Bāhilī 92, 92n171, 132, 173
Abū Ziyād 106, 106n225
Abyssinia, emigration to ~ 49n47; land of ~ 49, 148–149
ʿĀd 181, 181n393, 224, 275
Adam 41n21, 71n116, 150, 150n346, 211; children of ~ 268
Aden 181n393, 181n394, 276, 276n519
Adham b. Muḥriz al-Bāhilī 139–140, 140n330, 168, 173
Adherents, ~ of Christianity 145, 147, 176–177, 188, 190, 195–195 *see also* Christians; ~ of Islam 46–48, 65, 68, 71, 74, 82, 108, 121–122, 134, 154, 156, 163–165, 167–168, 170, 185, 190, 202, 207, 235, 241, 256, 261, 270, 280–281; ~ of Polytheism 82 *see also* adherents of the former religion; ~ of the former religion 10, 48; ~ of the Torah 262; ~ of the Truth 275
ʿAdī b. Ḥātim 67, 67n101
Afterlife, the 48–49, 56, 77, 79, 127, 134, 148, 160, 182, 202, 214, 239, 244, 271, 275, 277, 283
ahl 25, 27, 122, 149n343, 239; ~ al-dhimma 27, 196, 226 *see also* People of the Book; ~ al-ḥifāẓ 236; ~ al-najda wa-al-shidda 129; ~ al-quwwa wa-al-shidda 27, 107; ~ al-raʾy 221; ~ al-rāyāt 236; ~ al-sābiqa 86
Ahlwardt, Wilhelm 11
Aḥmas 116, 116n271
al-Ajlaḥ b. ʿAbdallāh 205, 205n424
Ajnādayn 3, 41n22, 93n173, 123n293; ~ as the first great battle in Syria 130; Battle of ~ 3, 32, 39n15, 41n20, 42n23, 45n35, 48n44, 50n50, 50n51, 56n66, 65n96, 70n111, 76n134, 88n162, 89n165, 116n267, 123–130, 131, 132, 175, 192, 215, 228n445, 272; people of ~ 125
akhbār (traditions) 4, 22–23; ~ historiography 4; *see also* khabar
al-ʿAlā b. Zuhayr, ~ 's brother 91n168
Aleppo 58n71, 59n76, 72n119, 116n272, 128n303, 172, 172n377, 188n400, 246n484, 249n489, 250; conquest of ~ 246; people of ~ 246, 250
ʿAlī b. Abī Ṭālib 44, 44n30, 48, 127n300, 256, 284
Allāhu akbar (God is the greatest) 27, 40n17, 114, 158, 162, 209, 247, 248, 263
Alms 268
amān 27, 42 *see also* Letter of protection
ʿĀmila 22, 144, 144n338, 157, 228, 236
amīr 27, 43 *see also* Commander
ʿĀmir, ʿAbd al-Munʿim 7–9, 12–13, 20
amīr al-muʾminīn 27, 136 *see also* Commander of the Believers
ʿĀmir al-Shaʿbī 105, 105n217, 205, 267
ʿAmmān 73, 73n128, 124n295
ʿAmmār b. Yāsir 260, 260n500
Amna bt. Abī Bishr b. Zayd al-Aṭwal al-Azdiyya 193, 193n410, 194
ʿAmr b. ʿAbd al-Raḥmān 138, 138n325, 246
ʿAmr b. al-ʿĀṣ 4, 89n165, 91–92, 123–126, 128, 132, 134, 141–143, 169, 172, 177, 183–185, 188–190, 211, 222–223, 227, 229, 239, 260, 269–270; ~ as chief commander 90; ~ 's appointment as commander 89; ~ 's appointment as commander of Syria 272–273; ~ 's brother 128; ~ 's great-grandfather 164n363; ~ 's letter

to the people of Jerusalem 186; ~ 's sister 239n471; ~ 's son 186
ʿAmr b. al-Ḥajjāj 232, 232n454
ʿAmr b. Mālik al-Qaynī 139, 139n329, 157, 160, 265
ʿAmr b. Muḥṣan b. Surāqa b. ʿAbd al-Aʿlā b. Surāqa al-Azdī 31–32, 64, 64n92, 80, 82, 110, 117, 119, 132, 163, 238
ʿAmr b. Saʿīd b. al-ʿĀṣ 65, 65n94, 163–166
ʿAmr b. Shuʿayb 91, 91n169
ʿAmr b. al-Ṭufayl b. ʿAmr b. Dhī al-Nūr al-Azdī 110, 110n245, 111, 207–209, 233–234
amwāl 39n13, 174
al-ʿAmwās 268n512; plague of ~ 32, 45n35, 50n51, 231n452, 268, 271n516, 272
Anacoluthon 26
Anas b. Mālik 51, 51n53, 52–54, 56
Anatolia 176n386, 246n484, 247, 250
al-Anbār 60n81, 103n205, 109n234, 109n236; raid on ~ 109
Angels 75, 200–201, 211, 225, 266
Antioch 3, 41n22, 59n76, 70n112, 72, 72n120, 73–74, 74n131, 75, 140–141, 174–175, 177, 189, 189n403, 244, 249; Heraclius's departure from ~ 246
Antiquity 26; late- ~ 1, 26, 237n467
Apostasy, ~ wars (ridda) 2, 39n15, 40n18
ʿaql (mind), creation of the ~ 214
Arab/s 2, 38, 38n12, 40, 46, 57, 60, 71–72, 84–86, 95, 103, 126, 140–141, 146, 151, 157, 160, 175–176, 187–190, 195–196, 207, 213–214, 216–217, 230, 237, 245, 252, 265; apostatising ~ 40; categories of the ~ 189–190; Christian ~ 56n66, 71, 75, 85, 99n196, 100–101, 107, 123, 141, 153, 190, 222–223, 245; coming of the ~ to Abū Bakr 80; ~ commander 187; ~ earthly paradise 175; ~ horse/s 236, 245; ~ horsemen 53, 54, 69, 100, 207; ~ian tribe/s 2, 39n14, 40n17, 45n33, 60n81, 72n122, 113n256; ~ land 82, 167; ~ noblemen 53n59, 59n76, 207, 227, 257; pagan ~ 42n23; northern ~ian tribe/s 47n41, 47n42, 54n62, 59n75, 59n78, 60n79, 68n106, 83n148, 84n151, 84n153, 84n154, 87n162, 97n187, 101n200, 111n247, 112n248, 112n249, 113n251, 116n270, 116n271, 144n336, 144n337, 144n338, 164n364, 165n369, 198n417, 233n458, 241n476, 249n489; ~ Prophet 245; southern ~ian tribe/s 57n68, 58n71, 58n72, 60n80, 80n142, 105n218, 112n249, 121n287, 144n336, 144n337, 144n338, 144n339, 164n365, 195n414, 228n444, 228n445, 228n446, 232n453, 233n457, 242n478, 265n509; ~ tribes 2, 39n14; Yemenite ~ 265
al-ʿAraba 79n139; Battle of ~ and al-Dāthina 2, 50n50, 76n134, 79, 92
Arak 116, 116n272
Armenia 176, 176n385, 176n386; ~ n Byzantine general 176n388; ~ n unit 41n19; people of ~ 199, 227; ruler of ~ 176, 222n432, 227, 236; Vardan as ~ n name 122n292
Asad 60, 60n80, 98n188, 198n417, 228
al-ʿashara al-mubashshara 39n14, 127, 127n300
al-Ashtar *see* Mālik b. al-Ḥārith al-Nakhaʿī
Aslam 84, 84n152
ʿAṭāʾ b. ʿAjlān 257, 257n495, 262, 264
awwābūn (penitents) 62
Ayfaʿ *see* Dhū al-Kalāʿ
Ayla 41n22, 70n113, 190, 190n406
ʿAyn al-Tamr 60n81, 93n173, 94n175, 109n236, 112; Battle of ~ 98n190, 99n194, 109–110; people of ~ 109
al-Azd 8, 22–23, 58, 58n72, 227, 232–234
al-Azdī *see* Abū Ismāʿīl Muḥammad b. ʿAbdallāh al-Azdī al-Baṣrī

Baalbek 3, 41n20, 58n71, 67n100, 93n173, 118n277, 140–143, 144, 170n375; conquest of ~ 169; fortress of ~ 169; people of ~ 118–119, 143, 169; raids on the region of ~ 143
Badr 45n38; Battle of ~ 45; battle-day of ~ 274
Bāhān 3, 176n388, 177, 188–189, 195–198, 207, 221, 225–227; ~ as chief commander 5, 176, 187, 194, 198, 210–213, 215, 226, 231, 245; ~ 's death 245; ~ 's debate with Khālid 212–219; ~ 's speech 194–195; ~ 's strategy in the Battle of al-Yarmūk 219–220; studies on ~ 22; ~ 's vision 221
Bajīla 116, 116n270, 116n271
Bakr b. Wāʾil 97, 97n187, 99, 99n195, 101n200, 108, 112, 120, 233n458
Balad (region) 102, 123

al-Balādhurī 23–24, 107n231, 117n276, 122n291
al-Balqā' 41n22, 50n50, 73n126, 73n127, 124, 124n295, 141n333, 150, 152, 183; ~ in a poem 237
Balty-Guesdon, Marie-Genevieve 9–11, 284n526
Banī Yāsīn, Yūsuf 2, 7, 9–11, 20–21, 25, 31, 33, 38n9, 43n26, 43n27, 52n55, 52n56, 52n57, 67n103, 69n107, 70n109, 76n135, 82n144, 91n168, 72n170, 93n172, 104n213, 106n222, 115n261, 116n267, 117n273, 139n327, 139n329, 159n354, 161n357, 163n361, 168n370, 170n376, 190n405, 195n413, 205n424, 205n425, 236n464, 236n465, 246n485, 257n496
Bānqiyā 98n190, 106n227; people of ~ 106–107
Banū 'Abs 249, 249n489
Banū 'Āmir b. Lu'ayy 54, 54n62
Banū 'Amr 68n106, 241, 241n476
Banū al-Aṣfar *see also* Byzantines, the 40n19, 46, 46n39, 51
Banū Buqayla 105, 105n218
Banū 'Ijl 101, 101n200, 102, 108
Banū Ka'b 84, 84n151
Banū Mashja'a 115, 115n262, 120
Banū Muḥārib b. Fihr 87n162, 113, 113n251, 173
Banū Numayr 198, 198n417, 199, 253
Banū al-Qayn 144n339, 157
Banū Sahm 165, 165n369
Banū Sa'īd b. al-'Āṣ 111, 111n247
Banū Sulaym 83, 83n148, 98n188, 115n264
Banū Taghlib 109, 112, 112n248, 113n256
Bashīr b. Sa'd al-Anṣārī 98, 98n190, 106–107, 109
Bashīr b. Thawr al-'Ijlī 108, 108n233
al-Baṣra 8, 60n81, 97n185, 99n195, 102n203; desert of ~ 113n256; land of ~ 60n81, 97–99
Battle-day/s (yawm/ayyām) 30, 39n14, 92, 207; ~ in a poem 209; ~ of Ajnādayn 131, 132, 192; ~ of al-'Araba and al-Dāthina 92; ~ of Badr 274; ~ of Fiḥl 157, 175, 192; ~ of Marj al-Ṣuffar 132; ~ of Mu'ta 106; ~ of al-Yarmūk 227, 238, 243
Battlefield 125–126, 200–201, 239
Baysān 70n112, 70n113, 143, 143n334, 144n335
Bayt al-Maqdis 7; Faḍā'il ~ 36n3; Jabal ~ 128n302 *see also* Jerusalem
Believer/s 41n21, 51, 56, 62–63, 69, 78, 86, 95, 110, 141, 154, 163, 166–167, 177, 200–201, 239, 252, 265, 271–272, 280; Commander of the ~ 27, 44n28, 136–137, 153, 154–155, 166–167, 171–172, 178–181, 190, 199–200, 203–204, 230, 242, 252, 255–256, 259–261, 264, 273, 276, 278–279, 282–283; Yemenite ~ 51
Berlin, manuscript 9767 11–13, 14, 16, 19, 20, 21, 37n8
bid'a (innovation) 28, 65, 79
Bilāl 50, 50n49, 78–79, 261; ~ 's dispatch 79
binā' (tent) 196
Binitarianism 42n23, 150, 187, 218
al-Biqā' *see* Bekaa 169n371
Biṣbahan b. Ṣalūbā 107, 107n231
Bishop/s 44n19, 199, 201, 205, 230–231
Bosra 41n20, 93n173, 106n222, 108n232, 116n267, 116n269, 118, 118n278, 122n290, 123–124, 181n393, 181n394, 228n445, 275; Battle of ~ 119–121, 275; conquest of ~ 3, 121; people of ~ 118–119, 121
Bow 62, 62n87, 151–152, 152n350, 157; ~men 41n19
Brockelmann, Carl 9–11
al-Bukhārī 33
Byzantine/s, the 2–3, 5, 10, 38, 40, 40n19, 42, 46–48, 50–51, 56–57, 72–73, 75, 78, 81–82, 89–90, 92, 107–108, 120, 123–127, 129, 132, 138–139, 141–146, 153–166, 168, 172–185, 188–213, 219–220, 222–224, 227–241, 243–248, 250–252, 272, 279, 281; a ~ grand man's vision 225–226; a ~ man's murder 226–227; Abū 'Ubayda's negotiation with ~ 151–153; ~ army 3, 120, 125, 129, 145, 161–162, 166, 175, 179, 187, 236, 250; ~ cavalry 132, 155–156, 158, 174, 198, 209; ~ chiefs 232, 281; ~ commanders 92, 119n282, 198, 215, 219; ~ corruption 3, 10, 40n19, 152, 174, 195–197; ~ decision makers (ahl al-ra'y) 221; ~ defeat 3, 70n112, 145, 156, 163, 176n388, 198, 209–210, 244; description of the ~ 46, 85, 156, 231; ~ Emperor 2, 29,

70, 70n112, 73–75, 77, 84–86, 131, 171–172, 174–175, 180, 187–189, 194, 210, 212, 221, 244; ~ Empire 29, 70n112, 74–75, 145, 175, 175n383, 176–177, 220–221; ~ encampment 3, 212–213, 220, 222–223; ~ fortress/es 40n19, 56–57, 77, 140–142, 148, 165–166, 168, 171, 178, 184–186, 192, 195, 215–216, 253, 256, 280–282; ~ grand man/men 41n19, 148, 156, 160, 174, 196–198, 210–212, 244–245, 247; ~ horsemen 120, 245; land of the ~ 68, 172, 178; Muʿādh's negotiation with ~ 147–151; ~ noblemen 71; ~s' children 72, 141, 177, 220, 230; ~ 's rule 217; ~ sovereigns 29, 183; the Mighty of ~ 27; ~ (white) clothes 216, 259

Caesar *see also* Heraclius and Byzantines Emperor 29, 70n112, 132, 132n314, 133, 138, 140–141, 143, 145, 174, 189, 219–220, 276; ~ in Antioch 140, 141; ~ 's reaction to the lost Battle of al-Yarmūk 244–245
Caesarea 45n37, 50n50, 56n66, 70n112, 70n113, 83n150, 84n155, 99n194 129, 129n310, 168–169, 174, 274n518; conquest of ~ 4, 32, 274, 276–282, 283; people of ~ 169, 175, 276–277, 280–282
Caetani, Leone 23
Cairo 11–12, 36n4, 37n6, 37n7, 120n285, 284n526; Mashhad al-Ḥusayn 284n527; Old ~ 15–16
Caliph 28, 172, 183; ~ ʿAbd al-Malik 225n442; ~ Abū Bakr 5; ~ ʿAlī 284; ~ Muʿāwiya 284; ~ ʿUmar 4–5, 254; *see also* khalīfa and khalīfat rasūl Allāh
caliphate (khilāfa) 29, 44n28, 44n29, 104n213, 134n319, 55, 254; ~ of ʿ Abd al-Malik b. Marwān 225; ~ of ʿUmar 284; ~ of ʿUthmān 284
Call, for prayers 79, 248, 261; ~er, for prayers 79, 248
Camel/s 54, 66, 114, 195n412, 216–218, 267; ʿAbdallāh b. Qurṭ al-Thumālī's riding ~ 202; Abū Bakr's female riding ~ 62; Saʿīd b. ʿĀmir b. Ḥudhaym's she-~ 79; she-~ 114, 118n280; ~ 's tar 260; ʿUmar's ~ 258–259
Caskel, Werner 33
Castle/s ; *see also* fortress/es 195, 229; ~ of al-Khawarnaq 237n468
Cavalry, Byzantine ~ 41n19, 119n282, 132, 155–156, 158, 198, 208–209, 213, 230, 280; Muslim ~ 40n17, 46–47, 54n59, 72, 83n150, 90, 93n173, 97n187, 98, 120, 125–127, 131–132, 138, 143, 146, 154–158, 160–163, 166, 169–170, 184, 187, 198, 206–210, 216, 227, 230, 235, 239, 214, 246–248, 250, 280, 282; ~man/men, Byzantine ~ 158, 174, 209, 250, 280; ~man/men, Muslim 46, 54n61, 110, 143, 159, 168–171, 209, 230, 247; Persian ~ 106; ~ raids 141; the blessed ~ 157; ~ unit/s (katība, khayl) 28, 29, 98
Chief/s, Byzantine 232, 281; ~ in a poem 238; Muslim ~ 29, 40n17, 68n106, 69, 142, 168, 172, 177–178, 190, 217, 241–243, 255
Chieftains 40n18; ~ in a poem 234
Chieftainship 68n105, 68n106, 241–242
Child/children 53, 55, 68, 71–72, 126, 141, 166, 168, 177, 193, 218, 220, 230, 276; Arabs as ~ of one mother and one father 46, 263; association of a ~ with God 42n23, 150, 218; ~ of Adam 268; ~ of al-Aṣfar 40n19, 46n39; the Byzantine sovereigns' ~ 177
Christian/s, the 22, 56, 56n66, 57, 144–145, 155, 189–190, 194, 195, 245, 258, 279; ~ Arabs 38n12, 40n19, 70n112, 75, 99n196, 101, 123, 141, 189–190, 190n404, 222, 223, 245; ~ as Polytheists 42n23; ~ foot-messenger 187–188; ~ 's conversion 10; ~ 's scripture 129,150; ~ spies 56n66, 133, 187
Christianity 10, 38n12, 58n71, 71, 85, 189–190, 195, 222
Clothes 104, 210; Byzantine white ~ 190n404, 216, 259; Muslims wearing white ~ 259
Commander/s (amīr) 27, 215, 262, 268; Byzantine ~ 3, 41n19, 70n112, 72, 75, 92, 199n282, 126, 140, 176, 196, 210, 219, 221, 222n432, 236, 244–245; Byzantine ~ of Damascus 133, 138 ; Byzantine ~ of Ḥimṣ 122; chief ~ 149; ~ in a poem 91, 237; Muslim ~ 2–5, 41n20, 43, 44n28, 48–50, 50n50, 50n51, 54–55, 57, 59, 59n76, 59n77, 67–69, 70n111, 78, 81–84, 84n155, 89, 89n165, 93, 97, 99, 100, 119, 124, 138, 151, 168–169, 200, 204, 206, 222,

227, 232, 241–242, 246, 248–249, 251, 260, 262, 274, 277–279; Muslim ~ of Damascus 274; Muslim ~ of Ḥimṣ 75n133, 251, 274; ~ of the Believers (amīr al-mu'minīn) 27, 44n28, 136–137, 153–155, 166–167, 171–172, 178–181, 190, 199–200, 203–204, 230, 242, 252, 255–256, 259, 260–261, 264, 273, 276, 278–279, 282–283; ~ of the districts 54, 260–261, 276; Sasanid ~ 94n175, 103, 106n228
Companion/s 42, 80, 81, 83, 93, 146, 148, 151, 152, 160, 164, 188, 202, 211, 212, 217, 261, 280; Abū Bakr's ~ 51; Abū 'Ubayda's ~ 125, 134, 142, 151, 183, 250, 253, 259; 'Amr b. al- 'Āṣ's ~ 143, 239; al-Ashtar's ~ 242, 248, 249, 250; Bāhān's ~ 3, 195–196, 197, 198, 212, 215, 219–221, 232; Bashīr b. Sa'd's ~ 106–107; al-Ḍaḥḥāk b. Qays's ~ 277–279; al-Durunjār's ~ 120–121, 236, 240; Heraclius's ~ 74, 245, 246; Khālid's ~ 97, 101, 116, 118–119, 125, 131, 156, 158, 209, 214; Maysara b. Masrūq's ~ 172, 247, 248, 250, 251; Mu'ādh b. Jabal's ~ 207, 270–271; Mukhaymis's ~ 4, 254; al-Muthannā b. Ḥāritha's ~ 95, 102, 108; ~ of the Prophet 2, 23, 39–40, 43, 43n26, 43n27, 47n44, 48n47, 51n53, 52n57, 58n69, 58n70, 59n73, 59n74, 59n76, 59n77, 60n82, 61, 67n100, 84, 92n171, 99n193, 101n201, 109n237, 185, 200, 201, 258, 268, 278; Shuraḥbīl b. Ḥasana's ~ 125; Suhayl b. 'Amr's ~ 88; Suwayd b. Quṭba's ~ 98; the Byzantines' ~ 243; 'Umar's ~ 257, 259, 261; Yazīd b. Abī Sufyān's ~ 238
Conduct, Muslims' 48, 65, 133, 135–136, 196, 222, 264, 278
Conrad, Lawrence 6–8, 21–23, 35n2, 36n3, 71n115
Constantinople 3, 70n112, 72n120, 175, 175n384; Heraclius's return to ~ 246
Conversion, to Islam 89, 101, 266; a Byzantine grand man's ~ 212, 220; Byzantines' ~ 219; Christians' ~ 10, 56n66, 194; Jirja's ~ 189; Ka'b b. Ḥabr's ~ 4, 262–264
Converts, Muslim 212
Cross/es 56, 56n66, 129, 149, 205, 208, 230
Crucify 110, 112n249
Crusades 6; ~ (period) 12, 19
Cyprus 87n159, 87n160, 87n161, 89, 89n163

al-Ḍaḥḥāk b. Qays 4, 84, 84n155, 206–207, 269, 277–279, 280; ~ 's cousin 278
Damascus 3–4, 8, 36n4, 37n8, 40n19, 41n22, 42n23, 45n35, 45n37, 48n44, 50n50, 56n66, 69n108, 70n112, 72, 72n118, 72n119, 89n165, 93n173, 115n265, 115n266, 116n269, 118n278, 118n279, 120n282, 121n288, 122, 122n291, 123, 125, 129, 132, 132n315, 137, 138n326, 139n328, 140n331, 141, 141n333, 169, 172–173, 173n378, 175, 176n388, 177, 179–180, 182–183, 187, 189, 199, 203, 208, 241, 251, 253, 283; ~ as one of the greatest cities in Syria 142; commander of ~ 133, 138; conquest of ~ 22, 32, 44n28, 138–139, 140–142, 143, 272; ~ in a poem 131, 139; land of ~ 118, 124, 182, 188, 243, 251; ~ manuscript 12–13, 20; Muslim commander of ~ 45n37, 274; Muslim people of ~ 275; people of ~ 116, 125, 131–132, 140, 182–183, 241, 275; raid on ~ 165, 169; ~ referred to as Dimashqa 131n313; ~ 's al-Jābiya Gate 122, 130, 132, 138; ~ 's Eastern Gate 93n173, 122, 130, 132, 138; siege of ~ 116, 130, 132, 137–138
Darādaka, Ṣāliḥ 7, 52n55
Dārayyā 138, 138n326; ~ in a poem 139
Dārim al-'Absī 74, 74n131; ~ 's son 74n131
al-Dāthina 79n140; Battle of al-'Araba and ~ 2, 50n50, 76n134, 79, 92–93
da'wa (call), religious 28, 87, 97, 147–149, 152, 210, 218, 251, 252, 267; Abū Bakr's ~ 48–49; ~ for support from people of Syria 85
Daws, in a poem 253, 253n457
Day; Dooms~ (yawm al-ma'ād) 111, 268; farewell ~ 62; ~ of Fear 111; ~ of Judgement 62n86, 135, 270; ~ of Resurrection (yawm al-qiyāma) 79, 96, 136, 263, 266, 275
Dayr al-Jabal 193, 193n409, 205
Dayr Khālid 7, 33, 122, 130
Dayr Misḥal 170, 170n375
Defeat; God's ~ 281; Muslims' ~ 230; *see also* Byzantines, the ~ defeat

de Goeje, Michaël 6, 9, 21–23, 120n282, 222n432
de Slane, Baron William Mac Guckin 9–11
Destruction 65, 138, 152, 162, 197, 200, 224, 252, 278
Dhāt al-Manār 73, 73n125, 144n337, 265
Dhāt al-Ṣanamayn 116, 116n269
dhikr (invocation of God) 55, 57, 210, 228, 228n447, 269, 271
dhimma (protection) 28, 105, 144, 166, 182, 186, 255, 260; ahl al-~ *see also* ahl al-dhimma and People of the Book; ~t Allāh 185, 257
Dhū al-Kalāʿ 52, 52n57, 53, 57, 171
Dhū al-Nūr al-Ṭufayl b. ʿAmr al-Azdī 110, 110n246, 128n308; ~ 's son 110, 128n308
Dionysius of Tellmaḥrē 17
Ḍirār b. al-Azūr 120, 120n283
Ḍirār b. al-Khaṭṭāb 91, 91n167
Disbelievers *see also* Unbeliever/s 100, 149, 163, 202
al-Durunjār 41n19, 119n282; ~ at Baalbek 141; ~ at Bosra 199; ~ at Fiḥl 146; ~ at Marj al-Ṣuffar 131; ~ at al-Yarmūk 222–223, 227, 232, 235–236, 240

Edessa 70n112, 246, 246n484
El Cheikh, Nadia 9, 22
Emigrant/s, the 31, 38n12, 40n17, 45, 45n36, 47, 47n44, 49, 61, 80, 82n145, 95, 116, 181, 200, 257; earliest ~ 67; early ~ 127, 278; noble ~ 86; prominent ~ 45
Encampment; Byzantine ~ 3, 127, 132, 145, 154, 156, 159, 162–163, 166, 181–182, 194, 198, 207, 210, 212–213, 219–220, 222–224, 231, 252; Muslims' ~ 4, 51, 53, 57, 80–81, 98–99, 118, 120, 133, 137, 142–144, 146, 156, 160, 164, 171, 174, 180, 186, 193, 199, 203–204, 210, 215, 222–223, 227, 230, 232, 235–236, 246, 250, 273, 276, 282
Esau 46n39

Farrukh-Shadād b. Hurmuz 106, 106n228, 107
Farwa b. Luqayṭ 168, 168n370, 173
fatḥ/futūḥ (conquest/s) 2–4, 28, 40, 43, 55, 57, 74–75, 77, 90–91, 95, 108, 119, 133, 138, 141, 149, 154, 167–168, 169, 174, 180, 202–203, 227, 252, 256, 267–268, 272, 276, 282–283; ~ literature 1
Fear, ~ of defeat 250; ~ of God 55, 142, 196
Fighter for the cause of God (mujāhid) 29, 43, 46, 62, 89, 111, 182, 201, 280
Fiḥl 3, 42n23, 44n28, 45n35, 54n59, 56n66, 75n133, 141n333, 144n335, 168, 174–175, 215; Battle of ~ 32, 50n51, 58n70, 58n71, 59n76, 65n94, 76n134, 111n247, 115n263, 121n287, 144–146, 153–166, 203; battle-day of ~ 175, 192; commander of ~ 120n282; conquest of ~ 48n44, 70n111, 144n336, 144n337, 144n338, 144n339; date of the Battle of ~ 272; people of ~ 157, 166; siege of ~ 93n173
Fire, the 111, 153, 218, 271–272, 275, 281; ~ pit 218; ~ worship 42n23, 218
fitna (first civil war) 284
Flag/s 153, 157, 159–160, 162–163, 173, 198, 202, 206–208, 210, 222, 227, 230, 232, 238, 282; followers of the ~ (ahl al-rāyāt) 236; ~holder/s 58n70, 58n71, 67n100, 92n171, 140n331, 173, 233n457, 234, 281; ~ in a poem 234; Muḥammad's ~ 39n14, 45n37, 274, 281; white ~ 122
Follower/s (tābiʿūn) 62, 72, 76, 153, 160, 195, 206–207, 230, 236, 265, 282; Ceasar's ~ 276; ~ of Muʿāwiya 80n141; ~ of Muḥammad's model 39n15; ~ of the truth 204; the ~ s 30, 52n57, 95, 181
Food 48, 210, 216, 259, 262
Fortress/es 40n19, 56–57, 77, 104, 140, 141–142, 148, 165–166, 168, 169, 171, 178, 184–186, 192, 195, 215–216, 230, 253, 256, 280–282

Gardens of Bliss 66, 153, 234, 239
Gaulmin, Gilbert 11
al-Ghadīr 116, 116n268
Ghassān 105n218, 121, 121n287, 121n288, 144, 157, 228, 236
ghazw (invasion) 90, 249n490
Ghifār 84, 84n153
ghilmān 65; *see also* Slave/s
al-Ghūṭa 93n173, 115n262, 115n266, 116, 116n267, 116n269, 121n288, 122, 122n291, 132n315, 138n326, 243; people of ~ 115, 115n265, 116; raid/s on ~ 116, 122

God (Allāh) ; ~ as the Lord (rabb) 29, 38, 42–43, 48, 51, 62, 68, 71, 75–76, 79, 84, 97, 107, 110, 148–150, 152, 155, 165, 167, 186, 196–197, 201–202, 218, 224, 227–229, 234, 243, 252–253, 259, 261, 268–270, 283–284 ; ~ as the King 135–136, 146, 149, 154, 172, 227, 275; ~ as the Supreme Speaker 95; ~ as Trustee (wakīl) 30, 56, 61, 180; eulogies of ~ 30; ~ leads (someone) to the conquest (fataḥa Allāh ʿalā yad) 43, 74, 90–91, 95, 108, 167–168, 174, 180, 227, 252, 282; ~ 's bestowal of victory (naṣr) 53, 55, 68, 75, 86, 91, 129–130, 145, 149, 154–155, 157, 165–166, 172, 182, 184–185, 192, 201–203, 216, 220, 252; ~ 's scripture 9n14, 71, 100, 149–150, 152, 228, 264, 275 *see also* Qurʾān; ~ 's son 150, 152, 187; the word of ~ 49, 53
Greed 71, 207, 216, 220–221, 276

Habbār b. Sufyān 128, 128n307
Ḥabīb b. Maslama 4, 83n150, 238–239, 280–281; ~ as commander of Ḥimṣ 251, 274; ~ as tax collector of Ḥimṣ 178–179; ~ 's conflict with al-Ḍaḥḥāk b. Qays 277–279; ~ 's cousin 83n150, 84n155; ~ 's dispatch ~ 83
Ḥābis b. Saʿd al-Ṭāʾī 58, 58n70, 146, 173
Ḥadas 265, 265n509
ḥadd (vehemence) 28; Byzantines' ~ 156, 230, 235, 279; Muslims' ~ 147, 210; ~ punishments 226
ḥadīth/s (tradition/s) 13, 17–18, 162, 258n498, 197, 235; prophetical ~ 7, 23, 39n14, 44n30, 48, 59n74, 127n300, 135n320, 162, 263n505, 271; ~ scholar 12, 70n109; transmitter of ~ 35n2, 36n3, 36n4, 37n6, 38n9, 52n56, 52n57
Ḥaḍramawt (tribe) 228, 228n446, 232
ḥajj (pilgrimage) 28, 203–204, 268, 271
al-Ḥajjāj b. ʿAbd Yaghūth b. Asad 58, 58n69, 232
al-Ḥajjāj b. Yūsuf al-Thaqafī 189n402
Ḥajr 95n178
al-Ḥakam b. Jawwās b. al-Ḥakam b. al-Mughaffal 238, 238n470
al-Ḥakam b. Saʿīd b. al-ʿĀṣ 65, 65n95, 164n363
ḥalāl (licit) 260
Hamdān 80, 80n142, 81, 228
Ḥamza b. ʿAlī 112, 112n250
Ḥamza b. Mālik al-Hamdānī 80, 80n141, 81
Haneberg, Daniel 8
Hāniʾ b. Qabīṣa al-Ṭāʾī 103, 103n212
Ḥanẓala b. Ḥawya 236, 236n466, 237–238; ~ 's son 236n465
ḥarām (illicit) 174, 260, 265, 267
ḥarīm (women's domiciles) 177; *see also* Woman/women's domiciles
al-Ḥārith b. ʿAbdallāh al-Azdī 205, 205n425, 106–210; ~ accompanying Khālid to the debate with Bāhān 214–215, 219; ~ as a friend of Khālid 213
al-Ḥārith b. al-Ḥārith b. Qays 165, 165n368
al-Ḥārith b. Hishām 87, 87n159, 88–90; ~ 's death 89
al-Ḥārith b. Kaʿb 43, 43n26, 116, 119, 192
al-Ḥasan b. ʿUbaydallāh 246, 246n485, 247–248
Hāshim b. ʿUtba b. Abī Waqqāṣ 70, 70n111, 71, 131, 157, 159–160, 206, 227; ~ 's dispatch 76–77; ~ 's uncle 77
Ḥassān b. Thābit al-Anṣārī 135, 135n322, 240; ~ 's nephew 135, 240
Ḥawrān 116n269, 118, 118n279, 121, 139n328, 240n474; the land of ~ 41n22, 119
Heraclius 3, 5, 22, 41n19, 70n112, 72n120, 73–75, 77, 81, 90, 123n292, 140, 149, 174–177, 187, 276 *see also* Caesar and Byzantine Emperor; ~ as supreme commander 145, 177, 180; ~ in a poem 91; ~ 's farewell greeting to Syria 246; ~ 's letter to the people of Syria 85; ~ 's reaction to the lost Battle of al-Yarmūk 244–245; ~ 's reaction to the Muslims' raids 69–71
Hereafter, the 62, 96, 202, 238
al-Ḥijāz 8, 47n41, 47n42, 47m43, 72n121, 72n122, 73, 73n124, 73n125, 86n158, 107, 191, 261
al-Ḥijr 72, 72n122, 72n123, 191–192
Hilāl b. Bashīr al-Namirī 110, 110n243
Ḥimṣ 3–4, 8, 22, 41n20, 42n23, 50n51, 53n57, 53n58, 58n70, 58n71, 59n76, 67n100, 70n112, 72, 72n119, 75n133, 83n150, 89n165, 92n171, 117n274, 118n276, 122n291, 125, 129, 132, 139n327, 140n330, 140n331, 172, 174, 175, 176n388, 177, 179–180,

182, 203–204, 208, 241, 243, 251; ~ as the best district in Syria 171; commander of ~ 122; conquest of ~ 142, 168–172; first newborn of ~ 173; ~ al-Jund al-Muqaddam 251; land of ~ 41n22, 137, 173, 174, 179, 182, 188–189; Muslim commander of ~ 45n37, 75n133, 83n150, 88n162, 251, 274; people of ~ 131, 143, 169–171, 178–179, 241, 274; ~ 's Eastern Gate 171; siege of ~ 93n173; ~ 's Rastan Gate 170–171
Ḥimyar 53, 53n58, 57, 170, 173, 227, 232; Kaʿb b. al-Ḥabr as belonging to ~ 265; people of ~ 57
al-Ḥīra 47n41, 58n71, 58n72, 60n81, 93n173, 98n188, 103, 103n210, 103n212, 105n218, 106, 106n222, 109, 109n236, 237n468; Battle of ~ 45n37; conquest of ~ 104; fortresses of ~ 104; people of ~ 103–104; trading in ~ 113
Hishām b. al-ʿĀṣ 128, 128n306
Hishām b. ʿUrwa b. al-Zubayr 266, 266n510
Hodgson, Marshall (on translation) 1, 25–27
Honour 147, 197, 218, 238, 256, 259, 260; God as possessor of ~ 172; man/men of ~ 69; Muḥammad as ~ for the Muslims 39n14, 186, 257; the Muslims' ~ 204; worldly ~ 90, 148
Horse/s 53, 54, 62, 66, 114, 119, 126, 127, 147, 157, 159, 162, 170–171, 193, 195, 198–199, 206, 209, 230–231, 237–238, 247, 261, 277, 281; Arab ~ 236, 245; ~ in a poem 139, 161; work~ 258–259
Horseman/horsemen 101, 108, 118, 125, 139n328, 142–143, 146, 174, 184, 198, 209, 231, 235, 246–247, 253; Arabs' renowned ~ 53–54, 69, 100, 207, 227; Byzantine ~ 120, 174, 192, 210, 230, 245, 279, 281–282; ~ in a poem 238; Khālid as ~ 213; ~ of Bakr b. Wāʾil 108; pre-Islamic renowned ~ 61; renowned Muslim ~ 129, 184, 247
Hour, the 48, 251, 272
Houris (al-ḥūr al-ʿayn) 234
Ḥudhayfa b. ʿAmr al-Tanūkhī 245, 245n483
Humphreys, Stephen 12, 17n43
al-Ḥumr Mountain 128, 128n302
Ḥumrān b. Abbān 110, 110n242; ~ 's cousin 110
Hurmuzjird 102, 102n204
al-Ḥusayn b. Ziyād al-Ramlī 14–16, 18–20, 31–32, 35, 35n2, 36n3, 38, 43, 52, 56, 60, 64, 66–69, 73, 76, 80, 82, 85, 91–93, 101, 104–106, 110, 112, 115–117, 119, 121–123, 127, 129–130, 132, 137–139, 156–157, 159–163, 168, 173–175, 179, 182, 189–192, 194–195, 197, 199–200, 203–205, 213, 219, 223, 225–227, 229, 232, 234, 236, 238, 243–244, 246, 257, 262, 264–267, 271–272, 274–275
Ḥuwārīn 117, 117n276, 118; people of ~ 119

Ibn Abī Quḥāfa *see* Abū Bakr al-Ṣiddīq
Ibn al-ʿAdīm 12, 19, 35n2, 37n8, 249n490
Ibn ʿAsākir 17, 18n45, 31, 33
Ibn Dhī al-Sahm al-Khathʿamī 68, 68n105, 241
Ibn Ḥajar 19–20
Ibn Ḥintima 44n28, 97 *see also* ʿUmar b. al-Khaṭṭāb
Ibn Ḥubaysh 6
Ibn al-Juʿayd 145, 145n340, 259–260
Ibn Khayr al-Ishbīlī 10, 16–18, 20
Ibn Qamīʾa al-Laythī 61, 61n84
Ibn Qanāṭir 41n19, 222, 222n432, 227, 236
Ibn Saʿd 33
Idol/s 42n23, 116n269, 218; ~ aters 49, 201
ijāza (permission of transmission) 13, 19
ʿIkrima b. Abī Jahl 87, 87n161, 88–90; ~ 's death 89
Īliyāʾ *see* Jerusalem
iltifāt (deictic shift) 26, 136n323
īmān (faith) 3, 39, 71, 86, 110, 111, 211, 257
imāra (command) 51, 140
Infantry, Byzantine ~ 41n19, 157–158, 209, 230, 248; Byzantine ~man/men 158, 169, 174, 247, 280; Muslim ~ 40n17, 72, 99, 120, 126, 131, 141, 155, 157–158, 160, 166, 187, 198, 206, 210, 216, 227, 230, 235, 280, 282; Muslim ~man/men 46, 50, 231, 243
Infidel/s, the 23, 99, 119, 127, 134, 187–188, 198, 243, 247–248, 258
Iram 224, 224n438
Iraq 2, 8, 32, 40n18, 42n23, 45n35, 47n41, 47n43, 60, 60n81, 93n173, 94, 94n175, 95–97, 97n187, 100, 101n200,

101n201, 102, 102n202, 102n203, 102n204, 103n205, 107–109, 109n235, 112n249, 113n255, 113n256, 115, 115n264, 115n265, 116, 116n268, 116n269, 117n276, 120, 176n385, 228; arable lands of ~ 60, 60n81, 94, 102; conquest of ~ 108; Khālid's activities in ~ 93–112; land of ~ 100, 104; people of ~ 95; Syria as a substitute for ~ 108
Islam 38–40, 46, 48–49, 55, 66, 67, 69, 74, 85, 86–89, 100–101, 104, 110, 111, 112, 121–122, 130, 138, 155, 168, 187, 189, 194, 207, 210–212, 218, 220, 223, 252, 257, 262, 264, 266, 277; abode of ~ *see* Abode of Islam; adherents of ~ 82, 108, 121–122, 134, 156, 163–165, 168, 170, 185, 190, 202, 207, 235, 241, 256, 261, 280–281; brother/ brethren in ~ 40n17, 63, 65, 68, 79, 81, 88, 122, 137–138, 152–153, 164, 165, 177, 198–199, 201, 206, 212, 219, 261, 269; he/she excelled at ~ (ḥasuna islāmuhū/hā) 28, 87, 122,155, 189, 194, 212, 220; sanctity of ~ 68, 223; ~ 's enemy 239
ʿiṣma (protection) 111
Ismāʿīl b. Abī Khālid 105–106, 106n221, 275
isnād/s (chain of transmitters) 4, 7–8, 10, 12–13, 18, 20, 21, 23; extended ~ 36n3; interpretation of the ~ 31–32, 52n54, 127n298, 163n361, 195n413
Israelites 264, 264n508, 269
izār (loincloth) 263

Jābān 94n175, 103, 103n206
al-Jābiya 50n49, 54n59, 69, 69n108, 111, 125, 130, 132, 138, 183; Abū ʿUbayda at ~ 73, 107, 116, 122; ~ Gate *see* Damascus; ʿUmar's speech at ~ 4, 44n28, 56n66, 257–258
al-jāhiliyya (pre-Islamic period) 25–26, 28, 53n59, 54, 61, 69
Jalūlāʾ, conquest of ~ 32, 282
Jamāl al-Dīn Abū al-Faḍl Yūsuf b. ʿAbd al-Muʿṭī b. Manṣūr b. Najā al-Muḥāmilī 11, 15, 18n45, 37n8
Jarīr b. ʿAbdallāh al-Bajalī 107, 107n230
al-Jazīra 60n81, 176, 176n385; people of ~ 176, 199
Jerusalem 4, 8, 10, 12, 19, 44n29, 44n30, 45n35, 50n51, 70n112, 71n113, 89n165, 129, 129n309, 186, 257n494, 266n511, 268n512, 284; book on the merits of ~ 36n3; commander of ~ 145n340; conquest of ~ 82n145, 267–268; land of ~ 185; people of ~ 25, 44n28, 168–169, 175, 184–188, 251–256, 259; siege of ~ 94n173, 253–255; ʿUmar at ~ 258–265; ʿUmar's takeover of ~ 22, 44n28, 259–260
Jesus 71, 71n116, 71n117, 100, 150, 189n403, 196; ~ as messenger of God 211–212; ~ as servant of God 71n116, 150, 211; ~ as son of Mary 71n116, 100, 211,
Jew/s 10, 262n503, 267; ~ish scholars 262
jihād (Fighting for the cause of God) 28, 39, 42, 42n23, 43, 49–51, 63, 74, 76, 78, 81, 87–88, 96, 202, 238, 253–254, 256, 259, 271
Jirjīs 176, 176n387, 222, 227, 236
jizya (tribute) 28, 43, 105, 140, 153, 166–169, 171, 218–219, 255–256, 279; bring/give ~ with humility (wa-hum saghirūn) 27, 43, 43n25, 51, 55, 149, 153, 185, 187, 210, 218–219, 251–252, 256, 277
Jordan, country 34, 80n141; Trans~ 73n126, 73n127, 106n223, 118n279, 124n295, 141n333; ~ valley 70n113, 73n128, 79n139, 143n334, 144n335
Jordan, the River 3, 141, 141n333, 175, 189n401, 251; arable lands of ~ 124n295, 145, 150, 152, 166; commander of the land of ~ 254; conquest of land of ~ 167; land/s of ~ 3, 41n22, 50n51, 54n59, 71n113, 89n165, 120n282, 141, 141n333, 143–144, 153, 166–169, 172, 177, 183–186, 188–189, 192, 198, 251, 268; people of ~ 166, 168, 185–187, 194
Judaism 4, 57n68
Judhām 144, 144n337, 157, 228, 236, 265n509, 282; watering place of ~ 265
Juice 260; inspissated ~ 260; non-alcoholic ~ 4
Jundab b. ʿAmr b. Ḥumama al-Dawsī 58, 59n73, 234
Jūsiya 170n373

Kaʿb al-Ḥabr 4, 262, 262n503, 263–265; ~ 's father 262–263; ~ 's father's funeral 263
Kaegi, Walter 7–9, 22, 71n115, 122n292, 176n387
Kaḥḥāla, ʿUmar 8

Kāle-Sprenger-manuscript 11–14, 16, 20, 37n8; *see also* Berlin, manuscript 9767
Kaskar 93n173, 102, 102n202, 237n468
katāʾib (military units) 28, 50, 56, 60
khabar (report) 28, 52, 174, 192, 195, 203
Khalek, Nancy 7–8, 22–23
Khālid b. Saʿīd b. al-ʿĀṣ 48, 48n47, 49, 50n50, 63–64, 111n247; ~ as a subordinate of Muḥammad 51; ~ 's brother/s 65; ~ 's dispatch ~ 64–66; ~ 's uncle 111n247
Khālid b. al-Walīd 2–5, 22, 44n28, 93, 93n173, 142, 172, 177, 182–183, 188–189, 192, 241, 243, 251, 253; ~ as chief commander 2, 107–108, 124, 126, 134; ~ as Sword of God 94n173, 129; ~ at Thaniyyat al-ʿUqāb 122; ~ in a poem 101; ~ raiding al-Ghūṭa 122; ~ 's battles in Iraq 97–107; ~ 's character 191; ~ 's conquest of Aleppo 246; ~ 's conquest of Baalbek 143, 169; ~ 's conquest of Bosra 119–121; ~ 's conquest of Damascus 130–131, 132, 138–139; ~ 's conquest of al-Ḥīra 106–107; ~ 's debate with Bāhān 210–219; ~ 's deployment to Syria 107–108; ~ 's deposition from chief command in Syria 137–138; ~ 's desert march to Syria 109–119; ~ 's dialog with ʿAbd al-Masīḥ b. ʿAmr b. Buqayla al-Azdī 104; ~ 's dialog with Abjar b. Bajīr 100–101; ~ 's dispatch to Iraq 95–97; ~ 's monastery *see* Dayr Khālid; ~ 's nephew 58n72, 110n245, 208; ~ 's participation in the Battle of Ajnādayn 123–130; ~ 's participation in the Battle of Fiḥl 155–166; ~ 's participation in the Battle of Marj al-Ṣuffar 131–132; ~ 's participation in the Battle of al-Yarmūk 198–241; ~ 's participation in the conquest of Ḥimṣ 169–171; ~ 's participation in the conquest of Jerusalem 253; ~ 's tent 126, 223
khalīfa (caliph) 28, 44n28, 172, 264
khalīfat rasūl Allāh (the successor of the Messenger of God) 28, 39n15, 41; *see also* caliph
Khathʿam 68, 68n106, 228, 236, 241
Khawla bt. Thaʿlaba b. Mālik b. al-Dakhshum 232, 232n456
Khawlān 228, 228n444, 232
Khusraw 70n112, 71, 71n114; -'s scouting units 103
khuṭba (speech) 4, 5, 22, 29, 194, 196, 211, 219; Abū al-Dardāʾ's exhortatory ~ 275–276; ʿUbāda b. al-Ṣāmit's exhortatory ~ 274–275; ʿUmar's ~ at al-Jābiya 257–258; 274
Kināna 59, 59n78, 84n153, 206, 228, 236
Kinda 98n188, 228, 228n445
al-Kūfa 8, 35n2, 43n27, 60n81, 98n188, 101n199, 106n227, 109n236, 113n254, 115n265; land of ~ 60n81, 98
Kurd ʿAlī, Muḥammad 7, 22
kuttāb (elementary school) 173

Lakhm 144, 144n336, 157, 228, 236
Lakhmid/s 47n41, 109n235, 237n468
Landau-Tasseron, Ella 6, 8, 35n2, 36n4, 37n6
Law/s 218; religious ~ 48n46, 244
Lees, William Nassau 7, 9, 11, 20–22, 33, 60n82, 64n91, 92n170, 105n215, 127n299, 179n389, 271n515
Letter of protection 27, 42, 44n28, 140, 150–151, 187, 254–255; ~ for the people in the arable land of the River Jordan 145; ~ for the people of Aleppo 246; ~ for the people of Baalbek 169; ~ for the people of Bānqiyā 107; ~ for the people of Damascus 138, 183; ~ for the people of Fiḥl 166; ~ for the people of Ḥimṣ 171–172, 182; ~ for the people of Hurmuzjird 102; ~ for the people of Jerusalem 259; ~ for the people of Qinnasrīn 251; ~ for the people of Zandaward 102
Lion/s 127, 163, 199, 202, 229, 238, 259; birds with talons like ~ 225; ~ by day 133, 222, 265; ~ in a poem 159, 233; Khālid is like a ~ 108; swords like ~ 119
al-Liwā 115, 115n264
Locusts, ~ as God's punishment 264n508, 269; Byzantines as black ~ 209, 222

Maʾāb 41n22, 73n127, 73n128; ~ as first conquered Syrian town 73; people of ~ 73
al-Madāʾin 94n175, 105n218, 105n219; date of the fights at ~ 32, 105; people of ~ 105
Madhḥij 57, 57n68, 228, 232, 242n478
Madhʿūr b. ʿAdī al-ʿIjlī 101, 101n201, 102, 120

maḥram (unmarriageable relative) 258
Makhaḍkhaḍ 113, 113n253
Makīla b. Ḥanẓala b. Ḥawya 236, 236n465
māl/amwāl (possession/s) 39, 39n13, 51, 56, 68, 74, 96, 112, 117–118, 127, 148, 168, 171, 178, 179, 187, 192, 194–195, 218, 220–221, 229–230, 232, 239, 250–251, 252, 255, 268, 270–271, 276
Malḥān b. Ziyād al-Ṭāʾī 67, 67n100, 169–170, 173; ~ 's brother 58n71, 67
Mālik b. al-Ḥārith al-Nakhaʿī 241, 241n477, 242–243, 246–247, 249; ~ 's cousin 242, 248; ~ 's rule 242
Mālik b. Qusāma b. Zuhayr 189, 189n402
Mālik al-Qaynī 160
Maʿn b. Yazīd b. al-Akhnas al-Sulamī 83, 83n147, 146
manzila (the standing) 87, 90, 128, 148, 259
Maqṭaʿ al-Turāb 256, 256n493
Marj al-Qabāʾil 59n76, 249, 249n490
Marj Rāhiṭ 121, 121n287, 121n288, 122n291
Marj al-Ṣuffar 132n315, 215; Battle of ~ 131; battle-day of ~ 132
Martyr/s 46, 49n47, 62, 96, 109, 153, 167, 201, 218, 234
Martyrdom 51, 66, 77, 79, 157, 165–167
al-Maṣṣīṣa 59n76, 249, 249n491
Master/s 30, 40n17, 45n37, 64, 69, 78, 111, 281; Muḥammad as ~ 84
Masʿūd b. Ḥāritha 94, 94n177, 100
mathal (example) 162
mawlā (client) 65, 92n170, 110
Maysara b. Masrūq al-ʿAbsī 3, 31, 59, 59n76, 156, 158, 161, 170, 172–173, 178, 182, 192, 207–209; ~ 's conflict with al-Ashtar 246–251; ~ 's duel with a Byzantine 162; ~ 's wife 212
Mecca 2, 47n40, 47n43, 61n85, 70n109, 86n158, 87n162, 165n366; Muḥammad in ~ 39n14, 263–264; people of ~ 86–87
Medina 40n17, 40n18, 41n20, 45n36, 45n37, 45n38, 47, 47n43, 49n47, 50n49, 56, 61n83, 61n85, 62, 65n94, 65n95, 65n96, 66, 68n106, 72n121, 73n125, 73n126, 80–81, 87n162, 90, 92, 104, 111n247, 134, 228n445, 237n467, 242; Abū Bakr in ~ 38n12, 53; Muḥammad in ~ 39n14, 263–264; people of ~ 81; ʿUmar in ~ 4, 76n134, 203, 265–267
Messenger of God, the *see also* Muḥammad (the Prophet) 25, 29, 39–40, 43, 51, 61–63, 65, 75, 79, 88, 100, 127, 164, 185, 201, 211, 217, 259, 261–263; flag holder of the ~ 281; mosque of the ~ 267; quotations from the ~ 48, 258, 266, 271–272; ~ 's high esteem for Abū ʿUbayda 61, 81; ~ 's injury during the Battle of Uḥud 61
Mikhnaf b. ʿAbdallāh b. Yazīd b. al-Mughaffal 194, 194n411, 200, 234
Miṣr 101n200, 101n201, 120, 120n285; Fusṭāṭ ~ 15, 37n8; *see also* Cairo
Monk/s 40n19, 56n66, 189, 199, 201, 205, 208, 230–231; Muslims as ~ by night 133, 222, 265
Moon, crescent ~ 262; ~ worshipping 42n23, 218
Moses 262, 262n504, 265
Motes 175, 195, 202
Mourad, Suleiman 7–8, 10–11, 16, 21–22, 33, 35n2, 36n3, 36n4, 36n5, 37n6, 37n7, 37n8, 43n26, 52n55, 69n107, 70n109, 76n135, 93n172, 122n289, 161n357, 190n405, 257n495
Muʿādh b. Jabal 3–4, 22, 50, 50n51, 134–137, 142, 152, 157, 183, 212, 254–255, 261, 270; ~ leads the people in prayer after Abū ʿUbayda's death 268–269; ~ 's appointment of ʿAmr b. al-ʿĀṣ as successor 272–; ~ 's death 273–274; ~ 's dispatch ~ 62–63; mourning for ~ 273; ~ 's negotiation with the Byzantines 147–151; ~ 's participation in the Battle of Ajnādayn 126–127, 131–132; ~ 's participation in the Battle of Fiḥl 157, 163; ~ 's participation in the Battle of al-Yarmūk 199, 206–207, 222–223, 227–229, 231; ~ 's son 22, 231, 270; ~ 's will 270
Muʿāwiya b. Abī Sufyān 4, 80n141, 282, 282n526; ~ as chief commander 283–284; ~ 's caliphate 284; ~ 's conquest of Caesarea 282–283; ~ 's rule over Syria 4, 284
Muḍar 47, 47n42, 59n75, 84n151, 84n154, 97n187, 164n364
al-Muhājir b. Ṣayfī al-ʿUdhrī 223, 223n433, 227
Muḥammad (the Prophet) 39, 39n14, 41n21, 49, 84, 88n162, 110, 135, 149, 161, 186, 201, 211, 224n437, 245, 257, 265, 284; ~ as cameleer 211; ~ as sayyid 84; ~ as servant of God

39n14, 52, 97, 218, 251, 272; ~ as the Messenger of God 52, 55, 62, 97, 100, 217–218, 251, 263, 272; ~ 's death 2; ~ 's prophethood 100, 150
Muḥammad b. Ibrāhīm al-Ghassānī 11, 284, 284n526
Muḥammad b. Sīrīn 109, 109n241
Muḥammad b. Yūsuf 52, 52n55, 56, 60, 93, 123, 130, 137, 163, 229, 232, 272
al-Muḥill b. Khalīfa 67, 67n99, 173
Muḥriz b. Ḥuraysh b. Ṣulay' 113, 113n252
Muḥriz b. Usayd al-Bāhilī 140, 140n331, 168, 173
al-Mujālid b. Sa'īd al-Hamdānī 104–105, 105n215, 267
Mukhaymis b. Ḥābis b. Mu'āwiya 4, 253, 253n492, 254
Mūsā b. 'Imrān *see* Moses
Musaylima al-Ḥanafī al-Kadhdhāb 93n173, 95, 95n179
al-Musayyab b. Najaba 120, 120n284
Muslim/s, the, ~ as servants of God 48–49, 51, 53–55, 79, 110, 126, 148, 152, 157, 160, 219, 228, 231, 249, 257–258, 268–269, 272; ~ chiefs 40n17, 69, 142, 168, 172, 177–178, 190, 217, 241–243, 255; ~ nobility 218; ~ 's children 53, 68, 71, 126, 177, 193; ~ 's sons 177; ~ spies 86, 125, 177, 180–181, 194
al-Mustanīr b. Zubayr b. Aflaḥ b. Ya'būb b. 'Amr b. Ḍarīs al-Mashja'ī 115, 115n261, 116, 121–122; ~ 's grandfather 115n261; ~ 's great-grandfather 116n267
Mu'ta, battle-day of 106, 106n223
al-Muthannā b. Ḥāritha 93–94, 94n174, 98, 102, 107–108, 110; ~ 's brother 94–95, 100; ~ 's cousin 101; ~ 's dispatch ~ 94–95; ~ 's rescue of Abjar b. Bajīr 100–101; ~ 's victory at Nahr al-Damm 103
Muzayna 84, 84n154

Nabateans of Syria 86n157
al-Naḍir b. Ṣāliḥ 161, 161n357, 162
al-Naḍir b. Shifā 170, 170n376
Nahr al-Damm 103, 103n207
Nahr 'Īsā 109n234
Nahr al-Ubulla 98n189
al-Nakha' 98n188, 242, 242n478, 243, 247, 249
al-Namir 112, 112n249
Nawā, in a poem 139, 139n328
Nawfal b. Masāḥiq al-Qurashī 91, 91n166, 162
al-Nibāj 97n187, 99, 99n195, 100
Nobility, religion as ~ 214
Nomads 92
non-Arabs 40n19, 190, 190n404, 259; ~ 's abode 230
Nu'aym b. Ṣakhr b. 'Adī al-'Adawī 128, 128n305
al-Nu'mān b. Maḥmiyya Dhū al-Anf al-Khath'amī 241, 241n475, 242
Nūr ad-Dīn 'Alī b. Mas'ūd al-Mawṣilī al-Dimashqī 12–13, 38, 38n10

Offspring, Byzantine ~ 195; captured ~ 109, 117, 143, 144, 185, 187, 196, 232, 251, 277; Muslim ~ 68, 178; ~ of the afterlife 275; ~ of the worldly life 275
Oneness of God (tawḥīd) 150, 152, 186
Oppressed, the 65, 197
Oppression 152, 197
Oppressor 196–197

Palestine 70, 70n113, 73n124, 79n140, 89n165, 123n293, 141n333, 175; land of ~ 41n22, 70n112, 124, 141, 169, 172, 177, 251; Muslim commander of ~ 260; people of the land of ~ 169, 174
Paradise, the 4, 39n14, 96, 127n300, 164, 167, 192, 202, 212, 214, 218, 228, 254, 258, 263, 271–273, 275, 281, 283; inhabitants of ~ 234n461, 275; people of ~ 212; ~s 283
Paris, ms 1664 9, 10–17, 20, 31 ; ~ ms 1665 11–13, 15–17, 20, 36n4, 36n5, 37n7, 37n8
Patrician/s, Byzantine ~ 28, 41n19, 56–57, 69, 156, 159, 162, 168, 192, 195, 198–199, 205, 208–210, 220, 226, 230, 232, 243, 245, 279, 281; ~ of the people of Jerusalem 186–187, 251, 259–260
Penitents (awwābūn) 62
People of (ahl al-), ~ precedence 86; ~ suffering and misery 195; ~ the Book 211, 264; ~ the hamlets 42; ~ the land/s 71, 153, 168, 193, 195–196, 260; tribes~ *see* Tribespeople
Persia 94n174, 94n175; land of ~ 148–149; ~n Gulf 47, 60n81; people of ~ 94, 104–105, 216 *see also* Persian/s, the

Persian/s, the 47n41, 60n79, 60n80, 60n81, 94, 95, 96, 100, 104–105, 107, 108–109, 149, 151, 190n404, 228; ~ Emperors 71n114; ~ Emperor's son 148; ~ finery 139; ~ grand men 103, 106
Polytheist/s, the 4, 31, 42, 42n23, 43, 49, 53, 55, 63, 68–69, 76, 80, 86, 90, 95, 98, 121, 129, 138, 141, 145, 152–154, 171–172, 185, 203, 207, 212, 218, 223, 229, 238–239, 250, 282; attacked ~ 160, 280; defeated ~ 156, 163, 209; fleeing ~ 132, 166; killed ~ 128, 173, 225; one Muslim man better than 1,000 ~ 74, 201; ~'s defeat in the Battle of al-Yarmūk 227, 252; ~ 's land 268
Prayer/s 53, 57, 79, 105, 133, 137, 143, 147, 149, 157, 174, 210–211, 224, 243, 248, 261, 264, 268–270; act/s of ~ (rakʿa) 29, 223, 223n435, 224, 267; afternoon ~ 55; call for ~ (ādhān) 79, 261; direction of ~ (qibla) 29, 105, 149; early morning ~ (ghadāt) 28, 55, 65, 180, 182, 223, 249, 257; funeral ~ 269–270, 272; noon ~ 55, 127; place of ~ 257; ritual ~ (ṣalāt) 80, 218, 271
Priest/s 40n19, 56n66, 199, 201, 205, 208, 230, 258
Prophethood, Jesus's ~ 100; Muḥammad's ~ 100, 150
Prophets, ~' scripture 262–263
Province/s (kuwar) 29, 274; ~ial governor/s (marzubān) 105; ~ial people 277

qaḍāʾ (God's decree) 38, 43, 62, 154, 221, 231, 267
qadar (fate) 273
Qanān b. Dārim al-ʿAbsī 248, 248n487, 249; ~ 's son 249n489
Qanān b. Ḥāzim al-Qaysī 169, 169n372
Qarḥāʾ 191, 191n407, 192
al-Qāsim b. al-Walīd 105, 105n216, 271
al-Qayn 144, 144n339 *see also* Banū al-Qayn
Qays 59, 59n75, 83n148, 206, 236, 238
Qays b. Abī Ḥāzim 106, 106n222, 116, 275; ~ 's participation in the Battle of Bosra 119–121
Qays b. ʿĀṣim 94, 94n176
Qays b. Hubayra b. Makshūḥ al-Murādī 53, 53n59, 54, 155–156, 158–159, 160–161, 198–199, 206–209, 230, 239–240; ~ 's citation of a poem 208–209; ~ 's counsel to Abū ʿUbayda 191–192; ~ 's dispatch ~ 69; ~ 's encounter with Amna bt. Abī Bishr 192–194
Qayṣar *see* Caesar
Qinnasrīn 45n35, 58n71, 59n76, 93n173, 176n388, 188n400, 247, 249n489; conquest of ~ 3, 251; etymology of ~ 247; land of ~ 41n22, 188–189, 243, 246; Muslim commander of land of ~ 251; people of ~ 251
qirāʾatan (by way of reading) 14, 38
Qubāth b. Ashyam 59, 59n77, 206, 227, 238; ~ 's citation of a poem 237
Quḍāʿa 84n152, 112n249, 115, 115n262, 115n263, 120, 144, 144n339, 157, 195n414, 228, 228n444, 236
Qudāma b. Ḥāzim 67, 67n104, 68
al-Qudāmī 17, 48n104
Qurʾān, the 23, 41n21, 43n25, 51, 62n86, 72n122, 80, 149, 181n393, 181n394, 224, 264, 275; ~icised language 23; reciter/s of ~ 37n7, 228; translation of ~ 33
Qurāqir Valley 113, 113n255, 115; ~ in a poem 114
Quraysh 48n47, 54n62, 59n78, 76n134, 87, 87n162, 90, 111n247, 113n251, 165; ~ite noblemen 87, 87n159, 87n160, 90; ~ite people 86
Quṣam 115, 115n262, 115n265, 116n268

Rabbis 262
Rabīʿa 47, 47n41, 47n42, 60, 96–97, 97n187, 112n248, 112n249, 228
Rabīʿa al-ʿAnzī 159, 159n354
Rāfiʿ b. ʿAmr al-Ṭāʾī 113, 113n257, 114, 120; ~ in a poem 114
raʾīs/ruʾūs (chief/s), ~ in a poem 238; *see also* Byzantine ~ and Muslim ~
Rāshid b. ʿAbd al-Raḥmān al-Azdī 223, 223n434, 224–225, 227
Rebels 95
Religion, Islamic ~ 267, 279; ~ of Jesus 100; ~ of the Muslims 122; ~ of truth 49, 201; other ~s 10, 48–49, 201; *see also* Islam
Repentants (tawwābūn) 62
Reward/s 51, 53, 61, 66, 77, 79, 88–89, 102, 157, 176, 185, 203, 221, 223, 229, 234, 250, 255–256; God's ~ 43, 46, 49, 51, 63, 69, 74, 77, 96, 111, 125, 127,

146, 152, 160, 165, 202, 207, 238, 273, 280; ~ of the Hereafter 202; ~ of this world 202; the earlier ~ 97; the later ~ 97; the martyrs' ~ 167
riwāya/s (chains of transmission) 1, 10–12, 13–20, 21, 32, 35–38, 85n165
Rule, ~ of the Book 51
Rūmīl 46n39
Rūmiyya 157n383 *see also* Byzantine Empire

Saʿd b. Abī Waqqāṣ 45, 45n34, 47, 127n300; ~ 's nephew 45n34, 70n111, 77
al-Sadīr, in a poem 237, 237n468
Ṣafwān b. al-Muʿaṭṭal al-Khuzāʿī 138–139, 139n327, 146, 170; ~ 's citation of a poem 139
Sahl b. Saʿd al-Anṣārī 60, 60n82, 61, 64, 66, 93, 123, 130, 163, 229, 232
Saʿīd b. ʿĀmir b. Ḥudhaym al-Jumaḥī 76, 76n134, 126–127, 181, 202–205; ~ 's dispatch ~ 78–79
Saʿīd b. ʿAmr b. Ḥarām al-Anṣārī 99, 99n193, 109
Saʿīd b. al-ʿĀṣ b. Abī Uḥayḥa 64, 64n93
Saʿīd b. al-Ḥārith b. Qays 165, 165n367; ~ 's brother 165
Saʿīd b. Zayd b. ʿAmr b. Nufayl 47, 47n44, 85, 87, 89, 126, 131–132, 134, 157, 212, 231, 238–240; as ʿUmar's grand cousin ~ 127, 127n299, 127n300; ~ 's appointment as commander of Damascus 251, 253
Salama b. Hishām al-Makhzūmī 128, 128n304
ṣalāt *see* Prayer/s, ritual
Ṣāliḥ (the Prophet) 72, 72n122, 72n123
Sālim b. Rabīʿa 161, 161n358, 162
al-Samāwa Desert 113, 113n254, 113n256
Ṣandawdāʾ 109, 109n235; commander of ~ 45n37, 99n193
Sand grouse, ~s' nests 55
al-Ṣaqʿab b. Zuhayr 91, 91n168, 223, 227
Sasanian, ~ commanders 94n175; ~ Emperor 70n112, 71n114; ~ Empire 94n175, 105n220; *see also* Persian/s, the
Satan (shayṭān) 30, 46, 55, 164, 221, 258
Sauvan, Yvette 9–11, 284n526
Ṣāyama, Ibtisām 22
sayyid (master) 30, 40n17, 64, 69, 78, 111, 281
Scabbards 225
Scheiner, Jens 7, 22–23
Scripture, holy ~ (anājīl) 263
Servant/s 147–148, 168, 171, 221; humans as ~ of God 146, 154
Sex 196; ~ual intercourse 226–227
Sezgin, Fuat 9, 10–11
al-Shaʿbī *see* ʿĀmir al-Shaʿbī
Shaddād b. Aws b. Thābit 135, 135n321, 137, 240, 275; ~ 's uncle 45n37, 135n322
Shāh Kālè 11
Shahr b. Ḥawshab 262, 262n502, 264
Shield/s (turs) 277, 277n521; God's ~ 68; leather ~ (daraqa) 160, 160n355, 228
Shoshan, Boaz 7–8, 22–23, 35n2
Shuraḥbīl (al-Ḥimyarī) 170, 170n374
Shuraḥbīl b. Ḥasana 4, 41, 41n20, 142, 177–178, 183; ~ 's appointment as commander 50; ~ 's dispatch 57; ~ 's fighting at Bosra 123–126; ~ 's participation in the Battle of al-Yarmūk 189, 222, 227, 239; ~ 's visions 42, 56–57
Sibṭ al-Silafī 19; ~ 's uncle 19
Ṣiffīn 173n379; Battle of ~ 52n57, 140n330, 173
al-Silafī *see* Abū Ṭāhir Aḥmad b. Muḥammad al-Silafī
Sin/s 66, 69, 125, 133, 138, 172, 196–197, 202, 205, 216, 234, 261, 263, 268–269, 273; ~ners 75
Sīrīn 109, 109n240; ~ 's son 109n241
Sivan, Emmanuel 6, 8
Slave/s 49, 65, 226–227; ~ girl 196, 226–227, 271
Spear/s 62n87, 78, 78n138, 89n164, 129, 152n350, 157–158, 160–161, 164, 225, 225n443, 228–229, 238, 281; ~man 158; ~tips 229
Speech platform 81, 97, 197, 261
Sprenger, Aloys 8–9, 11
Subordinate/s (ʿāmil/ʿummāl), Byzantine ~ 3, 176, 210, 212; Muslim ~ 27, 39n14, 51, 174, 252
Successor/s, ~ to the caliphate 254; ~ to the land 169, 228
Successorship 55
Sufyān b. ʿAwf b. Mughaffal al-Azdī 179, 179n391, 180–181, 203–204
Sufyān b. Sulaym al-Azdī 179, 179n390, 182, 203, 205, 213
Suhayl b. ʿAmr 87, 87n160, 88–90; ~ 's death 89

ṣulḥ (peace-making process) 30, 138–139, 152, 169, 185, 253
sulṭān (sovereignty) 110, 177–178, 196, 220
al-Summāq Mountain 128, 128n303
sunna (normative practices), God's ~ 185; Jesus's ~ 71, 71n117; the Prophet's ~ 30, 49, 65, 149
Supporter/s 44n31, 44n32, 45n34, 81, 195, 200, 228, 243; God as ~ 155, 172, 201, 218; noble ~ 86; ~ of Abū Bakr 44n29; ~ of God 228; ~ of Yazīd b. Abī Sufyān 83n150; the ~ s 31, 38n12, 40n17, 45, 45n37, 47, 49, 80, 86, 87n162, 95, 116, 181, 200, 257
Suqayf b. Bashīr al-ʿIjlī 101, 101n199
Suwā 113, 113n256, 115; ~ in a poem 114
Suwayd b. Kulthūm b. Qays b. Khālid al-Qurashī 173, 173n378, 182–183
Suwayd b. Quṭba 97, 97n186, 98–99
Sword/s (sayf) 40n19, 55, 62, 62n88, 69, 78, 96, 106, 112, 119, 129, 152, 157–158, 160–162, 165, 197–199, 202, 209, 213–214, 214n431, 225, 230, 233, 237–240, 243, 247–248, 281–282; ~ as an honour 214; ~ in a poem 163, 233, 238; Indian-made ~ 163, 163n360; ~men 41n19
Syria, country 34, 118n279
Syria, Greater 2–4, 38, 38n12, 40n19, 41, 41n22, 42n23, 44n28, 45n35, 50n50, 56n66, 70n112, 73n125, 73n127, 89n163, 93n173, 108, 109n235, 109n236, 113n254, 118n278, 119, 119n281, 133, 135, 137, 149, 169, 172, 172n377, 173, 176n385, 176n388, 178, 192, 202–205, 210, 228–229, 240n474, 246, 249, 251, 253, 257, 262, 264–266, 268, 274, 284; ~ as God's abode 155; ~ as the Arabs' earthly paradise 175; Byzantines in ~ 50, 51, 124; central ~ 3, 119, 174–176, 184, 193; conquest of ~ 2, 4, 34, 283; dispatch (of men) to ~ 2, 40n17, 43–44, 46, 48, 50–51, 55–57, 60, 64, 65, 67–68, 70, 72–73, 78–80, 82–84, 89–91, 93, 124, 205, 222, 230; farthest parts of ~ 77, 252; Khālid's march to ~ 107–117, 120; land/s of ~ 50, 68, 79, 179, 195, 200, 206–207, 252, 260, 272, 276, 283; map of ~ xii; Muslim districts in/of ~ 261, 276, 278–279; Muslim people in ~ 95, 110, 200; ~n cities 75, 84–86, 137, 142; ~n desert 3, 103n205, 115n265, 117n274; nearest parts of ~ 75, 81, 282; ~n provinces 274; ~n town/s 73, 74, 190n406; ~n village/s 118n276, 190; people of ~ 85–86, 86n157, 125, 138, 154, 187, 190n404, 195, 252, 254–255, 268, 277, 282; Polytheists in ~ 63; the whole of ~ 277, 283

ṭabīʿa (natural disposition) 133
tābiʿūn *see* Follower/s
Tadmur 93n173, 115n265, 166n272, 117, 117n274; ~ 's grand men 117
Ṭalḥa b. ʿUbaydallāh 44, 44n31, 47, 127n300
Tamīm 60, 60n79, 198n417, 228
Tanūkh 195, 195n414, 245
taqwā (fear of God) 55, 142, 231
tarjama (biographical sketch) 6, 8, 21, 117n273,
Tax (kharāj) 29, 39n14, 40n18, 43n25, 178–179, 183, 266; ~ officers 266; ~payers 4, 44n28, 266–267; the prescribed ~ (zakāt) 30, 39, 80, 219, 268, 271
Ṭayba 39n14, 263, 163n505; *see also* Medina
ṭaylasān (shawl-like garment) 107
Ṭayyiʾ 58, 58n71, 67, 116, 146, 173
Thābit al-Bunānī 52, 52n56, 56, 60, 93, 123, 130, 137, 163, 229, 232, 272–274
Thamūd 72n122,72n123, 181, 181n394, 224, 275
Thaniyyat al-ʿUqāb 122, 122n291, 243
Thaniyyat al-Wadāʿ 61, 61n85
Thaqīf 164, 164n364, 164n365
Thumāla 164, 164n365, 201
Tear/s 42–43, 204, 260–261
Tent 128, 196, 235; dome-like ~ (qubba) 212–213, 215, 219; ~ poles 230, 232, 236, 239
Throne 42–43
Torah 262, 265; adherents of the 262
Tribe/s 3, 23, 28, 33, 52, 60, 83, 93, 97, 98n188, 102, 115n263, 126, 157, 181n393, 181n394, 218, 224n438, 227, 232–233, 241, 249, 274; ~men 53, 81, 83, 94n174, 102, 120, 157, 164, 234, 238; ~people (qawm) 53n58, 58n69, 59n75, 89–90, 92, 94, 102, 115, 157, 241–243; sub~ (ḥayy) 28, 54n62, 59n75, 68n106, 76n134, 83n148, 84n151, 84n152, 84n153, 84n154, 87n162, 97n187, 101n200, 105n218, 111n247, 112n248, 112n249, 113n251,

115, 151n262, 115n263, 116n270, 116n271, 120, 121n287, 144, 144n337, 164n364, 164n365, 165, 165n369, 195n414, 198n417, 228n444, 233n457, 233n458, 241n476, 242n478, 249n489, 265n509; ~women, in a poem 209; *see also* Arabian tribe/s, northern Arabian tribe/s, southern Arabian tribe/s
Trinitarianism 42n23, 150, 187, 218
Turban 62, 128
Turks 70n112, 71, 71n115, 216

ʿUbāda b. al-Ṣāmit al-Anṣārī 4, 274n518, 280–281; ~ 's dispatch 274; ~ 's speech 274–275
ʿUbaydallāh b. al-ʿAbbās 244, 244n481
al-Ubulla 42n23, 60n81, 98n189; Battle of ~ 2, 98–99; people of ~ 98–99
ʿudda (equipment) 57, 99, 114, 125, 173, 186, 195, 213, 229, 252
Uḥud 39n14, 61n83; Battle of ~ 61
ʿulamāʾ (religious scholars) 14, 16–18, 36n3, 271
al-Ullays 94n175, 103n205, 112; district of ~ 103; people of ~ 103
ʿUmar b. al-Khaṭṭāb 3–5, 22, 44, 44n28, 46, 48, 51, 83, 94–95, 127, 140, 152, 163, 179–180, 200–205, 229, 272, 274, 276, 279, 280; ~ as Commander of the Believers *see* Commander of the Believers; ~ as *fārūq* 277, 277n520; ~ as servant of God 136, 137, 153, 155, 166, 167, 171, 181, 252, 255, 273, 283; ~ as supreme commander 152; ~ at Jerusalem 258–262; ~ converting a Christian 155; ~ 's appointment as caliph 133–135; ~ 's appointment of Abū ʿUbayda 137–138; ~ 's appointment of Muʿāwiya 284; ~ 's appointment of Yazīd b. Abī Sufyan 277; ~ 's conquest of Jerusalem 259–260; ~ 's cousin 44n28, 47n44; ~ 's grand cousin 127; ~ 's high esteem for Abū ʿUbayda 61; ~ 's journey back to Medina 265–268; ~ 's journey to Syria 253–257; ~ 's relation to ʿAmr b. al-ʿĀṣ 90; ~ 's relation to Kaʿb 264–265; ~ 's relation to Khālid b. al-Walīd 97, 108, 124; ~ 's rod 204; ~ 's rule 97n184, 133, 140, 272; ~ 's speech at al-Jābiya 257–258; ~ 's toughness against the Qurayshite noblemen 86–88; ~ 's whip 266
al-ʿUmarī, Akram 7, 8, 22–23
ʿUmar al-Ṭalamankī 6, 14, 17–18, 18n45
ʿUmayr b. Rabbāb b. Ḥudhayfa b. Hāshim b. al-Mughīra 109, 109n237
ʿUmayr b. Saʿd al-Anṣārī 99, 99n194, 110, 281
Umm Abbān bt. ʿUtba b. Rabīʿa 126, 126n297, 128
Umm Ḥabība bt. al-ʿĀṣ 239, 239n471
Umm al-Nuʿmān bt. Mālik b. al-Ḥārith al-Nakhaʿī 248, 248n486
umma (community) 3, 30, 41n21, 63, 76, 135–136, 183, 187, 210, 215–217, 263, 267, 273; bygone ~ies 71, 73, 219, 224; former ~ies 180
ʿumra (minor pilgrimage) 30, 268, 271
Unbeliever/s 49, 55, 62, 69, 78, 82, 106, 129, 141, 166, 200, 218, 265; ~ ' lands 42
ʿUqla, ʿIṣām 2, 7, 9–11, 20–21, 25, 31, 33, 38n9, 43n26, 43n27, 52n55, 52n56, 52n57, 67n103, 69n107, 70n109, 76n135, 82n144, 91n168, 72n170, 93n172, 104n213, 106n222, 115n261, 116n267, 117n273, 139n327, 139n329, 159n354, 161n357, 163n361, 168n370, 170n376, 190n405, 195n413, 205n424, 205n425, 236n464, 236n465, 246n485, 257n496
ʿUrwa b. al-Zubayr 266, 266n511; ~ 's son 266n511
ʿUthmān b. ʿAffān 44, 44n29, 47–48, 127n300, 255–256; ~ as caliph 284; mawlā of ~ 110

Vajda, Georges 9–10, 36n4, 36n5, 38n9
Van Ess, Josef 7–8, 22, 35n2, 36n3, 41n20, 92n171, 231n452
Victory 42, 51, 63, 107, 154, 156–157, 165, 177, 185, 245, 267; ~ in a poem 91

Wādī al-ʿAraba 79n139
Wādī al-Mūjib 124n295
Wādī al-Qurā 72, 72n121, 191n407, 237, 267
Wādī al-Zarqāʾ 124n295
wālī (close friend) 30, 49, 55, 63, 65–66, 76, 89, 92, 124, 130, 134, 137, 183, 256, 280, 284
wālī/awliyāʾ (God's close friend/s) 130, 148, 155, 160, 184, 186, 218, 238, 252
Wansleben, Johann Michael 11
al-Wāqūṣa 189n401, 240, 240n474 *see also* al-Yarmūk

Wardān 41n19, 122, 122n292, 123, 125; ~ as chief commander 126
Wāthila b. al-Asqaʿ 159, 159n353
Weapon/s 65, 78n138, 152, 152n350, 193, 199, 277n521, 281
Weaponry 40n19, 53, 62n87, 186, 195, 209
Wedding, ~ night 126
Woman/women 55, 71–72, 131, 141, 177, 220, 230, 258; ~ as rulers 148; ~ in poems 209, 233; Muslim ~ 40, 126, 192–194 230; ~ of Ḥimyar 53; ~ of Khathʿam 68; ~ 's domiciles 177, 216–217, 220; slave ~ 227; ~ 's participation in the Battle of al-Yarmūk 232, 236, 239; ~ 's virginity 74; two ~ living with a man 265–266
Worldly life, the 56, 62n86, 96, 127, 134, 138, 147–148, 160, 165, 196, 202, 210, 216–217, 221, 244–245, 261, 266, 268, 273–275, 277, 283
wuḍūʿ (ritual ablution) 30, 80

al-Yaʿbūb b. ʿAmr b. Ḍarīs al-Mashjaʿī 116, 116n267, 120, 128
Yaḥyā b. Hāniʾ b. ʿUrwa al-Murādī 68–69, 69n107, 161, 191
al-Yamāma 43n26, 93n173, 95, 95n178, 97, 99n195, 107
Yarfaʾ 134, 134n319
al-Yarmūk, river 41n22, 42n23, 56n66, 118n279, 189, 189n401, 198–200, 203–205, 208, 223, 225, 230; Battle of ~ 3, 32, 41n20, 44n28, 45n35, 47n41, 50n50, 50n51, 53n58, 57n67, 58n69, 58n72, 59n73, 59n74, 59n74, 59n76, 59n77, 60n79, 60n80, 68n106, 70n111, 70n112, 76n134, 80n142, 83n147, 83n148, 83n150, 89n165, 93n173, 110n245, 115n263, 120n282, 121n287, 135n321, 144n336, 144n337, 144n338, 175, 176n387, 176n388, 190n404, 195n414, 205n425, 222n432, 223n434, 227–243, 228n444, 228n445, 228n446, 231n452, 232n453, 233n457, 234n460, 240n474, 241n475, 242n478, 244, 245n483; battle-day of ~ 227, 238, 243; dating of the Battle of ~ 272; ~ gorge 3; people of ~ 252, 280; ~ region 193
Yashkur, in a poem 233, 233n458
Yathrib 47n43, 237, 237n467
yawm al-qiyāma *see* Day of Resurrection
Yazīd b. Abī Sufyān 2, 4–5, 50, 50n50, 56–57, 63–64, 68, 74–76, 79, 83–84, 123–125, 131, 134, 142, 177, 183, 190, 278, 279; ~ as chief commander 274, 276–279; mourning for ~ 283; ~ 's appointment as commander 50, 54; ~ 's appointment as commander of Damascus 253; ~ 's brother 4, 129n310, 282; ~ 's cousin 65; ~ 's character 130, 178, 278; ~ 's cousin 49n47, 50n50, 63, 64–65; ~ 's death 283; ~ 's dispatch 54–55; ~ 's fights at al-ʿAraba and al-Dāthina 92–93; ~ 's participation in the Battle of Ajnādayn 126; ~ 's participation in the Battle of al-Yarmūk 222–223, 227, 238–239; ~ 's participation in the conquest of Caesarea 276–277, 280–282; ~ 's participation in the conquest of Damascus 130, 132; ~ 's participation in the conquest of Jerusalem 253, 259, 261
Yazīd b. Yazīd b. Jābir 31–32, 110, 110n244, 117, 122–123, 132, 163
Yemen 47n40, 53n58, 57n68, 68, 73n124, 81, 128n302; Arab tribes of ~ 2, 23, 38n12, 228; farthest parts of ~ 47; ~i blade 106; people of ~ 51–53, 57, 60; tribes of ~ 23

Zādiba 71n114, 103, 103n208
zakāt *see* Tax (zakāt)
Zamʿa b. al-Aswad b. ʿĀmir 54, 54n61
Zandaward 93n173, 102, 102n203
Zaynab bt. Aḥmad b. ʿAbd al-Raḥīm al-Maqdisī, known as Bint al-Kamāl 19
Zīzāʾ 73, 73n126
Zoroastrian magi 71
Zubayd 232, 232n453
al-Zubayr b. al-ʿAwwām 44, 44n32, 47

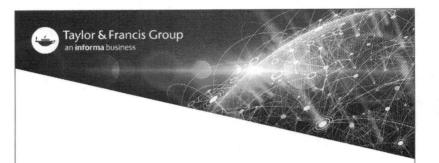

Printed in the United States
By Bookmasters